CSS

the missing manual®

The book that should have been in the box®

David Sawyer McFarland

O'REILLY®

Beijing | Boston | Farnham | Sebastopol | Tokyo

CSS: The Missing Manual

by David Sawyer McFarland

Published by O'Reilly Media, Inc.,
1005 Gravenstein Highway North, Sebastopol, CA 95472.

O'Reilly books may be purchased for educational, business, or sales promotional use. Online editions are also available for most titles (*http://safaribooksonline.com*). For more information, contact our corporate/institutional sales department: (800) 998-9938 or *corporate@oreilly.com*.

August 2006:	First Edition.
August 2009:	Second Edition.
December 2012:	Third Edition.
August 2015:	Fourth Edition.

Revision History for the Fourth Edition:

2015-08-05	First release
2015-10-09	Second release

See *http://oreilly.com/catalog/errata.csp?isbn=0636920036357* for release details.

ISBN-13: 978-1-491-91805-0

[LSI]

Contents

Part Two: **Applied CSS**

Part Four: **Advanced CSS**

Part Five: Appendixes

The Missing Credits

ABOUT THE AUTHOR

 David McFarland (author) is a web developer, teacher and author. He's been building web sites since 1995, when he designed his first website: an online magazine for communication professionals.

He's taught web design at the UC Berkeley Graduate School of Journalism, the Center for Electronic Art, the Art Institute of Portland, and Portland State University.

He's currently a Teaching Team Leader at the online education site, Treehouse (*http://teamtreehouse.com*).

ABOUT THE CREATIVE TEAM

Nan Barber (editor) is associate editor for the Missing Manuals series. She lives in Massachusetts with her husband and various electronic devices. Email: *nanbarber@gmail.com*.

Melanie Yarbrough (production editor and compositor) works and plays in Cambridge, Massachusetts, where she bakes up whatever she can imagine and bikes around the city. Email: *myarbrough@oreilly.com*.

Molly Ives Brower (proofreader) is a freelance editor and proofreader who has loved the Internet since she got a BITNET address in 1990. These days, though, she can be found online at *http://www.mjibrower.com* and on Twitter, where she goes by @vintagereader. Email: *molly@mjibrower.com*.

Ron Strauss (indexer) specializes in the indexing of information technology publications of all kinds. Ron is also an accomplished classical violist and lives in Northern California with his wife and fellow indexer, Annie, and his miniature pinscher, Kanga. Email: *rstrauss@mchsi.com*.

Rich Koster (beta reader) bought his first Mac, a 17-inch MacBook Pro, in 2009, and has never looked back toward the Dark Side (PCs). Rich served as the tech editor of David Pogue's *iPhone: The Missing Manual*, 3rd Edition. He's a husband, a father, and creator of the Disney Echo at *http://DisneyEcho.emuck.com*, which he has fun tending daily with his MacBook Pro!

ACKNOWLEDGEMENTS

Many thanks to all those who helped with this book, including the many students I've taught who always help me see complex concepts through beginner's eyes.

Thanks to my technical editors, Daniel Quinn and Jennifer Davis, who saved me from embarrassing mistakes. We all owe a big debt of gratitude to the many web designers who have broken new ground by using CSS in creative ways and shared their discoveries with the web design community.

Thanks to David Pogue, who got me started, many years ago on this long adventure. Thanks to Nan Barber for refining my writing, fixing my mistakes, and keeping me on track.

— David Sawyer McFarland

THE MISSING MANUAL SERIES

Missing Manuals are witty, superbly written guides to computer products that don't come with printed manuals (which is just about all of them). Each book features a handcrafted index and cross-references to specific pages (not just chapters). Recent and upcoming titles include:

- *Access 2013: The Missing Manual* by Matthew MacDonald
- *Adobe Edge Animate: The Missing Manual* by Chris Grover
- *Buying a Home: The Missing Manual* by Nancy Conner
- *Creating a Website: The Missing Manual, Third Edition* by Matthew MacDonald
- *CSS3: The Missing Manual, Third Edition* by David Sawyer McFarland
- *Dreamweaver CS6: The Missing Manual* by David Sawyer McFarland
- *Dreamweaver CC: The Missing Manual, Second Edition* by David Sawyer McFarland and Chris Grover
- *Excel 2013: The Missing Manual* by Matthew MacDonald
- *FileMaker Pro 13: The Missing Manual* by Susan Prosser and Stuart Gripman
- *Fire Phone: The Missing Manual* by Preston Gralla
- *Flash CS6: The Missing Manual* by Chris Grover
- *Galaxy Tab: The Missing Manual* by Preston Gralla
- *Galaxy S5: The Missing Manual* by Preston Gralla
- *Google+: The Missing Manual* by Kevin Purdy
- *HTML5: The Missing Manual, Second Edition* by Matthew MacDonald
- *iMovie: The Missing Manual* by David Pogue and Aaron Miller
- *iPad: The Missing Manual, Seventh Edition* by J.D. Biersdorfer
- *iPhone: The Missing Manual, Eighth Edition* by David Pogue
- *iPhone App Development: The Missing Manual* by Craig Hockenberry
- *iPhoto: The Missing Manual* by David Pogue and Lesa Snider

- *iPod: The Missing Manual, Eleventh Edition* by J.D. Biersdorfer and David Pogue

- *iWork: The Missing Manual* by Jessica Thornsby and Josh Clark

- *JavaScript & jQuery: The Missing Manual, Third Edition* by David Sawyer McFarland

- *Kindle Fire HD: The Missing Manual* by Peter Meyers

- *Living Green: The Missing Manual* by Nancy Conner

- *Microsoft Project 2013: The Missing Manual* by Bonnie Biafore

- *Motorola Xoom: The Missing Manual* by Preston Gralla

- *NOOK HD: The Missing Manual* by Preston Gralla

- *Office 2011 for Macintosh: The Missing Manual* by Chris Grover

- *Office 2013: The Missing Manual* by Nancy Conner and Matthew MacDonald

- *OS X Mavericks: The Missing Manual* by David Pogue

- *OS X Yosemite: The Missing Manual* by David Pogue

- *Personal Investing: The Missing Manual* by Bonnie Biafore

- *Photoshop CS6: The Missing Manual* by Lesa Snider

- *Photoshop CC: The Missing Manual, Second Edition* by Lesa Snider

- *Photoshop Elements 13: The Missing Manual* by Barbara Brundage

- *PHP & MySQL: The Missing Manual, Second Edition* by Brett McLaughlin

- *QuickBooks 2015: The Missing Manual* by Bonnie Biafore

- *Switching to the Mac: The Missing Manual, Mavericks Edition* by David Pogue

- *Windows 7: The Missing Manual* by David Pogue

- *Windows 8: The Missing Manual* by David Pogue

- *WordPress: The Missing Manual, Second Edition* by Matthew MacDonald

- *Your Body: The Missing Manual* by Matthew MacDonald

- *Your Brain: The Missing Manual* by Matthew MacDonald

- *Your Money: The Missing Manual* by J.D. Roth

For a full list of all Missing Manuals in print, go to *www.missingmanuals.com/library.html*.

Introduction

Cascading Style Sheets—CSS for short—give you creative control over the layout and design of your web pages. With CSS, dressing up your site's text with eye-catching headlines, drop caps, and borders is just the beginning. You can also arrange images with precision, create columns and banners, and highlight your links with dynamic rollover effects. You can even make elements fade in or out of view, move objects around the page, or make a button slowly change colors when a visitor mouses over it.

Anything that can do all that must be pretty complicated, right? *Au contraire*! The whole idea behind CSS is to streamline the process of styling web pages. In the next few pages, you'll learn about the basics of CSS.

■ What Is CSS?

CSS is a styling language. You use it to make HTML—the fundamental language of all web pages—look good. Well, hopefully, you'll use CSS to make your web pages look *better* than good. After you read this book, you'll be able to make your web pages beautiful, functional, and easy to use.

Think of HTML as the basic structure of your content, and CSS as a designer who takes your plain HTML and spruces it up with a fancy font, a border with rounded corners, or a bright red background.

But before you start learning about CSS, you need to understand HTML.

■ What You Need to Know

This book assumes you've already got some knowledge of HTML. Perhaps you've built a site or two (or at least a page or two) and have some familiarity with the sea of tags—<html>, <p>, <h1>, <table>—that make up the Hypertext Markup Language. CSS can't do anything without HTML, so you need to know how to create a web page by using basic HTML.

If you've used HTML in the past to create web pages, but feel like your knowledge is a bit rusty, the next section provides a basic refresher.

> **TIP** If you're just getting your feet wet learning HTML, then check out these free online tutorials: HTML Dog (*www.htmldog.com/guides/htmlbeginner*) and W3Schools (*www.w3schools.com/html*). If you're a printed-page fan, then you may want to pick up a copy of *HTML5: The Missing Manual*, Third Edition or *Head First HTML and CSS*, Second Edition (both O'Reilly).

■ HTML: The Barebones Structure

HTML (Hypertext Markup Language) uses simple commands called *tags* to define the various parts of a web page. For example, this HTML code creates a simple web page:

```
<!doctype html>
<html>
  <head>
    <meta charset="UTF-8">
    <title>Hey, I am the title of this web page</title>
  </head>
  <body>
    <p>Hey, I am a paragraph on this web page.</p>
  </body>
</html>
```

It may not be exciting, but this example has all the basic elements a web page needs. You'll notice something called a *doctype* declaration at the very beginning of the code, followed by <html> (with the brackets), a head, a body, and some stuff—the actual page contents—inside the body, ending in a final </html>.

■ Document Types

All web pages begin with a *doctype*—a line of code that identifies what flavor of HTML you used to write the page. Two doctypes have been used for years—HTML 4.01 and XHTML 1.0—and each of those doctypes has two styles: *strict* and *transitional*. For example, the HTML 4.01 transitional doctype looks like the following (the other doctypes for HTML 4.01 and XHTML 1.0 look similar):

```
<!DOCTYPE HTML PUBLIC "-//W3C//DTD HTML 4.01 Transitional//EN" "http://www.
w3.org/TR/html4/loose.dtd">
```

> **NOTE** For examples of all various doctypes, visit *www.webstandards.org/learn/reference/templates.*

If you look at the code for the sample HTML page in this section, you'll see that it uses a much more succinct doctype:

```
<!doctype html>
```

That's the HTML5 doctype. HTML5 is easier to use and more streamlined than its predecessors. This book uses the HTML5 doctype, which is supported by every popular browser (even the old Internet Explorer 6). There's no reason to use any doctype other than the simple HTML5 doctype.

> **NOTE** Just because the HTML doctype works in older browsers doesn't mean that those browsers understand all HTML5 tags or features. Internet Explorer 8 and earlier, for example, don't recognize the new HTML5 tags. To style tags with CSS for those versions of IE, you have to employ a little JavaScript. You'll learn how to get older browsers up to speed in the box on page 12.

The most important thing about a doctype, however, is to always use one. Without it, your pages will look different depending on your visitor's browser, since browsers display CSS differently if they don't have a doctype for guidance.

Each doctype requires you to write your HTML in a certain way. For example, the tag for a line break looks like this in HTML 4.01:

```
<br>
```

But in XHTML, it looks like this:

```
<br />
```

And there's another advantage of HTML5: It accepts either one.

How HTML Tags Work

In the simple HTML example on page XIV, as in the HTML code of any web page, most commands appear in pairs that surround a block of text or other commands. Sandwiched between brackets, these *tags* are instructions that tell a web browser how to display the web page. Tags are the "markup" part of the Hypertext Markup Language.

The starting (*opening*) tag of each pair tells the browser where the instruction begins, and the ending tag tells it where the instruction ends. Ending or *closing* tags always include a forward slash (/) after the first bracket symbol (<).

On any web page, you'll usually find at least these four elements:

- The first line of a web page is the **DOCTYPE declaration**, discussed in the previous section.

- The <html> tag appears once at the beginning of a web page and again (with an added forward slash) at the end: </html>. This tag tells a web browser that the information contained in this document is written in HTML, as opposed to some other language. All the contents of a page, including other tags, appear between the opening and closing <html> tags.

  If you were to think of a web page as a tree, the <html> tag would be its root. Springing from the trunk are two branches that represent the two main parts of any web page: the *head* and the *body*.

- The *head* of a web page contains the title of the page ("Izzie's Mail-Order Pencils"). It may also include other, invisible information, like a page description, that browsers and search engines use. You surround the head section with opening and closing <head> tags.

  In addition, the head section can include information that browsers use to format the page's HTML and to add interactivity. As you'll see, the <head> section can contain CSS code (like the kind you'll learn to write in this book) or a link to another file containing CSS information.

- The *body*, as set apart by its surrounding <body> tags, contains all the content that appears inside a browser window—headlines, text, pictures, and so on.

Within the <body> tag, you commonly find tags like these:

- You tell a web browser where a paragraph of text begins with a **<p>** (opening paragraph tag), and where it ends with a **</p>** (closing paragraph tag).

- The **<strong>** tag marks text as important. When you surround some text with it and its partner tag, **</strong>**, you get boldface type. The HTML snippet <strong> Warning!</strong> tells a web browser to strongly emphasize the word "Warning!"

- The **<a>** tag, or anchor tag, creates a *hyperlink* in a web page. When clicked, a hyperlink—or *link*—can lead anywhere on the Web. You tell the browser where the link points by putting a web address inside the <a> tags. For instance, you can type <a href="http://www.missingmanuals.com">Click here!</a>.

  The browser knows that when your visitor clicks the words "Click here!" it should go to the Missing Manual website. The href part of the tag is called an *attribute*, and the URL (the *Uniform Resource Locator*, or web address) is the *value*. In this example, http://www.missingmanuals.com is the *value* of the href attribute.

■ HTML5: More Tags to Choose From

HTML5—the current version of HTML—has been around for years now. Sometimes you'll hear the name used to describe things other than HTML tags, like local storage (a way to save data from a website to a visitor's computer), geolocation (a way to check where a visitor is in the world), and drawing to the web page using WebGL. Strictly speaking, those technologies aren't part of HTML, but they're new browser features that came onto the scene along with HTML5.

In this book, the term *HTML5* always refers to the HTML5 doctype as well as the new tags introduced as part of the HTML5 standard. HTML5 isn't radically different from its predecessors—it was created to make sure the Web continues to work the way it always has. Most of the basics of HTML are the same as they've always been; HTML5 adds a few new elements meant to support the way web designers currently build websites. For example, in HTML5, the <header> tag contains the content you usually find at the top of a page, such as a logo and sitewide navigation links; the new <nav> tag encloses the set of links used to navigate a site; and the <footer> tag houses the stuff you usually put at the bottom of a page, like legal notices, email contacts, and so on.

In addition, HTML5 adds new tags that let you insert video and audio into a page, new form tags that add sophisticated elements like sliders and pop-up date pickers, and built-in browser support for form validation (which ensures visitors correctly fill out your forms). You'll see HTML5 used throughout this book, especially in the next chapter.

■ Software for CSS

To create web pages made up of HTML and CSS, you need nothing more than a basic text editor like Notepad (Windows) or TextEdit (Mac). But after typing a few hundred lines of HTML and CSS, you may want to try a program better suited to working with web pages. This section lists some common programs, some free and some you have to buy.

> **NOTE** There are literally hundreds of tools that can help you create web pages, so the following isn't a complete list. Think of it as a greatest-hits tour of the most popular programs that CSS fans are using today.

Free Programs

There are plenty of free programs out there for editing web pages and style sheets. If you're still using Notepad or TextEdit, give one of these a try. Here's a short list to get you started:

- **Brackets (Windows, Mac, Linux;** *http://brackets.io/***).** Spearheaded by Adobe, this free, open-source text editor has many tools for working with HTML and CSS. It's written specifically for web designers and developers.

- **Atom (Windows, Mac, Linux;** *https://atom.io/***).** Another free, open-source text editor created by the people behind GitHub, the hugely popular code sharing and collaboration site. Like Brackets, this new text editor is aimed at web developers.

- **jEdit (Windows, Mac, Linux;** *http://jedit.org***).** This free, Java-based text editor works on almost any computer and includes many features that you'd find in commercial text editors, like syntax highlighting for CSS.

- **Notepad++ (Windows;** *http://notepad-plus.sourceforge.net***).** A lot of people swear by this fast text editor. It even has built-in features that make it ideal for writing HTML and CSS, like syntax highlighting—color-coding tags and special keywords to make it easier to identify the page's HTML and CSS elements.

Commercial Software

Commercial website development programs range from inexpensive text editors to complete website construction tools with all the bells and whistles:

- **EditPlus (Windows;** *www.editplus.com***)** is an inexpensive ($35) text editor that includes syntax highlighting, FTP, autocomplete, and other wrist-saving features.

- **skEdit (Mac;** *www.skedit.com***)** is an inexpensive ($30) web page editor, complete with FTP/SFTP, code hints, and other useful features.

- **Coda2 (Mac;** *www.panic.com/coda***)** is a full-featured web development toolkit ($99). It includes a text editor, page preview, FTP/SFTP, and graphic CSS-creating tools for creating CSS.

- **Sublime Text (Mac, Windows, Linux;** *www.sublimetext.com***)** is a powerful text editor ($70) beloved by many web coders. You'll find it frequently used in web design companies.

- **Dreamweaver (Mac and Windows;** *www.adobe.com/products/dreamweaver***)** is a visual web page editor (from $19.99 per month). It lets you see how your page looks in a web browser. The program also includes a powerful text editor and excellent CSS creation and management tools. Check out *Dreamweaver CC: The Missing Manual* for the full skinny on how to use this powerful program.

NOTE The various types of software discussed in this section are general-purpose programs that let you edit both HTML and CSS. With them, you need to learn only one program for your web development needs.

■ About This Book

The World Wide Web is really easy to use. After all, grandfathers in Boise and first graders in Tallahassee log onto the Web every day. Unfortunately, the rules that govern how the Web *works* aren't so easy to understand. The computer scientists and other techie types who write the official documentation aren't interested in explaining their concepts to the average Joe (or Joanne). Just check out *www.w3.org/TR/css3-transforms* to get a taste of the technical mumbo-jumbo these geeks speak.

People just learning CSS often don't know where to begin. And CSS's finer points can trip up even seasoned web pros. The purpose of this book is to serve as the manual that should have come with CSS. In its pages, you'll find step-by-step instructions for using CSS to create beautiful web pages.

CSS: The Missing Manual is designed to help readers at every technical level. To get the most out of this book, you should know the basics of HTML and maybe even a sampling of CSS. If you've never built a web page before, then check out the tutorial that starts on page 27. The primary discussions in these chapters are written for advanced beginners or intermediates. But if you're new to building web pages, special boxes labeled "Up to Speed" provide the introductory information you need to understand the topic at hand. If you're an advanced web jockey, on the other hand, then keep your eye out for similar boxes called "Power Users' Clinic." They offer more technical tips, tricks, and shortcuts for the experienced computer fan.

About the Outline

CSS: The Missing Manual is divided into five parts; the first four each contain several chapters while the last part contains appendixes.

- Part One, CSS Basics, shows you how to create style sheets and provides an overview of key CSS concepts like *inheritance*, *selectors*, and the *cascade*. Along the way, you'll learn the best HTML writing practices when working with CSS. Tutorials reinforce the part's main concepts and give you a good taste of the power of CSS.

- Part Two, Applied CSS, takes you into the real world of web design. You'll learn the most important CSS properties and how to use them to format text, create useful navigation tools, and enhance your page with graphics. You'll learn how to create simple animations with CSS. This section also provides advice on how to make attractive tables and forms.

- Part Three, CSS Page Layout, helps you with one of the most confusing, but most rewarding, aspects of CSS—controlling the layout of your web pages. You'll learn how to create common designs (like two- and three-column layouts) and how to add sidebars, and you'll learn about *floats* and *positioning*—two common CSS techniques for controlling page layout. You'll also learn how to craft websites that adapt to look good on desktop, tablet, and mobile browsers, as well as how to use flexbox, a powerful new way of laying out web pages.

- Part Four, Advanced CSS, delves into professional tips for improving your CSS, It also provides an introduction to Sass—a powerful and efficient way of authoring your style sheets.

- Part Five, Appendixes, includes two sets of resources. The CSS Property Reference summarizes each CSS property in small, easy-to-digest chunks so you can quickly learn about useful CSS properties you may not have seen before or brush up on what you already know. The second appendix covers tools and resources for creating and using CSS.

The Very Basics

To use this book, and indeed to use a computer, you need to know a few basics. You should be familiar with these terms and concepts:

- **Clicking.** This book gives you three kinds of instructions that require you to use your computer's mouse or trackpad. To *click* means to point the arrow cursor at something on the screen and then—without moving the cursor at all—to press and release the clicker button on the mouse (or laptop trackpad). A *right-click* is the same thing using the right mouse button. (On a Mac, press Control as you click if you don't have a right mouse button.)

  To *double-click* means to click twice in rapid succession, again without moving the cursor at all. And to *drag* means to move the cursor *while* pressing the button.

  When you're told to *Ctrl-click* something on a PC or *⌘-click* something on the Mac, you click while pressing the Ctrl or ⌘ key.

- **Menus.** The *menus* are the words at the top of your screen or window: File, Edit, and so on. Click one to make a list of commands appear, as though they're written on a window shade you've just pulled down. This book assumes that you know how to open a program, surf the Web, and download files. You should know how to use the Start menu (Windows) or the Dock or the Apple menu (Mac), as well as the Control Panel (Windows) or System Preferences (Mac OS X).

- **Keyboard shortcuts.** Every time you take your hand off the keyboard to move the mouse, you lose time and potentially disrupt your creative flow. That's why many experienced computer users use keystroke combinations instead of menu commands wherever possible. When you see a shortcut like Ctrl+S (⌘-S) (which saves changes to the current document), it's telling you to hold down the Ctrl or ⌘ key, and, while it's down, type the letter S, and then release both keys.

About→These→Arrows

Throughout this book, and throughout the Missing Manual series, you'll find sentences like this one: "Open the System→Library→Fonts folder." That's shorthand for a much longer instruction that directs you to open three nested folders in sequence, like this: "On your hard drive, you'll find a folder called System. Open that. Inside the System folder window is a folder called Library; double-click it to open it. Inside *that* folder is yet another one called Fonts. Double-click to open it, too."

Similarly, this kind of arrow shorthand helps to simplify the business of choosing commands in menus, as shown in Figure I-1.

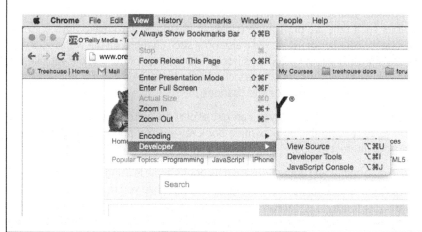

FIGURE P-1

In this book, arrow nota-tions help simplify menu instructions. For example, View→Developer→View Source is a more compact way of saying, "From the View menu, choose Developer; from the sub-menu that then appears, choose View Source."

About the Online Resources

As the owner of a Missing Manual, you've got more than just a book to read. Online, you'll find example files so you can get some hands-on experience, as well as tips, articles, and maybe even a video or two. You can also communicate with the Missing Manual team and tell us what you love (or hate) about the book. Head over to *www.missingmanuals.com*, or go directly to one of the following sections.

Living Examples

This book is designed to get your work onto the Web faster and more professionally. It's only natural, then, that half the value of this book lies on the Web.

As you read the book's chapters, you'll encounter a number of *living examples*— step-by-step tutorials that you can build yourself, using raw materials (like graphics and half-completed web pages) that you can download from *https://github.com/sawmac/css_mm_4e*. You may not gain very much by simply reading these step-by-step lessons while relaxing in your porch hammock. But if you work through them at the computer, you'll discover that these tutorials give you insight into the way professional designers build web pages.

You'll also find, in this book's lessons, the URLs of the finished pages, so that you can compare your work with the final result. In other words, you won't just see pic-tures of how the web pages *should* look; you'll find the actual, working web pages on the Internet.

About MissingManuals.com

At *www.missingmanuals.com*, you'll find articles, tips, and updates to *CSS: The Missing Manual*. In fact, we invite and encourage you to submit such corrections and updates yourself. In an effort to keep the book as up-to-date and accurate as possible, each time we print more copies of this book, we'll make any confirmed corrections you've suggested. We'll also note such changes on the website, so that you can mark important corrections into your own copy of the book, if you like. (Go to *www.missingmanuals.com/feedback*, choose the book's name from the pop-up menu, and then click Go to see the changes.)

Also on our Feedback page, you can get expert answers to questions that come to you while reading this book, write a book review, and find groups for folks who share your interest in CSS.

We'd love to hear your suggestions for new books in the Missing Manual line. There's a place for that on *missingmanuals.com*, too. And while you're online, you can also register this book at *www.oreilly.com* (you can jump directly to the registration page by going here: *www.oreilly.com/register*). Registering means we can send you updates about this book, and you'll be eligible for special offers like discounts on future editions of *CSS: The Missing Manual*.

Errata

In an effort to keep this book as up-to-date and accurate as possible, each time we print more copies, we'll make any confirmed corrections you've suggested. We also note such changes on the book's website, so you can mark important corrections into your own copy of the book, if you like. Go to *www.tinyurl.com/css4e-mm* to report an error and view existing corrections.

■ Safari® Books Online

Safari Books Online is an on-demand digital library that delivers expert content in both book and video form from the world's leading authors in technology and business.

Technology professionals, software developers, web designers, and business and creative professionals use Safari Books Online as their primary resource for research, problem solving, learning, and certification training.

Safari Books Online offers a range of plans and pricing for enterprise, government, education, and individuals.

Members have access to thousands of books, training videos, and prepublication manuscripts in one fully searchable database from publishers like O'Reilly Media, Prentice Hall Professional, Addison-Wesley Professional, Microsoft Press, Sams, Que, Peachpit Press, Focal Press, Cisco Press, John Wiley & Sons, Syngress, Morgan Kaufmann, IBM Redbooks, Packt, Adobe Press, FT Press, Apress, Manning, New Riders, McGraw-Hill, Jones & Bartlett, Course Technology, and hundreds more. For more information about Safari Books Online, please visit us online.

CSS Basics

HTML and CSS

C SS isn't anything without HTML. HTML provides web pages with content and meaningful structure, and while it may not be pretty by itself, the web wouldn't exist without it. So to get the most out of your CSS training, you need to know how to write HTML to create a solid, well-built foundation. This chapter introduces you to the basics of CSS and shows you how to write better, more CSS-friendly HTML.

The good news is that when you use CSS throughout your site, HTML actually becomes *easier* to write. You don't need to try to turn HTML into the design maven it was never intended to be. Instead, CSS offers most of the graphic design touches you'll likely ever want, and HTML pages written to work with CSS are easier to create, since they require less code and less typing. They'll also download faster—a welcome bonus your site's visitors will appreciate (see Figure 1-1).

■ HTML: Past and Present

HTML provides the foundation for every page you encounter on the Web. When you add CSS into the mix, HTML becomes simpler, because you don't need to use HTML tags (like the old `<font>` tag) to control how a web page looks. That job is for CSS. But before jumping into CSS, here's a quick walk through HTML's past (and present).

HTML Past: Whatever Looked Good

When a bunch of scientists created the Web to share technical documentation, nobody called in the graphic designers. All the scientists needed HTML to do was structure information for easy comprehension. For example, the `<h1>` tag indicates an important headline, while the `<h2>` tag represents a lesser heading, usually a subheading of the `<h1>` tag. Another favorite, the `<ol>` (ordered list) tag, creates a numbered list for things like "Top 10 reasons not to play with jellyfish."

FIGURE 1-1

CSS-driven web design makes writing HTML easier. The two designs pictured here look similar, but the top page is styled completely with CSS, while the bottom page uses only HTML. The size of the HTML file for the top page is only 4k, while the HTML-only page is nearly four times that size at 14k. The HTML-only approach requires a lot more code to achieve nearly the same visual effects: 213 lines of HTML code compared with 71 lines for the CSS version.

But as soon as people other than scientists started using HTML, they wanted their web pages to look good. So web designers started to use tags to control appearance rather than structure information. For example, you can use the `<blockquote>` tag (intended for material that's quoted from another source) on any text that you want to indent a little bit. You can use heading tags to make any text bigger and bolder—regardless of whether it functions as a heading.

In an even more elaborate workaround, designers learned how to use the `<table>` tag to create columns of text and accurately place pictures and text on a page. Unfortunately, since that tag was intended to display spreadsheet-like data—research results, train schedules, and so on—designers had to get creative by using the `<table>` tag in unusual ways, sometimes nesting a table within a table within a table to make their pages look good.

Meanwhile, browser makers introduced new tags and attributes for the specific purpose of making a page look better. The `<font>` tag, for example, let you specify a font color, typeface, and one of seven different sizes. (If you're keeping score at home, that's about 100 fewer sizes than you can get with, say, Microsoft Word.)

Finally, when designers couldn't get exactly what they wanted, they often resorted to using graphics. For example, they'd create a large graphic to capture the exact font and layout for web page elements and then *slice* the Photoshop files into smaller files and piece them back together inside tables to recreate the original design.

While all of the preceding techniques—using tags in creative ways, taking advantage of design-specific tag attributes, and making extensive use of graphics—provide design control over your pages, they also add a lot of additional HTML code. More code makes your site more difficult to build and much slower for your visitors to download.

HTML Present: Scaffolding for CSS

No matter what content your web page holds—the fishing season calendar, driving directions to the nearest IKEA, or pictures from your kid's birthday party—it's the page's design that makes it look like either a professional enterprise or a part-timer's hobby. Good design enhances the message of your site, helps visitors find what they're looking for, and determines how the rest of the world sees your website. That's why web designers went through the contortions described in the previous section to force HTML to look good. By taking on those design duties, CSS lets HTML go back to doing what it does best—structuring content.

Using HTML to control the look of text and other web page elements is obsolete. Don't worry if HTML's `<h1>` tag is too big for your taste or bulleted lists aren't spaced just right. You can take care of that later using CSS. Instead, think of HTML as a method of adding structure to the content you want up on the Web. Use HTML to organize your content and CSS to make that content look great.

Writing HTML for CSS

If you're new to web design, you may need some helpful hints to guide your forays into HTML (and to steer clear of well-intentioned, but out-of-date HTML techniques). Or if you've been building web pages for a while, you may have picked up a few bad habits that you're better off forgetting. The rest of this chapter introduces you to some HTML-writing habits that will make your mom proud—and help you get the most out of CSS.

Think Structure

HTML adds meaning to text by logically dividing it and identifying the role it plays on the page: For example, the <h1> tag is the most important introduction to a page's content. Other headers let you divide the content into less important, but related sections. Just like this book, a web page needs a logical structure. Each chapter in this book has a title (think <h1>) and several sections (think <h2>), which in turn contain smaller subsections. Imagine how much harder it would be to read these pages if the words just ran together as one long paragraph.

> **NOTE** For a tutorial on HTML, visit *www.w3schools.com/html/html_intro.asp*. For a quick list of all available HTML tags, visit the detailed (but a bit technical) reference at the Mozilla Developer network: *https://developer. mozilla.org/en-US/docs/Web/HTML/Element.*

HTML provides many other tags besides headers for *marking up* content to identify its role. (After all, the M in HTML stands for *markup*.) Among the most popular are the <p> tag for paragraphs of text and the <ul> tag for creating bulleted (non-numbered) lists. Lesser-known tags can indicate very specific types of content, like <abbr> for abbreviations and <code> for computer code.

When writing HTML for CSS, use a tag that comes as close as possible to matching the role the content plays in the page, not the way it looks (see Figure 1-2). For example, a bunch of links in a navigation bar isn't really a headline, and it isn't a regular paragraph of text. It's most like a bulleted list of options, so the <ul> tag is a good choice. If you're saying, "But items in a bulleted list are stacked vertically one on top of the other, and I want a horizontal navigation bar where each link sits next to the previous link," don't worry. With CSS magic you can convert a vertical list of links into a stylish horizontal navigation bar, as you'll see in Chapter 9.

More HTML Tags to Keep in Mind

HTML's motley assortment of tags doesn't cover the wide range of content you'll likely have on a web page. Sure, <code> is great for marking up computer program code, but most folks would find a <recipe> tag handier. Too bad there isn't one. Fortunately, HTML provides several "structural" tags that let you better identify and group content, and, in the process, provide "handles" that let you attach CSS styles to different page elements. Two of those tags—<div> and <span>—have been around nearly since the beginning of HTML. HTML5 introduced a much wider range of tags that let you group content that serves a particular function, like the <footer> tag, which you can use to group supplementary information like a copyright notice, contact information, or a list of resources.

```
<p>
<strong>
<font color="#0066FF" size="5" face="Verdana,
Arial, Helvetica, sans-serif">Urban Agrarian
Lifestyle</font></strong>
<br />
<font color="#FF3300" size="4" face="Georgia,
Times New Roman, Times, serif">
<em>
<strong>A Revolution in Indoor Agriculture
<br /></strong></em></font>
Lorem ipsum dolor sit amet...</p>
```

FIGURE 1-2

Old school, new school. Before CSS, designers had to resort to the <font> tag and other extra HTML to achieve certain visual effects (top). You can achieve the same look (and often a better one) with a lot less HTML code (bottom). In addition, using CSS for formatting frees you up to write HTML that follows the logical structure of the page's content.

The Urban Agrarian Lifestyle
A Revolution in Indoor Agriculture
Lorem ipsum dolor sit amet, consectetuer adipiscing elit, sed diam nonummy nibh euismod tincidunt ut laoreet dolore magna aliquam erat volutpat. Ut wisi enim ad minim veniam, quis nostrud exerci tation ullamcorper suscipit lobortis nisl ut aliquip ex ea commodo consequat. Duis autem vel eum iriure.

```
<h1>The Urban Agrarian Lifestyle</h1>
<h2>A Revolution in Indoor Agriculture</h2>
<p>Lorem ipsum dolor sit amet...</p>
```

■ UNDERSTANDING THE <DIV> AND <SPAN> TAGS

The <div> and <span> tags have been around for much of the life of the Web. They've traditionally been used to organize and group content that doesn't quite lend itself to other HTML tags. Think of them as like empty vessels that you fill with content. A *div* is a block, meaning it has a line break before it and after it, while a *span* appears inline, as part of a paragraph. Otherwise, divs and spans have no inherent visual properties, so you can use CSS to make them look any way you want. The <div> (for *division*) tag indicates any discrete block of content, much like a paragraph or a headline. But more often it's used to group any number of *other* elements, so you can insert a headline, a bunch of paragraphs, and a bulleted list inside a single <div> block. The <div> tag is a great way to subdivide a page into logical areas, like a banner, footer, sidebar, and so on. Using CSS, you can later position each area to create sophisticated page layouts (a topic that's covered in Part Three).

Simple HTML Is Search Engine Friendly

Once you ignore how plain HTML looks and instead think of it simply as the way to structure a document's content, and CSS as the tool for making that content look good, you'll discover additional benefits to writing lean, mean HTML. For one thing, you may boost your search-engine ranking as determined by sites like Google, Yahoo, and Bing. That's because when search engines crawl the Web, indexing the content on websites, they go through *all* the HTML on each page to discover the actual content. The old HTML way of using special tags (like <font>) and lots of tables to design a page gets in the way of the search engine's job. In fact, some search engines stop reading a page's HTML after a certain number of characters. When you use HTML just for design, the search engine may miss important content on the page or even fail to rank it at all.

By contrast, simple, structured HTML is easy for a search engine to read and index. Using an <h1> tag to indicate the

most important topic of the page (as opposed to just making the text big and bold) is a smart strategy: Search engines give greater weight to the contents inside that tag when they index the page.

What's more, CSS lets you control where content appears on the page. For example, although you may want a fancy navigation bar, a newsletter signup form, and a Contact Us button to appear at the top of your web page, you don't have to place that content at the top of your HTML file. You can place the page's most important content at the top of the HTML and let CSS control exactly where everything appears in the browser window.

To see Google's suggestions for building search-friendly websites, download their search engine start kit at *https://static. googleusercontent.com/media/www.google.com/en//webmasters/docs/search-engine-optimization-starter-guide.pdf.*

The <span> tag is used for *inline* elements: words or phrases that appear inside a larger paragraph or heading. Treat it just like other inline HTML tags, such as the <a> tag (for adding a link to some text in a paragraph) or the <strong> tag (for emphasizing a word in a paragraph). For example, you could use a <span> tag to indicate the name of a company, and then use CSS to highlight the name by using a different font, color, and so on. Here's an example of these tags in action, complete with a sneak peek of a couple of attributes—id and class—frequently used to attach styles to parts of a page.

```
<div id="footer">
    <p>Copyright 2015, <span class="bizName">SuperCo.com</span></p>
    <p>Call customer service at 555-555-5501 for more information.</p>
</div>
```

This brief introduction isn't the last you'll see of these tags. They're used frequently in CSS-heavy web pages, and in this book you'll learn how to use them in combination with CSS to gain creative control over your web pages.

ADDITIONAL TAGS IN HTML5

The <div> tag is rather generic—it's simply a block-level element used to divide a page into sections. One of the goals of HTML5 is to provide other, more *semantic* tags for web designers to choose from. Making your HTML more semantic simply means using tags that accurately describe the content they contain. As mentioned earlier in this section, you should use the <h1> (heading 1) tag when placing text that describes the primary content of a page. Likewise, the <code> tag tells you clearly what kind of information is placed inside—programming code.

HTML5 includes many different tags whose names reflect the type of content they contain, and can be used in place of the <div> tag. The <article> tag, for example, is used to mark off a section of a page that contains a complete, independent composition, like a blog post, an online magazine article, or simply the page's main body of text. Likewise, the <header> tag indicates a *header* or *banner*: the top part of a page, usually containing a logo, sitewide navigation, page title and tagline, and so on.

> **NOTE** To learn more about the new HTML tags, visit HTML5 Doctor (*http://html5doctor.com*) and *www. w3schools.com/html/html5_intro.asp* or grab a copy of the *HTML5 Pocket Reference* (O'Reilly).

Many HTML5 tags are intended to expand upon the generic <div> tag. Here are a few other HTML5 tags frequently used to structure the content on a page:

- The **<section>** tag contains a grouping of related content, such as the chapter of a book. For example, you could divide the content of a home page into three sections: one for an introduction to the site, one for contact information, and another for latest news.

- The **<aside>** tag holds content that is related to content around it. A sidebar in a print magazine is an example of the type of content that would go into an <aside>.

- The **<footer>** tag contains information you'd usually place in a page's footer, like a copyright notice, legal information, some site navigation links, and so on. You're not limited to just a single <footer> per page, though; you can put a footer inside an <article>, for example, to hold related information like footnotes, references, or citations.

- The **<nav>** element is used to contain primary navigation links.

- The **<figure>** tag is used for an illustrative image. You can place an <img> tag inside it, as well as another new HTML5 tag—the <figcaption> tag, which is used to display a caption explaining the photo or illustration within the <figure>.

> **TIP** Understanding which HTML5 tag to use—should your text be an <article> or a <section>?—can be tricky. For a handy flowchart that makes sense of HTML5's new sectioning elements, download the PDF from the HTML5doctor.com at *http://html5doctor.com/downloads/h5d-sectioning-flowchart.pdf*.

There are other HTML5 elements, and many of them simply provide a more descriptive alternative to the <div> tag. This book uses both the <div> tag and the new HTML5 tags to help organize web-page content. The downside of HTML5 is that Internet Explorer 8 and earlier don't recognize the new tags without a little bit of help (see the box on page 12).

In addition to letting you feel like you're keeping up with the latest web design trends, using HTML5 tags provides you with clues about a page's content, and may boost the site's search engine ranking. For example, using the <article> tag to hold the main story on a web page can highlight what's inside that tag, and is more descriptive (that is, *semantic*) than a plain old <div>. Even so, many web designers still use <div> tags even in places where an HTML5 tag makes sense, so there's no harm in continuing to use the <div> tag and avoiding the HTML5 sectioning elements if you like.

In addition, even with the HTML5 tags, sometimes you still need use <div> tags simply to group other HTML tags. You'd do this to provide a way to move that group to another spot on a page, to give the group a consistent background color, or to draw an outline and add a drop shadow.

Keep Your Layout in Mind

While you'll use the <h1> tag to identify the main topic of the page and the <p> tag to add a paragraph of text, you'll eventually want to organize a page's content into a pleasing layout. As you learn how to use CSS to lay out a page in Part Three, it doesn't hurt to keep your design in mind while you write the page's HTML.

You can think of web page layout as the artful arrangement of boxes (see Figure 1-3 for an example). After all, a two-column design consisting of two vertical columns of text is really just two rectangular boxes sitting side by side. A header consisting of a logo, tagline, search box, and site navigation is really just a wide rectangular box sitting across the top of the browser window. In other words, if you imagine the groupings and layout of content on a page, you'd see boxes sitting on top of, next to, and below one another.

FIGURE 1-3

This basic two-column layout includes a banner (top), a column of main content (middle, left), a sidebar (middle, right), and a footer (bottom). These are the main structural boxes making up this page's layout.

Getting IE8 to Understand HTML5

HTML5 gives you many HTML tags to play with, from tags that clearly describe the kind of content they hold, like the <nav> tag, to ones that provide added functionality, like the <video> tag for embedding videos and the <audio> tag for embedding sound and music.

Unfortunately, Internet Explorer 8 and earlier don't recognize these new tags, and won't respond to any CSS you apply to them. That's right—if you're using HTML5 and viewing web pages in IE8, this book is useless to you. Well...not exactly. There is a way to kick those old versions of IE into gear, so they'll understand all the CSS that applies to HTML5 tags.

Simply place the following code before the closing </head> tag at the top of your HTML file:

```
<!--[if lt IE 9]>
<script src="//html5shiv.googlecode.com/
svn/trunk/html5.js"></script>
<![endif]-->
```

This tricky bit of code uses what's called an "Internet Explorer conditional comment" (IECC for short) to embed a bit of JavaScript code that's only visible to versions of Internet Explorer earlier than IE9. In other words, only IE6, 7, and 8 respond to this code, and all other browsers (including newer versions of IE) simply ignore it. This code makes earlier versions of IE load a small JavaScript program that forces the browser to recognize HTML5 tags and apply the CSS that applies to those tags.

This code only affects how the browser displays and prints HTML5 tags; it doesn't make the browser "understand" an HTML5 tag that actually does something. For example, IE8 and earlier don't understand the <video> tag and can't play HTML5 video (even with the added JavaScript code).

If you're wondering whether you even need to worry about Internet Explorer 8 anymore, check out the box on page 13.

In your HTML, you create these boxes, or structural units, using the <div> tag, or one of HTML5's structural tags like <footer>, <header>, <article>, and <aside>. Simply wrap the HTML tags that make up the banner area, for example, in one div, a column's worth of HTML in another, and so on. If you're HTML5 savvy, you might create the design pictured in Figure 1-3, with a <header> tag for the top banner, an <article> tag for the main text, an <aside> or <section> tag for the sidebar, and a <footer> tag for the page's footer. In other words, if you plan to place a group of HTML tags together somewhere on a page, then you'll need to wrap those tags in a sectioning element like a <div>, <article>, <section>, or <aside>.

As you'll learn in Part Three, CSS provides powerful layout tools. You can literally place HTML anywhere in the browser window; recent developments like flexbox (Chapter 15) give you lots of freedom in how you structure your HTML. Still, it's always a good idea to group related content into some kind of container element like a <div> or an HTML5 structural tag.

FREQUENTLY ASKED QUESTION

Should I Care About IE8?

I know Internet Explorer 6 used to be a big headache for web designers. What versions of Internet Explorer should I be designing for now?

If you're a web designer, you've probably got the latest versions of Internet Explorer, Firefox, Safari, Chrome, and Opera on your computer. But you can't depend on your audience to update their web browsers; maybe they don't know how, or their computers are too old to use newer versions.

Fortunately, Internet Explorer 6 and 7 are pretty much gone from the planet, although they still exist and are used in pockets of China, India, and Venezuela (see *www.modern.ie/en-us/ie6countdown* for more). You may also be able to find them as part of a "history of computing" exhibit in a science museum somewhere.

However, as of this writing, Internet Explorer 8 is still used throughout the world. It's certainly not the most popular browser, but (depending on your source) it's still used by anywhere from around 2% to 19% of the world's web users. Two sites you can use to find browser usage are NetMarketShare (*www.netmarketshare.com/browser-market-share.aspx*) and the GlobalStats StatCounter (*http://gs.statcounter.com*).

However, even statistics that include the geographic region of your site's audience don't truly reflect what visitors to your site use. If you build a site aimed at tech-savvy web designers, odds are that you haven't had a visitor with IE 8 for quite some time. However, if your site's aimed at people in China, you may need to deal with IE 8 (and maybe even 6 and 7). The best way to find out how much of your traffic comes via any browser version is to look at your web server's log files or sign up for Google Analytics (*www.google.com/analytics*) so you can track your visitors' browsers (among many other things).

Microsoft says it will discontinue support for Internet Explorer 8 by January 2016. At that point, Windows fans will have more incentive to upgrade IE or switch to another browser, like Chrome or Firefox. *The* biggest problem with IE8 is that it doesn't understand HTML5 tags, which means you can't directly format these tags with CSS. If you're really worried about supporting Internet Explorer 8, either skip the HTML5 tags described on page 8 for structuring your HTML and stick to <div> tags, or use the quick JavaScript solution described in the box on page 12.

HTML to Forget

CSS lets you write simpler HTML for one big reason: There are many old HTML tags that you should abandon (if you're still using them). The <font> tag is the most glaring example. Its sole purpose is to add a color, size and font to text. It doesn't do anything to make the page's structure more understandable.

Here's a list of tags and attributes you can easily replace with CSS:

- **Ditch <font> for controlling the display of text.** CSS does a much better job with text. (See Chapter 6 for text-formatting techniques.)

- **Don't use the <b> and <i> tags to emphasize text.** If you want text to really be emphasized, use the <strong> tag, which browsers normally display as bold. For a slightly less emphatic point, use the <em> tag, which browsers display as italic. You can use CSS to make any text on a page italicized, bolded, or both.

While HTML 4 tried to phase the <b> and <i> tags out, HTML5 has brought them back. In HTML5 the <b> tag is meant to merely make text bold without adding any meaning to that text (that is, you just want the text to be bold looking but you don't want people to treat that text like you're shouting it). Likewise, the <i> tag is used for italicizing text, but not emphasizing its meaning.

NOTE To italicize a publication's title, the <cite> tag kills two birds with one stone. It puts the title in italics *and* tags it as a cited work for search engines' benefit. Of course, CSS lets you do anything you want with the tag, so if you want to reference a publication and not italicize it, you can still use the <cite> tag.

- **Skip the** <table> **tag for page layout.** Use tables only to display information like spreadsheets, schedules, and charts. As you'll see in Part Three, you can do all your layout with CSS for much less time and code than the table-tag tango.

- **Don't abuse the**
 tag. If you grew up using the <br> tag to insert a line break without creating a new paragraph, then you're in for a treat. (Browsers automatically—and sometimes infuriatingly—insert a bit of space between paragraphs, including between headers and <p> tags. In the past, designers used elaborate workarounds to avoid paragraph spacing they didn't want, like replacing a single <p> tag with a bunch of line breaks and using a <font> tag to make the first line of the paragraph *look like* a headline.) Using CSS's margin controls, you can easily set the amount of space you want to see between paragraphs, headers, and other block-level elements.

NOTE In Chapter 5, you'll learn about a technique called a "CSS Reset," which eliminates the gaps browsers normally insert between paragraphs and other tags (see page 109).

As a general rule, adding attributes to tags that set colors, borders, background images, or alignment—including attributes that let you format a table's colors, backgrounds, and borders—is pure old-school HTML. So is using alignment properties to position images and center text in paragraphs and table cells. Instead, look to CSS to control text placement (page 164), borders (page 194), backgrounds (page 231), and image alignment (page 229).

UP TO SPEED

Validate Your Web Pages

HTML follows certain rules: For example, the <html> tag wraps around the other tags on a page, and the <title> tag needs to appear within the <head> tag. It's easy to forget these rules or simply make a typo. Incorrect (or *invalid*, as the pros would say) HTML causes problems like making your page look different in different web browsers. More importantly, even valid CSS may not work as expected with invalid HTML. Fortunately, there are tools for checking whether the HTML in your web pages is correctly written.

The easiest way to check—that is, *validate*—your pages is on the W3C's website at *http://validator.w3.org* (see Figure 1-4). The W3C, or World Wide Web Consortium, is the organization responsible for determining the standards for many Web technologies and languages, including HTML and CSS. If the W3C validator finds any errors in your page, it tells you what they are.

The Web Developer extension for Chrome, Firefox, and Opera (*http://chrispederick.com/work/web-developer*) provides a quick way to test a page in the W3C validator.

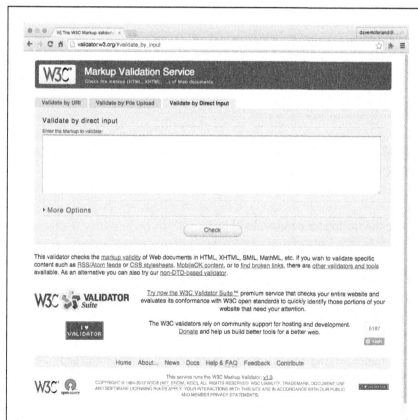

FIGURE 1-4

The W3C HTML validator located at http://validator. w3.org lets you quickly make sure the HTML in a page is sound. You can point the validator to an already existing page on the Web, upload an HTML file from your computer, or just paste the HTML of a web page into a form box and then click the Check button.

Tips to Guide Your Way

It's always good to have a map to get the lay of the land. If you're still not sure how to use HTML to create well-structured web pages, then here are a few tips to get you started:

- Use headings to indicate the relative importance of text. Again, think *outline*. When two headings have equal importance in the topic of your page, use the same level header on both. If one is less important or a subtopic of the other, then use the next-level header. For example, follow an <h2> with an <h3> tag (see Figure 1-5). In general, it's good to use headings in order and try not to skip heading numbers. For example, don't follow an <h2> tag with an <h5> tag.

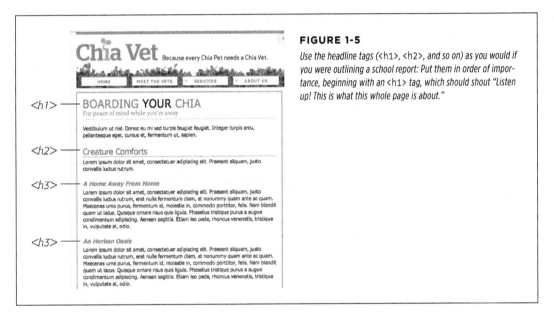

FIGURE 1-5

Use the headline tags (<h1>, <h2>, and so on) as you would if you were outlining a school report: Put them in order of importance, beginning with an <h1> tag, which should shout "Listen up! This is what this whole page is about."

- Use the <p> tag for paragraphs of text.

- Use unordered lists (<ul>) when you've got a list of several related items, such as navigation links, headlines, or a set of tips like these.

- Use numbered lists (<ol>) to indicate steps in a process or define the order of a set of items. The tutorials in this book are a good example, as is a list of rankings like "Top 10 websites popular with monks."

- To create a glossary of terms and their definitions or descriptions, use the <dl> (definition list) tag in conjunction with the <dt> (definition term) and <dd> (definition description) tags. (For an example of how to use this combo, visit *http://htmldog.com/guides/html/intermediate/definitionlists/*.)

- If you want to include a quotation like a snippet of text from another website, a movie review, or just some wise saying of your grandfather's, try the `<block-quote>` tag for long passages or the `<q>` tag to place a short quote within a longer paragraph, like this:

  ```
  <p>Mark Twain is said to have written <q>The coldest winter I ever spent
  was a summer in San Francisco</q>. Unfortunately, he never actually wrote
  that famous quote.</p>
  ```

- Take advantage of obscure tags like the `<cite>` tag for referencing a book title, newspaper article, or website, and the `<address>` tag to identify and supply contact information for the author of a page (great for a copyright notice).

- As explained in full on page 3, steer clear of any tag or attribute aimed solely at changing the appearance of a text or image. CSS, as you'll see, can do it all.

- When there isn't an HTML tag that fits the bill, but you want to identify an element on a page or a bunch of elements on a page so you can apply a distinctive look, use the `<div>` and `<span>` tags (see page 7). You'll get more advice on how to use these in later chapters.

- Don't overuse `<div>` tags. Some web designers think all they need are `<div>` tags, ignoring tags that might be more appropriate. For example, to create a navigation bar, you could add a `<div>` tag to a page and fill it with a bunch of links. A better approach would be to use a bulleted list (`<ul>` tag), After all, a navigation bar is really just a list of links. As discussed on page 8, HTML5 provides several new tags that can take the place of the `<div>` tag, like the `<article>`, `<section>`, and `<footer>` tags. For a navigation bar, you could use the HTML5 `<nav>` tag.

- Remember to close tags. The opening `<p>` tag needs its partner in crime (the closing **`</p>`** tag), as do all other tags, except the few self-closers like `<br>` and `<img>`.

- Validate your pages with the W3C validator (see Figure 1-4 and the box on page 15). Poorly written or typo-ridden HTML causes many weird browser errors.

◼ The Importance of the Doctype

HTML follows certain rules. You tell a web browser which version of HTML you're using (and which rules you're following) by including what's called a *doctype declaration* at the beginning of a web page. This doctype declaration is the first line in the HTML file, and defines what version of HTML you're using (such as HTML5 or HTML 4.01 Transitional).

If you mistype the doctype declaration or leave it out, you can throw most browsers into an altered state called *quirks mode*. Quirks mode is browser manufacturers' attempt to make their software behave like browsers did circa 1999 (in the Netscape 4 and Internet Explorer 5 days). If a modern browser encounters a page that's missing the correct doctype, then it thinks, "Gee, this page must have been written a long time ago, in an HTML editor far, far away. I'll pretend I'm a really old browser and display the page just as one of those buggy old browsers would display it." That's why, without a correct doctype, your lovingly CSS-styled web pages may not look as they should, according to current standards. If you unwittingly view your web page in quirks mode when checking it in a browser, you may end up trying to fix display problems that are related to an incorrect doctype and not the incorrect use of HTML or CSS.

NOTE For more (read: technical) information on quirks mode, visit *www.quirksmode.org/css/quirksmode. html* and *https://developer.mozilla.org/en-US/docs/Quirks_Mode_and_Standards_Mode*.

Fortunately, it's easy to get the doctype right. All you need to know is what version of HTML you're using. Almost everyone is using HTML5 now, and the doctype is simply:

```
<!doctype html>
```

Put this at the top of your HTML file and you're good to go. If you're still using older versions of HTML or XHTML such as HTML 4.01 Transitional and XHTML 1.0 Transitional, then the doctype is a lot more convoluted.

If you're using HTML 4.01 Transitional, for example, type the following doctype declaration at the very beginning of every page you create:

```
<!DOCTYPE HTML PUBLIC "-//W3C//DTD HTML 4.01 Transitional//EN" "http://www.
w3.org/TR/html4/loose.dtd">
```

The doctype declaration for XHTML 1.0 Transitional is similar. It's also necessary to add a little code to the opening <html> tag that's used to identify the file's XML type—in this case, it's XHTML—like this:

```
<!DOCTYPE html PUBLIC "-//W3C//DTD XHTML 1.0 Transitional//EN" "http://www.
w3.org/TR/xhtml1/DTD/xhtml1-transitional.dtd">
<html xmlns="http://www.w3.org/1999/xhtml">
```

If this entire discussion is making your head ache and your eyes slowly shut, keep your life simple by using the HTML5 doctype. It's short, easy to remember, works in all browsers, and what almost all new web pages use. You can use this doctype even if you don't touch any of the new HTML5 tags.

NOTE Most visual web page tools like Dreamweaver add a doctype declaration whenever you create a new web page, and many HTML-savvy text editors have shortcuts for adding doctypes.

■ How CSS Works

Now that you have a solid background on writing HTML for CSS, you're ready for what this book is all about. CSS is the styling language used to format HTML-based web pages. While HTML provides the page's structure, CSS works hand in hand with the web browser to make HTML *look* good on screen.

For example, you might use HTML to turn a phrase into a top-level heading, indicating that it introduces the content on the rest of the page. You'd use CSS to format that heading with, say, big and bold red type and position it 50 pixels from the left edge of the window. In CSS, that text formatting is a *style*—a rule describing the appearance of a particular portion of a web page. A *style sheet* is a set of these styles.

You can create styles to work with any HTML tag. For example, you can create styles specifically to format the images on a page. For instance, a style can align an image along the page's right edge, surround the image with a colorful border, and place a 50-pixel margin between the image and the surrounding text.

The web browser applies the styles you create to text, images, headings, and other page elements. For example, you can create a style that applies to a single paragraph on your page to instantly change the text's size, color, and font within that paragraph. You can create styles that apply to specific HTML tags, so, for example, a browser displays every first-level heading (<h1> tag) in your site in the same way, no matter where those headings appear. You can even create styles that apply only to specific tags that you've marked up in a special way in the HTML.

Creating styles is all about determining what you want to style (a single image, every image, every other item in a list, and so on) and how you want that selected element or elements to look. In fact, determining what you want to style is such a big topic, Chapters 3, 4, and 5 of this book are devoted to the subject. All of the different ways you can make page elements look is an even bigger topic, and is covered in Part Two.

The Different Flavors of CSS

Like operating systems and iPhone models, CSS spins off new versions continuously (well, maybe not as frequently as iPhones). CSS1, introduced in 1996, laid the groundwork for Cascading Style Sheets. The basic structure of a style, the selector concept (Chapter 3), and most of the CSS properties in this book were all in that very first version.

CSS2 added new features, including the ability to target your CSS to different printers, monitors, and other devices. CSS2 also added new selectors and the ability to precisely position elements on a web page.

CSS2.1, which is the currently accepted standard and implemented in all browsers, incorporates all of CSS1, adds several new properties, and corrects a few problems with the CSS2 guidelines. It wasn't a radical change from version 2, and most web browsers have adapted to the new rules just fine, thank you.

However, CSS3 has been around (and parts of it implemented in most browsers) for several years now. Unlike previous versions of CSS, CSS3 isn't actually one single standard. As CSS has grown in complexity, the W3C has split CSS up into separate modules—the Selectors module, the Values and Units module, the Box Alignment module, and so on. Since each module can develop independently of the others, there isn't any single standard called "CSS3." In fact, level 3 of the Selectors module is complete, and work on level 4 is underway.

In other words, what's known as CSS3 is really just a loose collection of different modules at various states of completion. Browser manufacturers have already incorporated many parts of these modules, but other modules aren't supported in many browsers. In the future, there won't be any CSS4; there will just be new versions of the different modules, each at a different level of work.

For these reasons, this book covers the core CSS2.1 (which has simply been rolled over into the various modules of CSS3), as well as the most exciting, popular, and widely supported new CSS properties.

Creating Styles and Style Sheets

E ven the most complex and beautiful websites, like the one in Figure 2-1, start with a single CSS style. As you add multiple styles and style sheets, you can develop fully formed websites that inspire designers and amaze visitors. Whether you're a CSS novice or a Style Sheet Samurai, you need to obey a few basic rules about how to create styles and style sheets. In this chapter, you'll start at square one, learning the basics of creating and using styles and style sheets.

> **TIP** Some people learn better by doing rather than reading. If you'd like to try your hand at creating styles and style sheets first and then come back here to read up on what you just did, turn to page 27 for a hands-on tutorial.

■ Anatomy of a Style

A single style defining the look of one element on a page is a pretty basic beast. It's essentially just a rule that tells a web browser how to format something on a web page—turn a headline blue, draw a red border around a photo, or create a 150-pixel-wide sidebar box to hold a list of links. If a style could talk, it would say something like, "Hey Browser, make *this* look like *that*." A style is, in fact, made up of two parts: the web page element that the browser formats (the *selector*) and the actual formatting instructions (the *declaration block*). For example, a selector can be a headline, a paragraph of text, a photo, and so on. Declaration blocks can turn that text blue, add a red border around a paragraph, position the photo in the center of the page—the possibilities are endless.

FIGURE 2-1

Every web page, no matter how complex-looking, is built using the basic building blocks of CSS. The body for this website (www.freshbooks.com), for example, includes a simple style:

```
body {
    font-family:
"Franklin-Book",
Helvetica, Arial,
sans-serif;

    color: #222;
}
```

NOTE Technical types often follow the lead of the W3C and call CSS styles *rules*. This book uses the terms "style" and "rule" interchangeably.

Of course, CSS styles can't communicate in nice clear English like the previous paragraph. They have their own language. For example, to set a standard font color and font size for all paragraphs on a web page, you'd write the following:

```
p { color: red; font-size: 1.5em; }
```

This style simply says, "Make the text in all paragraphs—marked with <p> tags—red and 1.5 ems tall." (An *em* is a unit of measurement that's based on a browser's normal text size. More on that in Chapter 6.) As Figure 2-2 illustrates, even a simple style like this example contains several components:

- **Selector.** As described earlier, the selector tells a web browser which element or elements on a page to style—like a headline, paragraph, image, or link. In Figure 2-2, the p selector refers to the <p> tag. This selector makes web browsers format all <p> tags using the formatting directions in this style. With the wide range of selectors that CSS offers and a little creativity, you'll be able to pinpoint any item on a page and format it just the way you want. (The next chapter covers selectors in depth.)

- **Declaration Block.** The code following the selector includes all the formatting options you want to apply to the selector. The block begins with an opening brace ({) and ends with a closing brace (}).

- **Declaration.** Between the opening and closing braces of a declaration block, you add one or more *declarations*, or formatting instructions. Every declaration has two parts: a *property* and a *value*. A colon separates the property name and its value, and the whole declaration ends with a semicolon.

- **Property.** CSS offers a wide range of formatting options, called *properties*. A property is a word—or a few hyphenated words—indicating a certain style effect. Most properties have straightforward names like font-size, margin-top, and text-align. For example, the background-color property sets—you guessed it—a background color. You'll learn about oodles of CSS properties throughout this book. You must add a colon after the property name to separate it from the value.

> **TIP** Appendix A: CSS Property Reference (page 637) has a handy glossary of CSS properties.

- **Value.** Finally, you get to express your creative genius by assigning a *value* to a CSS property—by making a background blue, red, purple, or chartreuse, for example. As upcoming chapters explain, different CSS properties require specific types of values—a color (like red, or #FF0000), a length (like 18px, 200%, or 5em), a URL (like *images/background.gif*), or a specific keyword (like top, center, or bottom).

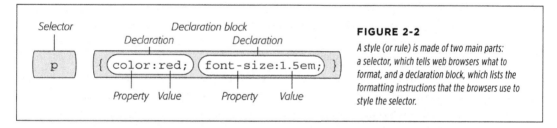

FIGURE 2-2

A style (or rule) is made of two main parts: a selector, which tells web browsers what to format, and a declaration block, which lists the formatting instructions that the browsers use to style the selector.

You don't need to write a style on a single line, as pictured in Figure 2-2. Many styles have multiple formatting properties, so you can make them easier to read by breaking them up into multiple lines. For example, you may want to put the selector and opening brace on the first line, each declaration on its own line, and the closing brace by itself on the last line, like so:

```
p {
    color: red;
    font-size: 1.5em;
}
```

Web browsers ignore spaces and tabs, so feel free to add them to make your CSS more readable. For example, it's helpful to indent properties, with either a tab or a couple of spaces, to visibly separate the selector from the declarations, making it easy to tell which is which. In addition, putting one space between the colon and the property value is optional but adds to the readability of the style. In fact, you can put as much white space between the two as you want. For example, `color:red`, `color: red`, and `color : red` all work.

> **NOTE** Don't forget to end each property/value pair with a semicolon:
>
>   color: red;
>
> Leaving off that semicolon can trip up browsers, breaking your style sheet and ruining the look of your web page. Don't worry, this mistake is very common—just make sure you use a CSS validator, as described in the box on page 27.

Understanding Style Sheets

Of course, a single style won't transform a web page into a work of art. It may make your paragraphs red, but to infuse your websites with great design, you need many different styles. A collection of CSS styles comprises a *style sheet*. A style sheet can be one of two types—*internal* or *external*, depending on whether the style information is located in the web page itself or in a separate file linked to the web page.

Internal or External—How to Choose

Most of the time, external style sheets are the way to go, since they make building web pages easier and updating websites faster. An external style sheet collects all your style information in a single file that you then link to a web page with just a single line of code. You can attach the same external style sheet to every page in your website, providing a unified design. It also makes a complete site makeover as easy as editing a single text file.

On the receiving end, external style sheets help web pages load faster. When you use an external style sheet, your web pages can contain only basic HTML—no byte-hogging HTML tables or <font> tags and no internal CSS style code. Furthermore, when a web browser downloads an external style sheet, it stores the file on your visitor's computer (in a behind-the-scenes folder called a *cache*) for quick access. When your visitor hops to other pages on the site that use the same external style sheet, there's no need for the browser to download the style sheet again. The browser simply downloads the requested HTML file and pulls the external style sheet from its cache—a significant savings in download time.

> **NOTE** When you're working on your website and previewing it in a browser, the cache can work against you. See the box on the next page for a workaround.

Don't Get Caught in the Cache

A browser's cache is a great speed-boost for Web surfers. Whenever the cache downloads and stores a frequently used file—like an external CSS file or an image—it saves precious moments traveling the highways of the Internet. Instead of re-downloading the next time it needs the same file, the browser can go straight to the new stuff—like a yet-to-be-viewed page or graphic.

But what's good for your visitors isn't always good for you. Because the web browser caches and recalls downloaded external CSS files, you can often get tripped up as you work on a site design. Say you're working on a page that uses an external style sheet, and you preview the page in a browser. Something doesn't look quite right, so you return to your web editor and change the external CSS file. When you return to the web browser and reload the page, the change you just made doesn't appear! You've just been caught by the cache. When you reload a web page, browsers don't always reload the external style sheet, so you may not be seeing the latest and greatest version of your styles.

To get around this snafu, you can *force reload* a page (which also reloads all linked files) by pressing the Ctrl (⌘) key and clicking the browser's Reload button; Ctrl+F5 also works for Chrome and Internet Explorer; Ctrl+Shift+R (⌘-Shift-R) is Firefox's keyboard shortcut; and Ctrl+R (⌘-R) works for both Safari and Chrome for the Mac.

■ Internal Style Sheets

An internal style sheet is a collection of styles that's part of the web page's code. It always appears between opening and closing HTML <style> tags in the page's <head> portion. Here's an example:

```
<style>
h1 {
  color: #FF7643;
  font-family: Arial;
}
p {
  color: red;
  font-size: 1.5em;
}
</style>
</head>
<body>

<!-- The rest of your page follows... -->
```

NOTE You can place the `<style>` tag and its styles anywhere after the `<title>` tag in the page's head, but web designers usually place them right before the closing `</head>` tag, as shown here. However, if you also use JavaScript, the style sheet should go before the JavaScript. Many JavaScript programs rely on CSS, so by adding your CSS first, you can make sure the JavaScript program has all the information it needs to get its job done.

The `<style>` tag is HTML, not CSS. But its job is to tell the web browser that the information contained within the tags is CSS code and not HTML. Creating an internal style sheet is as simple as typing one or more styles between the `<style>` tags.

Internal style sheets are easy to add to a web page and provide an immediate visual boost to your HTML. But they aren't the most efficient method for designing an entire website composed of many web pages. For one thing, you need to copy and paste the internal style sheet into each page of your site—a time-consuming chore that adds bandwidth-hogging code to each page.

But internal style sheets are even more of a hassle when you want to update the look of a site. For example, say you want to change the `<h1>` tag, which you originally decided should appear as large, green, bold type. But now you want small, blue type in the Courier typeface. Using internal style sheets, you'd need to edit *every* page. Who has that kind of time? Fortunately, there's a simple solution to this dilemma—external style sheets.

NOTE It's also possible to add styling information to an individual HTML tag without using a style sheet. The tutorial on page 28 shows you how to perform that maneuver by using an *inline* style. You shouldn't normally use inline styles to design your web pages; however, many JavaScript programmers do use inline styles when dynamically adding HTML content to a web page, so it's good to know how inline styles work and how to create them.

External Style Sheets

An external style sheet is nothing more than a text file containing all your CSS rules. It never contains any HTML code—so don't include the `<style>` tag in an external style sheet file. In addition, always end the file name with the extension .css. You can name the file whatever you like, but it pays to be descriptive. Use *global.css*, *site.css*, or simply *styles.css*, for example, to indicate a style sheet used by every page on the site, or use *form.css* to name a file containing styles used to make a web form look good.

Validate Your CSS

Just as you should make sure you've correctly written the HTML in your web pages using the W3C HTML validator (see the box on page 15), you should also check your CSS code to make sure it's kosher. The W3C provides an online tool for CSS checking as well: *http://jigsaw.w3.org/css-validator*. It operates just like the HTML validator: You can type the URL of a web page (or even just the address to an external CSS file), upload a CSS file, or copy and paste CSS code into a web form and submit it for validation.

It's easy to make a typo when writing CSS, and one small mistake can throw all of your carefully planned designs out of whack. When your CSS-infused web page doesn't look as you expect, a simple CSS error may be the cause. The W3C CSS validator is a good first step when troubleshooting your designs.

TIP If you have a page with an internal style sheet but want to use an external style sheet, then just cut all of the code between the `<style>` tags (without the tags themselves). Then create a new text file and paste the CSS into the file. Save the file with a .css extension—*styles.css*, for example—and link it to your page, as described next.

Once you create an external style sheet, you must connect it to the web page you wish to format. To do so, use the HTML `<link>` tag like this:

```
<link rel="stylesheet" href="css/styles.css">
```

The `<link>` tag has two required attributes:

- **rel="stylesheet"** indicates the type of link—in this case, a link to a style sheet.

- **href** points to the location of the external CSS file on the site. The value of this property is a URL and will vary depending on where you keep your CSS file. It works the same as the **src** attribute you use when adding an image to a page or the **href** attribute of a link pointing to another page.

TIP You can attach multiple style sheets to a web page by adding multiple `<link>` tags, each pointing to a different style sheet file. This technique is one way to organize your CSS styles, as you can see in Chapter 18.

■ Tutorial: Creating Your First Styles

The rest of this chapter takes you through the basic steps for adding inline styles, writing CSS rules, and creating internal and external style sheets. As you work through this book, you'll work through various CSS designs, from simple design elements to complete CSS-enabled web page layouts. To get started, download the tutorial files from *https://github.com/sawmac/css_mm_4e*. Download the zip archive containing the files. Each chapter's files are in a separate folder, named *02* (for Chapter 2), *03* (for Chapter 3), and so on.

NOTE In addition to a folder for each chapter's tutorial, you'll find another folder with the completed tutorial. For example, the *02_finished* folder contains the completed files for this chapter's tutorial. You can use this finished example if you get stuck and want to compare what you've written with the finished product.

Next, launch your favorite web page–editing software, whether it's a simple text editor like Notepad or TextEdit or a more full-featured editor like Sublime Text, Atom, or Dreamweaver.

Creating an Inline Style

When you type a CSS rule directly into a page's HTML, you're creating an *inline* style. Inline styles offer none of the time- and bandwidth-saving benefits of external style sheets, so the pros hardly ever use them. Still, in a pinch, if you absolutely must change the styling on a single element on a single page, then you may want to resort to an inline style. (For example, when creating HTML-formatted email messages, it's best to use inline styles. That's the only way to get CSS to work in Gmail, for one thing.) And if you do, you at least want the style to work properly. The important thing is to carefully place the style within the tag you want to format. Here's an example that shows you exactly how to do it:

1. **In your web page–editing program, open the file *02→index.html*.**

   This simple-but-elegant HTML5 file contains a couple of different headings, a few paragraphs, and a copyright notice inside an <address> tag. You'll start by creating an inline style for the <h1> tag.

2. **Click inside the opening <h1> tag and type style="color: #6A94CC;".**

   The tag should look like this:

   ```
   <h1 style="color: #6A94CC;">
   ```

   The style attribute is HTML, not CSS, so you use the equal sign after it and enclose all of the CSS code inside quotes. Only the stuff inside the quotes is CSS. In this case, you've added a property named color—which affects the color of text—and you've set that property to #6A94CC, a hexadecimal code for defining a color that's blue. (You'll learn more about coloring text on page 147.) The colon separates the property name from the property value that you want. Next, you'll check the results in a web browser.

3. **Open the *index.html* page in a web browser.**

   For example, start up your favorite web browser and choose File→Open File (or press Ctrl+O [⌘-O] and select the *index.html* file in the *02 tutorial* folder from your computer; or just drag the file from the desktop—or wherever you've saved the tutorial files—into an open browser window). Many HTML editors also include a "Preview in Browser" function, which, with a simple keyboard shortcut or menu option, opens the page in a web browser. It's worth checking your program's documentation to see if it includes this time-saving feature.

When you view the page in a browser, the headline is now blue. Inline styles can include more than one CSS property. You'll add another property next.

4. **Return to your HTML editor, click after the semicolon following** #6A94CC, **and then type** font-size: 3em;.

The semicolon separates two different property settings. The <h1> tag should look like this:

```
<h1 style="color: #6A94CC; font-size: 3em;">
```

5. **Preview the page in a web browser. For example, click your browser window's Reload button (but make sure you've saved the HTML file first).**

The headline is now much larger. And you've had a taste of how labor-intensive inline styles are. Making all the <h1> headings on a page look like this one could take days of typing and add acres of code to your HTML files.

6. **Return to your page editor and delete the entire style property, which returns the heading tag back to its normal** <h1>.

Next, you'll create a style sheet within a web page. (You'll find a finished version of this part of the tutorial in the *02_finished* folder in a file named *inline-style. html*.)

Creating an Internal Style Sheet

A better approach than inline styles is using a style sheet that contains multiple CSS rules to control multiple elements of a page. In this section, you'll create a style that affects all top-level headings in one fell swoop. This single rule automatically formats every <h1> tag on the page.

1. **With the file *index.html* open in your text editor, click directly after the closing** </title> **tag. Then hit Enter and type <style>.**

The HTML should now look like the following (the stuff you've added is in bold):

```
<title>CSS:The Missing Manual -- Chapter 2</title>
<style>
</head>
```

The opening <style> tag marks the beginning of the style sheet. It's always a good idea to close a tag right after you type the opening tag, since it's so easy to forget this step once you jump into writing your CSS. In this case, you'll close the <style> tag before adding any CSS.

2. **Press Enter twice and type </style>.**

Now, you'll add a CSS selector that marks the beginning of your first style.

3. **Click between the opening and closing** <style> **tags and type h1 {.**

The h1 indicates the tag to which the web browser should apply the upcoming style.

The weird bracket thingy after the h1 is called an *opening brace*, and it marks the beginning of the CSS properties for this style. In other words, it says, "The fun stuff comes right after me." As with closing tags, it's a good idea to type the closing brace of a style before actually adding any style properties.

4. **Press Enter twice and type a single closing brace:** }.

   As the partner of the opening brace you typed in the last step, this brace's job is to tell the web browser, "This particular CSS rule ends here." Now time for the fun stuff.

5. **Click in the empty line between the two braces. Hit the Tab key, and type color: #6A94CC;.**

   You've typed the same style property as the inline version—color—and set it to #6A94CC;. The final semicolon marks the end of the property declaration.

NOTE Technically, you don't have to put the style property on its own line, but it's a good idea. With one property per line, it's a lot easier to quickly scan a style sheet and see all the properties for each style. Also, the tab is another helpful visual organizing technique (you can also insert a few spaces instead). The indentation makes it easy to discern all of your rules at a glance, since the selectors (like h1 here) line up along the left edge, with the properties spaced a bit out of the way.

---

6. **Press Enter again and add two additional properties, like so:**

   ```
   font-size: 3em;
   margin: 0;
   ```

   Make sure you don't leave off the semicolon at the end of each line; otherwise, the CSS won't display correctly in a browser.

   Each of these properties adds a different visual effect to the headline. The first assigns a size and font to the text, while the second removes space from around the headline. Part Two of this book covers all these properties in detail.

   Congratulations—you've just created an internal style sheet. The code you've added should look like the bolded text:

   ```
   <title>CSS: The Missing Manual -- Chapter 2</title>
   <style>
   h1 {
    color: #6A94CC;
    font-size: 3em;
    margin: 0;
   }
   </style>
   </head>
   ```

7. **Save the page and preview it in a web browser.**

You can preview the page by opening it in a web browser as described in step 3 on page 28, or, if the page is still open in a browser window, just click the Reload button.

Next you'll add another style.

NOTE Always remember to add the closing `</style>` tag at the end of an internal style sheet. When you don't, a web browser displays the CSS style code followed by a completely unformatted web page—or no web page at all.

---

8. **Back in your text-editing program, click after the closing brace of the** h1 **style you just created, press Enter, and then add the following rule:**

```
p {
    font-size: 1.25em;
    color: #616161;
    line-height: 150%;
    margin-top: 10px;
    margin-left: 60px;
}
```

This rule formats every paragraph on the page. Don't worry too much right now about what each of these CSS properties is doing; later chapters cover these properties in depth. For now, just practice typing the code correctly and get a feel for how to add CSS to a page.

9. **Preview the page in a browser.**

The page is starting to shape up and should look like Figure 2-3. You can see what stylistic direction the page is headed in. You can see a completed version of this tutorial by opening the *02_finished→internal-stylesheet.html* file.

The process you've just worked through is CSS in a nutshell: Start with an HTML page, add a style sheet, and create CSS rules to make the page look great. In the next part of this tutorial, you'll see how to work more efficiently, using external style sheets.

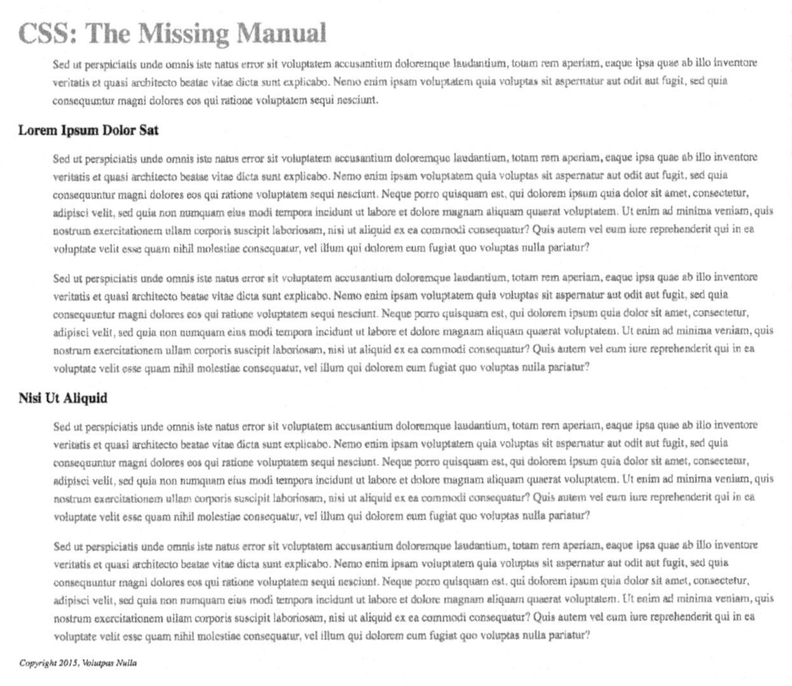

CSS: The Missing Manual

Sed ut perspiciatis unde omnis iste natus error sit voluptatem accusantium doloremque laudantium, totam rem aperiam, eaque ipsa quae ab illo inventore veritatis et quasi architecto beatae vitae dicta sunt explicabo. Nemo enim ipsam voluptatem quia voluptas sit aspernatur aut odit aut fugit, sed quia consequuntur magni dolores eos qui ratione voluptatem sequi nesciunt.

Lorem Ipsum Dolor Sat

Sed ut perspiciatis unde omnis iste natus error sit voluptatem accusantium doloremque laudantium, totam rem aperiam, eaque ipsa quae ab illo inventore veritatis et quasi architecto beatae vitae dicta sunt explicabo. Nemo enim ipsam voluptatem quia voluptas sit aspernatur aut odit aut fugit, sed quia consequuntur magni dolores eos qui ratione voluptatem sequi nesciunt. Neque porro quisquam est, qui dolorem ipsum quia dolor sit amet, consectetur, adipisci velit, sed quia non numquam eius modi tempora incidunt ut labore et dolore magnam aliquam quaerat voluptatem. Ut enim ad minima veniam, quis nostrum exercitationem ullam corporis suscipit laboriosam, nisi ut aliquid ex ea commodi consequatur? Quis autem vel eum iure reprehenderit qui in ea voluptate velit esse quam nihil molestiae consequatur, vel illum qui dolorem eum fugiat quo voluptas nulla pariatur?

Sed ut perspiciatis unde omnis iste natus error sit voluptatem accusantium doloremque laudantium, totam rem aperiam, eaque ipsa quae ab illo inventore veritatis et quasi architecto beatae vitae dicta sunt explicabo. Nemo enim ipsam voluptatem quia voluptas sit aspernatur aut odit aut fugit, sed quia consequuntur magni dolores eos qui ratione voluptatem sequi nesciunt. Neque porro quisquam est, qui dolorem ipsum quia dolor sit amet, consectetur, adipisci velit, sed quia non numquam eius modi tempora incidunt ut labore et dolore magnam aliquam quaerat voluptatem. Ut enim ad minima veniam, quis nostrum exercitationem ullam corporis suscipit laboriosam, nisi ut aliquid ex ea commodi consequatur? Quis autem vel eum iure reprehenderit qui in ea voluptate velit esse quam nihil molestiae consequatur, vel illum qui dolorem eum fugiat quo voluptas nulla pariatur?

Nisi Ut Aliquid

Sed ut perspiciatis unde omnis iste natus error sit voluptatem accusantium doloremque laudantium, totam rem aperiam, eaque ipsa quae ab illo inventore veritatis et quasi architecto beatae vitae dicta sunt explicabo. Nemo enim ipsam voluptatem quia voluptas sit aspernatur aut odit aut fugit, sed quia consequuntur magni dolores eos qui ratione voluptatem sequi nesciunt. Neque porro quisquam est, qui dolorem ipsum quia dolor sit amet, consectetur, adipisci velit, sed quia non numquam eius modi tempora incidunt ut labore et dolore magnam aliquam quaerat voluptatem. Ut enim ad minima veniam, quis nostrum exercitationem ullam corporis suscipit laboriosam, nisi ut aliquid ex ea commodi consequatur? Quis autem vel eum iure reprehenderit qui in ea voluptate velit esse quam nihil molestiae consequatur, vel illum qui dolorem eum fugiat quo voluptas nulla pariatur?

Sed ut perspiciatis unde omnis iste natus error sit voluptatem accusantium doloremque laudantium, totam rem aperiam, eaque ipsa quae ab illo inventore veritatis et quasi architecto beatae vitae dicta sunt explicabo. Nemo enim ipsam voluptatem quia voluptas sit aspernatur aut odit aut fugit, sed quia consequuntur magni dolores eos qui ratione voluptatem sequi nesciunt. Neque porro quisquam est, qui dolorem ipsum quia dolor sit amet, consectetur, adipisci velit, sed quia non numquam eius modi tempora incidunt ut labore et dolore magnam aliquam quaerat voluptatem. Ut enim ad minima veniam, quis nostrum exercitationem ullam corporis suscipit laboriosam, nisi ut aliquid ex ea commodi consequatur? Quis autem vel eum iure reprehenderit qui in ea voluptate velit esse quam nihil molestiae consequatur, vel illum qui dolorem eum fugiat quo voluptas nulla pariatur?

Copyright 2015, Voluptas Nulla

FIGURE 2-3

CSS easily formats text in creative ways, letting you change fonts, text colors, font sizes, and a lot more, as you'll see in Chapter 6.

Creating an External Style Sheet

Since it groups all of your styles at the top of the page, an internal style sheet is a lot easier to create and maintain than the inline style you created a few pages ago. Also, an internal style sheet lets you format any number of instances of a tag on a page, like every <p> tag, by typing one simple rule. But an external style sheet gets even better—it can store all of the styles for an *entire website*. Editing one style in the external style sheet updates the whole site. In this section, you'll take the styles you created in the previous section and put them in an external style sheet.

1. **In your text-editing program, create a new file and save it as *styles.css* in the same folder as the web page you've been working on.**

   External style sheet files end with the extension .css. The file name *styles.css* indicates that the styles contained in the file apply throughout the site. (But you can use any file name you like, as long as it ends with the .css extension.)

   Start by adding a new style to the style sheet.

2. **Type the following rule into the *styles.css* file:**

```
html {
  padding-top: 25px;
  background-image: url(images/bg_page.png);
}
```

This rule applies to the HTML tag—the tag that surrounds all other HTML tags on the page. The padding-top property adds space between the top of the tag and the content that goes inside it. In other words, what you just typed will add 25 pixels of space between the top of the browser window and the page's content. The background-image adds a graphic file to the page's background. The CSS background-image property can display the graphic in many different ways—in this case, the graphic will tile seamlessly from left to right and top to bottom, covering the entire browser window. You can read more about background image properties on page 231.

3. **Add a second rule following after the rule you just typed to the *styles.css* file:**

```
body {
  width: 80%;
  padding: 20px;
  margin: 0 auto;
  border-radius: 10px;
  box-shadow: 10px 10px 10px rgba(0,0,0,.5);
  background-color: #E1EDEB;
}
```

This rule applies to the <body> tag—the tag that holds all the content visible in a web browser window. There are a lot of different things going on in this style, and each of these properties is covered in-depth later in the book. But in a nutshell, this style creates a box for the page's content that's 80 percent the width of the browser window, has a little bit of space inside that moves text from the edge of the box (that's the padding property), and centers the box on the page (that's the margin property, and the particular trick of centering a page's content is discussed in the tutorial starting on page 81). Finally, the box gets a light blue background color and a transparent black drop shadow.

Instead of recreating the work you did earlier, just copy the styles you created in the previous section and paste them into this style sheet.

4. **Open the *index.html* page that you've been working on and copy all of the text inside the** <style> **tags. (Don't copy the** <style> **tags themselves.)**

Copy the style information the same way you'd copy any text. For example, choose Edit→Copy or press Ctrl+C (⌘-C).

5. **In the *styles.css* file, paste the style information by selecting Edit→Paste or pressing Ctrl+V (⌘-V).**

   An external style sheet never contains any HTML—that's why you didn't copy the `<style>` tags.

6. **Save *styles.css*.**

   Now you just need to clean up your old file and link the new style sheet to it.

7. **Return to the *index.html* file in your text editor and delete the `<style>` tags and all the CSS rules you typed in earlier.**

   You no longer need these styles, since they're in the external style sheet you're about to attach. In this tutorial, you'll take a dip into the exciting world of web fonts. You'll learn all about web fonts starting on page 126, but the basic idea is that you can use nearly any font you want in a web page—even a font that your site's visitors don't have installed on their own computers—simply by providing a link to that font file. There are many different ways to use web fonts, but in this example, you'll use Google's web font service.

8. **In the space where the styles used to be (between the closing `</title>` tag and the closing `</head>` tag), type the following:**

   ```
   <link href='http://fonts.googleapis.com/css?family=Varela+Round'
   rel='stylesheet'>
   ```

   Again, don't worry about the details yet. All you need to know for now is that when a web browser encounters this link, it downloads a font named Varela Round from a Google server, and your CSS styles can freely use it.

   Next, you'll link to the external style sheet you created earlier.

9. **After the `<link>` tag you added in the previous step, type:**

   ```
   <link href="styles.css" rel="stylesheet">
   ```

   The `<link>` tag specifies the location of the external style sheet. The `rel` attribute simply lets the browser know that it's linking to a style sheet.

NOTE In this example, the style sheet file is in the same folder as the web page, so using the file's name for the `href` value provides a simple "document-relative" path. If it were in a different folder from the page, then the path would be a bit more complicated. In either case, you'd use a *document-* or *root-relative* path to indicate where the file is. The routine is the same as when you create a link to a web page or set a path to an image file when using the HTML `<img>` tag. (For a brief primer on document- and root-relative links, visit *www.kirupa.com/html5/all_about_file_paths.htm*.)

---

10. **Save the file and preview it in a web browser.**

    You'll see the same text styles for the `<h1>` and `<p>` tags that you created in the internal style sheet on page 29. In addition, there's now a speckled, tan background (the background image you applied on the `<html>` tag), as well as a light-colored, greenish-blue box. That box is the <body> tag, and its width is 80 percent that of the browser window. Try resizing the browser window and notice that the box changes width as well. There's also a drop shadow on the box; you can see through the drop shadow to the speckled background. That's thanks to a special color type—rgba color—that includes a transparency setting (you'll read about it on page 149). Also notice that the corners of the box are rounded, thanks to the border-radius property.

NOTE If the web page doesn't have any formatting (for example, the top headline isn't big, bold, and dusty brown), then you've probably mistyped the code from step 6 or saved the *styles.css* file in a folder other than the one where the *index.html* file is. In this case, just move the *styles.css* into the same folder.

Now, you'll use the web font you linked to in step 8.

11. **In your text editor, return to the *styles.css* file. For the h1 style, add the following two lines:**

    ```
    font-family: 'Varela Round', 'Arial Black', serif;
    font-weight: normal;
    ```

    The finished style should look like this (additions in bold):

    ```
    h1 {
      font-family: 'Varela Round', 'Arial Black', serif;
      font-weight: normal;
      color: #6A94CC;
      font-size: 3em;
      margin: 0;
    }
    ```

    If you preview the page now, you'll see the new font, Varela Round, for the headline.

NOTE If you don't see the new font—it should have rounded tips on the ends of all the letters as pictured in Figure 2-4—then one of a couple of things could be wrong. If you're not connected to the Internet, you won't be able to download the font from Google; second, you may have mistyped either the <link> tag (see step 8 on the previous page), or the font-family declaration (line 2 above).

To demonstrate how useful it can be to keep your styles in their own external file, you'll attach the style sheet to another web page.

12. **Open the file *02→another_page.html*.**

    This page contains some of the same HTML tags—h1, h2, p, and so on—as the other web page you've been working on.

13. **Click after the closing </title> tag and press Enter.**

    You'll now link to both the web font and the external style sheet.

14. **Type the same** `<link>` **tags you did in steps 8 and 9.**

The web page code should look like this (the code you just typed appears in bold):

```
<title>Another Page</title>
    <link href='http://fonts.googleapis.com/css?family=Varela+Round'
rel='stylesheet'>
    <link href="styles.css" rel="stylesheet">
</head>
```

15. **Save the page and preview it in a web browser.**

Ta-da! Just two lines of code added to the web page is enough to instantly transform its appearance. To demonstrate how easy it is to update an external style sheet, you'll do so by editing one style and adding another.

16. **Open the** *styles.css* **file and add the CSS declaration** font-family: "Palatino Linotype", Baskerville, serif; **at the beginning of the** p **style.**

The code should look like this (the bold text is what you've just added):

```
p {
    font-family: "Palatino Linotype", Baskerville, serif;
    font-size: 1.25em;
    color: #616161;
    line-height: 150%;
    margin-top: 10px;
    margin-left: 60px;
}
```

In this case, you're not using a web font, but relying on the site visitor to already have one of the fonts listed on his machine (you'll learn all about using fonts on page 121). Next, create a new rule for the <h2> tag.

17. **Click at the end of the** p **style's closing** }, **press Enter, and add the following rule:**

```
h2 {
    color: #B1967C;
    font-family: 'Varela Round', 'Arial Black', serif;
    font-weight: normal;
    font-size: 2.2em;
    border-bottom: 2px white solid;
    background: url(images/head-icon.png) no-repeat 10px 10px;
    padding: 0 0 2px 60px;
    margin: 0;
}
```

Some of these CSS properties you've encountered already. Some are new—like the border-bottom property for adding a line underneath the headline. And some—like the background property—provide a shortcut for combining several different properties—in this case, the background-image and background-repeat—into a single property. Don't worry about the specifics of these properties; you'll learn them all in great detail in upcoming chapters (Chapter 6 covers font properties; Chapter 8 covers backgrounds; Chapter 7 covers padding and margins).

The styles you've created so far affect mainly tags—the h1, h2, and p—and they affect every instance of those tags. In other words, the p style you created formats every single paragraph on the page. If you want to target just one paragraph, you need to use a different kind of style.

18. **Click at the end of the** h2 **style's closing** }**, press Enter, and add the following rule:**

```
.intro {
  color: #666666;
  font-family: 'Varela Round', Helvetica, sans-serif;
  font-size: 1.2em;
  margin-left: 0;
  margin-bottom: 25px;
}
```

If you preview the *index.html* page in a web browser, you'll see that this new style has no effect...yet. This type of style uses a *class selector*, which formats only the specific tags you apply the class to. In order for this new style to work, you need to edit some HTML.

19. **Save the file** *styles.css* **and switch to the** *index.html* **file in your text editor. Locate the opening** <p> **tag following the** <h1> **tag and add** class="intro" **so the opening tag looks like this:**

```
<p class="intro">
```

You don't have to add a period before the word intro as you did when you created the style in step 18 (you'll learn why in the next chapter). This little extra HTML applies the style to the first paragraph (and only that one paragraph).

Repeat this step for the *another_page.html* file—in other words, add class="intro" to the first **<p>** tag on that page.

20. **Save all the files and preview both the** *index.html* **and** *another_page.html* **files in a web browser.**

Notice that the appearance of both pages changes, based on the simple edits you made to the CSS file. Close your eyes and imagine your website has a thousand pages. Aaaahhhhhhh, the power.

You've got one last change to make. If you look at the very bottom of the page in your browser, you'll see the copyright notice. It's a little small, and it isn't lined up with the paragraphs above. Also, it would look better if it shared the same formatting as the other paragraphs.

21. **In your text editor, return to the *styles.css* file. Locate the style that has the p selector. Type a comma, a space, and address.**

The style looks like this:

```
p, address {
    font-family: "Palatino Linotype", Baskerville, serif;
    font-size: 1.25em;
    color: #616161;
    line-height: 150%;
    margin-top: 10px;
    margin-left: 60px;
}
```

You haven't changed any of the style's properties—you've just changed the selector. In fact, you've just created a group selector. A group selector is a very efficient way to apply the same styling to a bunch of different page elements, and you'll learn more about them on page 49. In this case, the style applies to two tags: the <p> tag and the <address> tag.

22. **Close *styles.css* file and reload the *index.html* file in your web browser.**

The finished page should now look like Figure 2-4. (You'll find a completed version of this tutorial in the *02_finished* folder.)

For added practice, spend a few minutes playing around with the *styles.css* file. Try different values for the style sheet properties. For example, try a different number for the width property of the body style, or try different numbers for the font sizes.

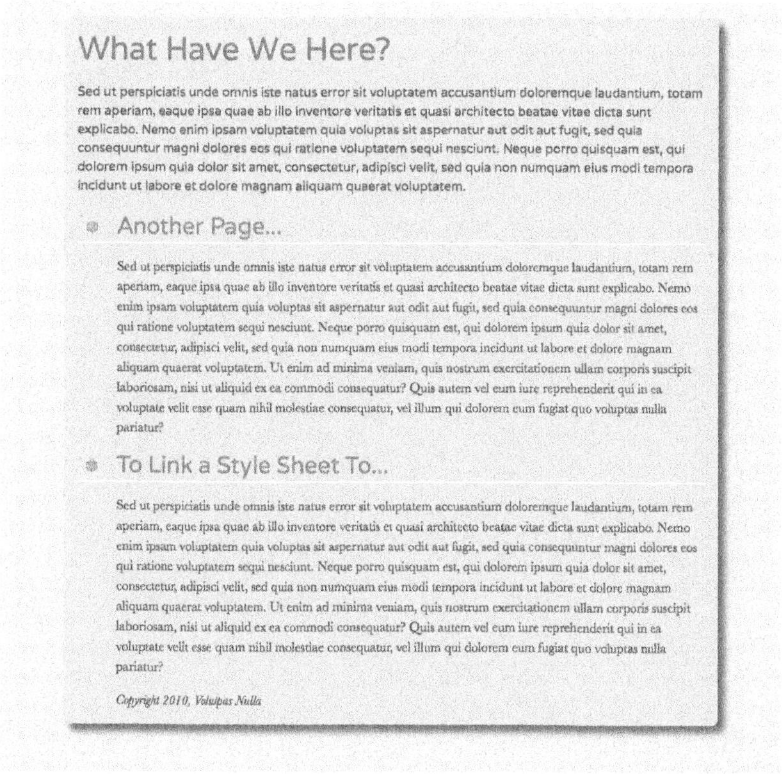

FIGURE 2-4

Using an external style sheet, you can update an entire site's worth of web pages by editing a single CSS file. In addition, by moving all of the CSS code out of an HTML document and into a separate file, you cut down on the file size of your web pages, so they load faster.

Selectors: Identifying What to Style

Every CSS style has two basic parts: a selector and a declaration block. (And if that's news to you, go back and read the previous chapter.) The declaration block carries the formatting properties—text color, font size, and so on—but that's just the pretty stuff. The ability to focus your styling on specific items lies in those first few characters at the beginning of every rule—the selector. By telling CSS *what* you want it to format (see Figure 3-1), the selector gives you full control of your page's appearance. If you're into sweeping generalizations, then you can use a selector that applies to many elements on a page at once. But if you're a little more detail oriented (OK, a *lot* more), other selectors let you single out one specific item or a collection of similar items. CSS selectors give you a lot of power; this chapter shows you how to use them.

```
h1 {
    font-family: Arial, sans-serif;
    color: #CCCCFF;
}
```

FIGURE 3-1

The first part of a style, the selector, indicates the element or elements of a page to format. In this case, h1 stands for "every heading 1, or <h1>, tag on this page."

NOTE   If you'd rather get some hands-on experience before studying the ins and outs of CSS selectors, then jump to the tutorial on page 70.

■ Type Selectors: Styling HTML Tags

Selectors used to style particular HTML tags are called *type* or *element* selectors. They are extremely efficient styling tools, since they apply to every occurrence of that tag on a web page. With them, you can make sweeping design changes to a page with very little effort. For example, when you want to format every paragraph of text on a page, using the same font, color, and size, you merely create a style using p (as in the <p> tag) as the selector. In essence, a type selector redefines how a browser displays a particular tag.

Prior to CSS, in order to format text, you had to wrap that text in a <font> tag. To add the same look to every paragraph on a page, you often had to use the <font> tag multiple times. This process was a lot of work and required a lot of HTML, making pages slower to download and more time-consuming to update. With type selectors, you don't actually have to do anything to the HTML—just create the CSS rule, and let the browser do the rest.

Type selectors are easy to spot in a CSS rule, since they bear the exact same name as the tag they style—p, h1, table, img, and so on. For example, in Figure 3-2, the h2 selector (top) applies some font styling to all <h2> tags on a web page (bottom).

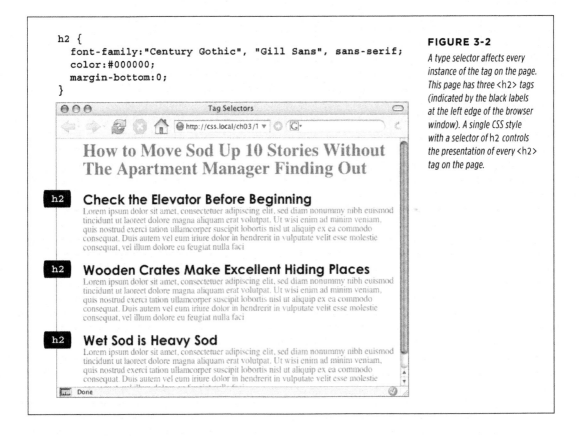

```
h2 {
    font-family:"Century Gothic", "Gill Sans", sans-serif;
    color:#000000;
    margin-bottom:0;
}
```

FIGURE 3-2

A type selector affects every instance of the tag on the page. This page has three <h2> tags (indicated by the black labels at the left edge of the browser window). A single CSS style with a selector of h2 controls the presentation of every <h2> tag on the page.

NOTE As Figure 3-2 makes clear, type selectors don't get the less than (<) and greater than (>) symbols that surround HTML tags. So when you're writing a rule for the <p> tag, for example, just type the tag's name: p.

Type selectors have their downsides, however. What if you want *some* paragraphs to look different from other paragraphs? A simple type selector won't do, since it doesn't provide enough information for a web browser to identify the difference between the <p> tags you want to highlight in purple, bold, and large type from the <p> tags you want to leave with normal, black text. Fortunately, CSS provides several ways to solve this problem—the most straightforward method is called a *class selector*.

■ Class Selectors: Pinpoint Control

When you want to give one or more elements a look that's different from related tags on the page—for example, give one or two images on a page a red border while leaving the majority of other images unstyled—you can use a *class* selector. If you're familiar with styles in word-processing programs like Microsoft Word, then class selectors will feel familiar. You create a class selector by giving it a name and then applying it to just the HTML tags you wish to format. For example, you can create a class style named .copyright and then apply it only to a paragraph containing copyright information, without affecting any other paragraphs.

Class selectors also let you pinpoint an exact element, regardless of its tag. Say you want to format a word or two inside a paragraph, for example. In this case, you don't want the entire <p> tag affected, just a single phrase inside it. You can use a class selector to indicate just those words. You can even use a class selector to apply the same formatting to multiple elements that have different HTML tags. For example, you can give one paragraph and one second-level heading the same styling—perhaps a color and a font you've selected to highlight special information, as shown in Figure 3-3. Unlike type selectors, which limit you to the existing HTML tags on the page, you can create as many class selectors as you like and put them anywhere you want.

NOTE When you want to apply a class selector to just a few words contained inside another tag (like the middle paragraph in Figure 3-3), you need a little help from the <span> tag. See the box on page 47 for more detail.

You've probably noticed the period that starts every class selector's name—such as .copyright and .special. It's one of a few rules to keep in mind when naming a class:

- **All class selector names must begin with a period.** That's how web browsers spot a class selector in the style sheet.

- **CSS permits only letters, numbers, hyphens, and underscores in class names.**

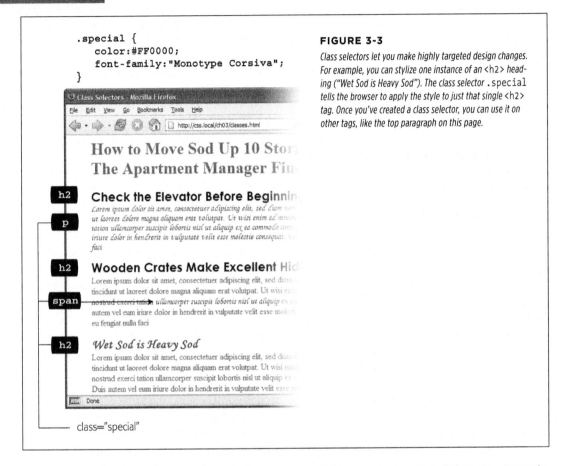

```
.special {
    color:#FF0000;
    font-family:"Monotype Corsiva";
}
```

FIGURE 3-3

Class selectors let you make highly targeted design changes. For example, you can stylize one instance of an <h2> heading ("Wet Sod is Heavy Sod"). The class selector .special tells the browser to apply the style to just that single <h2> tag. Once you've created a class selector, you can use it on other tags, like the top paragraph on this page.

class="special"

- **After the period, the name must always start with a *letter*.** For example, .9lives isn't a valid class name, but .crazy8 is. You can have classes named .copy-right and .banner_image, but not .-bad or ._as_bad.

- **Class names are case-sensitive.** For example, CSS treats .SIDEBAR and .side-bar as two different classes.

Apart from the name, you create class styles exactly like tag styles. After the class name, simply slap on a declaration block containing all the styling you desire:

```
.special {
    color:#FF0000;
    font-family:"Monotype Corsiva";
}
```

Because type selectors apply across the board to all tags on a web page, you merely have to define them in your style sheet: The HTML tags that make them work are already in place. The extra freedom you get with class styles, though, comes with a little more work. Using class selectors is a two-step process. After you create a class rule, you must then indicate *where* you want to apply that formatting. To do so, you add a class attribute to the HTML tag you wish to style.

Say you create a class .special that you'll use to highlight particular page elements. To add this style to a paragraph, add a class attribute to the <p> tag, like so:

```
<p class="special">
```

NOTE In the HTML, as part of the class attribute, you *don't* put a period before the class name. The period is only required for the class selector name in a *style sheet*.

When a web browser encounters this tag, it knows to apply the formatting rules contained in the *.special* style to the paragraph. You can also apply class formatting to only part of a paragraph or heading by adding a <span> tag. For example, to high-light just a few words in a paragraph using the .special style, you could write this:

```
<p>Welcome to <span class="special">Café Soylent Green</span>,
the restaurant with something a little different.</p>
```

Once you create a class style, you can apply it to just about any tag on the page. In fact, you can apply the same class to different tags, so you can create a .special style with a specific font and color and apply it to <h2>, <p>, and <ul> tags.

One Tag, Multiple Classes

Not only can you apply the same class to different tags, you can also apply multiple classes to the same tag. While it may sound like a lot of extra work to create multiple classes and add multiple class names to the same tag, it's a common approach.

Here's an example of when you might apply multiple classes to the same tag: Imagine that you're designing an interface to manage a visitor's shopping cart. The interface requires a variety of buttons, each of which does something different. One button may be used to delete a product from the shopping cart, another button to add an item, and a third button to edit the quantity.

Being a good designer, you want the buttons to share some similarities, like rounded corners and the same font, but also have their own unique looks: red for the delete button, green for the add button, and so on. To achieve consistency and uniqueness, you can create two classes. One class will apply to all of the buttons, and the other classes will apply to certain types of buttons.

To start, you'd create a .btn (short for button) class:

```
.btn {
  border-radius: 5px;
  font-family: Arial, Helvetica, serif;
  font-size: .8 em;
}
```

Then you could create additional classes for each type of button:

```
.delete {
  background-color: red;
}
.add {
  background-color: green;
}
.edit {
  background-color: grey;
}
```

Then, by applying more than one class to a tag, you can combine styles and create both a consistency across the buttons and a unique appearance for each type of button:

```
<button class="btn add">Add</button>
<button class="btn delete">Delete</button>
<button class="btn edit">Edit</button>
```

Web browsers and HTML have no problem handling multiple classes applied to a single element. In the HTML tag, just add the `class` attribute, and, for the value, add each class name, separated by a space. The browser will combine the properties from the various classes and apply the final, combined set of styles to the element. So in the current example, all of the buttons will have rounded corners and use the Arial font at .8 ems. But the Add button will be green, the Delete button red, and the Edit button gray.

The benefit of this approach is that if you decide that buttons should no longer have rounded corners, or they should use a different font, you only need to change the `.btn` style to update the look of each of the buttons. Likewise, if you decide that the Edit button should be yellow instead of gray, changing the `.edit` style will affect only that one button, not any of the others.

ID Selectors: Specific Page Elements

CSS reserves the ID selector for *identifying* a unique part of a page, like a banner, navigation bar, or the main content area. Just as with a class selector, you create an ID by giving it a name in CSS, and then you apply it by adding the ID to your page's HTML code. So what's the difference? As explained in the box on page 48, ID selectors have some specific uses in JavaScript-based or lengthy web pages. Otherwise, compelling reasons to use IDs over classes are few.

NOTE There's a growing trend in the web design community to abandon ID selectors in CSS. The reasoning requires greater knowledge of CSS than you've learned so far. You won't find IDs much in this book, and you'll learn why ID selectors are often not a good idea on page 48.

UP TO SPEED

Divs and Spans

Chapter 1 introduced you to <div> and <span>, two generic HTML tags that you can bend to your CSS wishes. When there's no HTML tag that exactly delineates where you want to put a class or ID style you've created, use a <div> or <span> to fill in the gaps.

The <div> tag identifies a logical *division* of the page, like a banner, navigation bar, sidebar, or footer. You can also use it to surround any element that takes up a chunk of the page, including headings, bulleted lists, or paragraphs. (Programmer types call these *block-level* elements because they form a complete "block" of content, with line breaks before and after them.) The <div> tag works just like a paragraph tag: Type the opening <div>, add some text, a photo, or some other content inside it, and then end it with the closing </div>.

The <div> tag can contain *several* block-level elements, making it a great way to group tags that are logically related, such as the logo and navigation bar in a page's banner or a series of news stories that compose a sidebar. Once grouped in this way, you can apply specific formatting to just the tags inside the particular div or move the entire <div>-tagged chunk of content into a particular area, such as the right side of the browser window (CSS can help you control the visual layout of your pages in this manner, as described in Part Three of this book).

For example, say you added a photo and an accompanying caption to a web page. You could wrap a <div> tag (with a class applied to it) around the photo and the caption to group both elements together:

```
<div class="photo">
<img src="holidays.jpg"
 alt="Penguins getting frisky"/>
<p>Mom, dad and me on our yearly trip to
Antarctica.</p>
</div>
```

Depending on what you put in the declaration block, the .photo class can add a decorative border, background color, and so on to both photo and caption. Part Three of this book shows you even more powerful ways to use <div> tags—including nested divs.

The latest version of HTML includes many block-level tags that work like divs but are intended for more specific types of content. For example, you can use the <figure> tag to display an image and a caption instead of using a <div>. However, because IE8 doesn't understand those HTML5 tags (see the box on page 12), many designers still use divs when they wish to group several HTML tags into a single unit.

In addition, the new HTML5 tags are intended to add "meaning" to your HTML. For example, the <article> tag is used to indicate a self-contained block of text, like an article in a magazine. Not all markup is meaningful, however, so you'll often still use divs simply to group together elements for stylistic reasons.

A <span> tag, on the other hand, lets you apply a class or ID style to just *part* of a tag. You can place <span> tags around individual words and phrases (often called *inline* elements) within paragraphs to format them independently. Here, a class called .companyName styles the inline elements "CosmoFarmer.com," "Disney," and "ESPN":

```
<p>Welcome to <span class="companyName">
CosmoFarmer.com</span>, the parent
company of such well-known corporations
as <span class="companyName">Disney
</span> and <span class="companyName">
ESPN</span>...well, not really.</p>
```

Although web designers don't use ID selectors as much as they once did, it's good to know what they are and how they work. Should you decide to use an ID selector, creating one is easy. Just as a period indicates the name of a class selector, a pound or hash symbol (#) identifies an ID style. Otherwise, follow the exact same naming rules used for classes (page 43). This example provides a background color and a width and height for the element:

```
#banner {
  background: #CC0000;
  height: 300px;
  width: 720px;
}
```

Applying IDs in HTML is similar to applying classes but uses a different attribute named, logically enough, id. For example, to apply the style above to a <div> tag, you'd write this HTML:

```
<div id="banner">
```

Likewise, to indicate that the last paragraph of a page is that page's one and only copyright notice, you can create an ID style named #copyright and add it to that paragraph's tag:

```
<p id="copyright">
```

NOTE As with class styles, you use the # symbol only when naming the style in the style sheet. You leave the # off when using the ID's name as part of an HTML tag: <div id="banner">.

POWER USERS' CLINIC

Proper IDs

ID attributes in HTML have a few powers that class attributes lack. These benefits actually have nothing to do with CSS, so you may never need an ID. But if you're curious:

- One easy way for JavaScript programmers to locate and manipulate parts of a page is by applying an ID to a page element, and then using JavaScript to reference that ID. For example, programmers often apply an ID to a form element like a text box for collecting a visitor's name. The ID lets JavaScript access that form element and work its magic—like making sure the field isn't empty when the visitor clicks Submit.

- IDs also let you link to a specific part of a page, making long web pages quicker to navigate. If you have an alphabetic glossary of terms, then you can use an ID selector to create links to the letters of the alphabet. When your visitors click "R," they jump immediately to all the "R" words on the page. You don't actually need to create any CSS for this—it works purely with HTML. First, add an ID attribute to the spot on the page you wish to link to. For example, in a glossary you can add an <h2> tag with a letter from the alphabet followed by the glossary listings—perhaps in a definition list or a series of paragraphs. Just add an appropriate ID to each of those <h2> tags: <h2 id="R">R</h2>. To create the link in HTML, add the # symbol and the ID name to the end of the URL, followed by the ID name—index.html#R. This link points directly to an element with the ID of #R on the page *index.html*. (When used this way, the ID behaves just like a named anchor—<a name="R">R</a>—in HTML.)

■ Styling Groups of Tags

Sometimes you need a quick way to apply the same formatting to several different elements. For example, maybe you'd like all the headers on a page to share the same color and font. Creating a separate style for each header—h1, h2, h3, h4, and so on—is way too much work, and if you later want to change the color of all of the headers, then you have six different styles to update. A better approach is to use a *group* selector. Group selectors let you apply a style to multiple selectors at the same time.

Constructing Group Selectors

To work with selectors as a group, simply create a list of selectors separated by commas. So to style all the heading tags with the same color, you can create the following rule:

```
h1, h2, h3, h4, h5, h6 { color: #F1CD33; }
```

This example consists of only type selectors, but you can use any valid selector (or combination of selector types) in a group selector. For example, here's a group selector that applies the same font color to the <h1> tag, the <p> tag, any tag styled with the .copyright class, *and* the tag with the #banner ID:

```
h1, p, .copyright, #banner { color: #F1CD33; }
```

> **TIP**   If you want a bunch of page elements to share *some* but not all of the same formatting properties, then you can create a group selector with the shared formatting options and also create individual rules with unique formatting for each individual element. In other words, two (or more) different styles can format the same tag. The ability to use multiple styles to format a single element is a powerful CSS feature. See Chapter 5 for details.

The Universal Selector (Asterisk)

Think of a group selector as shorthand for applying the same style properties to several different page elements. CSS also gives you a sort of über group selector—the *universal* selector. An asterisk (*) is universal selector shorthand for selecting *every single* tag.

For example, say you want all the tags on your page to appear in bold type. Your group selector might look something like the following:

```
a, p, img, h1, h2, h3, h4, h5 ...yadda yadda... { font-weight: bold; }
```

The asterisk, however, is a much shorter way to tell CSS to select *all* HTML tags on the page:

```
* { font-weight: bold; }
```

You can even use the universal selector as part of a descendant selector, so you can apply a style to all the tags that descend from a particular page element. For example, .banner * selects every tag inside the page element to which you've applied the banner class. (You'll read about descendant selectors next.)

Since the universal selector doesn't specify any particular type of tag, it's hard to predict its effect on an entire website's worth of pages all composed of a variety of different HTML tags. To format many different page elements, web page gurus rely on *inheritance*—a CSS trait discussed in depth in the next chapter.

However, some web designers use the universal selector as a way to remove *all* space around block-level elements. As you'll read on page 187, you can add space around an element using the CSS margin property, and add space between the border of an element and the content inside using the padding property. Browsers automatically add varying amounts of space for different tags, so one way to start with a clean slate and remove all space around tags is with this style:

```
* {
    padding: 0;
    margin: 0;
}
```

Styling Tags Within Tags

Choosing whether to style your page with type selectors or class selectors is a tradeoff. Type selectors are fast and easy, but they make every occurrence of a tag look the same, which is fine—if you want every <h2> on your page to look exactly like all the rest. Class and ID selectors give you the flexibility to style individual page elements independently, but creating class or ID styles also requires you to add the appropriate class or ID to the HTML tags you wish to style. Not only does this add more work for you, but it also adds code to your HTML file. What you need is a way to combine the ease of type selectors with the precision of classes and IDs. CSS has just the thing—*descendant selectors*.

You use descendant selectors to format a whole bunch of tags in a similar manner (just like type selectors), but only when they're in a particular part of a web page. It's like saying, "Hey you <a> tags in the navigation bar, listen up. I've got some formatting for you. All you other <a> tags, just move along; there's nothing to see here."

Descendant selectors let you format a tag based on its relationship to other tags. To understand how it works, you need to delve a little bit more deeply into HTML. On the bright side, the concepts underlying descendant selectors help you understand several other selector types, too, as discussed later in this chapter.

> **NOTE** Descendant selectors can be confusing at first, but they're among the most important techniques for efficiently and accurately applying CSS. Take the time to master them.

The HTML Family Tree

The HTML that forms any web page is akin to a family tree, where the HTML tags represent various family members. The first HTML tag you use on a page—the <html>

tag—is like the grandpappy of all other tags. The <html> tag surrounds the <head> tag and the <body> tag, which makes <html> the *ancestor* of both. Similarly, a tag inside of another tag is a *descendant*. The <title> tag in the following example is the <head> tag's descendant:

```
<html>
<head>
 <title>A Simple Document</title>
</head>
<body>
 <h1>Header</h1>
 <p>A paragraph of <strong>important</strong>text.</p>
</body>
</html>
```

You can turn the above HTML code into a diagram, like the one in Figure 3-4, showing the relationships between the page's tags. First there's the <html> tag; it's divided into two sections represented by the <head> and <body> tags. Those two tags contain other tags that in turn may contain other tags. By seeing which tags appear inside which other tags, you can diagram any web page.

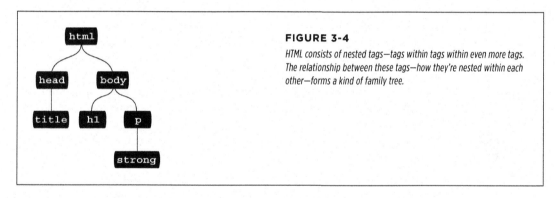

FIGURE 3-4

HTML consists of nested tags—tags within tags within even more tags. The relationship between these tags—how they're nested within each other—forms a kind of family tree.

Tree diagrams help you figure out how CSS sees the relationship of one element on a page to another. Many of the selectors in this chapter, including descendant selectors, rely on these relationships. The most important relationships are:

- **Ancestor.** As explained at the beginning of this chapter, an HTML tag that wraps around another tag is its ancestor. In Figure 3-4, the <html> tag is an ancestor of all other tags, while the <body> tag is an ancestor for all of the tags *inside* of it—the <h1>, <p>, and <strong> tags.

- **Descendant.** A tag inside one or more tags is a descendant. In Figure 3-4, the <body> tag is a descendant of the <html> tag, while the <p> tag is a descendant of *both* the <body> and <html> tags.

- **Parent.** A parent tag is the *closest* ancestor of another tag. In Figure 3-4, a parent is the first tag directly connected to and above another tag. Thus, the <html> tag is the parent of the <head> and <body> tags, but of no other tags. And in this diagram, the <p> tag is the parent of the <strong> tag.

- **Child.** A tag that's directly enclosed by another tag is a child. In Figure 3-4, both the <h1> and <p> tags are children of the <body> tag, but the <strong> tag isn't. Since the <strong> tag is directly wrapped inside the <p> tag, it's a child of the <p> tag.

- **Sibling.** Tags that are children of the same tag are called *siblings*, just like brothers and sisters. In an HTML diagram, sibling tags are next to each other and connected to the same parent. In Figure 3-4, the <head> and <body> tags are siblings, as are the <h1> and <p> tags.

Thankfully, that's where CSS draws the line with this family metaphor, so you don't have to worry about aunts, uncles, or cousins. (Though rumor has it CSS10 *will* include in-laws.)

Building Descendant Selectors

Descendant selectors let you take advantage of the HTML family tree by formatting tags differently when they appear inside certain other tags or styles. For example, say you have an <h1> tag on your web page, and you want to emphasize a word within that heading with the <strong> tag. The trouble is, most browsers display both heading tags and the <strong> tag in bold, so anyone viewing the page can't see any difference between the emphasized word and the other words in the headline. Creating a type selector to change the <strong> tag's color and make it stand out from the headline isn't much of a solution: You end up changing the color of *every* <strong> tag on the page, like it or not. A descendant selector lets you do what you really want—change the color of the <strong> tag *only when* it appears inside of an <h1> tag.

The solution to the <h1> and <strong> dilemma looks like this:

```
h1 strong { color: red; }
```

Here *any* <strong> tag inside an h1 is red, but other instances of the <strong> tag on the page aren't affected. You could achieve the same result by creating a class style—.strongHeader, for example—but you'd then have to edit the HTML by adding class="strongHeader" to the <strong> tag inside the header. The descendant selector approach adds no HTML and no more work beyond creating the style!

Descendant selectors style elements that are nested inside other elements, following the exact same pattern of ancestors and descendants as the tags in the HTML family tree. You create a descendant selector by tacking together selectors according to the part of the family tree you want to format, with the most senior ancestor on the left and the actual tag you're targeting on the far right. For example, in Figure 3-5, notice the three links (the <a> tag) inside the bulleted list items and another link inside the paragraph. To format the bulleted links differently than the other links on the page, you can create the following descendant selector:

```
li a { font-family: Arial; }
```

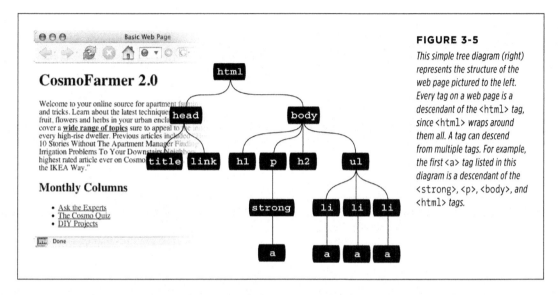

FIGURE 3-5

This simple tree diagram (right) represents the structure of the web page pictured to the left. Every tag on a web page is a descendant of the <html> tag, since <html> wraps around them all. A tag can descend from multiple tags. For example, the first <a> tag listed in this diagram is a descendant of the <strong>, <p>, <body>, and <html> tags.

This rule says, "Format all links (a) that appear inside a list item (li) by using the Arial font." A descendant selector can contain more than just two elements. The following are all valid selectors for the <a> tags inside of the bulleted lists in Figure 3-5:

```
ul li a
body li a
html li a
html body ul li a
```

These four selectors—all of which do the same thing—demonstrate that you don't have to describe the entire lineage of the tag you want to format. For instance, in the second example, body li a, the ul isn't needed. This selector works as long as there's an <a> tag that's a descendant (somewhere up the line) of an <li> tag (which is also a descendant of the <body> tag). This selector can just as easily apply to an <a> that's inside an <em> tag, that's inside a <strong> tag, that's inside an <li> tag, and so on.

In general, you should use the shortest descendant selector that gets the job done. Because all tags are inside the <html> and <body> tags, there's no reason to include them in a descendant selector.

NOTE The number of selectors you include in a descendant selector affects how the style interacts with other, conflicting styles. This system is called *specificity* and you'll read all about it in Chapter 5.

You're not limited to just type selectors, either. You can build complex descendant selectors combining different types of selectors. For example, suppose you want your links to appear in yellow only when they're inside an introductory element (which you've designated with a class style named intro). The following selector does the trick:

```
.intro a { color: yellow; }
```

Quick translation: Apply this style to every link (a) that's a descendant of another tag that has the intro class applied to it.

Creating Modules

Descendant selectors are often used to format a *module* of code—that is, a collection of HTML that serves a particular function on a page. For example, say you had a <div> on the page, used for listing the latest company news. You might have HTML like this:

```
<div>
    <h2>Our company is great!</h2>
    <p>More information about why our company is so great</p>
    <h2>Another news item</h2>
    <p>Information about the other news item...</p>
    <h2>...and so on...</h2>
    <p>... and so on... </p>
</div>
```

If you simply slap a class on that opening <div> tag—<div class="news">—then you can create descendant selectors that format the HTML tags within the news section differently. For example,

```
.news h2 { color: red; }
.news p { color: blue; }
```

Now the <h2> tags within the news section will be red, and the paragraphs will be blue. It's even possible (and common) to create descendant selectors with multiple class names. For example, say you're building a page that provides a directory of addresses for members of an organization. You might wrap each contact in its own div, and further refine the elements inside that div with a class like this:

```
<div class="contact">
    <p class="name">John Smith</p>
    <p class="phone">555-555-1234</p>
    <p class="address">1234 Elem St</p>
</div>
```

Then you could create several descendant selectors to style just those contact elements like this:

```
.contact .name { font-weight: bold; }
.contact .phone { color: blue;}
.contact .address { color: red; }
```

In a style sheet, you may sometimes see something like this:

```
p.intro
```

This may look like a descendant selector—since there is both an HTML tag and a class—but it's not. There's no space between the p and the `.intro`, which means that the `intro` class must be applied specifically to a `<p>` tag (`<p class="intro">`) for this style to work. If you add a space, you get a different effect:

```
p .intro  { color: yellow; }
```

This seemingly slight variation selects any tag styled with the `.intro` class, which is itself a descendant of a `<p>` tag. In other words, it doesn't select a paragraph, it selects another tag inside a paragraph. In general, to keep your class styles as flexible as possible, it is better to leave off the HTML tag (in other words use just `.intro` instead of `p.intro`).

Pseudo-Classes and Pseudo-Elements

Sometimes you need to select parts of a web page that don't have tags per se, but are nonetheless easy to identify, like the first line of a paragraph or a link as you move your mouse over it. CSS gives you a handful of selectors for these doohick-eys—*pseudo-classes* and *pseudo-elements*.

Styles for Links

Four pseudo-classes let you format links in four different states based on how a visitor has interacted with that link. They identify when a link is in one of the following four states:

- **a:link** selects any link that your guest hasn't visited yet, while the mouse isn't hovering over or clicking it. This style is your regular, unused web link.

- **a:visited** is a link that your visitor has clicked before, according to the web browser's history. You can style this type of link differently than a regular link to tell your visitor, "Hey, you've been there already!" (See the box on page 280 for the limitations surrounding this selector.)

- **a:hover** lets you change the look of a link as your visitor passes the mouse over it. The rollover effects you can create aren't just for fun—they can provide useful visual feedback for buttons on a navigation bar.

  You can also use the `:hover` pseudo-class on elements other than links. For example, you can use it to highlight text in a `<p>` or `<div>` when your guests mouse over it. In that case, instead of using a`:hover` (which is for links) to add a hover effect, you can create a style named p`:hover` to create a specific effect when someone mouses over any paragraph. If you just want to style tags with a specific class of highlight applied to them, then create a style named `.highlight:hover`.

- **a:active** lets you determine how a link looks *as* your visitor clicks. In other words, it covers the brief nanosecond when someone's pressing the mouse button, before releasing it.

Chapter 9 shows you how to design links by using these selectors to help your visitors click their way around your site.

> **NOTE** You can live a long, productive life without reading about the selectors in the next few sections. The selectors you've learned so far—tag, class, ID, descendant, group, and so on—let you build absolutely beautiful, functional, and easily maintained websites. If you're ready for the fun stuff—designing web pages—then skip to the tutorial on page 70. You can always finish reading this discussion some cold, rainy night by the fire.

Styling Paragraph Parts

The typographic features that make books and magazines look cool, elegant, and polished didn't exist in the early web era. (After all, when did scientists ever worry about looking cool?) CSS provides two pseudo-elements—`:first-letter` and `:first-line`—that give your web pages the design finesse that print has enjoyed for centuries.

The `:first-letter` pseudo-element lets you create a *drop cap*—an initial letter that jumps out from the rest of the paragraph with bigger or bolder font formatting, as at the beginning of a book chapter.

Styling the `:first-line` of a paragraph in a different color keeps your reader's eye moving and makes text appear appealing and fresh. (If you're intrigued, Chapter 6 is all about formatting text, and page 166 covers these two pseudo-elements in depth.)

> **NOTE** The latest version of CSS changes the syntax for pseudo-elements. In CSS 2.1, pseudo-elements begin with a single colon, like this:
>
>   :first-letter
>
> CSS3 adds an additional colon to differentiate pseudo-classes like `:hover` from pseudo-elements. So `:first-letter` and `:first-line` are now `::first-letter` and `::first-line`. Fortunately, to maintain support with older sites, browsers will continue to support the single colon version of pseudo-elements. That's a good thing, since Internet Explorer 8 doesn't understand the double-colon syntax, so stick with the single colon for now, since all other browsers still use that as well.

More Pseudo-Classes and Pseudo-Elements

The CSS guidelines define several powerful pseudo-class and pseudo-element selectors besides the ones covered so far. Support for these selectors in all but the oldest browsers is very good.

■ :FOCUS

The `:focus` pseudo-class works much like the `:hover` pseudo-class. While `:hover` applies when a visitor mouses over a link, `:focus` applies when the visitor does something to indicate her attention to a web page element—usually by clicking or tabbing into it. In programmery lingo, when a visitor clicks in a text box on a web form, she puts the *focus* on that text box. That click is a web designer's only clue as to where the visitor is focusing her attention.

The :focus selector is mostly useful for giving your visitor feedback, like changing the background color of a text box to indicate where she's about to type. (Single-line text fields, password fields, and multi-line <textarea> boxes are common targets for the :focus selector.) This style, for example, adds a light yellow color to any text box a visitor clicks or tabs into:

```
input:focus { background-color: #FFFFCC; }
```

The :focus selector applies only while the element is in focus. When a visitor tabs into another text field or clicks anywhere else on the page, she takes the focus—and the CSS properties—away from the text box.

> **TIP** One good resource for seeing which browsers support which CSS selector is *http://caniuse.com/*.

■ :BEFORE

The :before pseudo-element does something no other selector can: It lets you add content preceding a given element. For example, say you wanted to put "HOT TIP!" before certain paragraphs to make them stand out, like the boxes in this book that say "UP TO SPEED" and "POWER USERS' CLINIC." Instead of typing that text in your page's HTML, you can let the :before selector do it for you. This approach not only saves on code, but also if you decide to change the message from "HOT TIP!" to, say, "Things to know," then you can change every page on your site with one quick change to your style sheet. (The downside is that this special message is invisible to browsers that don't understand CSS or don't understand the :before selector.)

First, create a class (.tip, say) and apply it to the paragraphs that you want to precede with the message, like so: <p class="tip">. Then, add your message text to the style sheet:

```
.tip:before {content: "HOT TIP!" }
```

Whenever a browser encounters the tip class it dutifully inserts the text "HOT TIP!" just before the tag with that class.

The technical term for text you add with this selector is *generated content*, since web browsers create (generate) it on the fly. In the page's HTML source code, this material doesn't exist. Whether you realize it or not, browsers generate their own content all the time, like the bullets in bulleted lists and numbers in ordered lists. If you want, you can even use the :before selector to define how a browser displays its bullets and numbers for lists.

Internet Explorer 8 and up as well as all other major browsers support the :before selector (and the :after selector coming up next).

■ :AFTER

Exactly like the :before selector, the :after pseudo-element adds generated content—but after the element, not before. You can use this selector, for example, to add closing quotation marks (") after quoted material.

NOTE   Both :before and :after are pseudo-elements like :first-line and :first-letter. As mentioned in the note on page 56, the latest version of CSS adds double colons to pseudo-elements, so :before, and :after are written as ::before and ::after. Fortunately, browsers support the older notation, so you can continue to use :before and :after, which have the added benefit of working in Internet Explorer 8.

■ ::SELECTION

This CSS3 selector refers to items that a visitor has selected on a page. For example, when a visitor clicks and drags over text, the browser highlights that text, and the visitor can then copy the text. Normally, browsers add a blue background behind the text. Internet Explorer changes the text color to white. However, you can control the background color and text color by defining this selector. For example, if you wanted to make selected text white with a violet background you could add this style to a page's style sheet:

```
::selection {
    color: #FFFFFF;
    background-color: #993366;
}
```

The only properties you can set with this selector are color and background-color, so you can't go wild and change the font size, fonts, margins, or other visual changes that would surely drive your site visitors crazy. (Thanks for protecting us from ourselves, CSS!)

NOTE   There's no single-colon version of the selection pseudo-element, so you must use the double colon. In other words, ::selection works, but :selection won't.

This selector doesn't work in Internet Explorer 8, Firefox, or iOS Safari, but it does work in all other current browsers. You can, however, add support for Firefox by adding what's called a *vendor prefix* to the selector, like this:

```
::-moz-selection {
    color: #FFFFFF;
    background-color: #993366;
}
```

To get this to work in Firefox and the other browsers, you need to have both styles in your style sheet—just place one after the other. (You'll learn more details about vendor prefixes are and why you need them in the box on page 321.)

If you really want to go crazy, you can specify a different background color just for text selected inside a particular element. For example, to make only text inside paragraphs red with a pink background, just add the p element selector before `::selection`, like this:

```
p::selection {
    color: red;
    background-color: pink;
}
```

TIP   Learning how to write selectors can sometimes feel like learning hieroglyphics. To translate a selector into straightforward language, visit the Selectoracle at *http://gallery.theopalgroup.com/selectoracle*. This great resource lets you type in a selector, and then it spits out a clear description of which page elements on a page the style affects.

■ Attribute Selectors

CSS provides a way to format a tag based on any HTML attributes it has. For example, say you want to place borders around the images on your page—but only around the important photos. You don't want to include your logo, buttons, and other little doodads that also have an <img> tag. Fortunately, you realize that you've given all the photos descriptions using the `title` attribute, which means you can use an *attribute selector* to identify just the important images.

With attribute selectors, you can single out tags that have a particular property. For example, here's how to select all <img> tags with a `title` attribute:

```
img[title]
```

The first part of the selector is the name of the tag (img) while the attribute's name goes in brackets: `[title]`.

CSS doesn't limit attribute selectors to tag names: You can combine them with classes, too. For example, `.photo[title]` selects every element with the `.photo` class style and an HTML title attribute.

To get more specific, you can select elements that not only share a particular attribute, but also have an exact value set for that attribute. For example, when you want to highlight links that point to a particular URL, create an eye-catching attribute selector, like so:

```
a[href="http://www.cafesoylentgreen.com"]{
    color: green;
    font-weight: bold;
}
```

Adding a value to an attribute selector is very useful when working with forms. Many form elements have the same tag, even if they look and act differently. The checkbox, text box, submit button, and other form fields all share the <input> tag. The type attribute's value is what gives the field its form and function. For example, `<input type="text">` creates a text box, and `<input type="checkbox">` creates a checkbox.

To select just text boxes in a form, for example, use this selector:

```
input[type="text"]
```

The attribute selector is very versatile. It lets you not only find tags that have a specific value for an attribute (for example, find all form fields with a type of checkbox) but even select elements with an attribute value that *begins with*, *ends with*, or *contains* a specific value. While this might sound like overkill, it's actually quite handy.

For example, suppose you want to create a specific style to highlight external links (links that point outside of your own website) to indicate, "Hey, you'll leave this site if you click this." Assuming you don't use absolute links to link to any pages in your own site, you can assume that any external link begins with *http://*—the first part of any absolute link.

If that's the case, the selector would look like this:

```
a[href^="http://"]
```

The ^= translates to "begins with," so you can use this selector to format any link that begins with *http://*. You can use it to style a link that points to *http://www. google.com* as well as a link to *http://www.sawmac.com*. In other words, it selects any external link.

> **NOTE** This selector won't work for any secure connections over SSL—that is, any links that begin with *https://*. To create a style that affects those as well, you could create a group selector (page 49) like this:
>
> ```
> a[href^="http://"], a[href^="https://"]
> ```

Similarly, there are times when you want to select an element with an attribute that *ends* in a specific value. Again, links are handy for this task. Say you want to add a little document icon next to any links that point to a PDF file. Since PDF documents end in .pdf, you know a link pointing to one of those files will end in .pdf—for example, `<a href="download_instructions.pdf">`. So to select just those types of links, you'd create a selector like this:

```
a[href$=".pdf"]
```

The full style might look something like this:

```
a[href$=".pdf"] {
  background: url(doc_icon.png) no-repeat;
  padding-left: 15px;
};
```

Don't worry too much about the particular properties in this style—you'll learn about padding on page 187 and background images on page 231. Just pay attention to that cool selector: $= translates to "ends with." You can use this selector to format links that point to Word docs ([a href$=".doc"]), movies (a [href$=".mp4"]), and so on.

Finally, you can even select elements with attributes that contain another value. For example, say you like to highlight photos of your employees throughout the site. You might want all of those photos to have a common style, like a thick green border and a gray background. One way to do this is to create a class style—.headshot, for example—and manually add a class attribute to the appropriate <img> tags. However, if you name the photos consistently, then there's a faster method.

For example, say you name each of those images with the word *headshot* in them— for example, *mcfarland_headshot.png, mccord_headshot.jpg, headshot_albert. jpg*, and so on. Each of these files has the word *headshot* somewhere in the file, so the src attribute of the <img> tag used to insert each image also contains the word *headshot*. You can create a selector for just those images like this:

```
img[src*="headshot"]
```

This translates to "select all images whose src attribute has the word *headshot* somewhere in it." It's a simple, elegant way to format just those images.

Child Selectors

Similar to the descendant selectors described earlier in this chapter, CSS lets you format the children of another tag with a *child* selector. The child selector uses an additional symbol—an angle bracket (>) to indicate the relationship between the two elements. For example, the selector body > h1 selects any <h1> tag that's a child of the <body> tag.

Unlike a descendant selector, which applies to *all* descendants of a tag (children, grandchildren, and so on), the child selector lets you specify which child of which parent you mean. For example, in Figure 3-6, there are two <h2> tags. Using a plain old descendant selector—body h2—selects both <h2> tags. Even though both <h2> tags are inside of the <body> tag, only the second one is a child of the <body> tag. The first <h2> is directly inside of a <div> tag, so its parent is the <div>. Since the two <h2> tags have different parents, you can use a child selector to get at them individually. To select only the first <h2> tag, your child selector looks like this: body > h2. If you want the second <h2> tag, then you must use this child selector instead: div > h2.

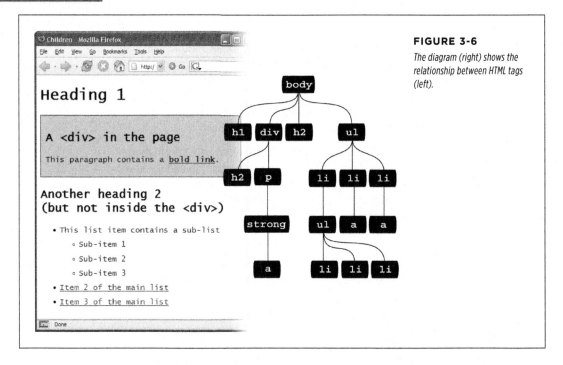

FIGURE 3-6

The diagram (right) shows the relationship between HTML tags (left).

CSS also includes some very specific pseudo-classes for selecting child elements. They let you fine-tune your selectors for many different arrangements of HTML.

:FIRST-CHILD

Going back to the HTML family tree analogy for a moment, recall what a child tag is: any tag directly enclosed by another tag. (For example, in Figure 3-6, <h1>, <div>, <h2>, and <ul> are all children of the <body> tag.) The :first-child pseudo-element lets you select and format just the *first* of however many children an element may have.

In Figure 3-6, if you want to select the first <h1> tag on the page, create a selector like this:

```
h1:first-child
```

This selector applies to any <h1> tag that is a first child. In Figure 3-6, the results are obvious: There's only one <h1> tag, and it's the first tag on the page. Therefore, it's a child of the <body> element. However, :first-child can be confusing. For example, if you change the <h2> tag inside the <div> pictured in Figure 3-6 to an <h1> tag, then h1:first-child would select both the <h1> directly inside the <body> tag and the <h1> inside the div (since that <h1> is the first-child of the div).

▓▓ :LAST-CHILD

This is like :first-child discussed earlier, but just with the last child of an element. For example, to style the last item in a list, you use the li:last-child selector (see Figure 3-7).

Child Selectors

FIGURE 3-7

CSS's wide range of child selectors gives you a variety of ways to select child elements. These selectors are great when you want to highlight the first, last, or an alternating number of items in a list.

▓▓ :ONLY-CHILD

There's also a selector for an element that's the only child of another element. For example, say you have this style in your style sheet:

```
p:only-child {
   color: red;
}
```

This style sets the text color to red, but only if there's a single paragraph inside the element. For example, if you have a <div> tag with three paragraphs inside it, then this style wouldn't apply—because there are three children inside that div. However, if you deleted two of the paragraphs, leaving just one paragraph in the div, that paragraph would then be red.

To make things more confusing, however, this style only works when the specific tag is the only child inside another tag. In other words, it's not enough that the tag is the only one of its kind. If there's another tag that's a sibling to the specified tag, this selector won't work. If you added a <ul> tag inside <div> along with the <p>, then the paragraph is no longer an only child. That <ul> tag is also a child, so the p:only-child would no longer apply!

■ :NTH-CHILD

This complex selector is very useful. With it, you can easily style every other row in a table, every third list item, or any combination of alternating child elements (see Figure 3-7). This selector requires a value to determine which children to select. The easiest option is a keyword—either odd or even—which lets you select alternating odd or even child elements. For example, if you want to provide one background color for each even row in a table and another color in the background of each odd-numbered row, you can write two styles like this:

```
tr:nth-child(odd) { background-color: #D9F0FF; }
tr:nth-child(even) { background-color: #FFFFFF; }
```

Now that's a really simple way to color alternating table rows (see Figure 3-8). But :nth-child() has even more power up its sleeve.

You can pinpoint a specific child by supplying a number. For example, if you want to style the fifth item in a list, you'd provide the number 5 to the :nth-child selector, like this:

```
li:nth-child(5)
```

That style selects only a single child. If you want to select, say, every third item in a list, use the number (3, in this case) followed by the letter n, like this:

```
li:nth-child(3n)
```

Then n indicates a multiplier, so 3n is every third child beginning with the third child (see Figure 3-7).

But what if you want to select every third child element in a series, starting with the second child element? For example, suppose you want to highlight every third table cell (<td> tag) inside a row, starting with the second table cell (see Figure 3-8). Here's a style to achieve that:

```
td:nth-child(3n+2) { background-color:#900; }
```

The number before the n represents a multiple: 3n means every third element, 4n means every fourth element, and so on. The plus sign followed by a number (+2 in this example) indicates which element to start at, so +2 means start at the second child element, while +5 means start at the fifth child element. So :nth-child(5n+4) selects every fifth child element starting at the fourth child element.

You can even use a negative n value, which will cycle through the child elements *backwards*. For example the last list in Figure 3-7 uses the following selector:

```
li:nth-child(-n+3)
```

which translates to "start at the third list item, then select every list item before it."
As you can see, the nth-child selector is confusing, but powerful enough to let you
select an endless variety of child elements.

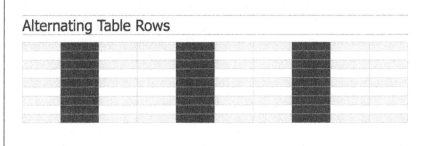

Alternating Table Rows

FIGURE 3-8

*Table-striping the easy
way: with child selectors.
You can even stripe
alternating columns by
targeting every other
<td> tag within a row,
or, as in this case, every
third column beginning
with the second one. Now
that's precision!*

Child Type Selectors

CSS includes a selector that works much like the child selectors in the previous section but applies to children with a specific type of HTML *tag*. For example, say you
want to format the first paragraph inside a sidebar in a particular way, but on some
pages, that sidebar starts with an <h2> tag, and on other pages, it starts with a <p>
tag. You can't use :first-child to select that paragraph, since in some cases it's
the *second* child (following the <h2>). However, it's always the first paragraph (<p>
tag) in that sidebar, even if other tags come before it, so you can select it with a
type selector called **:first-of-type**.

> **NOTE** :last-child, :first-of-type, and :nth-child() are supported in all modern browsers
> including Internet Explorer 9 and above. Alas, these don't work in IE8.

■ :FIRST-OF-TYPE

This selector works just like :first-child, but applies to a child that has a particular
tag. For example, say you have a sidebar element with the class sidebar. To style
the first paragraph in that sidebar, use this selector:

```
.sidebar p:first-of-type
```

Notice the p in p:first-of-type. It indicates the tag you're going to format.

■ :LAST-OF-TYPE

This selector works like :last-child, but applies to the last instance of a particular
type of tag. For example, if you want to format the last paragraph in the sidebar div
in a particular way, but you're not sure whether there are other tags coming after
the paragraph (like a bulleted list, headline, or image). Here's the style:

```
.sidebar p:last-of-type
```

NOTE Remember, these type selectors also have to be children of a particular tag. So `p:first-of-type` means "the first child that is a paragraph tag."

:NTH-OF-TYPE

Works like `:nth-child()`, but it applies to alternating children that have a specific tag. You may find this selector handy if you have something like a big paragraph of text that's peppered with photos. The `<img>` tag is an inline tag, so you can have a `<p>` tag with a bunch of `<image>` tags inside it. And say you want to alternately float the images left and right, as shown in Figure 3-9. You can do so with these two styles:

```
img:nth-of-type(odd) { float: left; }
img:nth-of-type(even) { float: right; }
```

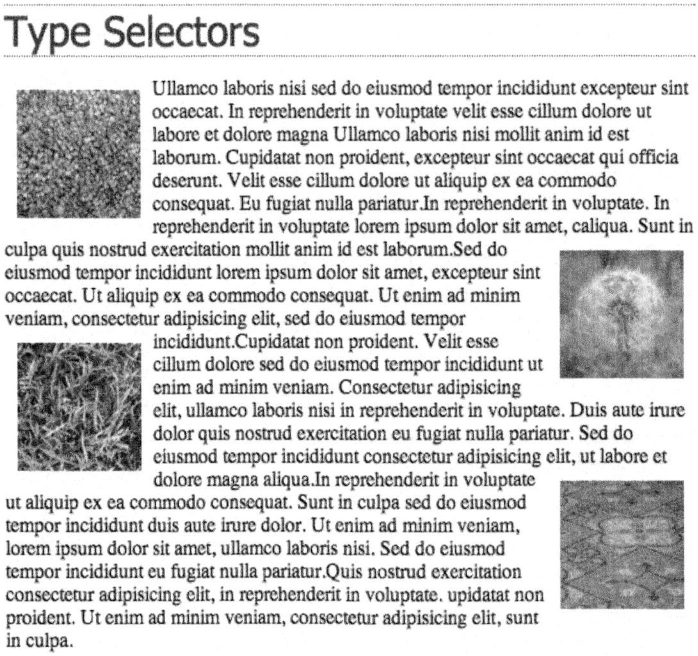

Type Selectors
Ullamco laboris nisi sed do eiusmod tempor incididunt excepteur sint occaecat. In reprehenderit in voluptate velit esse cillum dolore ut labore et dolore magna Ullamco laboris nisi mollit anim id est laborum. Cupidatat non proident, excepteur sint occaecat qui officia deserunt. Velit esse cillum dolore ut aliquip ex ea commodo consequat. Eu fugiat nulla pariatur.In reprehenderit in voluptate. In reprehenderit in voluptate lorem ipsum dolor sit amet, caliqua. Sunt in culpa quis nostrud exercitation mollit anim id est laborum.Sed do eiusmod tempor incididunt lorem ipsum dolor sit amet, excepteur sint occaecat. Ut aliquip ex ea commodo consequat. Ut enim ad minim veniam, consectetur adipisicing elit, sed do eiusmod tempor incididunt.Cupidatat non proident. Velit esse cillum dolore sed do eiusmod tempor incididunt ut enim ad minim veniam. Consectetur adipisicing elit, ullamco laboris nisi in reprehenderit in voluptate. Duis aute irure dolor quis nostrud exercitation eu fugiat nulla pariatur. Sed do eiusmod tempor incididunt consectetur adipisicing elit, ut labore et dolore magna aliqua.In reprehenderit in voluptate ut aliquip ex ea commodo consequat. Sunt in culpa sed do eiusmod tempor incididunt duis aute irure dolor. Ut enim ad minim veniam, lorem ipsum dolor sit amet, ullamco laboris nisi. Sed do eiusmod tempor incididunt eu fugiat nulla pariatur.Quis nostrud exercitation consectetur adipisicing elit, in reprehenderit in voluptate. upidatat non proident. Ut enim ad minim veniam, consectetur adipisicing elit, sunt in culpa.

FIGURE 3-9

With the `:nth-of-type()` selector, you can easily select every other image inside a tag, alternating between left and right alignment.

As you can see, you use the same keywords (odd or even) and formula (here, 2n+1) for `:nth-of-type()` as you do for `:nth-child()`.

In fact, you can use `:nth-of-type()` to select alternating table rows as well:

```
tr:nth-of-type(odd) { background-color: #D9F0FF; }

tr:nth-of-type(even) { background-color: #FFFFFF; }
```

In the case of CSS selectors, there's always more than one way to skin an HTML tag—there are usually five or more!

Making Lists Look Great

When would I ever use a child selector? Just from reading this chapter, I already know enough selectors to get at just about any page element, so why learn another?

There's one design challenge where child selectors can't be beat—and it comes up in more websites than you think. Any time you have an unordered list with one or more unordered lists nested inside (as in Figure 3-6), you can use child selectors to visually organize these categories and subcategories of information. You can format the first level of list items one way, and the second level of list items another way. Content presented in this manner looks neat, professional, and readable (and your visitors will love you for it).

First, create a class style for the outermost nested level in your list and call it, say, .mainList. For this top level, you might use a sans-serif font, a little larger than your other text, perhaps in bold or a different color. Subsequent categories can be smaller, in a serif font like Times for easiest reading. When

you have a lot of text, styling each subcategory level a bit differently helps visually orient your visitors in the material.

Apply the .mainList class style to the first <ul> tag: <ul class="mainList">. Then use a child selector (ul. mainList > li) to select just the first set of list items, and add your desired text styling for the first subcategory. This styling applies to the <li> tags that are children of the <ul> tag with the .mainList style applied to it. Then, to style the child <li> tags of any subsequent nested <ul> tags, use this selector, ul.mainList > li > ul > li. (A descendant selector like ul li, by contrast, selects the list items of all unordered lists on the page—nested ones and all.)

You'll need to keep a concept you'll learn in the next chapter—inheritance—in mind. Basically, certain CSS properties applied to one tag are inherited by tags inside them. So even if you use a child selector to target the children of one tag, properties may pass on to other tags inside that child. The :not() selector, discussed on page 69, is one way to avoid this.

◼ Siblings

Parent-child relationships aren't the only ones in the HTML family tree. Sometimes you need to select a tag based not on its parent tag but on its surrounding siblings—the tags that share a common parent. A tag that appears immediately after another tag in HTML is called an *adjacent sibling*. In Figure 3-6, the <div> tag is the adjacent sibling of the <h1> tag, the <p> tag is the adjacent sibling of the <h2> tag, and so on.

Using an adjacent sibling selector, you can, for example, give the first paragraph after each heading different formatting from the paragraphs that follow. Suppose you want to remove the margin that appears above that <p> tag so that it sits right below the heading without any gap. Or perhaps you want to give the paragraph a distinct color and font size, like a little introductory statement.

The adjacent sibling selector uses a plus sign (+) to join one element to the next. So to select every paragraph following each <h2> tag, use this selector: h2 + p (spaces are optional, so h2+p works as well). The last element in the selector (p, in this case) is what gets the formatting, but only when it's directly after its brother <h2>.

There's another sibling selector called the *general sibling combinatory selector* (say that three times fast). It's simply a ~ (tilde) and it means "select all siblings of this type." For example, while h2 + p selects a single <p> tag that immediately follows an <h2> tag, h2 ~ p selects *all* <p> tags that are siblings (that is, on the same level) of the h2. To be honest, you may never find a good use for this selector, but CSS is nothing if not thorough.

■ The :target Selector

The :target() selector is fun. It can let you create some really interesting effects, like applying a style to a page element *after* another element is clicked. That's the kind of interactivity usually reserved for JavaScript. The :target() selector relies on a particular use of ID attributes, as described in the box on page 48; you use IDs to link to a particular spot on a page.

For example, say you have a web page called *index.html*. On that page, you have a div with the ID of signupForm. If you have a link on this page (or another page) that points to index.html#signupForm, then the web browser jumps to that div. If that div is at the bottom of a very long web page, then the browser scrolls the page until that div is in view. These are sometimes called *in page* links, and they're often used on glossary-style web pages where visitors can click a letter and jump to the spot on the page where the glossary words beginning with that letter appear.

But you don't have to use this feature to jump to another spot on the page. Whenever a URL in the browser's location bar includes a # followed by an ID, the element with that ID becomes the target, so you can apply a specific style to an element only when the ID for that element is in the URL.

Here's an example of HTML showing how the :target selector works. Imagine this code appears near the top of a web page:

```
<button>
  <a href="#signupForm">Sign up for our newsletter</a>
</button>
<form id="signupForm">
  <label for="email">What's your email address?</label>
  <input type="email" id="email">
  <input class="btn" type="submit" value="Sign up">
</form>
```

When a visitor clicks the link—the <a> tag—the form is targeted. In other words, you can apply one style to the form in its regular state and another style when a visitor clicks that link. For example, you could start off by hiding the form (you'll learn more about CSS visibility properties on page 439) using this rule:

```
#signupForm {
  display: none;
}
```

This rule hides the form, so when the page loads, the visitor can't see it. But when the visitor clicks the "Sign up for our newsletter" button and the form is targeted, you can show it like this:

```
#signupForm:target {
   display: block;
}
```

In other words, if the URL in the browser's location bar is just the filename—index. html, for example—then the browser applies the first style and hides the form. But if the location looks like this—index.html#signupForm—then the target style applies and the form is made visible. Cool stuff.

NOTE For a really cool use of the :target selector, check out this all-CSS gallery: *http://benschwarz. github.io/gallery-css/.*

◼ The :not() Selector

The :not() selector, also called the *negation pseudo-class*, lets you select something that's not something else. For example, say you apply a class to a paragraph—<p class="classy">—and create a CSS class selector to format it, like this:

```
.classy { color: red; }
```

But what if you want to select all paragraphs *except* the classy paragraphs? That's where the :not() selector comes in. You put a CSS selector inside the parentheses to indicate what you *don't* want to select. For example:

```
p:not(.classy) { color: blue; }
```

This style makes the text color blue for all paragraphs that don't have the classy class.

The :not() selector can come in handy when you're using the attribute selectors discussed on page 59. For example, you saw on page 59 that you can use an attribute selector to pick all links that point outside your website, like this:

```
a[href^="http://"]
```

As you've probably noticed, that selector doesn't specifically select all links that point outside your site; it simply selects all links that use absolute URLs—that is, URLs beginning with *http://.* For many sites, that's the same thing. Many sites use document- or root-relative links to point to other pages within the site, and absolute URLs to link to other sites. However, in some cases, you may use absolute URLs to point to pages within your site.

For example, many content management systems (WordPress, for example) use absolute URLs to point to blog posts within the site. In this case, if you want to style links that point outside your site, you need to refine the basic attribute selector by also employing the :not() selector. For example, say your site's domain name is *mysite.com*. To select links that point outside your site, you'll want to select all absolute links that *don't* point to the domain *mysite.com*. Here's how you would do that:

```
a[href^="http://"]:not([href^="http://mysite.com"])
```

Translated into English, this selector says "Select all links whose href attribute begins with *http://,* but *not* ones that begin with *http://mysite.com.*" As you'll recall from page 60, in an attribute selector, ^= means "begins with." A shorter way to write the same thing would be this:

```
a[href^="http://"]:not([href*="mysite.com"])
```

In an attribute selector, *= means "contains," so this line would exclude any absolute URL that contains mysite.com. This would include *http://www.mysite.com* as well as *http://mysite.com.*

There are some limitations to the :not() selector:

- You can only use *simple selectors* with the :not() selector. In other words you can use element selectors (like html or p), the universal selector (* [see page 49]), classes (.footer, for example), IDs (#banner, for example), or pseudo-classes (:hover, :checked, :first-child, and so on). So the following are all valid:

```
.footnote:not(div)
img:not(.portrait)
div:not(#banner)
li:not(:first-child)
```

- You can't use descendant selectors (like div p a, pseudo-elements (like ::first-line), group selectors, or combinators (like the adjacent sibling selector h2 + p).

- You can't string multiple :not() selectors together. For example, the following is invalid:

```
a[href^="http://"]:not([href*="google.com"]):not([href="yahoo.com"])
```

In other words, you can only use :not() once with a selector.

▓ Tutorial: Selector Sampler

In the rest of this chapter, you'll create a variety of selector types and see how each affects a web page. This tutorial starts with the basic selector types and then moves on to more advanced styles.

To get started, you need to download the tutorial files located on this book's companion website at *https://github.com/sawmac/css_mm_4e*. Click the tutorial link and download the files. All of the files are enclosed in a zip archive, so you'll need to unzip them first. The files for this tutorial are contained inside the folder named *03*.

Keeping It Internal

Hey, what's up with the internal style sheet in this tutorial? Chapter 2 recommends using external style sheets for a bunch of reasons.

Think you're pretty smart, eh? Yes, external style sheets usually make for faster, more efficient websites, for all the reasons mentioned in Chapter 2. However, internal style sheets make your life easier when you're designing a single page at a time, as in this tutorial. You get to work in just one web page file instead of flipping back and forth between the external style sheet file and the web page.

Furthermore, you can preview your results without constantly refreshing your browser's cache; flip back to the box on page 25 for more on that quirkiness.

So, yes, you should use external style sheets for your sites. And if you were going to use the styles you created in this tutorial on more than just the single tutorial HTML file, you would. But just to keep things fast and simple as you learn CSS, you'll use a single HTML file and an internal style sheet for this exercise.

But, that was an excellent question! Keep up the good work.

1. **In your favorite text editor, open** *03→selector_basics.html.*

   This page is made of very basic HTML tags (see Figure 3-10). But you'll liven things up in this tutorial. First, you'll link to a Google font—the same one you used back on page 36.

2. **In the empty line below the closing** `</title>` **tag, type:**

   ```
   <link href='http://fonts.googleapis.com/css?family=Varela+Round'
   rel='stylesheet'>
   ```

   As described on page 36, this tag links to an external style sheet that Google hosts on its web servers. It downloads the Varela Round font and so you can use it on the page. (You'll learn more about using web fonts like this one from Google on page 140.) Next, you'll add the internal style sheet.

3. **After the** `<link>` **tag you added in the last step, hit Return and type <style>. Press Enter twice and then type </style>.**

   These are the opening and closing style tags—it's a good idea to type both tags at the same time, so you don't accidentally forget to add the closing `</style>` tag. Together, these two tags tell a web browser that the information between them is Cascading Style Sheet instructions. The HTML should now look like this (the stuff you added is in bold):

   ```
   <title>Selector Basics</title>
   <link href='http://fonts.googleapis.com/css?family=Varela+Round'
   rel='stylesheet'>
   <style>

   </style>
   ```

Type selectors—like the one you're about to create—are the most basic kind of selector. If you completed the tutorial in the last chapter, you've already created a few. Here, you'll add a background color to the page.

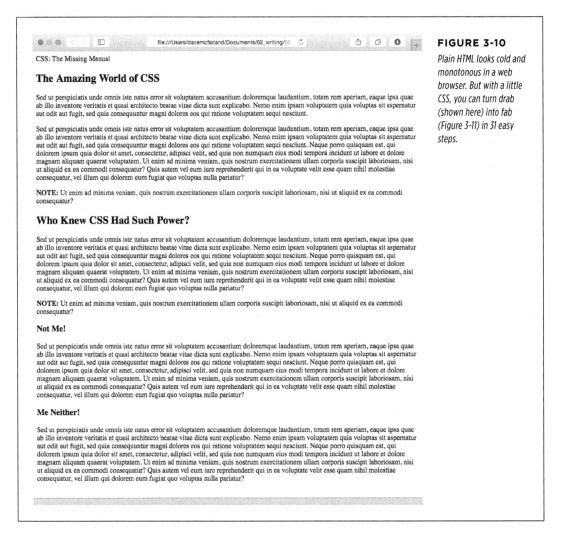

FIGURE 3-10

Plain HTML looks cold and monotonous in a web browser. But with a little CSS, you can turn drab (shown here) into fab (Figure 3-11) in 31 easy steps.

4. **Click between the opening and closing style tags you just added and type** body { **, hit Enter twice, and type the closing** }.

It's a good idea to always add the closing brace immediately after typing the opening brace, just so you don't forget. To create a tag selector, simply use the name of the HTML tag you wish to format. This style applies to the <body> tag. Now you can set the background color and the margin of space around the page.

5. **Click between** `<body>` **style's opening and closing braces ({ }) and add the following three CSS properties to supply the style's formatting—color, size, font, and left indent (as set by the padding):**

```
body {
  background-color: rgb(50,122,167);
  padding: 0 20px 20px 20px;
  margin: 0;
}
```

Press Enter to place each CSS property on its own line. It's also a good idea to visually organize your CSS code by indenting each property with the Tab key (some designers use two spaces instead of a tab—it's up to you).

The properties here change the background color of the page: `rgb()` is one way to specify a color's red, green, and blue values. In this case, the color is a dark blue. This background makes the black text hard to read, so you need to change the color of the paragraph tags.

NOTE These property names and their values may look unfamiliar. For now, just type them as is so you can get a taste of padding and margins work. You'll learn much more about these properties in Chapter 6.

6. **Add another style below the body style you just created:**

```
p {
    color: rgba(255,255,255,.6);
    font-size: 1em;
    font-family: "Varela Round", Arial, Helvetica, sans-serif;
}
```

With four CSS properties, this style supplies formatting for all paragraphs (all `<p>` tags)—color, size, and font. This time, the color is determined by an `rgba()` color value. With an extra "a" after the usual "rgb," this versatile value lets you create a color that's partially transparent. In this case, you've set the paragraph's text to white (which is 255,255,255 in rgb), but only 60 percent opaque (that's the .6 part). A bit of the blue background color shows through, so the paragraph text appears light blue.

Time for a look-see.

7. **Open the page in a web browser to preview your work.**

Unless you tinker with the preference settings, most browsers display black text in a standard serif font like Times. If your CSS style works properly, then you should see seven paragraphs using the Varela Round font in a light blue color.

Creating a Group Selector

Sometimes you'll want several different elements on a page to share the same look. For instance, you may want all your headings to have the same font and color for a consistent style. Instead of creating separate styles and duplicating the same property settings for each tag—<h1>, <h2>, and so on—you can group the tags together into a single selector.

1. **Return to your text editor and the *selector_basics.html* file.**

   Let's add a new style below the <p> tag style you just created.

2. **Click at the end of the closing brace of the** p **tag selector, press Enter to start a new line, and add the following code:**

   ```
   h1, h2, h3 {

   }
   ```

   As explained earlier in this chapter, a group selector is simply a list of selectors separated by commas. This rule applies the same formatting, which you'll add next, to all <h1>, <h2>, and <h3> tags on the page.

3. **Click in the empty line between the opening { and closing } and add five CSS properties:**

   ```
   color: rgb(255,255,255);
   font-family: Arial, "Palatino Linotype", Times, serif;
   border-bottom: 2px solid rgb(87,185,178);
   padding-top: 10px;
   padding-bottom: 5px;
   ```

   There's a lot going on here, but basically you're setting the color and font type for the headlines, adding a border line below the headlines for visual interest, and controlling the top and bottom spacing by using the padding property. The padding property adds space from the edges of an element without affecting a background or border—you're adding a bit of space above the headline, and inserting a bit of space between the bottom of that text and the border line below it.

4. **Save the file, and preview it in a web browser.**

   The <h1> heading near the top of the page and the <h2> and <h3> headings lower on the page all have the same font and font color as well as a greenish-blue border below them (see Figure 3-11). The <h1> tag looks a bit small, but you can easily bump up its size.

5. **Go back to your text editor and the *selector_basics.html* file. Add another style below the group selector style you just created:**

   ```
   h1 {
     font-size: 2em;
   }
   ```

   This style increases the size of the font. An em is the default browser font-size, so 2em is twice the normal text size. Notice, as well, that it's possible to have

more than one style apply to an element at the same time—the h1, h2, h3 rule
and the h1 rule in this case. Both the group selector and this new type selector
apply to h1 tags on this page. This process is the *cascade* in Cascading Style
Sheets. You'll learn all about how styles interact in Chapter 5.

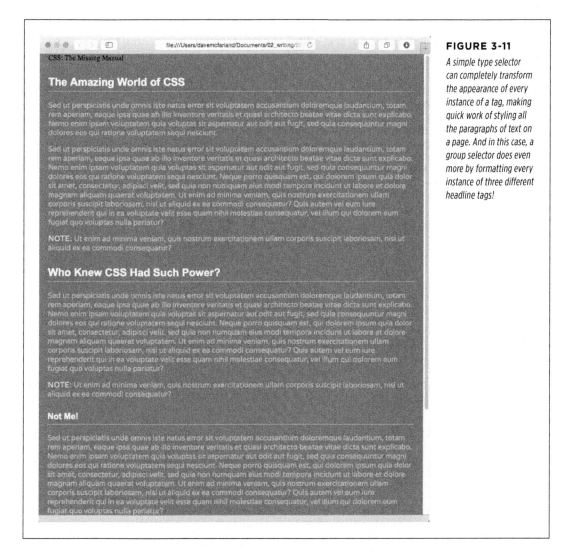

FIGURE 3-11

*A simple type selector
can completely transform
the appearance of every
instance of a tag, making
quick work of styling all
the paragraphs of text on
a page. And in this case, a
group selector does even
more by formatting every
instance of three different
headline tags!*

Creating and Applying an ID Selector

ID selectors are used to style a single tag. You create the style and add an ID attribute
to a tag on the page, and then the properties from that style are applied to that single
tag. You'll frequently use IDs to identify form elements, to create in-page links in a
page (see the box on page 48), and to use JavaScript to control elements on a page.

Although many web designers now shy away from ID selectors (you'll learn exactly why on page 108), it's still good to know how to use them.

In this exercise, you'll create a style that controls the look of the text that appears at the very top of the page: "CSS: The Missing Manual." This text is considered the page's logo, and you'll create a special ID style to format it.

1. **Return to your text editor and the _selector_basics.html_ file.**

   You'll add a new style below the h1 class style you created before.

2. **Click after the previous style's closing bracket (}), hit Enter to create a new line, and then type** #logo {.

   ID selectors always begin with the pound symbol (#). The style's name indicates that you'll apply this to a page element that's considered the site's logo.

3. **Hit Enter again, and then type:**

   ```
   font-family: Baskerville, Palatino, sans-serif;
   font-size: 2em;
   color: rgba(255,255,255,.8);
   font-style: italic;
   text-align: center;
   margin-bottom: 30px;
   background-color: rgb(191,91,116);
   border-radius: 0 0 10px 10px;
   padding: 10px;
   ```

   It looks like a long list of properties, but all it does it set some font properties, background color, and spacing for the logo text.

4. **Finish the style by typing the closing brace. The whole thing should look like this:**

   ```
   #logo {
      font-family: Baskerville, Palatino, sans-serif;
      font-size: 2em;
      color: rgba(255,255,255,.8);
      font-style: italic;
      text-align: center;
      margin-bottom: 30px;
      background-color: rgb(191,91,116);
      border-radius: 0 0 10px 10px;
      padding: 10px;
   }
   ```

   If you save the file and preview it in a web browser, you won't see any difference. That's because this style doesn't _do_ anything until you apply it. So you'll add an ID attribute to the page's HTML, indicating where you want the ID style to apply.

5. **Find the** `<div>` **tag near the opening** `<body>` **tag—it has the text "CSS: The Missing Manual" in it. Add** `id="logo"` **to the opening div so the HTML looks like this:**

```
<div id="logo">
  CSS: The Missing Manual
</div>
```

The `<div>` tag now reflects the formatting defined in the #logo style. As with all things CSS, there are many ways to arrive at the same destination: You could instead use a class style and apply it to the `<div>` tag. But in this case you're using an ID selector, since the point of this style—identifying the logo on the page—is in keeping with the general notion of ID selectors.

6. **Save the page, and preview it in a browser.**

Now the "CSS: The Missing Manual" text is centered, light-colored, and inside a small box at the top of the page (Figure 3-12).

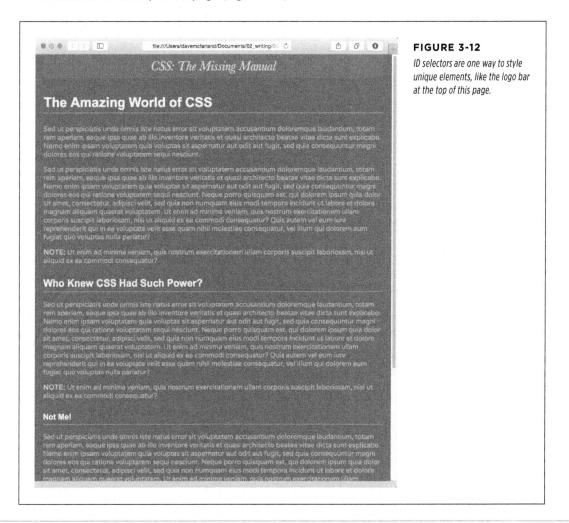

FIGURE 3-12

ID selectors are one way to style unique elements, like the logo bar at the top of this page.

Creating and Applying a Class Selector

Type selectors are quick and efficient, but they're a bit indiscriminate in how they style a page. What if you want to style a single <p> tag differently than all the other <p> tags on a page? A class selector is the answer.

1. **Return to your text editor and the *selector_basics.html* file.**

   Add a new style below the ID selector style you just created.

2. **Click at the end of the closing brace of the** #logo **selector, press Enter, and then type**

   ```
   .note {


   }
   ```

   This style's name, .note, indicates its purpose: to highlight paragraphs that contain extra bits of information for your site's visitors. Once you create a class style, you can apply it wherever these notes appear—like the third paragraph in this page.

3. **Click in the empty line between the opening { and closing } and add the following list of properties to the style:**

   ```
   color: black;
   border: 2px solid white;
   background-color: rgb(69,189,102);
   margin-top: 25px;
   margin-bottom: 35px;
   padding: 20px;
   ```

   Notice that you're not using the rgb() color values to color the font and border. CSS has several different ways to specify a color, including keywords like white, black, or orange. You'll learn about those on page 147.

   If you preview the page now, you see no changes. Like ID selectors, class selectors don't have any effect on a web page until you apply the style in the HTML code.

4. **In the page's HTML, there are two** <p> **tags that begin with the word "Note" inside** <strong> **tags.**

   To apply a class style to a tag, simply add a class attribute, followed by the class selector's name—in this case, the note style you just created.

5. **Click just after the** p **in the first** <p> **tag, and then type a space followed by** class="note". **The HTML should now look like this (what you just typed is in bold):**

   ```
   <p class="note"><strong>NOTE:</strong>
   ```

Be sure *not* to type `class=".note"`. In CSS, the period is necessary to indicate a class style name; in HTML, it's verboten. Repeat this step for the second paragraph (it's just above the `<h3>` tag with the text "Not Me!").

> **NOTE** There's no reason you can't add this class to other tags as well, not just the `<p>` tag. If you happen to want to apply this formatting to an `<h2>` tag, for example, then your HTML would look like this:
>
> ```
> <h2 class="note">
> ```

6. **Save and preview the web page in a browser.**

   The note paragraph is nicely highlighted on the page (see Figure 3-13).

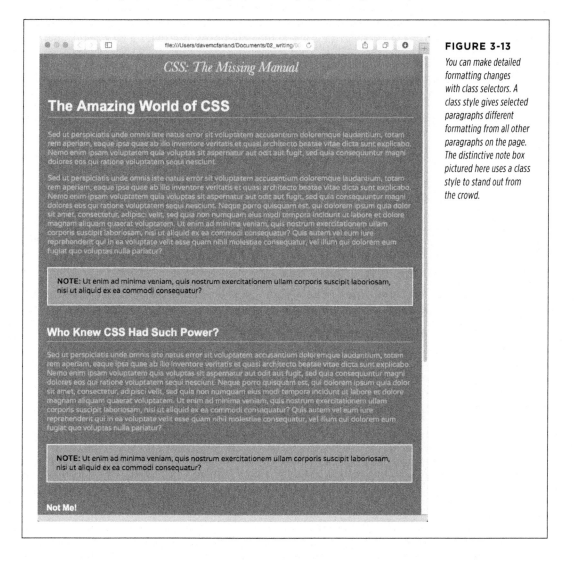

FIGURE 3-13

You can make detailed formatting changes with class selectors. A class style gives selected paragraphs different formatting from all other paragraphs on the page. The distinctive note box pictured here uses a class style to stand out from the crowd.

NOTE If your page doesn't look like Figure 3-13, then you may have mistyped the name of a property or its value. Double-check your code with the steps above. Also, make sure to end each declaration (property: value combination) with a semicolon and conclude the style with a closing brace at the very end. When your style is not working correctly, missing semicolons and closing braces are frequent culprits.

Creating a Descendant Selector

On the *selectors_basics.html* page, you applied the note class to two paragraphs. Each of those paragraphs begins with the word "Note:" in bold—actually the word is wrapped inside the HTML <strong> tag, which all browsers display as bolded text. But what if you want to format those bolded words in bright orange? You could create a tag style for the <strong> tag, but that would affect all <strong> tags on the page, and you only want to change the strong tag inside those note boxes. One solution would be to create a class style—.noteText, for example—and apply it to each of the <strong> tags inside the note boxes. But that's a lot of work, and you might forget to apply the class if you have a lot of pages with those notes.

A better method is to create a descendant selector (page 50), which targets only the <strong> tag when it's inside one of these note boxes. Fortunately, that's easy to do.

1. **Return to your text editor and the *selector_basics.html* file. Create a new empty line for the descendant selector style.**

    If you just completed the previous steps, click after the closing brace of the *.note* style, and then hit Enter.

2. **Type** .note strong {.

    The last tag in the selector—strong—is the element you ultimately want to format. In this case, the style formats the <strong> tag only when it's *inside* another tag with the class note applied to it. It has no effect on <strong> tags inside other paragraphs, lists, or heading tags, for example.

3. **Hit Enter, type** color: #FC6512;**, and then hit Enter again to create another blank line. Finish the style by typing the closing brace character.**

    The finished style should look like this:

    ```
    .note strong {
      color: #FC6512;
    }
    ```

4. **Save the page and preview it in a web browser.**

    The word "Note:" should appear in orange in each of the note boxes on the page.

Descendant selectors are among the most powerful CSS tools. Professional web designers use them extensively to target particular tags without littering the HTML with CSS classes. You'll learn a lot more about descendant selectors as they're used throughout this book.

Finishing Touches

The text on this page expands to fill the browser window. To see this in effect, preview the page and resize your browser window. You'll see the lines of text get wider as you stretch the window. If you have a large monitor, you'll see that the text becomes pretty hard to read past a certain width: The lines of text are too long to read comfortably. Fortunately, you can set a width for the page's content, so it doesn't get too wide to read.

1. **Return to your text editor and the *selector_basics.html* file. Create a new empty line for a new style.**

   If you just completed the previous steps, click after the closing brace of the .note strong descendant selector style, and then hit Enter.

2. **Add another style:**

   ```
   article {
     max-width: 760px;
   }
   ```

   This is another type selector. It applies to the HTML5 <article> tag, which is used to define the content that makes up an article like a blog post, or the content on this page.

   The max-width property sets the maximum width for the tag, meaning that the article tag will never get wider than 760 pixels. Save the file and preview it in a browser. If you widen the browser window, you'll notice that past 760 pixels, the window gets wider and the blue background of the page appears, but the text no longer expands.

   On the other hand, if you make the browser window smaller than 760 pixels, the text lines do get shorter. That's the power of the max-width property, which sets a maximum width, but no minimum. This property is extremely useful when you're designing sites that need to work on a variety of screen sizes—desktop computers, laptops, tablets, and smart phones. It's an important part of *responsive design,* which you'll learn about in Chapter 17.

   Now that you've limited how far the text can expand, it would be nice to keep the content centered on the screen instead of sticking to the left edge as the browser window expands.

3. **Add one more property to the** article **style so it looks like this (addition in bold):**

   ```
   article {
     max-width: 760px;
     margin: 0 auto;
   }
   ```

The margin property sets the space between an element and other elements around it. You'll read more about margins on page 187, but here this line sets the left and right margins to auto, which tells the web browser to automatically figure out how much space to add to the left and right sides of the article tag. Once the browser window gets past 760 pixels, the article element gets no wider, so the browser basically adds empty space to both the left and right of the tag, in essence centering it in the middle of the browser window.

For fun, you'll add one more advanced style—an adjacent sibling selector discussed on page 67—to format the paragraph immediately following the first headline on the page. (You can achieve the same effect by creating a class style and applying it to that paragraph, but the adjacent sibling selector requires no changes to your HTML.)

4. **Add one last style:**

```
h1+p {
  color: rgb(255,255,255);
  font-size: 1.2em;
  line-height: 140%;
}
```

This style will apply to any paragraph that *immediately* follows an <h1> tag—in other words, the first paragraph after the top headline on the page. It won't apply to the second or any subsequent paragraphs. This selector provides an easy way to create a unique look for an introductory paragraph to set it off visually and highlight the beginning of an article.

The style changes the font color and size. The line-height property (which you'll read about on page 163) controls the space between lines in a paragraph (also known as *leading*).

If you preview the page now, you'll see that the top paragraph is white and its text is larger, and there's more space between each line of text (see Figure 3-14). If you actually deleted this paragraph in the HTML, you'd see that the remaining paragraph would suddenly be white with larger text, since it would be the new adjacent sibling of the <h1> tag.

And there you have it: a quick tour through various selector types. You'll get familiar with all of these selectors (and more) as you go through the tutorials later in the book, but by now, you should be getting the hang of the different types and why you'd use one over the other.

NOTE You can see a completed version of the page you've just created in the *03_finished* folder.

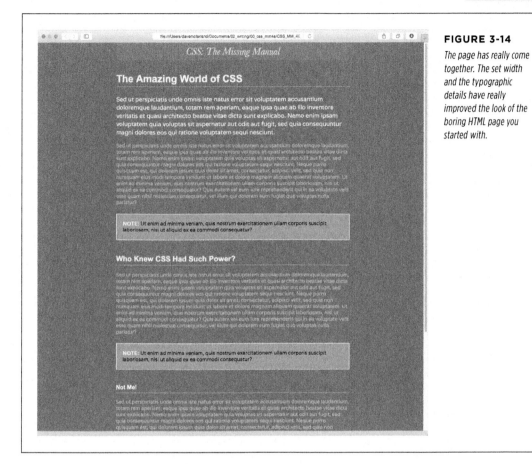

FIGURE 3-14

The page has really come together. The set width and the typographic details have really improved the look of the boring HTML page you started with.

Saving Time with Style Inheritance

Children inherit traits from their parents—eye color, height, male-pattern bald-ness, and so on. Sometimes we inherit traits from more distant ancestors, like grandparents or great-grandparents. As you saw in the previous chapter, the metaphor of family relations is part of the structure of HTML as well. And just like humans, HTML tags can inherit CSS properties from their ancestors.

■ What Is Inheritance?

Inheritance is the process by which some CSS properties applied to one tag are passed on to nested tags. For example, a <p> tag is always nested inside of the <body> tag, so properties applied to the <body> tag get inherited by the <p> tag. Say you created a type selector style (page 41) for the <body> tag that sets the color property to a dark red. Tags that are descendants of the <body> tag—that is, the ones inside the <body> tag—will inherit that color property. That means that any text in those tags—<h1>, <h2>, <p>, or whatever—will appear in that same dark red color.

Inheritance works through multiple generations as well. If a tag like the <em> or <strong> tag appears inside of a <p> tag, then the <em> and the <strong> tags also inherit properties from any style applied to the <body> tag.

> **NOTE** As discussed in Chapter 3, any tag inside of another tag is a *descendant* of that tag. So a <p> tag inside the <body> tag is a descendant of the <body>, while the <body> tag is an *ancestor* of the <p> tag. *Descendants* (think kids and grandchildren) inherit properties from ancestors (think parents and grandparents).

Although this may sound confusing, inheritance is a *really* big timesaver. Imagine if no properties were passed onto nested tags and you had a paragraph that contained other tags like a <strong> tag, an <em> tag to emphasize text and an <a> tag to add a link. If you created a style that made the paragraph text white and 32 pixels tall, using the Varela Round font, it would be weird if all the text inside the <em>, <strong> and <a> tags reverted to its regular, "browser boring" style (see Figure 4-1). You'd then have to create another style to format the <em> tag to match the appearance of the <p> tag. What a drag.

Inheritance doesn't just apply to tag styles. It works with any type of style, so when you apply a class style (see page 43) to a tag, any tags inside that tag inherit properties from the styled tag. The same holds true for ID styles, descendant selectors, and the other types of styles discussed in Chapter 3.

■ How Inheritance Streamlines Style Sheets

You can use inheritance to your advantage to streamline your style sheets. Say you want all the text on a page to use the same font. Instead of creating styles for each tag, simply create a tag style for the <body> tag. (Or create a class style and apply it to the <body> tag.) In the style, specify the font you wish to use, and all of the tags on the page inherit the font:

```
body {
 font-family: Arial, Helvetica, sans-serif;
}
```

You can also use inheritance to apply style properties to a *section* of a page. For example, like many web designers, you may use the <div> tag (page 47) to define an area of a page like a banner, sidebar, or footer; or if you're using HTML5 elements, you might use one of the sectioning elements like <header>, <aside>, <footer>, or <article>. By applying a style to that outer tag, you can specify particular CSS properties for all of the tags inside just that section of the page. If you want all the text in a sidebar to be the same color, you'd create a style setting the color property, and then apply it to the <div>, <header>, <article>, or other sectioning element. Any <p>, <h1>, or other tags inside inherit the same font color.

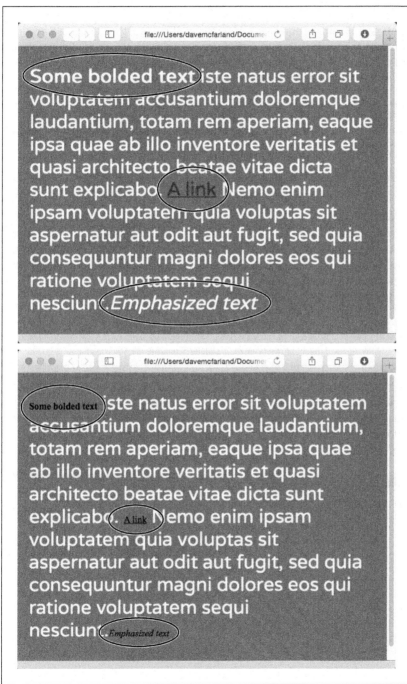

FIGURE 4-1

Inheritance lets tags copy properties from the tags that surround them.

Top: The paragraph tag is set with a specific font family, size, and color. The tags inside each paragraph—the <strong>, <a>, and <em> tags circled—inherit those properties so they look like the rest of the paragraph.

Bottom: If inheritance didn't exist, the same page would look like this figure. Notice how the <strong>, <em>, and <a> tags inside the paragraph (circled) retain the font-family, size, and color defined by the browser. To make them look like the rest of the paragraph, you'd have to create additional styles—a big waste of time.

■ The Limits of Inheritance

Inheritance isn't all-powerful. Many CSS properties don't pass down to descendant tags at all. For example, the border property (which lets you draw a box around an element) isn't inherited, and with good reason. If it were, then every tag inside an element with the border property would also have a border around it. For example, if you added a border to the <body> tag, then every bulleted list would also have a box around it, and each bulleted item in the list would also have a border (Figure 4-2).

> **NOTE** There's a list of CSS properties in Appendix A, including details on which ones get inherited.

Here are examples of times when inheritance doesn't strictly apply:

- As a general rule, properties that affect the placement of elements on the page or the margins, background colors, and borders of elements aren't inherited.

- Web browsers use their own inherent styles to format various tags: Headings are big and bold, links are blue, and so on. When you define a font size for the text on a page and apply it to the <body> tag, headings still appear larger than paragraphs, and <h1> tags are still larger than <h2> tags. It's the same when you apply a font color to the <body>; the links on the page still appear in good old-fashioned web-browser blue.

> **NOTE** It's usually a good idea to eliminate these built-in browser styles—it'll make designing sites that work consistently among different browsers easier. In Chapter 5, on page 109, you'll learn how to do that.

- When styles conflict, the more specific style wins out. In other words, when you've specifically applied CSS properties to an element—like specifying the font size for an unordered list—and those properties conflict with any inherited properties—like a font-size set for the <body> tag—the browser uses the font size applied to the <ul> tag.

> **NOTE** These types of conflicts between styles are very common, and the rules for how a browser deals with them are called the *cascade*. You'll learn about that in Chapter 5.

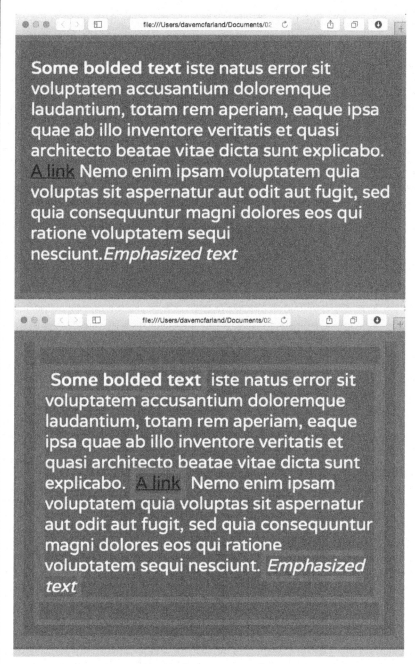

FIGURE 4-2

Fortunately, not all properties are inherited. The border applied to the body of this page (the thick red outline around the content) in the image at top isn't inherited by the tags inside the body. If they were, you'd end up with an unattractive mess of boxes within boxes within boxes (bottom).

■ Tutorial: Inheritance

In this three-part tutorial, you'll see how inheritance works. First, you'll create a simple tag selector and watch it pass its characteristics on to nested tags. Then, you'll create a class style that uses inheritance to alter the formatting of an entire page. Finally, you'll see where CSS makes some welcome exceptions to the inheritance rule.

To get started, you need to download the tutorial files located at *https://github.com/ sawmac/css_mm_4e*. Click the tutorial link and download the files. All of the files are enclosed in a zip archive, so you'll need to unzip them first. (Detailed instructions for unzipping the files are on the website.) The files for this tutorial are contained in the folder named *04*.

A Basic Example: One Level of Inheritance

To see how inheritance works, start by adding a single tag style and see how it affects the tags nested inside. The next two parts of this tutorial will build upon your work here, so save the file when you're done.

1. **Open the file *inheritance.html* in your favorite text editor.**

   This file already has an internal style sheet, with one type selector giving the `<body>` tag a background color.

> **NOTE** In general, it's better to use external style sheets for a website, for reasons discussed in Chapter 2 (page 26). But for a simple tutorial like this, it's easier to just work with one file.

2. **Add another style after the** `<body>` **style in the style sheet:**

   ```
   p {
     color: rgb(92,122,142);
   }
   ```

   As you've seen in the previous tutorials, the `color` property sets the color of text. Your style sheet is complete.

3. **Open the page in a web browser to preview your work.**

   The color of the page's four paragraphs has changed from black to a slate blue color (see Figure 4-3).

But notice how this `<p>` tag style affects *other* tags: Tags *inside* of the `<p>` tag also change color. For example, the text inside the `<em>` and `<strong>` tags inside each paragraph also changes from black to slate blue while maintaining its italic and bold formatting. This kind of behavior makes a lot of sense. After all, when you set the color of text in a paragraph, you expect *all* the text in the paragraph—regardless of any other tags inside that paragraph—to be the same color.

Without inheritance, creating style sheets would be very labor intensive. If the `<em>` and `<strong>` tags didn't inherit the color property from the `<p>` tag selector, then you'd have to create additional styles—perhaps descendant selectors like p em and p strong—to correctly format the text.

However, you'll notice that the link at the end of the first paragraph doesn't change color—it retains its link-blue color. As you'll learn on page 109, browsers have their own styles for certain elements, so inheritance doesn't apply. You'll learn more about this behavior in Chapter 5.

Using Inheritance to Restyle an Entire Page

Inheritance works with class styles as well—any tag with any kind of style applied to it passes CSS properties to its descendants. With that in mind, you can use inheritance to make quick, sweeping changes to an entire page.

1. **Return to your text editor and the *inheritance.html* file.**

   You'll add a new style below the <p> tag style you created.

2. **Click at the end of the closing brace of the p selector. Press Enter to create a new line, and then type** .content {. **Hit Enter twice, and type the closing brace:** }.

   You're about to create a new class style that you'll apply to the <body> tag, which surrounds the other tags on this page.

3. **Click between the two braces, and then add the following list of properties to the style:**

   ```
   font-family: "Helvetica Neue", Arial, Helvetica, sans-serif;
   font-size: 18px;
   color: rgb(194,91,116);
   max-width: 900px;
   margin: 0 auto;
   ```

   The whole thing should look like this:

   ```
   .content {
     font-family: "Helvetica Neue", Arial, Helvetica, sans-serif;
     font-size: 18px;
     color: rgb(194,91,116);
     max-width: 900px;
     margin: 0 auto;
   }
   ```

   This completed class style sets a font, font size, and color. It also sets a width and centers the style on the page (you saw this trick in the previous tutorial on page 81 for creating a fixed, centered area for a page's content).

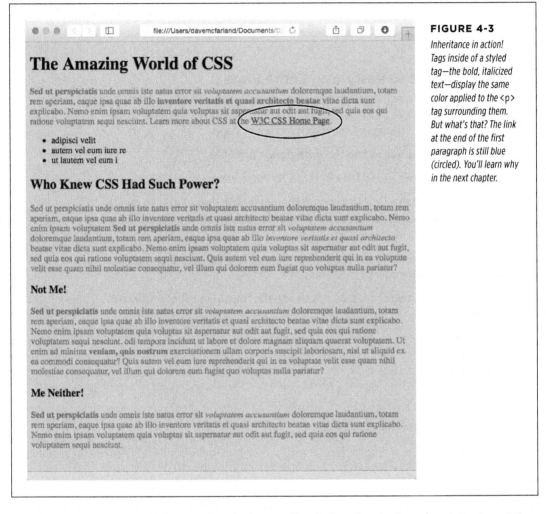

FIGURE 4-3

Inheritance in action! Tags inside of a styled tag—the bold, italicized text—display the same color applied to the <p> tag surrounding them. But what's that? The link at the end of the first paragraph is still blue (circled). You'll learn why in the next chapter.

4. **Find the opening** <body> **tag (just below the closing** </head> **tag), and then type** class="content".

   The tag should now look like this: <body class="content">. It applies the class to the <body> tag. Thanks to inheritance, all tags inside of the <body> tag (which are also all the tags visible inside a browser window) inherit this style's properties and therefore use the same font.

5. **Save and preview the web page in a browser.**

   As you can see in Figure 4-4, your class style has created a seamless, consistent appearance throughout all text in the body of the page. Both headings and paragraphs inside the <body> tag have taken on the new font styling.

The page as a whole looks great, but now look more closely: The color change affected only the headings and the bulleted list on the page, and even though the style specified an exact font size, the headline text is a different size than the paragraphs. How did CSS know that you didn't want your headings to be the same 18-pixel size as the body text? And why didn't the nested <p> tags inherit your new color styling from the <body> tag?

NOTE Why use a class—content—instead of a tag style—body—to redefine the look of the page? Well, in this case, a tag style would work fine. But applying a class to the <body> tag is a great way to customize the look of different pages on your site. For example, if all pages on your site share the same external style sheet, a body tag style would apply to the <body> tag of every page on your site. By creating different classes (or IDs) you can create a different style for the <body> tag for different sections of the site or different types of pages.

You're seeing the "cascading" aspect of Cascading Style Sheets in action. In this example, your <p> tags have two color styles in conflict—the <p> tag style you created in step 2 on page 90 and the class style you created here. When styles collide, the browser has to pick one. As discussed on page 80, the browser uses the more specific styling—the color you assigned explicitly to the <p> tag. You'll learn much more about the rules of the cascade in Chapter 5.

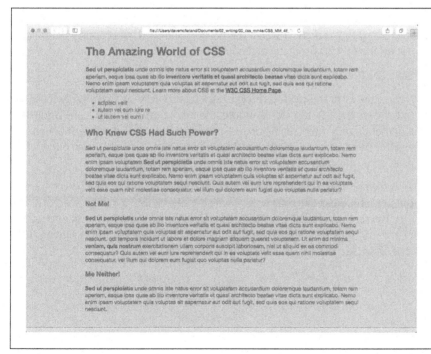

FIGURE 4-4

A style applied to the <body> tag passes its properties onto all the tags you see in the web browser, making it easy to apply global formatting effects to a page.

Inheritance In Action

Inheritance doesn't always apply, and that isn't necessarily a bad thing. For some properties, inheritance would have a negative effect on a page's appearance. You'll see another example of inheritance *in action* in the final section of this tutorial. Margins, padding, and borders (among other properties) don't get inherited by descendant tags—and you wouldn't want them to, as you'll see in this example.

1. **Return to your text editor and the *inheritance.html* file.**

   You'll expand on the p tag style you just created.

2. **Locate the** p **style, click at the end of the color property (**color: rgb(50,122,167);**), and then press Enter (Return) to create a new line.**

   You'll indent the paragraphs on the page by adding a left margin.

3. **Add two properties to the style so it looks like this:**

   ```
   p {
     color: rgb(50,122,167);
     padding-left: 20px;
     border-left: solid 25px rgba(255,255,255,.5);
   }
   ```

   These changes add a border to the left side of every paragraph, and move the text so that it doesn't touch the border: The padding property indents the paragraph text 20 pixels from the border.

4. **Save the file and preview it in a web browser.**

   Notice that all of the <p> tags have a thick light border on the left. However, the tags *inside* the <p> tag (for example, the <em> tag) don't have any additional indentation or border (see Figure 4-5). This behavior makes sense: It would look weird if there were an additional thick border and 20px of space to the left of each <em> and each <strong> tag inside of a paragraph!

   To see what would happen if those properties were inherited, edit the p selector so that it looks like this: p, p *, which makes it into a group selector (page 49). The first part is just the p selector you already created. The second part—p *—means "select all tags inside of a <p> tag and apply this style to them." (The *, or universal selector, is described on page 49.)

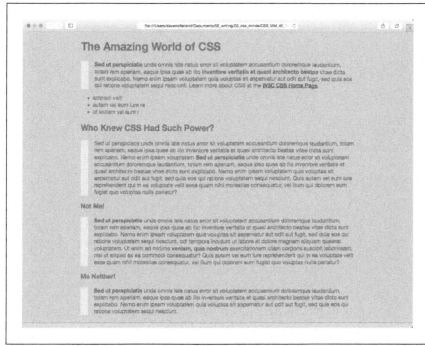

FIGURE 4-5

While most properties are inherited (like color), there are plenty—like margins, padding, and borders—that don't pass on to nested tags. The CSS Property Reference in Appendix A indicates which properties are and are not inherited.

NOTE You can find a completed version of the page you created in this tutorial in the *04_finished* folder.

Managing Multiple Styles: The Cascade

A s you create increasingly complex style sheets, you'll sometimes wonder why a particular element on a page looks the way it does. CSS's inheritance feature, as discussed in Chapter 4, creates the possibility that any tag on a page is potentially affected by any of the tags that wrap around it. For example, the <body> tag can pass properties on to a paragraph, and a paragraph may pass its own formatting instructions on to a link within the paragraph. In other words, that link can inherit CSS properties from *both* the <body> and the <p> tag—essentially creating a kind of Frankenstyle that combines parts of two different CSS rules.

Then there are times when styles collide—the same CSS property is defined in multiple rules, all applying to a particular element on the page (for example, a <p> tag style in an external style sheet and another <p> tag style in an internal style sheet). When that happens, you can see some pretty weird stuff, like text that appears bright blue, even though you specifically applied a class style with the text color set to red. Fortunately, there's actually a system at work: a basic CSS mechanism known as the *cascade*, which governs how styles interact and which styles get precedence when there's a conflict.

NOTE This chapter deals with issues that arise when you build complex style sheets that rely on inheritance and more sophisticated types of selectors like descendant selectors (page 50). The rules are all pretty logical, but they're about as fun to master as the tax code. If that's got your spirits sagging, consider skipping the details and doing the tutorial on page 111 to get a taste of what the cascade is and why it matters. Or jump right to the next chapter, which explores fun and visually exciting ways to format text. You can always return to this chapter later, after you're comfortable with the basics of CSS.

▪ How Styles Cascade

The *cascade* is a set of rules for determining which style properties get applied to an element. It specifies how a web browser should handle multiple styles that apply to the same tag and what to do when CSS properties conflict. Style conflicts happen in two cases: through inheritance, when the same property is inherited from multiple ancestors; and when one or more styles apply to the same element (maybe you've applied a class style to a paragraph and also created a <p> tag style, so both styles apply to that paragraph).

Inherited Styles Accumulate

As you read in the last chapter, CSS inheritance ensures that related elements—like all the words inside a paragraph, even those inside a link or another tag—share similar formatting. It spares you from creating specific styles for each tag on a page. But since one tag can inherit properties from *any* ancestor tag—a link, for example, inheriting the same font as its parent <p> tag—determining why a particular tag is formatted one way can be a bit tricky. Imagine a font family applied to the <body> tag, a font size applied to a <p> tag, and a font color applied to an <a> tag. Any <a> tag inside of a paragraph would inherit the font from the body and the size from the paragraph. In other words, the inherited styles combine to form a hybrid style.

The page shown in Figure 5-1 has three styles: one for the <body>, one for the <p> tag, and one for the <strong> tag. The CSS looks like this:

```
body { font-family: Verdana, Arial, Helvetica, sans-serif; }
p { color: #F30; }
strong { font-size: 24px; }
```

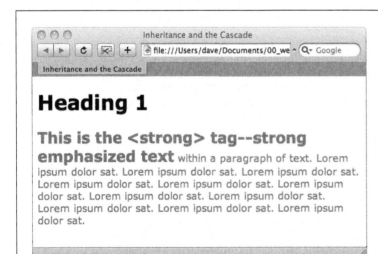

FIGURE 5-1

Thanks to inheritance, it's possible for multiple styles to affect the appearance of one tag. Here the <strong> tag has a specific color, font family, and font size, even though only a single property is applied directly to that tag. The other two formatting options were inherited from the tag's ancestors: the <body> and the <p> tags.

The `<strong>` tag is nested inside a paragraph, which is inside the `<body>` tag. That `<strong>` tag inherits from both of its ancestors, so it inherits the `font-family` property from the body and the `color` property from its parent paragraph. In addition, the `<strong>` tag has a bit of CSS applied directly to it—a 24px font size. The final appearance of the tag is a combination of all three styles. In other words, the `<strong>` tag appears exactly as if you'd created a style like this:

```
strong {
    font-family: Verdana, Arial, Helvetica, sans-serif;
    color: #F30;
    font-size: 24px;
}
```

Nearest Ancestor Wins

In the previous example, various inherited and applied tags smoothly combined to create an overall formatting package. But what happens when inherited CSS properties conflict? Think about a page where you've set the font color for the `<body>` tag to red and the paragraph tag to green. Now imagine that within one paragraph, there's a `<strong>` tag. The `<strong>` tag inherits from both the `<body>` and `<p>` tag styles, so is the text inside the `<strong>` tag red or green? Ladies and gentlemen, we have a winner: the green from the paragraph style. That's because the web browser obeys the style that's *closest* to the tag in question.

In this example, any properties inherited from the `<body>` tag are rather generic. They apply to all tags. A style applied to a `<p>` tag, on the other hand, is more narrowly defined. Its properties apply only to `<p>` tags and the tags inside them.

In a nutshell, if a tag doesn't have a specific style applied to it, then, in the case of any conflicts from inherited properties, the nearest ancestor wins (see Figure 5-2, number 1).

Here's one more example, just to make sure the concept sinks in. If a CSS style defining the color of text were applied to a `<table>` tag, and another style defining a *different* text color were applied to a `<td>` tag inside that table, then tags inside that table cell (`<td>`)—such as a paragraph, headline, or unordered list—would use the color from the `<td>` style, since it's the closest ancestor.

The Directly Applied Style Wins

Taking the "nearest ancestor" rule to its logical conclusion, there's one style that always becomes king of the CSS family tree—any style applied directly to a given tag. Suppose a font color is set for the body, paragraph, *and* strong tags. The paragraph style is more specific than the body style, but the style applied to the `<strong>` tag is more specific than either one. It formats the `<strong>` tags and only the `<strong>` tags, overriding any conflicting properties inherited from the other tags (see Figure 5-2, number 2). In other words, properties from a style specifically applied to a tag beat out any inherited properties.

This rule explains why some inherited properties don't appear to inherit. A link inside a paragraph whose text is red still appears browser-link blue. That's because browsers have their own predefined style for the <a> tag, so an inherited text color won't apply.

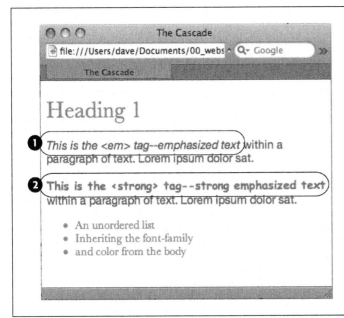

FIGURE 5-2

Here's how web browsers figure out which properties to display when inherited properties conflict: The <em> tag in the first paragraph (1) inherits the font family and color from both the <body> tag and the paragraph. But since the body and paragraph have different fonts and colors applied to them, the <em> tag uses the font and color specified for its closest ancestor—the <p> tag. When a style applies directly to a tag—the font family and color are specified for the <strong> tag (2)—browsers ignore conflicting inherited properties.

NOTE You can learn how to overcome preset styles for the <a> tag and change link colors to your heart's content. See page 279.

One Tag, Many Styles

Inheritance is one way that a tag can be affected by multiple styles. But it's also possible to have multiple styles apply *directly* to a given tag. For example, say you have an external style sheet with a <p> tag style and attach it to a page that has an internal style sheet that *also* includes a <p> tag style. And just to make things really interesting, one of the <p> tags on the page has a class style applied to it. So for that one tag, three different styles directly format it. Which style—or *styles*—should the browser obey?

The answer: It depends. Based on the types of styles and the order in which they're created, a browser may apply one or more of them at once. Here are a few situations in which multiple styles can apply to the same tag:

- **The tag has both a tag selector and a class style applied to it.** For example, a tag style for the <h2> tag, a class style named .leadHeadline and this HTML:

  ```
  <h2 class="leadHeadline">Your Future Revealed!</h2>
  ```

  Both styles apply to this <h2> tag.

NOTE Hold onto your hat if you're worried about what happens when these multiple styles conflict; details to follow.

- **The same style name appears more than once in the style sheet.** For example, you might have two styles—a group selector (page 49), like .leadHeadline, .secondaryHeadline, .newsHeadline and a class style .leadHeadline—in the same style sheet. Both of these rules define how any element with a class of leadHeadline looks.

- **A tag has both a class and an ID style applied to it.** Maybe it's an ID named #banner, a class named .news, and this HTML: <div id="banner" class="news">. Properties from both the banner and news styles apply to this <div> tag.

- **There's more than one style sheet containing the *same* style name attached to a page.** The same-named styles can arrive in an external style sheet and an internal style sheet. Or the same style can appear in multiple external style sheets that are all linked to the same page.

- **There are complex selectors targeting the same tag.** This situation is common when you use descendant selectors (page 50). For example, say you have a <div> tag in a page (like this: <div id="mainContent">), and inside the div is a paragraph with a class applied to it: <p class="byline">. The following selectors apply to this paragraph:

  ```
  #mainContent p
  #mainContent .byline
  p.byline
  .byline
  ```

If more than one style applies to a particular element, then a web browser combines the properties of all those styles, *as long as they don't conflict*. An example will make this concept clearer. Imagine you have a paragraph that lists the name of the web page's author, including a link to his email address. The HTML might look like this:

```
<p class="byline">Written by <a href="mailto:jean@cosmofarmer.com">Jean Graine
de Pomme</a></p>
```

Meanwhile, the page's style sheet has three styles that format the link:

```
a { color: #6378df; }
p a { font-weight: bold; }
.byline a { text-decoration: none; }
```

The first style turns all <a> tags powder blue; the second style makes all <a> tags that appear inside a <p> tag bold; and the third style removes the underline from any links that appear inside an element with the byline class applied to it.

All three styles apply to that very popular <a> tag, but since none of the properties are the same, there are no conflicts between the rules. The situation is similar to the inheritance example (page 98): The styles combine to make one überstyle containing all three properties, so this particular link appears powder blue, bold, *and* underline-free.

> **NOTE** Your head will really start to ache when you realize that this particular link's formatting can also be affected by inherited properties. For example, it would inherit any font family that's applied to the paragraph. A few tools can help sort out what's going on in the cascade. (See the box on page 104.)

■ Specificity: Which Style Wins

The previous example is pretty straightforward. But what if the three link styles above each had a *different* font specified for the font-family property? Which of the three fonts would a web browser pay attention to?

As you know if you've been reading carefully so far, the cascade provides a set of rules that helps a web browser sort out any property conflicts; namely, *properties from the most specific style win.* But as with the styles listed above, sometimes it's not clear which style is most specific. Thankfully, CSS provides a formula for determining a style's *specificity* that's based on a value assigned to the style's selector—a tag selector, class selector, ID selector, and so on. Here's how the system works:

- A tag selector is worth **1 point.**
- A class selector is worth **10 points.**
- An ID selector is worth **100 points.**
- An inline style (page 28) is worth **1,000 points.**

> **NOTE** The math involved in calculating specificity is actually a bit more complicated than described here. But this formula works in all but the weirdest cases. To read how web browsers actually calculate specificity, visit *www.w3.org/TR/css3-selectors/#specificity*.

The bigger the number, the greater the specificity. So say you create the following three styles:

- A tag style for the <img> tag (specificity = 1)
- A class style named .highlight (specificity = 10)
- An ID style named #logo (specificity = 100)

Then, say your web page has this HTML: <img id="logo" class="highlight" src="logo.gif" />. If you define the same property—such as the border property—in all three styles, then the value from the ID style (#logo) always wins out.

> **NOTE** A pseudo-element (like ::first-line for example) is treated like a tag selector and is worth 1 point. A pseudo-class (:link, for example) is treated like a class and is worth 10 points. (See page 55 for the deal on these pseudo-things.)

Since descendant selectors are composed of several selectors—#content p, or h2 strong, for example—the math gets a bit more complicated. The specificity of a descendant selector is the total value of all of the selectors listed (see Figure 5-3).

selector	id	class	tag	total
p	0	0	1	1
.byline	0	1	0	10
p.byline	0	1	1	11
#banner	1	0	0	100
#banner p	1	0	1	101
#banner .byline	1	1	0	110
a:link	0	1	1	11
p:first-line	0	0	2	2
h2 strong	0	0	2	2
#wrapper #content .byline a:hover	2	2	1	221

FIGURE 5-3

When more than one style applies to a tag, a web browser must determine which style should "win out" in case style properties conflict. In CSS, a style's importance is known as specificity and is determined by the type of selectors used when creating the style. Each type of selector has a different value, and when multiple selector types appear in one style— for example, the descendant selector #banner p—the values of all the selectors used are added up.

NOTE Inherited properties don't have any specificity. So even if a tag inherits properties from a style with a large specificity—like #banner—those properties will always be overridden by a style that directly applies to the tag.

The Tiebreaker: Last Style Wins

It's possible for two styles with conflicting properties to have the same specificity. ("Oh brother, when will it end?" Soon, comrade, soon. The tutorial is coming up.) A specificity tie can occur when you have the same selector defined in two locations. You may have a <p> tag selector defined in an internal style sheet and an external style sheet. Or two different styles may simply have equal specificity values. In case of a tie, the style appearing last in the style sheet wins.

Here's a tricky example using the following HTML:

```
<p class="byline">Written by <a class="email" href="mailto:jean@cosmofarmer.
com">Jean Graine de Pomme</a></p>
```

In the style sheet for the page containing the above paragraph and link, you have two styles:

```
p .email { color: blue; }
.byline a { color: red; }
```

Both styles have a specificity of 11 (10 for a class name and 1 for a tag selector) and both apply to the <a> tag. The two styles are tied. Which color does the browser use to color the link in the above paragraph? Answer: Red, since it's the second (and last) style in the sheet.

Get a Little Help

My head hurts from all of this. Isn't there some tool I can use to help me figure out how the cascade is affecting my web page?

Trying to figure out all the ins and outs of inherited properties and conflicting styles confuses many folks. Furthermore, doing the math to figure out a style's specificity isn't your average web designer's idea of fun, especially when there are large style sheets with lots of descendant selectors.

All current web browsers have built-in help in the form of an inspector. The fastest way to inspect an element on a page and all the CSS that affects it is to right-click (Control-click on a Mac) the element (the headline, link, paragraph, or image), and choose Inspect Element from the contextual menu. A panel will open (usually beneath the web page) showing the page's HTML, with your selected element's HTML highlighted. (To get this to work in Safari, you first need to turn on the Show Developer Menu option in the Preferences window→Advanced.)

On the right side of the panel, you'll see the styles applied to the element. There's usually a "computed" style—the sum total of all the CSS properties applied to the element through inheritance and the cascade, or the element's "Frankenstyle." Below that you'll find the style rules that apply to the element, listed in order of most specific (at the top) to least specific (at the bottom).

In the listing of styles, you'll probably see some properties crossed out—this indicates that the property either doesn't apply to the element, or that it's been overridden by a more specific style. For a couple of short tutorials on using Chrome's Developer's Tools for analyzing CSS, visit *https:// developer.chrome.com/devtools/docs/elements-styles* and *http://webdesign.tutsplus.com/tutorials/workflow-tutorials/ faster-htmlcss-workflow-with-chrome-developer-tools/.*

Now suppose the two styles swap position: the style sheet now looks like this:

```
.byline a { color: red; }
p .email { color: blue; }
```

In this case, the link would be blue. Since p .email appears after .byline a in the style sheet, its properties win out.

What happens if you've got conflicting rules in an external and an internal style sheet? In that case, the placement of your style sheets (within your HTML file) becomes very important. If you first add an internal style sheet by using the <style> tag (page 25) and *then* attach an external style sheet farther down in the HTML by using the <link> tag (page 26), then the style from the external style sheet wins. (In effect, it's the same principle at work that you just finished reading about: *The style appearing last wins.*) The bottom line: Be consistent in how you place external style sheets. It's best to list any external style sheets first, and only use an internal style sheet when you absolutely need one or more styles to apply to a single page.

Overruling Specificity

CSS provides a way of overruling specificity entirely. You can use this trick when you absolutely, positively want to make sure that a particular property can't be overridden by a more specific style. Simply insert !important after any property to shield it from specificity-based overrides.

For example, consider the two following styles:

```
.nav a { color: red; }
a { color: teal !important; }
```

Normally, a link inside an element with the class of nav would be colored red since the .nav a style is more specific than the a tag style.

However, including !important after a property value means that property always wins. So in the above example, all links on the page—including those inside an element with the nav class—are teal.

Note that !important works on an individual property, not an entire style, so you need to add !important to the end of each property you wish to make invincible. Finally, when two styles both have !important applied to the same property, the more specific style's !important rule wins.

Be careful using !important. Because it's so powerful, if you use it too often, your styles won't follow the normal rules of the cascade, leading to an "escalation" of the !important arms race. In other words, to overcome the power of !important in one style, you might add another !important in another style; then to overcome the second !important property, you might need to add !important to the same property in yet another style. So use !important infrequently, and before you do, try to figure out whether there's another way to overcome the conflict: Renaming or reordering styles in a style sheet might be all you need to do.

Controlling the Cascade

As you can see, the more CSS styles you create, the greater the potential for formatting snafus. For example, you may create a class style specifying a particular font and font size, but when you apply the style to a paragraph, nothing happens! This kind of problem is usually related to the cascade. Even though you may think that directly applying a class to a tag should apply the class's formatting properties, it may not if there's a style with greater specificity.

You have a couple of options for dealing with this kind of problem. First, you can use !important (as described in the box above) to make sure a property *always* applies. The !important approach is a bit heavy-handed, though, since it's hard to predict that you'll never, ever, want to overrule an !important property someday. Read on for two other cascade-tweaking solutions.

Changing the Specificity

The top picture in Figure 5-4 is an example of a specific tag style losing out in the cascade game. Fortunately, most of the time, you can easily change the specificity of one of the conflicting styles and save !important for real emergencies. In Figure 5-4 (top), two styles format the first paragraph. The class style—.intro—isn't as specific as the #sidebar p style, so .intro's properties don't get applied to the paragraph. To increase the specificity of the class, add the ID name to the style: #sidebar .intro.

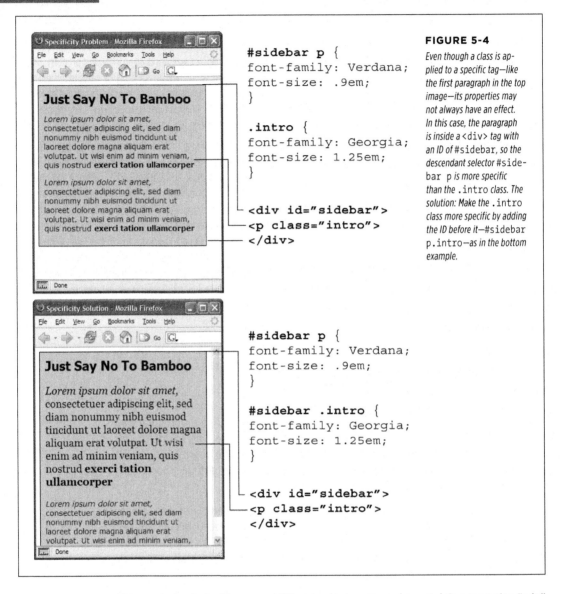

FIGURE 5-4

Even though a class is applied to a specific tag—like the first paragraph in the top image—its properties may not always have an effect. In this case, the paragraph is inside a <div> tag with an ID of #sidebar, so the descendant selector #sidebar p is more specific than the .intro class. The solution: Make the .intro class more specific by adding the ID before it—#sidebar p.intro—as in the bottom example.

```
#sidebar p {
    font-family: Verdana;
    font-size: .9em;
}


.intro {
    font-family: Georgia;
    font-size: 1.25em;
}


<div id="sidebar">
<p class="intro">
</div>
```

```
#sidebar p {
    font-family: Verdana;
    font-size: .9em;
}

#sidebar .intro {
    font-family: Georgia;
    font-size: 1.25em;
}

<div id="sidebar">
<p class="intro">
</div>
```

However, simply tacking on additional selectors to make a style's properties "win" can lead to what's been called *specificity wars*, where you end up with style sheets containing very long and convoluted style names like: #home #main #story h1. In fact, as you'll read on page 108, you should try to avoid these types of styles and aim to keep your selectors as short as possible.

NOTE If you're into math, the `#sidebar p` style has a specificity of 101 (100 for the ID, and 1 for the tag selector), while the `.intro` style has a specificity of 10 (10 points for a class selector). Since 101 is greater than 10, `#sidebar p` takes precedence. Changing `.intro` to `#sidebar .intro` changes its specificity to 110.

Selective Overriding

You can also fine-tune your design by *selectively* overriding styles on certain pages. Say you've created an external style sheet named *styles.css* that you've attached to each page in your site. This file contains the general look and feel for your site—the font and color of <h1> tags, how form elements should look, and so on. But maybe on your home page, you want the <h1> tag to look slightly different than the rest of the site—bolder and bigger, perhaps. Or the paragraph text should be smaller on the home page, so you can wedge in more information. In other words, you still want to use *most* of the styles from the *styles.css* file, but you simply want to override a few properties for some of the tags (<h1>, <p>, and so on).

One approach is to simply create an internal style sheet listing the styles that you want to override. Maybe the *styles.css* file has the following rule:

```
h1 {
    font-family: Arial, Helvetica, sans-serif;
    font-size: 24px;
    color: #000;
}
```

You want the <h1> tag on the home page to be bigger and red. So just add the following style in an internal style sheet on the home page:

```
h1 {
    font-size: 36px;
    color: red;
}
```

In this case, the <h1> tag on the home page would use the font Arial (from the external style sheet) but would be red and 36 pixels tall (from the internal style).

TIP Make sure you attach the external style sheet *before* the internal style sheet in the <head> section of the HTML. This ensures that the styles from the internal style sheet win out in cases where the specificity of two styles are the same, as explained on page 103.

Another approach would be to create one more external style sheet—*home.css* for example—that you attach to the home page in addition to the *styles.css* style sheet. The *home.css* file would contain the style names and properties that you want to overrule from the *styles.css* file. For this to work, you need to make sure the *home.css* file appears *after* the *styles.css* file in the HTML, like so:

```
<link rel="stylesheet" href="css/styles.css"/>
<link rel="stylesheet" href="css/home.css"/>
```

TIP Another way to fine-tune designs on a page-by-page basis is to use different class names for the <body> tag of different types of pages—for example .review, .story, .home—and then create descendant selectors to change the way tags on these types of pages look. This technique is discussed on page 582.

Avoiding Specificity Wars

Many web designers these days avoid ID selectors in favor of classes. One reason: ID selectors are very powerful, and therefore require more power to override. This often leads to specificity wars in which style sheets get loaded with unnecessarily long-winded and complicated selectors. This problem is best explained by example. Say, for instance, your page has this snippet of HTML:

```
<div class="article">
<p>A paragraph</p>
<p>Another paragraph</p>
<p class="special">A special paragraph</p>
</div>
```

You decide that you want to color the paragraphs inside the article div red, so you create a descendant selector like this:

```
#article p { color: red; }
```

But you want that one paragraph with the class of special to be blue. If you simply create a class selector, you won't get what you want.

```
.special { color: blue; }
```

As you read on page 102, when determining which properties to apply to a tag, a web browser uses a simple mathematical formula to deal with style conflicts: Browsers give an ID selector a value of 100, a class selector a value of 10, and a tag selector a value of 1. Because the selector #article p is composed of one ID and one element (a total of 101 specificity points), it overrides the simple class style—forcing you to change the selector:

```
#article .special {color: blue; }
```

Unfortunately, this change causes two more problems. First, it makes the selector longer, and second, now that blue color is applied only when the special class appears inside something with an ID of article. For example, if you copy the HTML <p class="special">A special paragraph</p> and paste it elsewhere in the page, it will no longer be blue. In other words, the use of the ID makes your selectors both longer and less useful.

Now look what happens if you simply replace all IDs with classes. The previous HTML would change to:

```
<div class="article">
<p>A paragraph</p>
<p>Another paragraph</p>
<p class="special">A special paragraph</p>
</div>
```

And you could change the CSS to this:

```
.article p { color: red; }
p.special { color: blue; }
```

The first style—.article p—is a descendant selector worth 11 points. The second style—p.special—is also worth 11 points (one tag and one class), and means "apply the following properties to any paragraph with the special class." Now if you cut that HTML and paste it anywhere else on the page, you'd get the blue styling you're after.

This is just one example, but it's not hard to find style sheets with ridiculously long selectors like #home #article #sidebar #legal p and #home #article #sidebar #legal p.special.

IDs can be useful. For example, many CMSes (Content Management Systems) use IDs to identify unique page elements, so using ID selectors makes sense. And the more powerful specificity they offer can make overriding other styles easier. But be careful using too many ID selectors. In most cases they don't provide anything that you can't accomplish with a simple class selector or tag selector, and their powerful specificity can lead you to unnecessarily complex style sheets.

> **NOTE** For a detailed discussion of why you should avoid ID selectors all together, visit *http://csswizardry. com/2011/09/when-using-ids-can-be-a-pain-in-the-class.*

Starting with a Clean Slate

Browsers apply their own styles to tags: For example, <h1> tags are bigger than <h2> tags, and both are bold, while paragraph text is smaller and isn't bold; links are blue and underlined; and bulleted lists are indented. There's nothing in the HTML standard that defines any of this formatting: Web browsers just add this formatting to make basic HTML more readable. However, even though browsers treat all tags roughly the same, they don't treat them identically.

For example, Chrome and Firefox use the padding property to indent bulleted lists, but Internet Explorer uses the margin property. Likewise, you'll find subtle differences in the size of tags across browsers, and an altogether confusing use of margins among the most common web browsers. Because of these inconsistencies, you can run into problems where, for instance, Firefox adds a top margin, while Internet Explorer doesn't. These types of problems aren't your fault—they stem from differences in the built-in browser styles.

To avoid cross-browser inconsistencies, it's a good idea to start a style sheet with a clean slate. In other words, erase the built-in browser formatting and supply your own. The concept of erasing browser styling is called *CSS reset*. This section gives you a working introduction.

In particular, there's a core set of styles you should include at the top of your style sheets. These styles set a baseline for properties that commonly are treated differently across browsers.

Here's a bare-bones CSS reset:

```
html, body, div, span, object, iframe, h1, h2, h3, h4, h5, h6, p, blockquote,
pre, a, abbr, acronym, address, big, cite, code, del, dfn, em, img, ins, kbd,
q, s, samp, small, strike, strong, sub, sup, tt, var, b, u, i, center, dl, dt,
dd, ol, ul, li, fieldset, form, label, legend, table, caption, tbody, tfoot,
thead, tr, th, td, article, aside, canvas, details, embed, figure, figcaption,
footer, header, hgroup, menu, nav, output, ruby, section, summary, time, mark,
audio, video {
    margin: 0;
    padding: 0;
    border: 0;
    font-size: 100%;
    vertical-align: baseline;
}

article, aside, details, figcaption, figure, footer, header, hgroup, menu,
nav, section {
    display: block;
}
body {
    line-height: 1.2;
}
ol {
    padding-left: 1.4em;
    list-style: decimal;
}
ul {
    padding-left: 1.4em
    list-style: square;
}
table {
    border-collapse: collapse;
    border-spacing: 0;
}
```

> **NOTE** The above CSS reset is adapted from Eric Meyer's well-known and influential CSS reset, which you can find at *http://meyerweb.com/eric/tools/css/reset*.

The first style is a very long group selector (page 49) that takes the most common tags and *zeros them out*—removing all the padding and margins, setting their base text size to 100%, and removing bold text formatting. This step makes your tags look pretty much identical (see Figure 5-5), but that's the point—you want to start at zero and then add your own formatting so that all browsers apply a consistent look to your HTML.

The second selector (article, aside, detail, and so on) is another group selector that helps older browsers correctly display the new HTML5 tags. The third selector (body) style sets a consistent line-height (space between lines in a paragraph). You'll learn about the line-height property in the next chapter.

> **NOTE** You don't have to type all this code yourself. You'll find a file named *reset.css* in the *05* tutorial folder that contains a basic CSS reset file. Just copy the styles from this file and paste them into your own style sheets. Another approach to resets is *normalize.css*, a free, open-source style sheet that makes different browsers display the same tags in a consistent manner. It's widely used by web designers. You can find it at: *http://necolas.github.io/normalize.css/*.

The fourth and fifth styles (the ol and ul tag styles) set a consistent left margin and style (page 168 introduces list styling), and the last style makes adding borders to table cells easier (you'll learn why this style is useful on page 363).

◼ Tutorial: The Cascade in Action

In this tutorial, you'll see how styles interact and how they can sometimes conflict to create unexpected results. First, you'll look at a basic page that has the CSS reset styles mentioned above plus a couple of other styles that provide some simple layout. Then you'll create two styles and see how some properties are inherited and how others are overruled by the cascade. Then you'll see how inheritance affects tags on a page, and how a browser resolves any CSS conflicts. Finally, you'll learn how to troubleshoot problems created by the cascade.

To get started, you need to download the tutorial files located at *https://github. com/sawmac/css_mm_4e*. Click the tutorial link and download the files. All of the files are enclosed in a zip archive, so you'll need to unzip them first. The files for this tutorial are contained inside the folder named *05*.

Resetting CSS and Styling from Scratch

First, take a look at the page you'll be working on.

1. **In a web browser, open the file *05→cascade.html* (Figure 5-5).**

    The page doesn't look like much—two columns, one with a blue background and a lot of same-looking text. There are a few styles already applied to this file, so open the CSS up in a text editor and have a look.

2. **Using your favorite text or web page editor, open the file *05→styles.css*.**

    This file is the external style sheet that the *cascade.html* file uses. It has several styles already in it—the first group is the CSS reset styles discussed on the previous page. They eliminate the basic browser styles, which is why all of the text currently looks the same. (You'll create your own styles to make this page look great soon.)

The last two styles—the class styles `.main` and `.sidebar`—create the two columns you see in Figure 5-5. The HTML is divided into two <div> tags, each with its own class. The class styles here essentially position the two divs so they appear side by side as columns (you'll learn how to control page layout and create columns in Part Three).

You'll first add a couple of styles to improve the page's basic appearance and its top headline.

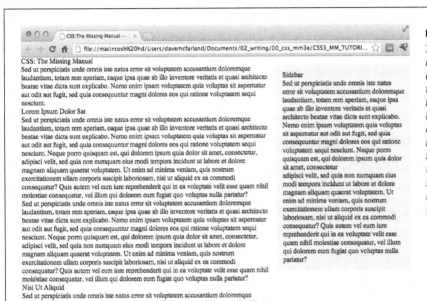

FIGURE 5-5

The basic "CSS reset" styles on this page eliminate the subtle differences in how different browsers display basic HTML tags. They also eliminate any difference between how the tags look. Your job is to take this empty canvas and style the tags so they look the way you want them to.

3. **In the *styles.css* file, add these two styles at the bottom of the style sheet following the last } of the** `.sidebar` **style:**

```
body {
  color: #B1967C;
  font-family: "Palatino Linotype", Baskerville, serif;
  padding-top: 115px;
  background: #CDE6FF url(images/bg_body.png) repeat-x;
  max-width: 800px;
  margin: 0 auto;
}
h1 {
  font-size: 3em;
  font-family: "Arial Black", Arial, sans-serif;
  margin-bottom: 15px;
}
```

The first style adds a background image and color to the page, and also sets a maximum width for the page. If you save this file and preview the *cascade.html* file in a web browser (see Figure 5-6), you'll notice that these attributes aren't inherited by the other tags—the same image, for example, isn't repeated behind the heading or paragraph tags.

FIGURE 5-6

Inheritance and the cascade in action: the <h1> tag at the top of this page inherits its font color from the <body> tag style, but gets its size and font family from the specific <h1> tag style.

The font-family and color properties, on the other hand, are inherited, so other tags on the page now use that font and have a brownish color. However, you'll see that although the top headline is the same color as the other text on the page, it uses a different font—here's the cascade in action. The h1 tag style doesn't have a color assigned to it, so that the heading inherits the brown color applied to the <body> tag. But since the h1 tag style specifies a font family, it overrides the inherited font from the <body> tag style.

Creating a Hybrid Style

In this example, you'll create two styles. One style formats all the second-level headlines of the page; another, more specific style reformats just those headings in the larger, main column of the page.

1. **In the *styles.css* file, add the following style to the end of the style sheet:**

```
h2 {
  font-size: 2.2em;
  color: #AFC3D6;
  margin-bottom: 5px;
}
```

This style simply changes the text color and increases the size of the <h2> tag and adds a little bit of space below it. If you view the file in a web browser, you'll see that the <h2> tags in the main column and the one <h2> tag in the right sidebar now look alike.

Next, you'll create a style to format *just* the second-level headlines in the main column.

2. **Return to your web page editor and the *styles.css* file. Click directly after the end of the new** <h2> **tag style, and then press Enter to create an empty line. Add the following style:**

```
.main h2 {
  color: #E8A064;
  border-bottom: 2px white solid;
  background: url(images/bullet_flower.png) no-repeat;
  padding: 0 0 2px 80px;
}
```

You've just created a descendant selector that formats all <h2> tags that appear *inside* a tag with a class of main applied to it. The two columns of text on this page are enclosed in <div> tags with different class names applied to them. The larger, left-hand column has the class main, so this particular style will only apply to the <h2> tags in that div.

This style is similar to the one you created in the tutorial for Chapter 2 in Step 17 on page 36—it adds an underline and a simple flower icon to the headline. This style also specifies an orange color for the text.

3. **Save the style sheet and preview the page once again in a web browser (Figure 5-7).**

You'll notice that all of the heading 2 tags (the two in the main column and one in the sidebar) are the same size, but the two in the main column also have the underline and flower icon.

Because the .main h2 style is more specific than the simple h2 style, if there are any conflicts between the two styles—the color property, in this case—the .main h2 properties win out. So, although the second-level headlines in the main column get a blue text color from the h2 style, the orange color from the more specific .main h2 style wins out.

However, since the .main h2 style doesn't specify a font size or bottom margin, the headlines in the main column get those properties from the h2 style.

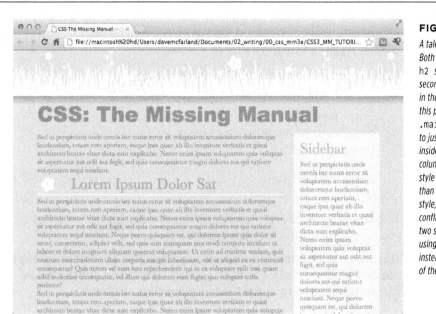

FIGURE 5-7

*A tale of two styles:
Both the h2 and .main
h2 styles apply to the
second-level headlines
in the left column of
this page. However, the
.main h2 style applies
to just those headlines
inside the main (left)
column. Also, since that
style is more powerful
than the basic <h2> tag
style, it overrides any
conflicts between the
two styles, in this case,
using an orange text color
instead of the blue color
of the <h2> tag style.*

Overcoming Conflicts

Because of how CSS properties sometimes conflict when several styles apply to
the same tag, you'll sometimes find your pages don't look exactly as you planned.

When that happens, you'll need to do a little work to find out why, and rejigger your
CSS selectors to make sure the cascade is working to produce the results you want.

1. **Return to your web page editor and the *styles.css* file.**

    You'll now create a new style to format just the paragraphs in the main column
    of the page.

2. **Add the following style to the end of the style sheet:**

```
.main p {
  color: #616161;
  font-family: "Palatino Linotype", Baskerville, serif;
  font-size: 1.1em;
  line-height: 150%;
  margin-bottom: 10px;
  margin-left: 80px;
}
```

Preview the page in a web browser and you'll see that this new style changes the color, size, and font of the text, spreads the lines of text out (the line-height property), and adjusts the bottom and left margins of the paragraphs.

Next, you'll make the first paragraph bigger and bolder so that it makes a more powerful message. One way to style just that one paragraph is to create a class style and apply it to that paragraph.

3. **Add one last style to the end of the style sheet:**

```
.intro {
  color: #6A94CC;
  font-family: Arial, Helvetica, sans-serif;
  font-size: 1.2em;
  margin-left: 0;
  margin-bottom: 15px;
}
```

This style changes the color, font, and size, and adjusts the margins a bit. All you have to do is apply the class to the HTML.

4. **Open the *cascade.html* file in your web page editor. Locate the <p> tag that appears after** <h1>CSS: The Missing Manual</h1> **and directly below** <div class="main">, **and then add the following class attribute:**

   <p class="intro">

5. **Preview the page in a web browser.**

   And...the paragraph is completely unchanged. What gives? Following the rules of the cascade, .intro is a basic class selector, while the .main p is a descendant selector composed of both a class and a tag name. These add up to create a more specific style, so its style properties overrule any conflict between it and the .intro style.

   In order to make the .intro style work, you need to give it a little juice by making its selector more powerful.

6. **Return to the *styles.css* file in your web page editor and change the name of the style from** .intro **to** p.intro.

   Make sure there's no space between the p and .intro. You've basically created a tie—.main p—is one class and one tag selector, and p.intro is one tag and one class. They both have a specificity value of 11, but because p.intro appears after .main p in the style sheet, it wins the battle, and its properties apply to the paragraph. (You could have created an even more specific style—.main .intro—to overcome the conflict.)

7. **Preview the page in a web browser (see Figure 5-8).**

Voila! The paragraph changes to blue, with bigger text, a different font, and no left margin. If you didn't have a clear understanding of the cascade, you'd be scratching your head wondering why that class style didn't work the first time around.

In this and the previous four chapters, you've covered the basics of CSS. Next, in Part Two, it's time to take that knowledge and apply it to real design challenges—making web pages look great.

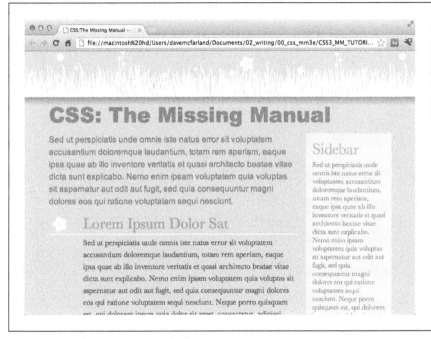

FIGURE 5-8

Even in a simple page like this one, with just a handful of styles, the look of any one tag is often a combination of properties from various styles.

Applied CSS

Formatting Text

Most websites still rely on words to get their messages across. Sure, people like to look at photos, movie clips, and animations, but it's the reading material that keeps 'em coming back. People are hungry for Facebook updates, news, gossip, how-to articles, recipes, FAQs, jokes, information lists, and even 140-character tweets. With CSS, you can—and *should*—make your headlines and body text grab a visitor's attention as compellingly as any photo.

CSS offers a powerful array of text-formatting options, which let you assign fonts, color, sizes, line spacing, and many other properties that can add visual impact to headlines, bulleted lists, and regular old paragraphs of text (see Figure 6-1). This chapter reveals all, and then finishes up with a tutorial where you can practice assembling CSS text styles and put them to work on an actual web page.

Using Fonts

The first thing you can do to make text on your website look more exciting is to apply different fonts to headlines, paragraphs, and other written elements on your pages. To apply a font to a CSS style, you use the `font-family` property and specify the font you wish to use. For example, say you want to use the Arial font for paragraphs on a page. You can create a p tag style and use the `font-family` property like this:

```
p {
  font-family: Arial;
}
```

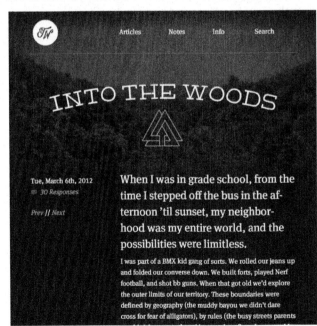

FIGURE 6-1

Good web typography makes sites that are easy to read and enjoyable to look at. Using too many fonts or too many typographic flourishes often leads to confusing and difficult to understand web pages (top). Using different type sizes, subtle style choices, and only a couple font variations makes a page easy to scan, and fun to read (bottom).

Originally, the `font-family` property only worked if your site's visitors had the same font installed on their computers. In other words, using the above example, if someone visiting your site didn't have the Arial font on their computer, the page's paragraphs would display with the web browser's default font (usually some variant of Times New Roman). Because of this, web designers were limited to a handful of fonts that come preinstalled on most computers.

More recently, web browsers began supporting *web fonts*—fonts that the browser downloads and uses while viewing your site. Web fonts use the `font-family` property as well, but require an additional CSS command called the `@font-face` directive, which instructs a web browser to download the specified font. Web fonts open up many exciting design possibilities, letting you choose from a wild array of typefaces. But, as you'll learn on page 126, they also come with their own set of challenges.

As a web designer, you can choose to stick with the tried-and-true font method—selecting fonts from the basic set installed on most computers—or use web fonts for greater design choice (at the cost of more work). You're not limited to one approach or the other, either. Many web designers mix the two—using standard fonts in some cases (like the main body text of a page) and web fonts in other cases (to create eye-catching headlines, for instance).

Choosing a Common Font

When you use the `font-family` property to specify a font, visitors to your site won't necessarily see the font you choose—they must either have it installed on their computers already or, in the case of web fonts, temporarily download the font to view the site. Because you can't always know whether your preferred font is available to a particular visitor, it's common practice to specify not only your main font, but also a couple of backup choices: This list of font options is called a *font stack*. If your viewer's computer has your first-choice font, then that's what she'll see. But when the first font isn't installed, the browser looks down the list until it finds a font that is. The idea is to specify a list of similar-looking fonts that are common to a variety of operating systems, like so:

```
font-family: Arial, Helvetica, sans-serif;
```

In this example, a web browser first looks to see if the Arial font is installed. If it is, then that font is used; if not, the browser next looks for Helvetica, and if that isn't installed, then it finally settles for a generic font—sans-serif. When you list a generic font type (like sans-serif or serif), the viewer's browser gets to choose the actual font. But at least you can define its basic character.

NOTE In your code, when you put a CSS property into action, you must, of course, include a selector and a set of braces to create a valid CSS rule. For example:

```
p { font-family: Arial, Helvetica, sans-serif; }
```

When you see examples in this book like `font-family: Arial, Helvetica, sans-serif;`, remember that's just the property in isolation, distilled down for your book-reading benefit.

Also, if the font's name is made up of more than one word, you must enclose it in quote marks:

```
font-family: "Times New Roman", Times, serif;
```

Here are some often-used combinations of commonly installed fonts organized by the type of font, including a generic font type at the end of each list.

▆ SERIF FONTS

Serif fonts are best for long passages of text, as it's widely believed that the serifs—those tiny "feet" at the end of a letter's main strokes—gently lead the eye from letter to letter, making text easier to read. Examples of serif fonts are Times, Times New Roman, and Georgia.

- "Times New Roman", Times, serif

- Georgia, "Times New Roman", Times, serif

- Baskerville, "Palatino Linotype", Times, serif

- "Hoefler Text", Garamond, Times, serif

Examples of these fonts are in Figure 6-2.

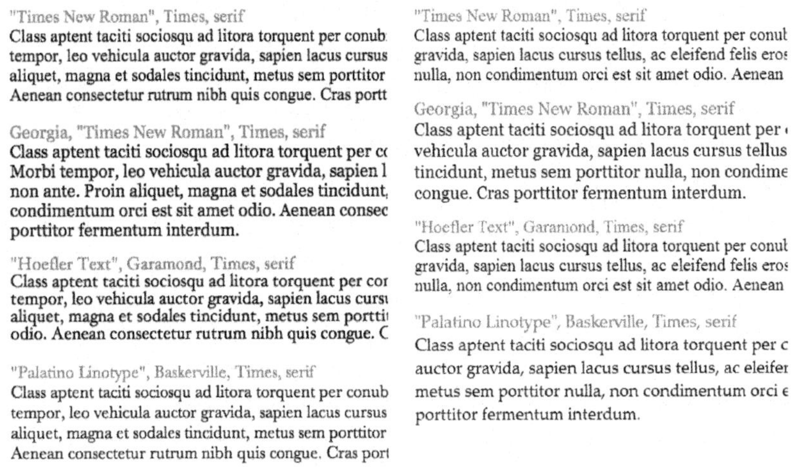

"Times New Roman", Times, serif
Class aptent taciti sociosqu ad litora torquent per conub tempor, leo vehicula auctor gravida, sapien lacus cursus aliquet, magna et sodales tincidunt, metus sem porttitor Aenean consectetur rutrum nibh quis congue. Cras portt

Georgia, "Times New Roman", Times, serif
Class aptent taciti sociosqu ad litora torquent per co Morbi tempor, leo vehicula auctor gravida, sapien l non ante. Proin aliquet, magna et sodales tincidunt, condimentum orci est sit amet odio. Aenean consec porttitor fermentum interdum.

"Hoefler Text", Garamond, Times, serif
Class aptent taciti sociosqu ad litora torquent per cor tempor, leo vehicula auctor gravida, sapien lacus curst aliquet, magna et sodales tincidunt, metus sem porttit odio. Aenean consectetur rutrum nibh quis congue. C

"Palatino Linotype", Baskerville, Times, serif
Class aptent taciti sociosqu ad litora torquent per conub tempor, leo vehicula auctor gravida, sapien lacus cursus aliquet, magna et sodales tincidunt, metus sem porttitor Aenean consectetur rutrum nibh quis congue. Cras port

"Times New Roman", Times, serif
Class aptent taciti sociosqu ad litora torquent per conul gravida, sapien lacus cursus tellus, ac eleifend felis eros nulla, non condimentum orci est sit amet odio. Aenean

Georgia, "Times New Roman", Times, serif
Class aptent taciti sociosqu ad litora torquent per vehicula auctor gravida, sapien lacus cursus tellus tincidunt, metus sem porttitor nulla, non condime congue. Cras porttitor fermentum interdum.

"Hoefler Text", Garamond, Times, serif
Class aptent taciti sociosqu ad litora torquent per conul gravida, sapien lacus cursus tellus, ac eleifend felis eros nulla, non condimentum orci est sit amet odio. Aenean

"Palatino Linotype", Baskerville, Times, serif
Class aptent taciti sociosqu ad litora torquent per c auctor gravida, sapien lacus cursus tellus, ac eleifer metus sem porttitor nulla, non condimentum orci e porttitor fermentum interdum.

FIGURE 6-2

Fonts don't always display the same on Mac (left) and Windows (right). The two systems come with different built-in fonts. In addition, antialiasing, which makes onscreen text look smoother, is better on the Mac than on Windows. Windows includes a technology called ClearType, which can improve the look of text on a screen. The quality of text on Windows depends on which ClearType settings your Windows computer has. You can learn more about ClearType at www.microsoft.com/typography/cleartype.

TIP The website CSS Font Stack (*www.cssfontstack.com*) provides a long list of fonts that are commonly installed on Macs and Windows computers, including detailed percentage breakdowns for each operating system. For example, you'll find the font Courier New on 99.73% of Windows computers and 95.68% of Macs.

▇ SANS-SERIF FONTS

Sans-serif fonts are often used for headlines, thanks to their clean and simple appearance. Examples of sans-serif fonts include Arial, Helvetica, and Verdana. The text in this book is set in a sans-serif font.

- Arial, Helvetica, sans-serif

- Verdana, Arial, Helvetica, sans-serif

- Geneva, Arial, Helvetica, sans-serif

- Tahoma, "Lucida Grande", Arial, sans-serif

- "Trebuchet MS", Arial, Helvetica, sans-serif

- "Century Gothic", "Gill Sans", Arial, sans-serif

Examples of sans-serif fonts are shown in Figure 6-3.

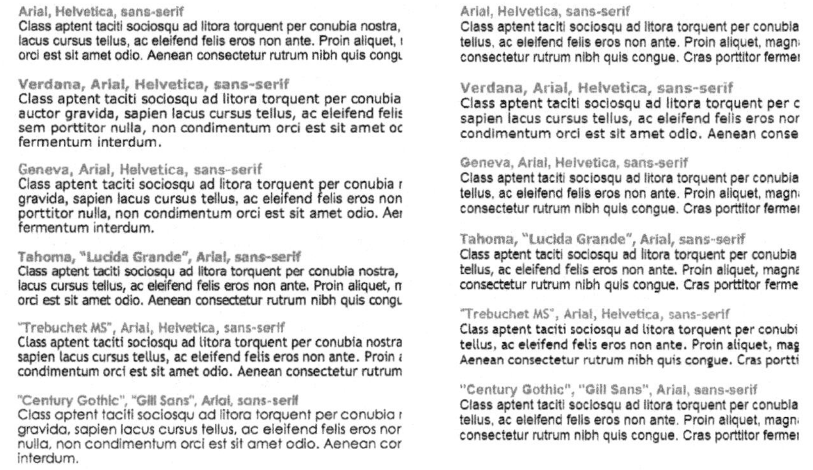

FIGURE 6-3

Sans-serif fonts on Mac (left) and Windows (right). Some people believe that you should use only sans-serif fonts on web pages because they think the delicate decorative strokes of serif fonts don't display well on the coarse resolution of a computer screen. However, high-density screens—newer screens that pack more pixels in per inch—don't have that problem. Their ultra-tiny pixels do an excellent job displaying small details like serifs. In the end, your aesthetic judgment is your best guide. Pick the fonts you think look best.

▇ MONOSPACED AND FUN FONTS

Monospaced fonts are often used to display computer code like the CSS snippets you see throughout this book. Each letter in a monospaced font is the same width (like the ones manual typewriters used).

- "Courier New", Courier, monospace

- "Lucida Console", Monaco, monospace

- "Copperplate Light", "Copperplate Gothic Light", serif

- "Marker Felt", "Comic Sans MS", fantasy

Examples of these font lists are pictured in Figure 6-4.

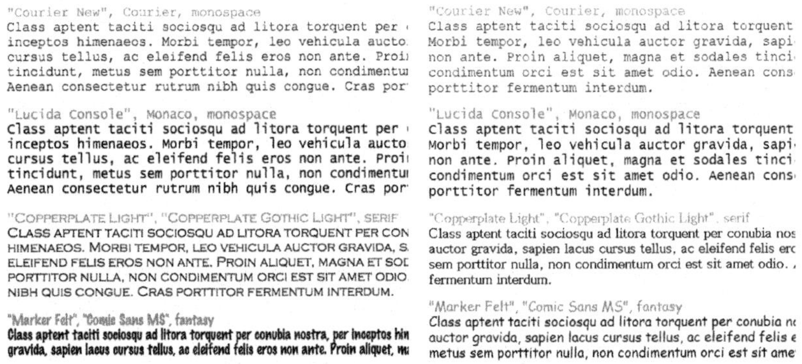

"Courier New", Courier, monospace
Class aptent taciti sociosqu ad litora torquent per
inceptos himenaeos. Morbi tempor, leo vehicula aucto
cursus tellus, ac eleifend felis eros non ante. Proi
tincidunt, metus sem porttitor nulla, non condimentu
Aenean consectetur rutrum nibh quis congue. Cras por

"Lucida Console", Monaco, monospace
Class aptent taciti sociosqu ad litora torquent per
inceptos himenaeos. Morbi tempor, leo vehicula aucto
cursus tellus, ac eleifend felis eros non ante. Proi
tincidunt, metus sem porttitor nulla, non condimentu
Aenean consectetur rutrum nibh quis congue. Cras por

"COPPERPLATE LIGHT", "COPPERPLATE GOTHIC LIGHT", SERIF
CLASS APTENT TACITI SOCIOSQU AD LITORA TORQUENT PER CON
HIMENAEOS. MORBI TEMPOR, LEO VEHICULA AUCTOR GRAVIDA, S
ELEIFEND FELIS EROS NON ANTE. PROIN ALIQUET, MAGNA ET SOD
PORTTITOR NULLA, NON CONDIMENTUM ORCI EST SIT AMET ODIO
NIBH QUIS CONGUE. CRAS PORTTITOR FERMENTUM INTERDUM.

"Marker Felt", "Comic Sans MS", fantasy
Class aptent taciti sociosqu ad litora torquent per conubia nostra, per inceptos him
gravida, sapien lacus cursus tellus, ac eleifend felis eros non ante. Proin aliquet, m

"Courier New", Courier, monospace
Class aptent taciti sociosqu ad litora torquent
Morbi tempor, leo vehicula auctor gravida, sapi
non ante. Proin aliquet, magna et sodales tinci
condimentum orci est sit amet odio. Aenean cons
porttitor fermentum interdum.

"Lucida Console", Monaco, monospace
Class aptent taciti sociosqu ad litora torquent
Morbi tempor, leo vehicula auctor gravida, sapi
non ante. Proin aliquet, magna et sodales tinci
condimentum orci est sit amet odio. Aenean cons
porttitor fermentum interdum.

"Copperplate Light", "Copperplate Gothic Light", serif
Class aptent taciti sociosqu ad litora torquent per conubia nos
auctor gravida, sapien lacus cursus tellus, ac eleifend felis erc
sem porttitor nulla, non condimentum orci est sit amet odio.
fermentum interdum.

"Marker Felt", "Comic Sans MS", fantasy
Class aptent taciti sociosqu ad litora torquent per conubia ne
auctor gravida, sapien lacus cursus tellus, ac eleifend felis e
metus sem porttitor nulla, non condimentum orci est sit ame

FIGURE 6-4

*Monospaced fonts on
Mac (left) and Windows
(right). Courier New
is the most common
monospaced font, but
you're far from limited to
it. Lucida Console is very
common on Windows,
and Monaco is installed
on every Mac.*

ADDITIONAL FONTS TO CONSIDER

There are literally thousands of fonts, and every operating system ships with many more fonts than are listed here. However, a few fonts are very common on both Macs and PCs, so you might want to give these a go:

- "Arial Black"

- "Arial Narrow"

- Impact

Be careful with Arial Black and Impact: They only have a single weight and don't include an italic version. Accordingly, if you use these fonts, make sure to set the font-weight and the font-style (coming up on page 156) to normal. Otherwise, if the text is bolded or italicized, the browser will make its best (read: ugly) guess at what the text should look like.

Using Web Fonts

The traditional way of using fonts in CSS is straightforward: Just specify the font you want, using the font-family property. However, you're limited to fonts your visitors are likely to have installed on their computers. Fortunately, as mentioned earlier, all major browsers now support web fonts. With web fonts, browsers actually download the font from a web server and use it to display text on the web page.

The CSS part of web fonts is pretty basic and requires just two CSS commands:

- The @font-face directive is responsible for telling a web browser both the name of the font and where to download the font from. You'll learn how this CSS command works on page 131, but for now just keep in mind that this is how you tell a browser to download the font.

- The font-family property is used with web fonts in the same manner as the already installed fonts described on page 121. In other words, once the @font-face directive instructs the browser to download the font, you can then assign that font to any CSS style by using the font-family property.

In theory, web fonts aren't all that difficult to use. However, when you dig into the details, you'll need to understand a few unique requirements to use them properly.

NOTE   Google offers a really easy method of using web fonts. Page 140 goes into all the details.

Font File Types

Believe it or not, Internet Explorer has had support for web fonts since version 5 (released over 15 years ago!). Unfortunately, it required a unique and difficult method to create font formatting. That is, you couldn't just take a regular font from your computer, slap it up on a web server, and be done. Instead, you needed to take a regular font and convert it to EOT—Embedded OpenType—format. That's still true for versions up through IE8.

There are still other font formats used for web fonts—some of which work in some browsers but not others. To make sure the largest number of visitors to your site can enjoy the fonts you specify, you'll need to provide those fonts in a variety of formats (you'll find the details on page 129).

Here's a list of the different font types and which browsers they work in.

- **EOT.** Embedded OpenType fonts work only in Internet Explorer. You need a special tool to convert a regular font to EOT format, but sites like FontSquirrel (page 129) can do this for you.

- **TrueType and OpenType.** If you look in your computer's Fonts folder, you'll probably find fonts in .ttf (TrueType) or .otf (OpenType), the most common formats for computer fonts. You can use them for word processing and desktop publishing as well as for web pages. This font type was once the most common font type used for web fonts and is still supported by most browsers. However, it's been passed by a leaner font format—WOFF.

- **WOFF.** Web Open Font Format was designed specifically for the Web. WOFF fonts are basically compressed versions of TrueType or OpenType fonts, which means they're generally smaller in file size and download more quickly than other fonts. WOFF format has wide browser support as well, including IE9 and later, Firefox, Chrome, Safari, Opera, BlackBerry Browser, iOS Safari version 5 and later, and Android Browser 4.4 and later.

NOTE   WOFF2 is a newer version of WOFF with up to 30 percent better compression, for even smaller, faster-loading fonts. However, at the time of this writing, it's not supported by Internet Explorer, Firefox, or Safari: *http:// caniuse.com/#search=woff2.*

- **SVG.** Scalable Vector Graphic format isn't a font format, per se. It's actually a way to create *vector graphics*—graphics that can scale without losing quality. Support for SVG fonts is very limited: Internet Explorer, Chrome, Opera, and Firefox don't support SVG fonts. Another problem with SVG is that it produces files that are often twice the size of TrueType and three times the size of WOFF fonts. The only real benefit of SVG is that it's the only font format understood by older versions of iOS running Safari version 4.1 or earlier, as well as Android Browser 4.3 and 4.1. If you're not targeting those older mobile devices, then you can skip SVG fonts.

You don't have to select just one font type and ignore all other browsers. As you'll read on the next page, you can (and usually will) specify multiple formats and let the browser download the one that works for it. In addition, you can download a font that's already been converted to formats, or even convert a regular TrueType font into these multiple formats.

NOTE   A single font file contains just one weight and style for that font. In other words, if you want text to be bold, italic, or bold and italic, you must download separate font files for each variation of the font. Some fonts, especially fun display fonts, only include one variant and are best used for headlines or text where you won't need italic or bold versions. See page 156 for more information on different font weights and styles.

Legal Issues with Web Fonts

The second hurdle to using web fonts is a legal issue. Individuals and companies create and sell fonts, like other software, to make their livelihood. When you upload a TrueType font to your web server for visitors to use while viewing your site, anyone can simply download the font and start using it on her own website or in her computer's word processing or page layout program. Most font companies don't like the idea of people pirating their creations, so many fonts have licenses that specifically prohibit their use on the Web.

In other words, even if you buy a font from Adobe, you can't simply start using it on your website. Many font companies are now offering different kinds of licenses (at different prices) to allow for use on the Web. This even applies to fonts that come supplied with your computer. You're allowed to use them with the programs you install on your computer, but you may not be allowed to place those same font files on your web server to use as a web font. If you don't know whether a font allows Web use, you're better off not using it and finding a font that can be used on the Web.

NOTE   To sidestep any legal issues, you can use a font service like Google Fonts (page 140) or TypeKit, a commercial web font service from Adobe (see the box on page 148).

Finding Web Fonts

When looking for web fonts, you're confronted with two issues: finding fonts that are legal to use on the Web and finding fonts in the font formats your visitor's web browsers need (EOT, WOFF, TrueType, and SVG). While some font companies have begun to offer web licenses for fonts you purchase, there is a wide assortment of free fonts available for web use. Here are a few of the many sources for free web fonts:

- **The League of Moveable Type (***www.theleagueofmoveabletype.com***).** Composed of a group of designers, this site was one of the first to offer free, hand-crafted fonts for web use. Their font, League Gothic, is widely used on the Web.

- **Exljbris font foundry (***www.exljbris.com***).** Provides classic, free fonts: Museo, Museo Sans, and Museo Slab.

- **The Open Font Library (***http://openfontlibrary.org***).** Over 400 free fonts (at the time of this writing) are available and all of them can be used on your websites (just don't use all 400 at once).

- **Font Squirrel (***www.fontsquirrel.com***).** A landmark site in the web font world offering more than a thousand fonts. In addition, Font Squirrel offers an online tool for converting a TrueType or OpenType font to other font formats including EOT, SVG, WOFF, and even WOFF2. You'll learn how to use this tool in the next section.

- **Google Fonts (***www.google.com/fonts***).** Google provides a simple and free way to include web fonts on your sites. You'll learn how to use this service on page 140.

Generating Multiple Font Formats

Most of the sites offering free fonts provide the font in a single format (usually TrueType (.ttf) or OpenType (.otf). While many browsers support TrueType and OpenType, not all do. In addition, the WOFF format is supported by all modern browsers and has the advantage of being smaller in file size than TrueType. The newer WOFF2 font is supported by a few browsers now, and will be adopted by all browsers at some point.

There are several approaches you can take when using web fonts on your own sites. First, you can be conservative and use fonts that work for old browsers and older mobile devices. This means including an EOT font (for IE8), TrueType fonts for older desktop browsers, WOFF fonts for current browsers, and SVG fonts for older phones and tablets.

Alternatively, since the WOFF file format is well supported by all modern browsers, you could simply use *just* WOFF fonts. Older browsers viewing the page will just skip the WOFF font, and choose the next font in the font stack (page 123).

And, finally, you can use just EOT and WOFF files. The EOT file will be for Internet Explorer 8, which is still in use (see the box on page 13). The WOFF file will be for all others current browsers (including IE9 and later.)

However you proceed, you'll need to create the font files. Fortunately, Font Squirrel provides a very useful online tool to help generate the required font formats. The Webfont Generator (located at *http://www.fontsquirrel.com/tools/webfont-generator*) provides a simple method for creating not only the proper fonts, but also a sample HTML file and a basic CSS style sheet.

To use Font Squirrel's Webfont Generator:

1. **Locate a TrueType (.ttf) or OpenType (.otf) font.**

   Use one of the sites listed in the previous section, or find a font from another site. Just make sure that the font is licensed for use as a web font. If it's not, or you're not sure, then skip it and find another font.

2. **Go to the Web font Generator at *www.fontsquirrel.com/tools/webfont-generator.***

   It's a simple page with just a few options (see Figure 6-5).

3. **Click the Upload Fonts button (#1 in Figure 6-5).**

   Your browser opens a "Select files" dialog box.

4. **Select one or more fonts from your computer, and then click the Open button.**

   Your browser uploads the file or files to the Font Squirrel server.

5. **Select a conversion option (#2 in Figure 6-5).**

   - *Basic* simply converts the font to EOT, WOFF, and SVG formats.

   - *Optimal* is a better choice, since it not only converts the font but also makes other enhancements to improve the performance and speed of the fonts.

   - *Expert* lets you tweak every last setting for the conversion. For example, it lets you create a *subset* of the font—that is, just a handpicked set of characters. In other words, you could exclude from the font file certain characters you're not using, like the semicolon, exclamation mark, or letters that use diacritical marks such as ü, é, or õ. In addition, you can use Expert to get just certain formats, like WOFF or WOFF2.

6. **Turn on the "Yes, the fonts I'm uploading are legally eligible for web embedding" checkbox (#3 in Figure 6-5).**

   As mentioned on page 128, fonts are intellectual property, and just slapping one up on a web server promotes software piracy. Make sure your fonts can be used on the Web; most of the ones listed in this section can.

7. **Click the Download Your Kit button (#4 in Figure 6-5).**

   Depending on the number of fonts you're converting and their complexity, the download process may take a while. The Font Squirrel server needs to take the font and perform its magic to generate each font format. When it's done, you'll download a folder containing the various font format files, a demo file, a CSS file, and a few other miscellaneous files. The most important are the font files you want to use (for example, .eot, .ttf, .woff, or .svg files).

Now that you've got the fonts you wish to use, it's time to learn how to use them with CSS's @font-face directive.

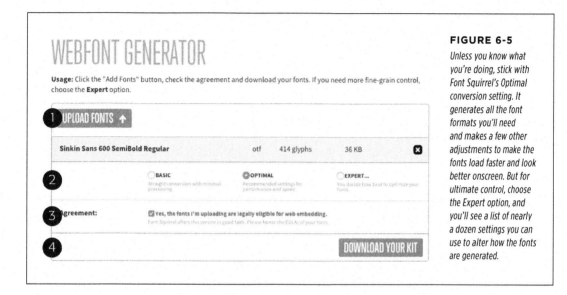

FIGURE 6-5

Unless you know what you're doing, stick with Font Squirrel's Optimal conversion setting. It generates all the font formats you'll need and makes a few other adjustments to make the fonts load faster and look better onscreen. But for ultimate control, choose the Expert option, and you'll see a list of nearly a dozen settings you can use to alter how the fonts are generated.

Using the @font-face Directive

Once you've downloaded the proper font files, it's time to use them. First, copy the files to the location on your computer where you keep the files for your website. Many web designers create a dedicated folder at the site root folder named fonts, _fonts, or web fonts. Alternatively, if you have a folder for your CSS files, you can place the font files there. It doesn't really matter where you put these files on your site, but it helps to be organized.

The secret to web fonts is a CSS command called the *@font-face directive*. This command at its most basic names the font and tells the browser where to find the font file for download. You place the @font-face directive in your style sheet, just like a regular style. For example, say you're using the League Gothic font. You have a TrueType file named *League_Gothic-web font.ttf* inside a fonts folder on your site. You'd instruct a browser to download this font by adding the @font-face directive to your style sheet, like this:

```
@font-face {
  font-family: "League Gothic";
  src: url('fonts/League_Gothic-web font.woff');
}
```

The first property, font-family, you've seen before, but here it has a different purpose. When used inside an @font-face directive, font-family assigns a name to the font. You then use that font name when you want to apply that font to a style. For example, say you want to use the League Gothic font for all paragraphs on a page. You could use this style:

```
p {
    font-family: "League Gothic";
}
```

> **NOTE** You use one @font-face directive for each font you wish to use. If you have three fonts—for example, regular, italic, and bold versions of a font—you need three @font-face directives. It's a good idea to keep them grouped together and place them at the top of your style sheet, so the browser can begin downloading them immediately.

The second attribute—the src property—tells the browser where to look for the font file on the server. You place the path from the style sheet to the font file on the system inside quote marks and inside url(). The path works just like other HTML file paths, like paths to images, links, and JavaScript files. For example, say you had a style sheet inside a folder named _styles, and a font file named my_font.woff inside a folder named _fonts. Both folders are in the root of your site. So the path from the style sheet to the font file is ../_fonts/my_font.woff. You'd write an @font-face directive for that font like this:

```
@font-face {
    font-family: "My Font";
    src: url('../_fonts/my_font.woff');
}
```

You've probably noticed that in the examples above, there's only a single font file— a WOFF font. That makes it easy to see how @font-face works in general, before jumping into more detail. As discussed earlier, @font-face lets you specify multiple files with different font types.

Unfortunately, if you want to support older browsers, phones, and tablets, the syntax that is a bit complicated. For example, say you want to use all the different font formats for League Gothic on your site. Here's how to rewrite the above code:

```
@font-face {
    font-family: 'League Gothic';
    src: url('fonts/League_Gothic-webfont.eot');
    src: url('fonts/League_Gothic-webfont.eot?#iefix') format('embedded-
opentype'),
        url('fonts/League_Gothic-webfont.woff2') format('woff2'),
        url('fonts/League_Gothic-webfont.woff') format('woff'),
        url('fonts/League_Gothic-webfont.ttf') format('truetype'),
        url('fonts/League_Gothic-webfont.svg') format('svg');
}
```

This all looks messy, and unfortunately, due to a bug in IE, it's unnecessarily complicated. Here's how it breaks down:

- Line 2 is the same as before. The font-family property supplies the name of the font—the same name you'll use when applying the font to your CSS styles.

- Line 3 is for Internet Explorer 9, but only when it's in Compatibility mode—a mode where IE9 acts like it's IE8. This weird feature was added to IE9 so that websites designed to correctly accommodate the bugs in IE 8 and earlier would look okay in IE9. A user has to purposely switch to compatibility mode in IE9, so you're probably safe leaving this out.

- Line 4 begins a second src property, which according to the rules of the @font-face directive, can have multiple font types specified. The first font is the .eot font again, but this time you'll see that at the end of the .eot file, you need to add ?#iefix. This is to accommodate yet more IE bugs—this time for IE6-8. If you don't add that little bit to the URL following the .eot, then the font may not display in IE8 or earlier correctly.

  You'll also notice that after the URL there's some new code:

  ```
  format('embedded-opentype')
  ```

  This indicates the font format, and you add this after each URL for a different font format.

- Lines 5-8 simply identify additional font formats. This is actually just one property—the src property—split over several lines for greater readability. For each font type you specify for the src property, you add a URL, a format, and a comma (for all but the last font):

  ```
  url('fonts/League_Gothic-web font.woff') format('woff'),
  ```

> **NOTE** At the end of the list of files for the src property, you add a semicolon to note that you've reached the end of the src property (line 7 above). Don't forget this final semicolon, or the @font-face directive won't work.

Even though a browser may understand different types of fonts (for example, Chrome can use WOFF2, WOFF, TrueType, and SVG fonts), it won't download all the font files. Instead, as it reads through the list of font types, the browser downloads only the first one it understands. In other words, if Chrome encountered the above code, it would skip the .eot file since it doesn't understand that font format, but it would download the .woff2 file. It would then skip the TrueType and SVG files entirely. That means the order in which you list the fonts is important. WOFF is generally preferred, since it's a smaller file that downloads more quickly. WOFF2 is an optimized version of WOFF, and thus has the smallest file size—but it's only supported in a few browsers. SVG is generally a much larger file. So you want to make sure that you list the fonts in a specific order to make sure browsers download the smallest font file that works for them: .eot, .woff2, .woff, .ttf, and .svg.

If you just need to support Internet Explorer 8 and more modern browsers, you can safely use just EOT, WOFF2, and WOFF files. In fact, if you're no longer worried about Internet Explorer 8 (see the box on page 13), you can get away with just WOFF files! Here are two alternative ways to specify the same @font-face directive as above:

```
@font-face {
  font-family: 'League Gothic';
  src: url('fonts/League_Gothic-webfont.eot?#iefix') format('embedded-
opentype'),
       url('fonts/League_Gothic-webfont.woff2') format('woff2'),
       url('fonts/League_Gothic-webfont.woff') format('woff');
}
```

And, if you're not worried about Internet Explorer 8 or earlier, you can simplify this even more:

```
@font-face {
  font-family: 'League Gothic';
  src: url('fonts/League_Gothic-webfont.woff2') format('woff2'),
       url('fonts/League_Gothic-webfont.woff') format('woff');
}
```

This book uses the last example, which aims to support only modern web browsers. But if you find that a significant portion of your website visitors use Internet Explorer 8, then you might wish to use the version that includes the .eot file as well. Likewise, if you need to support the older phones and tablets listed on page 132, you'll need to use the much more complex syntax shown on page 132.

> **NOTE** Just because you don't include web fonts for older browsers (like .svg, .ttf, or .eot) doesn't mean those older browsers won't see the content on your site. Remember, you'll use a font stack (page 123) when specifying a font, so that browsers that don't have an appropriate web font will use a fallback font—one that looks similar to the web font. Most of the time, it's all right if your site doesn't look exactly the same on every browser.

Creating Styles Using Web Fonts

The hardest part of web fonts is getting the font files in the proper format and setting up the @font-face directives. Once that's done, you use web fonts just as you would the preinstalled fonts discussed on page 121. In other words, when you create a new style, you simply use the font-family property and supply the name for the font you used in the @font-face directive. For example, in the previous code, the @font-face directive names the new font League Gothic. This is the name you use when applying this font to a style. To make all <h1> tags use the League Gothic font, you could write this style:

```
h1 {
  font-family: 'League Gothic';
  font-weight: normal;
}
```

Notice that there's a new property—font-weight—listed here. Browsers normally display <h1> tags as bold. Most browsers will artificially bold a web font when a bold version is required. This results in an ugly boldface. Setting the font-weight to normal tells the browser to just use the League Gothic font "as-is," and avoids trying to bold it. In the next section, you'll learn more about how to deal with font variants like bold and italic with web fonts.

It's also a good idea to include a list of backup, preinstalled fonts, in case the browser can't load the web font. This is the same technique described on page 123. For example:

```
h1 {
   font-family: 'League Gothic', Arial, sans-serif;
   font-weight: normal;
}
```

TIP   You can use fonts that contain symbols and icons on a web page, too. So rather than creating a graphic of a warning sign (for example) and placing it inside a paragraph of text, you can use the @font-face directive to load a font containing the warning sign icon and just use a simple letter (mapped to the icon in the font). *However,* before using icon fonts, you may want to check out the vast number of Unicode symbols that are really graphical icons, or use SVG (scalable vector graphics) for icons. You can learn more about those options at *https:// developers.google.com/web/fundamentals/media/images/use-icons?hl=en.*

Dealing with Bold and Italic Font Variants

The common fonts installed on computers include variations in style and weight, so when you apply a <strong> tag in HTML, a web browser uses the bold version of that font. Likewise, when you apply an <em> tag to text, the browser uses an italicized version of that font; and if you combine both tags, you'll see a bold and italic version of the font. These are actually different fonts contained in different font files. With the original method of using fonts in web pages (described on page 121), you never have to worry about these different fonts, since the browser uses the correct version automatically.

However, with web fonts, you need separate font files for each font variant. So for body text you'll need at least a regular version of a font, a bold version, an italic version, and a bold/italic version. Keep this in mind when finding a web font for your site; some fonts only have a single weight and no italic version. This could be fine for a headline, but not much use for long paragraphs of text, which most likely will have some italic and bold text. In addition, you must create separate @font-face directives for each font variant.

You have two choices when working with italic/bold versions of web fonts. One method is easier to implement, but doesn't work on Internet Explorer 8 or earlier (or IE9 in compatibility mode); the other is more labor intensive, but works on older versions of Internet Explorer.

■ THE EASY WAY TO ADD BOLD AND ITALIC

The easiest way to add bold and italic variants of your fonts is to add font-weight and font-style properties to the @font-face directive. Normally, the CSS font-weight property (page 156) tells a browser to display a font in bold, normal, or one of several other weights, while the font-style property (page 156) tells a browser to display a font as italic or normal. However, when used within the @font-face directive, font-style tells a browser to apply the font when the style asks for a particular variant of the font.

Say you have a font named PTSans. You start with the normal, non-bold, non-italic version of the font. The various font formats begin with PTSansRegular. In your style sheet, you'd add this @font-face directive:

```
@font-face {
  font-family: 'PTSans';
  src: url('PTSansRegular.woff2') format('woff2'),
       url('PTSansRegular.woff') format('woff'),
  font-weight: normal;
  font-style: normal;

}
```

> **NOTE** In the code above, no .eot font (required by IE8) is included, because this technique doesn't work with that browser. This example also ignores older versions of desktop, mobile, and tablet browsers. However, it will work with all current browsers, including Internet Explorer 9.

Notice the following:

- You use a generic name for the font family—PTSans in line 2 above—instead of the specific name for that font file—PTSansRegular.

- The font-weight is set to normal, since this isn't a bold version of the font (line 8).

- The font-style is set to normal, since this isn't an italic version of the font (line 9).

> **NOTE** The code examples here assume that the font files PTSansRegular.eot, PTSansBold.eot, and so on are in the same folder as the style sheet. If they were in different folders, you'd need to adjust the URL to accurately point to the location of the font files in relation to the style sheet.

Now, say you had an italicized version of the font—the file name begins with PTSansItalic. You'd then add this to your style sheet:

```
@font-face {
  font-family: 'PTSans';
  src: url('PTSansItalic.woff2') format('woff2'),
       url('PTSansItalic.woff') format('woff');
  font-weight: normal;
  font-style: italic;
}
```

You use the same `font-family` name in line 2—PTSans. However, you change the `font-style` to italic (line 6). This tells the browser that the font you're specifying is the italic version of the PTSans font. You'd add similar `@font-face` directives for the bold and the bold/italic versions like this:

```
@font-face {
  font-family: 'PTSans';
  src: url('PTSansBold.woff2') format('woff2'),
       url('PTSansBold.woff') format('woff');
  font-weight: bold;
  font-style: normal;
}

@font-face {
  font-family: 'PTSans';
  src: url('PTSansBoldItalic.woff2') format('woff2'),
       url('PTSansBoldItalic.woff') format('woff');
  font-weight: bold;
  font-style: italic;
}
```

In other words, you need four `@font-face` directives to cover all variants of bold, italic, and regular text. Notice that the `font-family` name is the same in each case; only the `src` properties change (to point to the different files) and the `font-weight` and `font-style` properties change.

The benefit of this method is that you can apply the regular font to text, apply `<em>` and `<strong>` tags to your HTML, and let the browser worry about which font file to load and use. In this example, if you want to use the PTSans font on all your paragraphs, you'd simply add this style to your style sheet:

```
p {
  font-family: PTSans;
}
```

Then you can mark up your paragraph tags with HTML. For example, you might have a paragraph like this:

```
<p>When I was younger, I could remember <em>anything</em>, whether it had hap-
pened or <strong>not</strong> -- <strong><em>Mark Twain</em>
</strong></p>
```

When the web browser reads the style sheet (with the four `@font-face` directives and the `p` tag style), it would display most of the paragraph using the PTSans-Regular font. However, the word "anything" contained inside the `<em>` tags would use the PTSansItalic font; the word "not" inside the `<strong>` tags would use the PTSansBold font; and "Mark Twain" inside both `<strong>` and `<em>` tags would use the PTSansBoldItalic font.

These directives even work for headlines. If you created a style to format all h1 tags with PTSans, you could create this style:

```
h1 {
    font-family: PTSans;
}
```

With this style in place, a web browser would actually use the bold version of PT-Sans, since headlines are normally displayed in bold. (When you use this technique involving multiple variations of a font, you should not add font-weight: normal;, as described on page 136.)

Unfortunately, Internet Explorer 8 and earlier don't understand this method and will use the PTSansRegular font for all of the text. IE will create faux-italic and faux-bold for the <em> and <strong> tags; that is, it will slant the PTSansRegular font on screen for italic, and make the PTSansRegular font thicker for bold. The resulting computer-generated bold and italic usually look pretty bad.

■ ADDING BOLD AND ITALIC AND SUPPORTING INTERNET EXPLORER 8

If you're still supporting Internet Explorer 8 (or earlier), the previous solution to bold and italic won't work. You can get font variants to work in IE8, but it requires a bit more work. To begin with, you still create four @font-face directives, one for each variant of the font. However, instead of giving them the same font-family name (PTSans, for example), you give each one its unique name (PTSansRegular, PTSansItalic, and so on). In other words, you'd rewrite the four @font-face directives like this:

```
@font-face { font-family: 'PTSansRegular';
    src: url('PTSansRegular.eot?#iefix') format('embedded-opentype'),
        url('PTSansRegular.woff2') format('woff2'),
        url('PTSansRegular.woff) format('woff');
}

@font-face { font-family: 'PTSansItalic';
    src: url('PTSansItalic.eot?#iefix') format('embedded-opentype'),
        url('PTSansItalic.woff2') format('woff2'),
        url('PTSansItalic.woff) format('woff');
}

@font-face { font-family: 'PTSansBold';
    src: url('PTSansBold.eot?#iefix') format('embedded-opentype'),
        url('PTSansBold.woff2') format('woff2'),
        url('PTSansBold.woff') format('woff');
}

@font-face { font-family: 'PTSansBoldItalic';
    src: url('PTSansBoldItalic.eot?#iefix') format('embedded-opentype'),
        url('PTSansBoldItalic.woff2') format('woff2'),
        url('PTSansBoldItalic.woff') format('woff');
}
```

Notice that each @font-face directive has its one family name—one that matches the font variant: PTSansRegular, PTSansItalic, PTSansBold, and PTSansBoldItalic.

In addition, notice that the font-weight and font-style properties used in the examples on pages 136–138 are gone. You don't need them here.

The hard part comes when it's time to apply the font. In the example on page 137, you merely applied the font-family to the style like this:

```
p {
    font-family: PTSans;
}
```

Now, unfortunately, you have to apply the different font names to the various tags—p for regular, em for italic, strong for bold, and a descendant selector to handle the case of bold and italic. So to get the different variants of the PTSans font to work, you need to create four styles, involving many lines of code, like this:

```
p {
    font-family: PTSansRegular;
    font-size: 48px;
    font-style: normal;
    font-weight: normal;
}

p em {
    font-family: PTSansItalic;
    font-style: normal;
    font-weight: normal;
}

p strong {
    font-family: PTSansBold;
    font-style: normal;
    font-weight: normal;
}

p strong em, p em strong {
    font-family: PTSansBoldItalic;
    font-weight: normal;
    font-style: normal;
}
```

First, notice there are four styles: the p style applies the PTSansRegular font; p em is a descendant selector that applies to an <em> tag that's inside a <p> tag—that style applies the PTSansItalic font; p strong is another descendant selector, which applies the PTSansBold font to the <strong> tag when it appears inside a paragraph; and finally, there's a group selector composed of two descendent selectors. The first descendant selector applies to an <em> tag that's inside a <strong> tag that's inside a `<p>` tag, whereas the second applies to a `<strong>` tag inside an `<em>` that's inside a `<p>`. You need both because you can nest `<em>` tags inside of `<strong>` tags and vice versa. You could end up with HTML like this:

```
<p>
  <em><strong>Hey!</strong></em>
  I'm talking to
  <strong><em>you</em></strong>
</p>
```

The single p strong em selector won't work for the "Hey!" above, since it's a `<strong>` tag inside an `<em>` tag.

NOTE In HTML5, the `<b>` (for bold) and `<i>` (for italic) tags are back. You should use them merely for presentational purposes—when you want text to be italic, but not add any real emphasis to the meaning of the text. For example, the titles of books are often italicized, so using the `<i>` tag is recommended:

```
<i>CSS: The Missing Manual</i>
```

Using `<em>` would emphasize the text and cause screen readers to read the text aloud in a different way than other text. At any rate, if you intended to use `<b>` and `<i>`, make sure you create styles that use the italic and bold variants of the font (again, you only need worry about that if you're using the IE8–safe way of specifying italics, not if you're using the method discussed on page 138).

Another thing to notice is that you have to set the font-weight and font-style to normal for all these styles. If you don't, many browsers (not just Internet Explorer) will try to bold the already bolded font, and italicize the already italic version of the font.

This second technique for supporting bold and italic variants is obviously a lot of work. It becomes even more work if you use more than one font with bold and italic versions on the same site. Which technique you use really depends on how important Internet Explorer 8 support is for you. At the time of this writing, IE 8 is still quite popular, ranging from 3.71% (*http://gs.statcounter.com/#browser_version_partially_combined-ww-monthly-201401-201501*) to 19% (*http://www.netmarketshare.com*) of web browsers in use.

NOTE Here's another approach to the problem of supporting bold and italic for IE8. Try the first method (page 136), and see how it looks in IE8. Some fonts, usually sans-serif fonts, don't always look that bad when IE does its faux-italic and -bold thing to them. You might find that the difference isn't that noticeable, and you can use the first method without much of a problem. Also, remember that IE8's market share will continue to decline as people buy new computers, switch to Chrome or another browser, or upgrade their operating systems.

Discovering Google Web Fonts

If the instructions for using web fonts discussed in the previous section sound too daunting to you, there's an easier way—although one with fewer font options. In addition to search, maps, email, and all the many services it offers, Google provides an easy-to-use web fonts service. Rather than downloading fonts, converting them to proper formats, and then placing them onto your web server, you simply include a single link to an external style sheet that indicates which fonts you'd like to use. Google's server sends the proper fonts to the visitor's web browser. No muss, no fuss.

Your only responsibilities are finding the fonts you want to use on the Google Fonts site, copying the necessary code (which Google provides) and adding it to your web page, and creating CSS styles using those fonts. Start by visiting the Google Fonts site at *www.google.com/fonts* (see Figure 6-6).

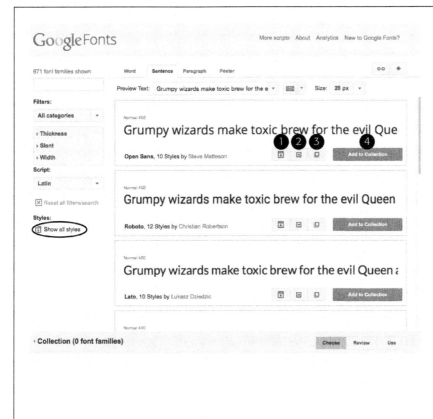

FIGURE 6-6

The Google Fonts site lists the fonts Google offers. Some fonts have multiple styles, such as bold, italic, thin, ultra-thin, and so on. To see all variants for a particular font, click the "Show all styles" link in the left sidebar (circled). Alternatively, to see just the different variants for a particular font, click the "See all styles" button (#1). To get started using a font right away, click the "Quick Use"(#2) button, which loads the Use panel described on page 144; the "Pop-out" button (#3) opens a new window with more information on the font as well as a specimen sheet demonstrating every letter in the font (it's a good way to see what the entire alphabet looks like and also to make sure that it has all the characters you need—such as unusual symbols or punctuation marks); lastly, the "Add to Collection" button (#4) adds the font to your collection. (A collection lets you select several fonts that you'd like to add to your site.)

Finding and Selecting Fonts

You select the fonts you wish to use by creating a *collection*. It's as easy as finding a font you like and clicking the "Add to Collection" button (see Figure 6-6). To find a font, you can scroll down the main web fonts page and see examples of the available fonts, but with over 670 fonts to choose from, it might take you a while to locate one you like. If you have a specific look already in mind, like a bold sans-serif font for headlines, use one of the filtering options on the left side of the page (see Figure 6-7).

- **Search by name.** If you know the name of the font you're interested in, then just type the name (or part of the name) in the Search field (#1 in Figure 6-7). The page then filters the list of fonts to show you the ones that match.

- **Filter by category.** The category menu (#2 in Figure 6-7) lets you show fonts that match one, two, three, four, or five categories: Serif, Sans Serif, Display, Handwriting, and Monospace. Just uncheck a box to hide that type of font, or turn on the box to show it. Display fonts are generally bold and stylish; they're not really good for long passages of text, but can make short headlines really jump out of the page. Handwriting fonts, or script fonts, look like someone wrote the text with a pen. They vary from elegant, wedding invitation-like scripts, to a hand-scrawled, "Give me the money if you want your cat back" ransom-note look.

- **Physical style.** Three sliders let you identify physical characteristics of fonts (#3 in Figure 6-7). The thickness slider lets you find fonts made of very thin lines (delicate lines that are often hard to read unless displayed at a large font size) to very thick lines (bold and chunky). The Slant slider identifies fonts with a "lean" to them: Generally this means italic versions of fonts, but also is relevant for handwritten fonts, which generally have a pronounced lean toward the right. Finally, use the Width slider to find fonts that are either narrower or more spread out. With wider fonts, you fit fewer letters on a single line but often make a bold statement in a headline.

- **Alphabet.** Lastly, the Script menu (#4 in Figure 6-7) lets you specify fonts for use with other languages. English and many European languages use the Latin alphabet, but if you need a font for Russian text, for example, you would choose Cyrillic. Pick the one that matches the language your text will appear in.

TIP To see a showcase of some of the best fonts available from Google, check out *http://hellohappy.org/beautiful-web-type/*.

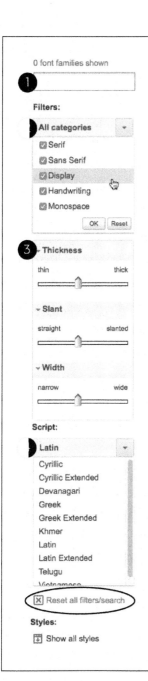

FIGURE 6-7

To help find the fonts that match your design, you can search Google's font directory, or filter down the list of fonts by specifying various criteria. If you try to use all of these filters, you'll most likely end up with no results. If so, click the "Reset all filters/search" link (circled) to return to the full list of Google web fonts.

As you find fonts that you'd like to use, you can click the "Add to Collection" button (#1 in Figure 6-8). The collection is kind of like a shopping cart, so you can add fonts to it and remove fonts from it.

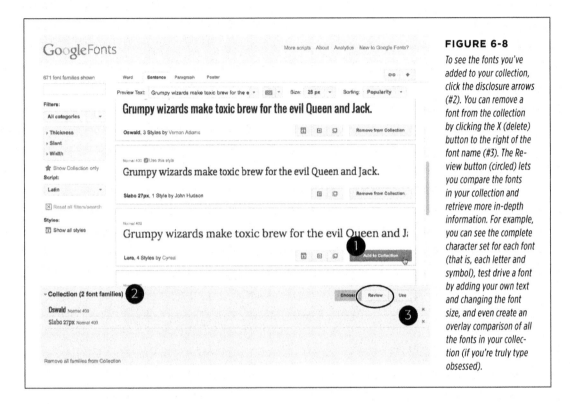

FIGURE 6-8

To see the fonts you've added to your collection, click the disclosure arrows (#2). You can remove a font from the collection by clicking the X (delete) button to the right of the font name (#3). The Review button (circled) lets you compare the fonts in your collection and retrieve more in-depth information. For example, you can see the complete character set for each font (that is, each letter and symbol), test drive a font by adding your own text and changing the font size, and even create an overlay comparison of all the fonts in your collection (if you're truly type obsessed).

Using Google Fonts

Once you've created a collection of fonts, you're ready to retrieve the code necessary to use them.

1. **At the bottom right of the Google Fonts screen (#1 in Figure 6-9), click the Use button.**

   A page opens with several options as well as the code you need to copy.

2. **Choose the style you want to use (#2 in Figure 6-9).**

   Some fonts include italic, bold, and other variants of the regular font. For body text, you'll usually want at least regular, italic, and bold. In the case of a headline, you can usually get away with just one font. You'll notice also that there's a "speed dial" on the right of this page. As you add more styles and fonts, the speed dial rotates clockwise indicating that it will take more time to download the fonts.

That's one drawback of web fonts. Since your site's visitors need to download them (as well as the web page, external style sheets, graphics, and other elements that make up your page), be careful not to go crazy and use too many fonts. Otherwise, people will have to wait a long time for the fonts to appear. The number on the dial indicates the number of milliseconds (on average) it will take to download the font files.

3. **Optionally, choose the character sets you want.**

This step isn't required and may not be available for all fonts. In addition, if you selected a character set other than Latin (see the last bullet point on page 142), then you may see other options besides Latin and Latin Extended. Latin Extended is a good choice if your text contains words in a language that uses particular accent characters like Turkish, Welsh, and Hungarian. For most Latin-based languages like French and Spanish, the normal Latin alphabet is all you need. You're better off not using the extended Latin if you don't need it, since using it adds file size and download time to the font.

> **NOTE** To see a list of the extra characters available in Latin Extended visit *http://en.wikipedia.org/wiki/Latin_Extended-A*.

4. **Copy the code in the "Add this code to your website" box (#3 in Figure 6-9).**

You have three options here.

- Standard provides a `<link>` tag that points to an external style sheet (this is the same as linking to any external style sheet, as described on page 26). However, this is actually a special link that points to Google's web server and provides the information Google needs to deliver the proper fonts. For instance:

  ```
  <link href='http://fonts.googleapis.com/css?family=Lato:300,400,300ital
  ic, 400italic|Oswald:400,700' rel='stylesheet' type='text/css'>
  ```

  Notice that at the end of the href attribute, the fonts and their styles are listed. In this example, the fonts are Lato and Oswald. And Google will load several styles of Lato: 300, 400, 300italic and 700italic. Those numbers are a way of indicating the weight (or thickness) of the font and are discussed in step 6 on page 147. In addition, a number plus "italic" (for example, "300italic") indicates an italicized version of that weight for that font.

> **NOTE** Even though the Google Fonts site suggests using "type='text/css'" as part of the <link> tag, you can leave it out. It's not needed in HTML5.

- Another option is @import. Click the @import tab under step 3 on the web page (see Figure 6-9) to see the code needed to use the @import directive. The benefit of this approach is that you can add @import to the beginning of another style sheet. For example, say you have a single external style sheet for your site, and you've linked all the pages in your site to it. The standard `<link>` method requires you to add that code to every page on your site. However, with the `@import` method, you can add the code to your single external style sheet and you're done.

FIGURE 6-9

When you're ready to use the Google fonts that you've added to your collection, click the Use button in the bottom right (#1), and then choose the styles you want (#2) and the method you'd like to use to attach those fonts to a page (#3). The most common way is to simply link to a style sheet that loads the fonts from Google's servers.

- Finally, you can choose a JavaScript approach. This book doesn't cover this method, since it requires a lot of code, and unless you know JavaScript really well, it's easy to make a mistake. In addition, it doesn't offer much benefit over the other options.

5. **Paste the code on your site's web pages.**

   In the case of the `<link>` method described in the previous step, you must paste the code onto every page you wish to use the fonts on. If you're just beginning the process of building your site, this isn't such a big deal, but if you already have lots of pages, this may end up being quite a bit of work. In that case, consider the @import method: You can place the @import code at the top of your site's external style sheet, and then all the pages that link to that style sheet will also download the proper fonts.

> **NOTE** The @import method can have a slight effect on your website's performance; that is, it can slow download speed.

6. **Create styles using the fonts.**

   Now that the fonts are loading, you can use them much like any other font. Just create a style, add the `font-family` property, and list the font. Google's Web Fonts page shows the font's name at the bottom of the Use page (#4 in Figure 6-9).

   If you're using multiple styles of a font, then you also need to add the `font-weight` and `font-style` properties to the style. Google doesn't use the regular normal or bold keywords to indicate a font's weight. Instead, it uses a numeric scale from 100 to 900. A value of 700 is bold, 400 is normal, and the other numbers indicate variations in thickness. For example, say you want to apply the regular italic version of the Gentium Book Basic font to the `<em>` tag. You can write this style:

```
em {
    font-family: "Gentium Book Basic", Palatino, serif;
    font-weight: 400;
    font-style: italic;
}
```

■ Adding Color to Text

Black and white is great for *Casablanca* and Woody Allen films, but when it comes to text, a nice sky blue looks snazzier than drab black. Coloring your text with CSS is easy. In fact, you've used the `color` property in a few tutorials already. You have several different ways to define the exact color you want, but they all follow the same basic structure. You type `color:` followed by a color value:

```
color: #3E8988;
```

In this example, the color value is a hexadecimal number indicating a muted shade of teal (more in a moment on what *hexadecimal* is).

TypeKit, a Google Alternative

Because of the technical and legal requirements for using web fonts, several companies have sprouted up that handle all the heavy lifting for you. Google Web Fonts is one example, but there are others. These *font services* let you select from a large collection of fonts hosted on their own web servers. In other words, you don't put the fonts on your server; you simply reference their servers by using a snippet of CSS or JavaScript. These services take care of sending the proper font format (EOT to IE8 and earlier, for example) to your visitors' browsers.

A commercial service from Adobe called TypeKit also provides a wide selection of fonts, but for a fee. Because it's part of Adobe (which makes fonts in addition to all the other software

they create), you have access to a wide range of professionally created fonts. With TypeKit, you create individual *kits*, or collections of fonts, and assign them to a website. You then add a snippet of JavaScript code to each page on your site. This code connects with the TypeKit servers, and delivers the fonts you requested to your site's visitors. TypeKit is a commercial service, though it does offer a free, limited trial version. Depending on how many fonts you want access to and how many people visit your website each month, you can end up spending from $24 a year up. You can also get access to these fonts if you subscribe to Adobe's Creative Cloud service: *https://www.adobe.com/creativecloud.html*.

Every graphics program from Fireworks to Photoshop to the GIMP lets you select a color using hexadecimal or RGB values. Also, the color pickers built into Windows and Mac let you use a color wheel or palette to select the perfect color and translate it into a hexadecimal or RGB value.

NOTE If your color design sense needs some help, you can find lots of attractive, coordinated collections of colors as well as great color-related resources at *www.colourlovers.com*. Another site, *http://paletton.com*, provides a handy web-based color and palette creation tool.

Hexadecimal Color Notation

The oldest color system used by web designers is hexadecimal notation. A color value like #6600FF actually contains three hexadecimal numbers—in this example 66, 00, FF—each of which specifies an amount of red, green, and blue, respectively. As in the RGB color system described next, the final color value is a blend of the amounts of red, green, and blue specified by these numbers.

TIP You can shorten the hexadecimal numbers to just three characters if each set contains the same two numbers. For example, shorten #6600FF to #60F, or #FFFFFF to #FFF.

▓ RGB

You can also use the RGB—red, green, blue—method used in computer graphics programs. The color value consists of three numbers representing either percentages (0–100 percent) or numbers between 0–255 for each hue (red, green, and blue). So when you want to set the text color to white (perhaps to set it off from an ominous dark page background), you can use this:

```
color: rgb(100%,100%,100%);
```

or

```
color: rgb(255,255,255);
```

> **NOTE** If all these numbers and digits have your head spinning, then you can always fall back on the classic HTML color keywords. (Just don't expect your site to win any awards for originality.) There are 17 colors—aqua, black, blue, fuchsia, gray, green, lime, maroon, navy, olive, orange, purple, red, silver, teal, white, and yellow. In CSS, you add them to your style like so: `color: fuchsia;`. In addition, most browsers support 147 SVG colors (also called X11 colors), so if you really want to show off, start using colors like linen, chocolate, khaki, and whitesmoke. You can find these colors listed at *https://developer.mozilla.org/en-US/docs/Web/CSS/color_value*. And you can find a list of the colors organized by hue at *http://html-color-codes.info/color-names/*.

■ RGBA

To add depth to a page, consider one of the newer color methods. RGBA stands for Red, Green, Blue, Alpha, and it works just like the RGB colors, with the addition of an *alpha* channel. That is, you can specify a level of opacity so that the color isn't solid, but see-through (see Figure 6-10). To the RGB colors, you add one last number: a value between 0 and 1. A value of 0 makes the color invisible, while 1 renders the color totally opaque (that is, you can't see through it):

```
color: rgba(255, 100, 50, .5);
```

You can create interesting visual effects by placing RGBA colored text over background images. For example, you can make the images seep through the color of the text a little (by using a high value like .9) or a lot (by using a low value like .1).

> **TIP** RGBA works particularly well with the `text-shadow` property discussed on page 160 and the `box-shadow` property discussed on page 201. Using RGBA, you can create even more subtle drop shadow effects by letting more of the background show through the shadow.

The downside? Internet Explorer 8 and earlier don't understand RGBA color. One solution is to declare a solid color first using hexadecimal notation, and then a second color property with RGBA color, like this:

```
color: rgb(255,100,50); /* for IE8 */
```

```
color: rgba(255,100,50,.5); /* for newer browsers */
```

All browsers interpret the first line; the second line overrides the first line, but only for browsers that understand RGBA color. In other words, IE8 applies the first color declaration and ignores the second, while IE9 and other browsers apply the RGBA color. You just won't get the transparency effect in IE8.

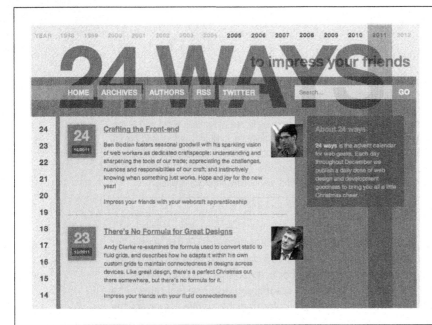

FIGURE 6-10

RGBA colors aren't just for text. You can use RGBA color with any CSS property that accepts a color value, like the background color of the search box in the top-right of this image, or the color of the navigation buttons: Home, Archives, Authors, and so on.

■ HSL AND HSLA

HSL stands for hue, saturation, and lightness (also sometimes labeled *luminance*). It's yet another way to specify color. It's not supported by Internet Explorer 8 or earlier, but works in all other browsers. If you're used to RGB or hex colors, you may find the HSL syntax a bit unusual. Here's an example of a bright red color:

```
color: hsl(0, 100%, 50%);
```

You supply three values inside hsl(). The first is a degree value from 0 to 360, which maps to a circle of hues. If you remember the order of the colors in a rainbow—red, orange, yellow, green, blue, indigo, and violet (ROYGBIV)—then you've got a basic idea of the values you'll need to specify a color. Red is 0 (it's also 360, since that's one full rotation around a circle), yellow is around 50, orange around 100, green around 150, and so on. Each color is separated by about 51 degrees.

The second is the saturation, or how pure the color is. You specify saturation in a percentage from 0% to 100%. A value of 0% is no saturation at all, or a dull gray. In fact, no matter what hue you specify, 0% will produce the same gray hue. A value of 100% is the pure color—bright and vibrant. The third value is the lightness value, specified in a percentage from 0% (completely black) to 100% (completely white). If you want to have a pure color, then you use a value of 50%.

HSL is supposed to be more intuitive then RGB or hexadecimal color values, but if you don't find it easy to understand, you don't have to use it. Instead, use a program like Fireworks or Photoshop or an online color picker to make picking an RGB or hex value easy.

> **NOTE** If you're interested in using HSL, you'll find an easy-to-use HSL color picker at *http://hslpicker.com*.

Just as RGB has its companion format, RGBA, HSL supports opacity with the HSLA format. It works similarly to RGB, described on page 148. You specify an opacity value from 0 (invisible) to 1 (totally opaque) to set the opacity value. This will create a bright red color with 50% opacity:

```
color: hsla(0, 100%, 50%, .5);
```

The examples in this book mostly stick with RGB and RGBA, but if you find HSL easier to understand, then use it!

■ Changing Font Size

Varying the size of text on a web page is a great way to create visual interest and direct your visitors' attention to important areas of a page. Headlines in large type sizes capture attention, while copyright notices displayed in small type subtly recede from prominence.

The font-size property sets text size. It's always followed by a unit of measurement, like so:

```
font-size: 1em;
```

The value and unit you specify for the font size (in this example, 1em) determine the size of the text. CSS offers a dizzying selection of sizing units: keywords, ems, exes, pixels, percentages, picas, points, and even inches, centimeters, and millimeters.

Units of measurement commonly used with printed materials—picas, points, inches, and so on—don't work well on web pages because you can't predict how they'll look from one monitor to the next. But you may have occasion to use points when creating style sheets for printer-friendly pages. Only a few of the measurement units—pixels, keywords, ems, rems, and percentages—make sense when you're sizing text for a computer monitor. The rest of this section explains how they work.

Using Pixels

Pixel values are the easiest to understand, since they're completely independent from any browser settings. When you specify, for example, a 36-pixel font size for an <h1> tag, the web browser displays text that's 36 pixels tall, period. Web designers cherish pixel values because they provide consistent text sizes across different types of computers and browsers.

To set a pixel value for the `font-size` property, type a number followed by the abbreviation px:

```
font-size: 36px;
```

> **NOTE** Don't include a space between the number and the unit type. For example, 36px is correct, but 36 px isn't.

Pixels and Retina Displays

When Apple introduced the iPhone with Retina display, iPhone owners rejoiced at the clarity and sharpness of the images. Apple's Retina display provides its clear image by cramming more pixels into a square inch. While regular computer displays range from 72–100 pixels per inch, the new Retina displays boast upward of 224 pixels per inch.

Apple has since added Retina displays to iPads and laptops. Other tablet and computer manufacturers are also jumping on the bandwagon, offering considerably more pixels per inch than older screens. What does this mean for web designers? Quite a bit. As you'll read in the box on "When Is a Pixel Not a Pixel?", these screens have considerable effect on images, and you'll need to do a bit of work to make great looking images for dense pixel displays.

When it comes to the pixels mentioned above, browsers on devices with Retina displays actually multiply a pixel value by 2. That is, if you specify text to be 16 pixels, a Retina-enabled web browser will actually use 32 pixels on the screen to draw the text. This is a good thing. If the browser only used 16 of its super-tiny pixels to display the text, then no one could read what you have to say.

In other words, although more dense displays are entering both the mobile and desktop computing world, they won't suddenly make the pixel-based type on your web pages appear microscopically small.

Using Keywords, Percentages, and Ems

Three ways of sizing text with CSS—keywords, percentages, and ems—work by either adding to or subtracting from the text size already on the viewer's browser screen. In other words, if you don't specify a text size using CSS, a web browser falls back on its preprogrammed settings. In most browsers, text inside a non-header tag is displayed 16px tall—that's called the *base text size*.

Web surfers can adjust their browsers by pumping up or dropping down that base size; however, changing the base font size requires fiddling with the browser's preference settings, a step most folks won't bother with.

> **NOTE** Most browsers have a *zoom* function that makes text, graphics, and the entire page smaller or larger. This setting doesn't really change the base text size as much as it magnifies the entire page. Ctrl++ (⌘-+) on most browsers zooms in on a page, while Ctrl+- (⌘--) zooms out. Pressing the Ctrl (Control) key and using the scroll wheel on a mouse also lets you zoom in and out of a page.

When you resize text with CSS, the browser takes the base text size (whether it's the original 16 pixels or some other size the viewer ordered) and adjusts it up or down according to your keyword, em, or percentage value.

KEYWORDS

CSS provides seven keywords that let you assign a size that's relative to the base text size: xx-small, x-small, small, medium, large, x-large, and xx-large. The CSS looks like this:

```
font-size: large;
```

The medium option is the same as the browser's base font size. Each of the other options decreases or increases the size by a different factor. In other words, while each size change is supposed to be a consistent increase or decrease from the previous size, it isn't. Basically, xx-small is the equivalent of 9 pixels (assuming you haven't adjusted the base font size in your browser); x-small is 10 pixels, small is 13 pixels, large is 18 pixels; x-large is 24 pixels, and xx-large is 32 pixels.

Keywords are pretty limited: You have only seven choices. When you want more control over the size of your text, turn to one of the other font-sizing options discussed next.

PERCENTAGES

Like keywords, percentage values adjust text in relationship to the font size defined by the browser, but they give you much finer control than just large, x-large, and so on. Every browser has a preprogrammed base text size, which in most browsers is 16 pixels. You can adjust this base size in your browser's preferences. Whatever setting has been chosen, the base text size for a particular browser is equivalent to 100%. In other words, for most browsers, setting the CSS percentage to 100% is the same as setting it to 16 pixels.

Say you want to make a particular headline appear two times the size of average text on a page. You simply set the font size to 200%, like so:

```
font-size: 200%;
```

Or, when you want the text to be slightly smaller than the default size, use a value like 90% to shrink the font size down a bit.

The above examples are pretty straightforward, but here's where it gets a little tricky: Font size is an inherited property (as discussed in Chapter 4), so any tags inside of a tag that has a font size specified inherit that font size. So the exact size of 100% can change if a tag inherits a font-size value.

For example, at the lower left of Figure 6-11, there's a <div> tag that has its font size set to 200%. That's two times the browser's base text size, or 32 pixels. All tags inside that <div> inherit that text size and use it as the basis for calculating their text sizes. In other words, for tags inside that <div>, 100% is 32 pixels. So the <h1> tag inside the <div> that has a font size of 100% displays at two times the base-text size for the page, or 32 pixels.

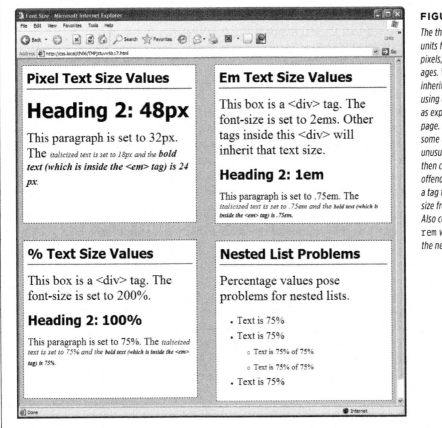

FIGURE 6-11

*The three most common
units for sizing text are
pixels, ems, and percent-
ages. Watch out for
inherited text sizes when
using ems or percentages,
as explained on the next
page. If you notice that
some text on a page looks
unusually large or small,
then check to see if the
offending text isn't inside
a tag that inherits a font
size from another tag.
Also consider using the
`rem` value described on
the next page.*

EMS

Once you understand percentages, you know everything you need to understand ems. The two work exactly the same way, but many web designers use ems because of its roots in typography.

The word *em* comes from the world of printed (as in paper) typography, where it refers to the size of a capital letter M for a particular font. As it's worked its way into the Web world, an em in CSS no longer means the same thing as in typography. Think of it as referring to the base text size. That is, a value of 1em means the same thing as a value of 100 percent, as described in the previous section. You can even say it the opposite way: A percentage value is just an em multiplied by 100: .5em is 50 percent, .75em is 75 percent, 3em is 300 percent, and so on.

For example, this CSS does the exact same thing as font-size: 200%;:

```
font-size: 2em;
```

NOTE As with pixel values, there's no space between the number and the word em. Also, even if you specify more than one em, you never add an *s* to the end: 2.5em, never 2.5ems.

When it comes to inheritance, ems also work just like percentage values (see the top-right of Figure 6-11 for an example). The bottom paragraph is set to .75em, which, since the <p> tag inherits the 2em (32px) setting from the <div> tag, works out to .75 x 32, or 24 pixels. Inside the <p> tag are two other tags that also have a font-size setting of .75em. The innermost tag, a <strong> tag, is set to .75em or, in essence, 75 percent of its *inherited* size. There's a lot of math to this one: 32 pixels (inherited from the <div> tag) x .75 (inherited from the <p> tag) x .75 (inherited from the <em> tag) x .75 (the <strong> tag's own font size). The result of this brainteaser is a text size of roughly 14 pixels.

Inherited font-size values can cause problems for nested lists. You can see an example in the bottom-right square of Figure 6-11. If you create a style like ul { font-size: 75% }, then a nested list (a <ul> tag inside of another <ul> tag) is set to 75 percent of 75 percent—making the text in the nested list smaller than the rest of the list.

To get around this conundrum, create an additional descendant selector style like this: ul ul {font-size: 100%}. This style sets any ul tag inside of a ul to 100 percent; in other words, 100 percent of the surrounding ul tag's font size. In this example, it keeps any nested lists to 75 percent of the base text size. There's another way to prevent this hall-of-mirrors, shrinking-text effect: the rem unit (discussed next).

▦ REMS

CSS includes another measurement unit called rem. No, it's not named after sleep patterns or a band. It stands for *root em*—meaning its value is based on the text size of the root element. In most cases this just means the base text size, so you can change the .75em shown in Figure 6-11 to this:

```
font-size: .75rem;
```

This style makes the font size .75 of the base text size, not the inherited font size (as is the case with ems). The root element in HTML is actually the html element you find at the beginning of a web page. When using rem values, you can set the base text size of the html element and then use rem units to set text to a size relative to that. For example, you can set the base text size to 20 pixels like this:

```
html {
  font-size: 20px;
}
```

Then use rem units to create fonts in relation to that 20-pixel base text size. For example, to then make all paragraphs 15 pixels in size, add this style:

```
p {
  font-size: .75rem;
}
```

The rem unit avoids the problems associated with inherited percentage and em font sizes. Percentages and ems are based on the font size of their parent element. A percentage font size applied to multiple nested elements will compound, making each successive font size a percentage of the previous element's font size. However, rem units are always based on the font size of the html element; in other words, a rem is always the same value even when nested inside elements that inherit different font sizes.

You should be aware, however, that while most browsers now understand the rem unit, Internet Explorer 8 and earlier don't.

TIP You can make type stand out on a page in many different ways. Making certain words larger than others or making some text darker, lighter, or brighter visually sets them apart from the surrounding text. Contrast is one of the most important principles of good graphic design; it can help highlight important messages, guide a reader's eye around a page, and generally make understanding a page easier. For a quick overview of typographic contrast, check out this page: *www.creativepro.com/article/dot-font-seven-principles-of-typographic-contrast*.

■ Formatting Words and Letters

Although you'll spend a lot of time fine-tuning the color, size, and fonts of the text on your web pages, CSS also lets you apply other common text-formatting properties (like bold and italic) as well as some less common ones (like small caps and letter spacing).

NOTE CSS lets you combine multiple text properties, but don't get carried away. Too much busy formatting makes your page harder to read. But worse, your hard work loses its impact.

Italicizing and Bolding

Web browsers display type inside the <em> and <i> tags in *italicized* type, and text inside the <strong>, <b>, <th> (table header), and header tags (<h1> and so on) in **bold** type. But you can control these settings yourself—either turn off bold for a headline or italicize text that normally isn't—using the font-style and font-weight properties.

To italicize text, add this to a style:

```
font-style: italic;
```

Alternatively, you can make sure text *isn't* italicized, like so:

```
font-style: normal;
```

> **NOTE** The font-style property actually has a third option—oblique—which works identically to italic.

The font-weight property lets you make text bold or not. In fact, according to the rules of CSS, you can actually specify nine numeric values (100–900) to choose subtle gradations of boldness (from super-extra-heavy [900] to nearly invisible-light [100]). Of course, the fonts you use must have nine different weights for these values to have any visible effect for your website's visitors. The only way to use the numeric values is with the web fonts discussed on page 126. In fact, Google Fonts (page 126) use the numeric values exclusively for specifying font weights.

> **NOTE** When using web fonts, you'll find that making text bold and italic requires a few other steps. See page 126 for the details.

To make text bold:

```
font-weight: bold;
```

And to make text un-bold:

```
font-weight: normal;
```

> **NOTE** Since headlines are already displayed as bold type, you may want to find another way of highlighting a word or words that are strongly emphasized or bolded inside a headline. Here's one way:
>
> ```
> h1 strong { color: #3399FF; }
> ```
>
> This descendant selector changes the color of any <strong> tags (usually displayed as bold) that appear inside a <h1> tag.

Capitalizing

Capitalizing text is pretty easy—just hit the caps lock key and start typing, right? But what if you want to capitalize every heading on a page, and the text you've copied and pasted from a Word document is lowercase? Rather than retyping the headline, turn to the CSS text-transform property. With it, you can make text all uppercase, all lowercase, or even capitalize the first letter of each word (for titles and headlines). Here's an example:

```
text-transform: uppercase;
```

For the other two options, just use lowercase or capitalize.

Because this property is inherited, a tag that's nested inside a tag with text-transform applied to it gets the same uppercase, lowercase, or capitalized value. To tell CSS *not* to change the case of text, use the none value:

```
text-transform: none;
```

■ SMALL CAPS

For more typographic sophistication, you can also turn to the font-variant property, which lets you set type as small-caps. In small cap style, lowercase letters appear as slightly downsized capital letters, like so: POMP AND CIRCUMSTANCE. While difficult to read for long stretches of text, small caps lend your page an old-world, bookish gravitas when used on headlines and captions. To create small-cap text:

```
font-variant: small-caps;
```

Decorating

CSS also provides the text-decoration property to add various enhancements to text. With it, you can add lines over, under, or through the text (see Figure 6-12), or for real giggles, you can make the text blink like a No Vacancy sign. Use the text-decoration property by adding one or more of the following keywords: underline, overline, line-through, or blink. For example, to underline text:

```
text-decoration: underline;
```

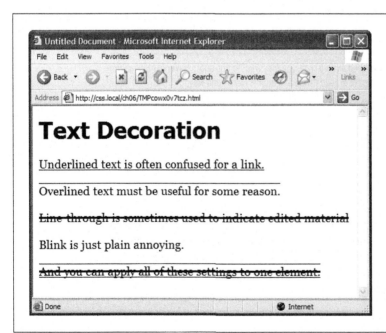

FIGURE 6-12

The text-decoration property in action. If this is what the people at CSS headquarters call "decorations," you'd best not ask for their design help on your next home remodel.

You can also combine multiple keywords for multiple effects. Here's how to add a line over and under some text:

```
text-decoration: underline overline;
```

But just because you *can* add these not-so-decorative decorations to text doesn't mean you should. For one thing, anyone who's used the Web for any length of time instinctively associates any underlined text with a link and tries to click it. So it's not a good idea to underline words that aren't part of a link. And blink is like a neon sign flashing "Amateur! Amateur! Amateur!" (That's probably why most browsers don't make text blink even if you ask for it.)

> **NOTE**   You can get a similar effect to underlining and overlining by adding a border to the bottom or top of an element (see page 194). The big advantage of borders is that you can control their placement, size, and color to create a more attractive design that doesn't look like a link.

The overline option simply draws a line above text, while line-through draws a line right through the center of text. Some designers use this strike-through effect to indicate an edit on a page where text has been removed from the original manuscript.

Finally, you can turn off all decorations by using the none keyword like this:

```
text-decoration: none;
```

Why do you need a text-decoration property that removes decorations? The most common example is removing the line that appears under a link. (See page 283.)

Letter and Word Spacing

Another way to make text stand out from the crowd is to adjust the space that appears between letters or words (see Figure 6-13). Reducing the space between letters using the CSS letter-spacing property can tighten up headlines, making them seem even bolder and heavier while fitting more letters on a single line. Conversely, increasing the space can give headlines a calmer, more majestic quality. To reduce the space between letters, you use a negative value like this:

```
letter-spacing: -1px;
```

A positive value adds space between letters:

```
letter-spacing: .7em;
```

Likewise, you can open up space (or remove space) between words using the word-spacing property. This property makes the space between words wider (or narrower) without actually affecting the spacing between the letters inside a word:

```
word-spacing: 2px;
```

With either of these properties, you can use any type of measurement you'd use for text sizing—pixels, ems, percentages—with either positive or negative values.

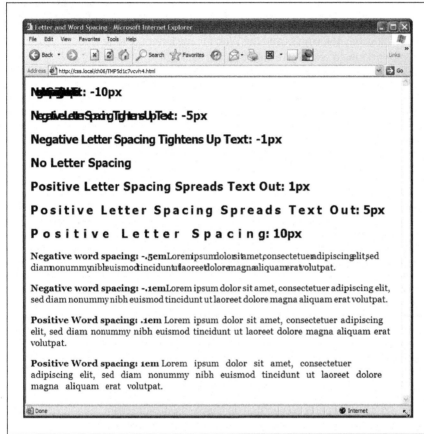

FIGURE 6-13

Use word and letter spacing judiciously. Too much or too little of either can make text difficult, if not impossible, to read.

Unless you're going for some really far-out design effect—in other words, totally unreadable text—keep your values small. Too high a negative value, and letters and words overlap. To keep the message of your site clear and legible, use both letter and word spacing with care.

■ Adding Text Shadow

CSS includes a property that lets you add drop shadows to text to add depth and interest to headlines, lists, and paragraphs (see Figure 6-14).

The text-shadow property requires four pieces of information: the horizontal offset (how far to the left or right of the text the shadow should appear), the vertical offset (how far above or below the text the shadow should appear), the blurriness of the shadow, and the color of the drop shadow. For example, here's the `text-shadow` property that creates the effect at the top of Figure 6-14:

```
text-shadow: -4px 4px 3px #999999;
```

FIGURE 6-14

Text shadows are a great way to add subtle (or, if you insist, not so subtle) depth to headlines and other text. While the text-shadow property works in all current browsers, it doesn't work in Internet Explorer 9 or earlier.

The first value, 4px, means "place the shadow 4 pixels to the left of the text." (A positive value here would place the shadow to the right of the text.) The second value, 4px, places the shadow 4 pixels below the text. (A negative value would place the shadow above the text.) The 3px value defines how blurry the shadow should be. A 0px value (no blur) results in a sharp drop shadow; the larger the value, the more blurry and indistinct the shadow. Finally, the last value is the drop shadow's color.

You can even add multiple drop shadows for more complex effects (see the bottom image in Figure 6-14): Just add a comma followed by additional drop shadow values, like this:

```
text-shadow: -4px 4px 3px #666, 1px -1px 2px #000;
```

There's no limit (except good taste) to the number of shadows you can add this way. Sadly, this effect doesn't work in Internet Explorer 9 or earlier. It does, however, work in all other current browsers (including later versions of Internet Explorer). In other words, *don't* rely on this effect to make text readable. The bottom image in Figure 6-14 shows you what not to do: The text color is white, and it's readable only because the drop shadows define the outline of the text. In Internet Explorer 9 and earlier, the text would be invisible—white text on a white background.

NOTE For some examples of beautiful ways to use text shadows, visit *http://webexpedition18.com/articles/ css3-text-shadow-property/*. You can also see a great example using multiple text shadows to create a 3-D text effect at *http://markdotto.com/playground/3d-text/*.

■ Formatting Entire Paragraphs

Some CSS properties apply to chunks of text rather than individual words. You can use the properties in this section on complete paragraphs, headlines, and so on.

Adjusting the Space Between Lines

In addition to changing the space between words and letters, CSS lets you adjust the space between lines of text using the `line-height` property. The bigger the line height, the more space that appears between each line of text (see Figure 6-15).

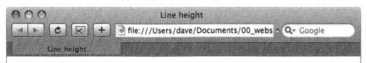

FIGURE 6-15

The line-height property lets you spread a paragraph's lines apart or bring them closer together. The normal setting is equivalent to 120 percent, so a smaller percentage tightens up the lines (top), while a larger percentage pushes them apart (bottom).

Line-height 75%: Lorem ipsum dolor sit amet, consectetuer adipiscing elit, sed diam nonummy nibh euismod tincidunt ut laoreet dolore magna aliquam erat volutpat. Lorem ipsum dolor sit amet, consectetuer adipiscing elit, sed diam nonummy nibh euismod tincidunt ut laoreet dolore magna aliquam erat volutpat.

Line-height 100%: Lorem ipsum dolor sit amet, consectetuer adipiscing elit, sed diam nonummy nibh euismod tincidunt ut laoreet dolore magna aliquam erat volatpat. Lorem ipsum dolor sit amet, consectetuer adipiscing elit, sed diam nonummy nibh euismod tincidunt ut laoreet dolore magna aliquam erat volutpat.

Line-height Normal: Lorem ipsum dolor sit amet, consectetuer adipiscing elit, sed diam nonummy nibh euismod tincidunt ut laoreet dolore magna aliquam erat volatpat. Lorem ipsum dolor sit amet, consectetuer adipiscing elit, sed diam nonummy nibh euismod tincidunt ut laoreet dolore magna aliquam erat volutpat.

Line-height 120%: Lorem ipsum dolor sit amet, consectetuer adipiscing elit, sed diam nonummy nibh euismod tincidunt ut laoreet dolore magna aliquam erat volatpat. Lorem ipsum dolor sit amet, consectetuer adipiscing elit, sed diam nonummy nibh euismod tincidunt ut laoreet dolore magna aliquam erat volutpat.

Line-height 200%: Lorem ipsum dolor sit amet, consectetuer adipiscing

elit, sed diam nonummy nibh euismod tincidunt ut laoreet dolore magna

aliquam erat volutpat. Lorem ipsum dolor sit amet, consectetuer adipiscing

elit, sed diam nonummy nibh euismod tincidunt ut laoreet dolore magna

aliquam erat volutpat.

■ LINE SPACING BY PIXEL, EM, OR PERCENTAGE

Just as with the `font-size` property, you can use pixels, ems, or percentages to set the size of line height:

```
line-height: 150%;
```

In general, percentages or ems are better than pixels, because they change according to, and along with, the text's font-size property. If you set the line height to 10 pixels and then later adjust the font size to something much larger (like 36 pixels), because the line height remains at 10 pixels, your lines then overlap. However, using a percentage (150% percent, say) means the line-height spacing adjusts proportionally whenever you change the font-size value.

The normal line-height setting for a browser is 120%. So, when you want to tighten up the line spacing, use a value less than 120%; to spread lines apart, use a value greater than that.

NOTE To determine the amount of space that appears between lines of text, a web browser subtracts the font size from the line height. The result—called *leading*—is the amount of space between lines in a paragraph. Say the font size is 12 pixels, and the line height (set to 150%) works out to 18 pixels. 18 - 12 = 6 pixels, so the browser adds 6 pixels of space between each line.

▉ LINE SPACING BY NUMBER

CSS offers another measurement method specific to line height, which is simply a number. You write it like this:

```
line-height: 1.5;
```

There's no unit (like em or px) after this value. The browser multiplies this number by the font size to determine the line height. So if the text is 1em and the line-height value is 1.5, then the calculated line height is 1.5em. In some cases, the effect may be no different from specifying a value of 1.5em or 150%.

However, because nested tags inherit the line-height value of their parent, you can often run into problems using an em or percentage value.

For example, say you set the line-height property of the <body> tag to 150%. All tags inside the page would inherit that value. However, it's not the percentage that's inherited; it's the *calculated* line height. So, say the font size for the page is set to 10 pixels; 150 percent of 10 is 15 pixels. Every tag would inherit a line height of 15 pixels, not 150 percent. So if you happened to have a paragraph with large, 36 pixel text, then its line height—15 pixels—would be much smaller than the text, making the lines squish together in a hard-to-read mess.

In this example, instead of using a line-height of 150% applied to the <body> tag, you could have all tags share the same basic proportional line height by setting the line-height to 1.5. Every tag, instead of inheriting a precise pixel value for line height from the body style, simply multiplies its font size by 1.5. So in the above example of a paragraph with 36-pixel text, the line height would be 1.5 x 36 or 54 pixels.

In other words, it's best to skip the ems and percentages for line heights and just use a simple numeric value.

Aligning Text

One of the quickest ways to change the look of a web page is with paragraph alignment. Using the `text-align` property, you can center a paragraph on a page, align the text along its left or right edge, or justify both left and right edges (like the paragraphs in this book). Normally, text on a page is left aligned, but you may want to center headlines to give them a formal look. Languages that read from right to left, like Hebrew and Arabic, require right-alignment. To change the alignment of text, use any of the following keywords—`left`, `right`, `justify`, `center`:

```
text-align: center;
```

Justified text looks great on a printed page—mainly because the fine resolution possible with printing allows for small adjustments in spacing, and because most programs used to lay out printed material can hyphenate long words (thus attempting to equally distribute the number of characters per line). This prevents large, unsightly gaps or rivers of white space flowing through the paragraphs. Web pages are limited to much coarser spacing because of the generally low resolution of monitors, and because web browsers don't know how to hyphenate long words. So when you use the `justify` option, the space between words can vary significantly from line to line, making the text harder to read. When you want to use the `justify` option on your web pages, test it thoroughly to make sure the text is attractive and readable.

Indenting the First Line and Removing Margins

In many books, the first line of each paragraph is indented. This first-line indent marks the beginning of a paragraph when there are no spaces separating paragraphs. On the Web, however, paragraphs don't have indents but are instead separated by a bit of space—like the paragraphs in this book.

If you have a hankering to make your web pages look less like other web pages and more like a handsomely printed book, take advantage of the CSS `text-indent` and `margin` properties. With them, you can add a first-line indent and remove (or increase) the margins that appear at the beginnings and ends of paragraphs.

■ FIRST-LINE INDENTS

You can use pixel and em values to set the first-line indent like this:

```
text-indent: 25px;
```

or

```
text-indent: 5em;
```

A pixel value is an absolute measurement—a precise number of pixels—while an em value specifies the number of letters (based on the current font size) you want to indent.

TIP You can use negative text-indent values to create what's called a *hanging indent*, where the first line starts further to the left than the other lines in the paragraph. (Think of it as "hanging" off the left edge.) You'll usually use a negative text indent along with a position margin value, so that the negative text indent doesn't stick outside the left side of a page, column, or layout box.

You can also use a percentage value, but with the text-indent property, percentages take on a different meaning than you've seen before. In this case, percentages aren't related to the font size; they're related to the width of the element containing the paragraph. For example, if the text-indent is set to 50%, and a paragraph spans the entire width of the web browser window, then the first line of the paragraph starts half the way across the screen. If you resize the window, both the width of the paragraph and its indent change. (You'll learn more about percentages and how they work with the width of elements in the next section.)

POWER USERS' CLINIC

A Shorthand Method for Text Formatting

Writing one text property after another gets tiring, especially when you want to use several different text properties at once. Fortunately, CSS offers a shorthand property called font, which lets you combine the following properties into a single line: font-style (page 156), font-variant (page 158), font-weight (page 156), font-size (page 151), line-height (page 163), and font-family (page 121). For example, consider the following declaration:

    font: italic bold small-caps 18px/1.5
    Arial, Helvetica, sans-serif;

It creates bold, italicized type in small caps, using 18px Arial (or Helvetica or sans-serif) with a line height of 150 percent. Keep these rules in mind:

- You don't have to include every one of these properties, but you *must* include the font size and font family:

      font: 1.5em Georgia, Times, serif;

- Use a single space between each property value. You use a comma only to separate fonts in the list at the end of the value like this:

      Arial, Helvetica, sans-serif

- When specifying the line height, add a slash after the font size followed by the line-height value, like this:

      1.5em/1.5

The last two properties must be font-size (or font-size/line-height) followed by font-family, in that order. All the other properties may be written in any order. For example, these two declarations are the same:

    font: italic bold small-caps 1.5em Arial;
    font: bold small-caps italic 1.5em Arial;

Finally, omitting a value from the list is the same as setting that value to normal. Say you create a <p> tag style that formats all paragraphs in bold, italics, and small caps with a line height of 2000 percent (not that you'd actually *do* that). You can then create a class style named .specialParagraph with the following font declaration:

    font: 1.5em Arial;

When you apply this style to one paragraph on the page, then that paragraph would *not* inherit the italic, bold, small caps, or line height. Omitting those four values in the .specialParagraph style is the same as writing this:

    font: normal normal normal 1.5em/normal
    Arial;

■ CONTROLLING MARGINS BETWEEN PARAGRAPHS

Many designers hate the space that every browser throws in between paragraphs. Before CSS, there was nothing you could do about it. Fortunately, you can now tap into the margin-top and margin-bottom properties to remove (or, if you wish, expand) that gap. To totally eliminate a top and bottom margin, write this:

```
margin-top: 0;
margin-bottom: 0;
```

To eliminate the gaps between *all* paragraphs on a page, create a style like this:

```
p {
  margin-top: 0;
  margin-bottom: 0;
}
```

As with text-indent, you can use pixel or em values to set the value of the margins. You can also use percentages, but as with text-indent, the percentage is related to the *width* of the paragraph's containing element. Because it's confusing to calculate the space above and below a paragraph based on its width, it's easier to stick with either em or pixel values.

NOTE Because not all browsers treat the top and bottom margin of headlines and paragraphs consistently, it's often a good idea to simply *zero out* (that is, eliminate) all margins at the beginning of a style sheet. To see how this works, turn to page 109.

For a special effect, you can assign a *negative* value to a top or bottom margin. For example, a –10px top margin moves the paragraph up 10 pixels, perhaps even visually overlapping the page element above it. (See step 4 on page 183 for an example.)

Formatting the First Letter or First Line of a Paragraph

CSS also provides a way of formatting just a part of a paragraph by using the ::first-letter and ::first-line pseudo-elements (see Figure 6-16). Technically, these aren't CSS properties, but types of selectors that determine what part of a paragraph CSS properties should apply to. With the ::first-letter pseudo-element, you can create an initial capital letter to simulate the look of a hand-lettered manuscript. To make the first letter of each paragraph bold and red you could write this style:

```
p::first-letter {
  font-weight: bold;
  color: red;
}
```

To be more selective and format just the first letter of a particular paragraph, you can apply a class style to the paragraph—.intro, for example:

```
<p class="intro">Text for the introductory paragraph goes here...</p>
```

Then you could create a style with a name like this: .intro::first-letter.

The ::first-line pseudo-element formats the initial line of a paragraph. You can apply this to any block of text, like a heading (h2::first-line) or paragraph (p::first-line). As with ::first-letter, you can apply a class to just one paragraph and format only the first line of that paragraph. Say you want to capitalize every letter in the first line of the first paragraph of a page. Apply a class to the HTML of the first paragraph—<p class="intro">—and then create a style like this:

```
.intro::first-line { text-transform: uppercase; }
```

FIGURE 6-16

The ::first-letter pseudo-element formats the first letter of the styled element, like the initial caps to the left. The ::first-line selector, on the other hand, styles the first line of a paragraph. Even if your guest resizes the window (bottom), the browser still styles every word that appears on a paragraph's first line.

NOTE For some strange reason, neither Chrome nor Safari understands the `text-transform` property (page 157) when it's used with the `::first-line` pseudo-element. In other words, you can't use CSS to capitalize the letters of a paragraph's first line in Chrome or Safari.

Styling Lists

The <ul> and <ol> tags create bulleted and numbered lists, like lists of related items or numbered steps. But you don't always want to settle for the way web browsers automatically format those lists. You may want to swap in a more attractive bullet, use letters instead of numbers, or even completely eliminate the bullets or numbers.

Types of Lists

Most web browsers display unordered lists (<ul> tags) using round bullets, and numbered lists (<ol> tags) using...well...numbers. With CSS, you can choose from among three types of bullets—disc (a solid round bullet), circle (a hollow round bullet), or square (a solid square). There are also six different numbering schemes—decimal, decimal-leading-zero, upper-alpha, lower-alpha, upper-roman, or lower-roman (see Figure 6-17). You select all these options using the *list-style-type* property, like so:

```
list-style-type: square;
```

or

```
list-style-type: upper-alpha;
```

Most of the time, you use this property on a style that's formatting an <ol> or <ul> tag. Typical examples include an ol or ul tag style—ul { list-style-type: square; }—or a class you're applying to one of those tags. However, you can also apply the property to an individual list item (<li> tag) as well. You can even apply different types of bullet styles to items within the same list. For example, you can create a style for a <li> tag that sets the bullets to square, but then create a class named .circle that changes the bullet type to circle, like this:

```
li {list-style-type: square; }
.circle { list-style-type: circle; }
```

You can then apply the class to every other item in the list to create an alternating pattern of square and circular bullets:

```
<ul>
<li>Item 1</li>
<li class="circle">Item 2</li>
<li>Item 3</li>
<li class="circle">Item 4</li>
</ul>
```

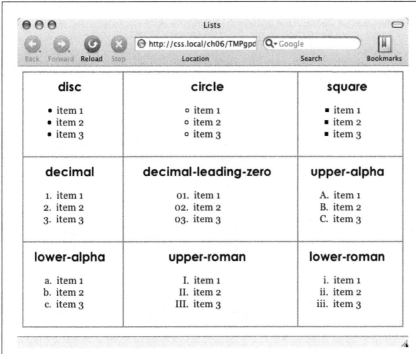

FIGURE 6-17

CSS provides many different ways to mark bulleted and numbered lists, from a handful of geometric shapes to many different numbering systems. If you feel like rushing a fraternity or sorority, you can also replace numbers with Greek letters—ά, β, χ—using the lower-greek option. In fact, there are a number of other numbering schemes including Armenian, Georgian, Katakana, and other regional variations. You can find out about them at https://developer.mozilla.org/en-US/docs/Web/CSS/list-style-type.

Or, using the nth-of-type selector (page 66) you could skip the class name entirely:

```
li {list-style-type: square; }
li:nth-of-type(odd) { list-style-type: circle; }
```

At times you'll want to completely hide bullets, like when you'd rather use your own graphic bullets (see page 171). Also, when a site's navigation bar is a list of links, you can use an <ul> list, but hide its bullets (see the example on page 290). To turn off the bullets, use the keyword none:

```
list-style-type: none;
```

Positioning Bullets and Numbers

Web browsers usually display bullets or numbers hanging to the left of the list item's text (Figure 6-18, left). With CSS, you can control the position of the bullet (somewhat) using the list-style-position property. You can either have the bullet appear outside of the text (the way browsers normally display bullets) or inside the text block itself (Figure 6-18, right):

```
list-style-position: outside;
```

or

```
list-style-position: inside;
```

> **TIP** You can adjust the space between the bullet and its text—increase or decrease that gap—by using the `padding-left` property. To use it, you create a style that applies to the `<li>` tags. This technique works only if you set the `list-style-position` property to the `outside` option (or don't use `list-style-position` at all).

In addition, if you don't like how web browsers indent a list from the left edge, then you can remove that space by setting both the `margin-left` and `padding-left` properties to 0 for the list. To remove the indent from all lists, you can create this group selector:

```
ul, ol {
    padding-left: 0;
    margin-left: 0;
}
```

Or you can create a class style with those properties and apply it to a particular `<ul>` or `<ol>` tag. The reason you need to set both the padding and margin properties is that some browsers use padding (Firefox, Mozilla, Safari) and some use margin (Internet Explorer) to control the indent. (You'll learn more about the margin and padding properties in the next chapter.)

FIGURE 6-18

Using the list-style-position *property, you can control the position of bullets and numbers in a list. The* outside *option (left) emphasizes the "listness" of your list. Use the* inside *option (right) if you need to maximize the width of your list.*

Browsers normally display one bulleted item directly above another, but you can add space between list items using the margin-top or margin-bottom properties on the particular list items. These properties work for spacing list items exactly the same way they work for spacing paragraphs, as explained on page 166. You just need to make sure that the style applies to the <li> tags by creating a class style and applying it individually to each <li> tag. Or, better yet, create an <li> tag style or descendant selector. The style should *not* apply to the <ul> or <ol> tag. Adding margins to the top or bottom of those tags simply increases the space between the entire list and the paragraphs above or below it—not the space between each item in the list.

Graphic Bullets

If you're not happy with squares and circles for your bullets, create your own. Using an image-editing program like Photoshop or Fireworks, you can quickly create colorful and interesting bullets. Clip art collections and most symbol fonts (like Webdings) provide great inspiration.

The CSS list-style-image property lets you specify a path to a graphic on your site, much as you specify a file when adding an image to a page by using the src attribute of the HTML <img> tag. You use the property like this:

```
list-style-image: url(images/bullet.gif);
```

The term url and the parentheses are required. The part inside the parentheses—images/bullet.gif in this example—is the path to the graphic. Notice that, unlike HTML, you don't have to use quotation marks around the path (though you can, if you like).

> **NOTE** When specifying a graphic in an *external* style sheet, the path to the image is relative to the style sheet file, not the web page. You'll learn more about how this works in the box on page 237, as you start to use images with CSS.

While the list-style-image property lets you use a graphic for a bullet, it doesn't provide any control over its placement. The bullet may appear too far above or below the line, requiring you to tweak the bullet graphic until you get it just right. A better approach—one you'll learn in Chapter 8—is to use the background-image property. That property lets you very accurately place a graphic for your bulleted lists.

> **NOTE** As with the font property (see the box on page 165), there's a shorthand method of specifying list properties. The list-style property can include a value for each of the other list properties—list-style-image, list-style-position, and list-style-type. For example, ul { list-style: circle inside; } formats unordered lists with the hollow circle bullet on the inside position. When you include both a style type and style image—list-style: circle url(images/bullet.gif) inside;—web browsers use the style type (circle in this example) if the graphic can't be found.

FREQUENTLY ASKED QUESTION

Customizing List Bullets and Numbers

I'd like the numbers in my numbered lists to be bold and red instead of boring old black. How do I customize bullets and numbers?

CSS gives you a few ways to customize the markers that appear before list items. For bullets, you can use your own graphics, as described previously. The cool, "I'm so CSS-savvy" way is to use what's called *generated content*. Basically, generated content is just stuff that isn't actually typed on the page but is added by the web browser when it displays the page. A good example is bullets themselves. You don't type bullet characters when you create a list; the browser adds them for you. With CSS, you can have a browser add content, and even style that content, before each <li> tag. You read about generated content on page 57, but just so you have the code at hand if you want to make regular bullets next to the list items red, add this CSS to your style sheet:

```
ul li {
    list-style-type: none;
}
ul li:before {
    content: counter(item, disc) " ";
    color: red;
}
```

And, if you wanted to make the items in a numbered list red, you can add this CSS:

```
ol li {
    list-style-type: none;
    counter-increment: item;
}
ol li:before {
    content: counter(item) ". ";
    color: red;
}
```

For a more in-depth explanation of styling numbered lists visit *http://blog.teamtreehouse.com/customize-ordered-lists-pseudo-element*.

■ Tutorial: Text Formatting in Action

In this tutorial, you'll gussy up headlines, lists, and paragraphs of text, using CSS's powerful formatting options.

To get started, you need to download the tutorial files from *https://github.com/sawmac/css_mm_4e*. Click the tutorial link and download the files. All of the files are enclosed in a zip archive, so you'll need to unzip them first. The files for this tutorial are contained inside the folder named *06*.

Setting Up the Page

First, you'll get your style sheet started, add the @font-face directive to load some web fonts, and add styles to format the body text.

1. **Launch your web browser and open the file *06→text.html* (see Figure 6-19).**

   It's not much to look at—just a collection of headlines, paragraphs and a lone bulleted list—but you'll turn it into something far better looking.

2. **Open the file *text.html* in your favorite text editor.**

You'll use a Google font as well as your own font files for this project. Start by adding a link to a Google font.

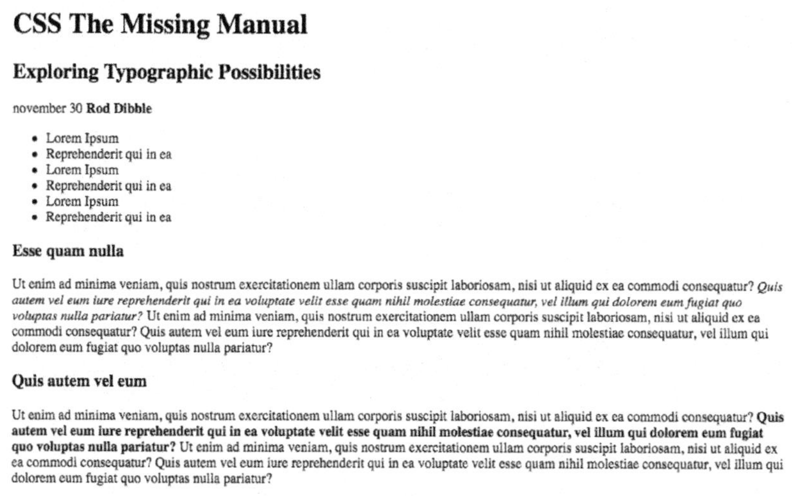

CSS The Missing Manual

Exploring Typographic Possibilities

november 30 **Rod Dibble**

- Lorem Ipsum
- Reprehenderit qui in ea
- Lorem Ipsum
- Reprehenderit qui in ea
- Lorem Ipsum
- Reprehenderit qui in ea

Esse quam nulla

Ut enim ad minima veniam, quis nostrum exercitationem ullam corporis suscipit laboriosam, nisi ut aliquid ex ea commodi consequatur? *Quis autem vel eum iure reprehenderit qui in ea voluptate velit esse quam nihil molestiae consequatur, vel illum qui dolorem eum fugiat quo voluptas nulla pariatur?* Ut enim ad minima veniam, quis nostrum exercitationem ullam corporis suscipit laboriosam, nisi ut aliquid ex ea commodi consequatur? Quis autem vel eum iure reprehenderit qui in ea voluptate velit esse quam nihil molestiae consequatur, vel illum qui dolorem eum fugiat quo voluptas nulla pariatur?

Quis autem vel eum

Ut enim ad minima veniam, quis nostrum exercitationem ullam corporis suscipit laboriosam, nisi ut aliquid ex ea commodi consequatur? **Quis autem vel eum iure reprehenderit qui in ea voluptate velit esse quam nihil molestiae consequatur, vel illum qui dolorem eum fugiat quo voluptas nulla pariatur?** Ut enim ad minima veniam, quis nostrum exercitationem ullam corporis suscipit laboriosam, nisi ut aliquid ex ea commodi consequatur? Quis autem vel eum iure reprehenderit qui in ea voluptate velit esse quam nihil molestiae consequatur, vel illum qui dolorem eum fugiat quo voluptas nulla pariatur?

FIGURE 6-19

The page begins with nothing but basic, drab, HTML.

---

3. **In the `<head>` of the web page, click directly after the closing `</title>` tag. Hit Enter (Return), and then type:**

```
<link href="http://fonts.googleapis.com/css?family=Slabo+27px"
rel="stylesheet">
```

This line tells Google to send you a font named Slabo 27px—a serif display font. Next, you'll link to an external style sheet that will hold the styles for this tutorial.

4. **After the `<link>` tag you just added, type the following line of code:**

```
<link href="css/styles.css" rel="stylesheet">
```

You've linked to an external style sheet in a folder named *css*. That folder holds an external style sheet and your web fonts.

5. **Open the file *css→styles.css*. This style sheet has a basic set of reset styles (see page 109).**

If you preview the *text.html* file in a web browser now, you'll see that all of the text on the page (headlines, paragraphs, and so on) looks nearly the same—in other words, all the basic HTML formatting the browser applied has been removed, so you can start with a clean slate.

Next, you'll add the necessary `@font-face` directives to load four web fonts. Actually, they are all the same font—PTSans—but include the bold, italic, and bold-italic variants.

6. **Add the following code to the top of the *styles.css* file (before the reset styles). (If you'd rather not type all this code, you can open the *at-font-face.css* file in the tutorial folder and just copy and paste that code into the *styles.css* file.)**

```css
@font-face {
  font-family: 'PTSans';
  src: url('fonts/PTSansRegular.woff2') format('woff2'),
       url('fonts/PTSansRegular.woff') format('woff');
  font-weight: normal;
  font-style: normal;
}
@font-face {
  font-family: 'PTSans';
  src: url('fonts/PTSansItalic.woff2') format('woff2'),
       url('fonts/PTSansItalic.woff') format('woff');
  font-weight: normal;
  font-style: italic;
}
@font-face {
  font-family: 'PTSans';
  src: url('fonts/PTSansBold.woff2') format('woff2'),
       url('fonts/PTSansBold.woff') format('woff');
  font-weight: bold;
  font-style: normal;
}
@font-face {
  font-family: 'PTSans';
  src: url('fonts/PTSansBoldItalic.woff2') format('woff2'),
       url('fonts/PTSansBoldItalic.woff') format('woff');
  font-weight: bold;
  font-style: italic;
}
```

In a nutshell, you've created a new font family named PTSans. You'll be able to use it in any new styles you create. You're using the method described on page 136 to add the bold-italic variants of the font. This method means that whenever you apply a normal bolded tag to text (like a headline, or the <strong> tag), the browser will automatically swap in the bold version of the font.

You placed the @font-face directive at the beginning of the external style sheet. That's not a requirement, though—it just feels neater to put all the fonts at the top and all of the regular styles after.

Next, you'll create a style that defines some general properties for all text on the page.

7. **At the bottom of the style sheet, after the reset styles, add a new line and type** `html {`.

This is a basic tag selector that applies to the `<html>` tag. As discussed in Chapter 4, other tags inherit the properties of this tag. You can set up some basic text characteristics like font, color, and font size for later tags to use as their starting point.

8. **Press Enter again, and then add the following two properties:**

   ```
   font-family: PTSans, Arial, sans-serif;
   font-size: 62.5%;
   ```

These two instructions set the font to PTSans (or Arial if the browser can't download PTSans), and the font size to 62.5 percent.

> **NOTE** Why set the page's base font to 62.5 percent? It just so happens that 62.5 percent times 16 pixels (the normal size of text in most web browsers) equals 10 pixels. With 10 pixels as a starting point, it's easy to compute what other text sizes will look like on the screen. For example, 1.5em would be 1.5 x 10 or 15 pixels. 2em is 20 pixels, and so on—easy multiples of ten. You can also use the `rem` unit (see page 155), which is similar to the em, but avoids the problem associated with nested inherited em units.

9. **Complete this style by pressing Enter and typing a closing bracket to mark the end of the style.**

At this point, your completed style should look like this:

   ```
   html {
      font-family: PTSans, Arial, sans-serif;
      font-size: 62.5%;
   }
   ```

Your style sheet is complete.

10. **Save the *styles.css* file, and open the *text.html* file in a web browser to preview your work.**

The text on the page changes font...it also gets really small. Don't worry, that's the 62.5 percent font size you set in step 8. That's just the starting point for all text, and you'll easily increase the size of text by defining em sizes for the other tags.

Formatting the Headings and Paragraphs

Now that the basic text formatting is done, it's time to refine the presentation of the headlines and paragraphs.

1. **Return to your text editor and the *styles.css* file. Click at the end of the closing brace of the HTML tag selector, add a new line, and then type** `.main h1 {`.

This is a *descendant selector* (page 50). It provides more specific direction than a basic HTML tag selector. In this case, the selector tells the web browser "apply the following formatting to any `<h1>` tag inside another tag with the class name main." If you look at the page's HTML, you'll see that there's a <div> tag with a class of main (<div class="main">). As you'll learn later, it's very common in CSS-based designs to group HTML tags inside of <div> tags. You can then position individual <div> tags to create columns and other complex page layouts. It's also common to use descendant selectors like this one to pinpoint your formatting choices by affecting just the tags in certain areas of the page.

2. **Hit Enter, and then type these three CSS properties:**

```
color: rgb(249,212,120);
font-family: "Arial Black", Arial, Helvetica, sans-serif;
font-size: 4em;
```

You've just changed the color of the <h1> tag as well as the font. This time, instead of using a web font, you're specifying a font that visitors must have installed on their computers. Many computers have Arial Black, but if the one visiting this page doesn't, it will fall back to Arial or Helvetica or just a generic sans serif. You've also set the font size to 4em, which for most browsers (unless the visitor has tweaked his browser's font settings) comes out to 40 pixels tall. That's all thanks to the 62.5% size you set for the body back at step 7. That smooth move made the base font size 10 pixels tall, so 4 × 10 comes out to 40 pixels. Next you'll add a text shadow to the headline.

3. **Complete this style by hitting Enter, adding the code in bold below (don't forget the closing brace):**

```
.main h1 {
  color: rgb(249,212,120);
  font-family: "Arial Black", Arial, Helvetica, sans-serif;
  font-size: 4em;
  text-shadow: 4px 4px 6px rgba(0,0,0,.75);
}
```

Here, you've added a text shadow (page 160), which is offset 4 pixels to the right, 4 pixels below, and is feathered out 6 pixels. In addition, you're using the RGBA color (page 149) to set the shadow to black with 75 percent transparency.

4. **Save the file and preview the *text.html* file in a web browser.**

Next, spruce up the appearance of the other headings and paragraphs.

NOTE Once a browser opens a file, it saves it in a type of easily accessible storage called a *cache*. If the browser needs that same file again, it plucks the cached version instead of wasting time downloading the file a second time. However, the cache can be a pain when designing locally. The browser may load the old version of your external style sheet from the cache instead of loading the one with your new changes. If the web page doesn't seem to get updated when you update an external style sheet, pressing F5 or Ctrl-Shift-R (⌘-Shift-R) will usually force the browser to load the new version of the file.

---

5. **Return to your text editor and the *styles.css* file. Click after the closing brace of the** `.main h1` **tag, hit Enter, and add the following style:**

```
.main h2 {
  font: normal 3.5em "Slabo 27px", Garamond, Times, serif;
  color: rgb(37,76,143);
  border-bottom: 1px solid rgb(200,200,200);
  margin-top: 25px;
}
```

Here you have another descendant selector that only applies to <h2> tags inside another tag with the class main (you're probably getting the hang of these now). The font property used here is shorthand that combines the more long-winded font-weight, font-size, and font-family (see the box on page 165). In other words, this one line makes the headline bold, 3.5ems tall, and specifies the Google font you linked to earlier.

In addition, this style adds a decorative border below the headline and a bit of space between the headline and the tag above it (in other words, it adds some space between the "CSS The Missing Manual" and the "Exploring Typographic Possibilities" headlines). You'll read more about borders and margins in the next chapter.

Time to tackle more headlines.

6. **Add another style below the one you added in the last step:**

```
.main h3 {
  color: rgb(241,47,6);
  font-size: 1.9em;
  font-weight: bold;
  text-transform: uppercase;
  margin-top: 25px;
  margin-bottom: 10px;
}
```

This style dishes out some of the usual formatting—color, size, boldness—and also uses the text-transform property (page 157) to make all of the text in the <h3> headlines uppercase. Finally, it adds a bit of space above and below the headlines by using the margin properties.

Next, you'll improve the look of the paragraphs.

7. **Add one more style to the page:**

```
.main p {
  font-size: 1.8em;
  line-height: 1.5;
  margin-left: 150px;
  margin-right: 50px;
  margin-bottom: 10px;
}
```

This style introduces the line-height property, which sets the spacing between lines. The number 1.5 is a multiplier: It calculates the line height by multiplying the font size (1.75em) and 1.5. Basically, it sets the line height to 1.5x or 150 percent of the font size. This adds a little more space between lines in a paragraph than you'd normally see in a web browser. This extra breathing room gives the text a lighter, airier quality and makes the sentences a little easier to read (but only if you speak Latin).

The style also increases the font size to 1.8em (18 pixels for most browsers) and indents the paragraph from the left and right edges of the page. You'll notice that there's a lot of typing going on for the margin properties—fortunately, as you'll read on page 189 in the next chapter, there's a margin shortcut property that requires much less typing to control the four margins of an element.

Time to try out a more advanced selector type.

8. **Add the following style to your style sheet:**

```
.main p::first-line {
  font-weight: bold;
  color: rgb(153,153,153);
}
```

The ::first-line pseudo-element (page 56) affects just the first line of a paragraph. In this case, just the first line of text for each of the paragraphs inside the main div will be bold and gray.

9. **Save the *styles.css* file and open the *text.html* file in a web browser to preview your work.**

At this point, the page should look like Figure 6-20.

Formatting Lists

This page has a single bulleted list. The plan is to move the list over to the right edge of the page and have the text following it wrap around it. CSS makes this little trick easy.

1. **Return to your text editor and the *styles.css* file. Add the following style at the end of the style sheet:**

```
.main ul {
  margin: 50px 0 25px 50px;
  width: 25%;
  float: right;
}
```

When formatting lists, you'll usually create styles for two different elements: the list itself (either the <ul> tag for bulleted lists or the <ol> tag for numbered lists) and the individual list items (the <li> tag). This style controls the entire list.

CSS The Missing Manual

Exploring Typographic Possibilities

november 30 Rod Dibble

- Lorem Ipsum
- Reprehenderit qui in ea
- Lorem Ipsum
- Reprehenderit qui in ea
- Lorem Ipsum
- Reprehenderit qui in ea

ESSE QUAM NULLA

Ut enim ad minima veniam, quis nostrum exercitationem ullam corporis suscipit laboriosam, nisi ut aliquid ex ea commodi consequatur? *Quis autem vel eum iure reprehenderit qui in ea voluptate velit esse quam nihil molestiae consequatur, vel illum qui dolorem eum fugiat quo voluptas nulla pariatur?* Ut enim ad minima veniam, quis nostrum exercitationem ullam corporis suscipit laboriosam, nisi ut aliquid ex ea commodi consequatur? Quis autem vel eum iure reprehenderit qui in ea voluptate velit esse quam nihil molestiae consequatur, vel illum qui dolorem eum fugiat quo voluptas nulla pariatur?

QUIS AUTEM VEL EUM

Ut enim ad minima veniam, quis nostrum exercitationem ullam corporis suscipit laboriosam, nisi ut aliquid ex ea commodi consequatur? **Quis autem vel eum iure reprehenderit qui in ea voluptate velit esse quam nihil molestiae consequatur, vel illum qui dolorem eum fugiat quo voluptas nulla pariatur?** Ut enim ad minima veniam, quis nostrum exercitationem ullam corporis suscipit laboriosam, nisi ut aliquid ex ea commodi consequatur? Quis autem vel eum iure reprehenderit qui in ea voluptate velit esse quam nihil molestiae consequatur, vel illum qui dolorem eum fugiat quo voluptas nulla pariatur?

FIGURE 6-20

The page is starting to come together. The headlines, paragraphs, and basic text settings are in place. Depending on which fonts you have on your computer, you may notice slight differences between your design and the one pictured here. For example, if your computer doesn't have Arial Black, the headline, CSS The Missing Manual, might not be as bold as is pictured here.

There are a few things happening in this style. First, the *margin* property uses the shorthand method. This one line sets all four margins around the list, replacing the four individual margin properties (`margin-top`, `margin-right`, and so on). The four values are ordered like this: top, right, bottom, left. So for this style, 50 pixels of space get added above the list, 0 space on the right, 25 pixels on the bottom, and 50 pixels on the left.

The `width` property (discussed in detail on page 204) makes the entire list 25% the width of the browser window. If any particular list item has more text than will fit within that space, it wraps to another line. The *float* property is the real magic—in this case, `float: right` means "move the list over to the right edge of the page." This property also causes the text following the list to wrap around the left side of the list. It's a cool trick, and you'll learn a lot more about floats on page 210.

You'll control the look of the individual list items next.

2. **Add one more style to the style sheet:**

```
.main li {
  color: rgb(32,126,191);
  font-size: 1.5em;
  margin-bottom: 7px;
}
```

Nothing new here: just changing the color and size and adding space below each list item. Time to check out your progress.

NOTE If you want to add space between list items, you need to add top or bottom margins to the `<li>` tag. Adding margins to the `<ul>` or `<ol>` tags simply adds space around the entire list.

3. **Save the page and preview it in a web browser.**

The page should now look like Figure 6-21.

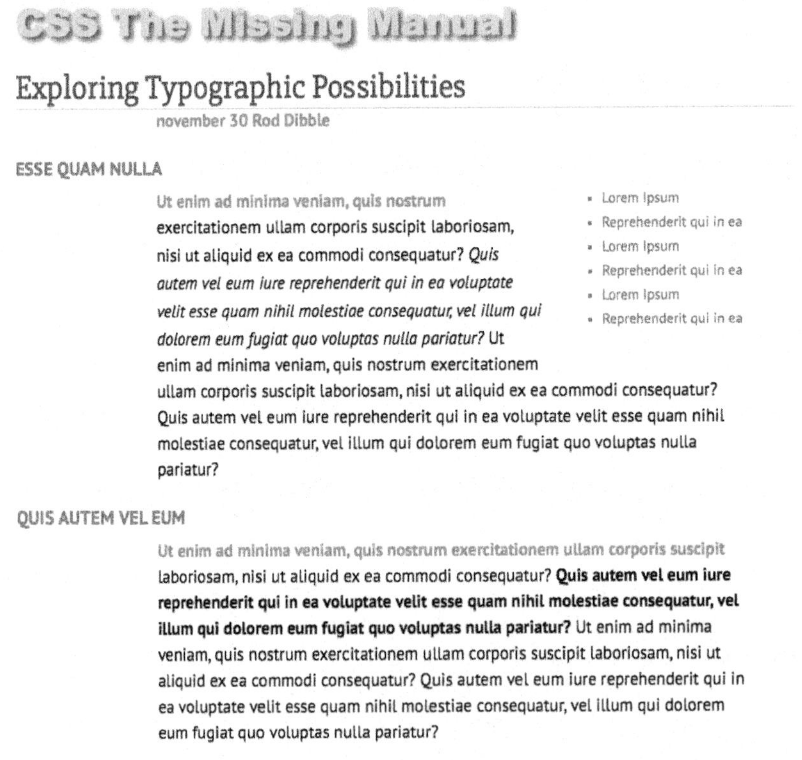

CSS The Missing Manual

Exploring Typographic Possibilities

november 30 Rod Dibble

ESSE QUAM NULLA

Ut enim ad minima veniam, quis nostrum exercitationem ullam corporis suscipit laboriosam, nisi ut aliquid ex ea commodi consequatur? *Quis autem vel eum iure reprehenderit qui in ea voluptate velit esse quam nihil molestiae consequatur, vel illum qui dolorem eum fugiat quo voluptas nulla pariatur?* Ut enim ad minima veniam, quis nostrum exercitationem ullam corporis suscipit laboriosam, nisi ut aliquid ex ea commodi consequatur? Quis autem vel eum iure reprehenderit qui in ea voluptate velit esse quam nihil molestiae consequatur, vel illum qui dolorem eum fugiat quo voluptas nulla pariatur?

- Lorem Ipsum
- Reprehenderit qui in ea
- Lorem Ipsum
- Reprehenderit qui in ea
- Lorem Ipsum
- Reprehenderit qui in ea

QUIS AUTEM VEL EUM

Ut enim ad minima veniam, quis nostrum exercitationem ullam corporis suscipit laboriosam, nisi ut aliquid ex ea commodi consequatur? **Quis autem vel eum iure reprehenderit qui in ea voluptate velit esse quam nihil molestiae consequatur, vel illum qui dolorem eum fugiat quo voluptas nulla pariatur?** Ut enim ad minima veniam, quis nostrum exercitationem ullam corporis suscipit laboriosam, nisi ut aliquid ex ea commodi consequatur? Quis autem vel eum iure reprehenderit qui in ea voluptate velit esse quam nihil molestiae consequatur, vel illum qui dolorem eum fugiat quo voluptas nulla pariatur?

FIGURE 6-21

The float *property gives you some interesting design options. In this case, the bulleted list is floated to the right edge of the page. In fact, the* float *property is so useful, you'll see that it's the main ingredient of CSS-based layouts, like the ones you'll learn about in Chapter 12.*

Fine-Tuning with Classes

Sometimes you want even more control over how a style is applied. For example, while you might want most paragraphs in one section of the page to look the same, you might also want one or two paragraphs to have their own unique look. In this tutorial, the paragraph of text near the top of the page—"November 30 Rod Dibble"—contains some unique information: a publication date and author. You want it to stand out from the other paragraphs, so you'll add a class to the HTML and create a class style.

1. **Open the *text.html* file in your text editor. Locate the HTML for that paragraph—** `<p>november 30 <strong>Rod Dibble</strong></p>`**—and add** `class="byline"` **to the opening** `<p>` **tag. The HTML should look like this:**

   ```
   <p class="byline">november 30 <strong>Rod Dibble</strong></p>
   ```

   Now it's a simple matter of creating a class style that overrides the generic formatting of the other paragraphs on the page.

2. **Open the *styles.css* file in your text editor. At the bottom of the style sheet, add a style for that paragraph:**

   ```
   .main .byline {
     font-size: 1.6em;
     margin: 5px 0 25px 50px;
   }
   ```

   This style tweaks the size and placement of just that one paragraph. Note that if you'd just named that style `.byline`—a basic class selector—it wouldn't work. Thanks to the rules of the cascade described in the last chapter, `.byline` is less specific (less powerful) than the `.main p` style you created in step 7 on page 177, so it wouldn't be able to override the size and margins specified by `.main p`. However, `.main .byline` is more specific.

   That paragraph still needs some work. It would be great if the name stood out more. The HTML in this case provides just the hook you need.

3. **Add another style to the style sheet:**

   ```
   .main .byline strong {
       color: rgb(32,126,191);
       text-transform: uppercase;
       margin-left: 11px;
   }
   ```

   If you look at the HTML in step 1 above, you'll see that the name—Rod Dibble—is inside a `<strong>` tag. The `<strong>` tag is used to emphasize text and mark it as important. But that doesn't mean you have to let it be bold, the way web browsers normally display that tag. Instead, this descendant selector targets the `<strong>` tag, but only when it appears inside another tag with the class

.byline, and only if all of that is inside yet another tag with the class main—whew, that's pretty specific.

This style turns the text blue, makes it uppercase, and adds a bit of space on the left side (nudging the name over just a bit from the "November 30" text).

Adding the Finishing Touches

For the last bit of design, you'll incorporate a few design touches that format the page and that main div so they both look better. Then you'll finish up with a cool bit of text formatting.

1. **Return to your text editor and the *styles.css* file.**

   First, you'll add a background color and image to the page.

2. **Locate the html style in the external style sheet—the first style that appears after the CSS reset rules—and add one new property so that it looks like this (changes are in bold):**

   ```
   html {
     font-family: PTSans, Arial, sans-serif;
     font-size: 62.5%;
     background: rgb(225,238,253) url(../images/bg_body.png) repeat-x;
   }
   ```

   The background property is a powerful tool for any web designer. You've already used it a couple of times in earlier tutorials; it lets you add color and insert and control the placement of an image to the background of any tag. You'll learn the ins and outs of this property on page 231, but for now this line changes the background color of the page to light blue and adds a dark blue stripe to the top of the page.

   Next you'll spruce up the main div.

3. **Add another style in between the html style and the .main h1 style:**

   ```
   .main {
     max-width: 740px;
     margin: 0 auto;
     padding: 0 10px;
     border: 4px solid white;
     background: transparent url(../images/bg_banner.jpg) no-repeat;
   }
   ```

   In other words, click after the closing } for the html style, hit Enter, and type the code above. You don't necessarily have to put the style in that spot for it to work, but for organizational purposes, putting the style that controls the div before the other styles that format tags inside that div makes sense.

   The max-width property sets a maximum overall width for this div. That is, the div could shrink to be smaller—great if a visitor is using a screen that's less than

740 pixels wide—but it will never stretch wider than 740 pixels. The `margin` property values—`0 auto`—put 0 pixels of space above and below the div and set the left and right margins to auto, which centers the div in the middle of the browser window. The `padding` property adds space inside the box, pushing content inside the div away from the border line. Finally, you've placed an image into the background of the div.

Those last two styles didn't have anything to do with text formatting, but if you preview the page, you'll see that they make it look a lot better...except for those two top headlines. The first headline isn't bold enough, and the second should fall below the newly added graphic.

4. **Add one last style right after the** `.main h1` **style:**

```
.main h1 strong {
  font-size: 150px;
  color: white;
  line-height: 1;
  margin-right: -.5em;
}
```

The HTML for the headline looks like this:

```
<h1><strong>CSS</strong> The Missing Manual</h1>
```

The "CSS" is enclosed inside `<strong>` tags, so this descendant selector formats only that text (in that sense, it's like the style you added in step 3 on page 181 that took advantage of a `<strong>` tag embedded within a paragraph). The text size is pumped way up, its color is changed, and the line height is adjusted so that it fits inside the top of the page. You'll notice that the line height is set to 1, so in this case, the line height will translate to 150 pixels—that's 1 times the font size of this style.

The one cool trick is the `margin-right` property, which is set to a negative value: `-.5em`. Since a positive margin pushes elements away, a negative margin actually pulls elements on top of each other. In this case, the rest of the text in the headline—"The Missing Manual"—is scooted over .5 em, which is .5 times the font size (150 pixels), on top of the "CSS" text.

NOTE Negative margins are perfectly legal (although tricky) CSS.

5. **Save the** *styles.css* **file and preview the** *text.html* **file in a web browser.**

It should look like Figure 6-22. You can compare your work to the finished *text.html* page located in the *06_finished* folder.

Congratulations! You've explored many of the text formatting properties offered by CSS and turned ho-hum HTML into an attractive, attention-getting design. In the next chapter, you'll explore graphics, borders, margins, and other powerful CSS design options offered by CSS.

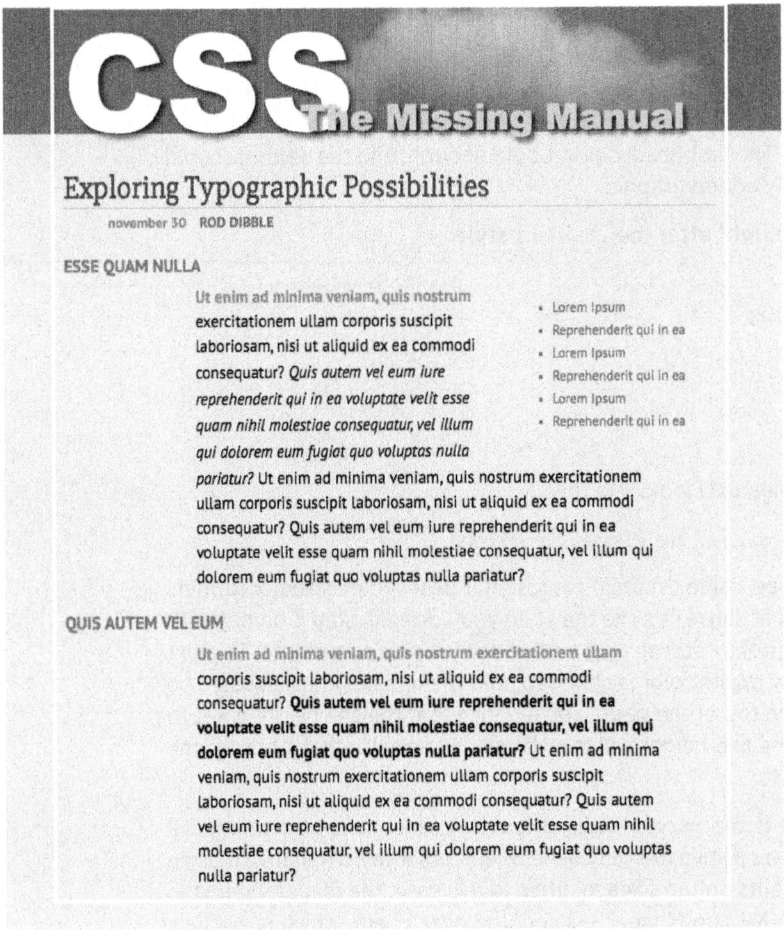

FIGURE 6-22

With a little CSS, you can turn plain text into a powerful design statement that helps guide readers through the information on your site.

Margins, Padding, and Borders

E very HTML tag is surrounded by a world of properties that affect how the tag appears in a web browser. Some properties—like borders and background colors—are immediately obvious to the naked eye. Others, though, are invisible—like padding and margin. They provide a bit of empty space on one or more sides of a tag. By understanding how these properties work, you can create attractive columns and decorative sidebars and control the space around them (what designers call *white space*) so your pages look less cluttered, lighter, and more professional.

Taken together, the CSS properties discussed in this chapter make up one of the most important concepts in CSS—the *box model*.

Understanding the Box Model

You probably think of letters, words, and sentences when you think of a paragraph or headline. You also probably think of a photo, logo, or other picture when you think of the <img> tag. But a web browser treats these (and all other) tags as little *boxes*. To a browser, any tag is a box with something inside it—text, an image, or even other tags containing other things, as illustrated in Figure 7-1.

Surrounding the content are different properties that make up the box:

- **padding** is the space between the content and the content's border. Padding is what separates a photo from the border that frames the photo.

- **border** is the line that's drawn around each edge of the box. You can have a border around all four sides, on just a single side, or any combination of sides.

- **background-color** fills the space inside the border, including the padding area.

- **margin** is what separates one tag from another. The space that commonly appears between the tops and bottoms of paragraphs of text on a web page, for example, is the margin.

For a given tag, you can use any or all of these properties in combination. You can set just a margin for a tag or add a border, margins, *and* padding. Or you can have a border and margin but no padding, and so on. If you don't adjust any of these properties, then you'll end up with the browser's settings, which you may or may not like. For example, although browsers usually don't apply either padding or borders to any tags on a page, some tags (like headings and paragraphs) have a preset top and bottom margin.

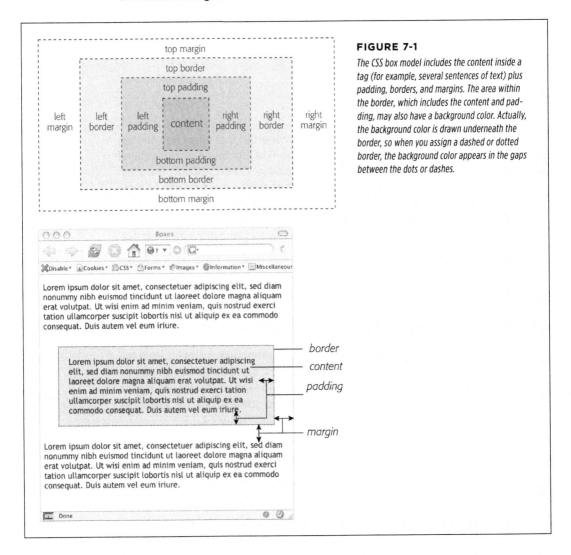

FIGURE 7-1

The CSS box model includes the content inside a tag (for example, several sentences of text) plus padding, borders, and margins. The area within the border, which includes the content and padding, may also have a background color. Actually, the background color is drawn underneath the border, so when you assign a dashed or dotted border, the background color appears in the gaps between the dots or dashes.

Controlling Space with Margins and Padding

Both margins and padding add space around content. You use these properties to separate one element from another—for example, to add space between a left-hand navigation menu and the main page content on the right—or to inject some white space between content and a border. You may want to move the border away from the edge of a photo (see Figure 7-2).

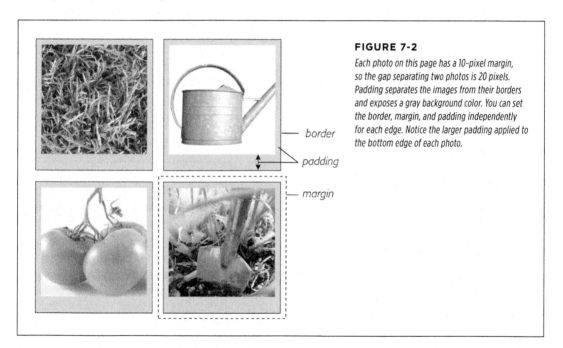

FIGURE 7-2

Each photo on this page has a 10-pixel margin, so the gap separating two photos is 20 pixels. Padding separates the images from their borders and exposes a gray background color. You can set the border, margin, and padding independently for each edge. Notice the larger padding applied to the bottom edge of each photo.

border

padding

margin

Padding and margin function similarly, and unless you apply a border or background color, you can't really tell whether the space between two tags is caused by padding or by a margin. But if you have a border around an element or a background behind it, then the visual difference between the two properties is significant. Padding adds space between the content and the border, and keeps the content from appearing cramped inside the box; it also includes the background area, so the space taken up by padding might be empty of content (like text or a photo), but it will still be filled with a background color or image. Margins, on the other hand, add white space (often called a *gutter*) between elements, giving the overall look of the page a lighter appearance.

You can control each side of the margin or padding for an element independently. Four properties control margin edges: margin-top, margin-right, margin-bottom, and margin-left. Similarly, four properties control padding: padding-top, padding-right, padding-bottom, and padding-left. You can use any valid CSS measurement to define the size of a margin or padding, like so:

```
margin-right: 20px;
padding-top: 3em;
margin-left: 10%;
```

Pixels and ems are commonly used and act just as they do with text (see page 151). A 20-pixel margin adds 20 pixels of space, and 3 ems of padding adds space equal to 3 times the font size of the styled element.

Percentage values are also commonly used. They let you add margins and padding that are flexible and change based on the width of the browser window, which makes them ideal for responsive designs (see Chapter 15).

NOTE To remove all the space for a margin or padding, use 0 (margin-top: 0 or padding-bottom: 0, for example). To remove space around all four edges of the browser window—to let a banner or logo or other page element butt right up to the edge without a gap—give the <body> tag a margin of 0 and a padding of 0: margin: 0; padding 0;.

POWER USERS' CLINIC

Margins, Padding, and Percentages

When you use percentages, web browsers calculate the amount of space based on the *width of the containing element*. On a simple web page, the containing element is the body of the page, and it fills the browser window. In this case, the percentage value is based on the width of the browser window at any given time. Say the window is 760 pixels wide. In that case, a 10% left margin adds 76 pixels of space to the left edge of the styled element. But if you resize the browser window, then that value changes. Narrowing the browser window to 600 pixels changes the margin to 60 pixels (10 percent of 600).

However, the containing element isn't always the width of the browser window. As you'll see in later chapters, when

you create more sophisticated layouts, you can introduce new elements that help organize your page.

You may want to add a <div> tag to a page in order to group related content into a sidebar area. (You'll see an example of this in the tutorial on page 223.) That sidebar might have a specified width of 300 pixels. Tags inside the sidebar consider the <div> tag their containing element. So a tag in the sidebar with a right margin of 10% will have 30 pixels of empty space to its right.

To make matters more confusing, top and bottom percentage values are also calculated based on the width of the containing element, not its height. So a 20% top margin is 20 percent of the width of the styled tag's container.

Margin and Padding Shorthand

You'll frequently want to set all four sides of a style's margin or padding. But typing out all four properties (margin-right, margin-left, and so on) for each style gets tedious. Fear not: You can use the shortcut properties named margin and padding to set all four properties quickly:

```
margin: 0 10px 10px 20px;
padding: 10px 5px 5px 10px;
```

> **NOTE** If the value used in a CSS property is 0, then you don't need to add a unit of measurement. For example, just type margin: 0; instead of margin: 0px;.

The order in which you specify the four values is important. It must be top, right, bottom, and left. If you get it wrong, you'll be in trouble. In fact, the easiest way to keep the order straight is to remember to stay out of **TR**ou**BL**e—top, right, bottom, and left.

If you want to use the same value for all four sides, it's even easier—just use a single value. If you want to remove margins from all <h1> tags, you can write this style:

```
h1 {
  margin: 0;
}
```

Similarly, use shorthand to add the same amount of space between some content and its border:

```
padding: 10px;
```

> **NOTE** When you're using the same value for both top and bottom and another value for both left and right, you can use two values. margin: 0 2em; sets the top *and* bottom margins to 0 and the left *and* right margins to 2 ems. Likewise, if the top and bottom margins (or padding) differ, but the left and right remain the same, you can use three values. For example, margin: 0 2em 1em; sets the top margin to 0, the left and right margins to 2 ems, and the bottom margin to 1 em.

Colliding Margins

When it comes to CSS, two plus two doesn't always equal four. You could run into some bizarre math when the bottom margin of one element touches the top margin of another. Instead of adding the two margins together, a web browser applies the larger of the two margins (Figure 7-3, top). Say the bottom margin of an unordered list is set to 30 pixels, and the top margin of a paragraph following the list is 20 pixels. Instead of adding the two values to create 50 pixels of space between the list and the paragraph, a web browser uses the *largest* margin—in this case 30 pixels. If you don't want this to happen, then use top or bottom padding instead (Figure 7-3, bottom).

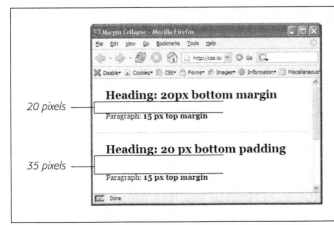

FIGURE 7-3

When two vertical margins meet, the smaller one collapses. Although the top headline has a bottom margin of 20 pixels, and the paragraph has a top margin of 15 pixels, a web browser adds only 20 pixels of space between the two elements. To get the full 35 pixels' worth of space that you want, use padding instead of margins, as shown in the bottom headline. Here, the heading has 20 pixels of bottom padding. Those 20 pixels get added to the 15-pixel top margin of the paragraph to form a 35-pixel gap.

Things get even weirder when one element is *inside* another element. This situation can lead to some head-scratching behavior. For example, say you add a "warning" box to a page (like a div tag to hold a warning message inside it). You add a 20-pixel top and bottom margin to separate the warning box from the heading above it and the paragraph of text below it. So far so good.

But say you insert a heading inside the warning box, and to put a little room between it and the top and bottom of the div, you set the heading's margin to 10 pixels. You may think you're adding 10 pixels of space between the heading and the top and bottom of the div, but you'd be wrong (Figure 7-4, top). Instead, the margin appears *above* the div. In this case, it doesn't matter how large a margin you apply to the headline—the margin still appears *above* the div.

> **NOTE** In the lingo of CSS, this phenomenon is known as *collapsing margins*, meaning two margins actually become one.

You have two ways around this problem: Either add a small amount of padding around the <div> tag or add a border to it. Since border and padding sit *between* the two margins, the margins no longer touch, and the headline has a little breathing room (Figure 7-4, bottom).

> **NOTE** Horizontal (left and right) margins and margins between floating elements don't collapse in this way. Absolutely and relatively positioned elements—which you'll learn about in Chapter 15—don't collapse either.

Removing Space with Negative Margins

Most measurements in CSS have to be a positive value—after all, what would text that's *negative 20 pixels* tall (or short) look like? Padding also has to be a positive value. But CSS allows for many creative techniques using negative margins.

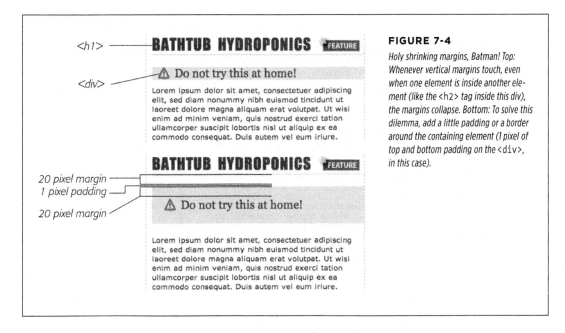

FIGURE 7-4

Holy shrinking margins, Batman! Top: Whenever vertical margins touch, even when one element is inside another element (like the <h2> tag inside this div), the margins collapse. Bottom: To solve this dilemma, add a little padding or a border around the containing element (1 pixel of top and bottom padding on the <div>, in this case).

Instead of adding space between a tag and elements around it, a negative margin *removes* space. So you can have a paragraph of text overlap a headline, poke out of its containing element (a sidebar or other layout <div>), or even disappear off an edge of the browser window. And, hey, you can even do something useful with negative margins.

Even when you set the margins between two headlines to 0, there's still a little space between the text of the headlines (thanks to the text's line height, as described on page 163). That's usually a good thing, since it's hard to read sentences that bunch together and touch. But, used in moderation, tightening the space between two headlines can produce some interesting effects. The second headline of Figure 7-5 (the one that begins "Raise Tuna") has a top margin of –10px applied to it. This moves the headline up 10 pixels so it slightly overlaps the space occupied by the headline above it. Also, the left and right borders of the "Extra! Extra!" headline actually touch the letters of the larger headline.

You can also use a negative margin to simulate negative padding. In the third headline of Figure 7-5, the one that begins with "The Extraordinary Technique," a line appears directly under the text. This line is actually the *top* border for the paragraph that follows. (You'll learn how to add borders on page 194.) But because that paragraph has a negative top margin, the border moves up and under the headline. Notice how the descending tail for the letter Q in the headline actually hangs *below* the border. Since padding—the space between content (like that letter Q) and a border—can't be negative, you can't move a bottom border up over text or any other content. But you get the same effect by applying a border to the following element and using a negative margin to move it up.

FIGURE 7-5

In this example, to make the last paragraph's top border look like it's actually the bottom border for the headline above it, add a little padding to the paragraph. Around 5 pixels of top padding moves the paragraph down from the border, while 4ems of left padding indents the paragraph's text, still allowing the top border to extend to the left edge.

TIP You can actually use a negative top margin on the paragraph or a negative bottom margin on the headline. Both have the same effect of moving the paragraph up close to the headline.

Inline, Block, and Other Display Settings

Although web browsers treat every tag as a kind of box, not all boxes are alike. CSS has two different types of boxes—*block boxes* and *inline boxes*—that correspond to the two types of tags—block-level and inline tags.

A *block-level* tag creates a break before and after it. The <p> tag, for example, creates a block that's separated from tags above and below. Headlines, <div> tags, tables, lists, and list items are other examples of block-level tags.

Inline tags don't create a break before or after them. They appear on the same line as the content and tags beside them. The <strong> tag is an inline tag. A word formatted with this tag happily sits next to other text—even text wrapped in other inline tags like <em>. In fact, it would look pretty weird if you emphasized a single word in the middle of a paragraph with the <strong> tag and that word suddenly appeared on its own line by itself. Other inline tags are <img> for adding images, <a> for creating links, and the various tags used to create form fields.

In most cases, CSS works the same for inline boxes and block boxes. You can style the font, color, and background and add borders to both types of boxes. However, when it comes to margins and padding, browsers treat inline boxes differently. Although you can add space to the left or right of an inline element using either left or right padding or left or right margins, you can't increase the height of the inline element with top or bottom padding or margins. In the top paragraph in Figure 7-6, the inline element is styled with borders, a background color, and 20 pixels of margin on all four sides. But the browser only adds space to the left and right sides of the inline element.

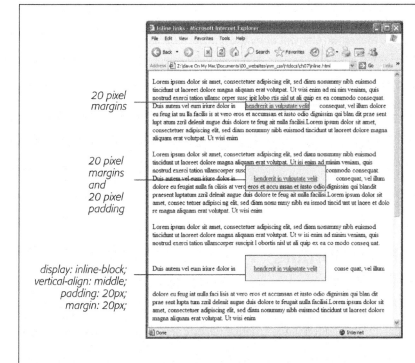

FIGURE 7-6

Adding top or bottom margins and padding doesn't make an inline element any taller, so you can run into some weird formatting. In the middle paragraph, the background and borders of a link overlap the text above and below. The background appears on top of the line before the styled inline text, but underneath the line following it because the browser treats each line as if it's stacked on top of the previous line. Normally, that isn't a problem since lines of text don't usually overlap. If you want top and bottom margins and padding to work for an inline element, you can use the `display:inline-block` *instruction (bottom). This leaves the item inline, but treats it like a box so padding, margins, borders, and width and height are all applied (and obeyed).*

20 pixel margins

20 pixel margins and 20 pixel padding

display: inline-block;
vertical-align: middle;
padding: 20px;
margin: 20px;

NOTE One exception to the rule that inline elements don't get taller when padding or margins are added is the <img> tag (even though it's an inline tag). Web browsers correctly expand the height of the image's box to accommodate any padding and margins you add.

At times, you may wish an inline element behaved more like a block-level element and vice versa. Bulleted lists present each item as its own block—each list item is stacked above the next. You may want to change that behavior so the list items appear side by side, all on a single line, as in a navigation bar (you can see an example of one in Figure 9-4 on page 290). Finally, you may want to treat an inline element like a block-level element. Maybe you want an image embedded in a paragraph to be on its own line, with space above and below.

Fortunately, CSS includes a property that lets you do just that—the display property. With it, you can make a block-level element act like an inline element:

```
display: inline;
```

Or you can make an inline element, like an image or link, behave like a block-level element:

```
display: block;
```

Finally, you can make an element act both like a block and an inline element. The inline-block setting makes an element sit on the same line as tags on either side of it, but also makes the element obey top and bottom margin and padding settings as well as height settings:

```
display: inline-block;
```

> **NOTE** The display property has a myriad of possible options, some of which don't work in all browsers. The inline-block value works in current browsers (see Figure 7-6). Another value, none, works in most browsers and has many uses. It does one simple thing—completely hides the styled element so it doesn't appear in a web browser. With a dab of JavaScript programming, you can make an element hidden in this way instantly become visible, simply by changing its display back to either inline or block. You can even make an element with a display of none suddenly appear using CSS.

■ Adding Borders

A border is simply a line that runs around an element. As shown back in Figure 7-1, it sits between any padding and margins you set. A border around every edge can frame an image or mark the boundaries of a banner or other page element. But borders don't necessarily have to create a full box around your content. While you can add a border to all four edges, you can just as easily add a border to just the bottom or any combination of sides. This flexibility lets you add design elements that don't necessarily feel like a border. For example, add a border to the left of an element, make it around 1em thick, and it looks like a square bullet. A single border under a paragraph can function just like the <hr> (horizontal rule) by providing a visual separator between sections of a page.

You control three different properties of each border: color, width, and style. The color can be any of the CSS color values discussed starting on page 148, such as a hexadecimal number, a keyword, or an RGB (or RGBA) value. A border's width is the thickness of the line used to draw the border. You can use any CSS measurement type (except percentages) or the keywords thin, medium, and thick. The most common and easily understood method is pixels.

Finally, the style controls the type of line drawn. There are many different styles, as you can see in Figure 7-7. You specify the style with a keyword. For example, solid draws a solid line and dashed creates a line made up of dashes. CSS offers these

styles: solid, dotted, dashed, double, groove, ridge, inset, outset, none, and hidden.
(None and hidden work the same way: They remove the border entirely. The none
value is useful for turning off a single border.)

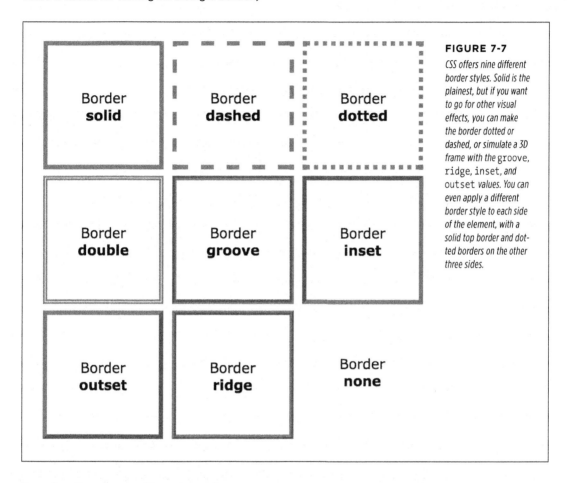

FIGURE 7-7

*CSS offers nine different
border styles. Solid is the
plainest, but if you want
to go for other visual
effects, you can make
the border dotted or
dashed, or simulate a 3D
frame with the* groove,
ridge, inset, *and*
outset *values. You can
even apply a different
border style to each side
of the element, with a
solid top border and dot-
ted borders on the other
three sides.*

Border Property Shorthand

If you've ever seen a list of the different border properties available in CSS, you may
think borders are really complex. After all, there are 20 different border properties,
which you'll meet in the following sections, plus a couple that apply to tables. But
all these properties are merely variations on a theme that provide different ways
of controlling the same three properties—color, width, and style—for each of the
four borders. The most basic and straightforward property is *border*, which simply
adds four borders:

```
border: 4px solid rgb(255,0,0);
```

The above style creates a solid, red, 4-pixel border. You can use this property to create a basic frame around a picture, navigation bar, or other item that you want to appear as a self-contained box.

> **NOTE** The order in which you write the properties doesn't matter: border: 4px solid rgb(255,0,0); works as well as border: rgb(255,0,0) solid 4px;.

Formatting Individual Borders

You can control each border individually using the appropriate property: border-top, border-bottom, border-left, or border-right. These properties work just like the regular border property, but they control just one side. The following property declaration adds a 2-pixel, red, dashed line below the style:

```
border-bottom: 2px dashed red;
```

You can combine the border property with one of the edge-specific properties like border-left to define the basic box for the entire style but customize a single border. Say you want the top, left, and right sides of a paragraph to have the same type of border, but you want the bottom border to look slightly different. You can write four lines of CSS, like this:

```
border-top: 2px solid black;
border-left: 2px solid black;
border-right: 2px solid black;
border-bottom: 4px dashed #333;
```

Or, you can achieve the same effect as the previous four lines of CSS with just two lines:

```
border: 2px solid black;
border-bottom: 4px dashed #333;
```

The first line of code defines the basic look of all four borders, and the second line redefines just the look of the bottom border. Not only is it easier to write two lines of CSS instead of four, but it also makes changing the style easier. If you want to change the color of the top, left, and right borders to red, then you only have to edit a single line, instead of three:

```
border: 2px solid red;
border-bottom: 4px dashed #333;
```

When you use this shortcut method—defining the basic look of all four borders using the border property and then overriding the look of a single border with one of the edge-specific properties like border-left—it's crucial that you write the code in a specific order. The more general, global border setting must come first, and the edge-specific setting second, like so:

```
border: 2px solid black;
border-bottom: 4px dashed #333;
```

Because the border-bottom property appears second, it overrides the setting of the border property. If the border-bottom line came before the border property, then it would be cancelled out by the border property, and all four borders would be identical. The last property listed can overrule any related properties listed above it. This behavior is an example of the CSS cascade you read about in Chapter 5.

You can also use this shortcut method to turn off the display of a single border with the none keyword. Say you want to put a border around three sides of a style (top, left, and bottom) but no border on the last side (right). Just two lines of code get you the look you're after:

```
border: 2px inset #FFCC33;
border-right: none;
```

The ability to subtly tweak the different sides of each border is the reason there are so many different border properties. The remaining 15 properties let you define individual colors, styles, and widths for the border and for each border side. For example, you could rewrite border: 2px double #FFCC33; like this:

```
border-width: 2px;
border-style: double;
border-color: #FFCC33;
```

Since you're using three lines of code instead of one, you'll probably want to avoid this method. However, each border edge has its own set of three properties, which are helpful for overriding just one border property for a single border edge. The right border has these three properties: border-right-width, border-right-style, and border-right-color. The left, top, and bottom borders have similarly named properties—border-left-width, border-left-style, and so on.

You can change the width of just a single border like this: border-right-width: 4px;. One nice thing about this approach is that if you later decide the border should be solid, you need to edit only the generic border property by changing dashed to solid.

In addition, you can specify individual values for each side of the border by using the border-width, border-style, and border-color properties. For example, border-width: 10px 5px 15px 13px; applies four different widths to each (top, right, bottom, and left) side.

Imagine that you want to have a 2-pixel, dashed border around the four edges of a style, but you want each border to be a different color. (Perhaps you're doing a website for kids.) Here's a quick way to do that:

```
border: 2px dashed;
border-color: green yellow red blue;
```

This set of rules creates a 2-pixel dashed border around all four edges, while making the top edge green, the right edge yellow, the bottom edge red, and the left edge blue.

NOTE You usually add padding whenever you use borders. Padding provides space between the border and any content, such as text, images, or other tags. Unless you want to put a border around an image, borderlines usually sit too close to the content without padding.

◼ Coloring the Background

It's a cinch to add a background to an entire page, an individual headline, or any other page element. Use the background-color property followed by any of the valid color choices described starting on page 148. If you want, add a shockingly bright green to the background of a page with this line of code:

```
body { background-color: rgb(109,218,63); }
```

Alternatively, you can create a class style named, say, .review with the background-color property defined, and then apply the class to the <body> tag in the HTML, like so: <body class="review">.

NOTE You can also place an image in the background of a page and control that image's placement in many different ways. You'll explore that in the next chapter. In addition, you can add a color gradient to the background of any element, another cool trick that you'll learn in the next chapter.

Background colors come in handy for creating many different visual effects. You can create a bold-looking headline by setting its background to a dark color and its text to a light color. Background colors are also a great way to set off part of a page like a navigation bar, banner, or sidebar.

And, don't forget about the RGBA color method described on page 149. With it, you can make the background partially transparent, letting underlying colors, textures, or images from other objects show through. For example, you can set the background color of the page to a tan color. Then, say you want a <div> tag inside that to be a lighter shade of that tan. Instead of placing a solid color in the background of that div, you can add the color white and then control the opacity of that color, so that various degrees of the tan color show through:

```
body {
  background-color: rgb(247,226,155);
}
.special-div {
  background-color: rgba(255,255,255,.75);
}
```

When you use background colors and borders, keep the following in mind: If the border style is either dotted or dashed (see Figure 7-7), the background color shows in the empty spaces between the dots or dashes. In other words, web browsers actually paint the background color *under* the borderline. However, you can get around that behavior by using the background-clip property and setting its value to padding-box like this:

```
background-clip: padding-box;
```

Creating Rounded Corners

As mentioned earlier, web browsers treat all elements as stark rectangular boxes. That becomes obvious when you put a border around a paragraph or div. Fortunately, you can soften the hard edges of those boxes by adding a rounded corner to your styles (see Figure 7-8). CSS includes the border-radius property to let designers add curves to one or more corners of an element. At its simplest, the border-radius property accepts a single value, which it then applies to all four corners of an element:

```
.specialBox {
  background-color: red;
  border-radius: 20px;
}
```

The browser uses the supplied radius value to draw a circle at each corner of the element. The value equals the distance from the center of the circle to its edge—its radius—as pictured in Figure 7-9. Pixels and ems are the most common measurements you'll use, but you can use percentages as well (though they behave a little differently than you might expect, as discussed in Figure 7-9).

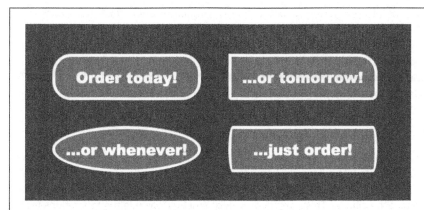

FIGURE 7-8

CSS lets you apply rounded corners to any element. Make sure you have a background color or border on the element, or else you won't be able to see any of that awesome rounded-ness.

With a single value, the browser draws the same radius for each corner of the element. For example, the top-left image in Figure 7-8 uses the following declaration:

```
border-radius: 30px;
```

However, you're not limited to the same value for each corner. You can supply separate values for each corner by providing four values. For example, the top-right box in Figure 7-8 has four different corners. The declaration is:

```
border-radius: 0 30px 10px 5px;
```

The numbers start at the top-left of the box and work their way around clockwise. In other words, the first value (0 in the example in Figure 7-8) applies to the top-left, the second (30px) to the top-right, the third (10px) to the bottom-right, and the fourth (5px) to the bottom-left corner. You can also supply just two values, in which case the first number applies to the top-left and bottom-right corners, while the second number applies to the top-right and bottom-left corners.

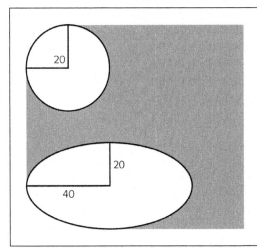

FIGURE 7-9

You can create either circular corners (top) or elliptical corners (bottom) by supplying either a single value—border-radius: 20px—or a combination of two values separated by /—border-radius: 40px/20px;. If you use a single percentage value, you'll most likely end up with an elliptical corner. That's because the browser calculates the horizontal radius by using a percentage of the element's width, and the vertical radius, using a percentage of the element's height. So, if you write something like border-radius: 20%, unless the element is a perfect square, the browser will calculate an elliptical corner more like this: border-radius: 20px/40px;.

In addition to the perfectly round (that is, circular) corners you've seen so far, it's also possible to apply an elliptical corner, like the ones in the two bottom examples in Figure 7-8. An elliptical path requires two radius values: The first is the radius from the center of the path to one of the left or right edges, while the second number is the distance from the center of the path to one of the top or bottom edges. For example, to add corners like the one pictured in the bottom-left corner in Figure 7-8, you'd create this declaration:

```
border-radius: 40px/20px ;
```

The 40px value is the horizontal radius; the 20px value is the vertical radius. The slash between them lets a browser know that you're creating an elliptical path. You can make all four corners have different oblong shapes by providing four values for each radius of the ellipsis. This is a bit confusing: You first provide the four values for the horizontal radius of each corner (starting in the top-left corner); then a forward slash (/) followed by four values for the vertical radius of each corner, like this:

```
border-radius: 40px 10px 20px 10px / 20px 30px 40px 20px;
```

To mix and match elliptical and circular corners you need to use this same syntax. Circular corners will have the same horizontal and vertical radii:

```
border-radius: 10px 10px 20px 10px / 10px 30px 40px 10px;
```

Finally, if you want to go the longhand route, you can use separate properties to define the appearance of each corner. For example:

```
border-radius: 1em 2em 1.5em .75em;
```

can also be written as:

```
border-top-left-radius: 1em;
border-top-right-radius: 2em;
border-bottom-right-radius: 1.5em;
border-bottom-left-radius: .75em;
```

NOTE Internet Explorer versions 8 and earlier don't understand the border-radius property, so they'll display square corners instead.

■ Adding Drop Shadows

As you read on page 160, you can create subtle (or not so subtle) drop shadows to text to make it pop from the page. The box-shadow property lets you add drop shadows to an element's bounding box so you can, for example, make a <div> appear to float above the page (see Figure 7-10). There are a few more options than with the text-shadow property. For example, you can make a shadow appear inside the box as at the bottom in Figure 7-10.

The basic syntax for the box-shadow property is pictured in Figure 7-11. The first value is a horizontal offset; that is, this value moves the shadow to the element's right or the left. A positive number moves the shadow to the right (Figure 7-10, top), and a negative number moves the shadow to the left.

The second value is the vertical offset—the position of the shadow either above or below the element. A positive element positions the shadow below the bottom edge of the box (Figure 7-10, top), while a negative value moves the shadow above the top edge of the box.

NOTE You must use pixels or ems for the drop shadow values. Percentages will not work.

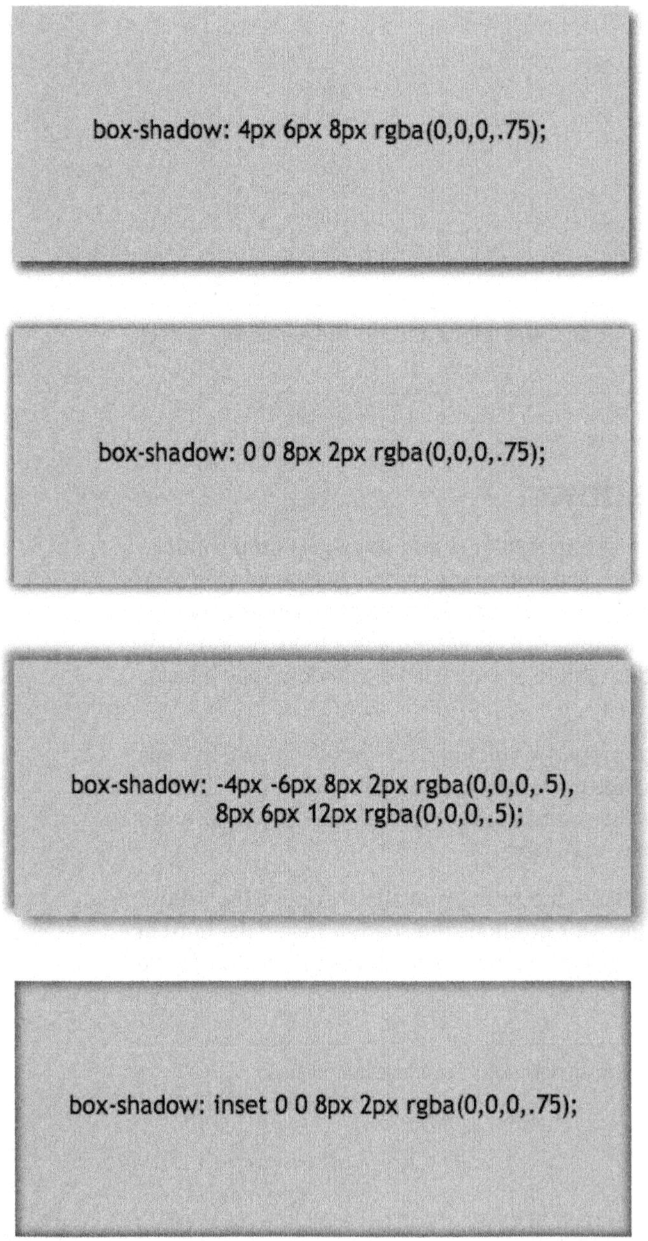

box-shadow: 4px 6px 8px rgba(0,0,0,.75);

box-shadow: 0 0 8px 2px rgba(0,0,0,.75);

box-shadow: -4px -6px 8px 2px rgba(0,0,0,.5),
8px 6px 12px rgba(0,0,0,.5);

box-shadow: inset 0 0 8px 2px rgba(0,0,0,.75);

FIGURE 7-10

The box-shadow property lets you add shadows to your elements to make them appear as though they're floating above the page. This property works in most current browsers, including Internet Explorer 9. Unfortunately, IE9 draws the shadows noticeably thinner than do other browsers. In addition, IE8 and earlier simply ignore the property and won't draw any shadows on elements.

The third value is the radius of the shadow. It determines how blurry and wide the shadow is. A value of 0 creates no blur, so the edges of the shadow are sharp. A large value creates more blur and a thicker shadow. Finally, the last value is the drop shadow's color. You can use any CSS color value, but RGBA values look particularly good since you can control the color's opacity to make it appear more translucent and shadow-like.

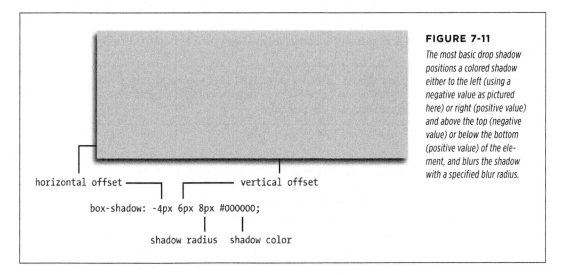

FIGURE 7-11

The most basic drop shadow positions a colored shadow either to the left (using a negative value as pictured here) or right (positive value) and above the top (negative value) or below the bottom (positive value) of the element, and blurs the shadow with a specified blur radius.

The box-shadow property includes two optional values: inset and a spread value. The inset keyword tells a browser to draw the shadow inside the box (Figure 7-10, bottom). Simply add inset as the first value of the box-shadow property to create an inset shadow:

```
box-shadow: inset 4px 4px 8px rgba(0,0,0,.75);
```

You can also add a *spread* as a fourth value (between the shadow radius and shadow color). The spread expands the shadow by the specified amount. In other words, if you add a spread value of 10px, a browser expands the shadow 10 pixels in each direction (basically making it 20 pixels wider and 20 pixels taller). The value also dictates when the blur radius is applied; when you add a spread value, the blurring of the shadow doesn't begin until after the spread value is applied. This is particularly useful when you want to add a shadow around the entire element—what a lot of image-editing programs call *glow*.

```
box-shadow: 2px 2px 10px #000000;
```

For example, at the second-from-top box in Figure 7-10, both the horizontal and vertical offsets are set to 0; the shadow radius is 8px; and the spread is 2px. The spread value pushes the shadow outward 2 pixels on all four sides of the box, and then the 8 pixels of shadow radius extends the blurring another 8 pixels. You can even use the spread value to create a second, different-colored border around an existing border. Here's an example of that:

```
border: 10px solid rgb(100,255,30);
box-shadow: 0 0 0 10px rgb(0,33,255);
```

Finally, you can even apply multiple shadows to a style (Figure 7-10, second from bottom). Just add a comma after the first set of shadow settings, and then add another shadow:

```
box-shadow: 10px 5px 8px #FF00FF,
            -5px -10px 20px 5px rgb(0,33,255);
```

You can add as many shadows as you want (and as common design sense allows).

> **NOTE** Drop shadows can force browsers to do a lot of re-rendering and redrawing. Use drop shadows carefully, and make sure you test the performance of pages with drop shadows in mobile devices, which lack the powerful CPUs of a desktop or laptop computer.

■ Determining Height and Width

Two other CSS properties that form part of the CSS box model are useful for assigning dimensions to an object, such as a table, column, banner, or sidebar. The height and width properties assign a height and width to the content area of a style. You'll use these properties often when building the kinds of CSS layouts described in Part Three of this book, but they're also useful for more basic design chores like assigning the width to a table, creating a simple sidebar, or creating a gallery of thumbnail images (like the one described in the steps on page 266).

Adding these properties to a style is very easy. Just type the property followed by any of the CSS measurement systems you've already encountered. For example:

```
width: 300px;
width: 30%;
height: 20em;
```

Pixels are, well, pixels. They're simple to understand and easy to use. They also create an exact width or height that doesn't change. An *em* is the same as the text size for the styled element. Say you set the text size to 24px; an em for that style is 24px, so if you set the width to 2em, then it would be 2 x 24 or 48 pixels. If you don't set a text size in the style, the em is based on the inherited text size (see page 152).

For the width property, percentage values are based on the percentage of the width of the style's containing element. If you set the width of a headline to 75% and that headline isn't inside any other elements with a set width, then the headline will be 75 percent of the width of the browser window. If the visitor adjusts the size of his browser, then the width of the headline will change. However, if the headline is contained inside a div (maybe to create a column) that's 200 pixels wide, the width of that headline will be 150 pixels. Percentage values for the height property work similarly, but are based on the containing element's height, instead of width.

Calculating a Box's Actual Width and Height

While the width and height properties seem pretty straightforward, there are a few nuances that can throw you for a loop. First of all, there's a difference between the value you set for a style's width and height and the amount of space that a web browser actually uses to display the style's box. The width and height properties set the width and height of the *content area* of the style—the place where the text, images, or other nested tags sit. (See Figure 7-1 for a refresher on where the content area sits within the overall box model.) The actual width—that is, the amount of screen real estate given by the web browser—is the total of the widths of the margins, borders, padding, and width properties, as illustrated in Figure 7-12.

Say you've set the following properties:

```
width: 100px;
padding: 15px;
border-width: 5px;
margin: 10px;
```

When the width property is set, you always know how much room is allocated just for your content—the words and images that fill the space—regardless of any other properties you may set. You don't need to do any math because the value of the width property is the room for your content (in the previous example, 100 pixels). Of course, you *do* have to perform a little math when you're trying to figure out exactly how much space an element will take up on a web page. In the preceding example, the width that a web browser allocates for the style's box is 160 pixels: 20 pixels for the left and right margins, 10 pixels for the left and right borders, 30 pixels for the left and right padding, and 100 pixels for the width.

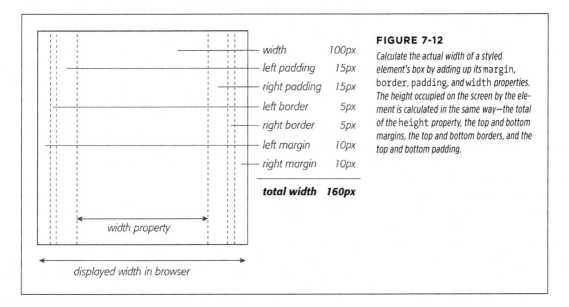

FIGURE 7-12

Calculate the actual width of a styled element's box by adding up its margin, border, padding, *and* width *properties. The height occupied on the screen by the element is calculated in the same way—the total of the* height *property, the top and bottom margins, the top and bottom borders, and the top and bottom padding.*

The general rule of thumb for setting heights on page elements is *don't*! A lot of budding CSS designers try to set heights on everything in an attempt to get pixel-perfect control. But unless you're totally sure of the exact dimensions of the content inside a tag, you can run into some unwanted results (see Figure 7-13). In this example, a pull-quote box used to highlight an interesting comment from an article has a set width and height of 100 pixels. When more text than fits into the 100-pixel height is added to the box, its contents spill out the bottom. Even if you make sure that the text you put inside a box with a fixed height fits, if a visitor increases the font size in her browser, the text might resize to a height larger than the box.

The `height` property is useful for controlling the height of a div containing images, for example, because you can correctly determine the height of the images; however, if you use the height for elements that have text, make sure to not only test your pages in the major browsers, but also test the page with different font sizes by increasing the font size in the web browser.

TIP The banner area of a page is another good candidate for a set height. Usually, the banner has limited content: a logo, search box, maybe some navigation buttons. Frequently, banners have a fair amount of white space (empty areas that help draw a visitor's attention to the key elements in the banner like the navigation bar), so specifying a height for a banner doesn't usually cause problems.

FIGURE 7-13

When you set the height of an element (like the right sidebar div here), but the content inside is taller than the element, browsers simply let the content spill out the bottom of the element below its edges.

Redefining Box Width with Box-Sizing

As mentioned on page 205, web browsers traditionally calculate the width of an element by adding together the border, padding, and width properties. Not only does this force you to (heaven forbid) do math to figure out an element's actual display width, it can cause other problems as well. This is especially true when you create float-based layouts using percentages. You'll learn the details of float layouts later in this book, but in a nutshell, CSS lets you place elements side by side using the float property, which lets you create multiple column layouts.

When using percentages with multiple columns, you can run into some weird problems. Say you have two columns (really, two tags, such as <div> tags), and you want each to be 50 percent of the width of the window. So you set the two columns to a width of 50%; however, the moment you add padding or a border to one of the columns, you'll increase its width to more than 50% (to be exact, it will be 50% plus the amount of left and right padding and the width of the left and right borders). In most cases, this will force the second column to drop *below* the first.

Fortunately, CSS offers a property that lets you change how a browser calculates the screen width (and height) of an element. The box-sizing property provides three options:

- The content-box option is the way browsers have always defined the screen width and height of an element, as described on page 205. That is, the browser adds the border widths and padding thicknesses to the values set for the width and height properties to determine the tag's onscreen width and height. Since this is the default behavior, you don't need to specify anything for content-box.

- The padding-box option tells a browser that when you set a style's width or height property, it should include the padding as part of that value. For example, say you give an element 20 pixels of left and right padding and set the width of the element to 100 pixels. The browser will consider the padding part of that 100-pixel value. In other words, the content area will be only 60 pixels wide (100 – 20 [left padding] – 20 [right padding]).

- The border-box value includes both the padding and the border thickness as part of the width and height values. This setting solves the problem of using percentage values for widths discussed above. For example, with the box-sizing property set to border-box, when you set an element's width to 50%, that element will take up 50 percent of the space, even if you add padding and borders to that element.

If you don't like the standard way browsers calculate element widths and heights, go with the border-box value. (Unless, of course, you have some unusual reason why you'd want to include the padding but not the border as part of the calculation.) To use the box-sizing property, simply supply one of the three values from the list. For example:

```
box-sizing: border-box;
```

Many web designers find the border-box setting so useful that they create a universal selector (page 49) style to apply it to every element on a page:

```
* {
  box-sizing: border-box;
}
```

As you'll read on page 416, the border-box property is very useful in overcoming common problems with certain types of CSS.

Controlling the Tap with the Overflow Property

When the content inside a styled tag is larger than the style's defined width and height, some weird things happen. As shown in Figure 7-13, browsers let the content spill out of the box (past the borders and often over other content).

Fortunately, you can control what a browser should do in this situation with the overflow property. Overflow accepts four keywords that control how content that overflows the edges of a box should be displayed:

- **visible.** This option is what browsers do normally. It's the same as not setting the property at all (Figure 7-14, top).

- **scroll.** Lets you add scroll bars (Figure 7-14, middle). It creates a kind of mini-browser window in your page and looks similar to old-school HTML frames, or the HTML <iframe> tag. You can use scroll to provide a lot of content in a small amount of space. Unfortunately, scroll bars *always* appear when you use this option, even if the content fits within the box.

- **auto.** To make scroll bars optional, use the auto option. It does the same thing as scroll but adds scroll bars only when needed.

- **hidden.** Hides any content that extends outside the box (Figure 7-14, bottom). This option is a bit dangerous—it can make some content disappear from the page.

Maximum and Minimum Heights and Widths

In case you haven't yet realized it, CSS offers a lot of flexibility. In addition to the standard width and height properties, you'll find four variations:

- The **max-width** property, not surprisingly, sets the maximum width for an element. That element can be thinner than the setting, but it can't be any wider than that setting. This option comes in handy when you want your page to resize to fit different display widths, but you don't want the page to get so wide that it's too hard to read on a really large monitor. For example, say you add this style to a page:

```
body {
  max-width: 1200px;
}
```

This style lets the page reflow to fit the width of smaller displays like smartphones and tablets. But on a really large desktop monitor, the page won't get wider than 1200 pixels, so the page can't grow unreadably wide.

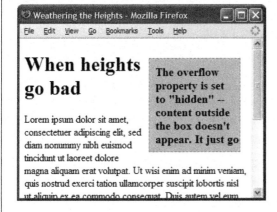

FIGURE 7-14

The overflow *property gives you three basic ways to deal with text that doesn't fit inside a box:* visible *displays the content anyway (top);* scroll *and* auto *add scroll bars (middle); and* hidden *just doesn't show anything that doesn't fit (bottom).*

- The **max-height** property works much like max-width, except it's for the element's height. As mentioned on page 206, however, it's usually best not to mess with the height of an element.

- The **min-width** property sets an element's minimum width. The element can stretch wider than the minimum width value, but it can never get thinner. If, for example, you notice that when you resize your browser window, the element's so thin that the layout falls apart, you can set a minimum width like this:

```
body {
  min-width: 760px;
}
```

If a visitor shrinks his browser window so it's only 500 pixels wide, then the browser will add a scrollbar rather than let the elements on the page get too narrow.

- The **min-height** property works like min-width, except for height. This property can solve the problem pictured in Figure 7-13. With a minimum height, you're telling a web browser to make the element at least a certain height. If the content inside the element is taller, then the browser will make the entire element taller as well.

■ Wrapping Content with Floating Elements

HTML normally flows from the top of the browser window down to the bottom, one headline, paragraph, or block-level element on top of another. This word-processor-like display is visually boring (Figure 7-15, top), but with CSS, you're far from stuck with it. You'll learn lots of new methods for arranging items on a web page in Part 3, but you can spice up your pages plenty with one little CSS property—float.

The float property moves an element to either the left or right. In the process, content below the floated element moves up and wraps around the float (Figure 7-15, bottom). Floating elements are ideal for moving supplemental information out of the way of the page's main text. Images can move to either edge, letting text wrap elegantly around them. Similarly, you can shuttle a sidebar of related information and links off to one side.

Although you can use floats in some complex (and confusing) ways, as you'll see in Chapter 13, the basic property is very simple. It takes one of three keywords—left, right or none—like so:

```
float: left;
```

- **left.** Slides the styled element to the left while content below wraps around the right side of the element.

- **right.** Slides the element to the right.

- **none.** Turns off the float and returns the object to its normal position. This property represents the element's normal behavior, so you'll only set this property if you want to override a left or right float that's applied from another style. (See Chapter 5 for rules about how multiple styles interact.)

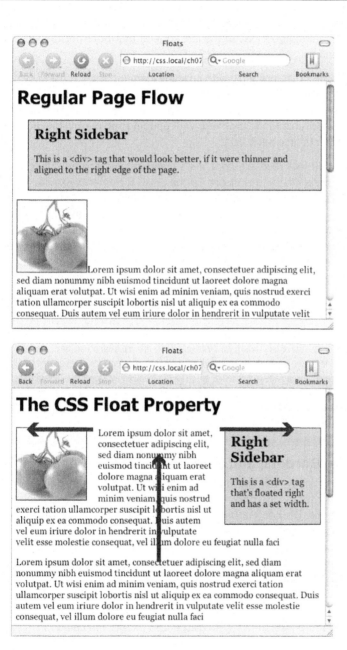

FIGURE 7-15

The regular flow of HTML is left to right, top to bottom, with one block-level element—headline, paragraph, div, and so on—stacked on top of the next. By letting you break up this uniformity, the float *property is one of CSS's most powerful tools. Its uses range from simply moving an image to one side of a paragraph to providing complete layout control over banners, sidebars, navigation bars, and other page elements.*

Floated elements move to the left or right edge of their *containing element*. In some cases, this just means that the element moves to the left or right edge of the browser window. However, if you float an element that's inside another tag with a set width or position on a web page, then the float will go to the left or right edge of that tag—the floated element's "container." For example, you may have a box on the page whose width is 30 percent of the browser window. That box is floated to the right edge of the browser window. Inside that box, you've got an image that floats to the left. That image slides to the left edge of that box—not the left edge of the browser window.

You can even use the float property with an inline element, such as the <img> tag. In fact, floating a photo to the left or right using CSS is a very common use of the float property. A web browser treats a floated inline element just like a block-level element, so you don't run into the problems with padding and margin that normally trouble inline elements (see page 192).

You can also float a block-level element like a headline or paragraph. A common technique is to float a <div> tag (or one of the HTML5 elements like <article>, <section>, or <aside>) containing other HTML tags and page content to create a kind of containing box. In this way, you can create sidebars, pull quotes, and other self-contained page elements. (You'll see an example of this in this chapter's tutorial.) When you float block-level elements, you should also set the width property for that element (in fact, CSS rules require setting the width for floated elements for all tags except images). This way, you can control how much horizontal space the block takes up and how much space is available for the content below it to move up and wrap around the block.

> **NOTE** The *source order*—the order in which you write your HTML—has a big impact on the display of floated elements. The HTML for the floated tag must appear *before* the HTML of any content that wraps around the floated element. Say you've created a web page composed of an <h1> tag followed by a <p> tag. Toward the end of that <p> tag, you've also inserted a photo using the <img> tag. If you float that photo to the right, say, then the <h1> tag and most of the content inside that <p> tag will still appear above the photo; only content that follows the <img> tag will wrap around the left side of the image.

Backgrounds, Borders, and Floats

To the frustration of many web designers, backgrounds and borders don't react to floated elements the same way content does. Say you float an element—a sidebar for example—to the right. The content below the sidebar moves up and wraps around it, just as it should. But if that content has a background or border set on it, then that background or border actually appears *underneath* the floated sidebar (Figure 7-16, left). In essence, a web browser wraps the text around the float, but not the border or background. Believe it or not, this is absolutely kosher and (according to the rules) how it's supposed to work. Of course, you may not want to follow these rules; you might want to have the border or background stop when it reaches the floated element (Figure 7-16, right). With a little CSS magic, you can do it.

First, you need to add one rule to the style that has background or borders running underneath the float. Once you locate the style, add this line: overflow: hidden;. The overflow property (page 407) makes any background or border that extends underneath the float disappear.

Another approach is to add a borderline around the floated element; when you make the borderline thick enough and match its color to the background color of the page, the border looks just like empty space—even though it's covering and hiding the background color and borderlines that are extending below it.

FIGURE 7-16

In this example, there's an <h1> tag with a background color and an <h2> tag with a border (left). Adding overflow: hidden; to the style for the <h1> tag (right) prevents the headline from appearing under the floating element (sidebar).

Stopping the Float

Sometimes you need a way to tell a tag to ignore a floated element. For example, you may have a copyright notice that should always appear at the bottom of the browser window. If you have a particularly tall sidebar that's floated to the left side of the page, the copyright notice might actually be drawn up the page and wrap around the float. Instead of appearing at the bottom of the page, the copyright is sitting farther up the page next to the sidebar. You want the copyright notice part of your page to refuse to wrap around the floated element and instead drop below it.

Other problems occur when you have several floated items close together. If the floated items aren't very wide, they float up and next to each other, and if they're of varying heights they can get into an unattractive logjam (see Figure 7-17, top). In this case, the floated elements *shouldn't* float next to each other. CSS provides the clear property for just these types of problems.

The clear property instructs an element to *not wrap* around a floated item. By clearing an element, you essentially force it to drop down below the floated item. Also, you can control which type of float (left or right) is cleared or force a style to simply ignore both types of floats.

The clear property accepts the following options:

- **left.** The style will drop below elements that are floated left, but will still wrap around right-floated objects.

- **right.** Forces a drop below right-floated objects, but still wraps around left-floated objects.

- **both.** Forces a drop below both left- and right-floated elements.

- **none.** Turns off clearing altogether. In other words, it makes an item wrap around both left- and right-floated objects, which is how web browsers normally work.

In the case of a copyright notice that must appear at the bottom of the page, you'd want it to clear both left- and right-floated objects—it should always be below other content, and should never wrap to the left or right of any other item. Here's a class style that would do just that:

```
.copyright {
 clear: both;
}
```

Figure 7-17 shows how the clear property can prevent floated items of varying heights from clumping together. All three photos in that figure have a right float applied to them. In the top figure, the photo of the tomatoes (1) is the first image on the page and appears at the far right edge. The second image (2) obeys the float set on the first image and wraps up to the left of it. The last photo (3) is too wide to sit next to the second photo (2) but still tries to wrap around both (1) and (2). It gets stuck in the process.

Using clear: right; on the images prevents the photos from sitting next to each other (Figure 7-17, bottom). The clear applied to the second photo prevents it from wrapping up next to the first image, while the last image's right clear property forces it to appear below the second image.

> **NOTE** This business of left floats, right floats, and how to clear them sounds complicated—and it is. This section gives you a basic introduction. You'll see the subject again in Chapter 13 and eventually learn how to use floats in more sophisticated ways.

FIGURE 7-17

Top: Sometimes you don't want an element to wrap around a floated object. Bottom: Applying the clear property (in this case clear: right;) to each image prevents them from sitting next to each other. The clear applied to photo (2) prevents it from wrapping up next to image (1). Applying clear: right; to photo (3) forces it to appear below photo (2).

▓ Tutorial: Margins, Backgrounds, and Borders

In this tutorial, you'll explore elements of the CSS box model, adjust the spacing around objects on a page, add colorful borders to items on a page, and control the size and flow of page elements.

To get started, you need to download the tutorial files located on this book's companion website at *https://github.com/sawmac/css_mm_4e*. Click the tutorial link and download the files. (All of the files are enclosed in a zip archive.

See detailed instructions for unzipping the files on the website.) The files for this tutorial are contained inside the *07* folder.

Controlling Page Margins and Backgrounds

You'll start with a very basic HTML file containing an internal style sheet with a basic CSS reset style. It's not much to look at right now (see Figure 7-18).

FIGURE 7-18

This web page is barebones HTML, with a single style that removes much of the built-in web browser styling. It'll look a lot better with a box model makeover.

NOTE For a sneak preview of the final result, check out Figure 7-21.

1. **In your favorite text editor, open *07→main.css*.**

   This style sheet is already linked to the *index.html* file, so the styles you add here will apply to that web page. The styles here (the same set of styles discussed on page 109) basically remove all margins, padding, and font size from the most common block-level elements and eliminate many of the cross-browser display problems you'll encounter related to these properties.

   Probably the most important properties are the margin and padding settings in the first style. There's enough cross-browser weirdness related to those two properties that many designers zero them out and start fresh. Another common alternative is a style sheet that eliminates cross-browser display differences, but still keeps some basic margins in place: *normalize.css* (*http://necolas.github.io/normalize.css/*) is one common choice.

   You'll start with something simple: a background color.

2. **At the bottom of the main.css file, click directly after the CSS comment** /* end reset styles */ **and add a tag selector style:**

   ```
   html {
     background-color: rgb(253,248,171);
   }
   ```

   This style adds a light yellow background color to the page. If you want to color the background of a web page, you can add the background-color property to either the <html> tag or the <body> tag. Next, you'll add some margins, borders, and other properties to the <body> tag.

NOTE You may be used to using hexadecimal colors (like #FDF8AB) instead of RGB colors. You can use a tool like the online convertor at *www.colorhexa.com* to convert between the two. Using RGB is a good idea because RGBA colors, with their optional transparency (page 149), are so useful, and it's easier to just stick with one color model (RGB) instead of mixing two (RGB and hex).

3. **Add another style to the style sheet:**

   ```
   body {
     background-color: rgb(255,255,255);
     border: 3px solid rgb(75,75,75);
   }
   ```

   This style adds a white background color to the <body> tag and a 3-pixel dark gray border. Because the <body> tag sits inside the <html> tag, a web browser considers it to be "on top" of the <html> tag, so the white background will cover the yellow color you added in the previous step. Next you'll give the <body> tag a width and adjust its padding and margins.

TIP Normally, if you add a background color property to the `<body>` tag, that color fills the entire browser window; however, if you also add a background color to the `<html>` tag, the body's background color fills only the area that has content. To see this in action, just preview the web page after completing step 4 above; then delete the `html` tag style, and preview the page again. A weird, but useful, bit of CSS trivia.

4. **Edit the body style you just created by adding five new properties (changes are in bold):**

   ```
   body {
      background-color: rgb(255,255,255);
      border: 3px solid rgb(75,75,75);
      max-width: 760px;
      margin-top: 20px;
      margin-left: auto;
      margin-right: auto;
      padding: 15px;
   }
   ```

   The `max-width` property constrains the body so that it never gets more than 760 pixels wide: If a visitor's browser window is wider than 760 pixels, then he'll see the background color from the `html` style and a 760-pixel box with the white background of the `<body>` tag. However, the browser window can get smaller than that, and the body will then shrink to fit the window, which makes viewing the page on a small tablet or phone easier.

   The `margin-top` property adds 20 pixels of space from the browser window's top edge—nudging the `<body>` tag down just a bit—while the left and right margin settings center the body in the middle of the browser window. "Auto" is just another way of telling a browser, "You figure it out," and since that `auto` value is applied to both the left and right margins, a browser simply provides equal space on the left and right side.

   NOTE You could also use the `margin` shorthand property (page 189) to condense those three lines of margin settings to just one, like this:

   ```
   margin: 20px auto 0 auto;
   ```

   Finally, to keep the content inside the `<body>` tag from touching the border line, 15 pixels of space are added to the inside of the body by using the `padding` property—in other words, the image and text are indented 15 pixels from all four edges. Next, you'll add a glow around the box using the `box-shadow` property.

5. **Edit the** body **style you just created by adding one last property after the border but before the width (changes are in bold):**

```
body {
    background-color: rgb(255,255,255);
    border: 3px solid rgb(75,75,75);
    box-shadow: 0 0 15px 5px rgba(44,82,100,.75);
    max-width: 760px;
    margin-top: 20px;
    margin-left: auto;
    margin-right: auto;
    padding: 15px;
}
```

This style adds a glow to the box by creating a 15-pixel shadow placed directly behind the box (the 0 0 part at the beginning indicates that the shadow isn't offset to the left/right or top/bottom; it's simply in the background). The 5px value is the spread value (page 203), and it pushes the shadow out 5 pixels around all four edges. Finally, the rgba value sets the color to a dark blue that's only 75 percent solid (that is, you can see through to the background yellow).

Your style sheet is pretty far along, and you're ready to check the page.

6. **Save the file and preview the page in a web browser.**

You should see a white box with an image, a bunch of text, and a gray outline with a bluish glow floating in a sea of yellow (see Figure 7-19). The text needs some loving attention. You'll take care of that next.

Adjusting the Space Around Tags

Since the CSS reset styles pretty much stripped the text on this page of all formatting, you'll need to create styles to make the headings and paragraphs look great. You'll start with the <h1> tag at the top of the page.

1. **Return to your text editor and the *main.css* file. Click at the end of the closing brace of the** <body> **tag selector, press Enter (Return) to create a new line, and then add the following style:**

```
h1 {
  font-size: 2.75em;
  font-family: Georgia, "Times New Roman", Times, serif;
  font-weight: normal;
  text-align: center;
  letter-spacing: 1px;
  color: rgb(133,161,16);
  text-transform: uppercase;
}
```

This style uses many of the text-formatting properties discussed in the previous chapter—the top headline is 2.75 ems tall (44 pixels in most browsers) and all uppercase, uses the Georgia font, and has a green color, with a little space between each letter. The text-align property makes sure the text is centered in the middle of the box. The real fun is adding a background color to really highlight the headline.

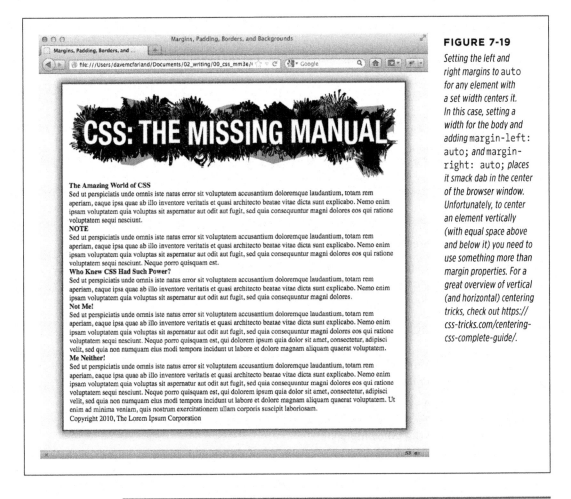

FIGURE 7-19

Setting the left and right margins to auto for any element with a set width centers it. In this case, setting a width for the body and adding margin-left: auto; and margin-right: auto; places it smack dab in the center of the browser window. Unfortunately, to center an element vertically (with equal space above and below it) you need to use something more than margin properties. For a great overview of vertical (and horizontal) centering tricks, check out https:// css-tricks.com/centering-css-complete-guide/.

> **TIP** Save the file and preview it in a web browser after each step in this tutorial. That way, you'll get a better understanding of how these CSS properties affect the elements they format. You may need to press the Ctrl or ⌘ key as you reload the web page to force the browser to reload the *main.css* file and not use the version that the browser stored in its cache. (See page 25 for more on how a browser's cache works.)

2. **Add one new property to the** h1 **tag style so that it looks like this (changes in bold):**

```
h1 {
  font-size: 2.75em;
  font-family: Georgia, "Times New Roman", Times, serif;
  font-weight: normal;
  text-align: center;
  letter-spacing: 1px;
  color: rgb(133,161,16);
  text-transform: uppercase;
  background-color: rgb(226,235,180);
}
```

If you preview the page now, you'll see that the headline has a light green background. When applied to a block-level element like a headline, the background fills the entire horizontal space available (in other words, the color doesn't just sit behind the text "The Amazing World of CSS," but extends all the way to the right edge of the box).

The headline text is a little cramped—the "T" that begins the headline touches the edge of the background. With a little padding, you can fix this.

3. **Add another property to the** h1 **tag style so that it looks like this (changes in bold):**

```
h1 {
  font-size: 2.75em;
  font-family: Georgia, "Times New Roman", Times, serif;
  font-weight: normal;
  text-align: center;
  letter-spacing: 1px;
  color: rgb(133,161,16);
  text-transform: uppercase;
  background-color: rgb(226,235,180);
  padding: 5px 15px 2px 15px;
}
```

The padding shorthand property provides a concise way to add padding around all four sides of the content—in this case, 5 pixels of space are added above the text, 15 pixels to the right, 2 pixels to the bottom, and 15 pixels to the left.

There's one other problem with the headline: Because of the padding added to the <body> tag (see step 4 on page 218), the headline (including its background color) is indented 15 pixels from the left and right edges of the gray border surrounding the body. The headline would look better if its background color touched the gray border. No problem; negative margins to the rescue.

4. **Add one last property to the** h1 **tag style so that it looks like this (changes in bold):**

```
h1 {
  font-size: 2.75em;
  font-family: Georgia, "Times New Roman", Times, serif;
  font-weight: normal;
  text-align: center;
  letter-spacing: 1px;
  color: rgb(133,161,16);
  text-transform: uppercase;
  background-color: rgb(226,235,180);
  padding: 5px 15px 2px 15px;
  margin: 0 -15px 20px -15px;
}
```

Here, the margin shorthand sets the top margin to 0, the right margin to –15 pixels, the bottom margin to 20 pixels, and the left margin to –15 pixels. The bottom margin just adds a bit of space between the headline and the paragraph that follows. The next trick is the use of negative values for the left and right margins. You can assign a negative margin to any element. This property pulls the element out toward the direction of the margin—in this case, the headline extends 15 pixels to the left and 15 pixels to the right, actually expanding the headline and pulling it out over the <body> tag's padding.

5. **Now, you'll add some formatting of the** <h2> **tags. Add the following style after the** h1 **tag style:**

```
h2 {
  font-size: 1.5em;
  font-family: "Arial Narrow", Arial, Helvetica, sans-serif;
  color: rgb(249,107,24);
  border-top: 2px dotted rgb(141,165,22);
  border-bottom: 2px dotted rgb(141,165,22);
  padding-top: 5px;
  padding-bottom: 5px;
  margin: 15px 0 5px 0;
}
```

This style adds some basic text formatting and a dotted border above and below the headline. To add a bit of space between the headline text and the lines, it puts a small bit of padding at the top and bottom. Finally, the margin property adds 15 pixels above the headline and 5 pixels below it.

6. **Save the file and preview the page in a web browser.**

The headlines are looking good (see Figure 7-20). Next, you'll create a sidebar on the right side of the page.

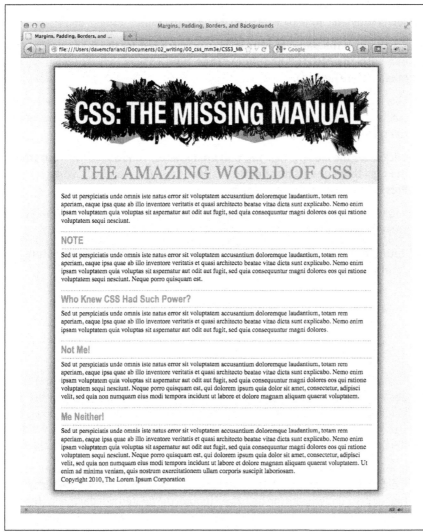

FIGURE 7-20

With just a few styles, you can add background colors, control margins throughout the page, and adjust the space between headlines and paragraphs.

Building a Sidebar

Sidebars are common elements in most types of print publications like magazines, books, and newspapers. They compartmentalize and highlight small chunks of information like a resource list, contact information, or a related anecdote. But to be effective, sidebars shouldn't interrupt the flow of the main story. They should, like the name says, sit unobtrusively off to one side, which you can easily make happen with CSS.

1. **Return to your text editor and open the *index.html* file.**

   First, you must isolate the region of the page that makes up the sidebar. The `<div>` tag is the perfect tool. You can enclose any amount of HTML into its own self-contained chunk by wrapping it in a `<div>` tag.

2. **Scroll down the page into the HTML and click *before* the first `<h2>` tag (the one with the "NOTE" headline). Then type** `<div class="sidebar">`, **and press Enter (Return).**

   This HTML marks the beginning of the sidebar and applies a class to it. You'll create the `.sidebar` class style soon, but first you need to indicate the end of the sidebar by closing the `<div>`.

3. **Click after the closing** `</p>` **tag that immediately follows the** `<h2>` **tag (this is the** `</p>` **that appears just before** `<h2>Who Knew CSS Had Such Power?</h2>`**). Press Enter, and then type** `</div>`.

   You've just wrapped a headline and paragraph inside a `<div>` tag. Next, you'll create a style for it.

4. **Return to the *main.css* file. Add the following style below the h2 style you created earlier:**

   ```
   .sidebar {
   width: 30%;
   float: right;
   margin: 10px;
   }
   ```

   This style sets the width of the content area (where the text appears) to 30 percent. In this case, the sidebar's width is 30 percent of the width of the container. The container is the `<body>` tag and its width will be up to 760 pixels (see step 4 on page 18.) The `float` property moves the sidebar to the right side of the box, and the `margin` property adds 10 pixels of space around the sidebar.

   If you preview the page in a browser, you'll see that the basic shape and placement of the sidebar are set, but there's one problem: The borders from the `<h2>` tags appear *underneath* the box. Even though the floated sidebar moves the text of the headlines out of the way, floats don't displace borders or backgrounds. Those just appear right under the floated sidebar. One way to fix this problem is to simply add a background color to the sidebar, so you can't see the h2 borders. (There's another technique, as well, which you'll use in step 9 on page 226.)

5. **Add two other properties to the** `.sidebar` **style so it looks like this (changes in bold):**

   ```
   .sidebar {
   width: 30%;
   float: right;
   margin: 10px;
   ```

```
    background-color: rgb(250,235,199);
    padding: 10px 20px;
    }
```

These properties add a light orangish color to the sidebar and indents the text from the sidebar's edges so it won't touch the borders you're about to add.

6. **Add two more properties to the** .sidebar **style so it looks like this (changes in bold):**

```
.sidebar {
  width: 30%;
  float: right;
  margin: 10px;
  background-color: rgb(250,235,199);
  padding: 10px 20px;
  border: 1px dotted rgb(252,101,18);
  border-top: 20px solid rgb(252,101,18);
  }
```

Here's an example of the handy technique described on page 197. If you want most of the borders around an element to be the same, you can first define a border for all four edges—in this case a 1-pixel, dotted, orange line around the entire sidebar—and then supply new border properties for the specific edges you want changed—in this example, the top border will be 20 pixels tall and solid. This technique lets you use just two lines of CSS code instead of four (border-top, border-bottom, border-left, and border-right).

Next, you'll add rounded corners and a drop shadow to really make this sidebar stand out.

7. **Finally, add two more properties to the** .sidebar **style so it looks like this (changes in bold):**

```
.sidebar {
  width: 30%;
  float: right;
  margin: 10px;
  background-color: rgb(250,235,199);
  padding: 10px 20px;
  border: 1px dotted rgb(252,101,18);
  border-top: 20px solid rgb(252,101,18);
  border-radius: 10px;
  box-shadow: 5px 5px 10px rgba(0,0,0,.5);
  }
```

The border-radius property (page 199) lets you create rounded corners. In this case, the 10-pixel setting provides a prominent-looking curve. The box-shadow property here adds a drop shadow below and to the right of the box, making it look as though it's floating above the page. You're almost done.

The headline inside the sidebar doesn't look quite right. It uses the same properties as the other <h2> tags (because of the h2 tag style you created in step 4). The border is distracting and the top margin pushes the headline down too much from the top of the sidebar. Fortunately, you can use a descendant selector to override those properties.

8. **After the** .sidebar **style, in the** *main.css* **style sheet, add a descendant selector:**

```
.sidebar h2 {
  border: none;
  margin-top: 0;
  padding: 0;
}
```

Because of the .sidebar, this style is more powerful—that is, it has greater *specificity* as described on page 102—than the basic h2 style. It erases the border from the original h2 tag style, along with the top margin and all the padding. However, since this style doesn't have a font size, color, or font family, those properties from the h2 style still apply—it's the cascade in action!

The page is looking good, but the borders on the <h2> tags still run up to and behind the sidebar. That just doesn't look good, but you can fix it easily.

9. **Locate the** <h2> **style and add the** overflow **property, like so:**

```
h2 {
  font-size: 1.5em;
  font-family: "Arial Narrow", Arial, Helvetica, sans-serif;
  color: rgb(249,107,24);
  border-top: 2px dotted rgb(141,165,22);
  border-bottom: 2px dotted rgb(141,165,22);
  padding-top: 5px;
  padding-bottom: 5px;
  margin: 15px 0 5px 0;
  overflow: hidden;
}
```

Setting the overflow property to hidden hides the borders that pass beyond the headline text and under the floating element.

10. **Save the file and preview the web page in a browser.**

The page should look like Figure 7-21.

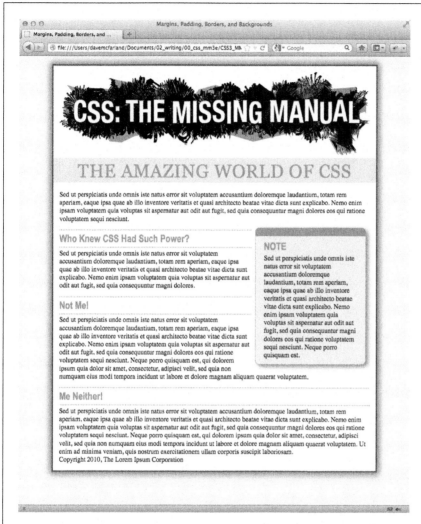

FIGURE 7-21

A handful of CSS styles add design elegance to ho-hum HTML. Notice how the floated sidebar both attracts attention and moves it out of the way of the main body of text.

Going Further

To try out your newfound skills, try this exercise on your own: Create a p tag style to add some pizzazz to the paragraphs on the page—try out some margin settings, font color, and so on. Next, create a class style for formatting the copyright notice that appears at the bottom of the *index.html* page (called, say, .copyright). In this style, add a border above the copyright notice, change its text color, shrink its font size, and change the type to uppercase. (Hint: Use the text-transform property discussed on page 157.) After you've created the style, add the appropriate class attribute to the <p> tag in the HTML.

Adding Graphics to Web Pages

No matter how much you gussy up your text or fiddle with borders and margins, nothing affects the appearance of your site more than the images you add to it. And once again, CSS gives you more image control than HTML ever dreamed of. You can work with graphics in CSS on two fronts: the <img> tag and the background-image property (which lets you place an image in the background of any tag on a page).

This chapter delves into some of the creative ways you can deploy images with CSS. The best way to learn how to use graphics in CSS is to see them in action, so this chapter has three—count 'em, three—tutorials. By creating a photo gallery web page and using images for overall page styling, you'll be an image-slinging pro in no time.

Discovering CSS and the <img> Tag

The venerable <img> tag has been the workhorse of photo-heavy websites since the beginning of the World Wide Web. Even sites without photos use it to add logos, navigation buttons, and illustrations. While CSS doesn't have any properties specifically aimed at formatting images, you can take advantage of the CSS properties you've already learned to enhance your site's graphics. For example, the border property is a quick and simple way to frame an image or unify the look of a gallery of photos. Here's a rundown of the CSS properties most commonly used with images:

- **Borders.** Use one of the many border properties (page 194) to frame an image. You'll see an example of this in the tutorial on page 261. Since each border side can be a different color, style, and width, you've got lots of creative options.

- **Padding.** The padding property (page 187) adds space between a border and an image. By putting a little breathing room between a photo and its frame, padding simulates the fiberboard mat that's used in traditional picture frames to surround and offset the image. And by setting a background color, you can even change the color of the mat.

- **Float.** Floating an image moves it to either the left or right edge of the page, or—if the image is contained in another layout element such as a sidebar—to the left or right edge of the image's containing element. Text and other page elements then wrap around the image. You can even float multiple images to create a flexible, multi-row image gallery. You'll see an example of this technique in the tutorial on page 266.

- **Margins.** To add space between an image and other page content, use the margin property. When you float an image, the text that wraps around it is usually uncomfortably close to the image. Adding a left margin (for right-floated images) or right margin (for left-floated images) adds space between text and the graphic.

- **Border-radius.** The border-radius property (which you learned about on page 199) lets you round the corners of elements, including images. It lets you take a rectangular photo and display it as if it has rounded, not square, corners.

In most cases, you won't create a style for the <img> tag itself. Formatting this tag is using too broad a brush, since it formats *all* images on your page—even those with very different functions, such as the logo, navigation buttons, photos, and even graphic ads. You wouldn't, after all, want the same black frame around all of those images. Instead, you should use a class style, such as .galleryImage or .logo, to apply the style selectively.

Another approach is to use a descendant selector to target images grouped together in one section of a page. If you have a gallery of photos, you can place all the photos inside a <div> tag with a class name of gallery, and then create a style for just the images inside that <div>, like this: .gallery img.

TIP Set the border-radius property to 50% to make an image appear to be circular. For example, you can create a class named round and apply it to any images you'd like to appear as circles:

```
.round { border-radius: 50%; }
```

■ Adding Background Images

The background-image property is the key to making visually stunning websites. Learn how to use it and its cousin properties, and you can make your site stand head and shoulders above the rest. For an example of the power of background images, check out *www.csszengarden.com* (Figure 8-1). The HTML for both the pages shown in Figure 8-1 is exactly the same; the most striking visual differences are accomplished by using different background images. How's that for CSS power?

If you've built a few websites, you've probably used an image for the background of a page—perhaps a small graphic that repeats in the background of the browser window creating a (hopefully) subtle pattern. That time-honored HTML method used the <body> tag's background attribute. But CSS does the same job better.

NOTE In the next few pages, you'll meet three background image properties by learning the individual CSS code for each one. Later in the chapter, you'll learn a shorthand method that'll save you a lot of typing.

The background-image property adds a graphic to the background of an element. To put an image in the background of a web page, you can create a style for the <body> tag:

```
body {
   background-image: url(images/bg.png);
}
```

The property takes one value: the keyword url, followed by a path to the graphic file enclosed in parentheses. You can use an absolute URL like this—url(http://www.cosmofarmer.com/image/bg.png)—or a document- or root-relative path like these:

```
url(../images/bg.png) /* document-relative */
url(/images/bg.png) /* root-relative */
```

As explained in the box on page 237, document-relative paths provide directions in relation to the style sheet file, *not* the HTML page you're styling. These will be one and the same, of course, if you're using an internal style sheet, but you need to keep this point in mind if you're using an *external* style sheet. Say you've got a folder named *styles* (containing the site's style sheets) and a folder named *images* (holding the site's images). Both these folders are located in the site's main folder along with the home page (Figure 8-2). When a visitor views the home page, the external style sheet is also loaded (step 1 in Figure 8-2). Now, say the external style sheet includes a style for the <body> tag with the background image property set to use the graphic file *bg.png* in the *images* folder. The document-relative path would lead from the style sheet to the graphic (step 2 in Figure 8-2). In other words, the style would look like this:

```
body {
   background-image: url(../images/bg.png);
}
```

This path breaks down like this: `../` means "go up one level" (that is, up to the folder containing the *styles* folder); `images/` means "go to the images folder"; and `bg.png` specifies that file.

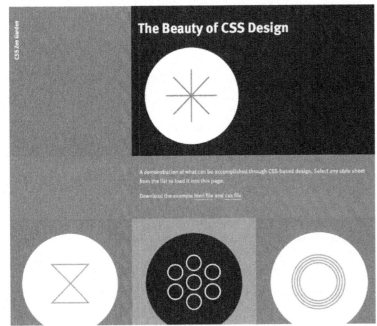

FIGURE 8-1

CSSzengarden.com showcases the power of CSS by demonstrating how you can transform a single HTML file into two utterly different-looking pages. The real secret to making each of the wonderful designs look unique is the extensive use of background images. (In fact, when you look at these pages' HTML code, you'll see there isn't a single `<img>` tag in it.)

GIFs, JPEGs, PNGs, and SVGs: The Graphics of the Web

Computer graphics come in hundreds of different file formats, with a mind-numbing assortment of acronyms: JPEG, GIF, TIFF, SVG, PNG, PICT, BMP, EPS, and so on.

Fortunately, graphics on the Web are a bit simpler. Today's web browsers work with three main bitmap graphics formats: GIF, JPEG, and PNG, each of which provides good *compression*. Through clever computer manipulation, compression reduces the graphic's file size so it can travel more rapidly across the Internet. Which you choose depends on the image you wish to add to your page.

GIF (Graphics Interchange Format) files provide good compression for images that have areas of solid color: logos, text, simple banners, and so on. GIFs also offer single-color transparency, meaning that you can make one color in the graphic disappear, permitting the background of a web page to show through part of the image. In addition, GIFs can include simple animations.

A GIF image can contain a maximum of only 256 shades, however, which generally makes photos look *posterized* (patchy and unrealistically colored, like a poster). In other words, that radiant sunset photo you took with your digital camera won't look so good as a GIF. (If you don't need to animate an image, the PNG8 format discussed later is a better choice than GIF.)

JPEG (Joint Photographic Experts Group) graphics, on the other hand, pick up where GIFs leave off. JPEG graphics can contain millions of different colors, making them ideal for photos. Not only do JPEGs do a better job on photos, they also compress multicolored images much better than GIFs, because the JPEG compression algorithm considers how the human eye perceives different adjacent color values. JPEG is the format many cameras use to save photos. When your graphics software saves a JPEG file, it runs a complex color analysis to lower the amount of data required to accurately represent the image. On the downside, JPEG compression makes text and large areas of solid color look blotchy.

Finally, the **PNG** (Portable Network Graphics) format includes the best features of GIFs and JPEGs, but you need to know which version of PNG to use for which situation. PNG8 is basically a replacement for GIF. Like GIF, it offers 256 colors and basic one-color transparency. However, PNG8 usually compresses images to a slightly smaller file size than GIF, so PNG8 images download a tiny bit faster than the same image saved in the GIF format. In other words, use PNG8 over GIF.

PNG24 and PNG32 (which is basically PNG24 with alpha transparency) offer the expanded color palette of JPEG images, without any loss of quality. This means that photos saved as PNG24 or PNG32 tend to be higher quality than JPEGs. But before you jump on the PNG bandwagon, JPEG images do offer very good quality and a *much* smaller file size than either PNG24 or PNG32. In general, JPEG is a better choice for photos and other images that include lots of colors.

Finally, PNG32 offers one feature that no other format does: 256 levels of transparency (also called *alpha* transparency), which means that you can actually see the background of a web page through a drop shadow on a graphic, or even make a graphic that has 50 percent opacity (meaning you can see through it) to create a ghostly translucent effect.

One more graphic format, SVG, is different from PNG, GIF, and JPEG, in that it's not a bitmapped image. Instead of being composed of tiny little pixels placed side by side and row upon row to create an image, SVG (or Scalable Vector Graphic), is defined by a set of mathematical instructions that describe how to draw the image on the screen. SVG and other vector format files aren't suitable photos or pictures, but instead are used for line art graphics like logos and icons. You can use Adobe Illustrator or a similar drawing program to create SVG files. The benefit of these files is that they are generally small in file size, but can be scaled up to any size and retain their sharpness and clarity. For a good list of SVG resources, visit: *https://css-tricks.com/mega-list-svg-information/*.

In the examples so far, the path isn't enclosed in quotes as in HTML, but quotes are fine, too. In CSS, all three of the following code lines are kosher:

```
background-image: url(images/bg.png);
background-image: url("images/bg.png");
background-image: url('images/bg.png');
```

NOTE You can use SVG files as background images in all browsers except Internet Explorer 8. Just store the SVG file on your site and reference it like any other graphic file:

```
background-image: url(images/icon.svg);
```

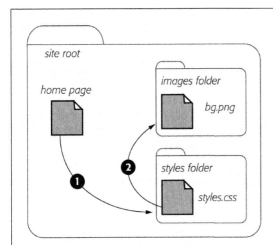

FIGURE 8-2

Document-relative paths are calculated in relation to the style sheet, not the web page being styled.

Controlling Repetition

If you use the background-image property by itself, the graphic always tiles, filling up the entire background of a web page. Fortunately, you can use the background-repeat property to specify how (or if) an image tiles:

```
background-repeat: no-repeat;
```

The property accepts four values: repeat, no-repeat, repeat-x, and repeat-y:

- **repeat** is the normal setting for background images that you want to display from left to right and top to bottom until the entire space is filled with a graphic (Figure 8-3).

- **no-repeat** displays the image a single time, without tiling or repetition. It's a very common option, and you'll frequently use it when placing images into the background of tags other than <body>. You can use it to place a logo in the upper corner of a page or to use custom graphics for bullets in lists, to name a couple of examples. (You'll see the bullet example in action in the tutorial on page 274.)

- **repeat-x** repeats an image horizontally along the x-axis (the horizontal width of the page, if your geometry is rusty). It's perfect for adding a graphical banner to the top of a web page (Figure 8-4, left) or a decorative border along the top or bottom of a headline.

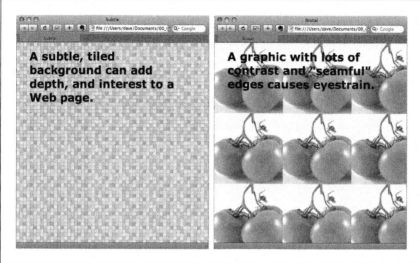

FIGURE 8-3

Be careful when tiling images in the background of a web page. Choose an image without a lot of contrast that tiles seamlessly (left). An image with too much contrast (right), makes text hard to read.

- **repeat-y** repeats an image vertically along the y-axis (the vertical length of the page). You can use this setting to add a graphic sidebar to a page (Figure 8-4, right) or to add a repeating drop shadow to either side of a page element (like a sidebar).

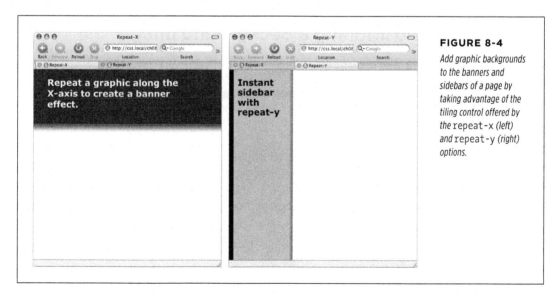

FIGURE 8-4

Add graphic backgrounds to the banners and sidebars of a page by taking advantage of the tiling control offered by the repeat-x *(left) and* repeat-y *(right) options.*

- **round** tiles an image like the repeat option, but it never clips the image. The images are scaled to fit side by side and row upon row with no clipping (see left image in Figure 8-5). Browsers will distort the image copies to make this happen, so the aspect ratio of the graphic is not preserved.

- **space** tiles an image like the repeat option, but it prevents the image from ever being clipped at the top or bottom. In other words, the space option always displays an image in its entirety. Accordingly, the browser will introduce space between the tiled copies of the image (see right image in Figure 8-5).

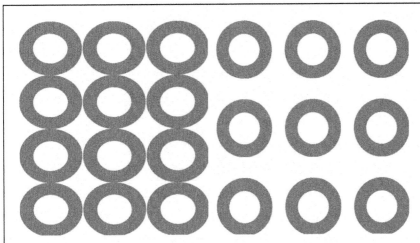

FIGURE 8-5

The round *(left) and* space *(right) settings for the* background-repeat *pattern make sure the browser doesn't clip any part of the repeated images. This combination of settings forces the browser to distort the aspect ratio of the image (left) or add extra space between the tiled images (right).*

■ Positioning a Background Image

Placing and tiling a background image is just half the fun. With the background-position property, CSS lets you control the exact placement of an image in a number of ways. You can specify both the horizontal and vertical starting points for a graphic in three ways—keywords, exact values, and percentages.

Keywords

You get two sets of keywords to work with. The first one controls the three horizontal positions—left, center, right—and the second controls the three vertical positions—top, center, bottom (Figure 8-6). Suppose you want to place a graphic directly in the middle of a web page. You can create a style like this:

```
body {
  background-image: url(bg_page.jpg);
  background-repeat: no-repeat;
  background-position: center center;
}
```

URL Types

In CSS, you need to specify a *URL* when you add a background image. A URL, or *Uniform Resource Locator*, is a path to a file located on the Web. There are three types of paths: *absolute path*, *root-relative path*, and *document-relative path*. All three simply indicate where a web browser can find a particular file (like another web page, a graphic, or an external style sheet).

An absolute path is like a postal address—it contains all the information needed for a web browser located anywhere in the world to find the file. An absolute path includes *http://*, the hostname, and the folder and name of the file. For example: *http://www.cosmofarmer.com/images/bluegrass.jpg*.

A *root-relative* path indicates where a file is located relative to a site's top-level folder—the site's root folder. A root-relative path doesn't include *http://* or the domain name. It begins with a / (slash) indicating the root folder of the site (the folder the home page is in). For example */images/bluegrass.jpg* indicates that the file *bluegrass.jpg* is located inside a folder named *images*, which is itself located in the site's top-level folder. An easy way to create a root-relative path is to take an absolute path and strip off the *http://* and the host name.

A *document-relative* path specifies the path from the current document to the file. When it comes to a style sheet, this means *the path from the style sheet to the specified file*, not the path from the current web page to the file.

Here are some tips on which type to use:

- If you're pointing to a file that's not on the same server as the style sheet, you *must* use an absolute path. It's the only type that can point to another website.

- Root-relative paths are good for images stored on your own site. Since they always start at the root folder, you can move the style sheet around without affecting the path from the root to the image on the site. However, they're difficult to use when first building your designs: You can't preview root-relative paths unless you're viewing your web pages through a web server—either your web server out on the Internet or a web server you've set up on your own computer for testing purposes. In other words, if you're just opening a web page off your computer using the browser's File→Open command, then you won't see any images placed using root-relative paths.

- Document-relative paths are the best when you're designing on your own computer without the aid of a web server. You can create your CSS files and then review them in a web browser simply by opening a web page stored on your hard drive. These pages will work fine when you move them to your actual, living, breathing website on the Internet, but you'll have to rewrite the URLs to the images if you move the style sheet to another location on the server.

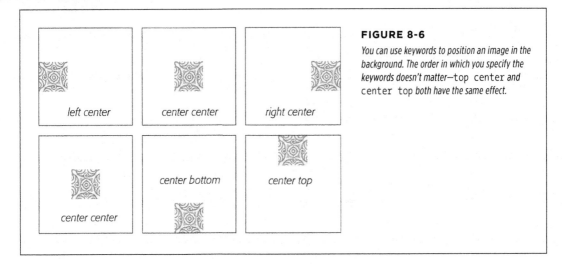

FIGURE 8-6

You can use keywords to position an image in the background. The order in which you specify the keywords doesn't matter—top center and center top both have the same effect.

To move that graphic to the top-right corner, just change the background position to this:

```
background-position: right top;
```

NOTE If you've decided to tile an image (by setting background-repeat to one of the values listed in the previous section), then the background-position property controls the *starting* point of the first tile. So, for example, if you use the repeat option, you'll still see the entire background filled by the image. It's just that the position of the *first* tile changes based on which background-position setting you used.

Keywords are really useful when you want to create vertical or horizontal banners. If you wanted a graphic that's centered on a page and tiled downwards in order to create a backdrop for content (Figure 8-7, left), then you'd create a style like this:

```
body {
   background-image: url(background.jpg);
   background-repeat: repeat-y;
   background-position: center top;
}
```

Likewise, using the bottom, center, or top keywords, you can position a horizontally repeating image by using repeat-x (shown back in Figure 8-4, left) in a particular place on the page (or within a styled element).

 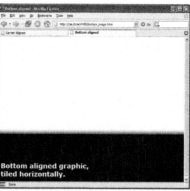

FIGURE 8-7

Use the background-position *property when tiling an image either vertically (left) or horizontally (right). In the left image, the graphic is a wide white box with drop shadows on the left and right edges. The page's background color is gray, so the text of the page looks like it's on a white piece of paper floating above the screen.*

TIP You can actually add a background image to both the `<html>` and `<body>` tags. If you tile both images horizontally and place the `<body>` tag's image at the top and the `<html>` tag's image on the bottom, you can achieve the effect of two stripes cutting across the top and bottom of the page—no matter how tall the page is.

BROWSER BUG

Bottoming Out

When displaying an image in the background of a web page, most browsers don't always vertically position the image in the way you'd expect. For example, if you set the vertical position to `bottom`, the image doesn't always appear at the bottom of the browser window. This happens when the content on a page is shorter than the browser window is tall.

If the web page has only a couple of paragraphs of text and it's displayed on a really large monitor, most browsers treat the height as the bottom of the last paragraph, not the bottom of the browser window. If you run into this annoyance, then just add this style to your style sheet:

```
html { height: 100%; }
```

Precise Values

You can also position background images by using pixel values or ems. You use two values: one to indicate the distance between the image's left edge and the container's left edge, and another to specify the distance between the image's top edge and the style's top edge. (Put another way, the first value controls the horizontal position, and the second value controls the vertical position.)

Say you want custom bullets for a list. If you add a background image to the `<li>` tag, the bullets often don't line up exactly (see Figure 8-8, top). So you can just nudge the bullets into place by using the `background-position` property (Figure

8-8, bottom). If the list would look better with, say, the bullets 5 pixels farther to the right and 8 pixels farther down, then add this declaration to the style defining the background image:

```
background-position: 5px 8px;
```

You can't specify distances from the bottom or right by using pixel or em measurements, so if you want to make sure an image is placed in the exact bottom-right corner of the page or a styled element, then use keywords (bottom right) or percentages, as discussed next. However, you can use negative values to move an image off the left edge or above the top edge, hiding that portion of the image from view. You may want to use negative values to crop out part of a picture. Or, if the background image has lots of extra white space at the top or left edge, you can use negative values to eliminate that extra space.

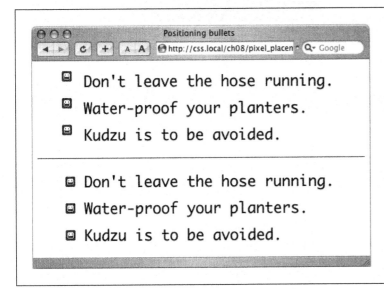

FIGURE 8-8

Using custom images for bullets sometimes requires careful positioning, so that the bullet graphic appears the correct distance from, and perfectly centered on, the list item's text.

Percentage Values

Finally, you can use percentage values to position a background image. Using percentages in this manner is tricky, and if you can achieve the effect you're after with the keyword or precise values discussed previously, then use them. But you have to use percentages to position an element in a spot that's proportional to the width of an element—say, if you want to place a graphic three-quarters of the way across a headline and you don't know the width of the element.

As with pixel or em values, you supply two percentages: one to indicate the horizontal position and the second to indicate the vertical position. What the percentage is measuring is a little tricky: In a nutshell, a percentage value aligns the specified percentage of the image with the same percentage of the styled element. What?

The best way to understand how percentage values work is to look at a few examples. To position an image in the middle of a page (like the one shown in the center of Figure 8-9) you'd write this:

```
background-position:50% 50%;
```

This declaration places the point on the image that's 50 percent from its left edge directly on top of the point that's 50 percent from the left edge of the page (or whatever element you've styled with the background image). The declaration also aligns the point on the image that's 50 percent from its top with the point that's 50 percent from the top edge of the page or styled element. In other words, the center of the image is aligned with the center of the element. This means that when using percentages, the exact point on the image that's being aligned can be a moving target. (That's because your styled element's positioning percentages can change if your visitors resize their browsers.)

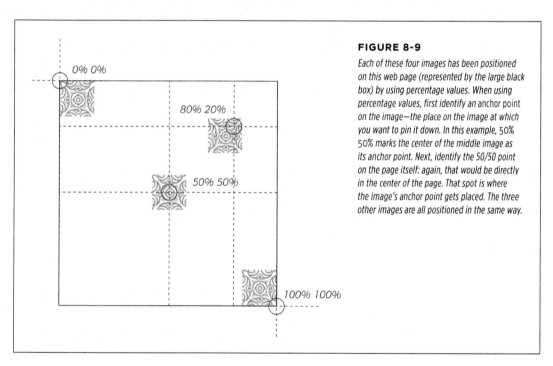

FIGURE 8-9

Each of these four images has been positioned on this web page (represented by the large black box) by using percentage values. When using percentage values, first identify an anchor point on the image—the place on the image at which you want to pin it down. In this example, 50% 50% marks the center of the middle image as its anchor point. Next, identify the 50/50 point on the page itself: again, that would be directly in the center of the page. That spot is where the image's anchor point gets placed. The three other images are all positioned in the same way.

NOTE Positioning an image vertically in the background of a page by using percentages won't necessarily put the image in the correct spot if the page content doesn't fill the entire height of the browser window. See the box on page 239 for the solution to this problem.

As with pixel and em values, you can specify negative percentage values, although the results can be hard to predict. You can also mix and match pixel/em values with percentage values. For example, to place an image that's 5 pixels from the element's left edge, but placed in the middle of the element's height, you could use this:

```
background-position: 5px 50%;
```

NOTE Although background images can raise the visual quality of your web pages, they usually don't show up if your visitor prints the page. Most browsers *can* print out the backgrounds, but it usually requires extra work on your visitor's part. If you plan to have your visitors print pages from your site, then you may want to keep using the `<img>` tag to insert mission-critical images like your site logo or a map to your store.

Fixing an Image in Place

Normally, if there's a background image on a web page and the visitor has to scroll down to see more of the page, the background image scrolls as well. As a result, any pattern in the background of the page appears to move along with the text. Furthermore, when you have a nonrepeating image in the background, it can potentially scroll off the top of the page out of view. If you've placed the site's logo or a watermark graphic in the background of the page, then you may *not* want it to disappear when visitors scroll.

The CSS solution to such dilemmas is the `background-attachment` property. It has two options—`scroll` and `fixed`. Scroll is the normal web browser behavior; that is, it scrolls the background image along with the text and other page content. Fixed, however, keeps the image in place in the background (see Figure 8-10). So if you want to place your company's logo in the upper-left corner of the web page, and keep it there even if the viewer scrolls, then you can create a style like this:

```
body {
    background-image: url(images/logo.gif);
    background-repeat: no-repeat;
    background-attachment: fixed;
}
```

The `fixed` option is also very nice when using a repeating, tiled background. When you have to scroll, the page's text disappears off the top, but the background doesn't move: The page content appears to float gracefully above the background.

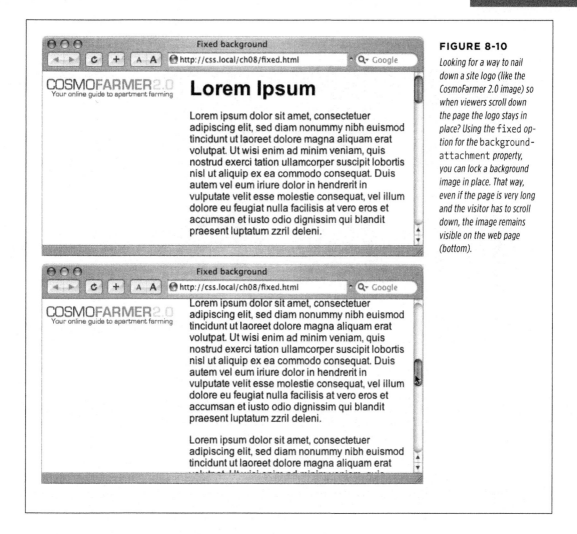

FIGURE 8-10

Looking for a way to nail down a site logo (like the CosmoFarmer 2.0 image) so when viewers scroll down the page the logo stays in place? Using the fixed *option for the* background-attachment *property, you can lock a background image in place. That way, even if the page is very long and the visitor has to scroll down, the image remains visible on the web page (bottom).*

Defining the Origin and Clipping for a Background

CSS includes the ability to tell a browser where the background image should begin in relation to the border, padding, and content of an element. For example, normally when you tile an image, it starts in the upper-left corner of the padding of an element (see the top, middle image in Figure 8-11). However, you can reposition that image's starting point, using the background-origin property. It takes one of three values:

- **border-box** places the image in the upper-left corner of the area assigned to the border (top-left in Figure 8-11).

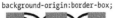

`background-origin:border-box;`

`background-origin:padding-box;`

`background-origin:content-box;`

FIGURE 8-11

The background-clip *property also applies to background colors. If you've added a non-solid border (like dotted, dashed, or double), the background color normally shows behind the border in the empty areas. However, to limit that color to just inside the border you would simply set the element's* background-clip *property to* padding-box.

`background-clip:border-box;;`

`background-clip:padding-box;`

`background-clip:content-box;`

- **padding-box** places the image in the upper-left corner of the area assigned to the padding (top-middle in Figure 8-11). This is normally where a browser places a background image.

- **content-box** places the image in the upper-left corner of the area assigned to the content (top-right in Figure 8-11).

Of course, this setting doesn't matter if there's neither a border nor any padding around an element; in addition, the effect can be very subtle, especially if you have a seamlessly tiling pattern.

NOTE Neither the background-origin nor the background-clip properties work in Internet Explorer 8 and earlier.

However, it can be noticeable if you're not repeating an image. For example, if you choose the no-repeat option (page 234) and the background image appears only a single time, you could place that image in the upper-left corner of the content area (inside any padding) like this:

```
background-image: url(logo.png);
background-repeat: no-repeat;
background-origin: content-box;
```

In addition, the background-origin property can be used effectively with another property—background-clip. The background-clip property limits the area where the background image appears. Normally, background images fill the entire area of an element including behind borders and padding areas (bottom-left in Figure 8-10). However, you can specify where the image appears with one of three values:

- **border-box** lets the image appear behind the content all the way behind any borders. You'll notice this only if you have borders with visible gaps like a dashed line (bottom-left in Figure 8-11). This is normally what browsers do, so there's no real reason to use this setting.

- **padding-box** limits any background to just the padding area and the element's content (bottom-middle in Figure 8-11). This is useful if you have a border that's dotted or dashed and you don't want the image to appear in the border's gaps.

- **content-box** limits the background to just the content area. The padding and the area behind the border will be free of any image (bottom-right in Figure 8-11).

By combining background-origin and background-clip, you can make sure that an image begins in the upper-left of the content area and appears only behind content like this:

```
background-origin: content-box;
background-clip: content-box;
```

Scaling Background Images

Normally, an image placed in the background of a page element is place at the size you created it. However, the background-size property lets you control the size of a background image. You have the option of using values or keywords to set the size:

- Supply a height and width value to set the size of the image. You can use an absolute value like a pixel value:

  ```
  background-size: 100px 200px;
  ```

  This code sets the background image to 100 pixels wide and 200 pixels tall. You can also set the value of just the width or height and set the other to auto:

  ```
  background-size: 100px auto;
  ```

  In this case, the background image is 100 pixels wide, and the browser automatically sets the height to keep the aspect ratio of the image intact (so it isn't distorted). You can also use percentage values. If you want the image to scale to completely fit the background, you can use 100% for both settings (Figure 8-11, left):

  ```
  background-size: 100% 100%;
  ```

- The contain keyword forces the image to resize to fit the background space of the page element while maintaining the aspect ratio of the image (Figure 8-10, middle). Depending on the shape of the image and the element, the image is stretched to fit either the width or height of the element.

  ```
  background-size: contain;
  ```

- The cover keyword forces the width of the image to fit the width of the element and the height of the image to fit the height of the element, without changing the aspect ratio of the image. (Figure 8-1, right).

  ```
  background-size: cover;
  ```

The background-size property almost always ends up resizing the original image: If the image is smaller than the elements, the browser scales the image up, usually resulting in noticeable pixelation and degradation of the image (as with the background images in Figure 8-12).

FIGURE 8-12

The background-size *property is the only way to change the size of a background image. Keep in mind that while most browsers understand this property, Internet Explorer 8 doesn't, so use it with care. (Or, if you don't care about IE8, then use it with reckless abandon).*

TIP Using the background-size property can be especially helpful when you're working with elements that are sized using percentages, such as the responsive designs discussed in Chapter 14. For example, if you put an image into the background of a banner that's 960 pixels when viewed on a desktop monitor but shrinks down to 480 when viewed on a phone, you can place a large background image in the banner and use this setting:

```
background-size: 100% auto;
```

This forces the web browser to resize the image to fit as the banner shrinks to a thinner size.

Bring Special Effects to Background Images

If you're a power user of photo-editing software like Photoshop, you've probably taken a look at the blend modes that let you transform how two layers interact visually. Here's an example of how they work: Imagine you have a photo placed in the background of an element. You've also set a background color for that element. Normally, any image that doesn't have any transparency will cover up the background color beneath.

But what if you could blend the image and background together? For example, say you wanted to let the background color show through but *only* in the white parts of the photo. The relatively new background-blend-mode lets you do just that. You apply the property to an element with a background color and image. The property takes one of 16 different blend mode values, each with a different effect on the mixture.

In another example, say you had a photo of a tomato placed into the background of a div and you want the orange color to mix with the photo. You could set the background color to orange and then set the blend mode like this:

```
background-image: url(tomato.png);
background-color: orange;
background-blend-mode: screen;
```

You can even use blend modes with multiple image backgrounds (page 249) to create some very interesting visual effects.

For a video explaining how blend-modes work in Photoshop, check out *www.youtube.com/watch?v=BnI1CJV17q4*. Even though this video is talking about Photoshop, they are the same blend modes with the same effects as the CSS background-blend-mode property.

For a visual demonstration on how blend modes work in CSS, visit *http://sarasoueidan.com/blog/compositing-and-blending-in-css/*. (No version of Internet Explorer supports this property yet.)

■ Using Background Property Shorthand

As you can see from the examples in the previous section, to really take control of background images you need to harness the power of several different background properties. But typing out each property—background-image, background-attachment, and so on—again and again can really take its toll on your hands. Fortunately, there's an easier way—the background shorthand property.

You can actually bundle all the background properties (including the background-color property) into a single line of streamlined CSS. Simply type background followed by the values for background-image, background-position, background-size, background-repeat, background-origin, background-clip, background-attachment, and background-color.

NOTE Internet Explorer 8 does not understand the background-size, background-origin, and background-clip properties. If you use them in the shorthand background property, IE8 will ignore the rule and not apply any background properties to the element.

The following style adds a graphic in the center of the page, resizes the image to 50% its size, places just one image (no-repeat), fixes the image into place (so if the page scrolls, the image stays) and sets the background color to white:

```css
body {
   background: url(bullseye.gif) center center / 50% no-repeat fixed #FFF;
}
```

If you specify a position (the center center, for example, in the code example directly above) and a background-size property (the 50% in the example), you separate them with a / character.

You don't need to specify all the property values either, and you usually won't. You can use one or any combination of them. For example, background: yellow is the equivalent of background-color: yellow. Any property value you leave out simply reverts to its normal behavior, so say you specify only an image:

```css
background: url(image/bullseye.gif);
```

That's the equivalent of this:

```css
background: url(image/bullseye.gif) left top / 100% repeat scroll border-box
border-box transparent;
```

This behavior of resetting non-defined values to their default values can lead you to some unexpected results. For example, say you add these two declarations to a style:

```css
background-color: yellow;
background: url(image/bullseye.gif) no-repeat;
```

You may expect to see a single bull's-eye image sitting atop a yellow background color. But you won't, because a browser resets the background-color to transparent (invisible) when it encounters the background property with no color specified. To get around this predicament, you need to specify the background-color second, like this:

```css
background: url(image/bullseye.gif) no-repeat;
background-color: yellow;
```

In addition, when multiple styles apply to the same element, you can inadvertently end up wiping out background images. For example, say you want to add a background image to every paragraph on a page, so you create a style like this:

```css
p {
   background: url(icon.png) left top no-repeat rgb(0,30,0);
}
```

You then decide you'd like the first paragraph after every h2 to have a blue background, so you create this:

```css
h2 + p {
   background: blue;
}
```

This second style uses the shorthand, which resets all the other background properties to their defaults. In the case of an image, the default is no image at all, so rather than simply adding a blue background to the paragraph and leaving the image in place, this style actually erases the image!

In other words, the background shorthand property can help you write less code, but it can also get you into trouble, so just keep this behavior in mind.

FREQUENTLY ASKED QUESTION

Finding Free Imagery

I'm not an artist. I can't draw, can't paint, don't even own a digital camera. Where can I find artwork for my site?

Thank goodness for the Web. It's the one-stop shop for creative geniuses who couldn't paint themselves into a corner if they tried. There are plenty of pay-to-download sites for stock photos and illustrations, but there are also quite a few completely free options.

Foter (*http://foter.com*) claims to let you access of 228 millions free stock photos. This site aggregates Creative Commons licensed photos from around the web. It even provides a free WordPress plug-in to make it easy to add stock images to your blogs. Unsplash (*https://unsplash.com*) doesn't have millions of photos, but the ones you find there are stunning—beautiful photos of nature, architecture, and animals for free.

morgueFile (*www.morguefile.com*), despite the grisly name, has many wonderful photos supplied free of charge by people who love to take pictures. Free Images (*www.freeimages.com*) is yet another excellent photographic resource. Openphoto (*http://openphoto.net*) also supplies images based on Creative Commons licenses, and you can use the search engine on the Creative Commons website to find images (and video and music) that can be used in personal and commercial projects:

http://search.creativecommons.org. In addition, you can use Flickr (*www.flickr.com/creativecommons*) to search for images that have a Creative Commons license applied to them. (Although they don't cost money, not all photos on these sites can be used in commercial projects. Make sure you read the fine print for any photo you wish to use.)

If you're looking for bullets to add to lists, icons to supercharge your navigation bar, or patterns to fill the screen, there are plenty of sites to choose from. Flaticon (*http://www.flaticon. com*) claims to provide access to the largest database of free vector icons available for use in illustration programs, but you can also use them in your web pages as PNG and SVG files. Some Random Dude (no, really, that's the name of the website) offers a set of 121 icons free of charge: *www.somerandomdude.com/work/sanscons/*. And if you're looking for interesting tiling patterns, check out the patterns on these sites: ColourLovers. com (*www.colourlovers.com/patterns*), Pattern4u (*www.koll-ermedia.at/pattern4u*), and Squidfingers (*http://squidfingers. com/patterns*). Or make your own tiled backgrounds with these online pattern creators: BgPatterns (*http://bgpatterns. com*), Stripe Generator 2.0 (*www.stripegenerator.com*), and PatternCooler (*www.patterncooler.com*).

Using Multiple Background Images

While one background image is fine, being able to layer multiple images in a background has its uses. For example, say you want to add a background image to a sidebar to make it look like a scroll (Figure 8-13). If you simply place a single image in the background, it might work at first (top-left in Figure 8-13), but if you add a lot of text inside that sidebar, it won't look so good (top-right in Figure 8-13). That's because the image is one size and it won't grow or shrink to accommodate the size of the sidebar.

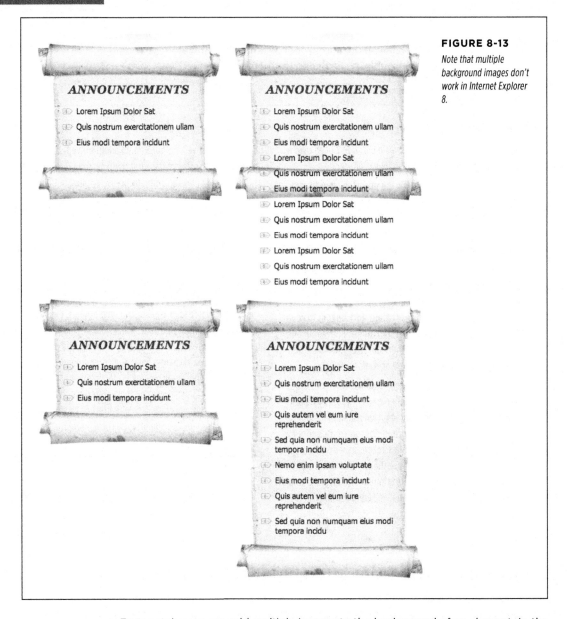

FIGURE 8-13

Note that multiple background images don't work in Internet Explorer 8.

Fortunately, you can add multiple images to the background of an element. In the scroll example, you can use three background images: one for the top of the scroll, one for the bottom of the scroll, and one for its text area. That last image is a seamlessly tiling image, so as the sidebar gets taller, the image simply tiles to fit the space.

Of course, you can use multiple images for simpler tasks as well. For example, say you want to add a colorful, richly textured image to the background of an element, and you also want to add a two-color logo. As discussed in the box on page 233, JPEG is a better format when an image has lots of colors, while PNG8 is better for areas of solid color like a logo. In this case, you can have the best of both worlds by using a JPEG for the colorful background and a PNG8 for the logo.

For multiple background images, simply use the background-image property with a comma-separated list of images, like this:

```
background-image: url(scrollTop.jpg),
                  url(scrollBottom.jpg),
                  url(scrollMiddle.jpg);
```

NOTE In this example code, each URL is listed on its own line, but you don't have to do it that way. You could type this all out in one single (really long) line. However, most designers find it easier to read if you place each image on its own line and use spaces (or tabs) to indent the following lines to line up. Just keep in mind that you need a comma after each image specified, except the last, which requires the usual semicolon necessary to end a declaration.

Because background images normally tile, you'll usually need to include a background-repeat property as well (if you don't, then the images would just tile one on top of the other, hiding all images underneath.) You can add other background properties as well, with a similarly comma-separated set of values, like this:

```
background-repeat: no-repeat,
                   no-repeat,
                   repeat-y;
```

When using multiple values like this, the first value (no-repeat in this example) goes with the first image listed in the background-image property (*scrollTop.png*); the second goes with the second image listed, and so on. Because this can get confusing quickly, many web designers use the shorthand method to specify multiple images, like this:

```
background: url(scrollTop.jpg) center top no-repeat,
            url(scrollBottom.jpg) center bottom no-repeat,
            url(scrollMiddle.jpg) center top repeat-y;
```

NOTE Multiple background images stack on top of one another, like layers in an image-editing program. The order in which you list the background images determines which image appears on top. The first image listed is on the element's top layer, the second is on the second layer, and the last is on the bottom layer. In the preceding example code, the top of the scroll (*scrollTop.jpg*) is above the bottom of the scroll (*scrollBottom.jpg*), which in turn sits above the text area of the scroll (*scrollMiddle.jpg*).

■ Utilizing Gradient Backgrounds

Gradients—smooth transitions of color from blue to red or black to white—are common staples of any image-editing program. Creating subtle shifts from one similar color to another creates a kind of misty quality; Apple uses gradients on buttons and other user interface elements in their OS X and iPhone software. It used to be that you had to open Photoshop and create a huge image file with the gradient you were after. Now you can let the browser create gradients for you.

CSS supports background gradients, which are, basically, images created on the fly by a web browser. In fact, you use the usual `background-image` property to create the gradient. You have several types of gradients to choose from.

Linear Gradients

The most basic type of gradient is a linear gradient. It moves along a straight line drawn across the element, transitioning from one color to another (see Figure 8-14). You specify a direction in either degrees, or using the keyword `to` followed by the keyword `top`, `bottom`, `right`, `left`, or a combination, like `to bottom left`.

FIGURE 8-14

Linear gradients let you bypass the old method of adding gradients to an element's background of an element: Create the gradient as a graphic in Photoshop or Fireworks, and then use the `background-image` *property to place that graphic in the background of the element.*

For example, to create a gradient that starts out with black on the left edge of an element and then transitions to white on the far right, you'd write this:

```
background-image: linear-gradient(to right, black, white);
```

To make the gradient start black at the top of the element and transition to white at the bottom of the element, use the `to bottom` keywords, like this:

```
background-image: linear-gradient(to bottom, black, white);
```

You can also paint a transition at an angle by using keywords like to bottom right to indicate the direction of the gradient. For example to draw a gradient that starts as orange in the top left of the element, then ends as red in the bottom right of the element, you'd write this:

```
background-image: linear-gradient(to bottom right, orange, red);
```

You can create a gradient by using any CSS color value (page 148), such as keywords like white or black, hexadecimal values like #000000, RGB values like rgb(0,0,0), and so on.

You're not limited to keywords, either. You can specify a degree value that specifies the direction of the gradient. Degrees are written with a number from 0 to 360 followed by deg and indicate where the transition ends (Figure 8-15). For example, 0deg is the top of the element, so the gradient starts at the bottom and ends at the top. In other words, this:

```
background-image: linear-gradient(to top, black, white);
```

is the same as:

```
background-image: linear-gradient(0deg, black, white);
```

The degree values continue clockwise, so 90deg is the right edge of the element (the same as to right), 180deg is the bottom of the element (the same as to bottom), and 270deg is the left side of the element (the same as to left).

When using a degree value, a browser draws an imaginary line through the middle of the element. The angle you specify is the angle of that line and also indicates where the gradient ends. For example, the gradient pictured in Figure 8-15, has a degree value of 48deg. The browser draws an imaginary line through the middle of the element, pointing to the 48-degree mark. This means the gradient starts at the element's bottom left, and moves upward to the top right.

For example, the gradient created in the bottom-left image in Figure 8-13 uses this declaration:

```
background-image: linear-gradient(135deg, rgb(0,0,0), rgb(204,204,204));
```

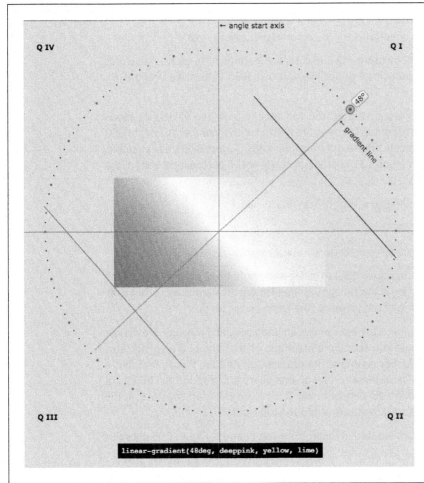

FIGURE 8-15

The degree value you supply for a linear gradient is used to create a line that passes through the middle of an imaginary point in the center of the element. The gradient is drawn along this line. The value dictates the slope of the gradient and where the gradient stops. You can use the interactive demo at http://codepen. io/thebabydino/full/ qgoBL to see how different degree values affect a gradient.

COLOR STOPS

The gradients you've seen so far use only two colors, but you can add as many as you like. The additional colors are called *color stops*, and they let the background transition from one color to a second color, then from that second color to a third color, and so on, until the final color ends the gradient. To add color stops, simply add more color values to the gradient. For example, the bottom-right image in Figure 8-14 contains three colors: black to white to black:

```
background-image: linear-gradient(to right, black, white, black);
```

Of course, you can use any color values (expressed as keywords, hexadecimal, or RGB) and even mix and match them, so you can even write the preceding line of code like this:

```
background-image: linear-gradient(to right, black, rgb(255,255,255), #FFFFFF,
HSL(0,0%,0%));
```

Web browsers evenly spread out the colors, so in this example the far left starts out black; the background of the middle of the element is white; and then the far right of the element is black. However, you can place the different color stops at more specific locations in the background by adding a second value after the color.

TIP You can get some really wild effects if you add the background-position property to an element with a gradient background. Essentially, you can change what the browser considers to be the starting point for the gradient. Try it out.

For example, say you want to start at a deep red, then quickly ramp up to a burnt orange about 10 percent into the element, stay at that orange color for most of the element, and then quickly ramp back down to deep red, like the top image in Figure 8-16. To do this, you'd use four color stops—red, orange, orange and red—and specify where the two white stops should be positioned:

```
background-image: linear-gradient(to right, #900, #FC0 10%, #FC0 90%, #900);
```

Notice that the 10% applies to the second color (the orange): This tells the browser that it needs to get to this color at 10 percent of the width of the element. Likewise, the 90% indicates that the browser needs to stay at that orange color until it's 90 percent across the element, and then begin the transition to the deep red at the far right of the element.

NOTE You don't have to use percentages to place color stops. You can use pixels or ems as well. However, percentages are more flexible and adapt as the width or height of an element changes. One exception is the repeating linear gradients discussed on page 257. Pixel values for stops are very useful for creating these types of tiled gradients.

You don't need to use any values for the first or last color, since the browser assumes that the first color starts at 0% and the last color ends at 100%. However, if you wanted to keep a solid starting color further into the element, you could provide a value after the first color. For example, the bottom image in Figure 8-16 is created with this declaration:

```
background-image: linear-gradient(to right, #900 20%, #FC0 30%, #FC0 70%, #900
80%);
```

Notice that the first color—#900—also has a position of 20%. This means that the first 20 percent of the element (from left to right) should be a solid red color. Then, at the 20 percent point, the gradient should begin transitioning to the orange color at 30 percent.

TIP You can use the keyword `transparent` for any color in a gradient if you want to see through the gradient to whatever lies below—like a background color set on the element, or even another linear gradient. Remember, you can have multiple background images on an element, so you can have multiple gradients on an element as well. For example, try out this code for an amazing effect:

```
background-image:
    linear-gradient(cyan,transparent),
    linear-gradient(225deg, magenta, transparent),
    linear-gradient(45deg, yellow, transparent);
```

FIGURE 8-16

You can specify where the color stops appear in a linear gradient. In the top example, a dark red color transitions quickly from the left to an orange color at 10 percent of the width of the element. To create a large solid color area in the middle, you need two color stops with the same color value. Basically, a gradient from one color to the same color is no gradient at all.

■ INTERNET EXPLORER SUPPORT

Gradients are not supported in Internet Explorer 9 and earlier. If you do choose to use gradients, then you should provide a backup color for IE9 and earlier. Find a solid color that matches the general tone of your gradient and declare it first, followed by the gradient declarations, like this:

```
background-color: #FC0;
background-image: linear-gradient(to bottom, #900, #FC0, #900);
```

IE9 will apply the background color, and since it doesn't understand linear gradients, it will skip the other declarations. Other browsers will apply the background color, but also create a gradient that covers the background color. If you're using RGBA colors with some level of transparency, then you won't want the background color to show through. In this case, use the background shorthand property instead, and the background-color will be overridden (thanks to the peculiar behavior of the background shorthand property discussed on page 247). So you can use this code for RGBA colors:

```
background-color: #FC0;
background: linear-gradient(to bottom, rgba(153,0,0,.5), #FC0,
rgba(153,0,0,.5));
```

Repeating Linear Gradients

Normally, a linear gradient fills the entire element with the first color at one point and the last color at the opposite edge of the element. However, it's possible to create repeating gradients so you can create gradient patterns. In essence, you define a gradient with specified color stops; the browser draws the gradient, and then repeats that pattern, tiling it in the background of the element. For example, to get the repeating gradient of the left image in Figure 8-17 you can write this code:

```
background-image: repeating-linear-gradient(45deg, #900 20px, #FC0 30px, #900
40px)
```

In cases like this, using pixel values for the color stops is very useful. In essence, the browser draws a gradient that starts at bottom-left; it starts with 20 pixels of deep red, then transitions to an orange at 30 pixels, and then goes back to deep red at 40 pixels. Once it's drawn that gradient, the browser simply tiles it in the background like a tiled image.

NOTE   There's plenty of room for experimentation with gradients. To see just a few of the amazing things that are possible, visit the CSS3 pattern gallery at *http://lea.verou.me/css3patterns/*, *www.standardista.com/cssgradients/*, the amazing use of gradients to create flags of the world at *www.standardista.com/CSS3gradients/flags.html*, and a see some amazing gradients used with the background-blend mode property discussed in the box on page 247 at *http://bennettfeely.com/gradients/*.

You can even use repeating gradients to create solid stripes without any of the fancy and subtle transitions between colors. For example, the image on the right in Figure 8-16 is created with this declaration:

```
background-image: repeating-linear-gradient(45deg, #900 0, #900 10px, #FC0
10px, #FC0 20px);
```

Here, you start with deep red (#900) at the 0 point, and go to red again at the 10px point. Since you're transitioning between the same colors, the browser draws this as a solid color. Next, you transition to orange (#FC0) at 10 pixels. Since that's the same spot at which the red ends, that's not a subtle transition; the pattern just goes from red to orange. Finally, the transition goes to the same orange at 20 pixels, creating another solid line. Because this is a repeating linear gradient, the browser simply tiles that pattern to fill the background of the element.

Again, repeating linear gradients work in most browsers, but not in IE9 and earlier. So it's a good idea to add a fallback background color:

```
background-color: #FC0;
background: repeating-linear-gradient(to bottom left, #900 20px, #FC0 30px,
#900 40px)
```

FIGURE 8-17

You can create striped patterns using CSS's repeating linear gradients. You can make stripes that form sharp lines, or that are fuzzy at the edges, by using different color stops.

Radial Gradients

CSS also provides a way of creating radial gradients—gradients that radiate outward in a circular or elliptical pattern (see Figure 8-18). The syntax is similar to linear gradients and at its most simple, you need only to provide a beginning color (the color at the middle of the gradient) and an ending color (the color at the end of the gradient). For example, the top-left image in Figure 8-18 is created with this code:

```
background-image: radial-gradient(red, blue);
```

This creates an elliptical shape that fits the height and width of the element, with the center of the gradient (the beginning red) in the center of the element.

You can also make circular gradients by adding a `circle` keyword before the colors. For example, the top-right image in Figure 8-19 is created with this code:

```
background-image: radial-gradient(circle, red, blue);
```

While a browser normally draws the center of a radial gradient in the center of the element, you can position the gradient's center by using keyword at followed by the same positioning keywords and values you use for the `background-position` property (page 236). For example, in the middle-left image in Figure 8-17, the radial gradient begins 20 percent over from the left edge of the element and 40 percent from the top of the element. The positioning values go before the color and shape keyword, like this:

```
background-image: radial-gradient(circle at 20% 40%, red, blue);
```

To dictate the size of the gradient, you can use one of four keywords:

- The **closest-side** keyword tells the browser to make the gradient extend from the center only as far as the side that's closest to the center. For example, in the middle-left image in Figure 8-18, the closest side to the center of the gradient is the top edge, so the radius of the circle travels from the center of the circle to this edge. This keeps the entire gradient within the element. Here is the code to produce this gradient:

  ```
  background-image: radial-gradient(closest-side circle at 20% 40%, red,
  blue);
  ```

  When `closest-side` is applied to an elliptical gradient, both closest sides (that is, the top or bottom and the left or right sides) are used to calculate the x and y radii of the ellipse.

- The **closest-corner** keyword measures the width of the gradient from its center to the corner of the element that's closest (middle-right in Figure 8-18). This can mean that the gradient may overflow the element. For example, the circle drawn on top of the middle-right image in Figure 8-17 demonstrates the actual size of the gradient. Part of the gradient extends beyond the element:

  ```
  background-image: radial-gradient(closest-corner circle at 20% 40%, red,
  blue);
  ```

- The **farthest-side** keyword measures the radius of a circle from its middle to the side of the element that's farthest away. In the case of an elliptical gradient, it's the distance from the center to either the farthest top or bottom side and the farthest left or right side. Here is the code to produce the image in the bottom-left of Figure 8-18:

  ```
  background-image: radial-gradient(farthest-side circle at 20% 40%, red,
  blue);
  ```

• The **farthest-corner** keyword measures the radius of a circle from its middle to the corner of the element that's farthest away. Here is the code to produce the image in the bottom-right of Figure 8-18:

```
background-image:  radial-gradient(farthest-corner circle at 20% 40%, red,
blue);
```

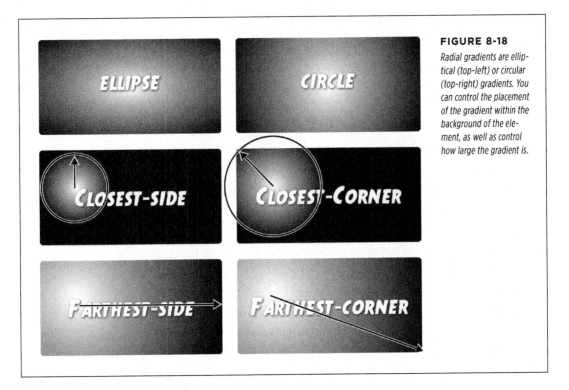

FIGURE 8-18

Radial gradients are elliptical (top-left) or circular (top-right) gradients. You can control the placement of the gradient within the background of the element, as well as control how large the gradient is.

As with linear gradients, you can use multiple color stops and set the placement of those color stops. For example, say you want a circular gradient that was composed of a bright red, an orange, and a yellow. You want the red to appear for a while before it transitions to orange, and then the orange lasts a while longer until the yellow appears at the end. You can use percentage values to dictate where the colors appear:

```
background-image: radial-gradient(circle at 20% 40%, red 20%, orange 80%, yel-
low);
```

Of course, as with linear gradients you can use any valid CSS color values, so you can rewrite this code as:

```
background-image: radial-gradient(circle at 20% 40%, rgb(255,0,0) 20%,
rgb(255,165,0) 80%, #FFFF00);
```

As with linear gradients, Internet Explorer 9 and earlier won't know what you're talking about if you use a radial gradient. You should add a backup background color:

```
background-color: red;
background: radial-gradient(circle at 20% 40%, red 20%, orange 80%, yellow);
```

Repeating Radial Gradients

As with linear gradients, you can create radial gradients that repeat—perfect for that bull's eye look, or when you wish to hypnotize your website visitors. You need to make sure you add either percentages or actual pixel or em values for the various color stops so the browser knows the size of a single radial gradient and can then repeat it. For example:

```
background-image: repeating-radial-gradient(circle, red 20px, orange 30px,
yellow 40px, red 50px);
```

Note that to create a smooth-looking repeating radial gradient, you should end with the same color you start with (red, in this example). This provides a smooth color change back to the original color. If you don't (for example, if you just ended with the yellow color in the above code), then there's a sharp line where the last color ends and the first color of the repeated gradient begins.

TIP Because web browsers treat linear and radial gradients simply as background images, you can use the other properties of background images, like background-size, background-position, and so on with them. In addition, you can have multiple comma-separated gradients on a single style, just as you can have multiple background images (page 249). In fact, you can mix images with gradients in the same element.

◼ Tutorial: Enhancing Images

A photo gallery is a perfect example of an eye-catching web page. This tutorial brings together a variety of image styling techniques. You'll format images with frames and captions, create a photo gallery that's flexible enough to look great in a variety of window sizes, and use the box-shadow property (page 201) to create professional-looking drop shadows.

To get started, you need to download the tutorial files located on this book's companion website at *https://github.com/sawmac/css_mm_4e*. Click the tutorial link and download the files. All of the files are enclosed in a zip archive, so you need to unzip them first. (There are detailed instructions on the website.) The files for this tutorial are in the *08* folder.

Framing an Image

You'll be working on a basic web page from the fictional (just in case you thought it was real) website CosmoFarmer.com (Figure 8-19). In this case, there's already an external style sheet attached to the page, adding some basic text formatting.

1. **Launch a web browser and open the file** *08→01_image_ex→image.html.*

FIGURE 8-19

Before and after—CSS, that is. If you rely just on HTML, images take up lots of space (top). With a little CSS (bottom) you can nicely frame an image and move it out of the way.

2. **Open the file *styles.css* in the *01_image_ex* folder in your favorite text editor.**

   This file is the external style sheet used by the *image.html* file. You'll start by adding a class style to this style sheet, and then applying a class to the <img> tag in the HTML file.

3. **Scroll to the bottom of the file, and then type the following:**

   ```
   img.figure {

   }
   ```

   The selector *img.figure* targets any <img> tag with the figure class applied to it. You'll use this to selectively format only the images you want. (You could also just name the style .figure—the only difference is that that style would then apply to *any* tag with the class figure, not just images.)

4. **Add float and margin properties to the style you just created, like so:**

   ```
   float: right;
   margin: 10px;
   ```

   The right float moves the image to the right side of the page, letting the text move up and wrap around the photo's left edge. The margins give the photo a little breathing room and move it away from the text, the side of the page, and the headline above. Next, you'll add a border, a background color, and some padding to make the image look more like a real snapshot.

5. **Add border, background color, and padding, so that the finished style looks like this:**

   ```
   img.figure {
     float: right;
     margin: 10px;
     border: 1px solid #666;
     background-color: #CCC;
     padding: 10px;
   }
   ```

   If you save this file and then preview the web page right now, you won't see a change, since the class style has no effect until you've added the class to a tag.

6. **Save and close the *styles.css* file and open the *image.html* file. Locate the <img> tag and add class="figure" so the tag looks like this:**

   ```
   <img src="../images/grass.jpg" alt="Apartment Grass" width="200"
   height="200" class="figure">
   ```

   Now that image takes on all of the formatting properties you defined for the .figure class style.

7. **Preview the page in a web browser. It should look like the bottom image in Figure 8-19.**

A picture may be worth a thousand words, but sometimes you still need a few words to explain a picture. So in the next part of this tutorial, you'll add a caption below the photo.

You'll frequently want to add a caption to an image or photo to provide more information about the subject, where the photo was taken, and so on. Instead of just floating the image, as you did in the previous exercise, you want the caption text to float as well. The best way to float both is to wrap the image and the text in a container that's floated as a single unit. This method keeps the photo and its related text together. If you decide later that you want to change their layout—perhaps float them to the left—no problem: You simply change the formatting for the entire container.

Fortunately, HTML includes two tags for just such a requirement: The <figure> tag is intended to enclose an image that's meant to be an illustrative figure. In addition, the <figcaption> tag can be used to enclose—you guessed it—a figure caption. First, you need to adjust some of the HTML.

8. **Return to your text editor and the *image.html* file. Locate the** <img> **tag in the code and remove the** class="figure" **that you added in step 6. Add** <figure> **before the** <img> **tag.**

This marks the beginning of the container. Now you'll add the caption and close the <figure> to indicate the end of the container.

9. **After the** <img> **tag, add the code in bold below, so the HTML looks like this:**

```
<figure>
<img src="../images/grass.jpg" alt="Creeping Bentgrass" width="200"
height="200">
<figcaption>Figure 1: Creeping Bentgrass is best suited for outdoor use
andshould be avoided by the indoor farmer.
</figcaption>
</figure>
```

10. **Return to the *styles.css* file. Scroll to the bottom of the file and delete the** img.figure **style you created earlier.**

You'll add a new style for the figure element.

11. **Add this style to the *styles.css* file:**

```
figure {
  float: right;
  width: 222px;
  margin: 15px 10px 5px 10px;
}
```

You've already used the float: right; property in the previous tutorial, and the margin adds a little white space around all four edges of the <figure> tag. But what's the *width* for, you ask. Although the photo has a set width (200 pixels), the caption paragraph doesn't. When you don't set a width, the paragraph makes the <figure> expand wider than the photo. In this case, you want the caption to be just as wide as the photo and its frame.

The 222-pixel value comes from a little math used to calculate the entire area taken up by the photo on the page: The photo is only 200 pixels wide. But in the next step you'll create a style that adds 10 pixels of left and right padding, as well as a 1-pixel left border and 1-pixel right border, to make the entire width of the photo 222 pixels from border to border (see page 204 for a refresher on how to calculate the width of an element).

12. **Add this style to the *styles.css* file:**

```
figure img {
  border: 1px solid #666;
  background-color: #CCC;
  padding: 10px;
}
```

This descendant selector affects any <img> tag *inside* a <figure> tag. Since you're using a descendant selector here, you don't need to add a class to the <img> tag. Next, you'll style the caption.

13. **Add the following style to the *styles.css* style sheet:**

```
figcaption {
  font: bold 1em/normal Verdana, Arial, Helvetica, sans-serif;
  color: #333;
  text-align: center;
}
```

This style uses some of the properties you learned about in Chapter 6 to create a center-aligned, bold, and gray caption using the Verdana font. Fortunately, the font shorthand property in the first line lets you roll four different properties into a single style declaration.

To make the caption stand out even more, add a background color and border.

14. **Add three properties to the** figcaption **style, like so:**

```
figcaption {
  font: bold 1em/normal Verdana, Arial, Helvetica, sans-serif;
  color: #333;
  text-align: center;
  background-image: linear-gradient(to bottom, #e6f3ff, white);
  border: 1px dashed #666;
  padding: 5px;
}
```

The purpose of the background-image, border, and padding properties should be clear—to create a colored box around the caption. We're using the linear gradient feature of the background-image property (page 231) to create a gradient that changes from light blue to white in the background of the caption. Now it's time to preview your work.

15. **Save both the *image.html* and *styles.css* files and preview the *image.html* file in a web browser.**

Now you see one reason why it's easier to develop a design using an internal style sheet—you need to work in and save only one file instead of two. The page should look like Figure 8-20. (You can find a completed version of this page in the *08_finished→01_image_ex* folder.)

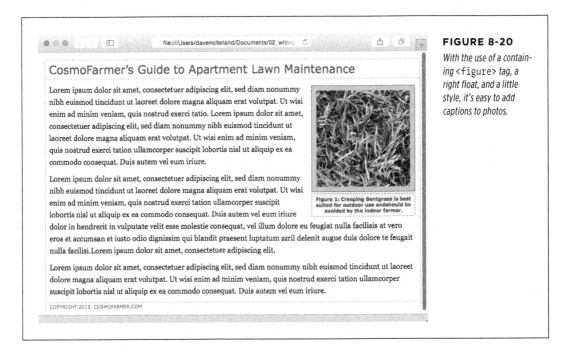

FIGURE 8-20

With the use of a containing <figure> tag, a right float, and a little style, it's easy to add captions to photos.

Tutorial: Creating a Photo Gallery

Folks used to rely on the HTML <table> tag to create rows and columns for holding the pictures in a photo gallery. But you can achieve the same effect with a little CSS and far less HTML.

1. **Open the file *08→02_gallery_ex→gallery.html*.**

First, a quick review of the HTML used to construct the photo gallery. The page contains six photos and photo captions. Each photo and caption is contained in a <figure>. The photo itself is an <img> tag and the caption is inside a <figcaption> tag.

```
<figure>
  <img src="../images/dandelion.jpg" alt="Dandelion" height="200"
width="200"/>
  <figcaption>Figure 6: The dandelion: scourge of the apartment farmer.
</figcaption>
</figure>
```

If you preview the page now, you'll see a series of photos stacked one on top of the next—not very attractive. The gallery would look nicer if the photos sat next to each other in rows upon rows. You can accomplish that with just a few styles.

2. **Open the *styles.css* file.**

This style sheet already contains a basic CSS reset and a few styles for the headline and other text. First you'll add a couple of styles for the photos and their captions.

3. **At the bottom of the *styles.css* file, add two new styles, as follows:**

```
figure img {
  border: 1px solid #666;
  background-color: #FFF;
  padding: 4px;
}

figcaption {
  font: 1.1em Arial, Helvetica, sans-serif;
  text-align: center;
  margin: 10px 0 0 0;
}
```

These two styles add a border to each image in the gallery, and set the font, alignment, and margins of the captions. The first is a descendant selector to target just the images inside the figures.

Next, place the photos side by side.

4. **Add the following style to the style sheet:**

```
figure {
  float: left;
  width: 210px;
  margin: 0 10px 10px 10px;
}
```

This style floats each photo/caption pair to the left. In effect, it places the photos side by side until there's no more room in the row. The browser then drops the next photos down a row, until all of the photos are displayed one row on top of the next. The width is the *total* width of the photo plus padding and borders. In this example, it's 200 pixels for the photo, 8 pixels for left and right padding, and 2 pixels for left and right borders.

5. **Save the *styles.css* file and preview the *gallery.html* page in a web browser. It should look like the left image in Figure 8-21.**

Adjust the width of your browser window to make it thinner and wider and watch how the images reflow into the space. Aha—something's not quite right. The second row of images has two empty spaces where photos should be. This problem occurs because the caption for the second image on the first line is taller than the other captions on the line. Images that jump down to another row bump into that caption and can't get by it. (You can read more about this float property snafu on page 414.) Fortunately, there's a simple fix to this dilemma.

FIGURE 8-21

Floating elements next to each other is one way to simulate the column and row appearance of a table. But it doesn't work well if the elements are of varying heights (left). Using display: inline-block *is another way to force elements to sit side by side (right) without the nasty dropping behavior pictured in the left image.*

6. **Return to your text editor and the *styles.css* file. Locate the** figure **style. Remove the** float:left **and add** display: inline-block; vertical-align: top. **The finished style should look like this:**

```
figure {
  display: inline-block;
  vertical-align: top;
  width: 210px;
  margin: 0 10px 10px 10px;
}
```

The display: inline-block property (page 192) treats each image/caption pair as a block (a box with height and width) but also as an inline element (so the blocks can sit side by side). In addition, the vertical-align property set to top makes sure that each <figure> tag aligns to the top of all the other <figure> tags in a row.

7. **Save the file and preview the page in a web browser. See the right side of Figure 8-21.**

If you resize the browser window, the gallery reformats itself. With a wider window you can fit four or even five images on a row, but if you make it smaller you'll see only one or two images per row.

Adding Drop Shadows

Your gallery looks good, but you can make it even more impressive. Adding drop shadows under each photo lends the page an illusion of depth and a realistic 3-D quality. But before you fire up Photoshop, you'll be glad to know there's no need to add individual drop shadows. Instead, you can make CSS automatically add a shadow to any image you want.

1. **In a text editor, return to the *styles.css* file you've been working on.**

You'll update the img style you created before.

2. **Add** box-shadow: 2px 2px 4px rgba(0,0,0,.5); **at the end of the** figure img **style so it looks like this (changes in bold):**

```
figure img {
  border: 1px solid #666;
  background-color: #FFF;
  padding: 4px;
  box-shadow: 2px 2px 4px rgba(0,0,0,.5);
}
```

You learned about the box-shadow property back on page 201. Here you've added a shadow that extends 2 pixels to the right of the image, 2 pixels below the image, and which spreads out 4 pixels. Using an RGBA color (page 149), you can set the shadow to 50 percent transparent black color.

3. **Save the file and preview the page. It should look like Figure 8-22.**

Each image has its own drop shadow, and you didn't even have to open Photoshop!

You can find a completed version of this tutorial in the *08_finished→02_gallery_ex* folder.

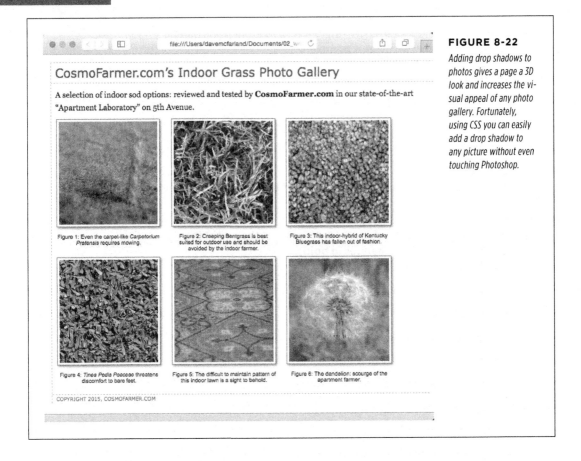

FIGURE 8-22

Adding drop shadows to photos gives a page a 3D look and increases the visual appeal of any photo gallery. Fortunately, using CSS you can easily add a drop shadow to any picture without even touching Photoshop.

■ Tutorial: Using Background Images

The CSS *background-image* property is the secret weapon of modern web design. It can turn a ho-hum, text-heavy web page into a dazzling swirl of imagery (see Figure 8-23). Since you can use it to add an image to the background of any HTML tag, the designs you can create are limited only by your imagination. The drop shadow example in the previous tutorial is just one example of creative background image use. Other common background image frills include applying a page background and adding custom bullets to unordered lists. You'll explore some of these common tasks in this tutorial.

Adding an Image to the Page Background

Whether it's an intricate pattern, a logo, or a full-screen photograph, images appear in the background of many web pages. In fact, adding an image to the background of a page is probably the most common application of the background-image property.

1. **In your text editor, open the file *08→03_bg_ex→bg_images.html.***

   This page is a basic two-column layout: a very simple page, with some text formatted on a white background (Figure 8-23, left). To start, you'll add a linear gradient to the page. The page has an external style sheet with the basic formatting. You'll use that style sheet to add new styles.

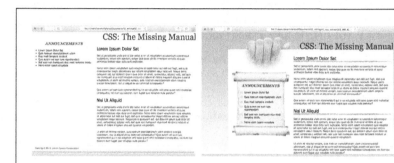

FIGURE 8-23

Using background images, you can make an already well-organized page (left) look much spiffier (right). Since you can add images to the background of any tag on a page, the possible placement of graphics on a page are nearly limitless.

2. **Open the *styles.css* file. At the bottom of the page, add the following style:**

   ```css
   html {
     background-image: linear-gradient(to bottom, rgb(176,194,213), white 700px);
   }
   ```

   This code adds a linear gradient (page 252) that transitions from a blue color at the top of the browser window to white 700px from the top.

3. **Save the CSS file and preview the *bg_images.html* file in a web browser.**

   Something weird is happening here. The gradient runs from blue to white, then repeats again, blue to white, which is not what you want. To prevent the image from tiling, you can tell the browser to make the HTML tag fill the browser window by setting its height to 100%.

4. **In the *styles.css* file add one more property (addition in bold):**

   ```css
   html {
     height: 100%;
     background-image: linear-gradient(to bottom, rgb(176,194,213), white 700px);
   }
   ```

Now, if you save the CSS file and preview the *bg_images.html* file, the background graphic's blue gradient drips down the page but doesn't repeat. Not bad looking, but the blue also appears in the text's background. You can make the text pop by giving its background a different color.

5. **Return to your text editor and the *style.css* file. Add another style for the <div> containing the content of the page:**

```
.wrapper {
  background-color: #FFF;
}
```

The wrapper div is a fixed width, centered in the middle of the page, containing all of the page's text. This style gives it a white background, but with the help of an image, you can do better than that.

6. **Edit the style you created in step 5 by adding a background image:**

```
.wrapper {
  background-color: #FFF;
  background-image: url(images/bg_main.jpg);
  background-position: left top;
  background-repeat: no-repeat;
}
```

These three lines of code add a background image to the top-left of the <div>; the no-repeat option for the background-repeat property means the image only appears a single time. If you save the file and preview it in a web browser, you'll now see the picture of a hand acting like it's holding the page. Very cool. The only problem is the text is too far up, covering up the image. You'll next push down the top headline and the left sidebar.

7. **Add two more styles to the style sheet:**

```
.banner {
 margin-top: 48px;
}
.announcement {
 margin-top: 115px;
}
```

The first line just adds a bit of padding, pushing down the banner containing the headline until it just touches the top of the white page, while the second style moves the left sidebar down enough to clear the picture of the hand. The page should now look like Figure 8-24.

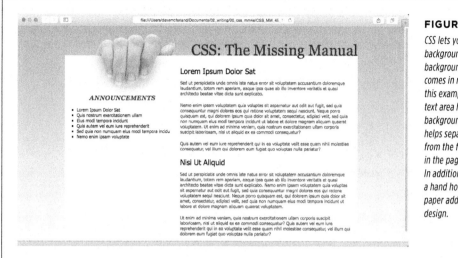

FIGURE 8-24

CSS lets you combine a background color and a background image, which comes in really handy in this example. The main text area has a white background color that helps separate the text from the fading gradation in the page's background. In addition, a graphic of a hand holding a piece of paper adds depth to the design.

Replacing Borders with Graphics

The border property is a useful tool in your design arsenal, but the limited number of border styles CSS offers can get boring. A hand-drawn line with a little texture would catch your visitors' attention better than a plain, straight one. You can skip the border property and add any kind of line you want as a background image—easy as pie. In this part of the tutorial, you'll replace the underline below each <h2> tag in the main text area with a custom graphic that looks like a hand-drawn line.

1. **Return to your text editor and the *styles.css* file. Add a style for the** <h2> **tags inside the main** <div> **tag:**

    ```
    .main h2 {
      background-image: url(images/underline.png);
      background-repeat: no-repeat;
    }
    ```

    The background-image property specifies which graphic to use in the background of <h2> tags inside any tag with a class of main, whereas the no-repeat value makes sure the graphic only appears a single time.

    If you preview the file now, you'll see that the underline doesn't exactly line up. In fact, it isn't *under* at all. It's above the headlines!

2. **Add the following style declaration to the** .main h2 **style below the** background-repeat **property:**

    ```
    background-position: left bottom;
    ```

You've changed the graphic's starting location so it appears at the left edge and bottom of the <h2> tags. If you preview the page now, though, you may not notice much improvement. The underline runs *into* the headline text.

But there's an easy fix. Since the bottom value used here puts the graphic at the bottom of the block created by the <h2> tag, you need only to increase the overall height of the block to move the line down a bit. You'll do this with a little bottom padding.

3. **Edit the** .main h2 **style one last time, so that it looks like this:**

```
.main h2 {
  background-image: url(images/underline.png);
  background-repeat: no-repeat;
  background-position: left bottom;
  padding-bottom: 7px;
}
```

Padding, as you'll recall from page 187, is the space between the border (the edge of the background as well) and the content. It also increases the overall height of the box—in this case, by adding 7 pixels of bottom padding. Now, the line graphic is placed at the bottom of the h2 block, but in the empty space created by the bottom padding.

4. **Save the style sheet and preview the** *bg_images.html* **file in a web browser.**

Each <h2> tag has the hand-drawn underline. Next you'll tackle the sidebar box, making it look a little less boxy and jazzing up the bulleted lists.

Using Graphics for Bulleted Lists

The average bullet used for unordered lists is a black dot—not very inspiring. But you can use the background-image property to replace those drab bullets with any image you want. The first step is to hide the bullets that normally appear beside list items.

1. **Return to your text editor and the** *styles.css file*. **Add a style for formatting the list items in the left sidebar.**

```
.announcement li {
  list-style: none;
}
```

The bulleted list is inside a <div> with a class of announcement, so this descendant selector targets just the list items (<li> tags) inside that div. The style removes the bullet. Now add the graphic.

> **NOTE** Applying list-style: none; to a style affecting the <ul> or <ol> tags will also remove all of the bullets (or numbers) from list items.

2. **Add the following two properties to the** .announcement li **style:**

```
background-image: url(images/bullet.png);
background-repeat: no-repeat;
```

You've seen these two properties before. They add an image to the background and turn off repeating so that the graphic appears only once.

If you preview the page, you'll see that the bullets currently overlap the list text and the list items are a little jammed together (Figure 8-25, top). A little padding and margin will fix this.

3. **Add two more properties to the** .announcement li **style:**

```
padding-left: 25px;
margin-bottom: 10px;
```

The left padding adds empty space, effectively moving the text out of the way in order to display the new bullet icon. The bottom margin adds just a bit of breathing room between each list item (Figure 8-25, middle).

There's just one final flaw. The bullet image is a tad too high on the line, causing the tip of the icon to stick out too far above the text. But you can easily fix that with the background-position property.

4. **Finish this style by adding** background-position: 0px 4px;. **The completed style should look like this:**

```
.announcement li {
  list-style: none;
  background-image: url(images/bullet.png);
  background-repeat: no-repeat;
  background-position: 0 4px;
  padding-left: 25px;
  margin-bottom: 10px;
}
```

This last style declaration positions the bullet icon to the far left (that's the 0) and 4 pixels from the top (4px) of the list item. It moves the icon down just a smidgen, enough to make the bullet look perfect.

NOTE As discussed on page 171, this kind of exact positioning is precisely why you should use the background property instead of the list-style-image property for adding graphic bullets to your lists.

---

5. **Save the file and preview the page in your browser.**

The list should now have 3D tabs with red exclamation marks instead of dreary black circles (Figure 8-25, bottom).

ANNOUNCEMENTS

Lorem Ipsum Dolor Sat
Quis nostrum exercitationem ullam
Eius modi tempora incidunt
Quis autem vel eum iure reprehenderit
Sed quia non numquam eius modi tempora incidu
Nemo enim ipsam voluptate

FIGURE 8-25

Replacing regular black bullets with your own graphics is easy. Just a few extra steps ensure the bullets and text are placed in the correct location.

ANNOUNCEMENTS

- Lorem Ipsum Dolor Sat

- Quis nostrum exercitationem ullam

- Eius modi tempora incidunt

- Quis autem vel eum iure reprehenderit

- Sed quia non numquam eius modi tempora incidu

- Nemo enim ipsam voluptate

ANNOUNCEMENTS

- Lorem Ipsum Dolor Sat

- Quis nostrum exercitationem ullam

- Eius modi tempora incidunt

- Quis autem vel eum iure reprehenderit

- Sed quia non numquam eius modi tempora incidu

- Nemo enim ipsam voluptate

Giving the Sidebar Personality

At this point, the sidebar looks pretty good. The text is nicely formatted, and the bullets look great, but the sidebar gets a little lost in the sea of white. Adding a background image can make the sidebar stand out in a whimsical way. You could use a single image—the scroll image pictured in the right image of Figure 8-23—in the background of the <div> tag, but in order to make sure the text fits exactly on the scroll, you'd have to limit the amount of content you put in the sidebar. Too much text and it won't fit on top of the single image (like at top-left, back in Figure 8-12); too little, and there will be too much empty space on the graphic.

A more flexible approach would let the image grow as the sidebar acquires more content (bottom-right in Figure 8-12). Fortunately, since CSS allows multiple background images, this trick is easy to pull off.

1. **Return to your text editor and the *styles.css* file. Locate the** .announcement **style you added in Step 7 on page 272 and add one additional property:**

```
.announcement {
    background: url(images/scroll_top.jpg) no-repeat center top,
      url(images/scroll_bottom.jpg) no-repeat center bottom,
      url(images/scroll_middle.jpg) repeat-y center top;
    margin-top: 115px;
}
```

Yes, that's only one property—the background property—but it has three different images. The order in which you list these images is important, since they stack on top of each other. In this case, the first image is the top of the scroll; it only appears once (no-repeat) at the top and center. The second image is the bottom of the scroll; it also only appears once, but at the bottom of the div. Finally, the middle part of the scroll—scroll_middle.jpg—will be layered underneath the other two images (since it appears last in the list), and it's repeated along the y-axis (up and down), so if the <div> gets taller, the image simply tiles to fill the space.

If you preview the page, you'll see a few problems. First, the text appears on top of the rolled up top and bottom parts of the scroll. A little padding will fix that.

2. **Update the** .announcement **style to add top and bottom padding. Make the changes listed in bold below:**

```
.announcement {
    background: url(images/scroll_top.jpg) no-repeat center top,
        url(images/scroll_bottom.jpg) no-repeat center bottom,
        url(images/scroll_middle.jpg) repeat-y center top;
    padding: 70px 0 60px 0;
    margin-top: 115px;
}
```

Another problem is that the bulleted list sticks out on both the left and right sides of the sidebar image. To make the bulleted list fit on the scroll, you need to add some left and right margin.

3. **Locate the** .announcement li **style you created earlier and add two proper-ties to the end so it looks like this:**

```
.announcement li {
    list-style: none;
    background-image: url(images/bullet.png);
    background-repeat: no-repeat;
    background-position: 0 4px;
    padding-left: 25px;
    margin-bottom: 10px;
    margin-left: 30px;
    margin-right: 40px;
}
```

These properties move both the left and right edges of each bulleted item in enough to clear the edges of the background image.

4. **Save the file and preview it in a web browser.**

The page should look like the right image in Figure 8-23. With just a few images and some CSS magic it's easy to bring boring web pages to life.

Sprucing Up Your Site's Navigation

I t's safe to say that without links there'd be no Web. The ability to be on one page, and then click something onscreen and suddenly see a page on a computer half a world away is what makes the Web so useful. Links are also how your visitors navigate their way around your website. That's why web designers agonize over making their links look good and work properly.

In this chapter, you'll learn how to style links to make them stand out from other text. You can also make your links provide visual cues so your site's visitors can see where they are—and where they've been. You'll learn how to use CSS to create onscreen buttons and navigation bars just like the pros use. And in the tutorial section, you'll get some hands-on experience creating a full set of navigation features that work in all browsers.

■ Selecting Which Links to Style

As always in CSS, you have to select something before you can style it. For links, you need to tell CSS not only *what* you want to style, but also *when* you want that style to apply. Web browsers keep track of how a visitor interacts with links, and then displays that link differently depending on the link's status, or *state*. When you use a CSS link selector, you can target a specific link state as well.

Understanding Link States

Most browsers recognize four basic link states: an unvisited link, a link that's been visited already (meaning the URL is stored in the browser's history), a link that the visitor's mouse is poised over, and a link that's being clicked. As described in Chapter

3, CSS gives you four pseudo-class selectors to accompany these states—:link, :visited, :hover, and :active. Using them, you can apply different formatting to each state, so there's no doubt in your visitors' minds whether they've been there or done that.

> **NOTE** Browsers also recognize a pseudo-class called :focus. Links get :focus when visitors use the keyboard to tab to them. This pseudo-class is also fun to use with form text fields, as you'll see in the forms tutorial on page 375.

Suppose you want to change the text color for an unvisited link from boring browser blue to vivid orange. Add this style:

```
a:link { color: #F60; }
```

Once someone has clicked that link, its state changes to visited, and its color changes to the purple used by most browsers. To change that color to deep red, use this style:

```
a:visited { color: #900; }
```

> **TIP** When you want to provide a style that applies to all link states—for example, use the same font and font size for all link states—then style the HTML <a> tag by creating a generic a selector. You can then use the specific link state styles—a:visited, for example—to change the color or in some other way customize the look of just that state.

WORD TO THE WISE

Limits on Visitation

Due to privacy concerns, browsers place severe limits on which CSS properties you can apply to the :visited pseudo class. As it turns out, years ago some nefarious types had figured out how to use JavaScript to read changes in the style of :visited links to determine which sites people had visited. For example, by loading a new background image for visited links, you can determine whether a visitor has been to Paypal.com,

eBay.com, BankofAmerica.com, or not-safe-for-work.com. Because of that potential problem, you're limited to styling the color, background-color, and border-color of visited links—and only if you've already given the normal states of those links a color, background color, or border color. In other words, you can't do much with the :visited pseudo-class.

The :hover pseudo-class offers many creative possibilities; you'll learn quite a few later in this chapter. It lets you completely alter the look of a link when a visitor moves her mouse over it. If you've used cumbersome JavaScript to make graphic buttons change when a mouse hovers over them, you'll love being able to create the same effect with CSS alone. But to start with a simple example, this style changes the color of a link as a mouse passes over it:

```
a:hover { color: #F33; }
```

TIP Be careful when adding CSS properties to the :hover pseudo-class. Properties that change the size of the hovered element might affect other elements around it. For example, if you increase the font size of a hovered text link, when moused over, the link text will grow, pushing other elements out of the way. The effect can be jarring.

And finally, if you're one of those obsessive-compulsive designers who leave no design stone unturned, you can even change the look of a link for the few milliseconds when a visitor is actually clicking it. Here's how:

```
a:active {color: #B2F511; }
```

In most cases, you'll probably have a generic a style, :visited, and :hover styles in your style sheets. For maximum design control you may want to style all the different states. But for that to work, you must specify the links in a particular order: link, visited, hover, and active. Use this easy mnemonic to remember it: **LoV**e/ **HA**te. So here's the proper way to add all four link styles:

```
a:link { color: #F60; }
a:visited { color: #900; }
a:hover { color: #F33; }
a:active {color: #B2F511; }
```

If you change the order, the hover and active states won't work. For example, if you put a:hover before a:link and a:visited, then the color change won't take effect when hovering.

NOTE Why does the order matter? That would be thanks to our friend the cascade (see Chapter 5). All those styles have the same specificity, so the order in which they appear in the code determines the style that wins out. A link can be both *unvisited* and *hovered over*. So if the a:link style comes last in the code, then it wins, and the color from a:hover never gets applied.

Targeting Particular Links

The styles in the previous section are basic <a> tag styles. They target certain link states, but they style *all* links on a page. What if you want to style some links one way and some links another way? A simple solution is to apply a class to particular link tags. Say you have a bunch of links within the body of an article, some of which point to sites that you want to highlight (for example, links to websites belonging to your friends, business associates, or sponsors). You may want to identify these links so people know they're special and are more likely to click them. In this case, you can apply a class to these external links, like this:

```
<a href="http://www.hydroponicsonline.com" class="sponsor">Visit this great
resource</a>
```

To style this link in its own way, you'd create styles like this:

```
a.sponsor { font-family: Arial, sans-serif; }
a.sponsor:link { color: #F60; }
a.sponsor:visited { color: #900; }
a.sponsor:hover { color: #F33; }
a.sponsor:active {color: #B2F511; }
```

Leaving off the a and only specifying the class works too:

```
.sponsor { font-family: Arial, sans-serif; }
.sponsor:link { color: #F60; }
.sponsor:visited { color: #900; }
.sponsor:hover { color: #F33; }
.sponsor:active {color: #B2F511; }
```

Now only those links with a class of "sponsor" will get this formatting.

> **NOTE** These examples change only the links' colors, but that's just to make it simple for demonstration purposes. You can use *any* CSS property to format links (except :visited links, as explained in the box on page 280). As you'll see in the next section, you have lots of creative ways to style links.

Grouping links with descendant selectors

If a bunch of links appear together in one area of a page, you can also save time by using *descendant selectors*. Say you have five links that lead to the main sections of your site. They represent your main navigation bar, so you want to give them a distinctive look. Just wrap those links in the HTML <nav> tag. Now you have an easy way to identify and format just those links:

```
nav a { font-family: Arial, sans-serif; }
nav a:link { color: #F60; }
nav a:visited { color: #900; }
nav a:hover { color: #F33; }
nav a:active {color: #B2F511; }
```

Alternatively, you can use a <div> tag and add a class to that div: <div class="mainNav">:

```
.mainNav a { font-family: Arial, sans-serif; }
.mainNav a:link { color: #F60; }
.mainNav a:visited { color: #900; }
.mainNav a:hover { color: #F33; }
.mainNav a:active {color: #B2F511; }
```

Using descendant selectors, it's easy to style links differently for different areas of a web page. (See page 582 in Chapter 18 for a thorough discussion of the power of descendant selectors.)

TIP It's very common to use bulleted lists to present links (you'll see an example of this technique on page 289). In this case, you can add an ID or class to the `<ul>` tag for the list—`<ul class="mainNav">`, for example—then create descendant selectors like `.mainNav a:link` to style them.

■ Styling Links

Now that you know how to create a selector that targets links, how should you style them? Any way you want! There aren't any CSS properties intended just for links. You have access to all CSS properties, so you're limited only by your imagination. Just make sure your links look like links. Not that they need to be blue and underlined, but links must look different from non-link text so visitors know they can click them.

If you make a link look like a button—adding a border, including a background, and making it change color when moused over—most people will understand they can click it. Or use a linear gradient (page 252) to add texture and depth to a link. Likewise, links that appear in long passages of text should look clearly distinct. You can make links stand out by bolding the text, keeping the traditional underline, coloring the background, or adding a hover style. You can even add a graphic (like an arrow) that provides a clear visual cue that clicking the text takes you somewhere else.

Underlining Links

Since the beginning of the Web, vibrant blue, underlined text has signaled, "Click here to go there." But that underline and color are often the first two things a designer wants to change. Underlines are such a common way to mark a link that they're boring (#1 in Figure 9-1). Fortunately, you can do several things to eliminate or improve on the standard underline, while still ensuring that your links are identifiable:

- **Remove the underline entirely.** To eliminate the regular underline, use the `text-decoration` property and the none value:

```
a {text-decoration: none;}
```

  Of course, removing the underline completely can confuse your visitors. Unless you provide other visual cues, your links look exactly the same as all the other text (#2 in Figure 9-1). So if you go this route, then make sure you highlight the links in some other way, like making link text bold (#3 in Figure 9-1), coloring the background, adding an informative graphic, or making the link look like a button (page 285).

- **Underline when mousing over.** Some designers remove underlines for all links, highlight them in some other way, and then add the underlines back when the visitor moves his mouse over the link (#4 in Figure 9-1). To do so, simply remove the underline for links, and then reintroduce it using the `:hover` pseudo-class:

```
a {
  text-decoration: none;
  background-color: #F00;
}
a:hover {
  background-color: transparent;
  text-decoration: underline;
}
```

Normal Link
Lorem ipsum dolor sit amet, consectetuer adipiscing elit, sed diam nonummy nibh euismod <u>tincidunt ut laoreet dolore</u> magna aliquam erat volutpat. Ut wisi enim ad minim veniam, quis nostrud exerci tation ullamcorper suscipit lobortis nisl ut aliquip ex ea commodo consequat. Duis autem vel eum iriure d

No Underline
Lorem ipsum dolor sit amet, consectetuer adipiscing elit, sed diam nonummy nibh euismod tincidunt ut laoreet dolore magna aliquam erat volutpat. Ut wisi enim ad minim veniam, quis nostrud exerci tation ullamcorper suscipit lobortis nisl ut aliquip ex ea commodo consequat. Duis autem vel eum iriure d

No Underline Highlight
Lorem ipsum dolor sit amet, consectetuer adipiscing elit, sed diam nonummy nibh euismod **tincidunt ut laoreet dolore** magna aliquam erat volutpat. Ut wisi enim ad minim veniam, quis nostrud exerci tation ullamcorper suscipit lobortis nisl ut aliquip ex ea commodo consequat. Duis autem vel eum iriure d

Underline on Hover
Lorem ipsum dolor sit amet, consectetuer adipiscing elit, sed diam nonummy nibh euismod **tincidunt ut laoreet dolore** magna aliquam erat volutpat. Ut wisi enim ad minim veniam, quis nostrud exerci tation ullamcorper suscipit lobortis nisl ut aliquip ex ea commodo consequat. Duis autem vel eum iriure d

Bottom Border
Lorem ipsum dolor sit amet, consectetuer adipiscing elit, sed diam nonummy nibh euismod tincidunt ut laoreet dolore magna aliquam erat volutpat. Ut wisi enim ad minim veniam, quis nostrud exerci tation ullamcorper suscipit lobortis nisl ut aliquip ex ea commodo consequat. Duis autem vel eum iriure d

Background Image
Lorem ipsum dolor sit amet, consectetuer adipiscing elit, sed diam nonummy nibh euismod tincidunt ut laoreet dolore magna aliquam erat volutpat. Ut wisi enim ad minim veniam, quis nostrud exerci tation ullamcorper suscipit lobortis nisl ut aliquip ex ea commodo consequat. Duis autem vel eum iriure d

FIGURE 9-1

You have plenty of ways to make the boring line (1) under links more exciting. Start by removing the link entirely (2, 3) and replacing it only when the visitor mouses over the link (4). Better yet, create a more stylized link by using the border *property (5) or a background image (6).*

- **Use a bottom border.** You can't control the color, width, or style of a regular link underline. It's always a solid, 1-pixel line in the same color as the link text. For greater variety, use the border-bottom property instead (#5 in Figure 9-1). Hiding the normal underline and adding a dashed-line border looks like this:

```
a {
  text-decoration: none;
  border-bottom: dashed 2px #9F3;
}
```

You can alter the style, width, and color of the border. To put more space between the text and the border, use the padding property.

- **Use a background image.** You can customize the look of links even further by using a graphical line. For example, #6 in Figure 9-1 uses a graphic that looks like a hand-drawn line. There's a similar technique for underlining headlines in the Chapter 8 tutorial (page 273). Start by creating an underline graphic using a program like Fireworks or Photoshop, which have brush tools that simulate the look of a crayon, felt-tip marker, or whatever. Next, create a style for the link that removes the normal underline and adds a background image. Make sure the graphic repeats horizontally and is positioned at the bottom of the link. You may also need to add a little bottom padding to position the line. Here's an example:

```
a {
  text-decoration: none;
  background: url(images/underline.gif) repeat-x left bottom;
  padding-bottom: 5px;
}
```

Creating a Button

You can also make links look like the buttons in the dialog boxes and toolbars you see in desktop programs. Buttons look great in navigation bars, but you can also use them for any small (one- or two-word) links on your pages. Your main allies in this task are the border, background-color, and padding properties. With them, it's easy to create a wide range of boxy-looking buttons (see Figure 9-2).

Say you added a class to a link that you'd like to style as a button: <a href="stale. html" class="button">Free Donuts Here!</a>. To add a basic black outline around this link (like the top-left image in Figure 9-2), you'd create this style:

```
a.button {
  border: solid 1px rgb(0,0,0);
}
```

You can get fancier by adding a background color as well, like so:

```
a.button {
  border: solid 1px rgb(0,0,0);
  background-color: rgb(51,51,51);
}
```

NOTE In these examples, both a.button or .button would work for style names. In the case of a.button, the style only applies to <a> tags with the class button, while .button applies to any tag with that class name. If you want to make sure the style only applies to a particular tag, then add the tag name to the beginning. Adding the tag name is also a helpful reminder when looking over your CSS code—it provides a valuable clue as to what the style is intended to format. When you see a.button, it's clear that the style is aimed at particular links.

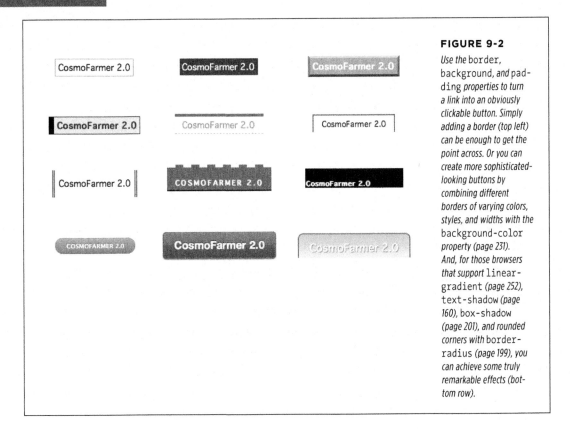

FIGURE 9-2

Use the border, background, *and* pad-ding *properties to turn a link into an obviously clickable button. Simply adding a border (top left) can be enough to get the point across. Or you can create more sophisticated-looking buttons by combining different borders of varying colors, styles, and widths with the* background-color *property (page 231). And, for those browsers that support* linear-gradient *(page 252),* text-shadow *(page 160),* box-shadow *(page 201), and rounded corners with* border-radius *(page 199), you can achieve some truly remarkable effects (bottom row).*

Mind you, all four borders don't need to be the same width, type, or color. You don't even have to have four borders. One common design technique is to add a beveled look to a button using four different border colors, as shown at top right in Figure 9-2. Creating the beveled look isn't difficult, but you need to remember what makes something look three-dimensional—the light source. Imagine a light shining on one of the four sides: That side is the lightest, while the side opposite is the darkest (since the raised button is blocking the light and putting that side into a "shadow"). The other two sides should have shades in between the "lit" and "shadow" borders. Here's the CSS used to create the beveled design in the top-right corner of Figure 9-2:

```
a.button {
    background: #B1B1B1;
    color: #FFF;
    font-weight: bold;
    border-width: 4px;
    border-style: solid;
    border-top-color: #DFDFDF;
    border-right-color: #666;
```

```
    border-bottom-color: #333;
    border-left-color: #858585;
}
```

Keep in mind that you can (and probably should) create a :hover state for your buttons as well. That way, your buttons can react when a visitor moves her mouse over the link, providing useful visual feedback. In the case of a beveled button, reversing the various colors—make a dark background lighter, a light border darker, and so on—is very effective.

Using linear gradients, rounded corners, or box and text shadows can really add depth to a button. For example, the button in the bottom middle of Figure 9-2 is created with this code:

```
background-color: #ee432e;
background-image: -webkit-linear-gradient(top, #ee432e 0%, #c63929 50%,
#b51700 50%, #891100 100%);
background-image: -moz-linear-gradient(top, #ee432e 0%, #c63929 50%, #b51700
50%, #891100 100%);
background-image: -o-linear-gradient(top, #ee432e 0%, #c63929 50%, #b51700
50%, #891100 100%);
background-image: linear-gradient(top, #ee432e 0%, #c63929 50%, #b51700 50%,
#891100 100%);
border: 1px solid #951100;
border-radius: 5px;
box-shadow: inset 0px 0px 0px 1px rgba(255, 115, 100, 0.4), 0 1px 3px #333333;
padding: 12px 20px 14px 20px;
text-decoration: none;
color: #fff;
font: bold 20px/1 "helvetica neue", helvetica, arial, sans-serif;
text-align: center;
text-shadow: 0px -1px 1px rgba(0, 0, 0, 0.8);
```

Line 1 sets a deep red background color; this color is provided for browsers that don't understand linear gradients (IE9 and earlier as well as other older browsers). Lines 2–5 set up a linear gradient for various browsers. Line 6 adds a simple border, while line 7 creates the rounded corners and line 8 adds a subtle inset shadow and a second drop shadow below the button; in other words, it applies two drop shadows, which is perfectly legal, as described on page 249. Line 9 adds padding to provide space around the button text and the button border, while line 10 removes the underline that normally appears below links. The last lines set properties for the text in the button, including its color, font, alignment, and text shadow.

TIP   Creating great-looking buttons often involves piling on the CSS properties (as you can tell from the above code). If you need a little help creating all that code, check out the not-so-humble Best CSS Button Generator at *http://www.bestcssbuttongenerator.com*. To see other great examples of CSS buttons, visit *http://www.freshdesign-web.com/css3-buttons.html* and *http://tympanus.net/codrops/2012/01/11/css-buttons-with-pseudo-elements/*.

Using Graphics

Adding graphics to links is one of the easiest and most visually exciting ways to spruce up your site's navigation. There are any number of possible techniques and designs, but none of the good ones involve an HTML <img> tag. Instead, you can easily add attractive and informative imagery to any link using the CSS background-image property. You can see several examples in Figure 9-3. (You'll also learn more advanced techniques for using images to create graphical buttons and rollovers starting on page 298.)

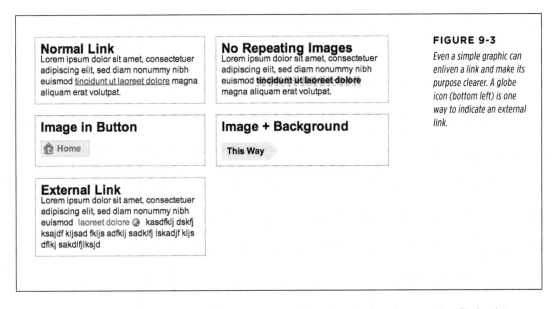

FIGURE 9-3

Even a simple graphic can enliven a link and make its purpose clearer. A globe icon (bottom left) is one way to indicate an external link.

If you need a refresher on background-image and related properties, flip back to page 231. Meanwhile, here are a few things to keep in mind when you use images with links:

- **Don't forget** no-repeat. Normally a background graphic tiles repeatedly in the background. With many graphics, that effect looks awful for links (top right, Figure 9-3). Unless you're using a subtle pattern like a gradient fill, remember to set the repeat option to stop the tiling like this: background-repeat: no-repeat;.

- **Control placement with** background-position. To place an image accurately in the background, use the background-position property (page 236). When you want to place an image on the far-right edge of a link but centered vertically on the line, use this CSS: background-position: right center.

For more accurate placement, use a specific value such as pixels or ems. These units of measurement make it easy to scoot a graphic a couple of pixels away from the left edge of the link. By combining these units with a percentage value, you can easily center a graphic vertically within a link but place it an exact amount away from the left edge: background-position: 10px 50%;.

TIP In positioning background images, the first value is the horizontal placement (left to right); the second is vertical placement (top to bottom).

Unfortunately, there's no way to exactly place an image from the right or bottom edges. So if you want to move an image in from the right edge a bit, then you have two options: First, in your image-editing program, you can add empty space to the right edge of the graphic. The amount of empty space you add should be equivalent to how much you want to indent that graphic from the right. Once you've created the graphic, use the `background-position` property to place the graphic on the right edge of the element: for example, `background-position: right top;`. Or you can use percentage values: `background-position: 90% 75%;` places the point that lies 90 percent from the left edge of the image on top of the point 90 percent from the left edge of the styled element. As you can imagine, this method doesn't provide complete accuracy, so you'll need to experiment a little. (See page 236 for more on how percentage positioning works.)

- **Padding gives you room.** If you're using an image or icon to mark a link, then make sure to add padding on the side the image is on to move the link text out of the way. For instance, the third example in Figure 9-3 has 30 pixels of left padding to prevent the word "Home" from overlapping the picture of the house, while a little right padding makes room for the globe in the bottom-left image.

NOTE Since the `<a>` tag is an inline element, adding top and bottom padding (or, for that matter, top and bottom margins) has no effect. See page 192 for the reason why. You can, however, turn a link into a block-level element (`display: block`) so it can accept top and bottom padding and margins, or use the `inline-block` setting (`display: inline-block`). You'll see both of these techniques later in this chapter.

- **Use the pseudo-classes.** Don't forget the `:hover` and `:visited` pseudo-classes. They can add great dynamic effects and provide helpful feedback about your links. You can swap in a *different* background graphic for any of these pseudo-classes. So you could, for example, have a dim lightbulb graphic in the background of a normal link but change that graphic to a lit bulb when the mouse travels over it.

Should you decide to use a graphic for a link's `:hover` state, keep in mind that browsers don't download the graphic until your visitor's mouse actually hovers over the link, so there'll be a noticeable delay before the graphic appears. Once the graphic is downloaded, however, the delay goes away. See page 298 for a technique to prevent this awkward problem.

Building Navigation Bars

Every site needs good navigation features to guide visitors to the information they're after—and help them find their way back. Most sites are organized in sections, such as Products, Contact Info, Corporate Blog, and so on. This structure lets visitors know what information to expect and where they can find it. Much of the time, you find links to a site's principal sections in a *navigation bar*. CSS makes it easy to create a great-looking navigation bar, rollover effects and all.

Using Unordered Lists

At heart, a navigation bar is nothing more than a bunch of links. More specifically, it's actually a *list* of the different sections of a site. Back in Chapter 1, you learned HTML's mission is to provide meaningful structure to your content. Accordingly, you should always use a tag that's appropriate to the meaning of that content. For a list of items, that's the <ul> or unordered list tag—the same one you use to create bulleted lists. It doesn't matter whether you want your list to have *no* bullets or to stretch horizontally across the top of the page: You can do all that by styling the <ul> tag with CSS. Figure 9-4 shows an example.

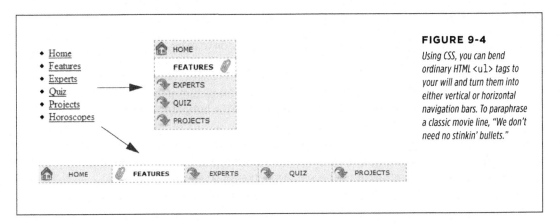

FIGURE 9-4

Using CSS, you can bend ordinary HTML <ul> tags to your will and turn them into either vertical or horizontal navigation bars. To paraphrase a classic movie line, "We don't need no stinkin' bullets."

The HTML for a nav bar is straightforward. There's a single link inside each individual list item. Also, you need a way to style just that unordered list. (You don't want *actual* lists of items to look like navigation bars.) Applying a class or id to the <ul> tag is a good approach:

```
<ul class="nav">
<li><a href="index.html">Home</a></li>
<li><a href="news.html">News</a></li>
<li><a href="reviews.html">Reviews</a></li>
</ul>
```

The CSS varies a bit depending on whether you want a horizontal or vertical navigation bar. In either case, you need to do two things:

- **Remove the bullets.** Unless the navigation bar is supposed to look like a bulleted list, remove the bullets by setting the list-style-type property to none:

```
ul.nav {
  list-style-type: none;
}
```

- **Eliminate padding and margins.** Since browsers indent list items from the left, you need to remove this added space as well. Some browsers do the indenting using padding, and others use margin, so you need to set both to 0:

```
ul.nav {
  list-style-type: none;
  padding-left: 0;
  margin-left: 0;
}
```

These two steps essentially make each list item look like any plain old block-level element, such as a paragraph or headline (except that a browser doesn't insert margins between list items). At this point, you can begin styling the links. If you want a vertical navigation bar, read on; for horizontal nav bars, see page 293.

Vertical Navigation Bars

A vertical navigation bar is just a bunch of links stacked one on top of the next. Removing the bullets, left margin, and padding (as explained in the previous section) gets you most of the way there, but you need to know a few additional tricks to get things looking right:

1. **Display the link as a block.**

   Since the <a> tag is an inline element, it's only as wide as the content inside it. Buttons with different length text (like Home and Our Products) are different widths. The staggered appearance of different width buttons stacked on top of each other doesn't look good, as you can see in #1 in Figure 9-5. In addition, top and bottom padding and margins have no effect on inline elements. To get around these limitations, style the link as a block element:

   ```
   ul.nav a {
     display: block;
   }
   ```

   The block value not only makes each button the same width, but it also makes the entire area of the link clickable. That way, when your visitors click areas where there's no link text (like the padding around the link), they still trigger the link.

2. **Constrain the width of the buttons.**

   Making links block-level elements also means they're as wide as the tag they're nested in. So when they're just sitting in a page, those links stretch the width of the browser window (#2 in Figure 9-5). You have several ways to make them a little narrower. First you can just set the width of the <a> tag. If you want each button to be 8 ems wide, for example, then add that to the width property:

   ```
   ul.nav a {
     display: block;
     width: 8em;
   }
   ```

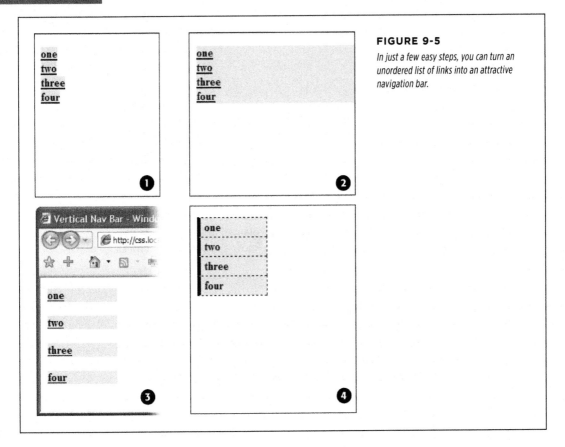

FIGURE 9-5

In just a few easy steps, you can turn an unordered list of links into an attractive navigation bar.

Setting a width for any of the tags that wrap around those links—such as the <li> or <ul> tags—also works.

If the button text occupies only one line, you can also center the text vertically so there's equal space above and below the link text. Just add a height to the link *and* set its line-height property to the same value:

```
a {
  height: 1.25em;
  line-height: 1.25em;
}
```

NOTE You may not need to set an explicit width if the nav bar is inside a page layout element that itself has a width. As you'll read in Part Three, it's easy to create a sidebar that hugs the left (or right) edge of a page. The sidebar has a set width, so plopping the unordered list nav bar inside it automatically constrains the width of the buttons.

Now that all this busywork is out of the way, you can style the buttons to your heart's content. Add padding, background colors, margins, images, or whatever tickles your artistic fancy. If you want to spread the buttons out so they don't touch, then add a bottom (or top) margin to each link.

Horizontal Navigation Bars

CSS lets you turn a set of stacked list items into a side-by-side presentation of links, like the one shown back in Figure 9-4. This section shows you two common ways to create a horizontal navigation bar from a list. The first—using the display: inline property—is easy, but it usually leads to a small gap between buttons. There's a way around this, but it involves fussing with your HTML. If you want a horizontal nav bar where buttons touch, then turn to the floated <ul> method described on page 296.

WORKAROUND WORKSHOP

When Borders Bump

In a vertical navigation bar, if the buttons touch, you'll see a double border between two buttons. In other words, the bottom border from one button touches the top border of the next button.

To get around this, add the border to only the *top* of each link. That way, you'll get just one border line where the bottom from each button touches the top from the next.

This workaround, however, leaves the entire nav bar borderless below the last link. To fix that problem, you can create a class with the correct bottom border style and apply it to the last link—but that makes you add more code to your HTML.

There are two better ways: first, you can add a bottom border to the <ul> tag that encloses the nav bar. Or, you can use the :last-of-type selector to format the bottom of just that last link (you'll see an example of this technique in the tutorial on page 311).

The same holds true when you have horizontal links. In this case the right and left borders of adjacent buttons touch. Just turn off the left borders on the buttons and add a left border to the containing tag—the <ul> tag, for example—or use the :first-of-type selector to select the first link in the bar and add a border to its left side.

Whichever method you use, start by removing the bullets and left space from the <ul> tag, as illustrated in #1 in Figure 9-6.

■ USING DISPLAY: INLINE AND DISPLAY: INLINE-BLOCK

The simplest method of creating a horizontal navigation bar involves changing the display property of the list items from block to inline. It's easy to do using CSS.

1. **Create a style for the unordered list to remove any padding, margins, and bullets.**

    ```
    ul.nav {
      margin-left: 0px;
      padding-left: 0px;
      list-style: none;
      border-bottom: 1px dashed #000;
    }
    ```

In this case, you've also added a bottom border, which will appear under the buttons (see #1 in Figure 9-6).

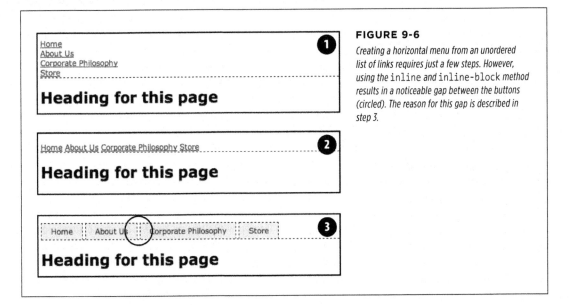

FIGURE 9-6

Creating a horizontal menu from an unordered list of links requires just a few steps. However, using the inline *and* inline-block *method results in a noticeable gap between the buttons (circled). The reason for this gap is described in step 3.*

2. **Make the list items inline elements.**

   Inline elements don't create a line break before or after them as block-level elements do. Setting the display property of the `<li>` tags to inline makes them appear one beside the other (#2 in Figure 9-6).

   ```
   .nav li { display: inline; }
   ```

   You need to make sure you don't have too many buttons, though. If they don't all fit side by side, some will drop down below the first row.

3. **Style the links.**

   You can remove the underline beneath the links and add a border around them instead. You can also add background color or a background image to provide visual depth. Add padding if you need more room around each link's text. If you want some space between each button, then apply a right margin. The following style gives links a button-like appearance, as shown in #3 in Figure 9-6:

   ```
   .nav a {
     display: inline-block;
     border: 1px dashed #000;
     border-bottom: none;
     padding: 5px 15px 5px 15px;
     background-color: #EAEAEA;
     text-decoration: none;
     color: #333;
   }
   ```

First, you need to set the `display` property of the links to `inline-block`. This makes sure that top and bottom padding and margins are obeyed (as described on page 192, normally inline elements ignore top and bottom padding and margins as well as width and height values). Then you can style the buttons to your heart's content. Here, you've added a border to the links and removed the bottom border so it doesn't double up on the bottom border applied to the unordered list.

TIP You can make the buttons all equal in size by setting the width of the links.

To make this horizontal nav bar appear in the center of the page, add `text-align: center;` to the `<ul>` tag's style. In fact, this is one benefit of this technique over the float technique described next—when you use `inline` and `inline-block`, you can center your nav bar, which you can't do with floats.

You will, however, notice that the buttons don't touch (see the circled area in Figure 9-6). That has to do with the way web browsers treat the white space between the `<li>` tags. For example, take this example HTML:

```
<ul class="nav">
<li><a href="index.html">Home</a></li>
<li><a href="news.html">News</a></li>
<li><a href="reviews.html">Reviews</a></li>
</ul>
```

Web browsers treat any white space (a tab, carriage return, or space character) between a closing `</li>` and the next `<li>` as a space. There are a couple of ways to remove this space:

- Put the closing `</li>` and opening `<li>` on the same line like this:

  ```
  <ul class="nav">
  <li><a href="index.html">Home</a></li><li>
  <a href="news.html">News</a></li><li>
  <a href="reviews.html">Reviews</a></li>
  </ul>
  ```

  This kind of code isn't normally written this way, and a program like Dreamweaver definitely wouldn't write it this way. To remove the space, you have to get in and change the code by hand.

- Add a negative right margin to the list items. For example, you could change the `li` style in step 2 above to this:

  ```
  .nav li {
      display: inline;
      margin-right: -5px;
  }
  ```

The negative margin value basically pulls the following list item over 5 pixels to close up the gap between the buttons. The problem with this technique is that the exact value you use will vary depending upon the size of the text—5 pixels may or may not work—so you'll need to experiment to get the proper value.

■ USING FLOATS FOR HORIZONTAL NAVIGATION

Another more popular technique is to float the list items. This method also places the links side by side. In addition, this technique doesn't suffer from the spacing problem of the inline method.

> **NOTE** Nav bars made up of floated elements are hard to center horizontally in the middle of a page. When you need to do that, the inline method described above or the flexbox method demonstrated on page 557 are better.

1. **Float the list items.**

   Adding a left float to the `<li>` tags removes them from the normal top-down flow of elements:

   ```
   .nav li { float: left; }
   ```

   The floated list items (along with their enclosed links) slide right next to each other, just like the images in the photo gallery tutorial on page 266. (You can just as easily float them right if you want those buttons to align to the right edge of the screen or containing sidebar.)

FREQUENTLY ASKED QUESTION

Pop-up Menus

How do I create those cool pop-up menus that display a sub-menu of links when someone rolls his mouse over a button?

Navigation bars that have multiple levels of menus that pop up or slide out are extremely popular. They're a perfect way to cram a lot of link options into a compact navigation bar. You can create them in a couple of ways.

First, there's the CSS-only approach. You can find a basic tutorial on the process at *http://blog.teamtreehouse.com/create-simple-css-dropdown-menu*. For a spiffy CSS menu that uses CSS transitions to animate the appearance and disappearance of the drop-down menus, check out *www.red-team-design.com/css3-animated-dropdown-menu*.

If you're not the do-it-yourself type, or if you're just in a hurry, you can use the free Pure CSS Menu generator—a wizard-like web page that produces the necessary HTML and CSS for you: *http://purecssmenu.com*.

The one disadvantage to most approach to CSS menus: sub-menus disappear instantly if your visitor's mouse strays. You can hope that all your visitors have excellent reflexes, or you can try a different approach. For an excellent tutorial that also includes how to use JavaScript to make your drop-down menus even more responsive, check out *https://css-tricks.com/drop-down-menus-with-more-forgiving-mouse-movement-paths*.

---

2. **Add** display: block **to the links.**

Links are inline elements, so width values (as well as top and bottom padding and margins) don't apply to them. Making a browser display the links as block elements lets you set an exact width for the button and add a comfortable amount of white space above and below each link:

```
.nav a { display: block; }
```

3. **Style the links.**

Add background colors, borders, and so on.

4. **Add a width.**

If you want the nav buttons to have identical widths, set a width for the <a> tag. The exact width you use depends on how much text is in each button. Obviously for a link like Corporate Philosophy, you need a wider button.

If you want each button to be simply the width of the text inside, don't set a width. You can, however, add left and right padding to give the text some breathing room.

TIP   To center the text in the middle of the button, add text-align: center; to the links' style.

---

5. **Add** overflow: hidden **to the** <ul> **tag style.**

If it has a border, background color, or image, you should need to "contain the float"—that is, the floated list items inside the <ul> will appear to pop out of the bottom of the list (and outside the <ul> tags border or background color).

```
.nav {
  overflow: hidden;
}
```

Here are the styles required to create the navigation bar pictured in Figure 9-7. Notice that the buttons are the same width, and the button text is centered.

```
.nav {
  margin: 0px;
  padding: 0px;
  list-style: none;
  border-bottom: 3px solid rgb(204,204,204);
  overflow: hidden;
}

.nav li {
  float: left;
}
```

```
.nav a {
  width: 12em;
  display: block;
  border: 3px solid rgb(204,204,204);
  border-bottom: none;
  border-radius: 5px 5px 0 0;
  padding: 10px;
  margin-right: 5px;
  background-color: rgb(95,95,95);
  background-image: -webkit-linear-gradient(rgb(175,175,175), rgb(95,95,95));
  background-image: -moz-linear-gradient(rgb(175,175,175), rgb(95,95,95));
  background-image: -o-linear-gradient(rgb(175,175,175), rgb(95,95,95));
  background-image: linear-gradient(rgb(175,175,175), rgb(95,95,95));
  text-decoration:none;
  color: white;
  text-align: center;
  font-family: Arial, Helvetica, sans-serif;
  font-weight: bold;
}
```

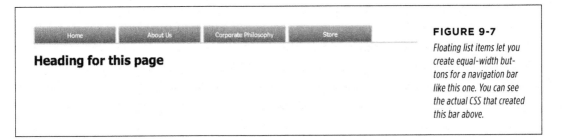

FIGURE 9-7

Floating list items let you create equal-width buttons for a navigation bar like this one. You can see the actual CSS that created this bar above.

CSS-Style Preloading Rollovers

In the bad old days, making a graphical link change to another graphic when moused over required JavaScript. With CSS, you can achieve similar effects with the :hover pseudo-class and a background image. However, there's one problem with the CSS method: Unless your visitor has already downloaded the rollover graphic, there's a noticeable delay while the browser sucks down the new graphic and displays it. The delay happens only the first time the visitor hovers over the link, but still, waiting for graphics to load is very 20th century.

The JavaScript solution can avoid this problem thanks to a technique called *preloading*, which automatically downloads the rollover graphic well before it's needed. But CSS doesn't give you that option, so you need to enlist another clever maneuver called *CSS sprites*, which utilizes a single graphic to create different states for the same button.

> **NOTE** CSS Sprites are used widely by companies like Yahoo and Google, not just for rollover effects but also to optimize the download speed of websites. You can learn more about them at *http://coding.smashingmagazine. com/2009/04/27/the-mystery-of-CSS-sprites-techniques-tools-and-tutorials/*. And for a list of tools, best practices and helpful applications for working with sprites, visit *http://webdesign.tutsplus.com/articles/css-sprite-sheets-best-practices-tools-and-helpful-applications--webdesign-8340*.

Here's how to implement the method:

1. **In your favorite image-editing program, create one image with different versions of the button.**

   You might create a regular state, a rollover state, and maybe even a "you are here" state. Place the images one on top of the other, with the regular link image on top and the rollover image below.

> **NOTE** There are many online tools to help you do this: SpritePad (*http://spritepad.wearekiss.com* and Sprite Cow (*www.spritecow.com*) are two examples.

2. **Measure the distances from the top of the entire graphic to the top of each image.**

   In Figure 9-8 (top), the rollover image's top edge is 39 pixels from the top of the graphic.

3. **Create a CSS style for the regular link. Include the image in the background and place it at the left top of the style (Figure 9-8, middle).**

   Your style may look something like this:

   ```
   a { background: #E7E7E7 url(images/pixy.png) no-repeat left top; }
   ```

4. **Create the :hover style.**

   Here's the trick: Use the `background-position` property to shift the graphic *upwards*, so the first image disappears and the rollover image becomes visible (Figure 9-9, bottom).

   ```
   a:hover { background-position: 0 -39px; }
   ```

Besides preventing the dreaded download delay, this technique helps you keep your navigation graphics organized in a single file.

> **NOTE** Some websites take this technique to the extreme. Yahoo, Amazon, and Google (among many others) often put together dozens of little images into a single file and display only the portion of the file containing the desired button. You can see an example from Amazon here: *www.flickr.com/photos/mezzoblue/3217540317*. Sites with millions of daily viewers benefit from complex sprites, since it's easier and faster for a web server to send a single (albeit bigger) image file than dozens of smaller files.

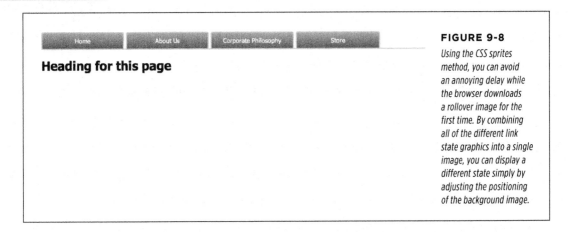

FIGURE 9-8

Using the CSS sprites method, you can avoid an annoying delay while the browser downloads a rollover image for the first time. By combining all of the different link state graphics into a single image, you can display a different state simply by adjusting the positioning of the background image.

Styling Particular Types of Links

Web designers link to all sorts of things: other web pages on their sites, web pages on other sites, PDFs, Word documents, and zip archive files, to name a few. To help guide your site's visitors, you might want to supply clues to let them know where a link leads before they click it. Advanced selectors are a great way to do just that.

Links to Other Websites

You can easily create a style that identifies links to other websites using an attribute selector. As you read on page 59, attribute selectors let you style HTML tags that have a particular attribute—for example, an <img> tag with the alt attribute set to *Our Company*. You can also style tags whose attributes *contain* certain values. Any link that points outside your site must be an absolute URL (see the box on page 237), meaning it must begin with either *http://* or *https://*—for example, *https:// css-tricks.com*.

> **NOTE** All major companies now use *SSL* (secure socket layer) on their sites, so links to those sites will always begin with *https://*. In fact, it's now considered an industry best practice for all sites to use SSL, so you probably now see more links that begin with *https://* than with *http://*.

Because you need to account for both http:// and https:// there are two approaches, each with a possible drawback. First, you can search the beginning of the href property for http, like this:

```
a[href^='http']
```

This will match URLs that begin with both http:// and https://. However, it will also select relative links that point to http.html, or http-information.html. If you don't plan on linking to any pages within your site that begin with http, then this will work fine.

Another method is to use the contains selector to look for :// anywhere within the URL like this:

```
a[href^='://']
```

This will match both http:// and https://, and because you won't have :// anywhere else in an href property, it should work for all external links.

You could style these any way you'd like, but one common technique is to add a small image next to the link—an icon indicating an external link. You'll see this in action on page 305 of this chapter's tutorial.

If you happen to use absolute links to point to other pages in *your* site, then you'll probably not want that same styling to appear for them. Fortunately, CSS's *negation* pseudo-class—:not()—makes this easy. With it, you can select absolute links that are *not* in your site:

```
a[href*='://']:not(a[href*='www.mysite.com']) {
  background: url(images/globe.png) no-repeat center right;
  padding-right: 15px;
}
```

Email Links

Email links are another special kind of link. Normally, email links look just like any other link—blue and underlined. However, they don't act like any other link. Clicking one launches a visitor's email program, and some people find starting up a new program while browsing a website really distracting, so let 'em know it's for email.

The same basic technique described for external links above applies. Since all email links begin with mailto:, you can create a selector like the following to create a style to format just email links:

```
a[href^='mailto:']
```

You'll see an example of this in action in the tutorial on page 305.

Links to Specific Types of Files

Some links point to files, not other web pages. You often see a company's annual report online as a downloadable PDF file or a zip archive of files (like the tutorials for this book) on a website. Links to those types of files usually force the browser to download the file to the visitor's computer, or, for PDF files, launch a plug-in that lets you view the file within the browser. It can be a real drag to click a link, only to find out that it's actually started a 100MB download!

You can identify specific file types in much the same way as external links or email links. But instead of looking for specific information at the beginning of the link's URL, you can find it at the end. For example, a link to a PDF document might look like this `<a href="annual_report.pdf">`, while a link to a zip archive could look like this: `<a href="tutorials.zip">`. In each case, the specific file type is identified by an extension at the end of the URL—.pdf or .zip.

CSS provides an attribute selector that lets you find attributes that end with specific information. So to create a style for links to PDF files, use this selector:

```
a[href$='.pdf']
```

`$=` means "ends in," so this selector means "select all links whose `href` attribute ends in .pdf." You can create similar styles for other types of files as well:

```
a[href$='.zip'] /* zip archive */
a[href$='.doc'] /* Word document */
```

You'll see examples of this technique in the tutorial on page 307.

■ Tutorial: Styling Links

In this tutorial, you'll style links in a variety of ways, like adding rollovers and background graphics.

To get started, download the tutorial files from this book's companion website at *https://github.com/sawmac/css_mm_4e*. Click the tutorial link and download the files. All the files are enclosed in a zip archive, so you need to unzip them first. The files for this tutorial are contained inside the *09* folder.

Basic Link Formatting

1. **Launch a web browser and open the file *09→links→links.html*.**

   This page contains a variety of links (circled in Figure 9-9) that point to other pages on the site, links to pages on other websites, and an email address. Start by changing the color of the links on this page.

2. **Open *links.html* in a text editor and place your cursor between the opening and closing `<style>` tags.**

   The page already has an external style sheet attached to it with some basic formatting, plus the `<style>` tags for an internal style sheet.

NOTE For this exercise, you'll put the styles in an internal style sheet for easy coding and previewing. But if you were creating the CSS for an entire site, you'd place the styles into a separate CSS file.

---

3. **Add a new style to the internal style sheet:**

```
<style>
a {
  color: #207EBF;
}
</style>
```

This style is about as generic as it gets. It will apply to all <a> tags on the page. It's a good place to start, since it sets up the overall look of links for the page. You'll add more styles that will let you pinpoint links in specific areas of the page. Now, time to remove that boring old underline beneath the link.

4. **Add** text-decoration: none; **to the style you just created.**

This removes the underline, but also makes the link less visible on the page. Remember, you should always do something to make links stand out and seem clickable to your site's visitors.

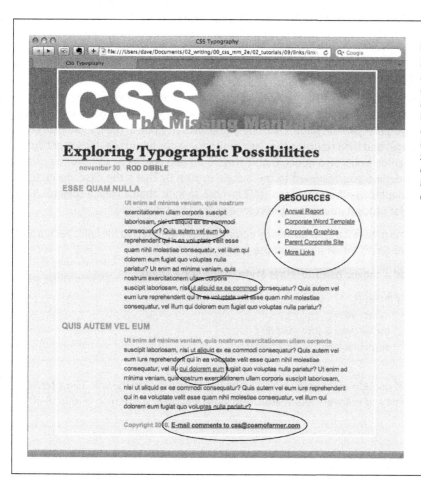

FIGURE 9-9

Here's a basic web page with links in their standard browser configuration—underlined and blue (or purple, if they're links to previously visited pages). In this case, some links point to other pages on the site, some point to other sites, and one is an email address. In this tutorial, you'll style each of these links differently.

5. **Add** font-weight: bold; **to the** a **style.**

   Now links appear in bold (other text may appear bold, too). Next you'll replace the underline, but you'll do it a bit more creatively, using a border instead of the text-decoration property.

6. **Add a** border **declaration to the style, so it looks like this:**

   ```
   a {
     color: #207EBF;
     text-decoration: none;
     font-weight: bold;
     border-bottom: 2px solid #F60;
   }
   ```

   The links really stand out, and using a border instead of the normal underline applied to links lets you change the line's color, size, and style (Figure 9-10, left). Now you'll change the look of visited links.

7. **Add a** :visited **pseudo-class style for visited links:**

   ```
   a:visited {
     color: #6E97BF;
   }
   ```

   This style changes the look of visited links to a lighter, grayer shade of the main link color—a subtle way to draw attention away from an already visited page. If you preview the page, click one of the links (try one in the middle part of the page) and then return to the *links.html* page. You should see the link get lighter in color. You'll also notice that it stays bold and continues to have the orange underline you assigned to the a style in step 6. That's the cascade in action (Chapter 5)—the a:visited style is more specific than a plain a selector, so its color property overrides the color assigned by the a style.

   Time to take it a step further by adding a rollover effect, so the link's background changes color when the mouse moves over it.

8. **Add a** :hover **pseudo-class style to the style sheet:**

   ```
   a:hover {
     color: #FFF;
     background-color: #6E97BF;
     border-bottom-color: #6E97BF;
   }
   ```

   This pseudo-class applies only when the mouse is over the link. The interactive quality of rollovers lets visitors know the link does something (Figure 9-10).

RESOURCES

- Annual Report
- Corporate Word Template
- Corporate Graphics
- Parent Corporate Site
- More Links

FIGURE 9-10

With a couple of styles, you can change the look of any link. With the :hover pseudo-class, you can even switch to a different style when the mouse moves over the link.

Adding a Background Image to a Link

The email link at the bottom of the page looks no different than the other links on the page (Figure 9-11, top). You have other plans for that `mailto:` link, however. Since it points to an email address, clicking it doesn't take a visitor to another page, but instead launches an email program. To provide a visual cue emphasizing this point, you'll add a cute little email icon.

1. **Add a descendant selector to the internal style sheet of the *links.html* file:**

   ```
   a[href^="mailto:"] {
     color: #666666;
     border: none;
     background: url(images/email.gif) no-repeat left center;
   }
   ```

   This is an advanced attribute selector, which selects any links that begin with `mailto:` (in other words, it selects email links). The `border: none` setting removes the underline defined by the a style you created in step 6—you're going for a subtle look here. The `background` property adds an image on the left edge of the link. Finally, the `no-repeat` value forces the graphic to appear just a single time. Trouble is, the graphic lies directly underneath the link, so it's hard to read the text (circled in the middle image in Figure 9-11).

2. **Add 20 pixels of left padding to the `attribute` style you just created:**

   ```
   padding-left: 20px;
   ```

   Remember that padding adjusts the space between content and its border. So adding some left padding moves the text over 20 pixels but leaves the background in place. One last touch: Move the entire link a little away from the copyright notice.

3. **Add 10 pixels of left margin to the style, so it finally ends up like this:**

```
a[href^="mailto:"] {
    color: #666666;
    border: none;
    background: url(images/email.gif) no-repeat left center;
    padding-left: 20px;
    margin-left: 10px;
}
```

This small visual adjustment makes it clear that the icon is related to the link and not part of the copyright notice (Figure 9-11, bottom).

Highlighting Different Links

At times you may want to indicate that a link points to another website. In this way, you can give your visitors a visual clue that there's additional information elsewhere on the Internet or warn them that they'll exit your site if they click the link. Also, you may want to identify links that point to downloadable files or other non-web-page documents.

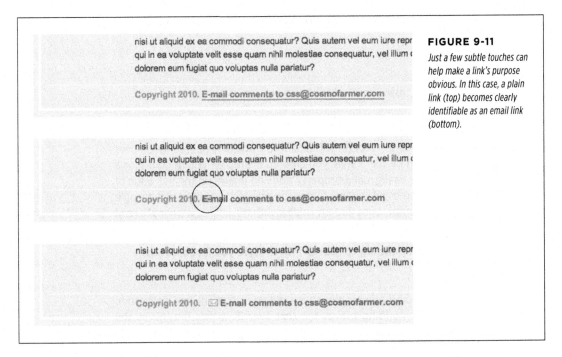

FIGURE 9-11

Just a few subtle touches can help make a link's purpose obvious. In this case, a plain link (top) becomes clearly identifiable as an email link (bottom).

On the web page you're working on, the right-hand "Resources" sidebar contains different types of links that you'll highlight with icons—a different icon for each type of link. First, you'll set up a basic style that applies to all of those links.

1. **Add this style to the *links.html* internal style sheet:**

```
.resources a {
  border-bottom: none;
}
```

Since all of the links you want to format are inside a div with the class resources, the descendant selector .resources a targets just those links. This style gets rid of the underline that the generic link style added.

Next, you'll add an icon next to external links.

2. **Add another style at the end of the *links.html* internal style sheet:**

```
.resources a[href*='://'] {
  background: url(images/globe.png) no-repeat right top;
}
```

This is a descendant selector style that uses the advanced attribute selector discussed on page 59. Basically, it targets any link that contains :// (but only those that are also inside the element with the class resources). As with the email link style you created earlier, this style adds a background image. It places the image at the right side of the link.

However, this style has a similar problem as the email link style—the image sits underneath the link's text. Fortunately, the solution is the same—just add some padding to move the image out of the way of the text. In this case, though, instead of adding left padding, you'll add right padding (since the icon appears on the right side of the link). In addition, since every link in the resources box will have a similarly sized icon, you can save some code by adding the padding to the .resources a style you created in Step 1.

3. **Edit the .resources a style so that it looks like this:**

```
.resources a {
  border-bottom: none;
  padding-right: 22px;
}
```

If you save the page and preview it in a web browser, you'll see small globe icons to the right of the bottom two links in the sidebar. Time to format the other links.

4. **Add three more styles to the internal style sheet:**

```
.resources a[href$='.pdf'] {
  background: url(images/acrobat.png) no-repeat right top;
}
.resources a[href$='.zip'] {
  background: url(images/zip.png) no-repeat right top;
}
.resources a[href$='.doc'] {
  background: url(images/word.png) no-repeat right top;
}
```

These three styles look at how the href attribute ends; identify links to either Adobe Reader files (.pdf), zip archives (.zip), or Word documents (.doc); and assign a different icon in each case.

5. **Finally, add a hover state for the resources links:**

```
.resources a:hover {
  color: #000;
  background-color: rgba(255,255,255,.8);
}
```

This style both changes the color of the text and adds a background color (see Figure 9-12).

You can find a finished version of this tutorial in the *09_finished/links/links. html* file.

RESOURCES

- Annual Report
- Corporate Word Template
- **Corporate Graphics**
- Parent Corporate Site
- More Links

FIGURE 9-12

Using advanced attribute selectors, you can easily identify and style different types of links—external links and links to PDF files, Word docs, and zip files.

■ Tutorial: Creating a Navigation Bar

In this exercise, you'll turn a plain old list of links into a spectacular navigation bar, complete with rollover effects and a "You are here" button effect.

1. **In a text editor, open *09→nav_bar→nav_bar.html*.**

   As you can see, there's not much to this file yet. There's an internal style sheet with the basic reset styles discussed on page 109, and one rule setting up some basic properties for the <body> tag. The HTML consists of an unordered list with six links. It looks like example #1 in Figure 9-13. Your first step is to add some HTML so you can target your CSS to format the links in this list.

2. **Locate the opening <ul> tag and add** class="mainNav" **to it, so it looks like this:**

   ```
   <ul class="mainNav">
   ```

   The class attribute identifies this list as the main navigation area. Use this class to build descendant selectors to format only these links—and not just any old link on the page.

3. **Below the body style in the internal style sheet, add a new style:**

```
.mainNav {
    margin: 0;
    padding: 0;
    list-style: none;
}
```

This style applies only to a tag with a class of mainNav—in this case, the `<ul>` tag. It removes the indent and bullets that browsers apply to unordered lists, as shown in #2 in Figure 9-13. Next, you'll start formatting the links.

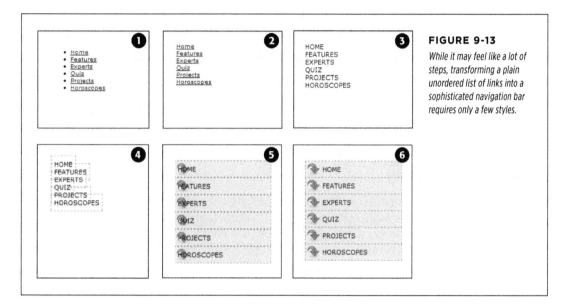

FIGURE 9-13

While it may feel like a lot of steps, transforming a plain unordered list of links into a sophisticated navigation bar requires only a few styles.

4. **Add a descendant selector to format the links in the list:**

```
.mainNav a {
    color: #000;
    font-size: 11px;
    text-transform: uppercase;
    text-decoration: none;
}
```

This style defines the basic text formatting for the links. It sets the color and font size, makes all letters uppercase, and removes the line usually found underneath links (#3 in Figure 9-13). Now start making the links look like buttons.

5. **To the** `.mainNav a` **style, add the following** border **and** padding **properties:**

```
border: 1px dashed #999;
padding: 7px 5px;
```

If you preview the file now, you'll see a few problems (#4 in Figure 9-13): The borders overlap and the boxes aren't the same width. That's because the <a> tag is an inline element, so the width of the box is just as wide as the text in the link. In addition, top and bottom padding don't add any height to inline boxes, so the borders overlap. (See page 192 for a discussion of inline boxes.) You can fix these problems by changing how a browser displays these links.

6. **Add** `display: block;` **to the** `.mainNav a` **style.**

You've changed the basic display of the <a> tag so it acts like a paragraph or other block-level element, with the links neatly stacked one on top of the other. The only problem now is that they also extend the full length of the browser window—a little too wide for a button. You can fix this by constraining the width of the <ul> tag's style.

7. **In the internal style sheet, locate the** `.mainNav` **style and add** `width: 175px;` **to it:**

```
.mainNav {
  margin: 0;
  padding: 0;
  list-style: none;
  width: 175px;
}
```

With the list's width now set to 175 pixels, the links still expand, but they're limited to the width of their container (the <ul> tag). In many cases, you'll have a list of links inside some layout element (like a sidebar) that already has a set width, so you'll be able to skip this step. (You'll learn how to add sidebars in Part Three.)

Now for the fun part.

8. **Add background properties to the** `.mainNav a` **style, like so:**

```
.mainNav a {
  color: #000;
  font-size: 11px;
  text-transform: uppercase;
  text-decoration: none;
  border: 1px dashed #999;
  padding: 7px 5px;
  display: block;
  background-color: #E7E7E7;
  background-image: url(images/nav.png);
  background-repeat: no-repeat;
  background-position: 0 2px;
}
```

These lines add a gray background color to the links and a non-repeating image at the left edge of each button (#5 in Figure 9-13). You still have a couple of things to fix: The link text overlaps the icon, and the border between each button is 2 pixels thick. (Technically, the borders are still just 1 pixel thick, but the bottom and top borders of adjoining links are creating a 2-pixel line.)

TIP Using the background shorthand property, you can write the code in step 8 like this: `background: #E7E7E7 url(images/nav.png) no-repeat 0 2px;`.

---

9. **Remove the bottom border and adjust the padding for the `.mainNav a` style, so it looks like this:**

```
.mainNav a {
  color: #000;
  font-size: 11px;
  text-transform: uppercase;
  text-decoration: none;
  border: 1px dashed #999;
  border-bottom: none;
  padding: 7px 5px 7px 30px;
  display: block;
  background-color: #E7E7E7;
  background-image: url(images/nav.png);
  background-repeat: no-repeat;
  background-position: 0 2px;
}
```

The text of each link sits clear of the icon and the borders look great...except for one thing. The last link's bottom border is now gone. (Sometimes CSS feels like two steps forward, one step back!) But you have a few ways to fix this snafu. One way is to apply a bottom border to the `<ul>` tag containing the list of links. (Since there's no padding on that tag, there's no space separating the top of the `<ul>` from the top of that first link.) But another way is to use the `:last-of-type` pseudo-class (page 65). You just need to select the link that's inside the last list item in the navigation bar, and give it a bottom border.

10. **Add the following style between** `.mainNav` **and the** `.mainNav a` **styles:**

```
.mainNav li:last-of-type a {
  border-bottom: 1px dashed #999;
}
```

This descendant selector styles the link (a) that's inside the last list item (`li:last-of-type`) or the navigation list (`.mainNav`).

There you have it: a basic navigation bar using borders, padding, background color, and images (#6 in Figure 9-13).

Adding Rollovers and Creating "You Are Here" Links

Now it's time to add some interactive and advanced features to this nav bar. First, you'll add a rollover effect to the buttons in your main navigation bar. That way, the buttons change to show your visitor which button she's about to click.

It's also considerate to let your visitor know which page of your site she's on. Using the same HTML nav bar you already have, you can make this bit of interactivity happen automatically. You simply make the button's format change to match the page's section. Sounds simple, but it does require a little planning and setup, as you'll see in the following steps.

The rollover effect is easy, so get that out of the way first:

1. **In the *nav_bar.html* file, add the following style to the end of the style sheet:**

   ```
   .mainNav a:hover {
     font-weight: bold;
     background-color: #B2F511;
     background-position: 3px 50%;
   }
   ```

   This style sets the button's hover state. It makes the text inside the button bold, and changes the background color to a vibrant green. In addition, it uses the CSS sprites technique discussed on page 298. The same image is used as in step 8 on page 310—however, that image actually holds three different icons (see Figure 9-14). In this case, the image is centered within the button, displaying the middle icon in the file.

   Now, moving the mouse over any of the buttons instantly changes its look. (Open the page in your web browser and try it yourself.)

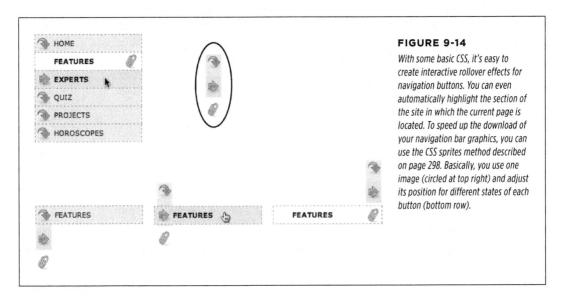

FIGURE 9-14

With some basic CSS, it's easy to create interactive rollover effects for navigation buttons. You can even automatically highlight the section of the site in which the current page is located. To speed up the download of your navigation bar graphics, you can use the CSS sprites method described on page 298. Basically, you use one image (circled at top right) and adjust its position for different states of each button (bottom row).

Next, make your navigation bar more informative by highlighting the button that matches the section in which the page is located. To do so, you need to identify two things in the nav bar's HTML: the section a page belongs to and the section each link points to. For this example, assume that the page you're working on is the home page.

> **NOTE** Alternatively, you can create a class style that changes the appearance of a link and apply it to the link representing the page's section. For a horoscope page, you'd apply the class to the Horoscope link in the nav bar: `<a href="/horoscopes/" class="current">Horoscopes</a>`.

2. **Locate the** `<body>` **tag, and then add** `class="home"`**, like so:**

   ```
   <body class="home">
   ```

   Now that you know what section this page belongs to, you can use a descendant selector to create special CSS rules that apply only to tags on pages within the Features section. Next, you need to identify the section each link applies to, which you accomplish by adding some classes to those links.

3. **In the nav bar's HTML code, locate the Home link, and then add** `class="homeLink"` **so the tag looks like this:**

   ```
   <a href="/index.html" class="homeLink">Home</a>
   ```

   This class identifies this link, providing the information you need to create a style that applies only to that link.

   You need to add a class to the other links in the navigation bar as well.

4. **Repeat step 3 for each of the other links using the following classes:** `featureLink`, `expertLink`, `quizLink`, `projectLink`, and `horoscopeLink`.

   You're done with the HTML part of this exercise. Now it's time to create some CSS. Because you've provided classes to identify the different links, it's easy to create a descendant selector to highlight the Home link.

5. **Add another style to the page's style sheet:**

   ```
   .home .homeLink {
     background-color: #FFFFFF;
     background-position: 97% 100%;
     padding-right: 15px;
     padding-left: 30px;
     font-weight: bold;
   }
   ```

   You've seen all these properties before. Again, you're using the CSS sprites method to adjust the position of the background image. This time, the image is moved over to the right 97 percent (that is, the point 97 percent across the image is matched up with the point 97 percent across the button), and the bottom of the image is placed at the bottom of the button. In other words, it displays the icon at the bottom of the image (see Figure 9-14). See page 240 for a discussion of how percentage values work with background-images.

The most interesting part is the selector—.home .homeLink. It's a very specific selector that applies only to a link with a class of homeLink that's *also* inside a <body> tag with a class of home. If you change the class of the page to quiz, for example, the link to the Home page is no longer highlighted.

Preview the page in a browser to see the effect: The Home link now has a white background and a paper clip icon. To make this work for the other links, you need to expand this selector a little...OK, make that a *lot*.

6. **Edit the selector for the style you just added, like so:**

```
.home .homeLink,
.feature .featureLink,
.expert .expertLink,
.quiz .quizLink,
.project .projectLink,
.horoscope .horoscopeLink{
   background-color: #FFFFFF;
   background-position: 97% 100%;
   padding-right: 15px;
   padding-left: 30px;
   font-weight: bold;
}
```

Yes, that's a lot of CSS. But your setup work here has a big payoff. This style now applies to every link in the nav bar, but only under certain conditions, which is exactly how you want it to behave. When you change the class attribute of the <body> tag to quiz, the link to the Quiz gets highlighted instead of the link to the Features section. Time to take your work for a test drive.

> **NOTE** This long-winded selector is an example of the group selector discussed on page 49.

7. **Change the** class **attribute of the** <body> **tag to** feature **like this:**

```
<body class="feature">
```

Preview the page, and wham! The Feature link is now highlighted with a white background and a paper clip icon (Figure 9-14). The secret at this point is to just change the class in the <body> tag to indicate which section of the site a page belongs to. For a horoscope page, change the class to class="horoscope" in the <body> tag.

> **NOTE** Ready to take this design further? Try adding a rollover effect to complement the style you created in step 6. (Hint: Use the :hover pseudo-class as part of the selector like this: .quiz .quizLink:hover.) Also try adding a different graphic for the Home link. (You have a *home.png* file in the images folder to use.)

To see the completed version of this navigation bar, see the file *09_finished→nav_ bar→nav_bar_vertical.html*.

From Vertical to Horizontal

Suppose you want a horizontal navigation bar that sits at the top of the page. No problem—you did most of the hard work in the last part of this tutorial. Just modify that page a little to spread the buttons along a single line. (You'll use the *nav_bar. html* file you just completed, so if you want to keep the vertical nav bar, then save a copy of the file before proceeding.)

1. **Make sure you've completed all the steps above to create the vertical navigation bar, and have the file *nav_bar.html* open in your text editor.**

   Now you'll see how easy it is to change the orientation of a navigation bar. Start by cleaning up some of the work you already did. You need to remove the width you set for the `<ul>` tag in step 7 on page 310. That width prevented the nav buttons from spanning the entire length of the page. But since the `<ul>` needs to spread out much wider to contain the side-by-side buttons, this width has to go.

2. **Find the** `.mainNav` **style, and then remove the** `width: 175px;` **declaration.**

   And now it's time for the big secret of horizontal nav bars—placing the buttons side by side.

3. **Add a new style to your style sheet (directly below the** `.mainNav` **style is a good spot):**

   ```
   .mainNav li {
     float: left;
     width: 12em;
   }
   ```

   This style applies to the `<li>` tag (the list items that hold each link). The first declaration floats the tag to the left. In this way, each `<li>` tag attempts to wrap around to the right side of the previous `<li>` tag. Also, setting the width of the `<li>` tag defines the width of each button. Here, a value of 12 ems provides enough space to contain the longest link name—Horoscopes. When you're working with longer links, you need to increase this value.

   If you preview the page now, you'll see the basics are complete. All that's left are some cosmetic enhancements (see the circled areas of #1 in Figure 9-15). Currently, there's no bottom border below the buttons, and the border where buttons touch doubles up (because the right border of one button combines with the left border of the link next to it), so you'll fix those issues next.

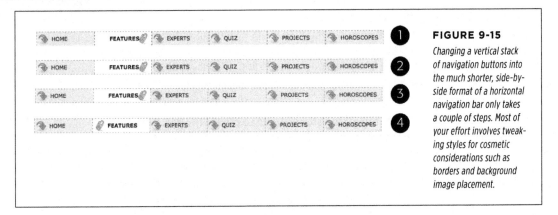

FIGURE 9-15

Changing a vertical stack of navigation buttons into the much shorter, side-by-side format of a horizontal navigation bar only takes a couple of steps. Most of your effort involves tweaking styles for cosmetic considerations such as borders and background image placement.

4. **In the** `.mainNav a` **style, change** `border-bottom: none;` **to** `border-right: none;`.

   This change removes the right border so the borders don't double up between buttons, and at the same time restores the border to the bottom of each button. But now the border on the right side of the last navigation button is missing (#2 in Figure 9-15). You can use the `:last-of-type` selector to fix that—you already have that style in place from the previous part of this tutorial.

5. **Change the** `border-bottom` **property of the** `.mainNav li:last-of-type a` **style to** `border-right` **like this:**

   ```
   .mainNav li:last-of-type a {
     border-right: 1px dashed #999;
   }
   ```

   This change adds a right border, but only to the last link in the navigation bar (#3 in Figure 9-15). Finally, that paper clip aligned to the right edge of the "You are here" button looks odd (#3 in Figure 9-15). You'll switch its position to the left edge of the button.

6. **Locate the "You are here" style you created in step 6 on page 314. (It's the one with the crazy, long-winded selector.) Change its background position from** `97% 100%` **to** `3px 100%`**. The style should now look like this:**

   ```
   .home .homeLink,
   .feature .featureLink,
   .expert .expertLink,
   .quiz .quizLink,
   .project .projectLink,
   .horoscope .horoscopeLink
   {
   ```

```
    background-color: #FFFFFF;
    background-position: 3px 100%;
    padding-right: 15px;
    padding-left: 30px;
    font-weight: bold;
}
```

Preview the page, and you'll find a fully functional horizontal navigation bar (#4 in Figure 9-15).

To see the finished version, open the file *09_finished→nav_bar→nav_bar_horizontal. html.*

NOTE You may want to center the text inside each button. If so, you need to do two things: Add `text-align: center;` to the `.mainNav a` style, and adjust that style's `left-padding` until the text looks absolutely centered.

CSS Transforms, Transitions, and Animations

For the short history of the Web, designers have had a few options for adding animation to their websites. The humble, goofy-looking animated GIF is perhaps the simplest way to provide basic animation within an image. Adobe Flash was once the number one tool for creating complex animations, and even games and web applications, but it has a number of drawbacks: Its learning curve was steep; it can't interact with the other HTML on your page, like the images, headlines, and paragraphs that make up most web content; and because Flash isn't available on many mobile devices, it's no longer as popular as it once was. JavaScript lets you animate anything on a web page, but at the cost of learning a full-fledged programming language. Fortunately, CSS provides a way to move, transform, and animate any HTML element on a page, without resorting to any of these other technologies.

Transforms

CSS includes several properties that transform a web page element, by either rotating it, scaling it, moving it, or distorting it along its horizontal and vertical axes (a process called *skewing*). You can use a transform, for example, to provide a slight tilt (rotation) to a navigation bar, or make an image get twice as big when a visitor mouses over it. You can even combine multiple transformations for some wild visual effects.

The basic CSS property to achieve any of these changes is the CSS `transform` property. You use this property by supplying the *type* of transformation you want and a value indicating *how much* to transform the element. For example, to rotate an element, you supply the keyword `rotate`, followed by the number of degrees to turn it:

```
transform: rotate(10deg);
```

The above declaration rotates the element 10 degrees clockwise.

Browser support for transforms is very good: Internet Explorer 9, Safari, Chrome, Firefox, and Opera all support transforms. However, to get transforms to work in Safari and Internet Explorer 9, you need to add a vendor prefix, as shown in the first two lines of the following code (also see the box on the opposite page):

```
-webkit-transform: rotate(10deg);
-ms-transform: rotate(10deg);
transform: rotate(10deg);
```

One strange feature of CSS transforms is that they don't affect other elements around them. In other words, if you rotate an element 45 degrees, it may actually overlap elements above, below, or to the side. Web browsers actually start by setting aside the space the element would normally take up (before the transformation), and then they transform the element (rotate it, enlarge it, move it, or skew it). This process is readily apparent when you increase the size of an element by using a transform: scale function (page 332). If you increase an element's size two times, the browser enlarges the transformed element but doesn't move any of the surrounding content out of the way, usually causing parts of the page to overlap (Figure 10-1). In other words, the web browser preserves all the other parts of the page just as they would appear if the element wasn't enlarged.

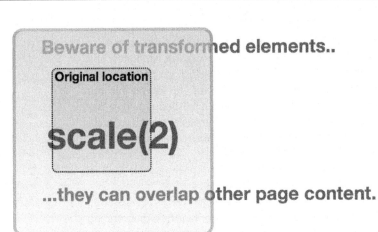

FIGURE 10-1

Get out of my way...or not. Transformed elements are pretty much ignored by other elements around them. Enlarging the `<div>` *here (the big square) simply makes it overlap the headline above and below it. The box in the middle, with the dotted outline, represents the* `<div>` *before it was scaled up by two.*

Vendor Prefixes

CSS is an always-evolving set of rules. Even as you build web pages today, there are smart people at the W3C (World Wide Web Consortium) working on new CSS properties, and other smart people adding support for new CSS properties in the web browsers they build. In fact, sometimes browser makers themselves come up with a new CSS property they think would be cool and add it to their browser. Other times, the W3C thinks up new CSS properties that the browser vendors gradually adopt.

During this period when new CSS properties and standards are developing, browser manufacturers move cautiously. They don't want to completely commit to CSS properties that may change. Likewise, as they experiment with CSS properties of their own design, browser makers hesitate to claim that they've come up with an agreed-upon standard. To mark a CSS property as experimental or not-yet-completely-agreed-upon, a browser manufacturer uses a prefix before the property name. Each of the major browser makers has its own prefix:

- -webkit- is used by Chrome, Safari, Opera, and other WebKit-based browsers
- -moz- is used by Mozilla Firefox
- -ms- is used by Microsoft Internet Explorer

When a property is in flux, a browser may support a vendor-prefixed version. For example, when the border-radius property was first proposed, Firefox supported a -moz-border-radius property, while Safari supported the -webkit-border-radius property.

When a property requires a vendor prefix, you usually write several lines of code to create the same effect: one for each vendor, and finally one with the non-prefixed version like this:

- ::-webkit-input-placeholder { color: red; }
- ::-moz-placeholder { color: red; }
- :-ms-input-placeholder { color: red; }
- :placeholder-shown { color: red; }

Usually, if the W3C CSS Working Group adopts a property and finalizes enough of its details, vendors drop the extension. For example, all major browsers simply support the border-radius property with no required vendor prefix. As you'll read throughout this book, the final details for some CSS properties are still being hammered out, so you may need to use a vendor prefix with them. This book will let you know when you need these prefixes and how to use them with a particular property.

Rotate

The transform property's rotate function is easy to understand: You give it a degree value from 0 to 360, and the browser rotates that element the specified number of degrees around a circle (see Figure 10-2). To specify a degree value, use a number followed by deg. For example, to rotate an element 180 degrees, add this declaration:

```
transform: rotate(180deg);
```

NOTE To save space, these examples don't include all the vendor prefixes here, but when you put this code into a style sheet, you need to add the -webkit-transform, -moz-transform, -o-transform, and -ms-transform properties as well.

You can even use negative numbers to rotate the element counter-clockwise. For example, the element in the top middle of Figure 10-2 is rotated 45 degrees counter-clockwise like this:

```
transform: rotate(-45deg);
```

The value 0deg provides no rotation, while 360deg is one complete rotation, and 720deg is two complete rotations. Of course, looking at an element that's been rotated once, twice, or three times will look just like an element that hasn't been rotated at all (top-left and bottom-right in Figure 10-2), so you're probably wondering why you'd ever use a value of 360 or higher. CSS provides a mechanism for animating changes in CSS properties. So, for example, you can make a button spin around four times when a visitor mouses over it by starting with an initial rotation of 0deg and adding a :hover style for that button that has a rotation of 1440deg.

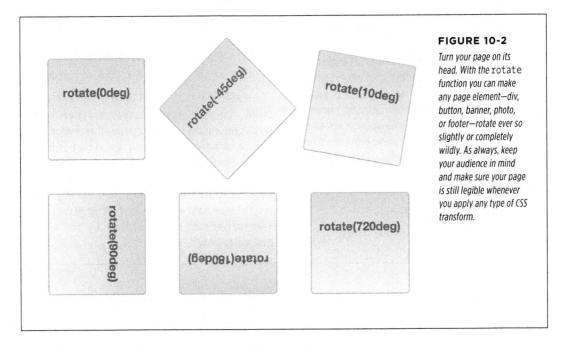

FIGURE 10-2

Turn your page on its head. With the rotate function you can make any page element—div, button, banner, photo, or footer—rotate ever so slightly or completely wildly. As always, keep your audience in mind and make sure your page is still legible whenever you apply any type of CSS transform.

Scale

You can also resize an element, making it bigger or smaller using the scale function (see Figure 10-3). For example, to make an element twice as big, you add this declaration:

```
transform: scale(2);
```

The number you supply inside the parentheses is a scaling factor—a number that's multiplied by the element's current size. For example, 1 is no scaling, .5 is half the current size, and 4 is four times the current size. In other words, a number between

0 and 1 shrinks an element, while a number larger than 1 makes it bigger (a value of 0 actually renders the element invisible on the page).

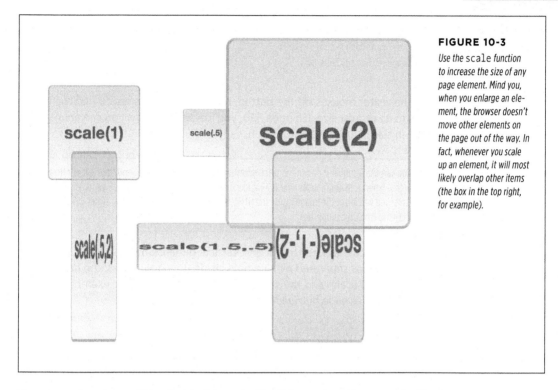

FIGURE 10-3

Use the scale function to increase the size of any page element. Mind you, when you enlarge an element, the browser doesn't move other elements on the page out of the way. In fact, whenever you scale up an element, it will most likely overlap other items (the box in the top right, for example).

The element and everything inside it is scaled by this number. For example, if you scale a <div> tag up by a factor of two, not only would that div be twice as wide and tall, but also the text inside would be twice as big, as would any images inside it.

Of course, you may be wondering why you'd ever use this. After all, you could just as easily increase or decrease the width and height of the element using the CSS width and height properties, and you can scale text size up or down using the font-size property. The most common use for scale is to make a visual change to an element dynamically on the page. For example, mousing over a button may make that button momentarily bigger. You could achieve this effect with the :hover state.

For example, say you have a link on a page with the .button class applied. You can create a simple style like this to format that button:

```
.button {
  font: .9em Arial, Helvetica, sans-serif;
  border-radius: .5em;
  background-color: rgb(34,255,23);
  border: 1px solid rgba(0,0,0,.5);
  padding: .5em;
}
```

To really emphasize that button, you can make it get slightly bigger when a visitor mouses over it, like this:

```
.button:hover {
  -webkit-transform: scale(1.2);
  -ms-transform: scale(1.2);
  transform: scale(1.2);
}
```

When the visitor mouses off the button, the transform is removed and the button returns to its regular size. On page 330, you'll even learn how you can animate this change in size by using CSS transitions.

> **TIP** You can use a similar idea for images. Display a gallery of small images, and then add a :hover style to them so that when a visitor mouses over the image, it grows larger. To make this look good, you should insert the final, enlarged version of the image inside the HTML, but set its size smaller by using either CSS or the <img> tag's width and height properties.

You can even scale the horizontal and vertical dimensions separately. To do this, supply two values separated by a comma inside the parentheses; the first number is the horizontal scale, and the second is the vertical scale. For example, to make an element half as wide but twice as tall, use this declaration:

```
transform: scale(.5,2);
```

You can see the effect at bottom left in Figure 10-3.

CSS also provides separate functions for horizontal and vertical scaling: scaleX scales along the horizontal axis, while scaleY scales vertically. For example, to make an element twice as tall without changing its width, you'd write this:

```
transform: scaleY(2);
```

> **NOTE** Again, to save space, this example shows only the un-prefixed version of the transform property. For this to work in Safari and Internet Explorer 9, you'll need to add the proper prefixes -webkit- and -ms-.

But to make an element three and a half times as wide, but not taller or shorter, you'd use:

```
transform: scaleX(3.5);
```

There's another visual trick that scaling offers: the ability to flip an element upside down and backwards. No one's quite sure what branch of mathematics the W3C used to come up with this system, but if you use a negative number with scale, you actually flip an element around. For example, here's how to flip an element upside down and left to right:

```
transform: scale(-1);
```

This produces the image pictured in Figure 10-4, left. You can also flip the element on only one axis. In the middle image in Figure 10-4, the image is flipped only on its horizontal axis. Flipping the element along its vertical axis produces the middle image:

```
transform: scale(-1,1);
```

It produces the effect of a mirror held to the side of the element, or like you've flipped the element over and are looking through its back. What fun!

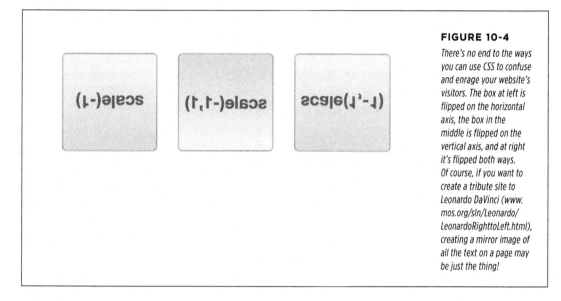

FIGURE 10-4

There's no end to the ways you can use CSS to confuse and enrage your website's visitors. The box at left is flipped on the horizontal axis, the box in the middle is flipped on the vertical axis, and at right it's flipped both ways. Of course, if you want to create a tribute site to Leonardo DaVinci (www.mos.org/sln/Leonardo/ LeonardoRighttoLeft.html), creating a mirror image of all the text on a page may be just the thing!

Translate

The `transform` property's `translate` function simply moves an element from its current position a set amount left or right and up or down. By itself, it's really not that useful. As you read on page 320, when a web browser transforms an element, it doesn't rearrange the page; it lays the page out as if the element had no transformation. Accordingly, when you move a div or other tag using the `translate` function, the browser leaves an empty space where the tag would normally appear, and then draws the element in its new position (see Figure 10-5). If you simply want to position an element on the page, you can use absolute or relative positioning, as described in Chapter 14.

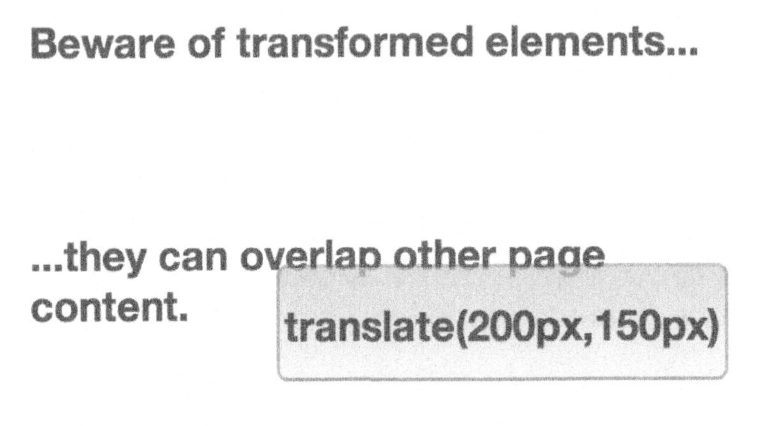

Beware of transformed elements...

...they can overlap other page content.

translate(200px,150px)

FIGURE 10-5

The translate function moves an element a set number of pixels, ems, or a percentage from its normal spot on a page. This often leaves an empty space: The blank area between the two headlines is where the outlined <div> tag would normally appear.

However, translate does come in handy when you want to make subtle movements in response to a hover or click. For example, in many user interface designs, when you click a button, it moves slightly down and to the left, simulating the look of a real 3D button being pressed into a keypad. You can simulate this effect using the translate function and the :active state of a link:

```
.button:active {
  -webkit-translate(1px,2px);
  -ms-translate(1px,2px);
  translate(1px,2px);
}
```

The translate function takes two values: The first specifies the horizontal movement, and the second the vertical movement. In this example, clicking an element with the .button class moves that element one pixel to the right and two pixels down. Use a negative number for the first value to move the element to the left; use a negative number for the second value to move the element up.

You're not limited to pixel values, either. Any valid CSS length value—px, em, %, and so on will work.

CSS also provides two additional functions for moving an element just to the left or right—translateX—and up or down—translateY. For example, to move an element up .5 ems, use the translateY function like this:

```
transform: translateY(-.5em);
```

The real fun with the `translate` function is when used with CSS transitions. With the CSS transition, you can then animate the movement of the element, so that it travels across the screen. You'll learn how to do that on page 330.

Skew

Skewing an element lets you slant it on its horizontal and vertical axes; this can give an element a three-dimensional feel (see Figure 10-6). For example, to slant all the vertical lines so that they lean to the left 45 degrees (as in the first image in Figure 10-6), you'd write this code:

```
transform: skew(45deg, 0);
```

To do the same along the y-axis (middle image in Figure 10-6), you'd write this:

```
transform: skew(0,45deg);
```

You can skew an element on both axes at once. For example, here is the code used to produce the third image in Figure 10-6:

```
transform: skew(25deg,10deg);
```

The first value is a degree value from 0deg to 360deg, proceeding in a counter-clockwise direction from the top of the element. For example, in the first image in Figure 10-6, the 45 degrees are represented by a line drawn from the center of the element and rotated 45 degrees counter-clockwise (bottom-left).

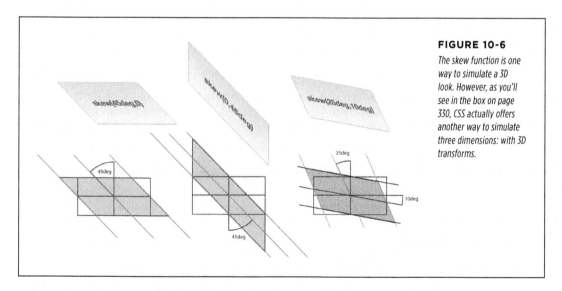

FIGURE 10-6

The skew function is one way to simulate a 3D look. However, as you'll see in the box on page 330, CSS actually offers another way to simulate three dimensions: with 3D transforms.

> **NOTE** Remember to add browser-prefixed versions of the `transform` property to your finished CSS: `-webkit-transform`, `-ms-transform`.

The second value is also a degree value from 0deg to 360deg. But this one proceeds in a clockwise position from the right of the element. So the middle image in Figure 10-6 shows a 45-degree slant of all of the horizontal lines.

TIP Visit *http://westciv.com/tools/transforms/index.html* to play with an online tool for visualizing CSS transforms.

As with translate and scale, CSS offers separate functions for the x- and y-axes: skewX and skewY.

NOTE CSS provides yet another transformation method called a *matrix*. A matrix is an array of numbers, as used in advanced algebra. They're pretty mind-bending and not at all intuitive unless you're Stephen Hawking. But if you want to learn how they work, visit *https://dev.opera.com/articles/understanding-the-css-transforms-matrix/* for as lucid an explanation as possible.

Multiple Transformations

You're not limited to just a single transformation. You can both scale an image and skew it; rotate it and translate it; or use any of the four different transform functions simultaneously. Simply add additional functions to the transform property, each separated by a space. For example, here's how you can rotate an element 45 degrees and enlarge it to twice its normal size:

```
transform: rotate(45deg) scale(2);
```

Here's an example with all four transformations applied at the same time:

```
transform: skew(45deg,0deg) scale(.5) translate(400px,500px) rotate(90deg);
```

The order in which you place the transform functions is the order in which the browser applies these effects. For example, in the second example, the element is first skewed, then scaled, then translated, and finally rotated. The order doesn't really matter unless you're using translate. Since translate actually moves the element, if you place it before a rotate, for example, the browser first moves the element and then rotates it. Since the element moved first, the point around which it rotates has changed. On the other hand, if you rotate it first, you're then moving the rotated element a certain amount from its center (which is now in a new location).

Origin

Normally, when you apply a transformation to an element, the web browser uses the center of the element as the transformation point. For example, when you rotate an element, the browser rotates it around its center point (Figure 10-7, left). However, CSS lets you change that transformation point, using the transform-origin property. It works just like the background-position property (page 236); you can supply keyword values, absolute values in pixels, and relative values in ems and percentages.

For example, to rotate a div around its top-left point (Figure 10-7, middle), you can use the left and top keywords, like this:

```
transform-origin: left top;
```

You can also use pixel values:

```
transform-origin: 0 0;
```

Or percentages:

```
transform-origin: 0% 0%;
```

Likewise, to rotate an element around its bottom-right corner (Figure 10-7, right), use the right and bottom keywords:

```
transform-origin: right bottom;
```

Which is also equivalent to:

```
transform-origin: 100% 100%;
```

When using pixel, em, or percentage values, the first number is the horizontal position, and the second is the vertical position.

> **NOTE** The transform-origin property has no effect on elements that are only moved using the translate function.

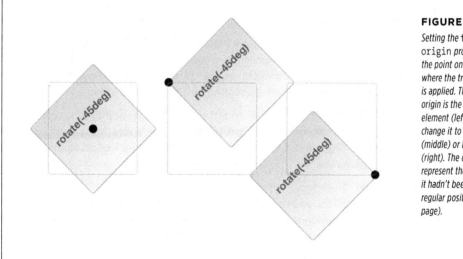

FIGURE 10-7

Setting the transform-origin property changes the point on the element where the transformation is applied. The default origin is the middle of the element (left), but you can change it to the top left (middle) or bottom right (right). The dotted squares represent the element if it hadn't been rotated (its regular position on the page).

3D Transforms

CSS also offers a much more complex type of transformation. 3D transforms let you simulate a three-dimensional space on the flat screen of a monitor, tablet, or phone.

For a short introduction to 3D transforms, visit *http://coding. smashingmagazine.com/2012/01/06/adventures-in-the-third-dimension-css-3-d-transforms/* and for a more detailed explanation with lots of examples, check out *http://desandro. github.io/3dtransforms/*. To see some great examples of 3D transforms in action, visit these sites:

- Apple's Morphing Power Cubes page (*www.webkit.org/ blog-files/3d-transforms/morphing-cubes.html*), one of the first examples of the power of 3D transformations, demonstrates a rotating cube, which you can change into a rotating set of tiles.

- Here's an example of a 3D "flip" effect: *http://davidwalsh. name/css-flip*—an animated effect that looks like you're turning over a card to show its back.

Transitions

While transforms can be fun (especially the rotate function), they really bring your page to life when coupled with a CSS transition. A *transition* is simply an animation from one set of CSS properties to another set over a specific amount of time. For example, you can make a banner rotate 360 degrees over the course of two seconds.

To make a transition work, you need a few things in place:

- **Two styles.** One style represents the beginning look of the element—a red nav button, for example—while the second style is the ending look—a blue nav button. The web browser will take care of the process of animating the change between the two styles (changing the button from red to blue, for example).

- **The** transition **property.** CSS adds the transition property—the secret sauce that makes the animation possible. In general, you apply the transition property to the original style, the style that defines the look of an element before the animation begins.

- **A trigger.** The trigger is the action that causes the change between the two styles. With CSS, you can use several pseudo-classes to trigger an animation. The most common is the :hover pseudo-class. With it, you can animate the change between an element's normal appearance and how it looks when a visitor mouses over it. You'll see an example of that in just a minute. In addition, you have :active (when the mouse is clicked on an element), :target (when an element is the target of link), and :focus (when a link is tabbed to, or a form field is clicked into or tabbed to). Beyond that, you can use JavaScript to dynamically change the style of any tag (see the box on page 335).

When the trigger no longer applies—when the visitor mouses off a navigation button, for example—then the browser returns the tag to its previous style *and* animates the entire process. In other words, you only need to set a transition to an element once, and the browser takes care of animating from one style to another and back to the original style.

A web browser can't animate every single CSS property, but you still have a long list of properties to choose from. In addition to the rotate, scale, translate, and skew transformations you just read about, you can also animate color, background-color, border-color, border-width, font-size, height, width, letter-spacing, line-height, margin, opacity, padding, and word-spacing; the positioning properties—top, left, right, and bottom—which you'll learn about in Chapter 15; and many other properties. You can find a complete list at *www.w3.org/TR/css3-transitions/#animatable-properties*.

NOTE CSS transitions work in most browsers. Unfortunately, when it comes to Internet Explorer, only version 10 and later understand CSS transitions. If you're still concerned about IE and earlier, use transitions simply as a way to add visual excitement. Mostly, this is just fine: IE9 and earlier will, in most cases, be able to switch between two styles (for example, show a :hover style) without animating that change.

Adding a Transition

At the heart of CSS transitions are four properties that control which properties to animate, how long the animation takes, the type of animation used, and an optional delay before the animation begins. Here's a simple example. Say you want a navigation button's background color to change from orange to blue when a visitor mouses over it. First, you start with the two styles needed to switch between these two colors. For example, you can apply a class of .navButton to the link and then create two styles, like this:

```
.navButton {
  background-color: orange;
}

.navButton:hover {
  background-color: blue;
}
```

These styles will work in any browser; hovering over the nav button will change its background from orange to blue. However, the change is instantaneous. To make the color animate over one second, add two new properties to the .navButton style, like this:

```
.navButton {
  background-color: orange;
  transition-property: background-color;
  transition-duration: 1s;
}
```

```
.navButton:hover {
    background-color: blue;
}
```

The transition-property specifies which properties to animate. You can specify a single property (as in the above example), use the keyword all to animate all CSS properties that change, or use a comma-separated list to specify more than one (but not all) properties. For example, say you create a :hover style so the text color, background color, and border color all change. You list out all three of those properties like this:

```
transition-property: color, background-color, border-color;
```

Or, to make it simple, use the all keyword, like this:

```
transition-property: all;
```

In most cases, using all works well, since every CSS change is animated, which creates a pleasing visual effect.

To specify how long the animation takes to complete, use the transition-duration property. This property takes a value in either seconds or milliseconds (thousandths of a second). For example, to make a transition take half a second to complete, you can use either:

```
transition-duration: .5s;
```

Or:

```
transition-duration: 500ms;
```

It's even possible to set separate timings for each animated property. For example, when a visitor mouses over a button, you may want the text color to change rapidly, the background color to change a little more slowly, and the border color to change really slowly. To do so, you need to list the animated properties, using transition-property and then list the times, using transition-duration, like this:

```
transition-property: color, background-color, border-color;
transition-duration: .25s, .75s, 2s;
```

The order in which you list the times must match the order in which you list the properties. So, in the above example, .25s goes with the color property, .75s with the background-color property, and 2s with the border-color property. If you move the properties around, then their timing changes.

Transition Timing

To have a working, animated transition, you only need to set transition-property and transition-duration. However, you can control the rate of the animation by using the transition-timing-function property. This property can be a little confusing: It doesn't control how long the animation takes (that's what the transition-duration property is for). Instead it controls the speed *during* the animation. For example, you can begin the animation slowly and then quickly complete it, creating an effect where the background color changes almost imperceptibly at first, and then quickly completes its color change.

The transition-timing-function property can take one of five keywords: linear, ease, ease-in, ease-out, and ease-in-out. If you don't specify a timing function, the browser uses the ease method, which begins the animation slowly, speeds up in the middle, and slows down at the end, providing a more organic change. The linear option provides a steady change along the entire length of the animation. No option is really any better than the other: they just provide different looks, so try them out to see which one you like best.

To use it, simply add the transition-timing-function property and the method you'd like to use:

```
transition-timing-function: ease-in-out;
```

> **NOTE** It's a lot easier to see the different timing functions than to describe them. Visit *www.the-art-of-web.com/css/timing-function/* to see an excellent side-by-side comparison of the five timing methods.

You can also use what's called a cubic-bezier value for the transition-timing-function property. The Bezier curve plots the progress of the animation over time (see Figure 10-8). If you've used a drawing program like Adobe Illustrator, you're probably familiar with Bezier curves. By adjusting two control points you can control how the line curves: the steeper the line, the faster the animation; the flatter the line, the slower. For example, the Bezier curve pictured in Figure 10-8 starts off steep (the animation begins quickly), then flattens in the middle (the animation slows down), and then grows steep again (the animation rapidly progresses to its final state). To create this kind of animation, add this line of code:

```
transition-timing-function: cubic-bezier(.20, .96, .74, .07);
```

Cubic Bezier curves aren't something you can come up with off the top of your head. You're better off using one of the many online tools for creating and testing different timing functions. Mathew Lein's Ceaser tool is one of the best: *http://matthewlein.com/ceaser/*.

As with the transition-duration property, you can apply different timings to different properties.

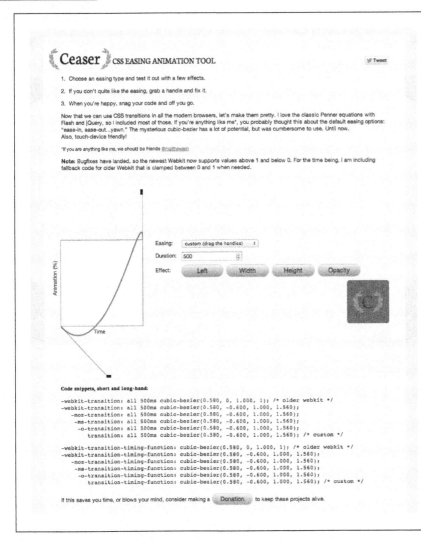

FIGURE 10-8

Creating a cubic Bezier curve lets you create a wide range of interesting timing functions for your animations. You can make them start really slowly and end quickly, or vice versa. The online Ceaser tool makes creating cubic Bezier curves a breeze: Just grab the control handle on the bottom-left point and drag to change the slope of the line, and then drag the control point on the top-right point. The steeper the line, the faster the progress of the animation at that stage. In this example, the line starts off relatively flat, meaning the animation will move slowly at first, then ramps up steeply at the end, meaning the animation will quickly progress to the finish at the end of the transition's duration.

Delaying a Transition's Start

Finally, you can prevent a transition from animating right away with the `transition-delay` property. For example, if you want to wait a half second before the animation begins, you can add this code:

```
transition-delay: .5s;
```

Using JavaScript to Trigger Transitions

CSS transitions are easy-to-use animations built right into web browsers (at least, *most* web browsers). You can create complex effects simply by defining a set of CSS properties to begin with, and a set of CSS properties to end with, and then step out of the way and let the web browser handle the rest.

Unfortunately, you're limited to just a handful of CSS selectors for triggering those transitions. Most commonly, you'll use the :hover pseudo-class to make an element change when moused over. You can also use the :focus pseudo-class on a form element to make it animate when a user clicks inside it (for example, you can make a multiline text area grow in height when focused, then shrink to just a few lines when a visitor clicks out of it).

For example, CSS doesn't have a :click pseudo-class, so if you want to trigger a transition when someone clicks on an element, you can't do it with CSS. Likewise, if you want to hover over one element but trigger an animation on another element, you're out of luck...if you're only using CSS. But CSS transitions work anytime a CSS property changes, even if you change the CSS property using JavaScript.

JavaScript is a programming language that lets you add interactivity to web pages, build dynamic user interfaces, and loads of other things. But you can also use JavaScript to simply add or remove a class from an element, or change any CSS property you'd like. Using JavaScript, you can add a class to an image when a visitor clicks a "Show bigger image" link. That new class simply scales up the image (using the scale transform discussed on page 322). By adding a transition to the image, you'll have an instant animation.

JavaScript is a big topic worthy of its own book... there just so happens to be *JavaScript & jQuery: The Missing Manual* by this author that's worth a read. But if you want to get started with the simplest way to use CSS transitions triggered by JavaScript, read this short tutorial: *https://css-tricks.com/controlling-css-animations-transitions-javascript/*.

Most of the time, you won't want to use a delay for all properties, since it kind of undermines the transition's potential for interactivity. After all, it's more like a cruel trick to make your visitors wait a second before they see any visual changes when they mouse over your button. However, if you're animating several properties, you may want to make one property wait until the others finish before its animation starts. For example, say you have a button whose background color and text color you want to change, and then have its border color change suddenly after the other two properties have finished. Here's how you might do that:

```
.navButton {
  color: black;
  background-color: #FF6603;
  border: 5px solid #660034;
  transition-property: color, background-color, border-color;
  transition-duration: 1s, 1s, .5s;
  transition-delay: 0, 0, 1s;
}

.navButton:hover {
  color: white;
  background-color: #660034;
```

```
    border-color: #FF6603;
}
```

As with the transition-duration property, you can specify different delay values for each property. The order in which you list the times must match the order of the properties listed for transition-property. For instance, in the preceding code, there's no delay for the transition between the color and background color, but there's a one-second delay before the border color changes.

TIP Usually you put the transition properties into the starting style (for example, .navButton on page 331), not the final style (.navButton:hover). However, here's a trick for use with CSS drop-down menus (see the box on page 296). One problem with drop-down menus in CSS is that they usually disappear very quickly if you accidentally mouse off the menu. However, you can make the menu appear quickly but disappear slowly using the transition-delay property. To do so, you add the following code to the original style:

```
transition-delay: 1s;
```

Then add no delay to the :hover style:

```
transition-delay: 0;
```

It's somewhat counterintuitive, but this code basically makes the :hover transition happen immediately, with no delay. But to return to the regular style (where the menu disappears) takes 1 second. During that time, a visitor has enough time to move his errant mouse back over the menu before it disappears.

Transition Shorthand

Writing out all the different properties—transition-property, transition-duration, transition-timing-function, and transition-delay—can get pretty tiring. Especially when you consider you need to also create vendor-prefixed versions of each of those as well. Fortunately, there's a faster way to create transitions—the transition property.

This property bundles all of the other properties into one. To use it, simply list the property, duration, timing function, and delay in a space-separated list. For example, to animate all CSS properties for one second using the ease-in timing function, with a half-second delay, write the following:

```
transition: all 1s ease-in .5s;
```

You need to list either all or a single CSS property and a duration, but the timing function and delay are optional. By default, the timing function is ease, and there's no delay. So if you simply want to animate the transition of all CSS properties for one second, then write this:

```
transition: all 1s;
```

If you only want to animate the change in the background color, then list that property:

```
transition: background-color 1s;
```

You can only list a single CSS property here, so if you wish to animate multiple CSS properties (but not all), then you can write a comma-separated list of space-separated transition properties. Take the example from page 335, where the border-color property is animated separately from the color and background color. You can rewrite that code like this:

```
transition: color 1s, background-color 1s, border-color .5s 1s;
```

To make the code easier to read, many web designers put each transition on a separate line, like this:

```
transition: color 1s,
            background-color 1s,
            border-color .5s 1s;
```

This is perfectly legal as long as you remember to separate them with a comma and end the whole shebang with a semicolon.

POWER USERS' CLINIC

Getting Smoother Animations

Animating many different properties can take a toll on a web browser. Whether you're using CSS transitions or CSS animations, browsers need to do a lot of work to animate changes in CSS properties. Too many animations and transitions going on at once can bring a browser to a crawl and even crash it. This is particularly true with mobile devices and tablets, which have significantly slower CPUs than desktop and laptop computers.

However, there are four things that browsers can animate without a lot of CPU power: opacity (page 671), and the translate, scale, and rotate options of the transform property (page 319). These four properties are treated more efficiently than other CSS properties, so any transitions or animations you create with them will be smoother. (To find out the technical details, check out: *http://www.html5rocks. com/en/tutorials/speed/high-performance-animations/*).

In addition, you can also force animations to be moved to a computer's *GPU*, or graphic processing unit. GPUs are really super-fast computers, and they can do specific types of calculations much more quickly than the computer's CPU. You can trick the browser into handing a style to the GPU by adding a 3D transform property to the style. For example, if you plan to animate the background color of an element when a visitor mouses over it, you could create the style with the original background color, like this:

```
. highlight {
    background-color: rgb(231,0,23);
    transition: background-color 1s;
    transform: translateZ(0);
}
.highlight:hover {
    background-color: rgb(0,0,255);
}
```

The transform: translateZ(0) line doesn't do anything visually. It tells the browser to move the element 0 pixels along a three dimensional z-axis; in other words, move it not at all. However, because it uses a 3D transformation, browsers give this style to the GPU to process. The upshot is that the animation might appear to play back more smoothly because of the GPU's greater horsepower.

But before you start slapping transform: translateZ(0) on every style, be aware that the GPU can only handle so much, and piling too many visual effects for it to handle can slow the browser to a crawl.

In addition, too many animations and transitions can have a very negative effect on a page's performance, especially on mobile devices. Make sure you test all of your transition and animation effects in multiple browsers and on a mobile phone to make sure your page works well.

◼ Animations

CSS provides another, more feature-rich mechanism for creating animations. With CSS transitions, you can only animate from one set of CSS properties to another. CSS *animations* let you animate from one set of properties to another set to another set, and so on. In addition, you can have an animation repeat, pause when a visitor mouses over it, and even reverse itself once the animation reaches its end.

CSS animations are a bit more complicated than transitions, but they have the added benefit of not necessarily needing a trigger to begin the animation. While you can add an animation to a :hover state so the animation plays when the mouse hovers over an element, you can also have an animation start when the page loads. This effect lets you draw attention to a banner or logo by animating it across the page when a visitor first enters your site.

> **NOTE** CSS animations, like transitions, don't work in Internet Explorer 9 or earlier. They're well supported in all current browsers, however.

The first step in creating an animation is creating a set of keyframes. In animation, a *keyframe* is a single frame of an animation that dictates how the scene looks. Suppose the first keyframe shows a ball on one side of a soccer field. By adding a second keyframe, you can define an ending point for the animation—like the ball inside the goal on the other side of the soccer field. A web browser then provides the animation between the two keyframes by drawing all of the intermediate steps—the ball traveling across the field on its way to the goal.

If you're thinking transitions use a similar idea, you're right. In a transition, you define two styles and let the browser animate the change from one style to another. In this way, you could think of each of those styles as a keyframe. However, CSS animations let you define *multiple* keyframes, so you can create much more complex animated effects: a soccer ball traveling from one side of the field, to a player, to another player, and then into the goal, for example.

There are two steps in creating an animation:

1. **Define the animation.**

   This involves setting up keyframes that list the CSS properties to animate.

2. **Apply the animation to an element.**

   Once defined, you can apply the animation to any number of elements on a page. You can even set up separate timings, delays, and other animation properties for each element. So you can use the same animation with slightly different settings multiple times on a page.

Defining Keyframes

The first step is to set up your keyframes. The syntax involved may look kind of strange, but here's the basic structure:

```
@keyframes animationName {
  from {
   /* list CSS properties here */
  }

  to {
    /* list CSS properties here */
  }
}
```

You start with @keyframes, followed by a name. The name is what you call the animation. You'll end up using that name later when you apply the animation to an element on the page, so make it descriptive, like "fadeOut" or "fadeIn."

> **NOTE** The term @keyframes isn't a CSS property, it's called an *at rule*. Other at rules in CSS include the @import statement for loading an external style sheet from another style sheet, and @media to define styles for different types of media such as a printer or different screen sizes and resolutions (page 465).

You then add at least two keyframes. In the current example, the keywords from and to are used to create the beginning keyframe (from) and the final keyframe (to). Inside each keyframe you add one or more CSS properties—just as if you were creating a style. In fact, you can think of each keyframe as just a CSS style filled with one or more CSS properties. For example, say you want to create an animation that fades an element into view. You could start with an opacity value of 0 (invisible), and end with a value of 1 (fully visible):

```
@keyframes fadeIn{
  from {
    opacity: 0;
  }
  to {
    opacity: 1;
  }
}
```

You're not limited to just two keyframes, either. You can use percentage values to define multiple keyframes. The percentage represents where in the overall length of the animation the change should occur. For example, say you want to create an effect where the background of an element changes from yellow to blue to red. You can write this:

```
@keyframes backgroundGlow {
  from {
    background-color: yellow;
  }
  50% {
    background-color: blue;
```

```
  }
  to {
    background-color: red;
  }
}
```

In this case, the blue background will appear halfway through the animation. If you want the yellow to last longer and the blue to appear after three-quarters of the animation is complete, use 75% instead of 50%. You can continue to add additional keyframes this way (for example, at 25%, 66%, and so on).

> **NOTE** You can replace the `from` keyword with 0% and the `to` keyword with 100%.

Nor are you limited to a single CSS property. You can place any number of animatable properties (page 331) inside each keyframe—background-color, opacity, width, height, and so on:

```
@keyframes growAndGlow {
  from {
    background-color: yellow;
  }

  50% {
    transform: scale(1.5);
    background-color: blue;
  }

  to {
    transform: scale(3);
    background-color: red;
  }

}
```

In the above example, not only does the background color cycle through three colors, it also scales up in size until it's three times its original size.

You can also get pretty tricky with the percentage values by adding multiple percentage values for one set of CSS properties. This is useful in a couple of cases: First, it's good if you want to animate to a certain point, pause, and then continue. For example, say you'd like to begin with a yellow background color for a <div> tag. Then you'd like to change that color to blue, stay at blue for a while, and then finish with a red color. In other words, you want a sort of pause in the middle while the background color stays constant before changing again. You can do that with this code:

```
@keyframes glow {
  from {
    background-color: yellow;
```

```
  }
  25%, 75% {
    background-color: blue;
  }
  to {
    background-color: red;
  }
}
```

Notice the 25%, 75% in line 5. That means 25% of the way through the animation, the background color of the element should be blue. However, it should be blue 75% of the way through as well. In other words, from the 25% mark to the 75% mark, the background will remain solid blue, before finally turning red. If this animation ran for 4 seconds, then for the middle 2 seconds of the animation, the element's background would remain solid blue.

You can also use percentages when you want to use the same set of CSS properties for different parts of the animation. For example, say you want to animate the background color again, but this time go from yellow to blue to orange to blue to orange to red. Blue and orange appear twice, so instead of writing their background-color properties multiple times, you can instead do this:

```
@keyframes glow {
  from {
    background-color: yellow;
  }
  20%, 60% {
    background-color: blue;
  }
  40%, 80% {
    background-color: orange;
  }
  to {
    background-color: red;
  }
}
```

In this case, the background color will turn blue at the 20% mark, orange at the 40% mark, then blue again at the 60% mark, and orange one last time at the 80% mark before finally turning red.

Unfortunately, as of this writing, to use CSS animations in Chrome, Safari, and Opera, you must also use the -webkit- vendor prefix (see the box on page 321). In other words, you need to create one animation for those browsers, and another animation (without any vendor prefix) for Firefox and Internet Explorer 10 and above:

```
@-webkit-keyframes fadeIn {
  from {
    opacity: 0;
```

```
    }
    to {
        opacity: 1;
    }
}

@keyframes fadeIn{
    from {
        opacity: 0;
    }
    to {
        opacity: 1;
    }
}
```

Notice the two hyphens—one between the @ and the vendor prefix and one between the vendor prefix and the word keyframes.

Applying an Animation

Once you've completed a set of keyframes, the animation is ready. However, to make it work, you need to apply it to an element on your page. You can add an animation to any style for any element on a page. If you simply add the animation to a style that applies immediately to an element—for example, an h1 tag style—the animation will apply when the page loads. You can use this technique to add an introductory animation to a page that makes a logo zoom into place in the page's upper-left, or make a particular box of content glow to draw attention to it.

In addition, you can apply an animation to one of the pseudo-classes, including :hover, :active, :target, or :focus to make an animation run when a visitor mouses over a link, for example, or clicks into a form field. Finally, you can apply the animation to a class style and use JavaScript to dynamically apply that class in response to a visitor clicking a button or some other page element (see the box on page 335).

CSS provides a handful of animation-related properties to control how and when an animation plays back (as well as a shorthand version that encompasses all the individual properties). At a minimum, to get an animation running, you need to supply the name you gave the original animation (in the @keyframes rule as discussed on page 338), and a duration for the animation.

Here's a simple example. Say you want a div with an important announcement to fade into view when the page loads. You've given that div a class name of announcement: <div class="announcement">.

1. **Create the fade-in animation with the** @keyframes **rule:**

```
@keyframes fadeIn {
    from { opacity: 0; }
    to { opacity: 1; }
}
```

If you're only animating a single property, it can be easier to read to if you put the keyframes on a single line:

```
from  { opacity: 0; }
```

However, if you're animating many properties, it's easier to read (and type) if you spread that code over several lines:

```
from {
  opacity: 0;
  color: red;
  width: 50%;
}
```

2. **Apply that animation to the style for the `<div>` tag:**

```
.announcement {
  animation-name: fadeIn;
  animation-duration: 1s;
}
```

The animation-name property simply tells the browser which animation to use. It's the same name you provided when you created the animation in step 1. The animation-duration property sets the time the animation takes from start to finish. In this example, these are the only two animation properties listed, but you can (and probably will) put other non-animation properties in the style as well. For example, in the real world, you'd probably add properties such as width, background-color, border, and so on to this .announcement style.

Putting the animation's name inside quotes—'fadeIn'—isn't technically required, and it's not done in this example, but doing so can prevent any conflicts that might arise if you use a CSS keyword for an animation name.

As with the @keyframes rule, each of the animation properties require the -webkit-vendor prefix to work in Chrome, Safari, and Opera, so the above .announcement style would need to be written like the following to work in as many browsers as possible:

```
.announcement {
  -webkit-animation-name: fadeIn;
  -webkit-animation-duration: 1s;
  animation-name: fadeIn;
  animation-duration: 1s;
}
```

It may seem a bit of a pain to define the animation in one place with the @keyframes rule and then apply it in another (the style); however, once you've defined the animation, you're free to use it any number of times in any number of styles. For example, you can create a generic fade-in type of animation and apply it to different elements. What's more, you can control the animation independently for each style—for example, make the header fade in over the course of half a second, but make another page element fade in for five seconds.

In addition, you can apply more than one animation to an element. Say you create one animation named fadeIn to make an element fade in and another animation named blink to make the background color blink wildly. To apply both animations to the element, you provide a comma-separated list of names like this:

```
animation-name: fadeIn, blink;
```

To give the animations separate timings, provide a list of comma-separated times:

```
animation-name: fadeIn, blink;
animation-duration: 1s, 3s;
```

The order in which you place the times applies to the animation name in the same order. For example, the first animation gets the first time listed. In the above example, fadeIn takes one second to complete, while blink takes three seconds.

You can apply several other useful animation properties as well. Read on.

Timing the Animation

You've already seen that the animation-duration property lets you control an animation's length. As with transitions, you can use milliseconds (750ms, for example) or seconds (.75s, for example) to specify the duration.

As with transitions, you can also set a specific type of timing function to control the rate of the animation throughout that duration. For example, you can start the animation slowly and end it quickly, using a cubic-Bezier curve (page 333) or using one of the built-in keyword methods: linear, ease, ease-in, ease-out, or ease-in-out. These work the same as the transition-timing-function property discussed on page 332.

You can use the animation-timing-function to control the entire animation or just specific keyframes. For example, to apply the ease-out timing function for the fadeIn animation presented earlier (step 1 on page 342), add the timing function to the .announcement style (step 2 on page 345):

```
.announcement {
  animation-name: fadeIn;
  animation-duration: 1s;
  animation-timing-function: ease-out;
}
```

However, you can also control the timing function for the animation between keyframes. For example, say you create an animation that has three keyframes with three different background colors. The web browser will animate from one color to another and then to a third. Perhaps you want it to slowly move from the first to the second color using a cubic Bezier curve, and then move in a uniform time from the middle to the end. You can do that by adding two timing functions, one to the first keyframe (which controls the animation from keyframe 1 to 2), and one at the second keyframe to control the animation from keyframe 2 to 3:

```
@keyframes growAndGlow {
  from {
    background-color: yellow;
    animation-timing-function: cubic-bezier(1, .03, 1, .115);
  }
  50% {
    transform: scale(1.5);
    background-color: blue;
    animation-timing-function: linear;
  }
  to {
    transform: scale(3);
    background-color: red;
  }
}
```

You can also delay the beginning of the animation using the animation-delay property. It works the same as the transition-delay property for transitions (page 334), and simply waits a specific number of milliseconds or seconds before the animation begins. For example, if you want to wait one second before the "announcement" div fades into view, you can rewrite that .announcement class like this:

```
.announcement {
  animation-name: fadeIn;
  animation-duration: 1s;
  animation-delay: 1s;
}
```

Adding a delay to an animation is a great way to catch people's attention and add surprise to a page.

> **NOTE** The animation-timing-function and animation-delay properties require the -webkit- vendor prefix for Chrome, Safari, and Opera, so make sure you add the appropriate -webkit-animation-timing-function, and so on to your animated styles.

Finishing the Animation

With CSS, you can control a few additional aspects of an animation, including whether to repeat an animation, which direction the animation runs if it's animated more than once, and how the browser should format the element when the animation is complete.

Transitions are animations that only run once—mouse over a button and the button grows, for example. Animations, however, can run once, twice, or continuously, thanks to the `animation-iteration-count` property. If you want an animation to run 10 times (fade in and out 10 times, perhaps), add this code to the style you're animating:

```
animation-iteration-count: 10;
```

Normally a browser only plays the animation once, and if that's all you're after, then leave off this iteration count property. If you want the animation to play continuously, the `animation-iteration-count` property accepts one keyword: `infinite`. So to run the `fadeIn` animation an infinite number of times on the announcement div, you can create this style:

```
.announcement {
  animation-name: fadeIn;
  animation-duration: .25s;
  animation-iteration-count: infinite;
}
```

That, however, would annoy your visitors to no end, so please don't do it. However, you could use a style like this for a simple "pulsing" effect where a "sign up today" button gently glows (by animating the `box-shadow` property discussed on page 201).

Normally, when an animation runs more than once, a web browser literally starts the animation over from the beginning. So if you animated a background color from yellow to blue and repeated it twice, the browser would show a yellow box turning blue, and then suddenly the yellow box would return and then animate to blue once again. This effect can be pretty jarring. In this case, it would look better if, for the second time through the animation, the browser simply reversed the effect. That's how transitions work. For example, when you mouse over an element, the browser animates the transition from the regular state to the rollover state. When you move the mouse off the element, the browser simply reverses the animation to return to the regular state. To make an animation move forward on odd runs and backward on even runs, use the `animation-direction` property and the `alternate` keyword. For example, to make an element fade out and then back in again, you can create an animation called fadeOut, like this:

```
@keyframes fadeOut {
  from { opacity: 1; }
  to { opacity: 0; }
}
```

Then, play that animation twice, reversing its direction on the second time:

```
.fade {
  animation-name: fadeOut;
  animation-duration: 2s;
  animation-iteration-count: 2;
  animation-direction: alternate;
}
```

This code tells the web browser to run the fadeOut animation on any element with the class of fade. The animation should run for two seconds and then repeat. Because of the alternate value for animation-direction, the animation will fade out the first time (go from totally opaque—an opacity of 1—to invisible—an opacity of 0), but will run backwards the second time (from 0 to 1 opacity), which makes it fade back into view.

TIP To have an animation run a number of times but end up back at the beginning state, use an even number of iterations and set the animation-direction property to alternate.

No matter how many times you have a web browser run an animation, once the animation is completed, the browser displays the animated element in its original, pre-animation state. For example, say you animate an image so it slowly grows to twice its size. Once the animation is completed, the web browser snaps the image back down to its original size, creating a jarring visual effect. Fortunately, you can tell the browser to keep the animated element formatted the same as when the animation ended by setting the animation-fill-mode property to forwards.

```
animation-fill-mode: forwards;
```

Apply this property to the element you're animating, along with the animation-name, animation-duration, and other animation properties.

Animation Shorthand

As you can see, there are a lot of animation properties, and writing all of them out in addition to all of the vendor-prefixed versions is a recipe for carpal tunnel syndrome. While you still need vendor-prefixed versions, you can simplify things by using the animation shorthand property. This single property combines animation-name, animation-duration, animation-timing-function, animation-iteration-count, animation-direction, animation-delay, and animation-fill-mode into a single property. For example, you can take this code:

```
.fade {
  animation-name: fadeOut;
  animation-duration: 2s;
  animation-timing-function: ease-in-out;
  animation-delay: 5s;
  animation-iteration-count: 2;
  animation-direction: alternate;
  animation-fill-mode: forwards;
}
```

And rewrite it like this:

```
.fade {
  animation: fadeOut 2s ease-in-out 5s 2 alternate forwards;
}
```

That's one line of code instead of seven! You should list the property values in the order used above: name, duration, timing function, count, direction, delay, and fill-mode. In addition, make sure each value is separated by a space. Only the name and duration are actually required. The other values are optional.

If you want to apply more than one animation to an element, simply use comma-separated lists of animation properties. For example, to apply two animations (say fadeOut and glow) to the .fade style, write this:

```
.fade {
  animation: fadeOut 2s ease-in-out 5s 2 alternate forwards,
             glow 5s;
}
```

Of course, in real usage you'd need to use the -webkit- vendor prefix as well:

```
.fade {
  -webkit-animation: fadeOut 2s ease-in-out 5s 2 alternate forwards,
                     glow 5s;
  animation: fadeOut 2s ease-in-out 5s 2 alternate forwards,
             glow 5s;
}
```

In general, you should opt to use the animation shorthand—it's much more concise and gentler on your fingers and the keyboard.

Pausing an Animation

CSS includes another animation property—animation-play-state—to control an animation's playback. It accepts only one of two keywords: running or paused. To pause an animation, simply apply this declaration to a style:

```
animation-play-state: paused;
```

There's only one way to really apply that using CSS, however—a pseudo-class. As with transitions, you need some kind of trigger to pause an animation. One way to do this is to pause any animation when a visitor mouses over the animation. Here's an example using the .fade class style:

```
.fade {
  animation: fadeOut 2s ease-in-out 2 alternate 5s forwards,
             glow 5s;
}
```

This code runs two animations—fadeOut and glow—on any element with the fade class applied to it. Say you want to let visitors pause this animation simply by mousing over it. You'd only need to add one more style:

```
.fade:hover {
  animation-play-state: paused;
}
```

Of course, you'll need all the -webkit- vendor prefixed version as well: -webkit-animation-play-state.

A more powerful way to pause an animation would be to dynamically apply the animation-play-state property to the element using JavaScript. In this way, you can create a complex animation and add a Pause button that pauses the animation when clicked. See the box on page 335 for more on JavaScript and CSS animations.

Animating on Hover

So far, the animations you've seen here would all run when the page loads. You have a few other options, including several pseudo-classes and using JavaScript, to trigger a CSS animation. The most common pseudo-class for animation is :hover. With it, you can run an animation when a visitor mouses over any element; for example, you can make a logo do fancy gymnastics, move off the page, and then move back again.

To animate an element when a visitor's mouse hovers over it, start by creating an animation with the @keyframes rule (step 1 on page 342). Then, create a :hover pseudo-class for whatever element you wish to animate. In that style, you simply add the animation properties (step 2 on page 343). Now the animation runs only when the visitor hovers over the element.

■ Tutorial

In this exercise, you'll add transformations, animation, and transitions to a banner.

To get started, download the tutorial files from this book's companion website at *https://github.com/sawmac/css_mm_4e*. Click the tutorial link and download the files. All the files are enclosed in a zip archive, so you need to unzip them first. (You'll find detailed instructions on the website.) The files for this tutorial are contained inside the *10* folder.

1. **In a text editor, open *10→styles.css*.**

   The *banner.html* file includes a banner with a logo graphic, headline, and set of navigation buttons (see Figure 10-9). The *styles.css* file is the style sheet attached to the *banner.html* page. First, you'll add a transformation so that when a visitor mouses over a button it scales up in size.

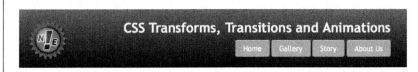

FIGURE 10-9

A normal, static banner just waiting to come to life with animation, transformations, and transitions.

2. **At the bottom of the _styles.css_ file add the following rule:**

```
nav a:hover {
  -webkit-transfrom: scale(1.5);
  -ms-transform:  scale(1.5);
  transform: scale(1.5);
}
```

The buttons on the page are contained inside an HTML nav element. This descendant selector targets links inside the <nav> tag in their hover state (that is, when a visitor mouses over the link). The style applies the scale function (page 322) to make the button slightly larger. Unfortunately, you need to add the -webkit- and -ms- vendor-prefixed versions for Safari and Internet Explorer 9.

3. **Save _styles.css_ and preview the _banner.html_ file in a web browser. Mouse over the links below the headline.**

When you mouse over a button, it grows larger, almost popping off the page (Figure 10-10). Very cool, but it would look even better if you added an animation to the effect.

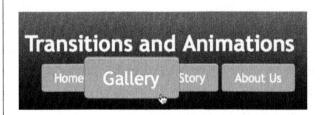

FIGURE 10-10

Pop goes the button. By adding a scale _transformation to a button's hover state, you can make it almost pop off the page. The enlarged button doesn't affect any of the content around it (for example, it doesn't push the other buttons out of the way). This is a unique aspect of all CSS transformations._

4. **Add another style before the** nav a:hover **style you just created:**

```
nav a {
  transition: all .5s;
}
```

Here, you're instructing the web browser to animate all changes to the CSS properties of the <a> tags inside the <nav> element, and to make the animation last half a second. To make things more interesting, you'll add a background color to the hover state.

5. **Locate the** nav a:hover **style and add** background-color: red;**, so the finished style looks like this:**

```
nav a:hover {
  background-color: red;
  -webkit-transform:scale(1.5);
  -ms-transform:  scale(1.5);
  transform: scale(1.5);
}
```

If you save the page and preview it now, you'll see that not only do the buttons grow larger when hovered over, they also fade to red. But now you'll add separate timings to these transitions, so the button first grows larger and then turns red.

6. **Delete the code inside the** nav a **style and add two new properties:**

```
nav a {
  -webkit-transition: -webkit-transform .5s,
                      background-color 1s ease-in .5s;
  transition: transform .5s,
              background-color 1s ease-in .5s;
}
```

You need to add two properties: one for Safari and one for all other browsers. Even though Safari understands the transition property (without a vendor prefix), you have to use the -webkit- vendor prefix because you're using the -webkit-transform property, and that wouldn't make sense to any other browser.

The second property—the plain transition property—is for all other browsers.

The first part—transform .5s—informs the browser that you want to animate any changes in the transform property over the course of half a second. The second part—background-color 1s ease-in .5s—indicates that you wish to animate the background color change over the course of one second, using the ease-in timing method (page 332), but wait half a second before starting. That .5s at the end is important, since it matches the .5s of the transform animation. In other words, the browser will wait until the transform transition is complete before changing the background color.

7. **Save *styles.css* and preview the *banner.html* file in a web browser.**

Mouse over a button. First, the button gets larger. Keep the mouse over the button, and it then turns red. You can of course, tweak the timing—for example, remove the delay for the background-color transition, and the color change will begin at the same time as the size change. However, since the color change lasts for one second, it will continue after the button has reached its final size.

Adding an Animation

Now it's time to try out CSS animations. You'll begin by simply spinning and scaling the logo image. The first step in creating a CSS animation is to use the @keyframes rule to set up the keyframes of the animation. This example starts you off with a simple animation and just two keyframes.

TIP Because CSS animations require a fair amount of code, it's a good idea to start by using only the vendor-prefix for the browser you most often use. Test the page in that browser, and once you've perfected the animation, then add the code for the other browsers. This example uses code that will work in Chrome, Safari, and Opera. If you prefer Firefox or Internet Explorer 10 or later, then leave off the -webkit- part for now.

---

1. **Open the *styles.css* file and add the following style to the bottom of that file, after the** `nav a:hover` **style:**

```
@-webkit-keyframes logo {
  from {
    -webkit-transform: rotate(0) scale(.5);
  }
  to {
    -webkit-transform: rotate(-720deg) scale(1);
  }
}
```

This example uses the WebKit syntax, which means it'll work in Chrome, Safari and Opera. If you're using Firefox or Internet Explorer (10 or later) as your main browser, replace `@-webkit-keyframes` with `@keyframes`.

This code is telling the browser that it should start the element with no rotation—`rotate(0)`—and at half its size—`scale(.5)`. It should then animate the change from that to the animation's "to" state—in this case rotating it –720 degrees, which is three counter-clockwise rotations—and scaling it back up to its normal size. In other words, this animation will spin an element and make it grow.

Now, you need to apply it to any element on the page.

2. **Create a new style after the one you just added:**

```
.logo {
    -webkit-animation: logo 1s;
}
```

The logo in the banner has a class of `logo` applied to it, so this class selector adds an animation to it. The `animation` property can take many values, but you only need the name and duration. Here, you're specifying the animation you created in the last step—`logo`—and telling a web browser to make the animation last one second.

3. **Save the *styles.css* file and preview *banner.html* in your browser.**

The logo should spin, grow in size, and then stop. If it doesn't, double-check your code and make sure you're previewing the page in the proper browser. If all goes according to plan, this animation should look great, but it would be even better if it moved in from off the page and then stopped in its proper spot in the banner. To do that, you'll simply animate the element's position on the page.

4. **Edit the** `@keyframes` **rule so it looks like this (addition in bold):**

```
@-webkit-keyframes logo {
  from {
    -webkit-transform: rotate(0) scale(.5);
    left: 120%;
  }
```

```
  to {
    -webkit-transform: rotate(-720deg) scale(1);
    left: 0;
  }
}
```

Here you begin the logo's position to the right of the banner and navigation buttons at the edge of the screen (basically, you're placing the logo's left edge 1.2x the width of the banner). To get this to work, you need to take advantage of the CSS `position` property. You'll learn about it in-depth in Chapter 15, but for now you just need to know that CSS gives you the power to position any element anywhere in the browser window—even outside the browser window. The final keyframe places the logo at the 0 position, where it normally would appear on the page at the left side of the banner.

5. **Save the *styles.css* file and preview the *banner.html* file in Chrome or Safari.**

Looking good. But you can still do better. Add another keyframe so the logo rolls into place and then rotates in the opposite direction as it gets bigger.

6. **Change the code you added in step 4 to look like this:**

```
@-webkit-keyframes logo {
  from {
    -webkit-transform: rotate(0) scale(.5);
    left: 120%
  }
  50% {
    -webkit-transform: rotate(-720deg) scale(.5);
    left: 0;
  }
  to {
    -webkit-transform: rotate(0) scale(1);
  }

}
```

Now you have three keyframes: one at the beginning, another right in the middle, and a third at the end. The browser will animate the properties as they change from frame 1 to frame 2 to frame 3.

The first keyframe is the same as in step 4: The logo is unrotated, half its size, and placed off to the right side. The second keyframe keeps the logo at the same size, rotates it three times, and moves it to the left side of the banner. Finally, once the logo is in the place, the browser scales it up while rotating it back from the –720 degree position to the 0 degree position; in other words, the logo now spins three times clockwise.

7. **Save the style sheet and preview the web page in Chrome or Safari.**

   The logo should roll in from the right side of the banner to the left, stop, grow, and spin clockwise. If it's not working, double-check your code against the code in step 6. At this point, though, the animation is a bit too fast. That's an easy fix.

8. **Edit the** `.logo` **style so the animation lasts for three seconds instead of one:**

   ```
   .logo {
     -webkit-animation: logo 3s;
   }
   ```

   Now you just need to duplicate this code and remove the -webkit- vendor prefix to have it work in Firefox and Internet Explorer 10 and later. You'll tackle the @keyframes rule first.

9. **Copy the vendor-prefixed** @keyframes **rule and paste a duplicate just below it. Remove the** -webkit- **prefix, so your code looks like this:**

   ```
   @-webkit-keyframes logo {
     from {
       -webkit-transform: rotate(0) scale(.5);
       left: 120%
     }
     50% {
       -webkit-transform: rotate(-720deg) scale(.5);
       left: 0;
     }
     to {
       -webkit-transform: rotate(0) scale(1);
     }
   }
   @keyframes logo {
     from {
       transform: rotate(0) scale(.5);
       left: 120%
     }

     50% {
       transform: rotate(-720deg) scale(.5);
       left: 0;
     }

     to {
       transform: rotate(0) scale(1);
     }
   }
   ```

At some point, in a beautiful future, all the browsers will use the single non-prefixed @keyframes rule and a non-prefixed transform property. But at this point, you're stuck duplicating a lot of code.

Fortunately, adding the @keyframes rule is the hardest part. Adding the animation to the .logo style isn't nearly as much work.

10. **Edit the** .logo **style by adding one new line:**

```
.logo {
  -webkit-animation: logo 3s;
  animation: logo 3s;
}
```

11. **Save** *styles.css* **and check it out in Firefox or Internet Explorer.**

The logo should roll along the page and enlarge on all of those browsers. Of course, in Internet Explorer 9 and earlier, you won't see any animation. However, the logo will still be correctly placed and the page will look just fine. You'll find a finished version of this tutorial in the *10_finished* folder.

To take this further, add an animation that makes one of the navigation buttons glow when the mouse is positioned over it. (Hint: create an animation that cycles through different box shadow values. Use the inset value to add the shadow inside the box as described on page 201. Then add that animation to the nav a:hover style so it only plays when the mouse hovers over a button.)

FIGURE 10-11

Books can do a lot, but they can't, unfortunately, show you the amazing animation that you just created. Here's what the page should look like when the animation has run its course and you mouse over the Home button.

Formatting Tables and Forms

The formatting powers of CSS go way beyond text, images, and links. You can make tables of information like schedules, sports scores, and music playlists easier to read by adding borders, backgrounds, and other visual enhancements. Similarly, you can use CSS to organize the elements of a form to help your visitors through the process of ordering items, signing up for your newsletter, or using your latest web application.

This chapter shows you how to display tables and forms with HTML and how to lay out and style them using CSS. In two tutorials at the end of the chapter, you'll create a table and a form, using the tricks you've learned along the way.

▓ Using Tables the Right Way

HTML tables have seen a lot of use in the short history of the Web. Originally created to display data in a spreadsheet-like format, tables became a popular layout tool. Faced with HTML's limitations, designers got creative and used table rows and columns to position page elements like banner headlines and sidebars. As you'll see in Part Three of this book, CSS does a much better job of laying out web pages. You can concentrate on using (and formatting) tables for their original purpose—displaying data (Figure 11-1).

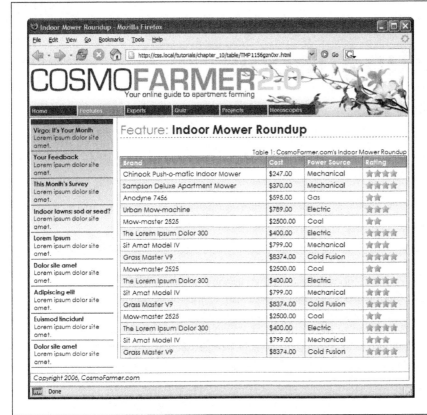

FIGURE 11-1

You can do all of your page layout and design with CSS and use tables for what they were intended—displaying rows and columns of information. CSS created the attractive fonts, borders, and background colors in this table about indoor lawn mowers, but the underlying structure is all thanks to HTML.

HTML (and XHTML) has a surprising number of tags dedicated to table building. This chunk of HTML creates the very simple table pictured in Figure 11-2.

```
<table>
<caption align="bottom">
   Table 1: CosmoFarmer.com's Indoor Mower Roundup
</caption>
<colgroup>
  <col class="brand" />
  <col class="price" />
  <col class="power" />
</colgroup>
 <thead>
 <tr>
 <th scope="col">Brand</th>
  <th scope="col">Price</th>
  <th scope="col">Power Source</th>
```

```
    </tr>
  </thead>
  <tbody>
    <tr>
      <td>Chinook Push-o-matic Indoor Mower</td>
      <td>$247.00</td>
      <td>Mechanical</td>
    </tr>
    <tr>
      <td>Sampson Deluxe Apartment Mower</td>
      <td>$370.00</td>
      <td>Mechanical</td>
    </tr>
  </tbody>
</table>
```

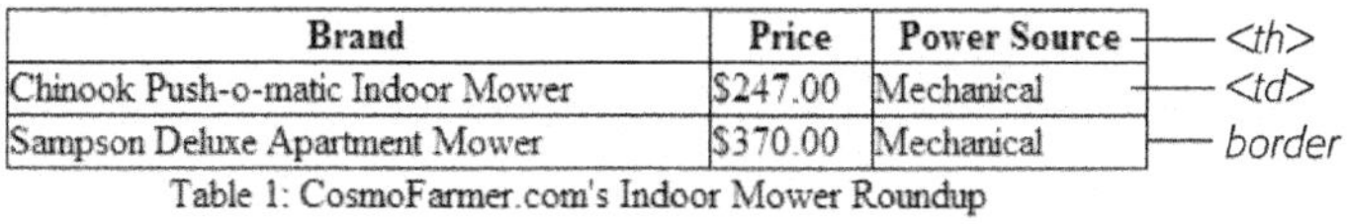

Even with only three rows and three columns, the table uses nine unique HTML tags: `<table>`, `<caption>`, `<colgroup>`, `<col>`, `<thead>`, `<tbody>`, `<tr>`, `<th>`, and `<td>`. In general, more HTML isn't a good thing, and you don't need all of these tags: You can get away with just the `<table>`, `<tr>`, and `<td>` tags (and usually `<th>` as well). However, a table's various tags give you lots of useful hooks to hang CSS styles on. The headers of each column—the `<th>` tags—can look different from other table cells if you create a `<th>` tag style, and you can use the `<colgroup>` tag as an easy way to set the width of a table column. This saves you the hassle of having to create lots of classes—like `.tableHeader`—and then apply them by hand to individual table cells. In the next section, you'll see examples of how you can use these different tags to your advantage.

Brand	Price	Power Source
Chinook Push-o-matic Indoor Mower	$247.00	Mechanical
Sampson Deluxe Apartment Mower	$370.00	Mechanical

Table 1: CosmoFarmer.com's Indoor Mower Roundup

FIGURE 11-2

Data tables, like this one, usually have headers created with the `<th>` tag. Header cells announce what type of information appears in a row or column. Price tells you that you'll find the cost of each lawn mower listed in the cells below. The actual data presented in a table is enclosed in `<td>` tags.

■ Styling Tables

You can use many of the CSS properties you've read about to dress up the appearance of a table and its contents. You can use the *color* property, for example, to set a table's text color, just like anywhere else. You'll find a few properties, however, that are particularly useful with tables, as well as a couple aimed specifically at formatting tables.

Because tables are composed of several HTML tags, it helps to know which tag to apply a particular CSS property to. Applying padding to a <table> tag, for example, has no effect. The next few sections cover CSS properties for formatting tables and which HTML tags they get along with.

Adding Padding

As you read on page 187, padding is the space between an element's border and its content. You can use padding to provide a little space between the edges of a paragraph's text and its border. When it comes to tables, the borders are the *edges* of a cell, so padding adds space around any content you've placed inside of a table cell (see Figure 11-2). Using padding, you can individually control space between a cell's content and each of its four edges.

You apply padding to either a table header or a table cell tag, but *not* to the <table> tag itself. So, to add 10 pixels of space to the inside of all table cells, use this style:

```
td, th { padding: 10px; }
```

You can also control the spacing separately for each edge. To add 10 pixels of space to the top of each table data cell, 3 pixels to the bottom of that cell, and 5 pixels on both the left and right sides, create this style:

```
td {
  padding-top: 10px;
  padding-right: 5px;
  padding-bottom: 3px;
  padding-left: 5px;
}
```

Or, use the padding shortcut property:

```
td {
  padding: 10px 5px 3px 5px;
}
```

Adjusting Vertical and Horizontal Alignment

To control where content is positioned *within* a table cell, use the text-align and vertical-align properties.

Text-align controls horizontal positioning and can be set to left, right, center, and justify (see Figure 11-3). It's an *inherited* property. (See Chapter 4 for more on inheritance.) When you want to right-align the contents of all table cells, create a style like this:

```
table { text-align: right; }
```

This property comes in handy with <th> tags, since browsers usually center-align them. A simple style like th { text-align: left; } makes table headers align with table cells.

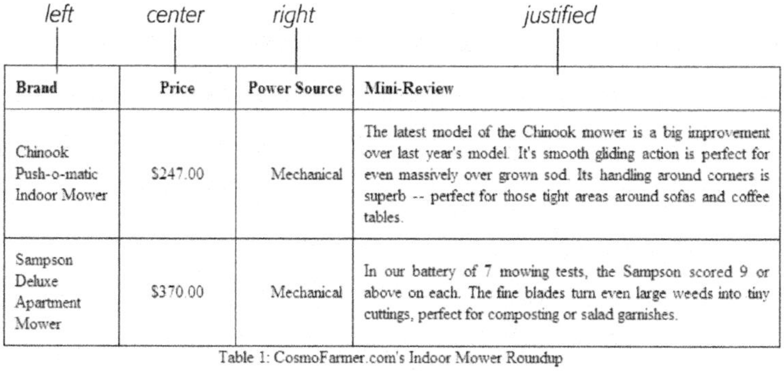

FIGURE 11-3

You can control which edge of a table cell its content aligns with by using the text-align *property. Be careful with the* justify *option, however. Browsers aren't very good at aligning text to both the left and right edges of an element. The result is often big, distracting chunks of empty space in the text.*

Table cells have a height as well. Web browsers normally align content vertically in the middle of a table cell (see the middle example in Figure 11-4). You can control this behavior by using the vertical-align property. Use one of these four values: top, baseline, middle, or bottom. Top pushes content to the top of the cell; middle centers content; and bottom pushes the bottom of the content to the bottom of the cell. Baseline works just like top, except the browser aligns the baseline of the first line of text in each cell in a row (Figure 11-4). Unless you're a real perfectionist, you won't even notice the subtlety of the baseline option. More importantly, neither will your visitors. Unlike text-align, the vertical-align property isn't inherited, so you can use it only on styles that apply directly to <th> and <td> tags.

NOTE So far, the table formatting you've learned applies to *all* your tables. When you want to style individual tables (or table cells), change the selector you use. To apply a special design to a certain table, give it a class name—<table class="stocks">—and create descendant selectors like .stocks td or stocks .th to uniquely format individual cells. If you want to style a particular cell differently than other cells in a table, then apply a class to the tag—<td class="subtotal">—and create a class style to format that cell.

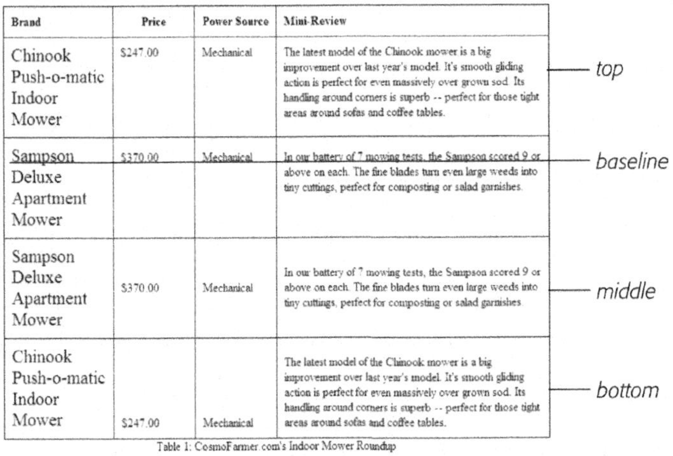

Brand	Price	Power Source	Mini-Review
Chinook Push-o-matic Indoor Mower	$247.00	Mechanical	The latest model of the Chinook mower is a big improvement over last year's model. It's smooth gliding action is perfect for even massively over grown sod. Its handling around corners is superb -- perfect for those tight areas around sofas and coffee tables.
Sampson Deluxe Apartment Mower	$370.00	Mechanical	In our battery of 7 mowing tests, the Sampson scored 9 or above on each. The fine blades turn even large weeds into tiny cuttings, perfect for composting or salad garnishes.
Sampson Deluxe Apartment Mower	$370.00	Mechanical	In our battery of 7 mowing tests, the Sampson scored 9 or above on each. The fine blades turn even large weeds into tiny cuttings, perfect for composting or salad garnishes.
Chinook Push-o-matic Indoor Mower	$247.00	Mechanical	The latest model of the Chinook mower is a big improvement over last year's model. It's smooth gliding action is perfect for even massively over grown sod. Its handling around corners is superb -- perfect for those tight areas around sofas and coffee tables.

Table 1: CosmoFarmer.com's Indoor Mower Roundup

— top
— baseline
— middle
— bottom

FIGURE 11-4

When padding is applied to a cell, the content never actually aligns to the any of the cell borders: There's always a gap equal to the padding setting.

Creating Borders

The CSS border property (page 194) works pretty much the same with tables as with other elements, but you need to keep a couple of things in mind. First, applying a border to a style that formats the <table> tag outlines just the table, not any of the individual cells. Second, applying borders to cells—td { border: 1px solid black; }—leaves you with a visual gap between cells, as shown in Figure 11-5, top. To gain control of how borders appear, you need to understand how web browsers normally draw table cells and the CSS border-collapse property.

- **Controlling the space between table cells.** Unless instructed otherwise, browsers separate table cells by a couple of pixels. This gap is really noticeable when you apply a border to table cells. CSS gives you the border-spacing property to control this space. Apply this property to the table itself, and if you wish to remove the space that browsers normally place between cells, then set the border-spacing property to 0:

```
table {
  border-spacing: 0;
}
```

Of course, if you like space between the cells, then add space:

```
table {
  border-spacing: 2px;
}
```

- **Eliminating double borders.** Even if you eliminate the cell spacing of a table, borders applied to table cells double up. That is, the bottom border of one cell adds to the top border of the underhanging cell, creating a line that's twice as thick as the border setting (Figure 11-5, middle). The best way to eliminate this (and eliminate cell spacing at the same time) is to use the `border-collapse` property. It accepts two values: `separate` and `collapse`. The `separate` option is normally how tables are displayed, with the cell spaces and doubled borders. Collapsing a table's borders eliminates the gaps and doubled borders (Figure 11-5, bottom). Apply the `collapse` value to a style formatting a table, like so:

```
table { border-collapse: collapse; }
```

> **NOTE** If you set the `border-collapse` property to `collapse`, `border-spacing` has no effect.

- **Rounded corners.** You can use the `border-radius` property (page 199) to add rounded corners to table cells (but not to tables themselves). For example, if you want to outline table cells and give them rounded corners, you can create this style:

```
td {
  border: 1px solid black;
  border-radius: 5px;
}
```

Note that if you set the `border-collapse` property to `collapse`, then browsers ignore any `border-radius` you've set for table cells; they'll just draw regular square corners.

> **NOTE** You can even apply the `box-shadow` property (page 201) to tables and to cells. If you apply it to a table, the shadow will appear outside the entire table, but if you apply the shadow to individual cells, then each cell will have its own drop shadow.

Styling Rows and Columns

Adding stripes (like the ones in Figure 11-6) is a common table design technique. By alternating the appearance of every other row of data, you make it easier for people to spot the data in each row. Fortunately, CSS does offer a way to do that. Using the `nth-of-type` selector, which you read about on page 64, you can add different backgrounds to odd and even rows:

```
tr:nth-of-type(odd) { background-color: red; }
tr:nth-of-type(even) { background-color: blue; }
```

If you don't want to apply the same background to the odd rows of all of your tables, simply add a class name to the table you wish to target (`products`, for a table with product information, for example), then use a descendant selector, like this:

```
.products tr:nth-of-type(odd) { background-color: red; }
.products tr:nth-of-type(even) { background-color: blue; }
```

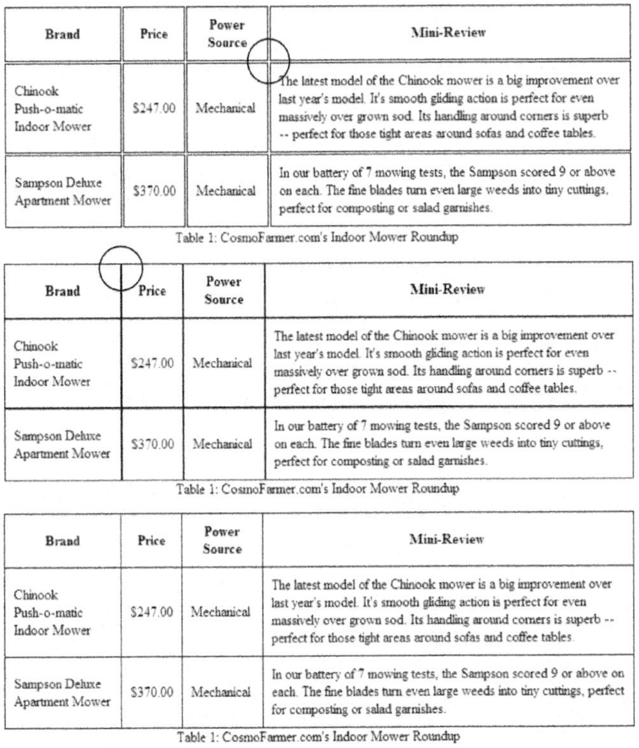

FIGURE 11-5

Browsers normally insert space between each table cell. (You probably won't notice this extra space unless you've added a border, as shown here at the top.) If you set the border-spacing *property to 0 to remove the extra space, you're left with double borderlines where adjoining borders touch (middle). The* border-collapse *property solves both dilemmas (bottom).*

You're not limited to colors either. You can use background images (see page 231) or even linear gradients (page 252) to create more sophisticated looks like the slight gradation in the table header row of Figure 11-6. (You'll see a similar example of this in the tutorial on page 374.) You can use a descendant selector to target cells in that row as well. This technique is great for when you style all of the cells in one column with their own look: <td class="price">, for example.

NOTE The nth-of-type selector isn't supported in Internet Explorer 8 or earlier.

Formatting columns is a bit trickier. HTML provides the <colgroup> and <col> tags to indicate groups of columns and individual columns, respectively. You include one <col> tag for each column in the table and can identify them with either a class or ID. (See the HTML code on page 358.) Only two sets of properties work on these tags: width and the background properties (background-color, background-image, and so on). But they can come in mighty handy. When you want to set the width of all of the cells in a column, you can skip any HTML attributes and just style the column, using a style applied to the `<col>` tag. For example, say you have this bit of HTML: `<col class="price">`. You can add this style to a style sheet to set the width of each cell in that column to 200 pixels:

```
.price { width: 200px; }
```

FIGURE 11-6

Alternating the background color from row to row in a table makes it easier to quickly identify the data for each row.

To highlight a column, you can use the background properties. Again, assume you have a `<col>` tag with a class of `price` applied to it:

```
.price { background-color: #F33; }
```

Keep in mind, however, that backgrounds for columns appear under table cells, so if you set a background color or image for `<td>` or `<th>` tags, the column's background won't be visible.

> **NOTE** Typically, web browsers display the border and background color of any empty table cell. If you want to hide those empty cells, CSS lets you. Just add `empty-cells:hide` to a style applied to a table:
>
> ```
> table {
>   empty-cells: hide;
> }
> ```

One caveat, however: If you set the `border-collapse` property (page 363) to `collapse`, browsers ignore the `empty-cells` property and show the borders and backgrounds of even empty cells.

Styling Forms

Web forms are the primary way visitors interact with a website. By supplying information on a form, you can join a mailing list, search a database of products, update your personal profile on Facebook, or order that *Star Wars* Lego set you've had your eye on.

There's no reason your forms need to look like all the others on the Internet. With a little CSS, you can style form fields to share the same formatting as other site elements like fonts, background colors, and margins. There only a few CSS properties specific to forms, but you can apply just about any property in this book to a form element.

> **TIP** For a great roundup of form designs, check out *www.sanwebe.com/2014/08/css-html-forms-designs*.

HTML Form Elements

A variety of HTML tags help you build forms. You can format some of them (like text fields) more successfully than others (radio buttons). Here are a few common form tags and the types of properties they get along with:

- **Fieldset.** The `<fieldset>` tag groups related form questions. Most browsers do a good job of displaying background colors, background images, and borders for this tag. Padding places space from the edges of the fieldset to the content inside it.

- **Legend.** The `<legend>` tag follows the HTML for the `<fieldset>` tag and provides a label for the group of fields. The legend appears vertically centered on the top borderline of a fieldset. If the form elements for collecting a shipping address appear inside the fieldset, you might add a legend like this: `<legend>Shipping Address</legend>`. You can use CSS to change the `<legend>` tag's font properties, add background colors and images, and add your own borders.

- **Text fields.** The <input type="text">, <input type"password">, and <textarea> tags create text boxes on a form. These tags give you the most consistent cross-browser CSS control. You can change the font size, font family, color, and other text properties for text boxes, as well as add borders, background colors, and images. You can set the width and height of these fields using the CSS width and height properties.

- **Buttons.** Form buttons—like <input type="submit">—let your visitors submit a form, reset its contents, or set off some other action. Most browsers let you go wild with text formatting, borders, backgrounds, drop shadows, and rounded corners. You can also align the button's text to the left, middle, or right using the text-align property. Linear gradients (page 252) look especially good on buttons.

- **Drop-down menus.** Drop-down menus created by the <select> tag also give you a fair amount of styling control. Most other browsers also let you set the font, font size, background color, image, and borders. However, backgrounds and background images aren't always added to the drop-down menu when it expands to show all of the menu's options.

- **Checkboxes and radio buttons.** Most browsers don't allow formatting of these elements, and the ones that do aren't consistent, so it's best to leave them alone.

POWER USERS' CLINIC

Attribute: The Ultimate Form Field Selector

When it comes to styling forms, tag styles just don't cut the mustard. After all, text boxes, radio buttons, checkboxes, password fields, and buttons all share the same HTML tag—<input>. While a width of 200 pixels makes sense for a text box, you probably don't want your checkboxes to be that big, so you can't use the <input> tag to format width. For now, the most cross-browser–friendly way of formatting only text fields would be to add a class name to each text field—like <input type="text" class="textfield" name="email">—and then create a class style to format it.

However, you can take advantage of the attribute selector (page 59) to fine-tune your form styling without resorting to classes.

An attribute selector targets an HTML tag based on one of the tag's attributes. The type attribute is responsible for determining what kind of form element the <input> tag produces. The type value for a form text field is text. To create a style that makes the background color of all single-line text fields blue, you'd create this selector and style:

```
input[type="text"] {
    background-color: blue;
}
```

Changing text in the above example to submit creates a style for submit buttons only, and so on.

All current browsers, even Internet Explorer 7, understand attribute selectors, so feel free to use them to style your forms with precision.

Laying Out Forms Using CSS

All it takes to create a form is adding a bunch of labels and other form elements to a web page. Visually, though, you may end up with a chaotic mess (see Figure 11-7, left). Forms usually look best when the questions and form fields are organized into columns (Figure 11-7, right).

You can achieve this effect in a couple of ways. The easiest approach is with an HTML table. Although form labels and fields aren't strictly table data, they lend themselves beautifully to a row/column format. Just put your labels ("First Name," "Phone Number," and so on) in one column, and form fields in a second column.

Using CSS, you can also create a two-column form like Figure 11-7 (with the added benefit of less HTML code). Here's the basic approach:

1. **Wrap each label in a tag.**

   The obvious choice for a tag is <label>, since it's designed to identify form labels. But you can't *always* use <label> tags for all labels. Radio buttons usually have a question like "What's your favorite color?" followed by separate <label> tags for each button. So what tag do you use for the question? In this case, you must resort to wrapping the question in a <span> tag: <span>What's your favorite color?</span>. Then add a class to each of these tags—<span class="label">—and also add the class to just those <label> tags you want to appear in the left-hand column (in Figure 11-8, that would be the labels for "First name," "Last name," and so on, but not the <label> tags for the radio buttons).

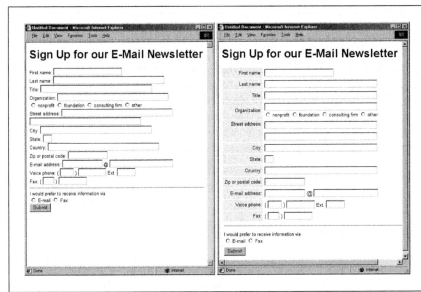

FIGURE 11-7

The different shapes and sizes of text boxes, radio buttons, and other form objects don't naturally align well with text, often causing an ungainly zigzag pattern. This form isn't just ugly; it's hard to read (left). The solution is to organize your forms into columns (right), using either an HTML table or CSS styles.

2. **Set the display property to** `inline-block`**, and set a width.**

Normally the `<label>` and `<span>` tags are inline elements, which ignore many of the settings available to block elements, including `width`, `height`, and `text-align`. However, if you make the label an `inline-block`, it can still sit next to (that's the "inline" part) the form field. The `width` value should provide enough space to accommodate the entire label on one line if possible. You can create a class style that looks something like this:

```
.label {
   display: inline-block;
   width: 20em;
}
```

The `width` and `inline-block` settings turn the labels into little evenly sized blocks and provide a clean left edge to which all the form fields align.

3. **Adjust the style.**

Just a couple more enhancements complete the job. You want to set the `vertical-align` property (page 360) to `top`, so the top of the label text aligns with the top of the form field. You also should align the label text to the right, so each label appears next to each form field. Finally, by adding a little bit of right margin, you can create a nice gutter of white space between the labels and form fields.

```
.label {
   float: left;
   width: 20em;
   vertical-align: top;
   text-align: right;
   margin-right; 15px;
}
```

At this point, you've got yourself a simple, neat form. You can make other enhancements if you wish, like making the labels bold and a different color. The tutorial that starts on the next page provides a step-by-step example of this technique.

Form Pseudo-Classes

There are a handful of pseudo-classes aimed at styling forms. The :focus pseudo-class lets you create a selector that changes the way a text field looks when a visitor clicks or tabs inside it (this is called giving the field *focus*). You can use this to change the size, background color, font, and other CSS properties of the field. You'll see an example of it in action in the tutorial on page 381.

The :checked pseudo-class works with radio buttons and checkboxes. It's intended to let you style those elements, but web browsers generally keep a tight visual rein on these fields, and most CSS properties do not apply. However, if you want to give them a try, you can simply create a style named :checked and add some CSS properties to it. Realize it will only apply to the radio buttons and checkboxes of a form. If you want to style a particular checkbox when it's checked, you can create a class style:

```
.special:checked
```

And then apply that class to just that checkbox:

```
<input type="checkbox" class="special" ...
```

Form elements can also be enabled or disabled. When disabled, the field can't be changed: For example, you can't type into

a disabled text field, or turn on a disabled checkbox. You can only change the state of a form element (from disabled to enabled, for example) using JavaScript, so you'll need to learn that to really take advantage of the :enabled or :disabled pseudo-classes. However, they can come in handy. For example, say you have an order form with both "billing" and "shipping" address fields. If you added a "same as billing address" checkbox next to the shipping address fields, a visitor can click this box. Using JavaScript, you can disable the shipping address fields so no one accidentally types into them. To make it clear that the user can't fill them out, you can change their style so they look "dimmed," or grayed out, like this:

```
:disabled {
    background-color: #333;
}
```

There are even more pseudo-classes intended to work with some of HTML's special form features, like built-in form validation or other special properties. To learn about these, visit *http://html5doctor.com/css3-pseudo-classes-and-html5-forms /*.

Tutorial: Styling a Table

HTML is great for building tables, but you need CSS to give them style. As you can see on page 358, it takes quite a bit of HTML to construct a simple table. Lucky for you, this book comes with a prebuilt HTML table for you to practice your CSS on. In this tutorial, you'll format the table's rows, columns, and cells, and give it an attractive font and background color.

To get started, download the tutorial files located on this book's companion website at *https://github.com/sawmac/css_mm_4e*. Click the tutorial link and download the files. All the files are enclosed in a zip archive, so you need to unzip them first. (Go to the website for detailed instructions.) The files for this tutorial are in the *11→table* folder.

1. **Launch a web browser and open the file *11→table→table.html*.**

   This page contains a simple HTML table. It has a caption, a row of table headers, and nine rows of data contained in table cells (Figure 11-8). In addition, the
   <col> tag is used three times to identify the three columns of data. As you'll
   see in a bit, <col> is a handy tag to style, since it will let you set the width of
   all cells in a column.

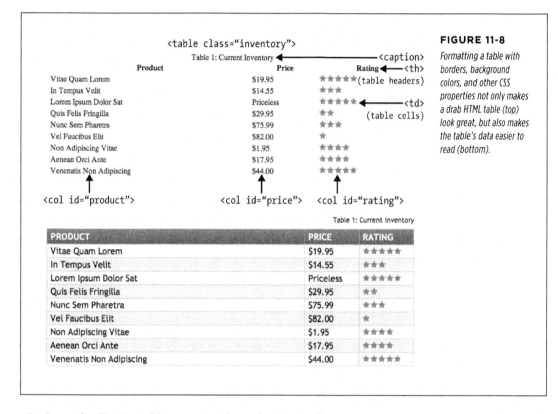

FIGURE 11-8

*Formatting a table with
borders, background
colors, and other CSS
properties not only makes
a drab HTML table (top)
look great, but also makes
the table's data easier to
read (bottom).*

2. **Open the file *11→table→css→main.css* in a text editor.**

   This external style sheet is attached to the *table.html* file. You'll start by creating
   a style that sets the table's width and text font. This table has a class of inven-
   tory applied to it, so you can use a class selector to format just this one table.

   NOTE   Browsers cache files, so if you make a change to the *main.css* file and it doesn't seem to be working,
   you may need to refresh you browser's cache. Check out this site, dedicated to teaching you just how to do that:
   www.refreshyourcache.com/en/home/.
   ---

3. **At the bottom of the *main.css* file add the following style:**

```
.inventory {
  font-family: "Trebuchet MS", Arial, Helvetica, sans-serif;
  width: 100%;
  margin-top: 25px;
}
```

Unless you set the width of a table, it grows and shrinks to fit the size of the content inside it. In this case, you've set a 100 percent width, so the table stretches to fit the entire width of its container. (In this case, it's the <body> tag itself, with a set width and auto left and right margins to center it in the browser window.) Setting the font family in the <table> uses inheritance to give all of the tags inside the table the same font—<caption>, table headers (<th>), table cells (<td>), and so on. Finally, the margin-top property scoots the table down from the headline above it.

Next you'll style the table's caption.

4. **Add another style below the table style you just created:**

```
.inventory caption {
  text-align: right;
  font-size: .85em;
  margin-bottom: 10px;
}
```

This descendant selector only affects the <caption> tag that appears inside another tag with the class of inventory (that's the <table> on this page). A <caption> tag indicates what a table is about. In this case, it shouldn't be the focus of attention, so you've kept the text small and moved it to the right edge, out of the way. The bottom margin adds a bit of space between the caption and the table.

When you read information across a table row, it's easy to lose track of which row you're looking at. Good visual guides are essential. Adding borders around the cells, which you'll do next, visually delineates the information.

5. **Add the following group style to the style sheet:**

```
.inventory td, .inventory th {
  font-size: 1.1em;
  border: 1px solid #DDB575;
}
```

This group selector formats the table header (<th>) and table cell (<td>) tags of this table with larger type and draws a border around each header and each cell. Browsers normally insert space between each cell, so at this point there are small gaps between the borders (Figure 11-9, circled). Between the gaps and the borders, the whole table looks too boxy. You'll fix that next.

6. **Add the** border-collapse **property to the table style you created in step 3 so that it looks like this:**

```
.inventory {
  font-family: "Trebuchet MS", Arial, Helvetica, sans-serif;
  width: 100%;
  margin-top: 25px;
  border-collapse: collapse;
}
```

The border-collapse property removes the spacing between cells. It also merges borders that touch, which prevents thick, unattractive borders. Without border-collapse, the bottom border of a table header and the top border of the table cell would double up to make a 2-pixel border.

If you preview the table now, you'll see the data is better organized visually, but the information in each cell looks a little cramped. Add some padding to fix that.

7. **Add padding to the group selector you created in step 5:**

```
.inventory td, .inventory th {
  font-size: 1.1em;
  border: 1px solid #DDB575;
  padding: 3px 7px 2px 7px;
}
```

Although the top table-header row stands out because of its boldface text, there are a few things you can do to make it stand out even more and improve its appearance.

8. **Create a new style below the** .inventory td, .inventory th **style for formatting just table head cells:**

```
.inventory th {
  text-transform:uppercase;
  text-align: left;
  padding-top: 5px;
  padding-bottom: 4px;
}
```

This style is a perfect example of effective cascading. The group selector td, th defines common formatting properties between the two types of cells. By introducing this th-only style, you can further tweak the look of *just* the table headers. For example, the padding-top and padding-bottom settings here override those same settings defined in the selector in step 7. However, since you don't override the left or right padding settings, the <th> tags will retain the seven pixels of left and right padding defined in step 7. This style also turns all of the text to uppercase and aligns it to the left edge of the table cell.

The table headers still don't have enough oomph, and the table seems to recede into the background of the page. A background graphic can provide the necessary boost.

Product	Price	Rating
Vitae Quam Lorem	$19.95	★★★★★
In Tempus Velit	$14.55	★★★
Lorem Ipsum Dolor Sat	Priceless	★★★★★
Quis Felis Fringilla	$29.95	★★
Nunc Sem Pharetra	$75.99	★★★
Vel Faucibus Elit	$82.00	★
Non Adipiscing Vitae	$1.95	★★★★
Aenean Orci Ante	$17.95	★★★★
Venenatis Non Adipiscing	$44.00	★★★★★

Product	Price	Rating
Vitae Quam Lorem	$19.95	★★★★★
In Tempus Velit	$14.55	★★★
Lorem Ipsum Dolor Sat	Priceless	★★★★★
Quis Felis Fringilla	$29.95	★★
Nunc Sem Pharetra	$75.99	★★★
Vel Faucibus Elit	$82.00	★
Non Adipiscing Vitae	$1.95	★★★★
Aenean Orci Ante	$17.95	★★★★
Venenatis Non Adipiscing	$44.00	★★★★★

FIGURE 11-9

When a browser displays a table, it normally inserts space between each cell (top). It also lets borders double up where cells touch. Setting the border-collapse *property to* collapse *solves both problems (bottom).*

9. **Edit the** th **style by adding a linear gradient to the background and changing the text color:**

```
.inventory th {
  text-transform:uppercase;
  text-align: left;
  padding-top: 5px;
  padding-bottom: 4px;
  background: rgb(229,76,16);
  background: linear-gradient(to bottom, rgb(229,76,16), rgb(173,54,8));
  color: white;
}
```

You start by simply adding an RGB color to the background; that way, Internet Explorer 9 and earlier (which don't understand gradients) at least have a solid color. The next three lines add the vendor-prefixed versions of the linear gradient, while the second-to-last line is the official linear-gradient syntax. Finally, the text color is changed to white.

When tables have lots of data stuffed into many rows and columns, it's sometimes hard to quickly identify which data belongs to each row. Thankfully, you can use the `nth-of-type` selector to quickly target alternating rows.

10. **Add another style to the *main.css* file:**

```css
.inventory tr:nth-of-type(even){
  background-color: rgba(255,255,255,.1);
}
.inventory tr:nth-of-type(odd){
  background-color: rgba(229,76,16,.1);
}
```

As you can read on page 66, the `nth-of-type` selector is used to select child elements that follow a numeric pattern; for example, every fifth paragraph. In this case, the first style selects every even `<tr>` tag, while the second selects every odd `<tr>` tag.

Finally, you'll adjust the width of the cells that fall under the Price and Rating columns. One technique is to meticulously add class names to those cells and create a class style with a set width. A better approach, however, is to take advantage of the `<col>` tag, which lets you assign a class or ID to a column's worth of cells. As you can see in Figure 11-8, those two columns have an ID of `price` and `rating`. You can easily set the width for these two columns with one group selector.

11. **Add one more style to the *main.css* file:**

```css
#price, #rating {
  width: 15%;
}
```

Save the style sheet and preview the *table.html* file in a web browser to see the results. Your page should look like the bottom image in Figure 11-8. You'll also find the completed exercise in the *11_finished→table* folder.

■ Tutorial: Styling a Form

This tutorial gives you some practice using CSS to organize a form and make it more attractive. If you open *11→form→form.html* in a web browser, then you'll see it contains a simple form for subscribing to the fictitious website, CosmoFarmer.com (Figure 11-10). The form asks several questions and uses a variety of form elements for input, including text boxes, radio buttons, and a pull-down menu.

As subscription forms go, it looks fine, but a little bland. In the steps on the following pages, you'll spruce up the fonts, line up the questions and boxes better, and add a few other improvements.

1. **Open the file *11→form→global.css* in a text editor.**

   You'll add your new styles to an external style sheet that's linked to the *form.html* file. Start by increasing the size of the type in the form to make it more readable.

2. **At the bottom of the style sheet, add the following style:**

```
.subform {
    font-size: 1.2em;
    color: white;
    font-family:Tahoma, Geneva, sans-serif;
}
```

   The subscription form has a class of subform applied to it, so this style sets the text size, color, and font for all text between the opening and closing <form> tags.

   Time to work on the layout. To better align the form elements, you'll create the appearance of two columns—one for the questions (labels) and another for the answers (form fields).

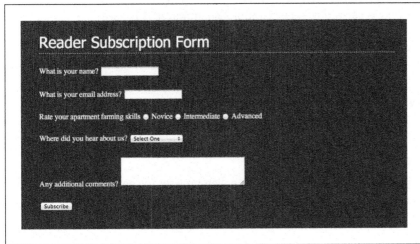

FIGURE 11-10

While the HTML <table> tag is one way to organize the questions of a form, you can also use CSS to make a disorganized jumble of labels and form fields (like the ones pictured here) and make a form's layout clearer and more attractive.

3. **Add another style to the style sheet:**

```
.subform .label {
    display: inline-block;
    width: 200px;
    vertical-align: top;
}
```

   This descendant selector identifies any element with a class of .label within this form. The style changes the labels from inline elements (which won't accept width values) to inline-block elements. The width setting sets the label area to 200 pixels wide, while the vertical align setting makes sure the label text aligns with the top of the form fields next to them. As a result, when you apply this style to each of the questions in the form, you create an even-width column. But in order to see the effect, you must first apply the class to the appropriate page elements.

4. **Open the file *form.html.* Locate the code** `<label for="name">` **and add** `class="label"`**, so the tag looks like this:**

   ```
   <label for="name" class="label">
   ```

   You must do the same for each question in the form, so...

5. **Repeat step 4 for the following pieces of HTML code:** `<label for="email">`, `<label for="refer">`, `<label for="comments">`**.**

   There's one additional question on the form—*Rate your apartment farming skills.* It isn't inside a `label` tag, since its purpose is to introduce a series of radio buttons, each of which has its own label. You need to add a `<span>` tag to this text so you can apply the `label` style to it.

6. **Find the text *Rate your apartment farming skills*, and then wrap it in a** `<span>` **tag with a class of** `label`**, like so:**

   ```
   <span class="label">Rate your apartment farming skills</span>
   ```

   Now the questions appear to be in a single column (Figure 11-11, top). But they'd look better if they stood out more and lined up with the corresponding form fields.

7. **In the *global.css* file, edit the** `.subform .label` **style you created in step 3, so it looks like this:**

   ```
   .subform .label {
   display: inline-block;
   width: 200px;
   vertical-align: top;
   text-align: right;
   margin-right: 10px;
   font-weight: bold;
   color: rgba(255,255,255,.5);
   }
   ```

   Preview the page in a web browser. The form should look like the bottom image in Figure 11-11.

   The form is shaping up, but that Subscribe button looks out of place over at the left edge. You'll align it with the other form elements next.

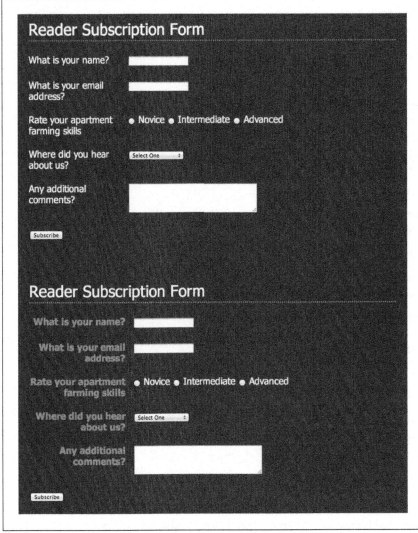

FIGURE 11-11

Sometimes small and subtle changes can make a form more readable. Making the questions on the form bold and aligning them with their corresponding form elements (bottom) immediately improves the look of the form.

8. **Add another style to the *global.css* file:**

```
.subform input[type="submit"]  {
  margin-left: 220px;
}
```

Since submit buttons are created by adding type="submit" to an <input> tag, you can simply use an attribute selector (page 59) to target them. This frees you from having to create a class style and applying it to the submit button.

Most browsers let you style buttons in other ways, too, so...

9. **Edit the Submit button style by adding a few more properties:**

```
.subform input[type="submit"] {
  margin-left: 220px;
  padding: 10px 25px;
  font-size: 1em;
  color: white;
}
```

Padding adds space between the text inside the button and the edges of the button, while the font-size and color properties affect the text on the button. Now you can get more creative and add a gradient to the button.

10. **Edit the Submit button style again:**

```
.subform input[type="submit"] {
  margin-left: 220px;
  padding: 10px 25px;
  font-size: 1em;
  color: white;
  background: rgb(0,102,153);
  background: linear-gradient(to bottom, rgba(255,255,255,.1) 40%,
rgba(255,255,255,.5));
}
```

Here you set a standard background color (for IE9 and earlier) followed by a linear gradient. There are two color stops: The first color runs from the top to 40 percent of the way into the button, then the gradient begins (for a recap of gradients and color stops, turn to page 252).

Finally, you'll tweak the look just a bit. You'll remove the standard border, round the corners, and add a glow around the box.

11. **Edit the Submit button style one last time (changes in bold):**

```
.subform input[type="submit"] {
  margin-left: 220px;
  padding: 10px 25px;
  font-size: 1em;
  color: white;
  background: rgb(0,102,153);
  background: linear-gradient(to bottom, rgba(255,255,255,.1) 40%,
rgba(255,255,255,.5));
  border-radius: 5px;
  box-shadow: 0 0 4px white;
}
```

Setting the border to none removes the border browsers normally draw around the button, while the border-radius property (page 199) rounds the button's corners. Finally, by adding a drop shadow with no horizontal or vertical offset (that's the 0 0 part), you can add a glow to an element. In this case, it looks like a slight white glow coming from behind the button.

NOTE You can take this button design even farther. Try creating a rollover style for it—.subform input[type="submit"]:hover—and change the background color. You can even animate that transition using what you learned in the previous chapter!

You've got the text labels and Subscribe button looking great, but why stop there? Time to jazz up the form fields. Begin by changing their font and background colors.

12. **Add a style for the form's Select menu:**

    ```
    .subform select {
      font-size: 1.2em;
    }
    ```

    This just pumps the text size up a bit. You could choose a font, add a background color, and make other changes. However, some browsers (like Safari) don't really let you style the drop-down menus much, so make sure you test out any style changes you make to drop-down menus.

    Now it's time to change the text fields.

13. **Create a new group selector for styling the three text boxes in the form:**

    ```
    .subform input[type="text"], .subform textarea {
        border-radius: 5px;
        border: none;
        background-color: rgba(255,255,255,.5);
        color: rgba(255,255,255,1);
        font-size: 1.2em;
        box-shadow: inset 0 0 10px rgba(255,255,255,.75);
    }
    ```

    This group style selects all input elements with the type of text as well as the multiline text boxes (the <textarea> tag). This adds various properties that you should be familiar with by now, like border-radius, background-color, font size, and box-shadow. The text boxes look a little small, so you'll set their widths and add a little bit of padding.

14. **Edit the style you just created by setting a width and padding (changes in bold):**

    ```
    .subform input[type="text"], .subform textarea {
      font-size: 1.2em;
      border-radius: 5px;
      border: none;
      background-color: rgba(255,255,255,.5);
    ```

```
color: rgba(255,255,255,1);

    font-size: 1.2em;
    box-shadow: inset 0 0 10px rgba(255,255,255,.75);
    width: 500px;
    padding: 5px;
}
```

You can make your form easier for your visitors to fill out by highlighting the active form element with the special :focus pseudo-class (page 56). You'll add that in the next step.

15. **At the end of the internal style sheet, add one last style for the pull-down menu and the three text fields:**

```
.subform input[type="text"]:focus, .subform textarea:focus {
    background-color: white;
    color: black;
}
```

Preview the page in a web browser. It should now look like Figure 11-12. You can find a completed version of this tutorial in the *11_finished→form* folder.

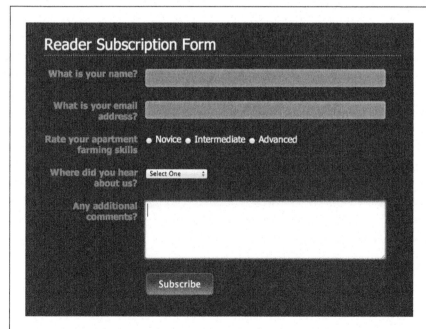

FIGURE 11-12

Using the :focus *pseudo-class, you can make your forms more interactive by highlighting the form fields the visitor uses. Here, you can see you're about to type in the Comments field because of its white background color.*

CSS Page Layout

Introducing CSS Layout

C SS leads a double life. As great as it is for formatting text, navigation bars, images, and other bits of a web page, its truly awesome power comes when you're ready to lay out entire web pages. While HTML normally displays onscreen content from top to bottom, with one block-level element stacked after another, CSS lets you create side-by-side columns and position images or text anywhere on the page (even layered on top of other page elements), so you can create much more visually interesting web pages.

There's a lot to CSS layout. This section of the book covers the most important CSS techniques in detail. This chapter provides a brief overview of the principles behind CSS layout and a handful of useful guidelines for approaching your own layout challenges.

Types of Web Page Layouts

Being a web designer means dealing with the unknown. What kind of browsers do your visitors use? Are they viewing your site on an Android phone or an iPad? The biggest issue designers face is creating attractive designs for different display sizes. Monitors vary in size and resolution, from 15-inch, 640×480 pixel notebook displays to 30-inch monstrosities displaying, oh, about 5,000,000×4,300,000 pixels. Not to mention the petite displays on mobile phones, and the small- to mid-range screens of tablets.

Web layouts offer several basic approaches to this problem. Nearly every page design you see falls into one of two types—*fixed-width* or *liquid*. Fixed-width designs give you the most control over how your design looks but can inconvenience visitors using devices that don't match the resolution of the screen you're designing for. Folks with really small monitors have to scroll to the right to see everything, and those with large monitors end up with wasted space that could be showing more of your excellent content. In addition, smartphone owners need to pinch and zoom to get to the content they're after. Liquid designs, which grow or shrink to fit browser windows, make controlling the design more challenging, but offer the most effective use of the browser window. A powerful approach to building web pages, called *responsive web design*, seeks to solve the problem of wildly varying screen widths, but at the cost of added complexity.

- **Fixed Width.** Some designers prefer the consistency of a set width, like the page in Figure 12-1, top. Regardless of the browser window's width, the page content's width remains the same. In some cases, the design clings to the left edge of the browser window, or, more commonly, it's centered in the middle. With the fixed-width approach, you don't have to worry about what happens to your design on a very wide (or small) monitor.

  Many fixed-width designs are below 1,000 pixels wide, letting the window and the space taken up by scrollbars and other parts of the browser's "chrome" fit within a 1024×768-pixel monitor. A very common width is 960 pixels. It used to be that *most* websites were fixed width, but that's changed significantly in the last few years, thanks to the widespread adoption of smartphones and tablets, which are often much narrower than the average fixed-width web page design. Because of that, fixed-width designs are falling out of favor and replaced with the responsive designs discussed next.

NOTE For an example of a fixed-width design, visit *www.nytimes.com* using a deskop browser. (The *New York Times* website provides a different version of the site for mobile devices, so use the desktop site for this example.)

- **Liquid.** Sometimes it's easier to roll with the tide instead of fighting it. A liquid design adjusts to fit the browser's width—whatever it may be—by assigning percentage widths instead of absolute pixel values. Your page gets wider or narrower as your visitor resizes the window (Figure 12-1, middle). While this type of design makes the best use of the available browser window real estate, it gives you the additional challenge of making sure your design looks good at different window sizes. On very large monitors, these types of designs can look ridiculously wide, creating very long, difficult to read lines of text. There are several different ways to implement liquid designs, such as floats (Chapter 13) and CSS flexbox (Chapter 14).

NOTE For an example of a liquid layout, check out *http://maps.google.com*.

- **Responsive web design (RWD).** Responsive web design, championed by web designer Ethan Marcotte, offers another way to address the problem presented by the wildly different screen sizes of smartphone, tablet, and desktop web browsers. Instead of presenting a single layout for all devices, responsive web design compensates for different browser widths by changing its presentation. For example, a responsive web page may shrink down from a wide, multicolumn layout for desktop monitors to a single-column layout for smartphones. In this way, responsive web design is very much like liquid layouts—the design uses percentages to grow or shrink in response to the width of the browser window. However, it goes one step further by using some tricky CSS—called *media queries*—to send different designs to different-width browsers, letting you create very different looking layouts depending on the device viewing the page.

In the tutorials at the end of the next chapter, you'll create a fixed-width design and a liquid design. In Chapter 15, you'll learn about a relatively new CSS property called `flexbox`. In Chapter 17, you'll dive into the techniques for creating responsive web designs.

NOTE The `max-width` and `min-width` properties offer a compromise between fixed and liquid designs. See page 208.

▓ How CSS Layout Works

As discussed in Chapter 1, in the early days of the Web, HTML's limitations forced designers to develop clever ways to make websites look good. The most common tool was the `<table>` tag, which was originally intended to create a spreadsheet-like display of information composed of rows and columns of data. Designers used HTML tables to build a kind of scaffolding for organizing a page's contents (see Figure 12-2). But because the `<table>` tag wasn't meant for layout, designers often had to manipulate the tag in unusual ways—like placing a table inside the cell of *another* table—just to get the effect they wanted. This method was a lot of work, added a bunch of extra HTML code, and made it very difficult to modify the design later. But before CSS, that's all web designers had.

HTML tables have one thing going for them: They provide a well-organized grid with a unified structure of individual cells. For CSS design, you use individual tags to contain content that you want to position in one area of the page. By grouping content into lots of individual containers and positioning those containers, you can create complex designs made up of columns and rows. The most common tag used to achieve this goal is the `<div>` tag.

FIGURE 12-1

You have several ways to deal with the uncertain widths of web browser windows and browser font sizes. You can simply ignore the fact that your site's visitors have different resolution monitors and force a single, unchanging width for your page (top), or create a liquid design that flows to fill whatever width window it encounters (middle). A responsive design literally reformats itself depending upon the browser window width. The Boston Globe (www.bostonglobe.com) site, for example, goes from one column (left), to two columns (middle), to three columns (right) as the browser window expands.

The <div> Tag

Web page layout involves putting chunks of content into different regions of the page. With CSS, one element commonly used for organizing content is the <div> tag. As you read on page 47, the <div> tag is an HTML element that has no inherent formatting properties (besides the fact that browsers treat the tag as a block with a line break before and after it). Instead, it's used to mark a logical grouping of elements or a *division* on the page.

You'll typically wrap a <div> tag around a chunk of HTML that belongs together. The elements that contain the logo and navigation bar in Figure 12-2 occupy the top of the page, so it makes sense to wrap a <div> tag around them. At the very least, you would include <div> tags for all the major regions of your page, such as the banner, main content area, sidebar, footer, and so on. But it's also possible to wrap a <div>

tag around one or more additional divs. One common technique is to wrap the HTML inside the <body> tag in a <div>. Then you can set some basic page properties by applying CSS to that *wrapper* <div>. You can set an overall width for the page's content, set left and right margins, center all of the page's content in the middle of the screen, and add a background color or image to the main column of content.

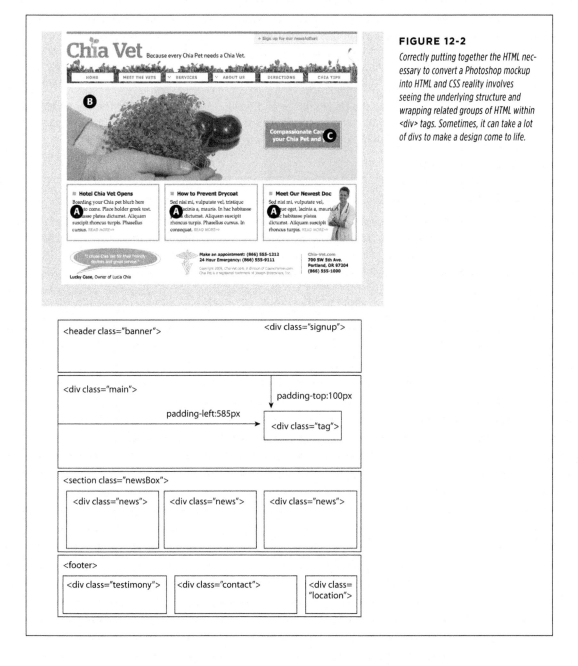

FIGURE 12-2

Correctly putting together the HTML necessary to convert a Photoshop mockup into HTML and CSS reality involves seeing the underlying structure and wrapping related groups of HTML within <div> tags. Sometimes, it can take a lot of divs to make a design come to life.

Once you've got your <div> tags in place, add either a class or ID to each one; that becomes your handle for styling each <div> separately. The <div> tag for a page's banner area might look like this: <div class="banner">. You can also use an ID, but you can use the same ID only once per page, so when you have an element that appears multiple times, use a class. If you have several divs that position photos and their captions, for example, you can wrap those tags in a div and add a class, like this: <div class="photo">. (For more on knowing when to use a div, read the box on page 47.) In addition, when it comes to the cascade (Chapter 5), IDs are very powerful and easily override other styles, often forcing you to create long-winded selectors like #home #banner #nav a just to override previously created selectors using IDs. For this reason, many web designers avoid IDs and stick with classes.

Once you have the divs in place and have accurately identified them with IDs or class names, you can then create CSS styles to position those divs on the page using floats (Chapter 13).

WORD TO THE WISE

A Delicate Balancing Act

Although divs are critical to CSS layout, don't go crazy pelting your page with divs. A common trap is to believe you must wrap *everything* on a web page in a <div> tag. Say your main navigation bar is an unordered list of links (like the one described on page 290). Because it's an important element, you may be tempted to wrap a <div> around it: <div class="mainNav"><ul>…</ul></div>.

But there's no reason to add a <div> when the <ul> tag is just as handy. As long as the <ul> contains the main navigation bar links, you can simply add your class to that tag: <ul class="mainNav">. An additional <div> is just unnecessary code.

Likewise, it doesn't make sense to use a <div> when another, more logical HTML tag is at hand. For example, say you want to add a pull quote to a long passage of text—a box aligned to the right edge of the page displaying an exciting quote pulled from the page. In this case, you can skip an extra <div> and simply use the HTML <blockquote> tag. You can position the blockquote tag using the float property as discussed on page 210.

That said, don't be afraid of divs either. Adding a few extra divs to a page is not going to substantially change the file size or slow the page's download speed. If a div helps you get the job done, and no other HTML tag makes sense, then by all means, use a div. Also, a div is the only way to go when you want to group a bunch of different HTML tags into a cohesive unit. In fact, it's not at all uncommon to see one div surround one or more other divs.

The basic rule of thumb is you should try to keep the amount of HTML on a page down to a minimum, but use as much HTML as is needed. If adding a few divs makes sense for the design—go for it. Alternatively, you can try the sectioning elements described in the next section.

HTML5 Sectioning Elements

Before HTML5, divs were the main way designers organized content. But the most recent version of HTML includes many HTML tags that are intended to group certain types of content. For example, the <article> tag is intended for content that makes up a single, self-contained composition—a blog post, for example. Likewise, the <header> tag is intended to provide headline, navigational aids, and other introductory material for a page or a section of page. Then there's the <footer> tag that's meant to contain concluding information like the copyright notice, the name of the website's creator, the date the page was published, and so on. In a nutshell, these tags take over the job of the <div> tag for specific types of content. (Visit *www. adobe.com/devnet/dreamweaver/articles/understanding-html5-semantics.html* for a quick introduction to these sectioning elements.)

Sectioning tags are intended to add *semantics* to a web page. That is, the name of the tag—<header>, for example—imparts identifying information about what's inside that tag. The <figure> tag is intended to enclose—you guessed it—a figure. In other words, if you want to enclose a particular type of content inside a tag, see if there's a tag that fits the bill. If the content is your page's footer, then use the <footer> tag instead of the plain old <div>. The <div> tag is still perfectly valid to use. But these days, it's generally used to group content for stylistic reasons—for example, if you'd like to add a border around a group of tags or move them over to the left side of the page using a float, then enclose those tags in a <div>. (You'll learn how to do just that in Chapter 13.)

That all said, beyond bragging rights at your next web designer meetup, there's no direct benefit to using these sectioning elements right now. In the future, software might look through your HTML and identify individual articles based on the presence of the <article> tag, or use these sectioning tags in some other way to better analyze your web page. However, if you've grown up using <div>, it's all right to just stick with the <div> tag for now.

Techniques for CSS Layout

The vast majority of web pages use the CSS float property for layout (see the box on page 393 for other CSS layout options). You've already encountered this seemingly simple property in Chapter 8, where the float property was introduced as a way of positioning an image within a column of text by either floating the image to the left or right side. The same concept applies to other tags: By setting the width of an element and floating it to the left or right, you can create a column (the text following the element ends up wrapping around the floated element as if it were another column). By using the float property with multiple divs or other tags, you're able to achieve multicolumn layouts. Taking this technique further, you can quickly create complex, multicolumn layouts by placing floated divs within floated divs.

Another CSS technique, *absolute positioning*, lets you place an element anywhere on the page with pixel-level accuracy. You can place an element 100 pixels from the top edge of the browser window and 15 pixels in from the left edge, for example. Desktop publishing programs like Adobe InDesign or Apple Pages work this way. Unfortunately, the fluid nature of web pages and some of the weird characteristics of absolute positioning make it difficult to achieve total layout control with this technique. As you'll read in Chapter 14, it is possible to lay out a page by using absolute positioning, but in general, this technique is better suited to smaller tasks like positioning a logo in a particular location on the page.

Don't worry if this sounds rather abstract right now—you'll see all of these techniques in action in the next three chapters.

■ Layout Strategies

Web page layout with CSS is more of an art than a science; there's no one formula to follow for marking up your content with HTML and creating your CSS. What works for one design might not for another. Although that might not be a comforting thought—"Hey, I bought this book to learn this darn stuff"—CSS layout is something you'll learn through experience, learning how the different CSS properties work (especially floats and absolute positioning), reading about different layout techniques, following tutorials like the ones in the next two chapters, and practicing—a lot.

However, there are definitely some strategies you can adopt as you approach CSS layout. These are more like guidelines than hard-and-fast rules, but as you begin to see your projects through the initial visual design, start with these tips in mind.

Start with Your Content

Many designers like to jump right into the good stuff—colors, fonts, icons, and images. But beginning with the visual design is putting the cart before the horse. The most important elements of a web page are the contents: headlines, paragraphs of text, stunning photographs, navigational links, videos, and such are what people will come to your site for. They want to read, learn, and experience what your site has to offer. Content is king, so think of what you want to say before you tackle how it should look. After all, it won't do you much good to create a fantastic, 3D-looking sidebar box if you don't have anything meaningful to put in it.

In addition, a page's message should dictate its design. If you decide that your home page needs to sell the services of your company and highlight the excellent customer service you offer, you might decide that a large photo of your friendly staff is important, as well as a quote from a satisfied customer. Since both of these elements are important to the page's message, you can craft the visual message by making both the picture and the quote prominent and compelling.

Mobile First

Along the same lines, the rise of smartphones and tablets has driven designers to think long and hard about winnowing down their content to just the key message and facts. This *Mobile First* movement is based on the limited screen size of smartphones as well as the limited attention of people on the go. Mobile-first design is about starting with your content, but it's also about getting rid of extraneous noise—including supplementary information that fits fine on a large desktop screen, but merely gets in the way on the smaller screen and detracts from the key information you're hoping to deliver.

Keep in mind that if your site will be visited by a significant number of people using smartphones or small tablets, not everyone will want to scroll through a long page of information (or pinch and zoom to see everything available on a page). Rather than trying to fill every last square inch of a 32" desktop monitor, think about simplifying your content so it's clear, direct, and easy to take in.

NOTE   The term *Mobile First* was coined by Luke Wroblewski. In fact, he wrote a fantastic short treatise on the subject: *www.abookapart.com/products/mobile-first*. For another short, but more recent, article explaining the Mobile First design approach, read: *www.sitepoint.com/making-case-mobile-first-designs/*.

POWER USERS' CLINIC

Other CSS Layout Options

Web designers initially used tables to create multicolumn layouts. Then the CSS float property came onto the scene and provided another, less code-intensive method to lay out a web page. And while most designers still use the float property to implement their designs, there are other options: some you can use today, and one that will be available in the future.

The CSS working group at the W3C is busily finalizing plans for several other techniques for CSS layout. For example, the CSS *multicolumn* layout module provides a way to take a long column of text and display it across multiple side-by-side columns. You'll learn about it in the next chapter, on page 409.

The *flexible box*, or flexbox, layout module provides yet another way to arrange boxes of content—vertically, horizontally, and in different directions and orders. And remarkably, this module is pretty well supported in many browsers today. You'll learn about flexbox in Chapter 15.

Finally, the *CSS grid* layout module is perhaps the most ambitious attempt to change how designers lay out web pages. This method lets you break up a page into a set of rows and columns, then accurately attach page elements to that grid. It's intended to make building web applications easier and more like building desktop *programs*. The CSS grid is pretty complicated and, at the time of this writing, not yet supported by most browsers. Surprisingly, Internet Explorer does support the grid, and was the first browser to do so. You can read more about the CSS grid layout module at *http://hugogiraudel.com/2013/04/04/css-grid-layout/*.

Start with a Sketch

Once you've figured out your content, you can think about organizing that content visually. Some designers start by hand-coding the HTML: creating divs, adding <header>, <article>, <footer> tags, and so on. This is a fine approach, often called "designing in the browser," since it gives you a head start on building your site by jumping right into the HTML.

However, before taking the leap into HTML, you should at least sketch out the placement of your content. You don't need anything fancy—paper and pencil work fine. Since web design is about placing content inside of boxes (divs and other HTML tags) and placing them on the page, simply sketching out a bunch of boxes, drawing columns, and so on, is a fast and easy way to try out different page layouts. You can quickly get a feel for where content should go, how big it should be, and the general color tone (light or dark).

TIP   Yahoo offers a free Stencil Kit (*http://developer.yahoo.com/ypatterns/wireframes*) that you can use in Illustrator, Visio, OmniGraffle, and other graphics programs to create web page mock-ups. The supplied user-interface elements, like buttons, form fields, windows, and navigation buttons can make sketching out a page layout as simple as dragging and dropping icons.

If you're comfortable with a graphics program like Photoshop, Illustrator, or Fireworks, you can use that to create a visual design. If you're not a whiz with graphics programs, even just drawing boxes to indicate different placement of page elements can help you refine your thinking about how the page should be laid out. It's a lot easier to change a two-column design to a four-column design by resizing boxes in Illustrator than by rewriting HTML and CSS.

However, if you do use a graphics program, don't spend too much time refining the graphic design. It's a lot of work to create the look of many CSS properties in Photoshop or Illustrator, and you'll only have to recreate that look using CSS code. In other words, try to refine a "lo-fi" look for your site on paper or in a graphics program, and then jump to your text editor to create the HTML to fit your content and use the CSS properties you've learned in this book to test out different styles.

Identify the Boxes

Once you've created a visual mock-up, it's time to think of how to create the HTML markup and CSS to achieve your design goal. This process usually involves envisioning the different structural units of a page and identifying elements that look like individual boxes. For example, in Figure 12-2, there are quite a few elements that look like boxes: most obviously, the three announcement boxes near the bottom (marked as A in Figure 12-2). Each box is usually a good candidate for a separate <div> tag (unless there's a more appropriate HTML tag, as discussed in the box on page 390).

Often a visual clue in your mock-up can help you decide if a div is needed. For example, a border line drawn around a headline and several paragraphs of text indicates you'll need to surround that group of HTML tags with a <div> tag that has a border applied to it.

In addition, whenever you see chunks of text sitting side by side (like the three chunks of content in the footer in Figure 12-2), you know you'll need to have each group in its own <div> tag—HTML tags don't usually sit side by side, so you have to use some layout mojo (like the float technique covered in the next chapter) to make that happen.

It's also common to group divs (or other tags) that sit side by side in columns within another div. For example, in the bottom half of Figure 12-2, you can see the basic set of <div> tags that provide the page's structure. The "news" <div> and the <footer> tag are containers for their own set of divs. While this isn't always a necessity, it can provide flexibility. For example, you can reduce the main area (the photo of the hand and the tagline) in width and move the news div to the right side to form its own column. The news items could then be stacked on top of each other rather than sitting side by side.

Go with the Flow

Tags don't normally sit side by side or layer on top of each other. Normally, HTML tags act pretty much like text in a word-processing program: filling the entire width of the page and flowing from top to bottom. Each block-level tag—headline, paragraph, bulleted list, and so on—stacks on top of the next block-level tag. Since that's the "business as usual" approach of HTML tags, you usually don't have to do any kind of positioning if you plan on stacking one div on the next.

For example, in Figure 12-2, four elements—the <header> tag, the "main" div, the <section> tag, and the <footer> tag—span the entire width of their container (the <body> tag) and sit one on top of the other. Because this is the normal way block-level tags work, you don't need to do anything special with the CSS for those four divs to stack on top of each other.

Remember Background Images

You've no doubt seen tiled images filling a web page's background, or subtle gradients adding depth to a banner. But the background-image property provides another way to add photos to a page without resorting to the <img> tag. Not only does putting an image into the background of an existing HTML tag save the few bytes of data required by the <img> tag, but it also simplifies some layout challenges.

For example, in Figure 12-2, the central image of the hands holding the Chia Pet (B) is actually just a background image. This makes placing another div—the one with the tagline "Compassionate care..." (C) really easy, since it's just sitting on top of the background of its parent div. Likewise, the picture of the doctor at the lower right of the page is just a background image placed in that div—adding some right padding pushes the text in that div out of the way of the photo.

> **NOTE** There are downsides to using photos in the background of divs (or any HTML tag). First, web browsers usually don't print backgrounds—so if you've got a page with a map containing driving directions to your business, insert the map with the <img> tag and not as a background image. Likewise, search engines don't search CSS, so if you think the image can help attract traffic to your site, use an <img> tag and include a descriptive alt attribute.

Pieces of a Puzzle

This tip can be filed under "creative problem solving" or "if I stare at this design long enough I'll come up with some crazy solution." Often, what looks like a single, unified whole is actually composed of multiple pieces.

You can see a simple example of this in Figure 12-2, even though at first glance it looks like one big white box full of content. Actually there are four stacked divs, each with a white background. So, if you're having trouble seeing how to put together one large element on a page—a very large graphic, a rainbow that spans several columns, or just a solid background color that appears to span multiple areas of a page—think about how you could achieve the same look by breaking the large unit into smaller pieces that are joined like parts in a jigsaw puzzle.

Layering Elements

If you're a Photoshop, Illustrator, or Fireworks fan, you're probably used to the notion of layers. Layers let you create separate canvases that float on top of each other to build one unified image. In these programs, it's easy to make a logo float on top of a headline of text, or place a photo over another photo. If you want a web page that has this kind of effect, you have a couple of choices.

Often the easiest way to layer something on top of a photo is to put the image into the background of another tag. Because the background image is behind the tag, anything inside that tag—text, another photo—will sit on top of the photo.

But what if you want to layer a photo on top of some text? In that case, you'll turn to the only CSS property that lets you layer elements—the position property. You'll learn all about that property in Chapter 14, since to position something on top of something else requires absolute positioning.

Don't Forget Margins and Padding

Finally, sometimes the simplest solution is the best. You don't always need fancy CSS to move a page element into place. Remember that padding and margins (page 187) are just empty space, and by using those properties, you can move elements around the page. For example, the tagline box (C in Figure 12-2) is positioned simply by setting the top and left padding of the parent div. As you can see in the diagram in the bottom half of Figure 12-2, the tagline is placed inside another div (<div id="main">). That div doesn't actually have any content besides the tagline—the photo is just a background image—so adding padding moves the tagline div down and to the right.

Building Float-Based Layouts

Float-based layouts take advantage of the float property to position elements side by side and create columns on a web page. As described in Chapter 7 (page 210), you can use this property to create a wraparound effect for, say, a photograph, but when you apply it to a <div> tag, float becomes a powerful page-layout tool. The float property moves a page element to one side of the page (or other containing block). Any HTML that appears below the floated element moves up on the page and wraps around the float.

The float property accepts one of three different values—left, right, and none. To move an image to the right side of the page, you could create this class style and apply it to the <img> tag:

```
.floatRight { float: right; }
```

The same property applied to a <div> tag full of content can also create a sidebar:

```
.sidebar {
  float: left;
  width: 25%;
}
```

Figure 13-1 shows these two styles in action.

NOTE The none value turns off any floating and positions the element like a normal, unfloated element. It's useful only for overriding a float that's already applied to an element. You may have an element with a particular class such as .sidebar applied to it, with that element floating to the right. But on one page you may want an element with that class to *not* float, but to be placed within the flow of the page, like this Note box. By creating a more specific CSS selector (see page 102) with float: none, you can prevent that element from floating.

FIGURE 13-1

You can use the `float` *property to lay out a web page with multiple columns. On this page, a block of content is floated to the left edge. The sidebar has a set width, but the main content doesn't, which makes this design a liquid layout. The main section of the page simply expands to fill the width of the browser window. In the upper right, the bathtub photo is floated to the right.*

A simple two-column design like Figure 13-1 requires just a few steps:

1. **Wrap each column in a** `<div>` **tag with an ID or class attribute.**

   In Figure 13-1, the news items listed in the left sidebar are wrapped in one div—`<div class="news">`—and the main content in another div—`<div class="main">`.

2. **Float the sidebar div either right or left.**

   When you work with floats, the source order (the order in which you add HTML to a file) is important. The HTML for the floated element must appear *before* the HTML for the element that wraps around it.

Figure 13-2 shows three two-column layouts. The diagrams on the left side show the page's HTML source order: a <div> for the banner, followed by a <div> for the sidebar, and lastly, a <div> for the main content. On the right side, you see the actual page layout. The sidebar comes *before* the main content in the HTML so it can float either left (top, bottom) or right (middle).

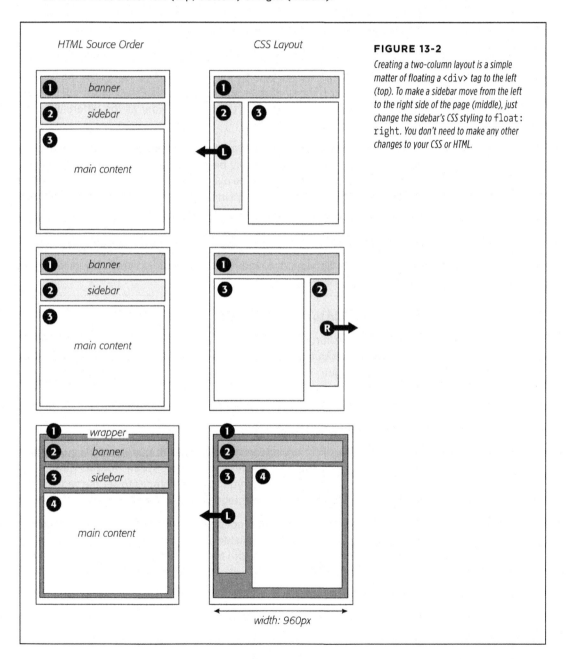

FIGURE 13-2

Creating a two-column layout is a simple matter of floating a <div> tag to the left (top). To make a sidebar move from the left to the right side of the page (middle), just change the sidebar's CSS styling to float: right. You don't need to make any other changes to your CSS or HTML.

3. Set a width for the floated sidebar.

Unless you're floating an image with a predefined width, you should always give your floats a width. This way, you create a set size for the floated element, letting the browser make room for other content to wrap into position.

The width could be a fixed size like 170px or 10em. You can also use percentages for a flexible design that's based on the width of the browser window. (See page 151 for more about the pros and cons of the different measurement units.) If the sidebar is 20 percent wide, and the browser window is 700 pixels wide, then the sidebar will be 140 pixels wide. But if your visitor resizes the window to 1000 pixels, then the sidebar grows to 200 pixels. Fixed-width sidebars are easier to design for, since you don't have to consider all the different widths the sidebar might stretch to.

However, percentages let you maintain the same proportions between the two columns, which can be more visually pleasing. In addition, percentages make your designs more flexible, since the overall proportion of the page can adjust to fit the screen size, something that's important when creating responsive web designs, which you'll learn about in the next chapter.

> **NOTE** When the overall page design is a fixed width (as described on page 386), percentage width values for the sidebar are based on the fixed-width containing element. The width isn't based on the window size and won't change when the browser window changes size.

4. Add a left margin to the main content.

If the sidebar is shorter than the other content on the page, the text from the main column wraps underneath the sidebar, ruining the look of two side-by-side columns (see Figure 13-2 for an example). Adding a left margin that's equal to or greater than the width of the sidebar indents the main content of the page, creating the illusion of a second column:

```
.main { margin-left: 27%; }
```

By the way, it's usually a good idea to make the left margin a little bigger than the width of the sidebar. This creates some empty space—a white gutter—between the two elements. So when you use percentages to set the width of the sidebar, use a slightly larger percentage value for the left margin.

Avoid setting a width for the main content div. It's not necessary, since browsers simply expand it to fit the available space. Even if you want a fixed-width design, you don't need to set a width for the main content div, as you'll see in the next section.

■ Applying Floats to Your Layouts

Now that you've learned a basic two-column liquid layout, you can adapt it in count-less ways. Converting it to a fixed-width layout is a snap. Simply wrap all the tags within the page's body inside *another* <div> (like <div class="wrapper">). Then create a style for that new container element that has a set width, such as 960 pixels (see Figure 13-2, bottom). That width setting constrains everything inside the container box.

> **TIP** It's also possible to create a fixed-width page without resorting to the extra wrapper div: set a width on the <body> tag. You already saw an example of this technique in the tutorial on page 33.

Expanding it into a three-column design isn't difficult, either (Figure 13-3). First, add another <div> between the two columns and float it to the right. Then add a right margin to the middle column, so that if the text in the middle column runs longer than the new right sidebar, it won't wrap underneath the sidebar.

The rest of this section explores more CSS layout techniques that use float-based layouts.

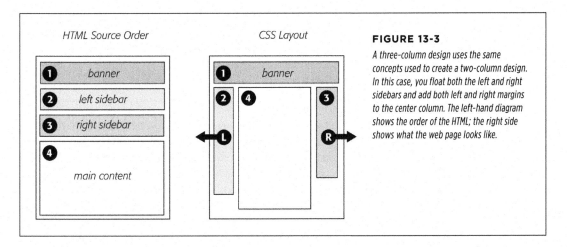

FIGURE 13-3

A three-column design uses the same concepts used to create a two-column design. In this case, you float both the left and right sidebars and add both left and right margins to the center column. The left-hand diagram shows the order of the HTML; the right side shows what the web page looks like.

Floating All Columns

It's perfectly possible to float *every* column, not just the left and right sidebars. You could float the first sidebar to the left, the middle column to the left, and the right sidebar to the right, as shown in Figure 13-4, top. This approach lets you put more than three columns in your design. You can float four or more columns, as long as there's room for all the floats to fit side by side.

When you float all columns in a design, you need to pay close attention to the widths of each column. If the total width of all the columns is more than the space avail-able—for example, if the browser window is smaller or the columns are placed inside another <div> with a set width—then the last column drops down below the others. (You can read a solution to this dropping float problem on page 414.)

In addition, floating more than just the sidebars lets you change the order of your divs in the HTML. Take, for example, the left diagram in Figure 13-3, which shows the order of the <div> tags for that page. Because of the way floated elements work, they must appear before any content that wraps around them, so in this example, the main content area must go *after* the sidebars.

You Don't Have to Reinvent the Wheel

If terms like *liquid layout* and *containing element* sound a little intimidating, don't give up. First of all, the tutorials beginning on page 417 walk you step by step through the process of laying out web pages with CSS. But there's no law saying you have to create your own CSS layouts from scratch. On the Web, you'll find plenty of pre-built and tested designs you can make your own. The LayoutGala site offers 40 different CSS designs that work in all common browsers (*http://blog.html.it/layoutgala/*). The designs are just basic skeletons consisting of <div> tags and the CSS that positions them. All you need to do is fill them with your own design touches like font styling and imagery.

For a bit more style, visit Templated (*http://templated.co*), which offers a collection of over 800 free CSS and HTML tem-

plates. These modern designs include images, background colors, and typographic touches to jumpstart your next site.

There are also quite a few *layout generators*—online tools that let you customize basic requirements like the number of columns you want, whether you're after a liquid or fixed layout, and so on. The Layout Generator (*http://www.pagecolumn.com*) provides a simple tool for creating a complex multicolumn designs. You can then download HTML and CSS files with the code created for you. In chapter 16, you'll learn how to use a *grid system*—a CSS file with specific method for laying out multiple column grids—to create complex page designs.

The order of the <div> tags in the HTML may not seem like a big deal until you try to browse the web page *without* CSS, which is the case for many alternative browsers, including screen readers that read a page's content aloud to visually impaired visitors. Without CSS, all the sidebar material (which often includes navigational elements, ads, or other information that's not relevant to the main topic of the page) appears before the content the visitor came to read in the first place. The inconvenience of having to scroll past the same sidebar content on each page will turn off some visitors. Furthermore, your page is less accessible to vision-impaired visitors, who have to listen to their screen readers read off a long list of links and ads before coming to any real information.

And if that doesn't sway you, you've got the search engines to worry about. Most search engines limit the amount of HTML they read when searching a site. On a particularly long web page, they simply stop at a certain point—possibly missing important content that *should* be indexed by the search engine. Also, most search engines give greater value to the HTML near the beginning of the file. So if you're worried about getting good placement in search engine results, it's in your best interest to make sure the important content is as close as possible to the top of the page's HTML code.

In the top-left diagram in Figure 13-4, the main content's HTML is between the left and right sidebars, which is better than having it after both sidebars. You can even put the main content before *both* sidebars' HTML by wrapping the main content and left sidebar in one <div>, floating that <div> left, and then floating the main content right and the left sidebar left *within* that <div> (Figure 13-4, bottom). Voilà—the main column's HTML falls before the other <div> tags.

Floats Within Floats

The bottom diagram in Figure 13-4 illustrates another useful technique—floating elements *within* floats. Imagine that the main content (3) and the left sidebar (4) divs didn't exist, and only the column wrapper (2) and the right sidebar (5) were left. You'd have just a basic two-column design, with one column floated left and another floated right. In fact, it's still a two-column design even with the two divs (3 and 4) placed back inside the column-wrapper div. The difference is that the left column is itself divided into two columns.

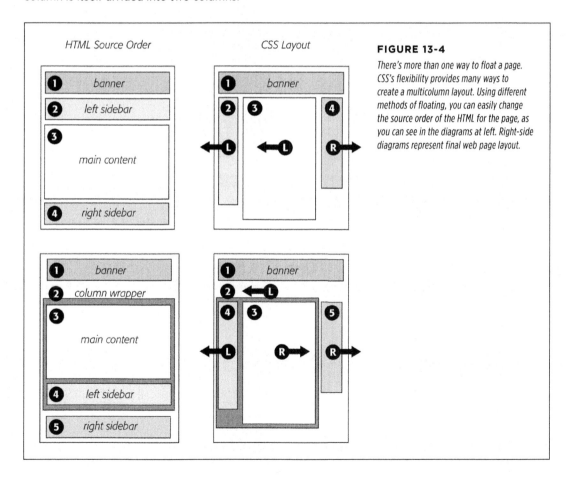

FIGURE 13-4

There's more than one way to float a page. CSS's flexibility provides many ways to create a multicolumn layout. Using different methods of floating, you can easily change the source order of the HTML for the page, as you can see in the diagrams at left. Right-side diagrams represent final web page layout.

Although this arrangement is a bit confusing, it's also helpful in a number of instances. First, it lets you add columns within a column. The three-column layout at the top of Figure 13-5 shows a small Tips box in the middle column that also has two columns inside it. By nesting floats inside floats, you can create some very complex designs.

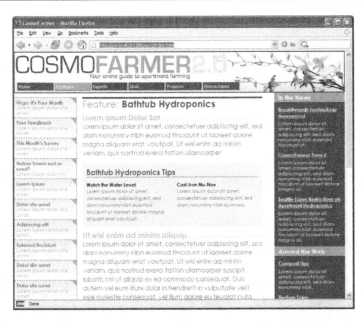

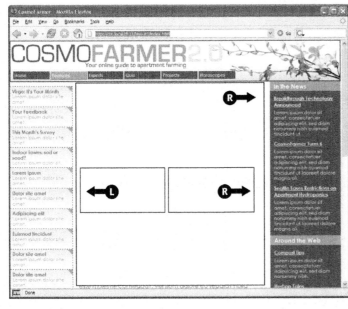

FIGURE 13-5

Top: Create columns within columns by floating elements inside other floated elements. In the middle column, the Tips box provides a simple two-column note that adds visual interest to the page. Bottom: It doesn't matter which direction the container is floated (in this instance, to the right)—you simply float the two additional columns left and right.

■ Overcoming Float Problems

As you get more adventurous with CSS, you'll probably encounter—like many web designers before you—some of the weird intricacies of working with floats. This section describes a few common problems and their solutions.

Clearing and Containing Floats

Floats are powerful design tools because they let content flow around them. Floating a photo lets text below it move up and wrap around the image (Figure 13-1). When you're creating float-based column designs, though, sometimes you *don't* want content to move up and next to a floated element. For example, you frequently want to keep copyright notices, contact information, or other housekeeping details at the bottom of your web page, below all other content.

In the two- and three-column designs you've seen so far, if the main column is shorter than either of the floated sidebar columns, a footer can move up and around the left floated column (Figure 13-6, left). To make the footer stay down below the sidebars, you can use the `clear` property. This property prevents an element from wrapping around floats. You can make an element drop below a left-floated object (`clear: left;`) or a right-floated object (`clear: right;`). For footers and other items that need to appear at the bottom of the page, you should clear *both* left and right floats, like this:

```
footer { clear: both; }
```

FIGURE 13-6

You don't always want an item to wrap around a floated element (left). Copyright notices and other material that belong at the bottom of a page usually need to clear any floats they encounter. To achieve this, use the `clear` *property for the copyright notice to force it to the bottom of the page below any floated elements.*

Another problem occurs when you float one or more elements inside a non-floated containing tag like a `<div>` tag. When the floated element is taller than the other content inside the div, it sticks out of the bottom of the enclosing element. This snafu is especially noticeable if that tag has a background or border. The top of the web page in Figure 13-7 shows a `<div>` tag that has an `<h1>` tag and two columns created by floating two divs. The background and border, which appear only around the <h1> tag, are actually applied to the entire enclosing <div>, including the area where the two columns are. However, since the columns are floated, they pop out of the bottom instead of expanding the borders of the box.

NOTE For a good explanation of why floated elements can break outside of their containing blocks, read www.complexspiral.com/publications/containing-floats.

A similar problem happens in the bottom example in Figure 13-7. In this case, each image is floated left inside a containing <div> that has a border. Because the images are taller than their boxes, they pop out of the bottom. Unfortunately, this example is even worse than the previous one, because each image causes the image below it to wrap to the right, creating an ugly staggered effect.

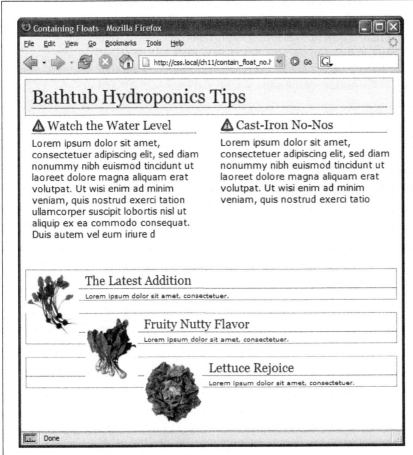

FIGURE 13-7

A floated element can escape its containing <div> if it's taller than the container itself. If the containing tag includes a background or border, then the escaping elements can look like they're not even part of the container (top of page). In addition, a floated element can bump into other elements—including other floats, thereby creating a "stair-stepped" effect (bottom of page) instead of the nicely stacked boxes in Figure 13-8.

You have many ways to tackle the problem of these renegade floating elements. It's good to have more than one solution at your fingertips, so here's a list of the most popular:

- **Add a clearing element at the bottom of the containing div.** This solution is the most straightforward. Simply add a tag—like a line break or horizontal rule—as the last item in the <div> containing the floated element (that is, right before the closing </div> tag). Then use the clear property to force that extra tag below the float. This trick makes the enclosing div expand, revealing its background and border. You can add a line break—
 (HTML) or
 (XHTML)—*before* the closing </div> tag and add a class to it: <br class="clear"/>. Then create a style for it, like this:

  ```
  br.clear { clear: both; }
  ```

  The problem with this technique is that it adds extra HTML.

- **Float the containing element.** An easier way is to just float the <div> containing the floated elements as well. A floated container <div> expands to fully contain any floated elements inside it. In Figure 13-8, top, the <div> containing the heading and two floated columns is floated to the left of the page. In the process, its entire box—background and borders—expands to fit everything inside it, including the floated elements. Strange, but true.

  If you go this route, make sure you add a clear property to whatever element follows the floated container to make sure the following element drops below the container.

- **Use overflow:hidden.** Another common technique is to add the following two properties to a style for the containing block:

  ```
  overflow: hidden;
  ```

  The overflow:hidden property is just another one of those weird CSS things: It forces the containing block to expand and contain the floated elements. In general, this technique works very well. However, if you have any absolutely positioned elements (see page 430) inside the container, they may not show up. You can get into this situation if you have a drop-down menu inside another tag and the drop-downs, when they appear, are supposed to appear outside the container element. If that's the case, use one of the other methods described on these pages.

- **Use the Micro Clear Fix.** With this technique, created by Nicolas Gallagher, you add just a few styles and a class name to the tag containing the floated element. This technique is the latest in a long evolution of methods that use the :after pseudo-class. To use it, add the following style to your style sheet:

  ```
  .clear:after {
    content: " ";
    display: table;
    clear: both;
  }
  ```

Once you've added that style to a style sheet, you simply add the class name to the div *containing* the escaping floats: <div class="clear">. If you're using HTML5 sectioning elements like <article> or <footer>, then add that class to them: <article class="clear">. (See the bottom of Figure 13-8.) This technique is very reliable; however, unlike the previous two techniques, you do have to add extra HTML (the class attribute) to the page.

FIGURE 13-8

Don't let a float escape! You have several ways to make floated elements stay inside the borders and backgrounds of their containing tag. Two methods are pictured here, though any of the four discussed would produce the same results. Floating the container works (top), as does a special combination of CSS (bottom). Both methods result in borders and backgrounds that surround the container and the floats inside.

POWER USERS' CLINIC

Multiple Columns: The Easy Way

CSS includes a *multicolumn layout* module: It lets you divide a single element (like a div full of text) into three, four, or more columns. It provides CSS properties to determine the number of columns and the space between columns, and to add a line (a *rule*) between the columns.

Multicolumns are intended to simulate the kind of columns you find in a newspaper or magazine, where one long story flows from the top to the bottom of one column, back to the top of the second column, down to the bottom of that column, and so on. In other words, it's not for placing columns of unrelated content next to each other (for example, a sidebar with links, and a main column containing an article). In addition, you can't set different widths for each individual column; they're all the same width.

Multiple columns work well in a magazine, where you have a set height and can see an entire page, making it easy to read to the bottom of a column and jump back to the top of the next. On a web page, however, you don't know the size of your visitors' monitors, so a long column of text might force a visitor to scroll down to get to the bottom, then scroll back up to read the next column. Unless you make sure you have very short columns, you might end up forcing people to scroll down and up to read one page—not very user friendly.

However, multiple columns are great for long bulleted lists with short items. Instead of one really long list of bullets, you can spread them across a page in multiple columns, saving precious vertical space. The basic syntax is pretty straightforward: You can use the column-count property to set the number of columns, the column-gap property to set the space between

columns, and the column-rule property to draw a line between the columns. To set the style, size, and color of the column rule, use the same syntax as for borders (page 194).

You apply these to the tag that contains the elements you wish to divide into columns. For example, say you have several paragraphs of text inside a `<div>` tag. You apply these properties to that div, and the paragraphs flow across multiple columns. If, for instance, you give that column a class called multicol, you can create the following style for a three-column design, with a 1 em gap and a dotted rule:

```
.multicol {
  column-count: 3;
  column-gap: 1em;
  column-rule: 1px dotted black;
}
```

Mind you, Internet Explorer 9 and earlier don't understand multiple columns. In addition, you need to use vendor prefixes (page 321) for Chrome and Safari (-webkit-column-count, -webkit-column-gap, and -webkit-column-rule) and for Firefox (-moz-column-count, -moz-column-gap, and -moz-column-rule). Opera, however, understands the non-prefixed version.

There are a few other properties for multicolumns, which you can read about at the official W3C page: *www.w3.org/TR/css3-multicol/*. In addition, there's a simple introduction to multicolumns at *http://dev.opera.com/articles/view/css3-multi-column-layout/* and an online tool for creating and previewing multiple columns at *www.aaronlumsden.com/multicol/*.

Creating Full-Height Columns

HTML tables aren't great for web page layout for several reasons. They add lots of code, they're difficult to update, and they don't work well on alternative browsers like those used by cellphones. But tables have one thing going for them in the layout department—the ability to create columns of equal height. Equal-height columns let you add a background color or graphic to one column and have it fill the entire height of the page. The backgrounds of the two sidebars in the top image of Figure 13-9 fill the screen height, creating solid, bold stripes on either side of the page.

CSS floats, on the other hand, fall a bit short in this regard. Table cells in a row are always the same height, which isn't true of divs. The height of a float is usually dictated by the content inside it; when there's not a lot of content, the float is not very tall. Since a background image or background color fills only the float, you can end up with solid-colored columns that stop short of the page bottom, as in the circled areas at the bottom of Figure 13-9.

NOTE The flexible box model fixes the problem of different height columns in a row. You'll learn about it in Chapter 15.

As with most problems related to CSS, there are several workarounds. The most tried-and-true method is the *faux column* technique first championed by CSS guru Dan Cederholm. The secret is to add background images to a tag that *wraps around* the stubby sidebar and the other columns on the page. Say your HTML has two <div> tags that contain the content for a left sidebar and the page's main content:

```
<div class="sidebar">Sidebar content here</div>
<div class="main">Main content for page, this column has a lot of text and is
much taller than the sidebar.</div>
```

The sidebar <div> is floated to the left edge of the page and has a width of 170 pixels. Because there's less content in the sidebar, it's shorter than the main text. Suppose you wrap that HTML in a wrapper <div> tag, like so:

```
<div class="wrapper">
<div class="sidebar">Sidebar content here</div>
<div class="main">Main content for page, this column has a lot of text and is
much taller than the sidebar.</div>
</div>
```

That outer div grows to be as tall as the tallest element inside it, so if the main div is very tall, that wrapper div will be just as tall. Here's the magic: Create a style for the wrapper div with a background image the width of the sidebar, in the background color you want for the sidebar. That way, if the background image tiles vertically, it forms a solid bar the height of the wrapper div (Figure 13-9, top).

```
.wrapper { background: url(images/col_bg.gif) repeat-y left top; }
```

Web browsers display that background image directly *under the sidebar*, creating the illusion that the sidebar has a background color.

NOTE You're not limited to solid colors either. Since you're using an image anyway, you can make a decorative pattern that tiles seamlessly down the left side of the page.

FIGURE 13-9

Full-height columns with bold background colors are a common design technique. The left and right sidebars (top) show how solid backgrounds can help visually define the different areas of a page. When a sidebar's background stops abruptly (circled at bottom), you get extra white space that's both distracting and unappealing.

Reproducing this result for two columns is just a little more involved. First, add two wrapper divs:

```
<div class="wrapper1">
<div class="wrapper2">
<div class="sidebar1">Sidebar content here</div>
<div class="sidebar2">Second sidebar</div>
<div class="main">Main content for page, this column has a lot of text and is
much taller than the two sidebars.</div>
</div>
</div>
```

> **NOTE** If the wrapper and each column are all fixed widths, you can create this faux-column look for both the left and right columns with just a single image and a wrapper div. Just make the graphic as wide as the wrapper, with the left side of the graphic being the color and width of the left sidebar, the right side of the graphic the color and width of the right sidebar, and the center part of the graphic matching the background color of the center column.

If the first sidebar appears on the left side of the page and the second sidebar appears on the right side, create two styles. Apply one style to the first wrapper <div> tag to add a background to the left sidebar; apply one to the second wrapper <div> to add a background to the right sidebar (Figure 13-10, bottom).

```
.wrapper1 { background: url(images/col1_bg.gif) repeat-y left top; }
.wrapper2 { background: url(images/col2_bg.gif) repeat-y right top; }
```

When adding a background image to the right-hand column, make sure you position the background image in the top right of the second wrapper, so that it falls underneath the second sidebar on the right side of the page.

One major problem with the faux-column technique is that it's very difficult to make it work when the columns are all percentage widths. If the widths of the sidebars are a percentage of the browser window, they can be thinner or wider depending upon a visitor's monitor. The faux-column technique requires placing a graphic in the background of the wrapper element. That graphic is a specific width and won't scale as the browser's width, and thus the column's width, changes.

One clever workaround uses linear gradients (page 252) to add a gradient to a wrapper element. The gradient becomes the background colors for the columns inside the wrapper element. Now, you may be thinking, "I like rainbows and all, but I want the background colors to each column to be solid, not a gradient that morphs from one color to the next." Well, fear not, you can get solid colors.

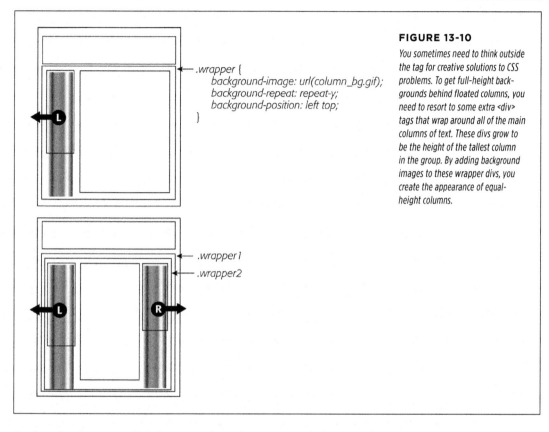

FIGURE 13-10

You sometimes need to think outside the tag for creative solutions to CSS problems. To get full-height backgrounds behind floated columns, you need to resort to some extra <div> tags that wrap around all of the main columns of text. These divs grow to be the height of the tallest column in the group. By adding background images to these wrapper divs, you create the appearance of equal-height columns.

As described on page 254, linear gradients let you set color stops—places where a new color is defined as part of the gradient. If the first stop is white, for instance, and the second stop is white, the gradient runs from white to white. In other words, there's no color change—it's just one solid color. In addition, you can set a color stop at the same spot as another color stop, which lets the second color begin immediately after the other with no subtle gradient effect.

Say you have a three-column design. The first column is 25 percent wide, the middle column is 50 percent wide, and the third column is 25 percent wide. You want the first column to have a background color of red, the middle white, and the third blue.

1. **Wrap all three columns in a wrapping element:**

```
<div class="wrapper">
  <div class="sidebar1"> ... content here ...</div>
  <div class="main"> ... content here ...</div>
  <div class="sidebar2"> ... content here ...</div>
</div>
```

The wrapper is the element in which you'll add the gradient. In addition, if you float all three of the columns inside the wrapper, you'll need to use one of the methods described on page 405 for containing those floats.

2. **Add a linear gradient, with color stops that match the width of the columns:**

```
.wrapper {
  background-image: linear-gradient(left,
    red 0%,
    red 25%,
    white 25%,
    white 75%,
    blue 75%,
    blue 100%);
}
```

Red runs from 0% (far left of the wrapper) to 25%. It's the same color, so there's no gradient. Then white begins at 25%—the same point at which red ended—so again there's no gradient. White continues until the 75% mark—just a solid white stretch. Then blue begins exactly where white ends and continues to the 100% mark (the right side of the wrapper). In other words, you have three solid-color columns whose widths change with the browser width. Perfect.

The downside of using a linear gradient is that it only works with solid colors (or, of course, gradients, if you'd like to do that), so you can't use a graphic in the background or borders around each column. In addition, Internet Explorer 9 and earlier don't understand gradients at all.

NOTE There are even a few other ways to make columns appear to be equal height. Check out this blog post by CSS expert Chris Coyier for an overview of the different techniques: *http://css-tricks.com/fluid-width-equal-height-columns/*.

NOTE Another clever technique uses the :before pseudo-class to create an element that's placed behind the floated column. You can read about it at *http://webdesign.tutsplus.com/tutorials/quick-tip-solving-the-equal-height-column-conundrum--cms-20403*.

Preventing Float Drops

Suddenly, one of your columns simply drops down below the others (Figure 13-11, top). It looks like there's plenty of room for all the columns to coexist perfectly side by side, but they don't. You've got the dreaded *float drop*.

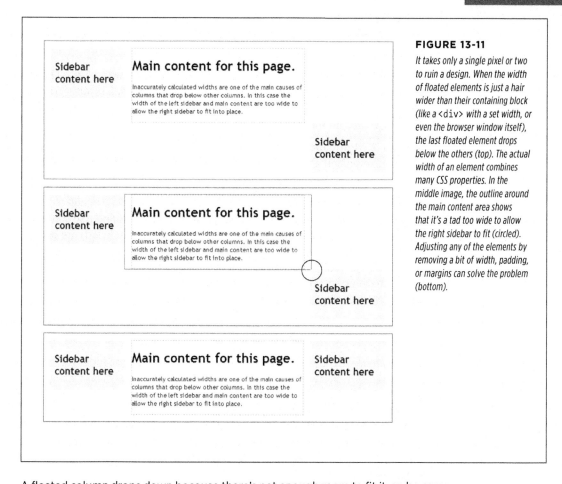

FIGURE 13-11

It takes only a single pixel or two to ruin a design. When the width of floated elements is just a hair wider than their containing block (like a <div> with a set width, or even the browser window itself), the last floated element drops below the others (top). The actual width of an element combines many CSS properties. In the middle image, the outline around the main content area shows that it's a tad too wide to allow the right sidebar to fit (circled). Adjusting any of the elements by removing a bit of width, padding, or margins can solve the problem (bottom).

A floated column drops down because there's not enough room to fit it, so be careful if you set widths for *each* column. If the available space in the browser window (or the containing block in a fixed-width design) is less than the *total* widths of the columns, then you're asking for a float drop. Also, keep the CSS box model in mind: As discussed on page 205, the width of an element displayed in the browser window isn't the same as its `width` property. The displayed width of any element is a combination of its width, left and right border sizes, left and right padding, and left and right margins. For the columns to fit, the browser window (or containing block) must accommodate the combined total of all those widths.

Take, for example, the simple three-column layout in Figure 13-11. As you can see in the top example, the three columns don't fit. Here's a breakdown of the math behind the problem:

- **Wrapper div.** A fixed-width wrapper `<div>` tag encloses the entire design. Its width property is set to 760 pixels, so all three columns can't total more than that.

- **Sidebar 1 (left side).** Its width is 150 pixels, but it also has 10 pixels of padding, making its total onscreen width 170 pixels. (150 + 10 pixels of left padding + 10 pixels of right padding.)

- **Main content.** The main content `<div>` is 390 pixels wide, with a 1-pixel border and 15 pixels of left and right margin for a total width of 422 pixels. (You may need a calculator for this one: 390 + 1 [left border] +1 [right border] + 15 [left margin] + 15 [right margin].)

- **Sidebar 2 (right side).** This element has a width property set to 150 pixels, with 10 pixels of left and 10 pixels of right padding: 170 pixels, just like Sidebar 1.

The actual widths of each element add up to a grand total of 762 pixels. That's two pixels more than the width of the wrapper div. The middle image of Figure 13-11 shows an outline around the main content div indicating its total width plus margins. Just those measly two extra pixels of width (circled) are enough to cause a column to drop down. The solution: Remove 2 pixels of space from any of the elements. Changing the main content div's left and right margins from 15 to 14 pixels buys you the extra room needed for all three columns to fit side by side (bottom).

Bottom line: Float drops are always caused by not enough room to hold all of the columns.

Another way to make the math easier is to never set the border or padding on column divs or elements. In this way, if you set three columns to 20%, 60%, and 20% widths, respectively, you'll know they fit side by side, since they total 100%, and there's no padding or border to mess that up. If you do want padding, you can simply add padding to the elements inside the column: for example, give the same left and right padding to the headlines, paragraphs, and other elements inside the div. This requires more work, but it prevents potential float drops caused by column widths totaling more than 100%.

If you want borders as well, another technique is to nest divs like this:

```
<div class="column1">
  <div class="innerColumn">
    ...content goes here ...
  </div>
</div>
```

You then set the width on the outer div—column1 in this case—and add the padding and borders to the inner div—innerColumn—in the above code. Don't set a width on the inner div; it will automatically fill the width of the outer column.

Preventing Float Drops With Box-Sizing

The main culprit responsible for float drops is the wacky way browsers calculate the actual screen width for an element. You set the width to 100 pixels, for example, but the browser draws it as 122 pixels, because you've also added 10 pixels of left and right padding and a 1-pixel border around the whole thing. Fortunately, one CSS property lets you sidestep these headache-inducing calculations.

The CSS box-sizing property lets you tell a web browser to use a different model for calculating the actual screen width of an element. You can give it one of three values:

- The **content-box** value is how browsers normally work: The width of an element on the screen is the combined value of the left and right border thicknesses, left and right padding, and the CSS width property.

  ```
  box-sizing: content-box;
  ```

- The **padding-box** value tells a browser to include the left and right padding. In other words, the display width of an element is the total of the CSS width and the left and right padding. It doesn't include any borders around the element.

  ```
  box-sizing: padding-box;
  ```

- Finally, the **border-box** property includes padding, borders, and CSS width. In general, this is the one you want to use. It keeps the math simple and helps prevent float drops, especially when you're using percentage-based widths along with pixel-based units for the border width and padding:

  ```
  box-sizing: border-box;
  ```

The very good news is that almost all browsers support this scheme, including Internet Explorer 8. However, while those browsers support the content-box and border-box value, not all browsers support the padding-box value (see *http://caniuse.com/#search=box-sizing*). That's all right, though, because for use the most important value is border-box.

Some web designers suggest setting all elements to the border-box setting, so that every tag will be measured in the same way. To do so, use the * selector, which selects every element on the page, at the top of your style sheet along with your CSS reset:

```
* {
  box-sizing: border-box;
}
```

■ Tutorial: Multiple-Column Layouts

In this tutorial, you'll create a multicolumn, float-based layout. In the process, you'll create a three-column liquid design, as well as a fixed-width design. In addition, you'll learn a couple of different techniques for doing it.

To get started, download the tutorial files located on this book's companion website at *https://github.com/sawmac/css_mm_4e*. Click the tutorial link and download the files. All the files are in a zip archive, so you need to unzip them first, as detailed on the website. The files for this tutorial are in the *13* folder.

Structuring the HTML

The first step in creating a CSS-based layout is identifying the different layout elements on the page. You do this by wrapping chunks of HTML inside of <div> tags, each of which represents a different part of the page.

1. **Open the *index.html* file in a text editor and click in the empty line following the HTML comment:** <!-first sidebar goes here-->**.**

   As you can see, some of the HTML work is already done: Currently, there's a banner and footer. Before you create any styles, you need to add the structure and content for the page. You'll next add an <aside> tag to create the left sidebar.

2. **Add an opening** <aside> **for the sidebar:** <aside class="sidebar1">**. Then press Enter (Return) to create a new, empty line.**

   You're using the HTML5 <aside> tag, but you could just as easily use a <div> tag to create this column.

   If you were creating a web page from scratch, at this point you'd add the HTML for the page's sidebar, perhaps a list of articles on the site, links to related websites, and so on. In this case, the HTML is already taken care of. The code for an unordered list of links is waiting for you in another file. You just need to copy and paste it into this page.

3. **Open the file *sidebar1.txt*, copy all of the contents, and then return to the *index.html* file. Paste the HTML after the** <aside> **tag you created in step 2 (or your** <div> **tag, if you went that route).**

   The HTML for the sidebar is nearly complete. You just need to close the <aside> tag.

4. **Immediately after the code you just pasted, type </aside>.**

   You've just added the first layout element on the page. In a little bit, you'll style this HTML so that it looks like a column. But first, you need to add some more content.

5. **Place your cursor in the empty line after this HTML comment:** <!--main content goes here-->**, and then type <article class="main">.**

   This div holds the page's main content. You'll get that HTML from another file, too.

6. **Open the file *main.txt*, copy all of the contents, return to the *index.html* file, and then paste the code after the** <article> **tag you just created. Add the closing** </article> **tag exactly as in step 4. Save the HTML file.**

   That's all the HTML you need to create your design for now. Next, it's time to turn your attention to building the CSS.

Creating the Layout Styles

If you preview the page now, you'll see that the banner, navigation buttons, and text are already styled. That's because this page has an external style sheet attached to it with some basic formatting. Next, you'll create styles to format the page's columns:

1. **In a text editor, open the *styles.css* file.**

   Since the web page uses an external style sheet, you'll add all the new styles to it. You're now managing two files, the HTML file and the CSS file, so make sure you save both before previewing your work in a web browser.

2. **Scroll to the bottom the CSS file. You'll see a CSS comment that reads** /* add tutorial styles below here */**. Below that, add this style:**

   ```
   .sidebar1 {
     float: left;
     width: 20%;
   }
   ```

   This class style floats the sidebar div to the left of the page, and gives it a width of 20%. The width property is important in this style: Unless you're floating an image that has a set width, you should always set a width for a floated element. Otherwise, the browser sets the width based on the content inside the float, leading to inconsistent results. Here, the width is percentage-based, meaning it's determined by the width of its container. In this case, the container is the <body> tag, and it fills the entire browser window width. So the sidebar's onscreen width will depend on the width of the visitor's browser window.

3. **Save the HTML and CSS files and preview the *index.html* file in a web browser.**

   The sidebar now forms a left-hand column...sort of. When the text in the main column reaches the bottom of the sidebar, it wraps around the bottom of the sidebar, as shown in Figure 13-12. While that's normally how floats work, it's not what you want in this case. To make the main body text appear like a column of its own, you have to add enough left margin to indent the main text beyond the right edge of the sidebar.

4. **Create a style for the second column:**

   ```
   .main {
     margin-left: 22%;
   }
   ```

   Since the sidebar is 20 percent wide, a margin of 22 percent indents the main content an additional 2 percent, creating a gutter between the two columns. This additional white space not only makes the text easier to read, but also makes the page look better.

   Preview the page now, and you'll see you've got yourself a two-column layout.

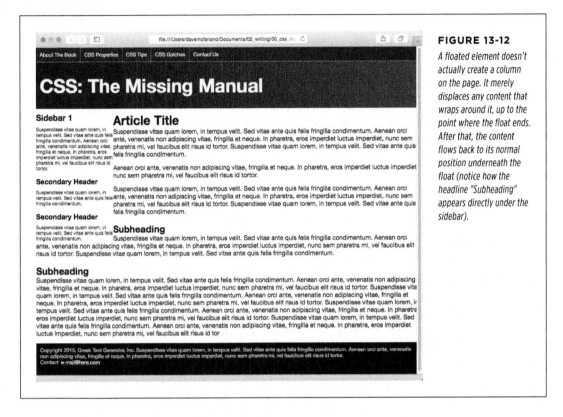

FIGURE 13-12

A floated element doesn't actually create a column on the page. It merely displaces any content that wraps around it, up to the point where the float ends. After that, the content flows back to its normal position underneath the float (notice how the headline "Subheading" appears directly under the sidebar).

Adding Another Column

As you can see, a two-column design isn't hard. Adding a third column so you can treat your visitors to even more information isn't any harder. In fact, the steps are quite similar to the previous part of this tutorial.

1. **Open the file *sidebar2.txt*. Copy all the HTML from that file, and then return to the *index.html* file.**

   The HTML for this column goes after the `<article>` tag containing the page's main text.

2. **Locate the HTML comment `<!-- second sidebar goes here -->` near the bottom of the file. Click in the empty line below it.**

   It's often hard to find the right closing `</div>` when you use a lot of divs to structure a page. That's why HTML comments—like this one—can really help you identify and keep track of the HTML in your page.

3. **Type** `<aside class="sidebar2">`**, press Enter, and then paste the HTML you copied in Step 1. Hit Enter again, and then type** `</aside>`**. Save the HTML file.**

When you close the `<aside>` tag, you've completed the HTML for the page's third column. Start styling it next.

4. **In your text editor, return to the *styles.css* file. Below the** `.main` **style you created in Step 4 on the previous page, add a new style:**

```
.sidebar2 {
  float: right;
  width: 20%;
}
```

You're floating this column to the right side of the page to flank the main content with sidebars on either side.

5. **Save all the files and preview the *index.html* file in a web browser.**

Right away, you'll notice something strange. The second sidebar appears below the main content and even runs over the footer. The problem has to do with the HTML's source order. When you float an element, only HTML that comes after that element wraps around and appears next to the floated element. In other words, since the second sidebar's HTML is after the main content, it doesn't appear *next* to the main content, only after it.

There are a couple of ways to get around this situation. You could move the second sidebar's HTML (the second `<aside>` element) before the main content's HTML (the `<article>` element). Then the first sidebar would float to the left and the second to the right; the main content would just scoot up in between them.

Alternatively, you could simply float the main column as well. If you set its width so all three columns add up to no more than 100 percent, then the three columns will sit side by side. For this example, you'll try that approach.

6. **Edit the** `.main` **style so that it looks like this:**

```
.main {
  float: left;
  width: 60%;
}
```

If you save the CSS file and preview the *index.html* file in a browser, you'll notice another problem—suddenly, everything's turned black! Remain calm: That's the footer trying to wrap around all the floats and causing a mess. As you read above, when you float an element and another element wraps around it, the background color and borders for that element actually extend underneath the floated element. Strange, true...and frustrating. To fix it, you simply need to make the footer drop below—that is, *clear*—the floats.

7. **Add one more style after the** `.sidebar2` **style:**

```
footer {
  clear: both;
}
```

As described on page 405, the `clear` property forces an element to drop below floated elements. In this case, it pushes the footer down below the columns, as shown in Figure 13-13.

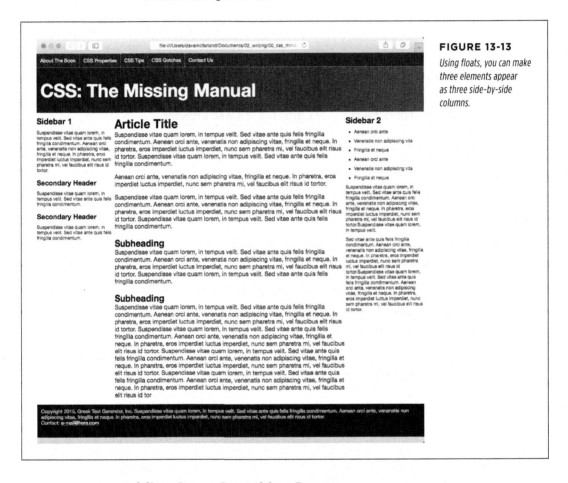

FIGURE 13-13

Using floats, you can make three elements appear as three side-by-side columns.

Adding Some Breathing Room

You've got three columns, but the text is a little jammed together. The three columns practically touch, and the text on the right sidebar hugs too closely to the edge of the browser window. A little padding can help fix this.

1. **Add padding to the** `.sidebar1`, `.main`**, and** `.sidebar2` **styles, so the styles look like this:**

```
.sidebar1 {
  float: left;
  width: 20%;
  padding: 0 20px 0 10px;
}

.main {
  float: left;
  width: 60%;
  padding: 0 20px 0 20px;
}

.sidebar2 {
  float: right;
  width: 20%;
  padding: 0 10px 0 20px;
}
```

Here, you're using the `padding` shorthand property (page 189). The numbers represent the top, right, bottom, and left padding. So in the `.sidebar1` style, you're adding 0 top padding, 20 pixels of right padding, 0 bottom padding, and 10 pixels of left padding.

If you save the *styles.css* file and preview the *index.html* file in a browser, you'll notice a problem—the dreaded float drop (page 414). By adding padding, you've essentially increased the width of each column, and since the total widths of the columns (20% + 60% + 20%) already totaled 100%, that extra padding forces the third column down below the other two. It just can't fit!

There are a couple of ways to handle this problem. First, you can remove the padding from these styles, and add it to all the elements inside. In other words, add 10 pixels of left and right padding to the <h2>, <h3>, <p>, and <ul> tags. That's a lot of work.

Second, you could remove the padding from the styles in the CSS file and then, in the *index.html* file, add a <div> inside each of the columns, something like this:

```
<aside class="sidebar1">
  <div class="innerColumn">
  ... content goes here ...
  </div>
</aside>
```

Then, in the *styles.css* file, simply create a style to add the padding:

```
.innerColumn {
  padding: 0 20px 0 10px;
}
```

Because there's no width set on the .innerColumn style, it simply grows to fill the column, while the padding scoots everything inside of it (the headings, paragraphs, and so on) in by 10 pixels. The downside of this approach is you need to add additional HTML.

There's another way, that's a lot easier, more flexible, and widely supported by web browsers.

2. **Add the following style to the top of the style sheet (just below the** /* reset browser styles */ **comment):**

```
* {
  box-sizing: border-box;
}
```

This style takes advantage of the universal selector (page 49). It applies the box-sizing property to every element on the page. By setting this property to border-box, you're instructing web browsers to use the size of the padding and border properties as part of the CSS width value. In other words, the padding doesn't add to the CSS widths you set earlier. This prevents any float drop, since the columns now only add up to 100 percent of the browser window width.

Finally, you'll add a border line to separate the columns.

3. **Edit the** .main **style by adding a left and right border so that it looks like this:**

```
.main {
  float: left;
  width: 60%;
  padding: 0 20px;
  border-left: dashed 1px rgb(153,153,153);
  border-right: dashed 1px rgb(153,153,153);
}
```

These properties add two lines, one on either side of the main content section. If you preview the page in a web browser now, it should look like Figure 13-14.

Fixing the Width

Currently, the page is a liquid design, meaning that it expands to fill the entire width of the browser window. But say you'd rather have the page stay the same width all the time—because you hate how it looks on cinema display monitors, or you don't like what happens to the design when the browser window is shrunk too small. Changing a liquid design to a fixed-width design is easy. Start by adding a little more HTML.

1. **Return to your text editor and the *index.html* file. Directly after the opening** <body> **tag, add a new** <div> **tag:**

```
<body>
<div class="pageWrapper">
```

You're wrapping the entire page inside a div, which you'll use to control the page's width. You need to make sure that tag is closed.

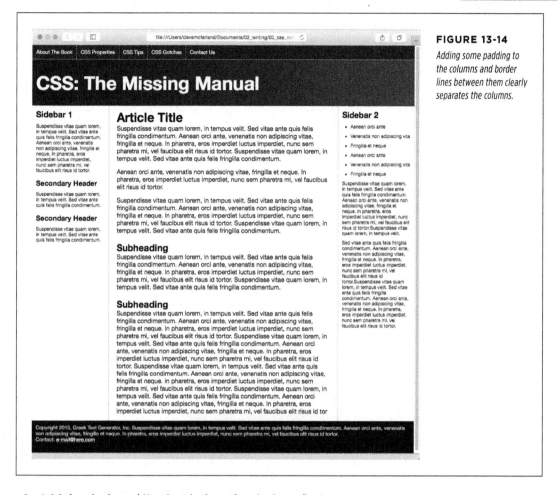

FIGURE 13-14

Adding some padding to the columns and border lines between them clearly separates the columns.

2. **Add the closing** </div> **just before the closing** </body> **tag:**

   ```
   </div>
   </body>
   ```

   Now that there's a div surrounding all of the content on this page, you can control the page's width by setting a width for this tag.

3. **Save the HTML file, and switch to the *styles.css* file. Add another style:**

   ```css
   .pageWrapper {
   width: 960px;
   }
   ```

If you save the CSS and HTML files and preview the *index.html* file in a browser, you'll see that the page is indeed locked in at 960 pixels. If you make the browser window thinner than 960 pixels, you'll get scroll bars.

You don't have to set an exact width, however. If, you want the page to fit into a browser window that's thinner—say 760 pixels—you're better off avoiding an exact width. The real problem is that the page becomes hard to read when the browser is really wide. Another approach is to use the max-width property, which prevents the div from getting larger than a particular value, but doesn't prevent it from getting thinner to fit smaller screens. While you're at it, you'll also center the div within the browser window.

4. **In the *styles.css* file, change the** .pageWrapper **style you just created so it looks like this:**

```
.pageWrapper {
  max-width: 1200px;
  margin: 0 auto;
}
```

The max-width property provides a liquid layout, but only up to a point. In this case, when the browser window is wider than 1200 pixels, the div won't get any wider. The margin setting here—0 auto—provides 0 margin for the top and bottom, and auto margins for left and right. That auto setting tells the browser to automatically figure out the margin, splitting the space evenly between left and right and centering the div in the browser window. The page should now look like Figure 13-15.

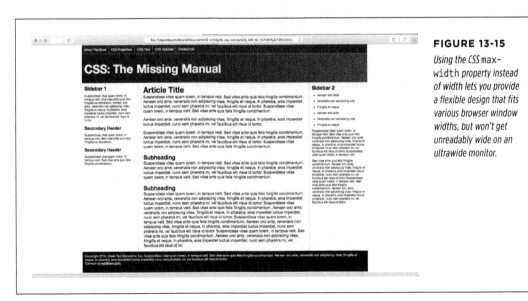

FIGURE 13-15

Using the CSS max-width property instead of width lets you provide a flexible design that fits various browser window widths, but won't get unreadably wide on an ultrawide monitor.

Mixing Liquid and Fixed Design

The page looks pretty good, but it might look better if the black background for the nav bar at the top, the footer at the bottom, and the dark purple gradient in the banner extended all the way across the page (see Figure 13-16). Because the nav, banner, and footer are inside the pageWrapper div, those backgrounds stop when the browser window is wider than 1200 pixels. Instead, you want to keep some parts of the page—the tags with the background colors—liquid, while limiting the width of the tags containing any content.

The background color for the navigation is applied to a <nav> element in the HTML; the purple gradient is applied to a <header> element; and the black background in the footer is applied to the <footer> element. In order for their backgrounds to extend the width of the page, they can't be constrained by the pageWrapper div. So the first step is removing that style.

1. **In the *styles.css* file, delete the** .pageWrapper **style you just created.**

   You can leave the pageWrapper div in the HTML. It won't hurt to have that little bit of extra HTML, and you may want to use it later to hang styles on.

   The page is back to its fully liquid form. Now you want to constrain just the nav, banner text, footer text, and main content so they don't get any wider than 1200 pixels. To do so, you need to dig into the HTML a bit and see what elements you have to play with.

   Look in the HTML for the *index.html* file and find the <nav> tag. Inside it, you'll see that the navigation buttons are created with a simple unordered list. Bingo. You can set the maximum width of that list to 1200 pixels and center it on the page, while leaving the <nav> tag (and its black background) to extend the entire browser window width. Likewise, the text inside the banner—*CSS: The Missing Manual*—is inside an <h1> tag. You can set its maximum width and margin as well. In the footer, you've got a <p> tag you can control.

2. **In the *styles.css* file, add one more style:**

   ```
   nav ul, header h1, footer p {
     max-width: 1200px;
     margin: 0 auto;
   }
   ```

   This group selector targets the navigation bar, banner, and footer text, but not their containing elements. If you save the CSS file and preview *index.html* now, you'll see that the navigation, title, and footer text don't get wider than 1200 pixels. However, the main content region still fills the entire browser window. To fix that, you need to wrap the three columns in another div to create a group that you can size and center.

NOTE Another approach is to insert another `<div>` inside the `<header>` tag and wrapped around the `<nav>` and `<h1>` tags, and another `<div>` inside the `<footer>` tag. You can let the `<header>` and `<footer>` stay full width while constraining the width of those nested divs.

3. **Open the *index.html* file in your text editor. Just before the comment that introduces the first sidebar—**`<!-- first sidebar goes here -->`**—add** `<div class="contentWrapper">`**:**

   ```
   <div class="contentWrapper">
   <!-- first sidebar goes here -->
   ```

   Now, you need to close that div.

4. **Scroll down near the bottom of the HTML file. Between the closing** `</aside>` **tag and opening** `<footer>` **tag, add a closing** `</div>` **so the HTML looks like this:**

   ```
   </aside>
   </div>
   <footer>
   ```

   Finally, you can add this new class name to the style you created in step 2.

5. **In the *styles.css* file, add the new class to the group selector, like this:**

   ```
   nav ul, header h1, footer p, .contentWrapper {
     max-width: 1200px;
     margin: 0 auto;
   }
   ```

   The finished page should look like Figure 13-16. A completed version of this tutorial is in the *13_finished* folder.

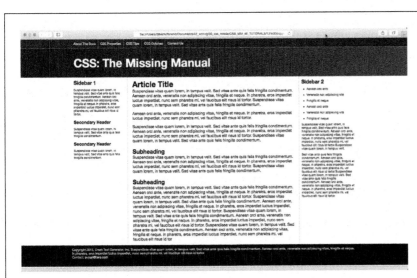

FIGURE 13-16

Creating a multicolumn design is no harder than floating HTML tags: three columns, three floated elements. You can add more columns simply by adding more HTML containers (`<div>`, `<article>`, `<aside>`, and so on) and floating them to the left and right. Just make sure to remember to adjust their widths so there's enough room for them to fit side by side.

Positioning Elements on a Web Page

When the World Wide Web Consortium introduced *CSS Positioning*, some designers understandably thought they could make web pages look just like print documents created in desktop publishing programs. With just a couple of CSS properties, CSS Positioning lets you position an element in a precise location on a page—say 100 pixels from the top of the page and 200 pixels from the left edge. Pixel-accurate placement seemed to promise that, at last, you could design a page simply by putting a photo here, a headline there, and so on.

Unfortunately, the level of control designers expected from CSS Positioning never materialized. There have always been differences in how various browsers display CSS-positioned elements. But, even more fundamentally, the Web doesn't work like a printed brochure, magazine, or book. Web pages are much more fluid than printed pages. Once a magazine rolls off the press, readers can't change the page size or font size. About the only way they can change the look of the magazine is to spill coffee on it.

Web visitors, on the other hand, can tinker with your handcrafted presentation. They can increase their browser's font size, potentially making text spill out of your precisely placed and sized layout elements. In addition, since these days people browse the Web using phones, tablets, and even televisions, you can't predict the dimensions and use them to determine the exact placement of onscreen elements. But the news isn't all bad: As long as you don't try to dictate the exact width, height, and position of *every* design element, you'll find CSS's positioning properties powerful and helpful. You can use these properties to make a text caption appear on top of a photo, place a logo anywhere on the page, and much more.

◼ How Positioning Properties Work

The CSS position property lets you control how and where a web browser displays particular elements. Using position, you can, for example, place a sidebar anywhere you wish on a page or make sure a navigation bar at the top of the page stays in place even when visitors scroll down the page. CSS offers four types of positioning:

- **Absolute.** Absolute positioning lets you determine an element's location by specifying a left, right, top, or bottom position in pixels, ems, or percentages. (See Chapter 6 for more on picking between the different units of measurement.) You can place a box 20 pixels from the top and 200 pixels from the left edge of the page, as shown in Figure 14-1, middle. (More in a moment on how you actually code these instructions.)

  In addition, absolutely positioned elements are completely detached from the flow of the page as determined by the HTML code. In other words, other items on the page don't even know the absolutely positioned element exists. They can even disappear completely underneath absolutely positioned items, if you're not careful.

> **NOTE** Don't try to apply both the float property and any type of positioning other than static (explained below) or relative to the same style. The float property and absolute or fixed positioning can't work together on the same element.

- **Relative.** A relatively positioned element is placed relative to its current position in the HTML flow. So, for example, setting a top value of 20 pixels and left value of 200 pixels on a relatively positioned headline moves that headline 20 pixels down and 200 pixels from the left *from wherever it would normally appear.*

  Unlike with absolute positioning, other page elements accommodate the old HTML placement of a relatively positioned element. Accordingly, moving an element with relative positioning leaves a "hole" where the element would have been. Look at the dark strip in the bottom image of Figure 14-1. That strip is where the relatively positioned box *would have* appeared, before it was given orders to move. The main benefit of relative positioning isn't to move an element, but to set a new point of reference for absolutely positioned elements that are nested inside it. (More on that brain-bending concept on page 435.)

- **Fixed.** A fixed element is locked into place on the screen. It does the same thing as the fixed value for the background-attachment property (page 242). When a visitor scrolls the page, fixed elements remain onscreen as paragraphs and headlines, while photos disappear off the top of the browser window.

  Fixed elements are a great way to create a fixed sidebar or lock a navigation bar to the top or bottom of the browser window. You can read about how to create this effect on page 446.

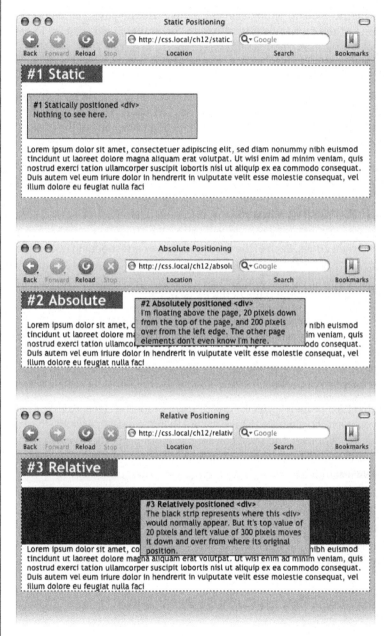

FIGURE 14-1

CSS offers several ways to affect an element's placement. The static option, top, is the way browsers have presented content since the beginning of the Web. They simply display the HTML in top-to-bottom order. Absolute positioning (middle) removes an element from the page flow, placing it on top of the page, sometimes overlapping other content. Relative positioning (bottom) places an element relative to where it would normally appear on the page and leaves a hole (the dark background here) where that element would have been without relative positioning.

- **Static** positioning simply means the content follows the normal top-down flow of HTML (see Figure 14-1, top). Why would you want to assign an element static positioning? The short answer: You probably never will.

To change the positioning of any element, simply use the position property followed by one of the four keywords: absolute, relative, fixed, static. To create an absolutely positioned element, add this property to a style:

```
position: absolute;
```

Static is the normal positioning method, so unless you're overriding a previously created style that already has a position of absolute, relative, or fixed, you won't need to specify that. In addition, static elements don't obey any of the positioning values discussed next.

Setting a positioning value is usually just part of the battle. To actually place an element somewhere on a page, you need to master the various positioning properties.

Setting Positioning Values

The display area of a web browser window—also called the viewport—has top, bottom, left, and right edges. Each of the four edges has a corresponding CSS property: top, bottom, left, and right. But you don't need to specify values for all four edges. Two are usually enough to place an item on the page. You can, if you want, place an element 10 ems from the left edge of the page and 20 ems from the top.

To specify the distance from an edge of a page to the corresponding edge of the element, use any of the valid CSS measurements—pixels, ems, percentages, and so on. You can also use negative values for positioning, like left: –10px; to move an element partly off the page (or off another element) for visual effect, as you'll see later in this chapter (page 444).

After the position property, you list one or more properties (top, bottom, left, or right). If you want the element to take up less than the available width (to make a thin sidebar, for example), then you can set the width property. To place a page's banner in an exact position from the top and left edges of the browser window, create a style like this:

```
.banner {
  position: absolute;
  left: 100px;
  top: 50px;
  width: 760px;
}
```

This style places the banner as pictured in Figure 14-2, top.

NOTE If you don't specify a vertical positioning value (for left or right), the browser places the element in the same place on the page vertically as it would if there were no positioning. The same is true for horizontal settings (top or bottom). In other words, if you simply set an element to a position of absolute but don't provide any placement values for top, right, bottom, or left, the browser simply keeps the element in the same place on the page, but stacked above other content.

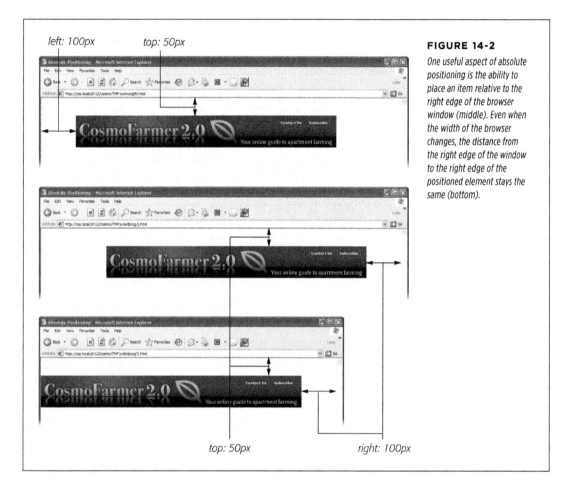

left: 100px *top: 50px*

FIGURE 14-2

One useful aspect of absolute positioning is the ability to place an item relative to the right edge of the browser window (middle). Even when the width of the browser changes, the distance from the right edge of the window to the right edge of the positioned element stays the same (bottom).

top: 50px *right: 100px*

Here's another example: placing an element so it always remains a fixed distance from the right side of the browser. When you use the right property, the browser measures the distance from the right edge of the browser window to the right edge of the element (Figure 14-2, middle). To position the banner 100 pixels from the right edge of the window, you'd create the same style as above, but simply replace left with right:

```
.banner {
  position: absolute;
  right: 100px;
  top: 50px;
  width: 760px;
}
```

Since the position is calculated based on the right edge of the browser window, adjusting the size of the window automatically repositions the banner, as you can see in Figure 14-2, bottom. Although the banner moves, the distance from the right edge of the element to the right edge of the browser window remains the same.

You can even specify *both* left and right position properties as well as both top and bottom, and let the browser determine the width and height of the element. Say you want a central block of text positioned 10 percent from the top of the window and 10 pixels from both the left and right edges of the window. To position the block, you can use an absolutely positioned style that sets the top, left, and right properties to 10%. In a browser window, the left edge of the box starts from the left edge of the window to 10 percent of the window's width, and the right edge extends to 10 percent from the right edge (Figure 14-3). The exact width of the box, then, depends on how wide the browser window is. A wider window makes a wider box; a thinner window, a thinner box. The left and right positions, however, are always 10 percent of the browser window's width.

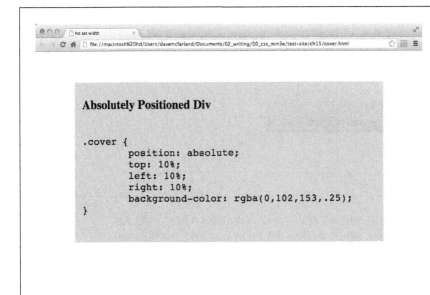

FIGURE 14-3

You can let a browser figure out an element's width simply by setting both the left and right values of an absolutely positioned element.

The width and height properties, which you learned about in Chapter 7, work exactly the same way for positioned elements. To place a 50×50-pixel gray box in the top-right corner of the browser window, create this style:

```
.box {
  position: absolute;
  right: 0;
  top: 0;
  width: 50px;
  height: 50px;
  background-color: #333;
}
```

The same caveat mentioned on page 206 applies here as well: Be careful with setting heights on elements. Unless you're styling a graphic with a set height, you can't be sure how tall any given element will be on a page. You might define a sidebar to be 200 pixels tall, but if you end up adding enough words and pictures to make the sidebar taller than 200 pixels, then you end up with content spilling out of the sidebar. Even if you're sure the content fits, a visitor can always pump up the size of her browser's font, creating text that's large enough to spill out of the box. Furthermore, when you specify a width and height in a style and the contents inside the styled element are wider or taller, strange things can happen.

When Absolute Positioning Is Relative

So far, this chapter has talked about positioning an element in an exact location in the browser window. However, absolute positioning doesn't always work that way. In fact, an absolutely positioned element is actually placed *relative* to the boundaries of its closest positioned ancestor. Simply put, if you've already created an element with absolute positioning (say a <div> tag that appears 100 pixels down from the top of the browser window), then any absolutely positioned elements with HTML *inside* that <div> tag are positioned relative to the div's top, bottom, left, and right edges.

NOTE   If all this talk of parents and ancestors doesn't ring a bell, then turn to page 50 for a refresher.

In the top image of Figure 14-4, the light gray box is absolutely positioned 5 ems from the top and left edges of the browser window.

There's also a <div> tag nested inside that box. Applying absolute positioning to that div positions it *relative to its absolutely positioned parent*. Setting a bottom position of 0 doesn't put the box at the bottom of the screen; it places the box at the bottom of its parent. Likewise, a right position for that nested div refers to the right of the edge of its parent (Figure 14-4, bottom).

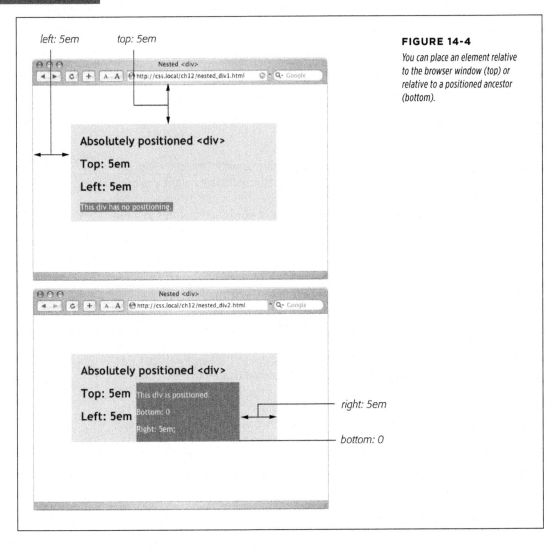

Whenever you use absolute positioning to place an element on the page, the exact position depends upon the positioning of any other tags the styled element is nested in. Here are the rules in a nutshell:

- **A tag is positioned relative to the browser window** if it has an absolute position *and* it's not inside any other tag that has either absolute, relative, or fixed positioning applied to it.

- **A tag is positioned relative to the edges of another element** if it's inside another tag with absolute, relative, or fixed positioning.

When (and Where) to Use Relative Positioning

You get one big benefit from placing an element relative to another tag: If that tag moves, the positioned element moves along with it. Say you place an image inside an <h1> tag, and you want the image to appear on the right edge of that <h1> tag. If you simply position the image in an exact spot in the browser window on the left edge of the <h1> tag, you're taking your chances. If the <h1> moves, the absolutely positioned image stays glued to its assigned spot. Instead, what you want to do is position the image relative to the <h1> tag, so that when the headline moves, the image moves with it (bottom two images in Figure 14-5).

> **NOTE** You can use the background-image property to place an image into the background of an <h1> tag. But if the graphic is taller than the <h1> tag, or you want the graphic to appear *outside* the boundaries of the headline (see the example third from the top in Figure 14-5), then embed the image with the <img> tag and use the relative positioning technique described in this section.

You could use the position property's relative value to place the image, but that has drawbacks, too. When you set an element's position to relative and then place it—maybe using the left and top properties—the element moves the set amount from where it would normally appear in the flow of the HTML. In other words, it moves relative to its current position. In the process, it leaves a big hole where it would've been if you hadn't positioned it at all (Figure 14-1, bottom). Usually, that's not what you want.

A better way to use relative positioning is to create a new positioning context for nested tags. For instance, the <h1> tag in the example at the beginning of this section is an ancestor of the <img> tag inside it. By setting the position of the <h1> tag to relative, any absolute positioning you apply to the <img> tag is relative to the four edges of the <h1> tag, not the browser window. Here's what the CSS looks like:

```
h1 { position: relative; }
h1 img {
  position: absolute;
  top: 0;
  right: 0;
}
```

Setting the image's top and right properties to 0 places the image in the upper-right corner of the headline—not the browser window.

In CSS, the term *relative* doesn't exactly mean the same thing it does in the real world. After all, if you want to place the <img> tag relative to the <h1> tag, your first instinct may be to set the image's position to relative. In fact, the item that you want to position—the image—gets an absolute position, while the element you want to position the element *relative to*—the headline—gets a setting of relative. Think of the relative value as meaning "relative to me." When you apply relative positioning to a tag, it means "all positioned elements inside of me should be positioned relative to my location."

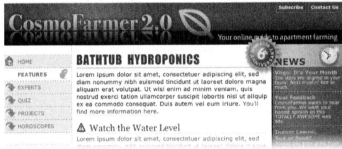

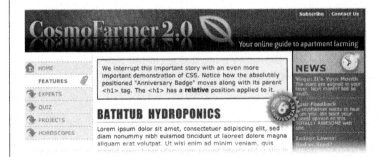

FIGURE 14-5

Top: A graphical button (circled) is placed inside an <h1> tag. Second from top: Adding absolute positioning to the button— right: -35px; top: -35px;—moves it outside of the <h1> tag area and places it in the top-right corner of the browser window (circled). (In fact, it's placed a little outside of the browser window, thanks to the negative positioning values.) Third from top: Adding position: relative to the <h1> creates a new positioning context for the <img> tag. The same top and right values move the <img> tag to the <h1> tag's top-right corner. Bottom: When you move the heading down the page, the graphic goes along for the ride.

> **NOTE** Because you'll often use relative positioning merely to set up a new positioning context for nested tags, you don't even need to use the left, top, bottom, or right settings with it. The <h1> tag has position: relative, but no left, top, right, or bottom values.

Stacking Elements

As you can see in Figure 14-6, absolutely positioned elements sit "above" your web page and can even reside on top of (or underneath) other positioned elements. This stacking of elements takes place on what's called the z-index. If you're familiar with the concept of layers in Adobe Photoshop, Sketch, or Adobe Illustrator, then you know how the z-index works: It represents the order in which positioned elements are stacked on top of the page.

To put it another way, think of a web page as a piece of paper and an absolutely positioned element as a sticky note. Whenever you add an absolutely positioned element to a page, it's like slapping a sticky note on it. Of course, when you add a sticky note, you run the risk of covering up anything written on the page below.

Normally, the stacking order of positioned elements follows their order in the page's HTML code. On a page with two absolutely positioned <div> tags, the <div> tag that comes second in the HTML appears *above* the other <div>. But you can control the order in which positioned elements stack up by using the CSS z-index property. The property gets a numeric value, like this:

```
z-index: 3;
```

The larger the value, the closer to the top of the stack an element appears. Say you have three absolutely positioned images, and parts of each image overlap. The one with the larger z-index appears on top of the others (see Figure 14-6, top). When you change the z-index of one or more images, you change their stacking order (Figure 14-6, middle).

You can even use negative z-index numbers, which can come in handy when you want to position an element underneath its parent or any of its ancestors. For example, in the top image in Figure 14-6, the <div> tag is relatively positioned. If you wanted to place one of the images behind the <div>, you could use a negative z-index value:

```
z-index: -1;
```

> **NOTE** It's perfectly OK to have gaps in z-index values. In other words, 10, 20, 30 does the exact same thing as 1, 2, 3. In fact, spreading out the numerical values gives you room to insert more items into the stack later. And, when you want to make sure nothing ever appears on top of a positioned element, give it a really large z-index, like this: z-index: 10000;. But don't get too carried away; some browsers can only handle a maximum z-index of 2147483647.

Hiding Parts of a Page

Another CSS property often used with absolutely positioned elements is visibility, which lets you hide part of a page (or show a hidden part). Say you want a label to pop into view over an image when a visitor mouses over it. You make the caption invisible when the page first loads (visibility: hidden), and switch to visible (visibility: visible) when the mouse moves over it.

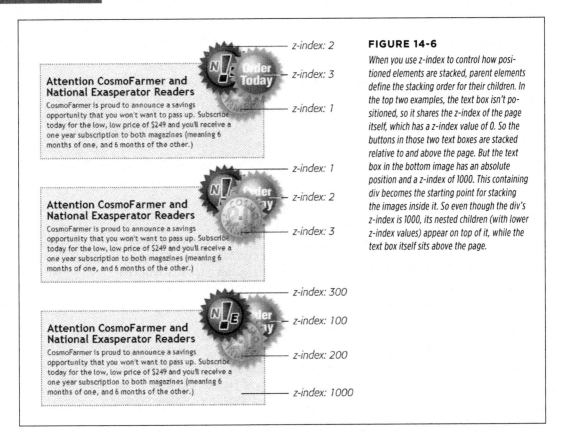

FIGURE 14-6

When you use z-index to control how positioned elements are stacked, parent elements define the stacking order for their children. In the top two examples, the text box isn't positioned, so it shares the z-index of the page itself, which has a z-index value of 0. So the buttons in those two text boxes are stacked relative to and above the page. But the text box in the bottom image has an absolute position and a z-index of 1000. This containing div becomes the starting point for stacking the images inside it. So even though the div's z-index is 1000, its nested children (with lower z-index values) appear on top of it, while the text box itself sits above the page.

The visibility property's hidden value is similar to the display property's none value, but there's a fundamental difference. When you set an element's display property to none, it literally disappears from the page without a trace. However, setting the visibility property to hidden prevents the browser from displaying the element's contents, but leaves an empty hole where the element would have been. When applied to absolutely positioned elements that are already removed from the flow of the page, visibility: hidden and display: none behave identically. Most developers simply use the display: none method and skip the visibility property entirely.

There's yet another way to hide an element—set its opacity to 0 like this:

```
opacity: 0;
```

To make it reappear, you can set its opacity back to 1:

```
opacity: 1;
```

The benefit of using opacity is that it's one of the CSS properties that a browser can animate. This means you can use the CSS transitions you learned about in Chapter 10 to animate changes in opacity. For example, you can make an element appear to fade into view by changing its opacity from 0 to 1 and adding a transition.

The most common way to switch an element from hidden to displayed and back again is with JavaScript. But you don't have to learn JavaScript programming to use the visibility property (or, for that matter, the display property). You can use the :hover pseudo-class (see page 55) to make an invisible element visible. For example, say you wanted to place a caption over an image, but you only want that caption to show up when a visitor mouses over the image (see Figure 14-7). You could do that following these steps:

1. **Create the HTML for the image and caption.**

   One way to do this would be to use the HTML <figure> and <figcaption> tags, like this:

   ```
   <figure class="hat">
   <img src="hat.jpg" width="100" height="100">
    <figcaption>A picture of a hat</figcaption>
   </figure>
   ```

   Here you're applying a class—hat—to the <figure> tag so you can style just that one figure.

2. **Position the caption.**

   To place the caption on top of the image, you use absolute positioning. To place the caption in relation to the img, you should set its parent (the <figure> tag) to relative, and also give the parent a set width that matches the dimensions of the photo.

   ```
   .hat {
     position: relative;
     width: 100px;
     height: 100px;
   }

   .hat figcaption {
     position: absolute;
     bottom: 0
     left: 0;
     right: 0;
     background-color: white;
   }
   ```

   The caption is placed at the bottom of the figure (bottom: 0). With its left and right values set to 0, it will span the entire width of the figure.

3. Hide the caption.

With the current code, a browser would display the caption on top of the image, but you want that to happen only when someone's mouse hovers over the image. To hide it, add either visibility: hidden; or display: none; to the .hat figcaption style.

```
.hat figcaption {
  display: none;
  position: absolute;
  bottom: 0
  left: 0;
  right: 0;
  background-color: white;
}
```

4. Make the caption appear when a visitor mouses over the image.

To do this, you'll employ a little trick with the :hover pseudo-class (page 55). You want to make the caption visible when the visitor mouses over the image. Unfortunately, there's no way to create a style that affects the caption when the mouse moves over the image. However, since the caption is inside the <figure> tag, you can craft a descendant selector that affects the caption when the mouse moves over the figure:

```
.hat:hover figcaption {
  display: block;
}
```

This descendant selector basically says "target any <figcaption> tag that's inside an element with the class of hat, but only when the mouse is over that element." This selector only works because the figcaption tag is a descendant of the element being hovered over.

You can elaborate on this idea to create CSS-based pop-up tooltips. For a basic CSS method of adding pop-up tooltips—additional information that appears when someone mouses over a link—check out *www.menucool.com/tooltip/css-tooltip*. You also have many JavaScript options to choose from. For example, the jQuery qTip[2] plug-in is a full-featured and easy-to-use JavaScript tooltip based on the jQuery framework: *http://craigsworks.com/projects/qtip2/*.

As mentioned earlier, you can also use the opacity setting to hide and show an element, as well as use a transition to animate this effect. To do that, you can change the previous styles to look like this:

```
.hat figcaption {
  opacity: 0;
  transition: opacity .5s ease-in;
  position: absolute;
  bottom: 0
  left: 0;
```

```
    right: 0;
    background-color: white;
  }
  .hat:hover figcaption {
    opacity: 1;
  }
```

You'll see this in action in the tutorial on page 454. Remember, however, that transitions don't work in Internet Explorer 9 or earlier. That's OK in this case; your visitors will still see the caption appear, it just won't fade in and out of view smoothly.

FIGURE 14-7

Now you don't see it, now you do. You can place an absolutely positioned element over another element, but hide it (left) until a visitor mouses over a parent element (right).

■ Powerful Positioning Strategies

As explained at the beginning of this chapter, you can run into trouble when you try to use CSS positioning to place *every* element on a page. Because it's impossible to predict all possible combinations of browsers and settings your visitors will use, CSS-controlled positioning works best as a tactical weapon. Use it sparingly to provide exact placement for specific elements.

In this section, you'll learn how to use absolute positioning to add small but visually important details to your page design, how to absolutely position certain layout elements, and how to cement important page elements in place while the rest of the content scrolls.

Positioning Within an Element

One of the most effective ways to use positioning is to place small items relative to other elements on a page. Absolute positioning can simulate the kind of right alignment you get with floats. In the first example in Figure 14-8, the date on the top headline is a bit overbearing, but with CSS you can reformat it and move it to the right edge of the bottom headline.

In order to style the date separately from the rest of the headline, you need to enclose the date in an HTML tag. The `<span>` tag is a popular choice for applying a class to a chunk of inline text to style it independently from the rest of a paragraph.

```
<h1><span class="date">Nov. 10, 2006</span> CosmoFarmer Bought By Google</h1>
```

Now it's a matter of creating the styles. First, you need to give the containing element—in this example, the `<h1>` tag—a relative position value. Then, apply an absolute position to the item you wish to place—the date. Here's the CSS for the bottom image in #1 of Figure 14-8:

```
h1 {
    position: relative;
    border-bottom: 1px dashed #999999;
}

h1 .date {
    position: absolute;
    bottom: 0;
    right: 0;
    font-size: .5em;
    background-color: #E9E9E9;
    color: black;
    padding: 2px 7px 0 7px;
}
```

Some of the properties listed above, like `border-bottom`, are just for looks. The crucial properties are bolded: `position`, `bottom`, and `right`. Once you give the headline a relative position, you can position the `<span>` containing the date in the lower-right corner of the headline by setting both the `bottom` and `right` properties to 0.

Breaking an Element Out of the Box

You can also use positioning to make an item appear to poke out of another element. In the second example in Figure 14-8, the top image shows a headline with a graphic. That is, the `<img>` tag is placed inside the `<h1>` tag as part of the headline. Using absolute positioning and negative `top` and `left` property values moves the image to the headline's left and pushes it out beyond the top and left edges. Here's the CSS that produces that example:

```
h1 {
    position: relative;
    margin-top: 35px;
    padding-left: 55px;
    border-bottom: 1px dashed #999999;
}
```

```
h1 img {
  position: absolute;
  top: -30px;
  left: -30px;
}
```

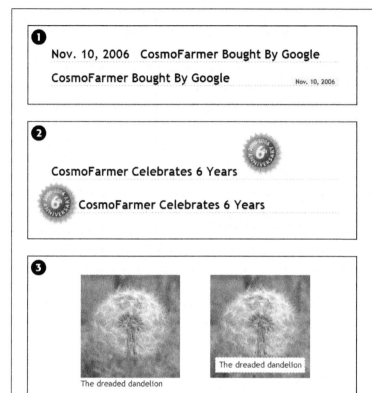

FIGURE 14-8

Absolute positioning is perfect for simple design details like placing a date in the lower-right corner of a headline (top), punching an image out of its containing block (middle), or placing a caption directly on top of a photo (bottom). (You'll learn the caption trick in the tutorial on page 452.)

The basic concept is the same as the previous example, but with a few additions. First, the image's top and left values are negative, so the graphic actually appears 30 pixels above the top of the headline and 30 pixels to the left of the headline's left edge. Be careful when you use negative values. They can position an element partially (or entirely) off a page or make the element cover other content on the page. To prevent a negatively positioned element from sticking out of the browser window, add enough margin or padding to either the body element or the enclosing, relatively positioned tag—the <h1> tag in this example. The extra margin provides enough space for the protruding image. In this case, to prevent the image from overlapping any content above the headline, add a significant top margin. The left padding of 55 pixels also moves the text of the headline out from under the absolutely positioned image.

Creating CSS-Style Frames Using Fixed Positioning

Since most web pages are longer than one screen, you may want to keep some page elements constantly visible—like a navigation panel, search box, or your site logo. HTML frames were once the only way to keep important fixtures handy as other content scrolled out of sight. But HTML frames have major drawbacks. Since each frame contains a separate web page file, you have to create several HTML files to make one complete web page (called a *frameset*). Not only are framesets time-consuming for the designer, they also make your site hard for search engines to search. And HTML framesets can also wreak havoc for visitors who use screen readers due to vision problems or those who want to print pages from your site.

Nevertheless, the idea behind frames is still useful, so CSS offers a positioning value that lets you achieve the visual appearance of frames with less work. You can see a page created using the *fixed* value in Figure 14-9.

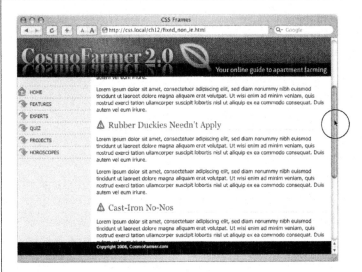

FIGURE 14-9

Revisit the Web of yesteryear, but with a lot less code. Using the position *property's* fixed *value, you can emulate the look of HTML frames by fixing some elements in place but still letting visitors scroll through the content of a very long web page. The scrollbar (circled) moves only the large text area; the top and bottom banners and the sidebar stay fixed.*

Fixed positioning works much like absolute positioning in that you use the left, top, right, or bottom properties to place the element. Also like absolutely positioned elements, fixed positioning removes an element from the flow of the HTML. It floats above other parts of the page, which simply ignore it.

Here's how you can build the kind of page pictured in Figure 14-9, which has a fixed banner, sidebar, and footer, and a scrollable main content area:

1. **Add** <div> **tags with class (or ID) attributes for each section of the page.**

   You can have four main <div> tags with classes (or IDs) like banner, sidebar, main, and footer (Figure 14-10). The order in which you place these tags in the HTML doesn't matter. Like absolute positioning, fixed positioning lets you place elements on a page regardless of their HTML order.

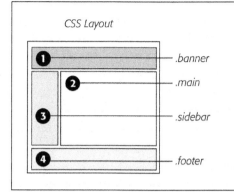

CSS Layout

FIGURE 14-10

With fixed positioning, you can lock any number of page elements in place, so they're always in view when your visitor scrolls. In this example, the header (1), sidebar (3), and footer (4) are fixed, while the content in the main area of the page (2) is free to scroll.

2. **Add your material to each div.**

In general, use the fixed divs for stuff a visitor should always have access to in the areas you wish to be locked in place. In this example, the banner, sidebar, and footer contain the site logo, global site navigation, and copyright notices.

The main content goes into the remaining <div> tag. Don't add too much information to a fixed div, however. If a fixed sidebar is taller than the visitor's browser window, he won't be able to see the entire sidebar. And since fixed elements don't scroll, there'll be no way (short of buying a bigger monitor) for that visitor to see the sidebar content that doesn't fit in his browser window.

3. **Create styles for all fixed elements.**

The left, right, top, and bottom values are relative to the browser window, so just determine where on the screen you'd like them to go and plug in the values. Specify a width for the elements as well.

> **NOTE** Unlike absolute positioning, fixed positioning is *always* relative to the browser window, even when an element with fixed positioning is placed inside another tag with relative or absolute positioning.

The styles to position the elements numbered 1, 3, and 4 in Figure 14-10 look like this:

```
.banner {
  position: fixed;
  left: 0;
  right: 0;
  top: 0;
}
```

```
.sidebar {
  position: fixed;
  left: 0;
  top: 110px;
  width: 175px;
}
.footer {
  position: fixed;
  bottom: 0;
  left: 0;
  right: 0;
}
```

4. **Create the style for the scrollable content area.**

   Since fixed-position elements are removed from the flow of the HTML, other tags on the page have no idea the fixed-position elements are there. So, the <div> tag with the page's main content, for example, appears underneath the fixed items. The main task for this style is to use margins to move the contents clear of those areas.

```
.main {
  margin-left: 190px;
  margin-top: 110px;
}
```

   Fixed positioning is well supported in browsers: Internet Explorer 8 and up, as well as all other major browsers (including the latest iOS and Android mobile browsers) support fixed positioning.

Tutorial: Positioning Page Elements

This tutorial lets you explore a few different ways to use absolute positioning, like creating a three-column layout, positioning items within a banner, and adding captions on top of photos. Unlike the previous chapter, where you wrapped chunks of HTML in <div> tags and added class names to them, in these exercises, most of the HTML work has already been done for you. You can focus on honing your new CSS skills.

To get started, download the tutorial files located on this book's companion website at *https://github.com/sawmac/css_mm_4e*.

Enhancing a Page Banner

First, you'll make some small but visually important changes to a page banner. You'll create styles that refer to HTML tags with classes applied to them. (Again, that part has been taken care of for you.)

1. **Launch a web browser and open the file _14→index.html_.**

   On this web page (Figure 14-11), start by repositioning several parts of the banner.

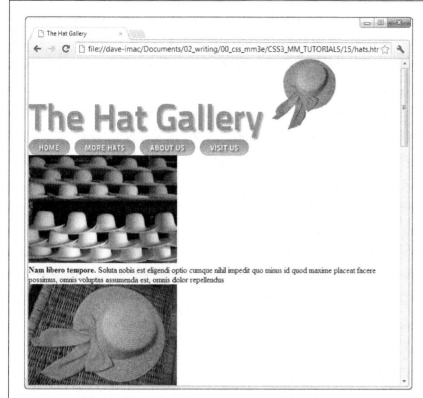

FIGURE 14-11

This page has a lot of stuff—logo graphic, banner, nav bar, and a gallery of images and captions. But there's not much visual structure. Just normal, static HTML with everything running from top to bottom of the page. You can make it more readable and interesting with some absolute positioning.

2. **Open the _styles.css_ file in a text editor.**

   This file already includes some basic formatting. You'll add the styles for this tutorial to the bottom.

   You'll start by moving the small hat image to the left side of the banner. To help break up the boxy look that's typical of CSS designs, break this graphic out of the banner's borders, so it looks like a slapped-on sticker.

3. **At the bottom of _styles.css_, add this new style:**

   ```
   header .badge {
     position: absolute;
     top: -20px;
     left: -90px;
   }
   ```

The graphic is inside of an HTML `<header>` tag, and the graphic itself has a class of badge. This style positions the top-left corner of the graphic 90 pixels to the left and 20 pixels above the top of the page.

Preview the page now, and you'll see a couple of problems. First, the graphic hangs off the edge of the page, but you really want it to hang off the edge of the banner area. You'll tackle that problem now.

4. **Add this style above the one you just created:**

   ```
   header {
     position: relative;
   }
   ```

   It's good practice to place the CSS code for styles that control a general section of a page (like this header style) above the code for styles that format just parts of that section (like the style you created in step 3). Also, grouping styles for related sections makes it easier to find styles when you need to analyze or edit a page's CSS. In this case, the header style goes first because it applies to a large chunk of HTML. But you should keep the header .badge style near it as you add more styles to the page. (You can read more about techniques for organizing your CSS on page 570.)

   The header style creates a new positioning context for any nested tags. In other words, the relative setting makes any other positioned elements inside this tag place themselves relative to the edges of the banner. This change in positioning shifts the placement of the style you created in step 3. Now it's 20 pixels above and 90 pixels to the left of the banner box. The badge still hangs off the page just a little bit, so you'll add some margin to the header to move it down a bit.

5. **Edit the header style by adding the two bolded lines below:**

   ```
   header {
     position: relative;
     margin-top: 20px;
     padding: 20px 0 0 10px;
   }
   ```

   This margin adds enough space above the header to move it and the graphic down. In addition, the padding adds space inside the header so the headline (and the soon to be repositioned nav bar) don't feel so cramped. But now you have another problem—"The Hat Gallery" headline is partially hidden underneath the badge. Overlapping elements is one of the hazards of absolute positioning. In this case, you can fix the problem by changing the badge's z-index and moving it behind the text.

6. **Add z-index: -1 to the** header .badge **style:**

   ```
   header .badge {
     position: absolute;
     top: -20px;
   ```

```
   left: -90px;
   z-index: -1;
 }
```

The -1 value places the absolutely positioned element behind its parent—in this case, behind the text (see Figure 14-12). Next, you'll use absolute positioning to move the navigation bar to the right side of the header.

7. **Add another style after the** header .badge **style.**

```
header nav {
  position: absolute;
  right: 0;
  top: 45px;
}
```

Although you could position the navigation bar by floating the <h1> tag, in this case, it's a lot easier to use absolute positioning. Here, you've created a tag style for the HTML <nav> tag, when it's also inside a <header> tag. Remember, in step 4, you gave the header a relative position, which means any tags inside it—like the <nav> tag—are positioned in relation to it, so the right value of 0 in this style places the right edge of the navigation bar on the right edge of the banner (see Figure 14-12).

FIGURE 14-12

Absolute positioning is a big help in placing small elements like the hat graphic and the navigation bar. Unlike floats, the exact position of the image and the navigation bar in the HTML code isn't important, giving you a lot of layout flexibility. You can achieve the same effect without absolute positioning, but it would be harder.

Placing Captions on the Photos

In Chapter 8, you learned one way to add a caption to a photo (page 264). In the examples from that chapter, the captions sat underneath the photos, which is what you want most of the time. But someday, you may want to add a caption directly *on* a photo, like the subtitles TV news shows love to display across the lower third of the screen.

1. **Open *index.html* in your text editor.**

   There is a gallery of photos on this page. The HTML for one image looks like this:

   ```
   <figure>
     <img src="images/file00079963469.jpg" width="300" height="210"
   alt="Panama">
     <figcaption><strong>Nam libero tempore.</strong> Soluta nobis est eli-
   gendi
       optio cumque nihil impedit quo minus id quod maxime placeat facere pos-
   simus,
       omnis voluptas assumenda est, omnis dolor repellendus
     </figcaption>
   </figure>
   ```

   This example uses the HTML `<figure>` and `<figcaption>` tags. The `<figure>` tag is normally a block-level tag, but since you want the images to sit side by side, start by changing them to inline elements.

2. **Add another style below the** header nav **style you added earlier.**

   ```
   .gallery figure {
     display: inline-block;
     width: 300px;
     height: 210px;
     margin: 15px;
     position: relative;
   }
   ```

   This HTML creates a descendant selector. The `<figure>` tags are all grouped inside a `<div>` tag with the class of gallery applied to it. You're using a descendant selector since you may add other figures to this page that aren't part of the gallery and should be formatted differently. This descendant selector targets just the `<figure>` tags you're after at the moment.

   By making the figure tag an `inline-block` element, the figures can all sit side by side. The width and height values match the width and height of the images. In other words, you want the `<figure>` tag to only be large enough to hold the images. The margin value adds a little space around the figures so they don't bump into each. Finally, the `position: relative` declaration sets a new positioning context, so you can position each caption in relation to its figure.

   Now it's time to position the captions.

3. Add one more style below the one you just added:

```
.gallery figcaption {
    position: absolute;
    top: 15%;
    bottom: 15%;
    left: 0;
    right: 0;
    background-color: rgba(153,153,153,.9);
}
```

The `<figcaption>` tags are absolutely positioned using all four positioning quadrants: top, bottom, left, and right. Basically, the captions will span the entire figure, but be placed a bit below the top and above the bottom (in fact, 15 percent below and above). Using all four settings means that you don't need to worry about setting a width or a height for the captions; instead, you leave it up to the browser.

Finally, the `background-color` declaration places a semi-transparent background atop each figure, which means you can see the image through the caption's background.

Now for some simple text enhancements.

4. Edit the style you just created by adding the bolded code below:

```
.gallery figcaption {
    position: absolute;
    top: 15%;
    bottom: 15%;
    left: 0;
    right: 0;
    background-color: rgba(153,153,153,.9);
    padding: 20px;
    font-family: Titillium, Arial, sans-serif;
    font-weight: 400;
    font-size: .9em;
    color: white;
}
```

The padding just provides a little breathing room for the text, while the other properties set a font, size, and color.

If you preview the page now, you'll see that the captions appear on top of all of the images. Next, you'll change the style so the captions appear only when a visitor mouses over an image. Start by hiding the captions.

5. **Add opacity: 0; to the style:**

```
.gallery figcaption {
    position: absolute;
    top: 15%;
    bottom: 15%;
    left: 0;
    right: 0;
    background-color: rgb(153,153,153);
    background-color: rgba(153,153,153,.9);
    padding: 20px;
    font-family: Titillium, Arial, sans-serif;
    font-size: .9em;
    font-weight: 400;
    color: white;
    opacity: 0;
}
```

Setting the opacity to 0 makes the caption invisible. You may also use display: none; or visibility: hidden; to hide the captions, but this way you can animate the opacity value by using a CSS transition—in fact, you'll add that effect in a moment. But first, you need to add a :hover state so when a visitor hovers over the image, its caption appears.

6. **Add the following to the style sheet:**

```
.gallery figure:hover figcaption {
  opacity: 1;
}
```

This tricky bit of CSS can be translated to "when the mouse moves over the figure element (figure:hover) inside an element with the class gallery (.gallery), set the opacity of the caption to 1." In other words, moving the mouse over the <figure> tag makes the descendant <figcaption> tag visible. Save the page and try it out. When you mouse over the figure, the caption should appear. We can animate this effect by adding a transition to the .gallery figcaption style.

7. **Edit the** .gallery figcaption **style so that it looks like this (additions are in bold):**

```
figcaption {
    position: absolute;
    top: 15%;
    bottom: 15%;
    left: 0;
    right: 0;
    background-color: rgb(153,153,153);
    background-color: rgba(153,153,153,.9);
    padding: 20px;
```

```
    font-family: Titillium, Arial, sans-serif;
    font-size: .9em;
    font-weight: 400;
    color: white;
    opacity: 0;
    transition: opacity .75s ease-out;
}
```

You've added the transition property. While Internet Explorer 9 and earlier don't understand transitions, that's OK; the captions will still appear in those browsers. They'll just appear and disappear instantly instead of fading in and out smoothly.

Finally, you'll make the copyright notice stick to the bottom of the browser window, using fixed positioning.

8. **Add one last style to the style sheet:**

```
footer {
    position: fixed;
    bottom: 0;
    left: 0;
    right: 0;
    padding: 10px;
    background-color: black;
    color: white;
}
```

As you read on page 430, fixed positioning lets you "stick" an element to a specific spot in the browser window. In this case, it's fixed to the bottom of the page (bottom: 0) and extends the entire width of the page (thanks to the left: 0 and right: 0 declarations). The last three declarations simply add a bit of space around the footer, giving it a black background and white text.

9. **Save the *styles.css* file, and preview the *index.html* file.**

The final page should look like Figure 14-13. You'll find a completed version of this tutorial in the *14_finished* folder.

FIGURE 14-13

With some clever CSS, you can make captions fade into view when mousing over an image (circled).

Responsive Web Design

Web designers have always had to contend with designing for various screen sizes—from 760-pixel-wide laptops to gargantuan widescreen displays. However, the rise of smartphones and tablets has now made it even more imperative to design for a wide range of screen widths and heights. Some companies go so far as to create separate, mobile-only websites (see the top images in Figure 15-1). However, unless you have the time, money, and technical expertise to develop two sites and program your web server to provide the proper site to the proper device, a mobile-only website is probably out of reach.

Fortunately, there's another, simpler approach that lets you build a single site that adapts to different device widths (see bottom images in Figure 15-1). Called *responsive web design*, this technique uses several different tricks to make a page change its layout based on the width of the browser screen. On a smartphone, for example, you can lay out a page in a single, easy-to-read column to fit the narrow width of the screen (bottom-left image), while maintaining a multicolumn layout on wider monitors (bottom-right image).

■ Responsive Web Design Basics

It's very hard to read a four-column web page on a phone whose screen is just 320 pixels wide. It's just as difficult to read a single column of text that's spread across the 2560 pixels of a large desktop monitor. *Responsive web design*, a term coined by web design pioneer Ethan Marcotte, is an attempt to solve that problem. Responsive web design, or RWD for short, lets you change the entire layout of a page based on browser window width (among other factors), so you can create the most readable presentation for each device, without having to create multiple versions of the same website. RWD is not a single technology or technique. Instead, it brings together several CSS and HTML methods to create web pages whose layouts adapt to different screens.

FIGURE 15-1

Many large companies, like Amazon and Target, create mobile versions of their sites, optimized for display on handheld devices like the iPhone (top). Fortunately, using responsive web design techniques, you can craft one HTML file that displays differently on different-width devices (bottom). On a phone, the page may appear as one long column, while in a desktop browser, the same page takes advantage of the wider screen to include multiple columns and larger photos.

> **NOTE** Ethan Marcotte lays out his steps for RWD in his book *Responsive Web Design* (A Book Apart). (There's nothing better than a straightforward title.) You can also read Ethan's original article about RWD at *www.alistapart. com/articles/responsive-web-design.*

RWD combines three main ideas: flexible grids for layout, flexible media for images and video, and CSS media queries to create different styles for different screen widths. With flexible grids, you skip fixed-width layouts. Since smartphone screens come in a wide variety of widths, it makes no sense to create a page at a fixed width;

instead, you want the page to grow or shrink to fit the particular device (this is the liquid layout concept discussed on page 386). Creating flexible media lets your images and videos scale to fit the appropriate screen real estate...big photos for big monitors, smaller photos for small screens, and so on.

Finally, media queries are a CSS technology that lets you send different styles to a browser based on current conditions in the browser. For example, you can send one set of styles when the screen is less than 480 pixels wide and another set when the window is more than 760 pixels wide. You're not just limited to width, either; you can craft styles that only apply to tablets in landscape view or to devices with high-pixel density (like the Retina display on iPhone and iPads).

Setting Up a Web Page for RWD

If you have a smartphone, like an iPhone or Android phone, take a look at it. Open a web browser and visit *www.nytimes.com*. You'll get shuffled off to a version of the site specifically aimed at mobile devices: mobile.nytimes.com. However, there's a View Desktop Version link that leads to the actual site you'd see in a desktop browser. You should see (unless the *New York Times* has made its site responsive since this writing) something like Figure 15-2. It's a large, multicolumn design smashed into the tiny screen space of the phone. Because phone manufacturers know that most websites are built for desktop screens, they've made their browsers behave a little differently than what you may be used to. Mobile browsers don't just display the page at 100 percent; if they did, then a fixed-width, 960-pixel-wide page would not fit the screen, and you'd see only one portion of the page at a time. You'd then have to swipe around to see all of the page. Instead, phone browsers zoom out to fit the page on screen. The exact amount they zoom out varies from phone to phone. Safari on the iPhone, for example, acts like the screen is really 980 pixels wide, so it shrinks the page down to fit within 980 pixels.

In general, this behavior of mobile browsers works well for the majority of sites, but not so well with a responsive web design. Because responsive sites are intended to look good on phones, you don't want the display to zoom out, which would make the text too small to read. Fortunately, there's a simple way to override this behavior of mobile browsers. Simply add the following code to the <head> section of your web page (directly above the <title> tag is a good spot for it):

```
<meta name="viewport" content="width=device-width">
```

HTML meta tags provide extra information about the page's content and can give browsers extra instructions about how to display the page. In this case, the viewport refers to the browser screen, and the content attribute sets the width of the browser to the width of the phone's. In other words, on mobile browsers that tend to zoom out, you're telling them not to zoom out, but to just make the screen's width match the actual display of the phone.

FIGURE 15-2

Websites designed for desktop browsers, like the New York Times site pictured here, tend to look like tiny postage stamps on phones. Visitors are forced to zoom in and drag around the screen to read everything.

Media Queries

CSS includes a concept called *media queries*, which let you assign styles to a page based on the destination browser's width and height. With this method, you can create custom styles for mobile phones, tablets, and desktop browsers, and, in turn, customize your site's presentation so it looks its best on each type of device.

The whole point of responsive design is to give your site's visitors the most readable and attractive presentation possible. This usually means customizing the design to look its best at different browser widths. Many designers think of three target screens related to the three most common web browsing devices: smartphones, tablets, and desktop computers. Granted, there's a wide variety of widths for these devices...you can have small phones, large phones, 7" tablets, 10" tablets, and so on, so there's no one width for all of these devices. Just keep in mind that the goal is to make a page look good at varying widths; you can simply test out different designs and different window widths to see when a four-column design needs to become a two-column or a one-column design.

Strategies for Using Media Queries

Although we recommend trial and error to determine what changes you need to make to a design so that it looks the best on different devices, there are a few common design changes that are routinely targeted by media queries:

- **Adjust columns.** Multiple side-by-side columns look great on a big monitor (and even on a tablet in landscape mode), but not so much on a phone. In addition, four columns is probably too many for most tablets in portrait mode, so bringing the page down to 2 or 3 columns is probably a good idea for media queries targeting tablets. Avoiding floats in mobile-targeted media-query styles lets you stack a page's content containers one on top of the other. You'll try out this technique in the tutorial on page 487.

- **Flexible widths.** You can use a fixed-width design for a desktop browser—that's how designers have done it for years—but for narrower screens like those on tablets and phones, a fixed design won't fit the window. A 960-pixel-wide page is just too much for a phone's 320 or 480 pixels. For phones and tablets, a good approach is setting the widths of your content divs to auto or 100%. This setting converts your page from a fixed-width design to a liquid, or flexible, design. In other words, no matter how wide a phone's screen, the divs will fit 100 percent of it. If a person holds an iPhone in portrait mode (so the screen width is 320 pixels) and then suddenly turns the phone horizontally (changing the screen width to 480 pixels), divs set to auto or 100% simply resize to fit the new space.

- **Tighten up white space.** Ample space between headlines, graphics, and other page elements adds breathing room to a design on a 23-inch monitor, but creates a scattered design and wasted space on a phone's small screen, forcing visitors to scroll excessively. Shrinking margin and padding values lets you fit more onto those small screens.

- **Adjust font sizes.** Contrast between big, bold headlines and small body type looks great on a desktop monitor, but overly large headlines waste screen space and are hard to read on a handheld device. Likewise, making body type a bit larger on phones can often make it easier to read. In other words, pay attention to font sizes as you create media-query styles.

- **Changing navigation menus.** You might have a beautifully designed horizontal navigation bar that spans the top of your web page, with a dozen buttons to take visitors to different sections of your site. Unfortunately, as the browser window becomes thinner, those buttons may no longer fit across the screen.

Instead, they'll break into two, three, or more lines on the screen. You'll see an example of this in the tutorial on page 476. It may be all right if the navigation bar becomes a few lines instead of just one, or it might take up too much of the top of the screen, forcing viewers to scroll down just to get to the first bit of actual content.

Unfortunately, there's no straightforward CSS solution. Many sites use JavaScript to dynamically change the navigation menu into an HTML drop-down menu, so it only takes up a small bit of space (to learn how to do that, visit *http://css-tricks. com/convert-menu-to-dropdown/*). There are other solutions as well. For an overview of different approaches some sites take to this problem, read *http:// exisweb.net/incredibly-useful-list-of-responsive-navigation-and-menu-patterns* and *http://bradfrostweb.com/blog/web/complex-navigation-patterns-for-responsive-design/.*

- **Hide content on handheld devices.** Many designers strip away content from mobile versions of sites. While it's easy to scan several columns and hundreds of lines of text on a desktop monitor, too much information on a phone can be overwhelming. You can use CSS to simply hide content that you think is superfluous for mobile users by setting the CSS display property to none.

  However, keep in mind that whenever you hide content, you're keeping a visitor away from information your site provides. This can be particularly shocking if someone visits your site using their desktop computer, then later visits the site on her phone only to find that important information she was looking for is now gone. In addition, even though you hide that content with CSS, the HTML is still there, forcing the mobile phone to waste time and bandwidth downloading HTML that it doesn't use.

- **Use background images.** If you put a 960-pixel banner on a page, no phone will display it without zooming out. One approach is to make sure your images are small enough to fit inside a phone's screen, or to use CSS background images instead. For example, you can create a div and add a class to it like this: `<div class="logo">`. Then, in the style sheet for the desktop browser, set the div's width and height to match the size of the large logo, using the background-image property to insert the image into the background. For example:

  ```
  .logo {
      width: 960px;
      height: 120px;
      background-image: url(images/large_logo.png)
  }
  ```

  You could then put another style inside the style sheet used for mobile phones that resizes that div and uses a different background image:

```
.logo {
    width: 100%;
    height: 60px;
    background-image: url(images/small_logo.png)
}
```

On page 472, you'll learn how to scale images that you've inserted into the HTML using the <img> tag, so they fit different browser widths.

Creating Breakpoints

Media queries let you send different styles to browsers based on their screen widths. For example, you can tell a browser "If your screen is no larger than 480 pixels, apply these styles," or, "If your screen is more than 480 pixels but less than 769 pixels, then use these styles." The different width values you specify—480, 769, and so on—are often called *breakpoints* in responsive design. Basically, at which value does the design start to break down?

An easy way to determine this is to take a completed desktop design and open it in a web browser. Grab the browser window's sizing handle and slowly make the window narrower. At a certain point, the design will probably start to look terrible. Those four columns, for example, will get mighty cramped. The point at which the design starts to look bad is a good candidate for a breakpoint; in other words, it's a good size at which to define a new media query and load some new styles to remove a column or two.

It's common to create three sets of media queries for three different breakpoints—one for smartphones, one for tablets, and one for desktop monitors. The exact breakpoint you use will vary from design to design (as well as from device to device), but here's a common starting point: A screen less than 480 pixels gets one set of styles, a screen between 481 and 768 gets another set of styles, and anything over 768 gets the desktop design. However, it's up to you. Some designers make the tablet design go up to 1024 pixels, and send desktop styles to browsers wider than 1024.

Some designers even go so far as designing four or five different breakpoints so their designs look best in a wide range of screen widths. The exact details on how you create these breakpoints using media queries is coming up on page 464.

Desktop First or Mobile First?

Another thing to consider is which device you're designing for first. You don't need to create three separate sets of styles, one for each width device you're targeting. You can, and should, start with a *default* design; that is, a design that works without media queries. You can then create media-query styles to override the default styles and reformat the page for the particular screen width. There are two main approaches:

- **Desktop first.** You can design your site with the desktop in mind. Throw in all the columns you want. Polish and finalize the design so it looks great on a large monitor. This becomes your base design, and you can put all of these styles into an external style sheet and link it to the pages of your site as you normally would.

Then you add media queries for tablets and phones. Those media-query styles will tweak the base desktop design—remove columns, make headline text smaller, and so on.

- **Mobile first.** You can flip that approach on its head by designing first for mobile browsers. This time, you put the basic small-screen styles in a regular external style sheet, and then refine the design for tablets and desktops by adding columns and other adjustments for larger screens in media queries.

Whichever method you choose, you should use a regular external style sheet linked to the web page as you normally would. In that style sheet, include all the styles that are common *across* the different devices. For example, you'll still want the same color palette and the same fonts across all versions of the site. You may also keep the same styling for links, images, and other HTML elements consistent. In other words, you don't need to create three entirely separate sets of styles for each device; start with one set that applies across phones, tablets, and desktop browsers, then refine the design for the media-query-targeted devices.

Creating Media Queries

A *query* is just a question asked of a web browser: "Is your screen 480 pixels wide?" If the answer is Yes, the browser launches a style sheet for just that size device (a style sheet that you supply, as explained on the previous page). The code that makes this happen looks pretty much the same as that for any external style sheet:

```
<link href="css/small.css" rel="stylesheet" media="(width: 480px)">
```

The one addition to this standard style sheet link is the media attribute, which sets up the conditions under which a browser uses a particular sheet. In the example above, a browser loads the *small.css* external style sheet when someone views your site with a browser whose width measures 480 pixels. The parentheses around the query—(width: 480px)—are required. If you leave them out, the browser will ignore the query.

Because 480 pixels is very precise—what if someone's using a phone with a smaller screen, say one that's just 300 pixels wide?—it's best to use a range of values in your media query. For example, you might want to apply a particular style for screens that are *less than or equal to* 480 pixels wide. You do that like this:

```
<link href="css/small.css" rel="stylesheet" media="(max-width:480px)">
```

The notation (max-width:480px) is the same as saying "for screens that are at most 480 pixels wide." So the styles inside the *small.css* file apply to screens that are 480 pixels wide, 320 pixels wide, and 200 pixels wide, for example.

Likewise, there's a min-width option that determines whether a browser is *at least* a certain width. This is useful when you target a device that's bigger than a mobile phone or tablet. For example, you can write this link to apply styles to screens wider than the 768 pixels of many tablets:

```
<link href="css/large.css" rel="stylesheet" media="(min-width:769px)">
```

To use this style sheet, a browser window must be at least 769 pixels wide—that's 1 pixel wider than 768, the width of some tablets.

And finally, you can set *both* max widths and min widths to target devices that *fall between* phones and desktop browsers. For example, to create a set of styles for a tablet that's 768 pixels wide, you could use this CSS code:

```
<link href="css/medium.css" rel="stylesheet" media="(min-width:481px) and
(max-width:768px)">
```

In other words, the browser's screen must be at least 481 pixels wide, but not more than 768 pixels wide. This *medium.css* file wouldn't apply to a 320-pixel-wide smartphone, nor would it apply to a desktop browser with a screen width of 1024 pixels.

> **NOTE** CSS media queries can do more than just check the width of a browser. The current media query standard states that you can check for height, orientation (whether a visitor holds a mobile phone in portrait or landscape mode), and even whether a device uses a color or monochrome screen. There are a few other browser characteristics you can check with media queries, but not all browsers support the queries. You can learn more about media queries at the W3C website: *www.w3.org/TR/css3-mediaqueries.*

Including Queries Inside a Style Sheet

The technique demonstrated above provides one way to use media queries by using the `<link>` tag to load different style sheets for different screen sizes. However, you can also add media queries within a single style sheet. You may want to do this so you don't have to add multiple `<link>` tags to an HTML file, for example, or you may want to keep your media-query styles together with your main style sheet. Most web designers use this approach, rather than using separate files for each media query.

There are a couple of ways to add media queries to a style sheet:

- **Use the** `@import` **directive.** The @import directive lets you load additional external style sheets within either an internal or external style sheet. You can also use @import with a media query. For example, say you want to load an external style sheet named *small.css* containing styles for displays that are 320 pixels or smaller. To do that, add the @import directive directly to a style sheet:

```
@import url(css/small.css) (max-width:320px);
```

> **NOTE** You must place @import directives at the beginning of a style sheet. They can't come after any styles. As a result, you may run into problems with the cascade, where styles you defined in an external style sheet and loaded using @import can be overridden by later styles in the style sheet. You can get around it by simply having one external style sheet that only contains @import directives. The first loads a basic style sheet for all devices, and the second and third load style sheets using media queries, like this:

```
@import url(css/base.css); /* no media query, applies to all */
@import url(css/medium.css) (min-width:481px) and (max-width:768);
@import url(css/small.css) (max-width: 480px);
```

- **Embed the media query in the style sheet.** You can also embed a media query directly inside a style sheet, like this:

```
@media (max-width: 480px) {

    body {

        /*style properties go here*/

    }

    .style1 {

        /*style properties go here*/

    }

}
```

The @media directive acts as a kind of container for all of the styles that match the query. So in this example, the body and .style1 styles only apply to devices whose screen is no wider than 480 pixels. By using embedded @media directives like this, you can keep all of your styles organized into one style sheet. A good approach is to start your external style sheets with styles that aren't contained in a media query using either the desktop-first or mobile-first approach, and then add media queries for the remaining devices. This is the most common approach used by web designers.

A Basic Style Sheet Structure

As you can tell, there are many different ways to use media queries to target different devices: desktop first, mobile first, separate style sheets, a single style sheet, and so on. As you gain more experience, you'll figure out which approach is best for which project. But as a starting point, you can always create a single external style sheet that includes styles for desktop displays, and then add media queries to modify that base-level design for tablets and phones. Here's a skeletal structure for just such a file:

```
/* Put your reset styles here */
/* Put styles for desktop and basic styles for all devices here */
body {
  /* properties for body here */
}

/* medium display only */
@media (min-width: 481px) and (max-width:768px) {
  body {
    /* properties that only apply to tablets */
  }
```

```
  }
/* small display only */
@media (max-width:480px) {
  body {
    /* properties that only apply to phones */
  }

}
```

You'll see this structure in action in the tutorial starting on page 476, and you'll find a basic starter style sheet called *desktop_first.css* in the *15* folder in this chapter's tutorial folder (*https://github.com/sawmac/css_mm_4e*). Remember that even though this file includes media queries, it's still just a regular style sheet and is linked to a web page the usual way. For example, if you save the this file as, you'd add this HTML to the <head> of a web page:

```
<link href="styles.css" rel="stylesheet">
```

Mobile First

If you decide to go the mobile-first route, you first create a set of styles aimed at mobile browsers, and then add media queries to alter the design for tablets, and then desktop browsers. Here's a basic style sheet structure for that approach:

```
/* Put your reset styles here */
/* Put styles for mobile and basic styles for all devices here*/
body {
  /* properties for body here */
}

/* medium display only */
@media (min-width: 481px) and (max-width:768px) {
  body {
    /* properties that only apply to tablets */
  }

}

/* large display only */
@media (min-width:769px) {
  body {
    /* properties that only apply to phones */
  }

}
```

You'll find a basic starter style sheet called *mobile_first.css* in the *15* folder in this chapter's tutorial folder.

■ Flexible Grids

You may be tempted to design fixed-width layouts to match your phone—for example, a style sheet with a 375-pixel width for an iPhone 6; another at 768 pixels to match the width of an iPad in portrait (tall) mode; and finally, one 1,000 pixels wide for desktop monitors. Don't do it. While the iPhone 6 is very popular, it's far from the only phone out there. Other iPhones have different pixel widths, and Android phones come in all sorts of shapes and sizes, and therefore, widths. You'll undoubtedly see many other unusually sized devices, and tablets come in a wide array of widths. In other words, there is no universal width for smartphones and tablets, so the best approach is to create flexible-width pages.

Flexible grids are a core component of responsive web design. They're nothing much more than the liquid layout discussed on page 386, in which the page's overall width resizes to fit different width screens. In most cases, that means you set the width to 100%. However, for desktop displays, you may want to use the max-width property (page 208) to make sure the page isn't absurdly wide on large desktop monitors.

In addition, the individual columns within a design should be percentage-based, instead of set with a fixed pixel- or em-based measurement. Individual columns also need to grow wider or narrower to fit the changing page width.

> **TIP** In the next chapter, you'll learn about some of the prepackaged flexible grid systems available for free to web designers. In fact, you'll use one of the most popular, Skeleton, to easily create multicolumn flexible grid-based web pages.

For example, say you want to create a two-column design where the first column is one-third the width of the page and the second is two-thirds. You may start with some simple HTML, like this:

```
<div class="columns">
  <div class="one-third">
  ...content goes here...
  </div>
  <div class="two-thirds">
  ...content goes here...
  </div>
</div>
```

You can then use several CSS styles to create the fluid layout:

```
.columns {
  width: auto; /* same as 100% */
  max-width: 1200px;
}
.columns:after {
  content: "";
  display: table;
```

```
    clear: both;
}
.one-third {
    float: left;
    width: 33%;
}
.two-thirds {
    float: left;
    width: 67%;
}
```

The first style—`.columns`—sets the width of the div containing the columns. Setting the width property to a value of `auto` is the same as setting it to 100%, while the `max-width` property will keep the box from getting too wide. The second style—`.columns:after`—helps contain the two floated columns (for more detail on how that works, see page 407). Finally, the last two styles just set the widths of the two divs to 33% (one-third the width of its container) and 67% (two-thirds) and floats them left so they appear side by side.

The Importance of HTML Source Order

When you're holding a phone upright in your hand, there's simply not enough room to have two, let alone three, columns in a row and still have a readable page, so many designers simply lay out a page in one long column for display on a mobile phone. To do so, just remove any floats from the columns you've created. For example, if you create a three-column design for desktop display using floats to position the columns side by side, simply set the `float` property to `none` on those elements. They then display as HTML normally does—one block-level tag on top of the other.

This makes the HTML source order very important. For example, a page may have two sidebars, one with a list of links to related sites, the other with ads for products your company sells. A middle column contains the main content—the stuff your audience is really after when they visit the page. One way to lay this out in columns is to float the first sidebar left and the second sidebar right, and let the main column simply wrap around the two and sit in the middle.

In terms of HTML, this would mean the two sidebar divs appear first, followed by the tag containing the main content. If you made this page mobile-friendly by removing the floats on these sidebars, you'd end up with the two sidebars appearing *above* the main content. Your audience would be faced with scrolling down past the ads and links just to get to the content they're after.

A more user-friendly approach is to place the main content container above the sidebars. As discussed on page 403, this method can require adding some additional containers and floating all the elements, including the main content div.

In short, be aware of how you order your HTML before you try to lay out a multicolumn design for the desktop. The easiest way to see what's going on is to view the web page without any CSS applied. You can then see all the divs and other block-level elements stacked on top of each other, and get a good idea of what the page will look like as a single column on a phone.

> **NOTE** The tutorial on page 476 demonstrates how you can create a three-column desktop design while keeping the most important content near the top of the page.

Reset the Box Model

As explained on page 414, when you use percentage-based widths, you run into the danger of float drops, where the total width of columns in a row exceeds 100 percent, so the last column drops down below the others. Because of the way browsers calculate the widths of elements, adding a border around a div, or padding inside it, will make the div's onscreen width greater than the width you set in the CSS.

For example, if you make one column 33 percent wide and another 67 percent wide (as in the example on the previous page), they'd fit perfectly next to each other, since their combined widths are 100%. However, if you add a 1-pixel border to the column, their combined width would be 100% + 2 pixels (the left and right borders). They'd now be too large to fit in the window, and the second column would drop down below the first.

There are a couple of ways to deal with this predicament, and they're detailed on page 416. But the most straightforward solution is to tell the web browser to *include* the border and padding widths and heights as part of its box model calculation. In other words, you can make the browser include the border and padding as part of the CSS width property, so adding more padding or a border doesn't increase an element's width (or height). Since that's a good thing for all elements, it's best to use a universal selector so you can reset the box model on every element on a page:

```
* {
  box-sizing: border-box;
}
```

A good place to put this style is in the page's CSS reset (page 109).

Converting Fixed Width to Flexible Grids

If you're starting with a brand new design, thinking in terms of percentages shouldn't be too hard. After all, if you wanted four equal-width columns, you'd set each to 25%:

```
width: 25%;
```

However, if you've already got a fixed-width website design and you want to convert it to a fluid design, things get a little trickier. To start with, say you design a page with a fixed width of 960 pixels. You either wrap the page in a <div> tag and give that div a width of 960 pixels, or simply set the <body> tag to that width. In either case, you now want that container to be completely fluid. That's easy: Just change

```
width: 960px;
```

to

```
width: auto;
```

Setting an element's width to auto is much the same as setting it to 100%; its width will be as wide as its container.

Next, you need to convert any column widths from pixel values to percentages. Ethan Marcotte, the champion of responsive web design, has come up with a nifty formula to make this relatively easy to figure out: *target / context = result*. In English, it means, "take the width (in pixels) of the element you wish to convert and divide it by the width of its container (in pixels)." The result is a fractional value that you convert to percentages.

Here's an example. Suppose that inside that 960-pixel-wide page, you have two columns: a sidebar that's 180 pixels wide and a main column that's 780 pixels wide. In your CSS file, you have some code like this:

```
.sidebar {
  float: left;
  width: 180px;
}
.main {
  float: left;
  width: 780px;
}
```

Of course, you'd have a lot of other CSS in there like borders, background colors, and so on, but for this exercise, you're just concerned about the widths. Starting with the sidebar, you'd take its width—180 pixels—and divide it by its container's width—960 pixels. The result—.1875—multiplied by 100 gives you the percentage value: 18.75%. Likewise, for the main column, you'd divide 780 by 960 to get .8125. Multiply that by 100 to get 81.25%. In other words, you end up changing the widths of those styles like this:

```
.sidebar {
  float: left;
  width: 18.75%;
}
.main {
  float: left;
  width: 81.25%;
}
```

Don't round up the new values. In other words, don't turn 18.75% into 19%; doing so will most likely cause the columns to no longer sit side-by-side, resulting in a float drop. Browsers can handle decimal values just fine. In fact, feel free to use all the numbers that your calculator returns. A width of 25.48488% is perfectly acceptable.

The same applies to a column inside another column. For example, say in the main column above you have one section of two floated divs that create two additional columns within the main column. Both divs share the same width—390 pixels—so to calculate their width in percentages you take their current width in pixels—390—and divide it by their container's width—in this example, the main column is 780 pixels. The result is .5. Multiply that by 100 to get 50%. (But you don't really need to do the math. After all, if you have two equally sized columns sitting side by side, you know that each takes up half the available space, or 50%.)

As you recreate your design and figure out percentage values, keep in mind that the total width of all columns in a single row can't exceed 100%.

TIP You can use the same formula to convert pixel-sized type to ems. Say you have paragraph text that's 18 pixels (the target). The default size of regular text (the context) is 16 pixels. Just divide 18 by 16 to get the new size in ems: 1.125em.

■ Fluid Images

While a flexible layout creates a design that works in a wide range of browser window widths, you'll encounter a problem if you've inserted images in your pages. Although columns in a flexible design shrink as the window gets smaller, images usually don't. This can lead to graphics overflowing their bounds and no longer fitting within the width of a column (see Figure 15-3).

Fortunately, there's a way to make images flexible as well. It requires two steps: a new CSS style and some changes to your HTML.

1. **First, in your style sheet, add the following style:**

   ```
   img { max-width: 100%; }
   ```

   This sets the maximum width of any image to 100 percent of the width of its container. In other words, an image can never be bigger than a column, div, or any HTML element that it sits inside of.

   This alone isn't enough to make an image flexible. Usually, when you insert an <img> tag, you also add the height and width for that image. That's the size the browser uses when displaying the image. With the max-width property in place, the image won't get wider than the column, but its height is still locked to the value set in the HTML. In other words, the image will conform to the width of the column, but its height won't change, resulting in a distorted image. The solution is straightforward: Just remove the width and height attributes from the HTML.

FIGURE 15-3

When a column gets thinner than an image inside it, that image overflows the bounds of the column, usually overlapping other columns and content.

2. **Locate every** `<img>` **tag in the page and remove the** height **and** width **attributes.**

   In other words, turn this HTML:

   ```
   <img src="bunny.jpg" width="320" height="200" alt="bunny">
   ```

   into this:

   ```
   <img src="bunny.jpg" alt="bunny">
   ```

   Many text editors have search-and-replace features that can speed up the process of finding and removing these attributes.

This approach assumes, of course, that you want all your images to fill the column they're in. In many cases, you'll want images to be smaller than that; for example, a photo that's floated to the right of the main column, with text wrapping around it. To deal with differently sized images, you can create different classes, with different max-width settings, and apply those classes to particular `<img>` tags within the HTML.

For example, say you want to float an image to the left of a column and size it to 40 percent of the column. First create a class style:

```
.imgSmallLeft {
  float: left;
  max-width: 40%;
}
```

Then apply that class to the `<img>` tag:

```
<img src="bunny.jpg" alt="bunny" class="imgSmallLeft">
```

A more flexible approach is to break the size and the float into separate classes:

```
.imgSmall {
  max-width: 40%;
}

.imgLeft {
  float: left;
}
```

Then apply both classes to the image:

```
<img src="bunny.jpg" alt="bunny" class="imgSmall imgLeft">
```

By using two classes, you can apply the `imgSmall` class to any image, even ones you decide to float right or not float at all.

> **NOTE** You can resize background images by using the `background-size` property discussed on page 245.

The Downside of Fluid Images

Fluid images have one major problem. When the page is viewed on a phone, the column widths and images can shrink to a width that's much smaller than on a desktop browser. This means the images are actually shrunk on screen. While the image quality won't suffer, you're forcing users of mobile phones to download image files that are much larger than really necessary. They're wasting their bandwidth on unnecessarily large image files. Unfortunately, there's no great solution to this problem yet; in fact, champions of responsive web design recognize this as one of the biggest problems with RWD.

Testing Responsive Designs

Since responsive designs are intended to adapt to the screens of different browsing devices, you'll need to find a way to view your pages at different screen widths. The easiest way to test your media queries is to view the page on a desktop browser and resize the browser window. Drag it in to make it thinner, and view what happens at each breakpoint or media query that you set. This technique works pretty well, but not all browsers let you scale the window down to the 320-pixel width of some phones.

In addition, Google Chrome provides a simple tool that lets you choose various devices and see what your page looks like when stuffed into the width and height of the device's screen. Choose View→Developer→Developer Tools to open the Chrome Developer Tools window. Then click the phone icon in the top left of the Developer Tools window to open a new view of the current web page. Use the Device menu at the top of the page to choose a new device—like an iPhone 6 or Motorola Droid Razr HD. When you're done, close the Developer Tools window to return to regular web browsing mode.

There are also several web-based tools that let you preview your pages inside windows of different dimensions. The responsivepx site (*http://responsivepx.com*) lets you enter a URL for a page on the Web, then input different screen heights and widths. The site opens the page in an <iframe> of the set width. The browser applies any media queries that pertain to that width screen, so you can preview the effect of your media queries.

The Responsinator (*www.responsinator.com*) comes with several preset window widths that match popular devices like iPhone, Samsung Galaxy, iPad, Kindle, and others. Just enter your site's URL, and its page will appear inside simulated screens. The Responsinator only works with files that you've uploaded to a web server on the Internet.

If you have a smartphone or tablet, you can preview a page directly from your computer on those devices, using Adobe's Edge Inspect tool (*https://creative.adobe.com/products/inspect*). This sophisticated tool is a great way to preview your working design in progress. Alternatively, you can just put your design up on a web server, whip out your phone, and visit that page to see what it looks like. Of course, unless you have dozens of smartphones, you won't know exactly what all people using mobile browsers will experience.

Finally, you can pay for a service like BrowserStack (*www.browserstack.com*) which lets you preview a page as it actually appears on different operating systems, browsers, and devices, including mobile phones and tablets. This clever service literally runs your web page through the device you select and lets you see the results.

There are many people and organizations working on ways to solve this problem, including the W3C. For a rundown on some of the currently popular solutions, read this article: *http://alistapart.com/article/responsive-images-in-practice*. Unfortunately, there is no solution that works in all browsers, so in the meantime, you may choose not to worry about the larger image files for mobile and wait for a solution to arrive—perhaps one already has by the time you're reading this. Or try a very good, but somewhat complicated solution called *adaptive images*. It uses JavaScript and PHP to send images of the appropriate size to each device. In other words, a small, handheld browser receives smaller image files for its smaller screen, while desktop browsers download larger images. To learn more about it, visit *http://adaptive-images.com*.

Videos and Flash

If you use the HTML video tag or embed Flash content, you can also use the max-width trick to make those elements scale with their containers as well. Simply add this style to your style sheet:

```
img, video, embed, object {
  max-width: 100%;
}
```

Unfortunately, this style doesn't do anything to help with videos that are embedded using iframes (the most common way to add a YouTube or Vimeo video to a page). For embedded YouTube videos, read this article—*http://demosthenes.info/ blog/649/Responsive-Design-Create-Fluid-YouTube-and-Vimeo-Content*—or simply use the Embed Responsively service (*http://embedresponsively.com*). Just give this website the URL of the YouTube or Vimeo video, and it will generate the HTML code you need to embed a responsive version of the video on a web page.

UP TO SPEED

When Is a Pixel Not a Pixel?

Most people think of a pixel as a single dot on a screen or monitor. And it is. But thanks to new high-density pixel displays like Apple's Retina displays, you now have to think of pixels in two different ways. A device like an iPhone 6 Plus has a resolution of 2208px×1242px. That's a lot of pixels, and the iPhone squishes those pixels into a smaller area than most other screens. It crams 326 pixels into every inch of the screen. Desktop monitors usually have around 100 pixels per inch. In other words, the iPhone puts three times as many pixels into one inch of its screen than many desktop monitors. The result is very clear, sharp images.

This poses a problem for web designers, however. If you give your text a size of 16 pixels, that would look fine on a desktop monitor (about .16 inches tall), but would be unreadable in a phone with a high-density screen—.04 inches tall.

Fortunately, that's not what browsers with high-density displays do. They actually make a single CSS pixel fill *multiple* pixels on its screen, so text that's 16 pixels tall is actually displayed using *more* than 16 pixels. Phones and other devices with high-density pixel displays make a distinction between a *device pixel*—an actual dot on a screen—and a *CSS pixel*.

A CSS pixel is a calculation based on the screen's pixel density and its distance from the viewer. Since a phone is held closer to your face than a monitor, items on its screen appear bigger than similarly sized items on a monitor that's 28 inches away.

On an iPhone, 1 CSS pixel is actually represented by 4 device pixels. So 16-pixel-tall type is actually 32 device pixels tall. Different devices like Android phones have different pixel densities and so use different calculations to determine how many screen pixels to use to display a single CSS pixel.

■ Responsive Web Design Tutorial

In this tutorial, you'll take the layout you created in Chapter 13 (with the addition of a few images) and turn it into a responsive web design. You'll use a desktop-first approach—so the basic CSS styles work best in a desktop browser—and then you'll add media queries to change the look for medium-size screens (like tablets) and small screens (like phones).

To get started, download the tutorial files located on this book's companion website at *https://github.com/sawmac/css_mm_4e*. Click the tutorial link and download the files. All the files are in a zip archive, so you need to unzip them first. The files for this tutorial are in the *15* folder.

Changing the HTML Source Order

In creating a layout for a small screen, you'll turn your three-column design into a single-column layout with each block of content stacked one on top of the other. One problem with the HTML from the page you worked on in the previous tutorial is that the left sidebar appears first in the source order, so if you turn this into a single-column design, that sidebar will appear before the main content.

It would be better for the site's visitors if they can get directly to the main content first, then scroll down to see the supplemental information from the sidebars. To achieve that, you have to add a little HTML and move some already-existing HTML. You'll use the technique described on page 401 in the last chapter (see in Chapter 13, Figure 13-4): move the main content container up above the first sidebar, and then wrap the main content and the sidebar in a new <div> tag. You'll float that new div left, the main content right, and the sidebar left. This arrangement will maintain the same visual layout for desktop displays—first sidebar on the left, main content in the middle, and second sidebar on the right—but then stack the main content above the two sidebars for the mobile design.

1. **Open the file *index.html* in the *15* folder.**

   This page is the same as the completed page from Chapter 13's tutorial. First, you'll move the main content up.

2. **Locate the HTML comment** <!-- main content goes here -->**, and select it and all the HTML down to and including the closing** </article> **tag.**

   In other words, select that comment and everything down to the <!-- second sidebar goes here --> comment.

3. **Cut that text to the clipboard, using Edit→Cut (or using whatever method your text editor provides).**

   Next, you'll paste that code above the first sidebar.

4. **Locate the** <div class="contentWrapper"> **tag toward the top of the file. Add an empty line after it, but before the** <!-- first sidebar goes here --> **comment, and choose Edit→Paste to paste the main content above the sidebar.**

   Now you need to add a <div> tag to enclose the main content and the first sidebar.

5. **After the** <div class="contentWrapper"> **tag, add** <div class="columnWrapper">**. The HTML should look like this:**

   ```
   <div class="contentWrapper">
   <div class="columnWrapper">
   <!-- main content goes here -->
   ```

Next, you'll close that div.

6. **Locate the closing** </aside> **for the first sidebar. It's just before the** <!--
second sidebar goes here --> **comment. Add** </div> **after the** </aside> **so
that the HTML looks like this:**

```
</aside>
</div>
<!-- second sidebar goes here -->
```

That's it for the HTML changes for now. You can find a file called *new-source-order.html* in the *15* folder with all of these HTML changes, if you got lost or want to check your work.

If you preview this page in a web browser, you'll see there's a three-column layout, but the main content's on the left side, and the first sidebar is in the middle (Figure 15-4). You can fix that with some CSS.

7. **Open the file** *styles.css* **in the** *15* **folder.**

This file contains the CSS you created in the last chapter. You'll first need to add a new style for the column wrapper and float it left so it sits next to the right sidebar.

8. **Near the bottom of the file, before the** .sidebar1 **style, add the following
style:**

```
.columnWrapper {
    float: left;
    width: 80%;
}
```

The width setting here is the combined widths of the left sidebar (20%) and the main column (60%). What you're actually doing is creating a two-column layout: The first column is this new <div> tag, and the second column is the right sidebar. The main content container and the left sidebar are actually two columns inside this column wrapper div—in other words, columns within a column, as described on page 401 and pictured in Figure 13-4.

Next, you'll adjust the floats and widths of the main column and first sidebar.

9. **Change the width value of the** .sidebar1 **style to** 25%**. The style should look
like this:**

```
.sidebar1 {
  float: left;
  width: 25%;
  padding: 0 20px 0 10px;
}
```

Originally, this sidebar took up 20% of the entire page width, but now that it's inside the column wrapper div, you need to adjust the sidebar and main content columns' widths to fit within the 80% width of the column wrapper. In other words, the percentage width you're specifying isn't a percentage of the entire page; it's a percentage of the column wrapper, which only takes up 80% of the page.

To figure out the new percentage, take the older percentage—20%—and divide it by the width of its container—80%—and then multiply by 100. So 20 divided by 80 is .25. Multiply that by 100 and you get 25%. You'll use the same technique to change the width of the main content.

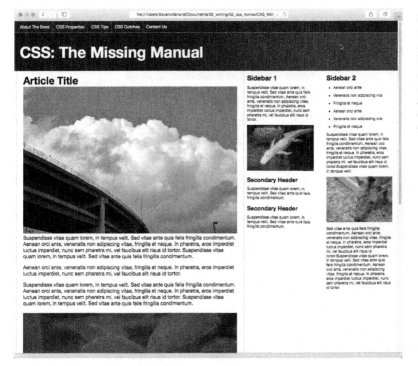

FIGURE 15-4

The page is still a three-column design, but now the main content is on the left and the left sidebar is in the middle. A couple of simple styles can get those columns back into their original positions.

10. **Locate the** `.main` **style, and change the float to** `right` **and the width to** 75%, **so the style looks like this:**

```
.main {
  float: right;
  width: 75%;
  padding: 0 20px;
  border-left: dashed 1px rgb(153,153,153);
  border-right: dashed 1px rgb(153,153,153);
}
```

You're floating this element to the right, so it appears to the right of the first sidebar, which places the main content in the middle again. You calculate the width by taking the old width and dividing it by the width of its container: 60/80 = .75, or 75%. If you save the files and preview the *index.html* file in a web browser, it should look like Figure 15-5.

NOTE This particular design won't get wider than 1200 pixels, thanks to the `max-width` set in the group selector `nav ul`, `header h1`, `footer p`, `.contentWrapper`. If you want this design to fill the browser window, no matter how wide it is, just remove the `max-width 1200px;` declaration from that group selector.

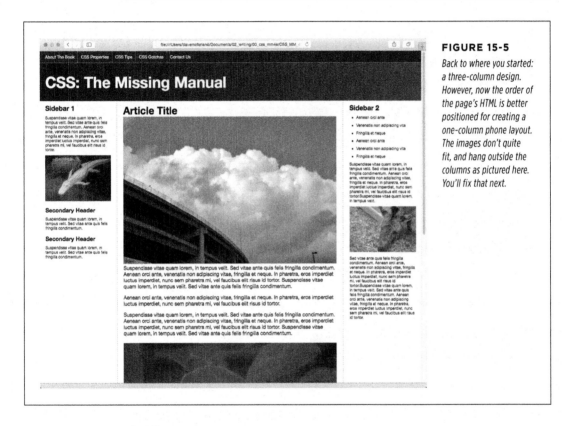

FIGURE 15-5

Back to where you started: a three-column design. However, now the order of the page's HTML is better positioned for creating a one-column phone layout. The images don't quite fit, and hang outside the columns as pictured here. You'll fix that next.

Fluid Images

You've successfully created a fluid layout. If you preview the page now and resize the browser window, you'll notice that as you make the window narrower, the columns get smaller. Unfortunately, some of the images are wider than the columns and they pop out of the design. As you read on page 472, part of responsive web design is making your images respond to changes in the width of the browser window as well. To make that work, you need to add some CSS and remove some HTML.

1. **Switch to the *styles.css* file in your text editor. At the bottom of the style sheet, add a style for the** `img` **tag:**

```
img {
  max-width: 100%;
}
```

This style makes the maximum width of an image equal to 100 percent of its container's width. So for a column that's 200 pixels wide on screen, the image will be 200 pixels wide. If a visitor resizes the browser window, and the column shrinks in size, the image will shrink to fit the column.

This only works, however, if you remove the image's width and height properties in the HTML.

2. **Delete the** height **and** width **attribute for each of the four** `<img>` **tags in the *index.html* file.**

There are four graphics—*clouds.jpg, jellyfishy.jpg, gator.jpg,* and *mule.jpg.* Remove the width and height attribute—for example:

```
<img src="imgs/clouds.jpg" alt="Clouds" width="678" height="452">
```

should become

```
<img src="imgs/clouds.jpg" alt="Clouds">
```

If you save the CSS and HTML files and preview the page in a web browser, you'll see that the images do change size as you make the page thinner. However, the two images in the main column are *really* big. Using max-width: 100% for the <img> tag does create flexible images, but in many cases, you won't want all images to be as wide as their column. In the case of the two images in the main column, they'd look a whole lot better if they were only half the size of the main column. You can do that by applying some classes to those tags and adding some styles.

3. **In the *styles.css* file, add the following styles to the bottom of the style sheet:**

```
img.half {
    max-width: 50%;
}

img.left {
    float: left;
    margin: 0 10px 10px 0;
}

img.right {
    float: right;
    margin: 0 0 10px 10px;
}
```

The first style sets the max-width to just 50%—half the column width. The other two styles let you float an image to the left or the right of the column, to let text wrap around them. To make use of these class styles, you need to add a bit of HTML to the images

4. **In the *index.html* file, locate the `<img>` tag for the *clouds.jpg* image—`<img src="imgs/clouds.jpg" alt="Clouds">`—and add class="half right" so it looks like this:**

   ```
   <img src="imgs/clouds.jpg" alt="Clouds" class="half right">
   ```

   It's common and often useful to apply more than one class to an element. In this way, you can combine simpler, modular styles to create more complex designs. In this case, the half class resizes the images, while the right class floats the image to the right. Simply by changing right to left you can move the image to the left of the column, while still maintaining the sizing property of the half style.

5. **For the *jellyfish.jpg* image, add class="half left" so its HTML code looks like this:**

   ```
   <img src="imgs/jellyfish.jpg" alt="Jellyfish" class="half left">
   ```

   Now the images are all sized. The page should look like Figure 15-6. If you want, you can create additional styles for other sizes, and even specify pixel sizes to allow particular images to resize to their full widths, but no more.

Adding Styles for Tablet Screens

The design at this point works the same in every device: desktop, tablets, and mobile phones. It's a flexible design that shrinks or grows to fit the browser window. But at a certain point, the sidebar columns are just too thin to be readable. The first media query you'll add will target screens that are between 480 and 768 pixels and will move the right sidebar to the bottom of the page, converting the three-column design into a more readable two-column design.

1. **Open the *styles.css* file in your text editor. Scroll to the bottom of the file and add:**

   ```
   @media (min-width: 481px) and (max-width:768px) {

   }
   ```

   Here's the first media query. It targets screens that are at least 481 pixels, but no more than 768 pixels. In the next part of this tutorial, you'll craft a media query for devices that are no more than 480 pixels wide. So this media query excludes those devices, but also excludes devices that are more than 768 pixels. In other words, any styles you place in this section of the style sheet won't apply to desktop browsers (unless you resize the window so that it's very thin); nor will they apply to most phones.

   The first thing you'll do is remove the float from the right sidebar.

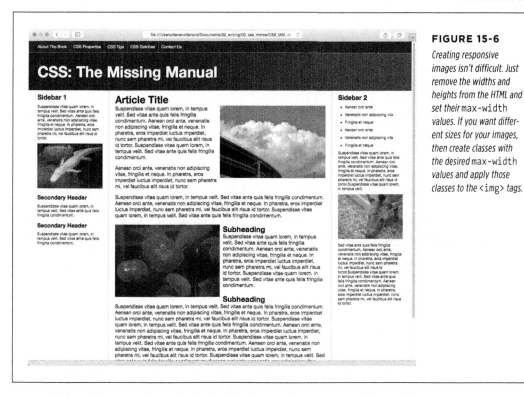

FIGURE 15-6

Creating responsive images isn't difficult. Just remove the widths and heights from the HTML and set their max-width *values. If you want different sizes for your images, then create classes with the desired* max-width *values and apply those classes to the* <img> *tags.*

2. **Inside the media query you added in the last step, add the following style (in bold):**

```
@media (min-width: 481px) and (max-width:768px) {
  .sidebar2 {
    float: none;
    width: auto;
  }
}
```

This removes the float from that sidebar, and sets its width to auto (overriding the 20% width from the .sidebar2 style earlier in the style sheet). However, this doesn't make the sidebar drop down below the other two columns. Because the column wrapper div is also floated left, the second sidebar wraps around it (see page 401 for more on how floats work). You'll need to make the sidebar clear those floats.

3. **Edit the style you added in the last step by adding the code in bold:**

```
.sidebar2 {
    float: none;
    width: auto;
    clear: both;
    border-top: 2px solid black;
    padding-top: 10px;
}
```

The clear property (discussed on page 405) makes this sidebar drop down below the other two columns. You've also added a distinctive top border to further visually separate this container from the above columns.

If you preview the page now and resize your browser window so that it's just less than 768 pixels, you'll see that the two columns don't span the entire width of the page (see Figure 15-7). That's because earlier in step 8 on page 478, you set that column wrapper to 80% of the page width. You need to reset that style inside the tablet media query.

4. **After the** .sidebar2 **style (but still within the media query), add the following:**

```
.columnWrapper {
  width: auto;
}
```

Make sure that style goes inside the media query. It resets the column wrapper's width to auto (the same as 100%) so it spans the entire width of the page. You don't need the float on this element any more either, since the sidebar2 column has dropped below. Because there are now only two columns, you can remove the right border that's applied to the main content column.

5. **Add one last style after the** .columnWrapper **style. The complete media query should now look like this (changes in bold):**

```
@media (min-width: 481px) and (max-width:768px) {
  .sidebar2 {
    float: none;
    width: auto;
    clear: both;
    border-top: 2px solid black;
    padding-top: 10px;
  }

  .columnWrapper {
    width: auto;
  }
  .main {
    border-right: none;
```

```
        }
    }
```

file:///Users/davemcfarland/Documents/D

About The Book   CSS Properties   CSS Tips   CSS Gotchas   Contact Us

CSS: The Missing Manual

Sidebar 1

Suspendisse vitae quam lorem, in tempus velit. Sed vitae ante quis felis fringilla condimentum. Aenean orci ante, venenatis non adipiscing vitae, fringilla et neque. In pharetra, eros imperdiet luctus imperdiet, nunc sem pharetra mi, vel faucibus elit risus id tortor.

Secondary Header

Suspendisse vitae quam lorem, in tempus velit. Sed vitae ante quis felis fringilla condimentum.

Secondary Header

Suspendisse vitae quam lorem, in tempus velit. Sed vitae ante quis felis fringilla condimentum.

Article Title

Suspendisse vitae quam lorem, in tempus velit. Sed vitae ante quis felis fringilla condimentum. Aenean orci ante, venenatis non adipiscing vitae, fringilla et neque. In pharetra, eros imperdiet luctus imperdiet, nunc sem pharetra mi, vel faucibus elit risus id tortor. Suspendisse vitae quam lorem, in tempus velit. Sed vitae ante quis felis fringilla condimentum.

Aenean orci ante, venenatis non adipiscing vitae, fringilla et neque. In pharetra, eros imperdiet luctus imperdiet, nunc sem pharetra mi, vel faucibus elit risus id tortor.

Suspendisse vitae quam lorem, in tempus velit. Sed vitae ante quis felis fringilla condimentum. Aenean orci ante, venenatis non adipiscing vitae, fringilla et neque. In pharetra, eros imperdiet luctus imperdiet, nunc sem pharetra mi, vel faucibus elit risus id tortor. Suspendisse vitae quam lorem, in tempus velit. Sed vitae ante quis felis fringilla condimentum.

Subheading

Suspendisse vitae quam lorem, in tempus velit. Sed vitae ante quis felis fringilla condimentum. Aenean orci ante, venenatis non adipiscing vitae, fringilla et neque. In pharetra, eros imperdiet luctus imperdiet, nunc sem pharetra mi, vel faucibus elit risus id tortor. Suspendisse vitae quam lorem, in tempus velit. Sed vitae ante quis felis fringilla condimentum.

6. **Save the *styles.css* file and preview the *index.html* file in a web browser. Resize the browser window until only two columns appear.**

The page should look like Figure 15-8.

Sidebar 1

Suspendisse vitae quam lorem, in tempus velit. Sed vitae ante quis felis fringilla condimentum. Aenean orci ante, venenatis non adipiscing vitae, fringilla et neque. In pharetra, eros imperdiet luctus imperdiet, nunc sem pharetra mi, vel faucibus elit risus id tortor.

Secondary Header

Suspendisse vitae quam lorem, in tempus velit. Sed vitae ante quis felis fringilla condimentum.

Secondary Header

Suspendisse vitae quam lorem, in tempus velit. Sed vitae ante quis felis fringilla condimentum.

Article Title

Suspendisse vitae quam lorem, in tempus velit. Sed vitae ante quis felis fringilla condimentum. Aenean orci ante, venenatis non adipiscing vitae, fringilla et neque. In pharetra, eros imperdiet luctus imperdiet, nunc sem pharetra mi, vel faucibus elit risus id tortor. Suspendisse vitae quam lorem, in tempus velit. Sed vitae ante quis felis fringilla condimentum.

Aenean orci ante, venenatis non adipiscing vitae, fringilla et neque. In pharetra, eros imperdiet luctus imperdiet, nunc sem pharetra mi, vel faucibus elit risus id tortor.

Suspendisse vitae quam lorem, in tempus velit. Sed vitae ante quis felis fringilla condimentum. Aenean orci ante, venenatis non adipiscing vitae, fringilla et neque. In pharetra, eros imperdiet luctus imperdiet, nunc sem pharetra mi, vel faucibus elit risus id tortor. Suspendisse vitae quam lorem, in tempus velit. Sed vitae ante quis felis fringilla condimentum.

Subheading

Suspendisse vitae quam lorem, in tempus velit. Sed vitae ante quis felis fringilla condimentum. Aenean orci ante, venenatis non adipiscing vitae, fringilla et neque. In pharetra, eros imperdiet luctus imperdiet, nunc sem pharetra mi, vel faucibus elit risus id tortor. Suspendisse vitae quam lorem, in tempus velit. Sed vitae ante quis felis fringilla condimentum.

Subheading

Suspendisse vitae quam lorem, in tempus velit. Sed vitae ante quis felis fringilla condimentum. Aenean orci ante, venenatis non adipiscing vitae, fringilla et neque. In pharetra, eros imperdiet luctus imperdiet, nunc sem pharetra mi, vel faucibus elit risus id tortor. Suspendisse vitae quam lorem, in tempus velit. Sed vitae ante quis felis fringilla condimentum. Aenean orci ante, venenatis non adipiscing vitae, fringilla et neque. In pharetra, eros imperdiet luctus imperdiet, nunc sem pharetra mi, vel faucibus elit risus id tortor. Suspendisse vitae quam lorem, in tempus velit. Sed vitae ante quis felis fringilla condimentum. Aenean orci ante, venenatis non adipiscing vitae, fringilla et neque. In pharetra, eros imperdiet luctus imperdiet, nunc sem pharetra mi, vel faucibus elit risus id tor

Sidebar 2

- Aenean orci ante
- Venenatis non adipiscing vita
- Fringilla et neque
- Aenean orci ante
- Venenatis non adipiscing vita
- Fringilla et neque

Suspendisse vitae quam lorem, in tempus velit. Sed vitae ante quis felis fringilla condimentum. Aenean orci ante, venenatis non adipiscing vitae, fringilla et neque. In pharetra, eros imperdiet luctus imperdiet, nunc sem pharetra mi, vel faucibus elit risus id tortor.Suspendisse vitae quam lorem, in tempus velit.

Sed vitae ante quis felis fringilla condimentum. Aenean orci ante, venenatis non adipiscing vitae, fringilla et neque. In pharetra, eros imperdiet luctus imperdiet, nunc sem pharetra mi, vel faucibus elit risus id tortor.Suspendisse vitae quam lorem, in tempus velit. Sed vitae ante quis felis fringilla condimentum. Aenean orci ante, venenatis non adipiscing vitae, fringilla et neque. In pharetra, eros imperdiet luctus imperdiet, nunc sem pharetra mi, vel faucibus elit risus id tortor.

Copyright 2015, Greek Text Generator, Inc. Suspendisse vitae quam lorem, in tempus velit. Sed vitae ante quis felis fringilla condimentum. Aenean orci ante, venenatis non adipiscing vitae, fringilla et neque. In pharetra, eros imperdiet luctus imperdiet, nunc sem pharetra mi, vel faucibus elit risus id tortor.
Contact: e-mail@here.com

FIGURE 15-8

The design now responds to the browser window's width. Three columns turn into two columns, followed by the second sidebar, which sits underneath. The entire design fits the browser width and makes sure the columns don't get too narrow to read on smaller devices.

Adding Phone Styles

Finally, it's time to add styles for devices that are no wider than 480 pixels.

1. **Go back to the *styles.css* file in your text editor. Scroll to the bottom of the file and add another media query:**

   ```css
   @media (max-width:480px) {


   }
   ```

   Make sure this goes after the other media query, not inside it. Here we'll target devices that are no wider than 480 pixels. The first step is to *linearize* the layout; that is, remove all of the floats so the content is stacked in a single column for easy reading on a small screen.

2. **Inside that media query, add the following style:**

   ```css
   .columnWrapper, .main, .sidebar1, .sidebar2 {
       float: none;
       width: auto;
   }
   ```

   This removes the float from the column wrapper and all the columns. Setting the width to auto makes them fill their container completely. So now the three columns are simply block-level elements stacked one on top of the other, with the main content on top and the two sidebars underneath.

   The main content area still has borders from the styles earlier in the style sheet. These left and right borders provide visual separation from the left and right sidebars in the three-column layouts, but you don't need them in this stacked layout, so you can remove them. On the other hand, adding visual separation between the now-stacked content blocks would be nice to have.

3. **After the style you just added (and still inside the 480-pixel media query), add these two styles:**

   ```css
   .main {
     border: none;
   }
   .sidebar1, .sidebar2 {
     border-top: 2px solid black;
     margin-top: 25px;
     padding-top: 10px;
   }
   ```

   The second group selector here adds a border above each sidebar as well as some top margin and padding to clearly mark off the different content regions on the page.

Save the CSS file and preview the *index.html* page in a web browser. Drag the browser window so it's less than 480 pixels wide. You'll now see the one-column design. If you view this page on a phone, you'll notice that the headline looks really big (Figure 15-9). In addition, the navigation buttons look a little out of control. You'll fix those two problems next.

4. **Add a style for the** <h1> **tag inside the 480-pixel media query:**

```
header h1 {
  font-size: 1.5em;
}
```

This style reduces the text size in the <h1> tag so it now fits on a single line. It's often a good idea to reduce the size of headlines when converting a desktop design to one viewed on a little phone screen. You may also find that you should *increase* the font size for body text to make it easier to read. There are a lot of ways you can tweak the phone design of your page, and it's up to you to figure out what looks best.

Now you'll tackle the navigation bar. The dashed borders separating the buttons look bad and jumbled. In addition, the buttons are aligned to the left, creating an out-of-balance asymmetry. They'll look better centered and without those borders.

5. **Add another style after the** header h1 **style you added in the previous step:**

```
nav {
  text-align: center;
}
```

The nav buttons are contained inside an HTML <nav> element. By setting the text-align value to center, all text inside that nav should be centered. However, the buttons are actually floated to the left, so this is only the first step. (You can turn to page 293 for more information on using floats to create a horizontal navigation bar.)

6. **Add two more styles after the** nav **style:**

```
nav li {
  float: none;
  display: inline-block;
}

nav a {
  float: none;
  display: inline-block;
  border: none;
}
```

You're removing the floats from both the list items and the links. In addition, you turn these elements into inline blocks. As described on page 293, using `inline-block` on navigation elements lets you place links side by side, while still preserving padding and margins. In addition, the `inline-block` method is the only way to center these buttons.

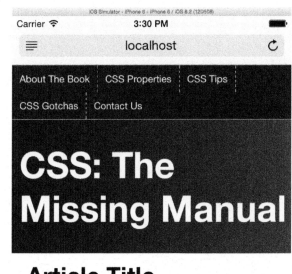

FIGURE 15-9

Even when you get the width of a page correctly sized for a mobile phone, there's still work to do. Here, a headline, which is the perfect size for a desktop browser, is an oversized monster on the phone, taking up way too much valuable screen space.

7. **The final 480-pixel media query should look like this:**

```
@media (max-width:480px) {
  .columnWrapper, .main, .sidebar1, .sidebar2 {
    float: none;
    width: auto;
  }
}
```

```
.main {
  border: none;
}

.sidebar1, .sidebar2 {
  border-top: 2px solid black;
  margin-top: 25px;
  padding-top: 10px;
}

header h1 {
  font-size: 1.5em;
}

nav {
  text-align: center;
}

nav li {
  float: none;
  display: inline-block;
}

nav a {
  float: none;
  display: inline-block;
  border: none;
}

}
```

Save all of your files and preview the *index.html* file in a web browser. Resize the browser window so it's less than 480 pixels to see the phone design; resize the window until the two-column design pops into view; and then again until you see the three-column desktop version. You should see designs like those pictured in Figure 15-10. You'll find a completed version of this tutorial in the *15_finished* folder.

FIGURE 15-10

One, two, and three columns, all in a single web page. Thanks to responsive web design techniques, you can transform a single web page to best fit any width device.

Using a CSS Grid System

So far you've learned a number of layout techniques, like how to create float-based layouts to create multiple side-by-side columns and how to create responsive designs that change their layout based on the width of the device displaying the web page. But when your site will appear on screens of all different shapes and sizes, you need all the control you can get.

This chapter expands on the concepts in the previous few chapters and shows you the most precise, yet responsive, page design technique of all—the CSS layout grid. A layout grid is a systematic arrangement of rows and columns used as an organizational tool for laying out content. In the world of CSS, a grid system is a predefined style sheet with styles that make it easy for web designers to add a layout grid to their pages. Grid systems use class names added to <div> tags in a page's HTML to create consistently sized columns.

How Grids Work

Grids have a long history in graphic design and traditional page layout. There are various theories about how to best organize content using grids to create beautiful designs, but most of them rely on the unchanging nature of print design and don't translate well to the flexible nature of browsers.

In web design, a grid acts as a way to organize content into rows and columns using consistent column widths. A page's width is divided into a set number of "units" that group easily to create columns of different widths. A common number of units is 12, since 12 divides easily into halves, thirds, and quarters. Because grids use a set number of units, columns tend to align better and look better because they share a consistent rhythm.

For example, the web page pictured in the top image in Figure 16-1 is organized in rows and columns using a CSS grid system. The page looks well balanced and well aligned because its grid creates consistent column widths. In this example, the underlying grid is composed of 12 units, and the page is divided into five rows. The first row has two columns: The first column, containing the company name, is four units wide; the second, with the navigation bar, is eight units wide. In most grid systems, there's always a gutter, or empty space, separating columns. In this case, there's a single gutter between the two columns.

The second and third rows each hold a single column 12 units wide; the fourth row has three columns, four units wide each, with a gutter between each column; and the bottom row has two columns, one four units wide and the other eight units wide (the same as the first row).

As you may have guessed by now, a "unit" isn't any precise measurement. It's a relative measure, like a percentage value. In fact, in most CSS grid systems, the width of those units is defined using percentage values. So one unit is around 1/12 of the total width of the page—the exact value varies based on the number of columns and gutters in the row. As you read on page 461, relative widths are the key to creating responsive designs, so the onscreen width of a 3-unit-wide column will vary based on the width of the browser window. If you resize the browser window, the precise width of a column in pixels will change, but its relative width will always be the same—3 units.

And therein lies the beauty of a grid system. Remember all that math you needed to calculate the percentage value for a div's width using responsive design (page 470)? That math is already done for you and baked into the CSS file for the grid system. In addition, as you can see in Figure 16-1, using consistent unit values makes page elements line up nicely. For example, the second column in row 4 starts at the same left position as the second column in the bottom row, so they're perfectly aligned. What's more, column widths are consistent for different unit values: The three columns in row 4, for example, are all the same width, because of the consistent and accurate calculations in the grid system.

FIGURE 16-1

Many websites use a grid system to lay out their pages using rows and columns with predefined widths. While visitors just see well-designed and visually pleasing pages (top), web designers know that the underlying grid provides organization, balance, and alignment (bottom). Grids are divided into rows that run horizontally across the page (numbered), and columns that divide the rows into smaller units. In addition, grids usually include gutters or extra space on the sides of a row (left and right spaces in the bottom image) and between columns.

Structuring Your HTML for Grids

Individual web designers—and big companies like Twitter—have created dozens of CSS grid systems to choose from. You can read about a sampling of them in the box on page 497. These systems rely on one or more CSS files designed to create the kind of columns described in the previous section. Most of these systems use a similar approach for structuring the HTML to create a grid, relying on a series of nested <div> tags to form three different types of page elements:

- **Containers.** A container div holds one or more rows. The container helps set a width for the entire grid system, and often uses the max-width property (page 208) to keep the content from growing absurdly wide on large monitors. Containers are also usually centered in the middle of the browser window.

- **Rows.** A row is another `<div>` tag, placed within a container, and the row holds more divs that make up the columns within it.

- **Columns.** A column is a `<div>` tag within a row. Each row has one or more columns.

To define a container, a row, or a column, you simply add a class name to each div. The name you use will vary from one CSS grid system to another, but many use some variation of the words *container, row,* and *column.* For example, say you wanted to start by creating a page with two rows. The first row contains two columns: one column for a logo and another for the site navigation. The second row holds one column to display the text of an article. The HTML markup for this grid system might look like this:

```
<div class="container">
  <!-- row #1 -->
  <div class="row">
    <!-- 3 unit wide column -->
    <div class="three columns">
      <!-- logo here -->
    </div>
    <!-- 3 unit wide column -->
    <div class="nine columns">
      <!-- navigation here -->
    </div>
  </div>
  <!-- row #2 -->
  <div class="row">
    <!-- 12 unit wide column -->
    <div class="one columns">
        <!-- article text here -->
    </div>
  </div>
</div>
```

There's nothing terribly complicated going on here. In fact, this HTML is very similar to the HTML used in the layout techniques described in Chapter 13. The main difference is that someone else wrote the CSS styles used for laying out the page, saving you a lot of time. All you have to do is download the CSS files for the grid system, attach the style sheet to your web pages, and structure your pages' HTML according to the rules defined by that grid system. This chapter uses a particular grid system (called Skeleton), but you have many CSS grid systems to choose from (see the box below).

Common CSS Grid Systems

This chapter uses a simple but powerful CSS grid system called Skeleton (*http://getskeleton.com*). But it's certainly not your only choice.

- Simple Grid (*http://thisisdallas.github.io/Simple-Grid/*) is another lightweight grid system. It's *barebones*: It doesn't provide any CSS except for creating the grid. It's also responsive, meaning that the page layout adjusts automatically to changing browser widths. So on a mobile device, for example, any multicolumn design instantly changes into a single column design that's easy to read on a phone.

- Pure.css (*http://purecss.io*) is more of a CSS *framework*, meaning it supplies CSS styles that make it easy not only to create a grid, but also to format buttons, tables, menus, and forms. Pure.css is a project of Yahoo, so you know it has some smart people working on it.

- Foundation (*http://foundation.zurb.com*) is another

responsive CSS framework. It's very popular, but it's also a lot more complex than most other grid systems. It's great for building web applications and interactive websites because it includes not only CSS, but also JavaScript code for creating drop-down menus, accordions, tooltips, and modal dialog boxes.

- Bootstrap (*http://getbootstrap.com*) is the most popular CSS framework (which explains why a lot of sites look very similar). Created by Twitter, Bootstrap is used in thousands of websites. It includes a CSS grid system, but like Foundation, it also includes everything but the kitchen sink. Bootstrap's CSS includes rules for styling buttons, tables, alerts, badges, labels, and even a large display container called the *jumbotron* (*http://getbootstrap.com/components/#jumbotron*). In addition, there are lot of JavaScript components to choose from, such as tooltips, a carousel, and modal dialog boxes.

Using the Skeleton Grid System

In this chapter, you'll learn how to work with Skeleton, a simple, responsive CSS grid system. You'll also see a few additional CSS rules to help with basic styling of buttons, forms, and tables. Skeleton gets all this work done in 400 lines of code, so it makes for a nice small file. It's built to work really well with mobile devices, and best of all, it's easy to use.

Skeleton is considered a responsive grid system because, while it allows for multiple columns on a page, it collapses those columns to stacked divs when the browser window's width is below 550 pixels. On mobile phones, space is at a premium, and displaying text or any other content in columns makes no sense; it's just too hard to read that way. So most mobile web designers choose to display content in one long column—one div stacked on top of another.

Skeleton lets you build a complex grid layout so your page is neatly structured into multiple columns on tablets, laptops, and desktop displays. On a phone, however, Skeleton's CSS automatically removes the side-by-side columns and forces content into an easy-to-read, single-column design. You don't have to do anything; responsive design is built right into Skeleton's CSS.

To start, visit the Skeleton website (*http://getskeleton.com*) and click the Download button (Figure 16-2). You'll end up with a folder containing a few other folders and files, but the only ones you really need to worry about are in the CSS folder: *normalize.css*, which provides a basic CSS reset (page 579) so all browsers will style HTML tags the same way; and *skeleton.css*, the file containing all the stuff you need to create a well organized layout.

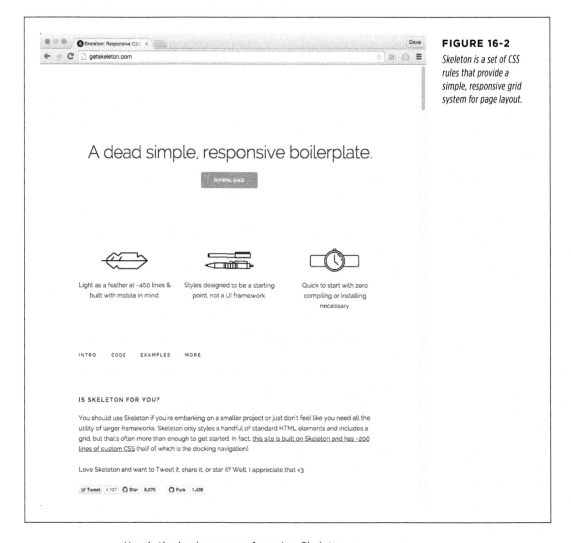

FIGURE 16-2

Skeleton is a set of CSS rules that provide a simple, responsive grid system for page layout.

Here's the basic process for using Skeleton:

1. **Attach the CSS files.**

   You can link to the *normalize.css* and the *skeleton.css* files like so:

   ```
   <link rel="stylesheet" href="css/normalize.css">
   <link rel="stylesheet" href="css/skeleton.css">
   ```

Skeleton's basic CSS styles use a Google Font (page 140) called Raleway. It's a beautiful font, so if you want to use it on your site, you should also link to those font files by adding another style sheet link to your web pages:

```
<link href="https://fonts.googleapis.com/css?family=Raleway:400,300,600"
rel="stylesheet" type="text/css">
```

2. **Add container divs.**

   As described earlier in this chapter, in a grid system a container div is used to hold rows and columns. A page might have just a single container, but there are times when multiple containers are necessary to create a particular design effect (more on that on page 503). A container in Skeleton is simply a div with the class container:

   ```
   <div class="container">

   </div>
   ```

   Don't put any HTML directly inside a container div, except for the row divs described next.

3. **Add divs for rows.**

   Inside each container, you'll have one or more rows. These are simply <div> tags nested inside the container div. They have the class row:

   ```
   <div class="container">
     <div class="row">

     </div>
   </div>
   ```

   You can put any number of rows inside a single container. In fact, unless you require the particular design effect described on page 503, you might only use a single container for the page containing multiple rows and columns:

   ```
   <div class="container">
     <div class="row">

     </div>
     <div class="row">

     </div>
     <div class="row">

     </div>
   </div>
   ```

4. **Add column divs.**

Skeleton uses a 12-unit grid, so each div you add to a row must be at least one unit wide (that's quite small) or 12 units wide (the entire width of the container). In addition, if you have more than one row, their total width must come to exactly 12 units. For example, if you have three columns, they each might be four units wide, or one might be two units wide, while the other two are five units wide.

You define a div as a column by adding the name `columns` to the class attribute. You then set that column's width using a number from one to twelve. Remember that CSS class names can't start with literal numbers like 1, 2, or 12, so you have to spell out these numbered class names. For example, to add three equal-width columns to a row you'd add three divs like this:

```
<div class="container">
  <div class="row">
    <div class="four columns">

    </div>
    <div class="four columns">

    </div>
    <div class="four columns">

    </div>
  </div>
</div>
```

> **TIP** If you want to create a single column within a row, don't add another div inside the row. Just add your content like this:
>
> ```
> <div class="row">
> <p>This text will fill the entire width of the container. It's a single
> column.</p>
> </div>
> ```

5. **Add content inside the column divs.**

The container and row divs are just structural elements used to contain your columns. The actual content—the good stuff like words, photos, and videos—goes inside each of the column divs.

6. **Create your own styles.**

Skeleton doesn't provide much more than an underlying structure for your content, hence the term "skeleton." To make it look great, you'll need to add your own styles to decorate your site with colors, fonts, background images, and so on. It's a good idea to create another CSS file named something like *custom.css* for these styles, and link it to your web page after the *skeleton.css* file:

```
<link rel="stylesheet" href="css/normalize.css">
<link rel="stylesheet" href="css/skeleton.css">
<link rel="stylesheet" href="css/custom.css">
```

Skeleton uses a mobile-first approach to its CSS (page 463), so you'll use media queries to refine your design for multiple browser widths, starting with the narrow screen of a phone. (You'll learn how to do that on page 507.)

▇ Creating and Naming Columns

Skeleton uses a 12-unit grid (Figure 16-3). You can create columns of different widths ranging from a single unit to 12. To create a column, you assign two class names to a div. One class is the unit width—one, two, three, and so on—while the other is columns. Keep in mind that this isn't a single CSS class name: You must add two class namess and the names must be separated from each other by a space. Each name refers to a different CSS rule in the Skeleton style sheet.

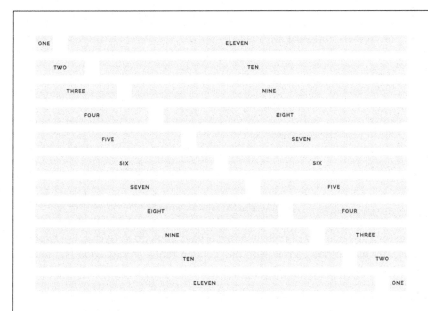

FIGURE 16-3

Skeleton's 12-unit grid system lets you create multiple combinations of column widths. As you can see, a single unit is not very wide at all, so it's unlikely that you'll ever create a column that thin. But since twelve divides into multiple combinations, you can create columns of a variety of different widths.

Take a look at the following two examples. Say you wanted to create a row with two columns of equal width. You'd simply add two divs, each six units wide, inside a row div and container div like this:

```
<div class="container">
  <div class="row">
    <div class="six columns">

    </div>
    <div class="six columns">

    </div>
  </div>
</div>
```

To create a design with four equal-size columns, add four divs, each with a unit size of three:

```
<div class="container">
  <div class="row">
    <div class="three columns">

    </div>
    <div class="three columns">

    </div>
    <div class="three columns">

    </div>
    <div class="three columns">

    </div>
  </div>
</div>
```

Columns don't need to be the same width. However, make sure that whatever width you use, the total number of units in a row always adds up to twelve. For example, it's perfectly fine to have a row with one column that's 4 units wide and another that's 8 units wide:

```
<div class="container">
  <div class="row">
    <div class="four columns">

    </div>
    <div class="eight columns">
```

```
     </div>
    </div>
   </div>
```

One really helpful aspect of Skeleton is that its CSS automatically (and correctly) calculates the gutters needed for multiple columns. That is, you don't need to figure out how much space to place between two columns. If you have just a single column in a row, Skeleton won't add any gutter; if you have two columns in a row, it'll add one gutter to separate the two; and if you have six columns, it'll add five gutters—all calculated automatically in the Skeleton CSS file!

TIP Skeleton provides shorthand class names to create columns that are half, one-third, and two-thirds the container width. Just use the names half, one-third, or two-thirds along with the class name column. For example, to create two columns, one that's one-third the width of the container, and another that's two-thirds the width of the container, you'd add two divs inside a row, like this:

```
<div class="row">
  <div class="one-third column">

  </div>
  <div class="two-thirds column">

  </div>
</div>
```

Creating Full Width Sections

The container div you add to a page holds rows and columns. Skeleton's CSS doesn't extend the width of the container style to fill the browser window for tablet, laptop and desktop screens. The container's width is set to different widths using media queries, but they never extend all the way to the edges of the window. In some cases this is fine, but if you want to add a background color or image to a container your design might not look perfect (see Figure 16-4). In this case, you frequently want to extend the background to the edges of the browser window (as in the bottom image in Figure 16-4).

FIGURE 16-4

Skeleton's container class doesn't extend to fill the browser window (top). If you set a background image or color on one of those containers, that background will cover only the container. In many cases, a design looks better if the background color or image extends to the edges of the browser window (bottom). The solution: add a <div> around each container, and add the background color or image to those wrapper divs.

Fortunately, this is really easy to do. Since the default width of any block-level element like a <div> tag is 100%, you just wrap the container div with yet another div and set the background color to that outermost div. For example, in the bottom image, the top area of the page has a large photo that fills that header portion from edge to edge. Here's the HTML for that section:

```
<div class="section header">
  <div class="container">
    <div class="row">
      <div class="three columns">
        <p class="logo">My Company</p>
      </div>
      <div class="nav nine columns">
        <a class="button button-primary" href="#">Home</a>
        <a class="button" href="#">Our Clients</a>
        <a class="button" href="#">About Us</a>
        <a class="button" href="#">Careers</a>
      </div>
    </div>
    <div class="row action">
      <h1>We do great things</h1>
      <h2>Donec pulvinar ullamcorper metus</h2>
      <a href="#" class="button button-primary">Learn More</a>
    </div>
  </div>
</div>
```

The critical part is the outermost <div>. This div surrounds the container div (lines 2 and 19). By adding a class name to that div, you can easily set a background image using CSS:

```
.header {
  background-image: url(../imgs/header.jpg);
  background-size: cover;
}
```

Now, since the width of that outer div is always 100%, its background will always extend the full width of the browser window.

As mentioned on page 503, you may only need a single container div for an entire web page. However, you may want to include different backgrounds on different rows, and have *those* backgrounds fill the entire width of the window.

For example, in the bottom image in Figure 16-4, a photo fills the top part of the page, and a black strip fills the bottom, so there are two different backgrounds for two different sections of the page. In this case, you need to include multiple containers: one for the top section (the photo), one for the middle section (the white area), and one for the bottom footer (the black strip). In addition, each of those containers must be wrapped with its own <div> tag. These are the divs that will fill the width of the browser window, and you style each of those separately. You'll see an example of creating this full-width background effect in the tutorial on page 509.

Styling Buttons

While Skeleton is mainly a grid system, it does provide a couple of fun and attractive styles for formatting other types of page elements. In particular, Skeleton creates cool-looking buttons (see Figure 16-5).

The Skeleton CSS file automatically styles certain HTML elements to look like the buttons pictured in Figure 16-5. For example, it styles the HTML <button> element, as well as form input fields with the type submit or button, like the white buttons pictured in the top of Figure 16-5. Say you have this HTML on a page:

```
<button>Button Element</button>
```

Skeleton's CSS automatically styles it as a white button with rounded corners and a gray border. Now suppose you want to style other HTML elements like this. For example, if you have a series of links forming a navigation bar, you may want each link to look like a Skeleton button. To do so, add the button class name to the link:

```
<a href="index.html" class="button">Home</a>
```

Skeleton includes another class—.button-primary—that creates a blue highlighted button (the bottom blue buttons in Figure 16-5). To turn an HTML button element, for example, into one of these blue Skeleton buttons, add a class to the HTML like this:

```
<button class="button-primary">Button Element</button>
```

If you want to turn a plain link into one of these flashy blue buttons, you have to add two classes: one to turn the link to a button and another to make it bright blue, like this:

```
<a href="index.html" class="button button-primary">Home</a>
```

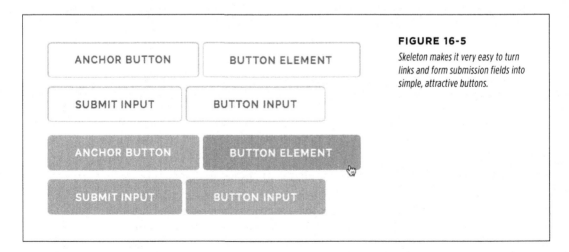

FIGURE 16-5

Skeleton makes it very easy to turn links and form submission fields into simple, attractive buttons.

Mobile First

Skeleton takes a mobile-first approach to CSS. Mobile first, which you read about on page 463, means starting with a design that looks good on small mobile devices like phones. Using media queries, you then add styles that improve the appearance of the page at different screen widths. Each media query defines a new, wider screen width, and you add styles to refine the design at each of these "breakpoints" (widths).

Mobile-first CSS involves using `min-width` settings in the `@media` directive (page 460). In other words, each media query adds new styles that apply when the screen is a minimum width. Take this media query, for example:

```
@media (min-width: 400px) {


}
```

The styles you add here will only work when the browser window is at least 400 pixels wide. If the screen is only 320 pixels wide, the styles inside this media query won't apply to the page. However, the styles will apply when the width of the browser window is 400 pixels or wider. The mobile-first approach adds successively wider media queries; each query applies to not only its `min-width` setting, but also to browsers that match queries with a larger `min-width` setting.

A good approach for creating a mobile-first design with Skeleton is to start with another style sheet. Name it something like *custom.css* or *site.css* and attach it to your web page after the Skeleton CSS files:

```
<link rel="stylesheet" href="css/normalize.css">
<link rel="stylesheet" href="css/skeleton.css">
<link rel="stylesheet" href="css/custom.css">
```

Within this CSS file, you'll add rules to refine the look of the site, adding colors, fonts, backgrounds, and so on. To create a mobile-first design, you need to start with some basic media queries in place. The creator of Skeleton recommends setting media queries to a number of different break points, like the following:

```
* Mobile first queries */
/* applies to ALL widths */

/* Larger than mobile */
/* applies to all widths 400px and greater */
@media (min-width: 400px) {

}
/* Larger than phablet (also point when grid becomes active) */
/* applies to all widths 550px and greater */
@media (min-width: 550px) {

}
```

```
/* Larger than tablet */
/* applies to all widths 750px and greater */
@media (min-width: 750px) {

}
/* Larger than desktop */
/* applies to all widths 100px and greater */
@media (min-width: 1000px) {

}
/* Larger than Desktop HD */
/* applies to 1200px and greater */
@media (min-width: 1200px) {

}
```

In mobile-first design, you'll want to add styles that apply to all devices (mobile or not) *outside* the media queries. For example, if you want to apply the same font, font color, and background colors to page elements regardless of browser width, then add those CSS rules here.

In addition, you should add the styles that make your site look great on a mobile device here. You can use Chrome's Developer Tools (page 104) to help you see what the page will look like on a mobile device.

Once the mobile version looks good, expand your browser window (or use Chrome's Dev Tools again) to see what your page looks like at the first break point of 400 pixels (line 6 in the code above.) If the page looks perfectly fine at this width (they often do), you can skip this breakpoint and expand your browser window to the next one (550 pixels).

If the design doesn't look great—maybe there's not enough empty space around page elements—then add new styles at this breakpoint until it looks good. Remember, any addition you make within the media query won't apply to earlier breakpoints. So, for example, if you add a style that increases padding around headlines within the media query with the min-width of 550 pixels, that padding won't be added to the headlines when the browser window is less than 550 pixels wide. In other words, changes you make inside this media query won't affect how the design looks on a phone.

You can continue this process by checking how your site looks at each breakpoint, adding any styles within the appropriate breakpoint to improve the look at that browser width. Although the code starting on page 507 has five media queries with five different breakpoints, don't feel you have to add styles at each breakpoint. You'll probably find that you only need to adjust the look of page elements for a few different widths. In addition, you may find that the min-width values supplied in this code don't work with your particular design. For example, your page design might look great all the way up to 650 pixels, but beyond that, page elements don't seem to fit or look as good. In this case, just change the `min-width` value for a particular breakpoint and add your styles inside that media query (for instance, change 550px to 650px). In fact, you probably won't need all of the media queries listed in the code starting on page 507, so feel free to remove them from the style sheet.

The best way to understand mobile-first design is to see it in action, which you'll get a chance to do in the tutorial coming up next.

■ Tutorial: Using a Grid System

This tutorial shows you how to apply a grid system to a web page using Skeleton. You'll start with some basic HTML, add the required CSS files, add and structure your HTML to create grids, and finally, add custom CSS rules to make the page look great—including on mobile devices.

To get started, download the tutorial files located on this book's companion website at *https://github.com/sawmac/css_mm_4e*.

Adding a Grid

To get started, you'll attach the required CSS files and add some basic HTML to create a grid container with rows and columns.

1. **In your text editor, open the file *16→index.html*.**

   This is a basic HTML file. It has a head and body, but no HTML in the body yet. Before you add HTML, however, add links to a few CSS files. There's already a link to a Google Font (page 140), but you also need links to the Skeleton files.

2. **On the empty line just before the closing** `</head>` **tag, add the following three lines.**

   ```
   <link rel="stylesheet" href="css/normalize.css">
   <link rel="stylesheet" href="css/skeleton.css">
   <link rel="stylesheet" href="css/custom.css">
   ```

   The first line of code loads the *normalize.css* file. *normalize.css* is a very popular CSS reset file (page 579) and is used in many projects. The second file is the basic *skeleton.css* file, which includes the CSS for the grid system. The final CSS file, *custom.css*, is mostly empty; it has a few media queries to add styles for different screen widths. You'll use this file to add styles to customize the look of the page.

   Next, you'll add a Skeleton container.

3. **Just below the HTML comment** `<!-- top section -->` **add the following HTML:**

   ```
   <!-- top section -->
   <div class="container">

   </div>
   ```

As explained on page 495, Skeleton uses the class name container to define the div that holds the rows you'll add to a page. You can have any number of containers on a page, or use just a single container div for all of your rows. As you'll see in a minute, there's a benefit of having more than one container.

Time to add your first row.

4. **Inside the** <div> **you just added, insert two divs to create two rows (additions are in bold):**

```
<!-- top section -->
<div class="container">
  <div class="row">

  </div>
  <div class="row">

  </div>
</div>
```

These divs create two rows. To the first row, you'll add two columns—one for the site name and the other for navigation.

5. **Inside the first** <div> **with the class** row**, type the following HTML:**

```
<div class="four columns">
  <p class="logo">My Company</p>
</div>
<div class="eight columns nav">

</div>
```

The Skeleton grid system divides a row into 12 units. You can divide those units to make individual columns, so here you have two columns, one 4 units and the other 8 units. Visually, you have one column that's 1/3, or around 33%, of the container width; the second is 2/3, or around 66%, of the container width.

The second column is wider, because it's going to hold a navigation bar. In fact, notice that there's a class name—nav—added to this tag. That's not a requirement of the Skeleton framework; you're adding it now so you can use it later to style the navigation bar.

6. **Open the file** *01-nav.html.* **Copy the HTML inside it and paste it into the 9-unit-wide div so the HTML looks like this (additions in bold):**

```
<div class="eight columns nav">
  <a href="#">Home</a>
  <a href="#">Our Clients</a>
  <a href="#">About Us</a>
  <a href="#">Careers</a>
</div>
```

These are just simple links and don't look like much. However, Skeleton includes some very fine-looking styles to format any element as a button. You simply add a class name to the <a> tags.

7. **Add a class attribute to each link, and assign a** button **class, like this:**

```
<div class="eight columns nav">
  <a class="button" href="#">Home</a>
  <a class="button"href="#">Our Clients</a>
  <a class="button" href="#">About Us</a>
  <a class="button" href="#">Careers</a>
</div>
```

Skeleton also includes a special class named button-primary that assigns a special look to a button. It's a great way to make the link for the current page stand out from the others, so visitors can tell what page they're on. The page you're working on is the home page, so you'll add that special class to the Home link.

8. **Add the class name** button-primary **to the first** <a> **tag:**

```
<div class="eight columns nav">
  <a class="button button-primary" href="#">Home</a>
  <a class="button" href="#">Our Clients</a>
  <a class="button" href="#">About Us</a>
  <a class="button" href="#">Careers</a>
</div>
```

There's one last row that needs content. This one is simple, because you want just a single row that spans the entire width of the container.

9. **Open the file** *02-action.html.* **Copy the HTML, return to the** *index.html* **file, and paste it inside the second row div inside the container div.** The final HTML of the container div will look like this (additions from this step are in bold):

```
<!-- top section -->
<div class="container">
  <div class="row">
    <div class="four columns">
      <p class="logo">My Company</p>
    </div>
    <div class="eight columns nav">
      <a class="button button-primary" href="#">Home</a>
      <a class="button" href="#">Our Clients</a>
      <a class="button" href="#">About Us</a>
      <a class="button" href="#">Careers</a>
    </div>
  </div>
  <div class="row">
    <h1>We do great things</h1>
    <h2>Donec pulvinar ullamcorper metus</h2>
```

```
<a href="#" class="button button-primary">Learn More</a>
  </div>
</div>
```

The content in this row will span the entire width of the container—in other words, there's only a single column. In this case you don't add any additional divs; you just put the HTML inside the row div.

10. **Add a class,** action, **to the last row:**

```
<div class="row action">
  <h1>We do great things</h1>
  <h2>Donec pulvinar ullamcorper metus</h2>
  <a href="#" class="button button-primary">Learn More</a>
</div>
```

You'll use that class name later when you style this area of the page. The name, action, doesn't have anything to do with Skeleton—it's just a class name you can use can style this section of the page.

11. **Save the *index.html* file and preview it in a web browser.**

The page should look like Figure 16-6. At this point it doesn't look like a marvelously organized grid layout. But it will. Let's add another row and three columns this time. To keep your fingers from going numb, we'll supply you with the basic HTML for the main content on this page.

FIGURE 16-6

Skeleton provides not only a grid layout system, but also some basic typographic styles and well-designed buttons.

12. **Open the file *03-info.html*. Copy the HTML and, in the *index.html* file, paste it just below the comment** <!-- info section -->.

This is just a basic set of nested divs. There's one <div> that represents a container for rows, and two <div> tags inside that represent rows. In the first row there's only an <h2> tag, which will be a single column that spans the entire container. In the second row are three additional divs, which will be three columns.

The HTML doesn't yet have any of Skeleton's class names—the secret sauce that applies the grid layout—so you'll add those next.

13. **Add** class="container" **to the first** <div> **in the HTML you just pasted into the page.**

```
<!-- info section -->
<div class="container">
```

This applies Skeleton's container style to the tag, creating a place to insert rows. Next you'll add some rows.

14. **Add** class="row" **to the next two divs inside the container, like this (additions in bold):**

```
<div class="container">
  <div class="row">
    <h2>Graeco feugiat intellegam at vix</h2>
  </div>
  <div class="row">
```

Now that you've created the rows, you need to create three columns in that second row. You can do so by adding a class attribute with two class names: The first name is the number of units the column should take up, and the second is the name columns.

15. **Add** class="four columns" **to each of the** <div> **tags inside the second row within the "info" section of this page. While you're at it, add the button class to the three links in each column.** The finished HTML for the "info" section should look like this:

```
<!-- info section -->
<div class="container">
  <div class="row">
    <h2>Graeco feugiat intellegam at vix</h2>
  </div>
  <div class="row">
    <div class="four columns">
      <p>Mei te possit instructior…</p>
      <p><a href="#" class="button">More info</a></p>
    </div>
    <div class="four columns">
      <p>Mei te possit instructior…</p>
      <p><a href="#" class="button">More info</a></p>
    </div>
    <div class="four columns">
      <p>Mei te possit instructior..</p>
      <p><a href="#" class="button">More info</a></p>
    </div>
  </div>
</div>
```

(The HTML shown here has been condensed by not including all of the Latin gibberish in each column.) Finally, you'll add a footer to the page.

16. **Open the file *04-footer.html*. Copy the HTML and, in the *index.html* file, paste it just below the comment** `<!-- footer -->`.

This HTML contains the proper Skeleton classes already in place (by now you probably know how Skeleton works, and don't need any more practice typing it all out). The HTML you've just added inserts another container with one additional row and two columns—one 8 units wide and the second 4 units wide.

17. **Save the *index.html* file and preview it in a browser.**

The page should look like Figure 16-7. The design is coming together: There are two columns in the header (the logo and navigation), three columns of main text, and two columns in the footer.

If you resize your browser window as thin as it will go, you'll notice that the columns eventually collapse and stack on top of each other. You're watching the responsive part of the Skeleton framework in action. It uses media queries, just like the ones you read about in the previous chapter, to create a single-column design for mobile devices.

FIGURE 16-7

With just some well-structured HTML, a handful of class names, and the Skeleton CSS file, creating multicolumn layouts is a breeze.

Adding Style

Skeleton takes your designs a long way toward an organized visual presentation, but it's rather plain. To add skin and clothes to this structure, you need to add your own CSS. In this section of the tutorial, you'll add a few design touches.

1. **In your text editor, open the file 16→css→custom.css.**

   This is a mostly empty CSS file. It only includes media queries set to different breakpoints—the screen widths at which you might want to change the size and look of page elements. For example, on a phone you'll probably want to decrease the size of headlines and eliminate excessive margins and padding.

   You'll start by seeing what happens if you add a background color to a container.

2. **On the empty line following the** /* Mobile first queries */ **comment, add the following style:**

   ```
   /* Mobile first queries */
   /* applies to ALL widths */
   .container {
     background-color: pink;
   }
   ```

   Remember that your page has several <div> tags with the class container. These are the tags that contain rows.

3. **Save the *custom.css* file. Preview the *index.html* file in a browser.**

   The page should look like Figure 16-8. Notice that the pink color is constrained to the width of the content, and is centered in the browser window. If you look back at the final design in Figure 16-4, you'll see that you want a photo in the background of the header area, and that photo should extend the entire width of the browser window. Skeleton containers don't do that, so you need to add another div that will span the entire width of the browser window.

4. **Open the *index.html* file in a text editor. Locate the** <!-- top section --> **comment and add another div, just below it:**

   ```
   <!-- top section -->
   <div class="section header">
     <div class="container">
   ```

   Here, you're beginning to wrap that container div with another div. You've given it a couple of class names—section and header—so you can style this area separate from other parts of the page. Now you need to close the div.

5. **Add a closing** </div> **just *before* the** <!-- info section --> **comment:**

   ```
   </div>
   <!-- info section -->
   ```

Now there's a new div that wraps around the container. By default, like all block-level elements, divs have a width of 100%. That is, they stretch to fill their parent element, which in this case is the page's body. So this new div will fill the browser window. Now you can add a photo that will fill the width of the browser window, but only sit inside the header section.

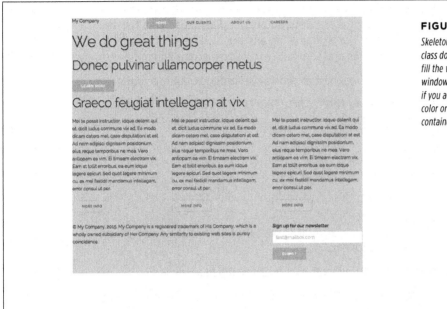

FIGURE 16-8

Skeleton's container class doesn't extend to fill the width of a browser window. This is a problem if you add a background color or image to the container.

6. **Save the *index.html* file, and return to the *custom.css* file in your text editor. Delete the** `.container` **rule you added in step 2 above, and replace it with this rule:**

```
/* Mobile first queries */
/* applies to ALL widths */
.header {
  padding: 50px 0 70px 0;
  background-image: url(../imgs/header.jpg);
  background-size: cover;
}
```

The `padding` property just adds a little breathing room at the top and bottom of this region of the page. The `background-size` property (discussed on page 245) scales the image added by the `background-image` property so it always fills the background. If you save the files now and preview the *index.html* file, you'll notice that the picture does span the browser window but only fills the header area.

Now you can format that header area.

7. **Just below the** `.header` **style, add a style for the logo:**

```
.logo {
  font-weight: 600;
  color: rgb(255, 209, 143);
}
```

This page uses a Google font (page 140) named Raleway, which includes three font weights. As you read on page 157, you can use numbers to indicate different font styles from very thin to very heavy and bold. 600 is a bold version of the font.

Next, you'll align the navigation to the right side of the page and improve the way the buttons look against the photo background.

8. **Add three more styles after the** `.logo` **style:**

```
.nav {
  text-align: right;
}
.button {
  background-color: rgba(255,255,255,.5);
}
.button:hover {
  background-color: rgba(255,255,255,.3);
}
```

The .nav style formats the column containing the navigation buttons. In step 5 on page 510, you added nav to the class attribute for that div. The other two styles change the appearance of the buttons so that they stand out better from the photo background.

Lastly, you'll center the text and button that appears below the navigation area.

9. **Add three more styles below the button styles you just added:**

```
.action {
  text-align: center;
  padding-top: 75px;
}
.action h1 {
  margin: 0;
}
.action h2 {
  margin: 0 0 20px 0;
}
```

You added the action class in step 10 on page 512. Here, you're centering the content in that area, and removing some of the spacing around the headlines.

10. **Save the files and preview the *index.html* file in a browser.**

The page should look like Figure 16-9.

FIGURE 16-9

An image and a few styles of your own add some skin to Skeleton's bones.

The Mobile Design

As you read on page 507, Skeleton uses a mobile-first approach to its CSS. That is, you start with a design for small mobile devices like phones. Then you add styles inside a series of media queries that define progressively wider screen widths. Each set of styles from the previous query applies to the current query and all other queries with greater `min-width` values.

Think about a few enhancements you could make for visitors using mobile phones. Figure 16-10 shows what the current page would look like in an iPhone 5: There's a lot of space at top of the screen. You can fix the logo style to put the company name at the top of the screen, and fix the navigation buttons to fit better.

1. **In your text editor, open the file *16→css→custom.css*.**

The styles you added to this file earlier in this tutorial are at the top of the file, outside any media queries. In keeping with the mobile first approach, the styles here will apply regardless of the browser width, on both small and super-wide desktop displays.

First, you'll refine the `.logo` style so that it looks best on a small phone.

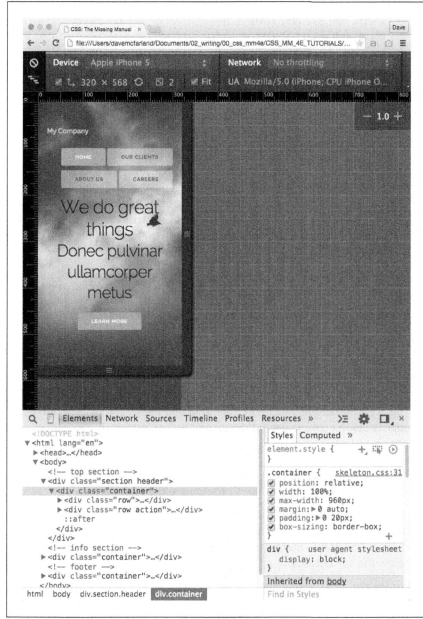

FIGURE 16-10

Using Google Chrome's Developer Tools, you can simulate the screen size of many different devices, including an iPhone 5 (pictured). See page 475 for more information on this cool tool built into Chrome.

2. **Locate the** `.logo` **style and add seven new declarations (additions in bold):**

```
.logo {
  font-weight: 600;
  color: rgb(255, 209, 143);
  background-color: black;
  position: fixed;
  top: 0;
  left: 0;
  right: 0;
  padding-left: 10px;
  z-index: 100;
}
```

The background-color setting makes the company name stand out. The position, top, left, and right settings fix this element to the top of the browser window. The padding setting adds a little breathing room on the left of the screen. Finally, the z-index setting (page 439) makes sure that as a visitor scrolls down the page, the logo sits above and on top of other page content (Figure 16-11, left).

The navigation buttons would look better if they were the same width and didn't have so much space around them.

3. **Below the** `.nav` **rule in the** *custom.css* **file, add the following style:**

```
.nav .button {
  width: 48%;
  margin: 2px 0;
}
```

This style makes the buttons in the navigation bar all the same width. It also adjusts the margins so the buttons don't touch (Figure 16-11, top right).

There's still too much space at the top of the page.

4. **Locate the first style in the** *custom.css*—**the** `.header` **rule—and change the** padding **values to** 30px 0 20px 0; **to remove the space at top.**

Now the navigation and logo fit better on a small screen, and there's not so much space below the "Learn More" button (Figure 16-11, bottom left). Lastly, it would be good to make that big headline a tad smaller and add more space below the nav buttons.

5. **Locate the** `.action` **rule and change its** padding-top **value to** 37px.

This adds some space between the first headline and the nav buttons. Now to shrink the font size of those headlines.

FIGURE 16-11

*Creating a mobile-first design
requires constant iteration—
adjusting styles to adjust
spacing, font size, and element
placement for different types
of devices with different screen
sizes.*

6. **In the *custom.css* file, after the** .action h2 **rule, add the following two styles:**

```
h1 {
  font-size: 3rem;
}
h2 {
  font-size: 2.5rem;
}
```

If you save the file and preview it using an iPhone 5 setting in Chrome's dev tools you'll see something like the bottom right image in Figure 16-11.

Styling a Breakpoint

So far you've made a great start on a mobile-friendly design. It even looks good on screens up to around 550 pixels. In other words, you don't need to worry about adding any styles to the first media query—the one with the min-width value of 400 pixels. However, at 550 pixels, the design starts to look a little weird. This is the point at which Skeleton's built-in grid kicks in, and the design changes from stacked divs to columns.

As you can see in Figure 16-12, the navigation buttons take up a lot of space and aren't aligned. It's time to make your design look better on progressively wider screens.

1. **Open the *custom.css* file in your text editor. Locate the media query with a** min-width **of** 550px **and add the following styles inside it (additions in bold):**

```
@media (min-width: 550px) {
  .header {
    padding: 40px 0 50px 0;
  }
  .logo {
    position: static;
    background-color: transparent;
    font-size: 2rem;
    line-height: 1;
  }
  .nav .button {
    width: auto;
  }
  h1 {
    font-size: 5rem;
  }
  h2 {
    font-size: 4.2rem;
  }
}
```

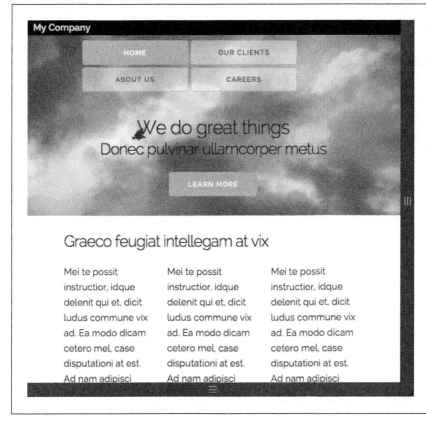

FIGURE 16-12

Skeleton's CSS grid springs into action at 550 pixels. This is when a media query kicks in and the styles inside it follow the column settings you specified in the HTML.

These styles reset the spacing in the header section of the page; change the logo so it's no longer fixed on the screen; adjust the width of the buttons; and increase the font size of the headlines (Figure 16-13, top right).

Finally, you'll just pump up the size of the logo text.

2. **In the media query with a** min-width **of** 750px**, add one last style:**

```
/* applies to all widths 750px and greater */
@media (min-width: 750px) {
  .logo {
    font-size: 3rem;
    position: relative;
    top: 5px;
  }
}
```

This changes the size of the company name and moves it over slightly.

FIGURE 16-13

Skeleton's responsive grid system makes it easy to create web pages that adjust to a variety of different browser widths, from phones to television screens.

3. **Save the *custom.css* file. Open the *index.html* file in a web browser, and shrink the window to less than 550 pixels wide. Then widen it slowly.**

The page design when the browser window is less than 550 pixels looks like the top-left image in Figure 16-13. As you widen the browser, the page will change two times: once at 550 pixels (top right) and once again at 750 pixels (bottom).

There's a lot more you can do to perfect this design at different breakpoints. Play around by adding different styles at the different media query breakpoints and see how you can improve this design.

You'll find the finished design in the *16_finished* folder inside the tutorials folder.

As you can see, a grid system is a handy tool that makes creating consistent column widths easy. However, underneath the hood, you'll find the same principles you learned earlier in this section of the book: floats, percentage widths, and so on. If you spend some time looking at the *skeleton.css* file, you can learn all about how it works.

TIP For a great discussion on how to build your own grid system with CSS read the article at *https://css-tricks.com/dont-overthink-it-grids/*.

Modern Web Layout with Flexbox

D esigners have used a number of different techniques for laying out web pages during the short life of the Web. At first, they relied on HTML tables to orga- nize content into rows and columns. Since the HTML <table> tag was never intended for page layout, though, designers found creative (and complicated) ways to use the <table> tag to achieve the designs they wanted.

Later, CSS and float-based layouts (like the type described in Chapter 13) provided a simpler, more logical way to control page design. Float-based layouts are still the most common type, and designers continue to refine their use. For example, the simple grid system you learned in the previous chapter is a sophisticated tool for creating layouts, but it still uses floats to make the magic happen.

However, the Web is always evolving, and the CSS Working Group at the W3C is working on new ways to give designers flexible and powerful CSS-layout properties. One of the newer methods that also has fairly broad browser support is *flexbox*.

■ Introducing Flexbox

Flexbox adds another layout mode to CSS. You've already read about block-level and inline-block level (page 192) elements. Tables and positioned elements (page 430) are also CSS layout modes. Flexbox, short for *flexible box*, adds another layout mode called *flex layout*.

Flexbox provides a very useful set of properties that let you lay out items in a row without floating them or using the inline-block value. In fact, the "flexible" part of flexbox lets the items inside a flex container adjust their widths automatically, very much like floated page elements using percentage values.

But flexbox is a lot easier than using floats, and it can provide all of the same layout advantages, as shown in Figure 17-1. The biggest downside is that not all browsers support it. Fortunately, the newest browsers—from Internet Explorer 11 and up, Chrome, Safari, Opera, and Firefox—all support flexbox properties; and only Safari still requires a vendor prefix.

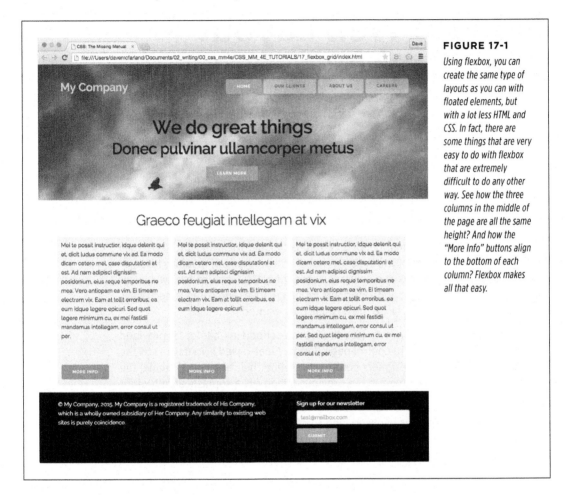

FIGURE 17-1

Using flexbox, you can create the same type of layouts as you can with floated elements, but with a lot less HTML and CSS. In fact, there are some things that are very easy to do with flexbox that are extremely difficult to do any other way. See how the three columns in the middle of the page are all the same height? And how the "More Info" buttons align to the bottom of each column? Flexbox makes all that easy.

Flexbox Basics

On the surface, flexbox is pretty simple. There are only two components you need to make it work:

1. **The Flex container.**

   Any HTML element can be a flex container, but usually you'll use a `<div>` or some other structural HTML tag. The tag you use for the flex container will contain children and other tags that make up the second part of the flexbox model.

2. Flex items.

Tags nested directly inside the flex container element are called *flex items*. Every direct child of the container element is automatically turned into a flex item. You can place any HTML tag inside the flex container. What's more, the child tags don't even have to be of the same type. For example, you could have one paragraph and four divs inside a flex container, and each of those will be a flex item.

Keep in the mind that only children of the flex container turn into flex items. If you had a <div> tag that you turned into a flex container and placed an unordered list inside it, only the <ul> tag would be a flex item. The <li> tags nested inside the <ul> tag would not be flex items.

In other words, as you're probably used to by now, flexbox is as easy as adding a <div> to a page and nesting additional divs inside it. For example, here's some simple HTML that can easily be used to create a row of items using flexbox:

```
<div class="container">
  <div>A flex item</div>
  <div>Another flex item</div>
  <div>A third flex item</div>
</div>
```

The outer div is the container, and the divs inside are the child elements. A browser will display this series of divs as block-level items, filling the entire width of the outer div and stacked one on top of the other as pictured in the top image in Figure 17-2.

However, you can easily transform the outermost div into a flex container using the display property and setting its value to flex like this:

```
.container {
    display: flex;
}
```

That single line of CSS gives you the second image from the top in Figure 17-2. Each of the child divs are converted automatically into flex items and placed side by side in a row: no floats or inline-blocks needed.

Unfortunately, at the time of this writing, Safari requires a vendor prefix for this property, so to make the above CSS work in all current browsers including Safari, you would write:

```
.container {
    display: -webkit-flex;
    display: flex;
}
```

Finally, you can make the divs inside the container the same width and fill up the container by simply giving those divs a `flex` property with a value of 1, like this:

```
.container div {
    flex: 1;
}
```

Again, to work in Safari, you'll need the vendor-prefixed version as well:

```
.container div {
    -webkit-flex: 1;
    flex: 1;
}
```

You'll learn more about the `flex` property in the next part of this chapter, but, in a nutshell, this line of code tells the browser to make sure each div (flex item) is the same width. This leads to the image second from the bottom in Figure 17-2.

TIP Autoprefixer (*https://github.com/postcss/autoprefixer*) is a tool that automatically adds vendor prefixes to your CSS code. Just write normal CSS, run it through Autoprefixer tool, and your style sheet will contain all the necessary vendor prefixes.

Because flex items automatically touch, you might want to add some space to separate each of them. There are many ways to do that, but here's one simple solution for this particular example:

```
.container div:nth-of-type(1n+2) {
    margin-left: 20px;
}
```

This nth-of-type selector (page 66) simply selects every div starting at the second one, and sets its left margin to 20 pixels (this handy trick makes sure the first div doesn't get a margin that indents it 20 pixels from the edge of the container). This results in the bottom image in Figure 17-2.

Conceptually, flexbox is pretty simple. As you can see, there's not a lot of CSS required to achieve this effect. Best of all, you don't have to worry about items escaping from their containers as you do with floated elements (page 405), and you can easily create equal-height columns. The only thing that makes flexbox difficult is understanding the large number of flexbox properties and imagining the almost limitless combinations of them all.

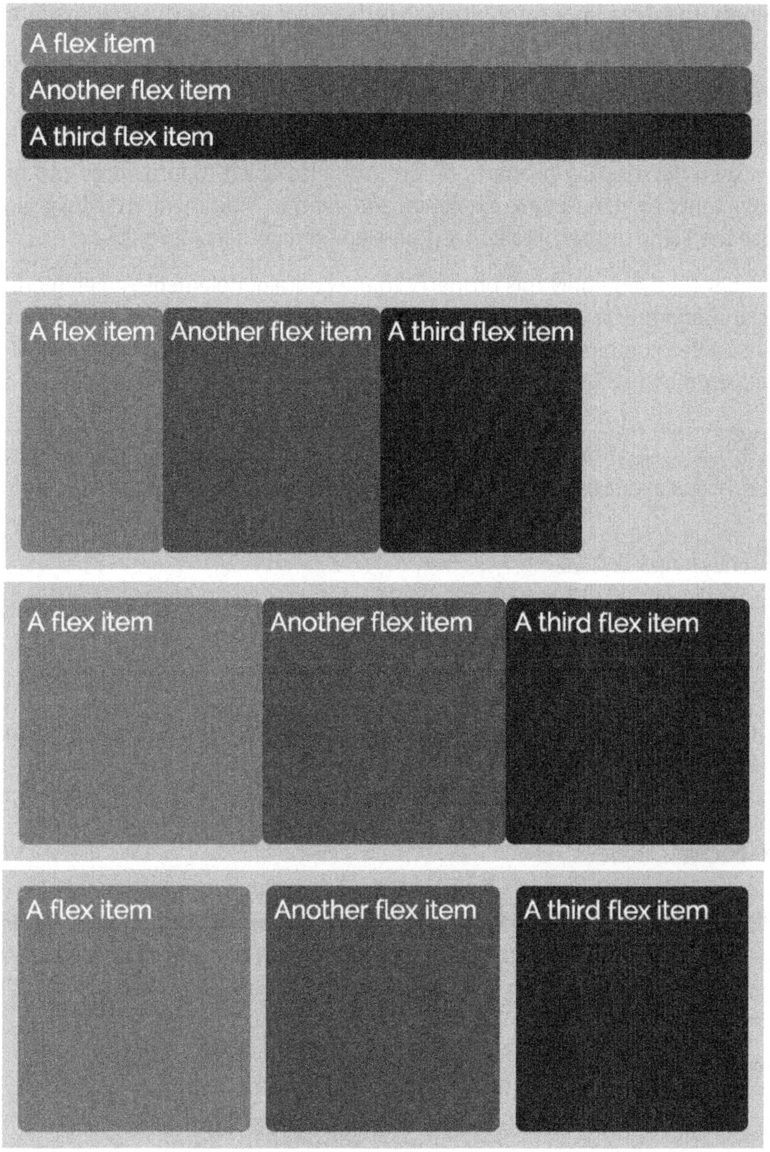

FIGURE 17-2

Flexbox makes it very easy to create equal-sized, equal-height, side-by-side columns without any floats. The extra empty space you see around the items (the lightest gray color) is simply padding added to the flex container.

Flex Container Properties

Both flex containers and flex items have their own set of CSS properties that control how a browser displays them. There are a handful of properties specific to just flex containers, the most important of which is the display property. To transform any HTML tag into a flex container:

```
display: -webkit-flex
display: flex;
```

You've seen the display property before. You also use it to turn items into block-level elements or inline-block elements, and even to hide them: display: none;. You use the same property to convert an element into a flex layout.

Remember that you apply this property to the container element—an element that wraps around other tags, which will become the flex items. You can even turn a flex item into a flex container for some interesting effects. You'll see an example of that technique on page 559.

> **NOTE** The examples in this chapter will include Safari's vendor-prefixed versions of each of the flexbox properties. To create a flex container in Safari, you need to use the display property and set its value to -webkit-flex:
>
> ```
> display: -webkit-flex;
> ```
>
> All other Safari-specific flex properties use the standard flex property name, with -webkit- at the beginning. For example, the flex-flow property for Safari looks like this:
>
> ```
> -webkit-flex-flow: column wrap;
> ```
>
> By the time you read this, these vendor prefixes may no longer be required. Consult *http://caniuse. com/#search=flexbox* to determine if you still need to include them.

Flex-Flow

Flex items, by default, are placed side by side as items in a row. In addition, a browser will display those flex items in a single row, without wrapping. In other words, no matter how narrow you make the browser window, the browser will keep those items side by side without dropping one below another—even if this makes content flow outside of a flex item (Figure 17-3, left).

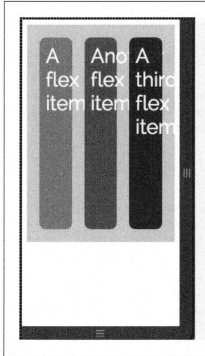 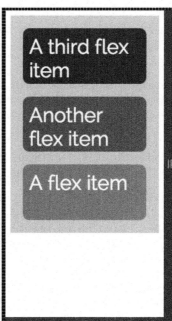

FIGURE 17-3

Flex items normally don't wrap, and if the browser window is made narrow enough, content inside a flex item will spill outside of its borders (left). But you can also display flex items as stacked on top of each other, and even reverse the order in which they are displayed (right).

The flex-flow property lets you control both the direction in which the items are displayed and whether or not they can wrap onto the next line. Flex-flow requires two values, separated by a space. The first is the direction and the second is whether the item can wrap. For example:

```
.container {
    display: -webkit-flex;
    display: flex;
    -webkit-flex-flow: column-reverse nowrap;
    flex-flow: column-reverse nowrap;
}
```

The first property value is the direction, and there are four possible settings:

- row is the normal setting. It displays flex items side by side, with the first item in the HTML source code being the left-most item, and the last item in the HTML source on the right (Figure 17-3, left).

- row-reverse also displays the flex items side by side, but reverses their order on screen. In other words, the last item to appear in the HTML source appears on the leftmost side of the container, and the first item in the HTML source appears at the right side of the container.

- column displays the flex items as stacked blocks one on top of the other. This is the normal way a group of divs would be displayed, so you might not use this setting often. However, it does come in handy when using media queries (page 460) and designing for mobile devices. You can convert the display of flex items as side-by-side items in a row (for larger screens) or into stacked divs for mobile devices by switching the direction to column within a media query for a small mobile screen (you'll see an example of this in the tutorial, in step 2 on page 564).

- column-reverse is the just like the column setting, except that the display order of the items is reversed. The item that appears *last* in the HTML source appears at the top of the container (Figure 17-3, right).

The second property controls whether flex items will wrap onto a new row (when using the row direction option) or onto a new column (when using the column direction option.) There are three possible values:

- nowrap is the normal behavior of flex items inside a flex container. The browser will keep the items in the same row no matter how narrow the browser window (Figure 17-3, left). In the case of columns, the browser will stacks the items one on top of the other (Figure 17-3, right).

- wrap lets items that don't fit inside the container's width drop down to a new row (or over to a new column) as pictured in the top image in Figure 17-4. In order for flex items to wrap onto new rows (or columns), you'll also need to set some values on the flex items as described on page 552.

- wrap-reverse is like the wrap option, but wraps items in a reverse order (Figure 17-4, bottom).

Flex items can be placed side by side in a row or stacked on top of each other in a single column, depending on which direction property you set (row or column). However, since the row option is most useful for page layout, the examples in the rest of this chapter on flexbox will apply to flex items laid out in a row.

NOTE   The flex-flow property is shorthand for two other flex-related CSS properties: flex-direction and flex-wrap. For example

```
flex-flow: row wrap;
```

is the same as

```
flex-direction: row;
flex-wrap: wrap;
```

Because flex-flow requires less code, it's the method recommended in this book.

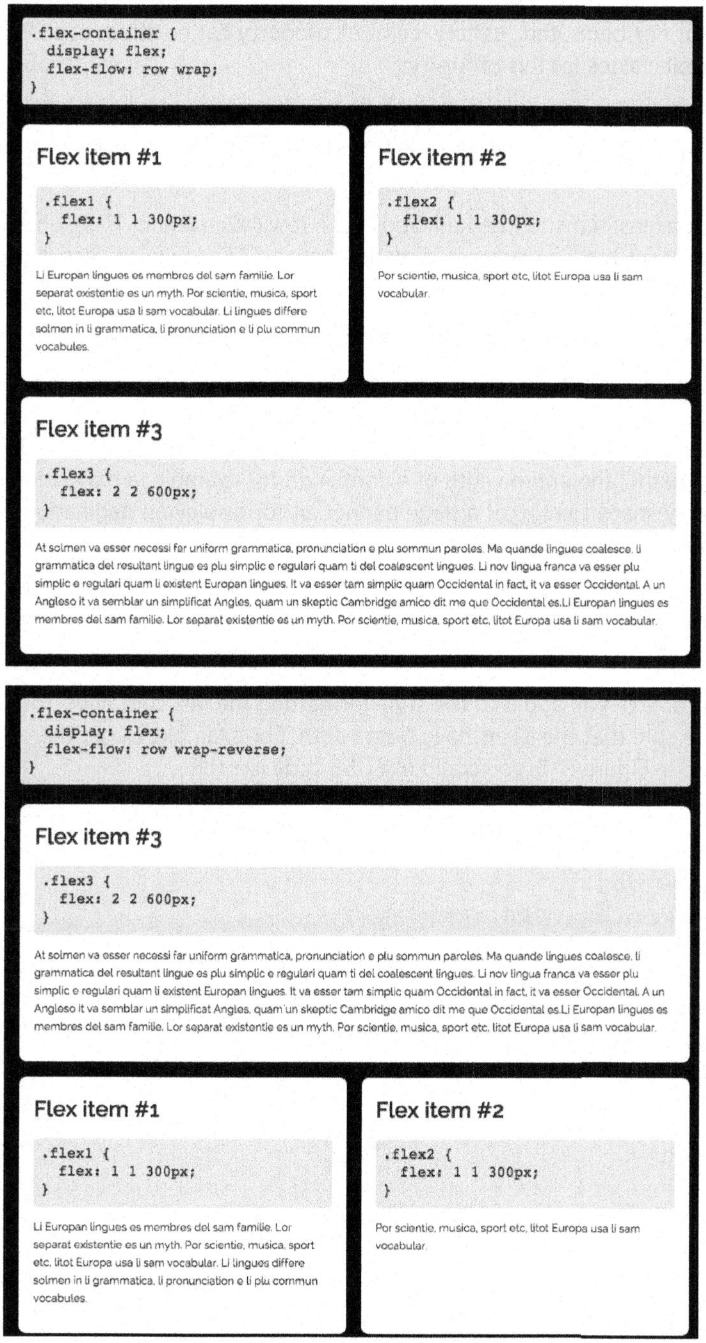

```
.flex-container {
  display: flex;
  flex-flow: row wrap;
}
```

FIGURE 17-4

Flex items that don't fit within the width of a flex container can wrap onto a new row. The wrap *option simply drops the last item down to a new row (top), but the* wrap-reverse *option places the wrapped item above the other items in the row.*

Flex item #1

```
.flex1 {
  flex: 1 1 300px;
}
```

Li Europan lingues es membres del sam familie. Lor separat existentie es un myth. Por scientie, musica, sport etc, litot Europa usa li sam vocabular. Li lingues differe solmen in li grammatica, li pronunciation e li plu commun vocabules.

Flex item #2

```
.flex2 {
  flex: 1 1 300px;
}
```

Por scientie, musica, sport etc, litot Europa usa li sam vocabular.

Flex item #3

```
.flex3 {
  flex: 2 2 600px;
}
```

At solmen va esser necessi far uniform grammatica, pronunciation e plu sommun paroles. Ma quande lingues coalesce, li grammatica del resultant lingue es plu simplic e regulari quam ti del coalescent lingues. Li nov lingua franca va esser plu simplic e regulari quam li existent Europan lingues. It va esser tam simplic quam Occidental in fact, it va esser Occidental. A un Angleso it va semblar un simplificat Angles, quam un skeptic Cambridge amico dit me que Occidental es.Li European lingues es membres del sam familie. Lor separat existentie es un myth. Por scientie, musica, sport etc, litot Europa usa li sam vocabular.

```
.flex-container {
  display: flex;
  flex-flow: row wrap-reverse;
}
```

Flex item #3

```
.flex3 {
  flex: 2 2 600px;
}
```

At solmen va esser necessi far uniform grammatica, pronunciation e plu sommun paroles. Ma quande lingues coalesce, li grammatica del resultant lingue es plu simplic e regulari quam ti del coalescent lingues. Li nov lingua franca va esser plu simplic e regulari quam li existent Europan lingues. It va esser tam simplic quam Occidental in fact, it va esser Occidental. A un Angleso it va semblar un simplificat Angles, quam un skeptic Cambridge amico dit me que Occidental es.Li European lingues es membres del sam familie. Lor separat existentie es un myth. Por scientie, musica, sport etc, litot Europa usa li sam vocabular.

Flex item #1

```
.flex1 {
  flex: 1 1 300px;
}
```

Li Europan lingues es membres del sam familie. Lor separat existentie es un myth. Por scientie, musica, sport etc, litot Europa usa li sam vocabular. Li lingues differe solmen in li grammatica, li pronunciation e li plu commun vocabules.

Flex item #2

```
.flex2 {
  flex: 1 1 300px;
}
```

Por scientie, musica, sport etc, litot Europa usa li sam vocabular.

Justify-content

The justify-content property determines where a browser should place the flex items within the row. This property only works if the flex items have set widths and if the total width of the items is less than the flex container. If you're using flex widths (page 546) for flex items, the justify-content property has no effect at all. There are five possible values for this property:

- flex-start aligns items to the left of the row (#1 in Figure 17-5). Confusingly, if you choose the row-reverse direction (page 533), the flex-start option aligns all items to the left.

- flex-end aligns items to the right side of the row (#2 in Figure 17-5), unless of course you set the row-reverse direction (page 533), in which case it aligns items to the left.

- center centers the flex items in the middle of the container (#3 in Figure 17-5).

- space-between evenly spaces out the flex items, dividing the space between them equally while aligning the leftmost item to the left and the rightmost item to the right (#4 in Figure 17-5). This is a great option for displaying a series of buttons that fill the entire width of a container: for example, a navigation bar that evenly spans the top of a page banner, or for displaying pagination links at the bottom of a blog post.

- space-around evenly distributes the leftover space within the container around all the items adding space to the left- and rightmost items as well (#5 in Figure 17-5).

To use this property you add it to the style formatting the flex container. You also need to make sure that the items have a set width. For example, to get the layout pictured in #5 in Figure 17-5, you could use CSS code like this:

```
.container {
    display: -webkit-flex;
    display: flex;
    -webkit-justify-content: space-around;
    justify-content: space-around;
}
.container div {
    width: 200px;
}
```

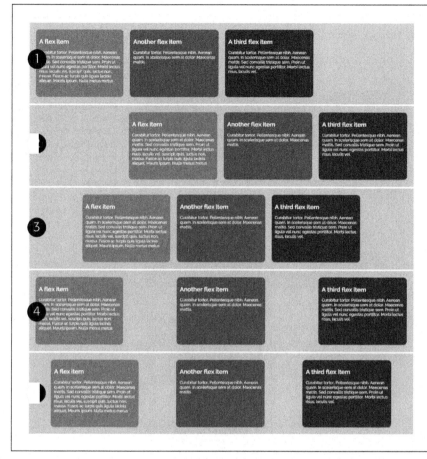

FIGURE 17-5

The justify-content *property is useful when the width of the container is greater than the widths of the items inside. It lets you determine where the items are placed and how they are distributed within the container.*

Align-items

The align-items property determines how flex items of different heights are vertically placed within a flex container. By default, flex items stretch to fit the container, so are all equal heights (see #5 in Figure 17-6). However, there are several other options:

- flex-start aligns the tops of all flex items to the top of the container (#1 in Figure 17-6).

- flex-end aligns the bottoms of all flex items to the bottom of the container (#2 in Figure 17-6).

- center aligns the vertical centers of all flex items to the vertical center of the container (#3 in Figure 17-6).

- `baseline` aligns the baseline of the first element within each flex (#4 in Figure 17-6).

- `stretch` is the normal behavior of flex items. It stretches each item in the container to the same height (#5 in Figure 17-6). This is a particularly difficult effect to achieve using other CSS techniques.

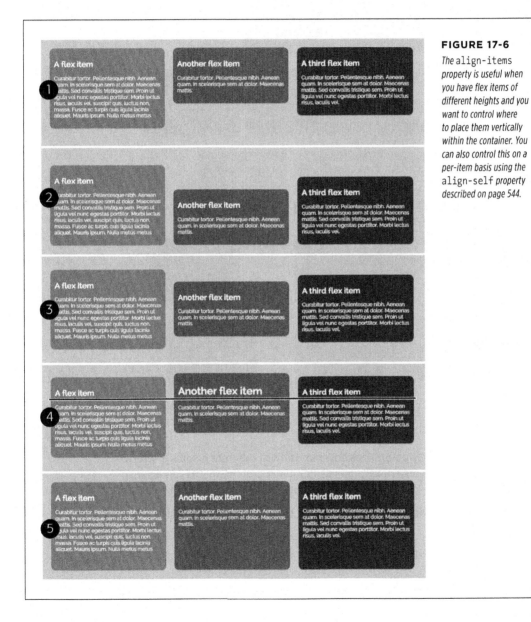

FIGURE 17-6

The `align-items` property is useful when you have flex items of different heights and you want to control where to place them vertically within the container. You can also control this on a per-item basis using the `align-self` property described on page 544.

These settings have a different effect when a flex container's direction is column (page 532). In that case, the align-items property controls where stacked flex items of different widths are placed horizontally within the flex container.

To use the align-items property, add it to the style formatting the flex container. For example, to get the layout pictured in #2 in Figure 17-6, you could use CSS code like this:

```
.container {
    display: -webkit-flex;
    display: flex;
    -webkit-align-items: flex-end;
    align-items: flex-end;
}
```

Align-content

The last property you can apply to a flex container is the align-content property. This property dictates how a browser places flex items that span over multiple lines. This property only works if two conditions are true: First, the flex container must have wrap turned on (page 532); second, the flex container must be taller than the rows of flex items. In other words, there must be additional vertical space inside the container that's greater than the combined heights of the rows of items. This isn't that common a situation, but you may find a time when you'll need it.

This align-content property supports six values:

- flex-start places the rows of flex items at the top of the flex container (#1 in Figure 17-7).

- flex-end places the flex item rows at the bottom of the container (#2 in Figure 17-7).

- center aligns the vertical center of all rows to the vertical center of the container (#3 in Figure 17-7).

- space-between evenly distributes extra vertical space between the rows, placing the top row at the top of the container and the bottom row at the bottom of the container (#4 in Figure 17-7).

- space-around evenly distributes space on the top and bottom of all rows. This adds space above the top row and below the bottom row (#5 in Figure 17-7).

- stretch is the normal behavior of rows of flex items. It stretches each item within a row to match the height of the other items in the row. Note that depending on how much content is in each item, rows may be of different heights. For example, in example #6 in Figure 17-7, the bottom row items have less content than the items in the top row, and are slightly shorter because of that.

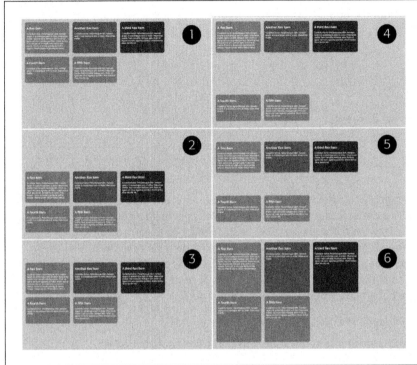

FIGURE 17-7
The align-content *property is only useful if your flex container and flex items meet specific conditions: you've turned on wrapping for the container, you have multiple rows of flex items, and the height of the container is greater than the height of the flex rows. In other words, you won't need this property often.*

To use the align-content property, add it to the style formatting the flex container. You also need to make sure that the flex-flow property (page 532) includes the wrap option, and that the height of the container is greater than the height of the rows of items. For example, to get the layout pictured in #5 in Figure 17-6, you could use CSS code like this:

```
.container {
  display: -webkit-flex;
  display: flex;
  -webkit-flex-flow: row wrap;
  flex-flow: row wrap;
  -webkit-align-content: space-between;
  align-content: space-between;
  height: 600px;
}
```

NOTE   Flex containers are not block-level elements, so some properties don't apply to flex containers or items. For example, the column property (page 409) doesn't apply to flex containers, and the float and clear properties (page 405) don't apply to flex items.

■ Flex Item Properties

Setting properties on the flex container element is just the beginning. There are a handful of additional properties that you can apply to flex items—the direct children of the flex container—which control the order in which those items are displayed, their widths, and how they are aligned within the container.

The Order Property

At the beginning of the Web, content was displayed from the top of the browser window to the bottom, following the same order the HTML appeared within the file. This linear approach was great when all you wanted was to post the text of a scientific paper. As graphic designers got hold of the Web, they started organizing content into rows and columns using the techniques you've see in this book: first tables, and then CSS floats.

However, even though designers have come up with clever ways to break the single-column, top-down flow that's the default presentation of any web page, they've always been trapped by the source order of the HTML in the file. For example, if you want to create a three-column design—a sidebar, a main column of text, and another sidebar—the most common approach is to create three divs and use floats to turn them into columns:

```
<div class="sidebar1">
  <!-- navigation and stuff here -->
</div>
<div class="main">
  <!—the main article, the reason people are here, the most important content
-->
</div>
<div class="sidebar2">
  <!—more (less important) stuff here -->
</div>
```

The problem with this approach is that the first sidebar—which might be stuffed with navigation, notes, and even advertisements—comes first in the source order of the file. That means that as Google's search spiders visit the page, they have to wade through a lot of side content before getting to the heart of the page—the main content in that second div. In addition, screen-readers used by visually impaired web surfers also have to climb over that mass of ancillary content before getting to the main article.

There are some tricky ways around this, like using negative margin values to pull columns into a new order, but they're all hacks that involve some precise CSS. There should be a better way. And indeed there is, thanks to flexbox. The order property lets you assign a numeric value to a flex item which dictates where within the row (or column) this item should appear. The HTML source order doesn't matter at all: You can make the last block of HTML appear first in the row, or the first block last (Figure 17-8, bottom).

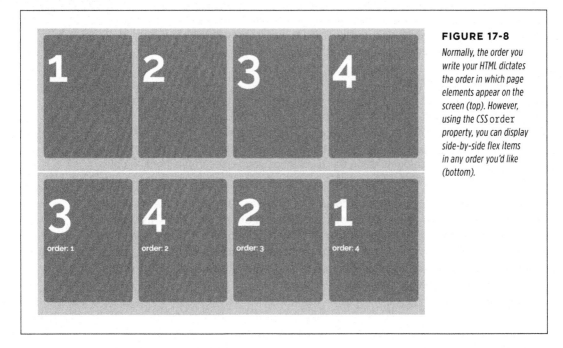

FIGURE 17-8

*Normally, the order you
write your HTML dictates
the order in which page
elements appear on the
screen (top). However,
using the CSS order
property, you can display
side-by-side flex items
in any order you'd like
(bottom).*

For example, say you wanted to recreate the three-column design—a sidebar on the
left, main content in the middle, and a sidebar on the right. You could reorganize
your HTML to be more search-engine and screen-reader friendly by placing the
main content first:

```
<div class="content">
  <div class="main">
    <!—the main article, the reason people are here, the most important con-
tent -->
  </div>
  <div class="sidebar1">
    <!-- navigation and stuff here -->
  </div>
  <div class="sidebar2">
    <!—more (less important) stuff here -->
  </div>
</div>
```

You could then turn the outer div—the "content" div here—into a flex container and use the order property to arrange the divs inside into any order on the page you'd like:

```
.content {
    display: -webkit-flex;
    display: flex;
}
.sidebar1 {
  -webkit-order: 1;
  order: 1;
}
.main {
  -webkit-order: 2;
  order: 2;
}
.sidebar2 {
  -webkit-order: 3;
  order: 3;
}
```

Now, even though the main div is listed first in the HTML, it appears between the two sidebars, while the first sidebar appears at the left side of the flex container. Simple!

The numbers you use for the order property work similarly to the z-index value (page 439). That is, you don't need to use the numbers 1, 2, or 3. A browser will simply arrange the items in order from smallest number to largest. For example, in the above example, you could replace the 1, 2, and 3 with 10, 20, and 30 or 5, 15, and 60. For sanity's sake, however, you should use an easy-to-understand system; ordering those items using 1, 2, 3, 4, and so on makes the most sense.

However, sometimes you might want to just move one column to the far left or far right of a row. In that case, you can simply set the order on that particular item, but not on any others. For example, you could simplify the above code and still move the first sidebar to the far left like this:

```
.content {
    display: -webkit-flex;
    display: flex;
}
.sidebar1 {
  -webkit-order: -1;
  order: -1;
}
```

Using -1 moves the item to the left side of the flex container, before all of the other rows. Conversely, you could move that same sidebar to the far right by setting its order number to 1, while leaving the other elements' order properties unset.

> **NOTE** When setting the flex container's flex direction to column, the order property will adjust how the flex items stack from top to bottom: A flex item with a lower order number will appear above a flex item with a larger order number. In addition, there are direction options for column-reverse and row-reverse that place the rows and columns in reverse order, so in those cases you need to adjust your numbers to account for the fact that those containers are listed in reverse order.

Align-self

The align-self property works just like the align-items property used for flex containers. However, whereas align-items applies to all the flex items within a container, align-self applies to just the individual flex item. You apply the property to an item (not the container) and it overrides any value for the align-items property. In other words, you could align all of the flex items inside a container to the top of the container, but have just a single item align to the bottom.

The possible values for align-self are the same as align-items (see page 537) and produce the same effect, but just for individual flex items (see Figure 17-9).

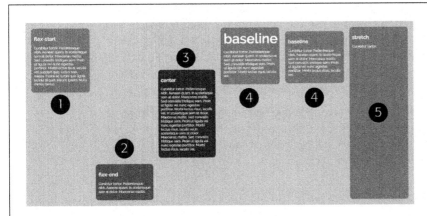

FIGURE 17-9

The align-self *property is similar to the* align-items *property, but only applies to individual flex items. In addition, the* baseline *option only makes sense if you have more than one item whose* align-self *property is* baseline *(#4).*

Mini-Tutorial: Auto Margins for Flex Items

Here's another amazing feature of flex items: Flex item margins don't collapse. That may not sound so amazing at first, but this handy property means you can use auto margin settings to add margins that adjust to the available space. You've seen something similar when you learned how to use margin: 0 auto; to center a web page on page 30.

To best understand how auto margins work and why they're so amazing, follow this brief tutorial. To get started, download the tutorial files located on this book's companion website at *https://github.com/sawmac/css_mm_4e*.

1. **In your text editor, open the file** *17→nav-bar→nav-bar.html.*

   This is a basic HTML file. It has a head and a body, and some simple HTML representing a banner. There's already a style sheet that contains basic styling, so the page looks like the top image in Figure 17-10. The HTML you're interested in is the following:

   ```
   <div class="banner">
       <p class="logo">Our Company</p>
       <a href="#">Our Clients</a>
       <a href="#" class="highlight">About Us</a>
       <a href="#">Careers</a>
   </div>
   ```

   There's a div, inside of which is a paragraph and three links. First, turn the div into a flex container.

2. **In the page's** head **section, there's an empty set of** `<style>` **tags. Click between the opening and closing** `<style>` **tags and add one style:**

   ```
   .banner {
      display: -webkit-flex;
      display: flex;
   }
   ```

   This turns the banner div into a flex container, and turns the paragraph and links inside it into flex items. If you save and preview the page now, it'll look like the second-from-top image in Figure 17-10. The navigation buttons are really tall, because the normal behavior of flex items is to grow until all items are the same height. You can change that and align the buttons to the bottom at the same time using the `align-items` property.

3. **Update the** `.banner` **style to include the both the WebKit and un-prefixed versions of the** `align-items` **property:**

   ```
   .banner {
      display: -webkit-flex;
      display: flex;
      -webkit-align-items: flex-end;
      align-items: flex-end;
   }
   ```

   The `flex-end` value (page 537) aligns the bottom of the flex items with the bottom of the flex container. The navigation bar looks like the image third from the top in Figure 17-10. Now, you could achieve something similar to this by floating the paragraph with the company name in it, but you'd have to do a lot of tricky

CSS to get those buttons aligned to the bottom like that. With flexbox, it's just a single property.

Finally, you'll use an auto margin to quickly achieve a common design requirement—aligning the company logo to the left of the banner and the navigation buttons to the right.

4. **Add one more style to the internal style sheet on the page. The finished style should look like this (additions in bold):**

```
<style>
.banner {
    display: -webkit-flex;
    display: flex;
    -webkit-align-items: flex-end;
    align-items: flex-end;
}
.logo {
    margin-right: auto;
}
</style>
```

With flex items, an auto margin tells the browser to automatically set the margin size based on the available space. In this case, the logo and three nav buttons don't fill the entire banner, so giving the logo a right margin of auto tells the browser to use whatever empty space is available inside the banner and place it to the right of "Our Company." This has the effect of pushing the navigation buttons all the way to the other side of the banner. Amazing!

The finished banner should look like the bottom image in Figure 17-10. You could have achieved the same effect by assigning the auto value to the first button's left margin. That would have added all the available space to the left of that first button, pushing all the other buttons the right.

NOTE For a more advanced design that uses flexbox and media queries to create a mobile-friendly navigation bar, look in the tutorial files: *17_finished→nav-bar-responsive→nav-bar.html.*

Flex

You can do a lot with the basic properties you've already learned. However, the flex property is what gives the flexbox its flexibility. This property is the key to controlling the width of flex items; it lets you easily create columns that "flex," or change width to match the size of their container, even when the size is unknown or dynamic. In this way, the flex property can let you create responsive web designs, like the ones you read about in Chapter 15, in a fraction of the time, and with far less math.

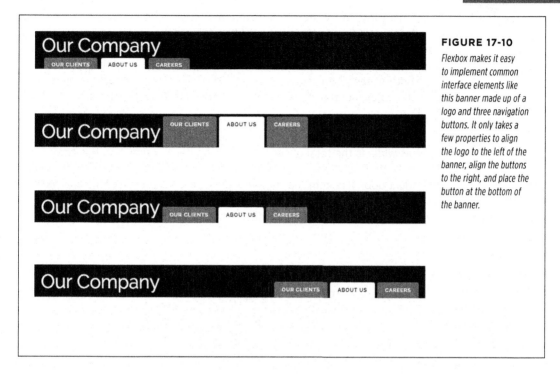

FIGURE 17-10

Flexbox makes it easy to implement common interface elements like this banner made up of a logo and three navigation buttons. It only takes a few properties to align the logo to the left of the banner, align the buttons to the right, and place the button at the bottom of the banner.

Unfortunately, the flex property can be a bit confusing, since it's really a shorthand property that combines three other flex properties. This chapter will take each property one at a time to build your knowledge gradually.

The first value you supply to flex is a number that indicates the relative width of that flex item. For example, if you have three divs inside a flex container, you can set each of their flex values to 1 to make them all the same width:

```
.container {
   display: -webkit-flex;
   display: flex;
}
.container div {
  -webkit-flex: 1;
  flex: 1;
}
```

Since all three divs have the same value, they will be the same width as each other (Figure 17-11, top). The number you supply for the flex value is simply a relative unit, not an absolute measure. In the top example, each flex item is about 33% the width of the container. However, if one of those divs has a flex value of 2, then the widths change (Figure 17-11, middle). The two divs on the left are each one unit, while the one on the right is two units. In other words, it's twice as wide as the other divs, so it now takes up half of the space in the flex container.

The actual width of the flex item, therefore, depends on both the flex value you provide in your CSS and the number of flex items in the container. For example, in the top and bottom images in Figure 17-11, the flex items all have a flex value of 1. However, in the top example, each item takes up around 33% of the container, and in the bottom each item takes up around 50% of the container width. They have the same flex value, but the number of items dictates the exact width of each.

The second value you can set for the flex property is also a number, but it represents the flex-shrink property. This property comes into play when the container is not as wide as the total of the widths of the items inside it. In this case, flex-shrink controls how narrow a flex item can be, or how much it can shrink, and it's dependent upon flex items having set widths, which is the job of the final value of the flex property. The next section will discuss that value first, and then return to how the flex-shrink property works.

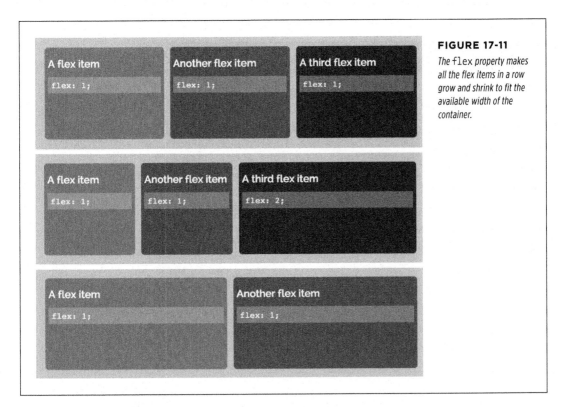

FIGURE 17-11

The flex property makes all the flex items in a row grow and shrink to fit the available width of the container.

NOTE For examples of great uses for flexbox check out the "Solved by Flexbox" site at *http://philipwalton.github.io/solved-by-flexbox/*.

The last value is the flex-basis property, which sets a base width for a flex item. You can use an absolute value like 100px or 5em, or a percentage value like 50%. You can think of the flex-basis value as a kind of minimum width for a flex item. When you set the flex-basis value, it sets a width for that item, but depending on other flex settings, the flex item may grow larger (or smaller) than the flex-basis value.

For example, in the top image in Figure 17-12, the flex-basis value for each item is 250px. The first value is 0—that's the value that determines how much the item flexes or grows. When it's set to 0, it doesn't grow, so the item's width matches the flex-basis value of 250 pixels.

However, whenever you provide a number greater than 0 for that first value, the entire width of the row will be filled. So in the middle image in Figure 17-12, although the flex-basis value for each item is 250px, the actual width of the items varies, because the flex-grow values are different—1, 2, and 4, respectively.

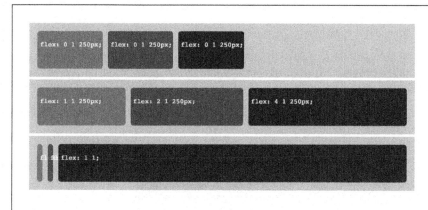

FIGURE 17-12

If you don't set a flex-basis value, and you set the flex-grow value to 0, then the item shrinks to as thin as it can be. For example, the first two items in the bottom image are set to flex: 0 1;. *There's no minimum width set, and there's no* flex-grow *value, so they shrink. The last item on the right, however, has a flex value of 1, so it's flexible, and grows to fill the remaining space available in the row.*

Digging into the Math

So how exactly does the browser figure out how wide a flex item should be when both a flex-grow and flex-basis value are set? Strap in, 'cause it's time to do a bit of math. It isn't all that difficult, but you will have to wade through a bunch of addition, subtraction, division, and multiplication.

Take a look at Figure 17-13. It's a single flex container holding three flex items. Because each item has a flex-grow property value greater than 0, those items will grow to fill the entire width of the container, which is 1000 pixels wide. They also have different flex-basis values: 300, 200, and 100 pixels. Start by totaling those minimum widths:

300 + 200 + 100 = 600

This value, 600, is the total amount of space the items want to take up. However, the container is wider than that—it's 1000 pixels wide. So you can determine how much extra space remains by subtracting the item widths from the container width:

1000 - 600 = 400

In other words, the browser has 400 pixels of extra space that it has to figure out what to do with. So, it looks at the various flex-grow values—1, 3, and 4—and determines how to divide the remaining space. 1 + 3 + 4 is 8, so the first item should get 1/8 of the leftover space. 1/8 of 400 (which is the same as 400/8) is 50. The first item's width is the total of its flex-basis value and its share of the leftover space:

300 + 50 = 350 pixels

The second item should get 3/8 of the remaining space added to its flex-basis value:

200 + (50 * 3) = 350 pixels

And the last item receives ½ of the 400 pixel leftovers, so its width is

100 + 200 = 300 pixels

There is some method to all of this math madness, and as you can see, there's a lot of work the browser has to do to set the width of flex items. You'll find some simple rules of thumb for choosing values for the flex property on page 553.

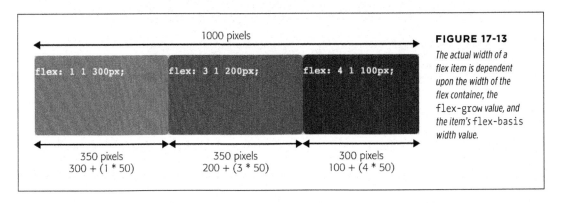

FIGURE 17-13

The actual width of a flex item is dependent upon the width of the flex container, the flex-grow value, and the item's flex-basis width value.

Returning to the Flex-Shrink Property

The second value for the flex property determines how much a flex item may shrink if the total of the widths of the items is wider than the container. This value is only important if the container has the nowrap setting (page 552), so that all of the items must sit next to each other in a single row.

For example, the flex containers for the examples pictured in Figure 17-14 are 1000 pixels wide. Because the flex-basis value of each item is 400 pixels (totaling 1200 pixels for all three), they can't fit within the container without shrinking. In the first row, the items all share the same flex-shrink value: 1. This means they'll all shrink (decrease in width) by the same amounts.

Understanding Flex Default Values

If you don't set the `flex` property on flex items within a flex container, browsers provide a default setting, which is the equivalent of:

```
flex: 0 1 auto;
```

With this setting, the width of each flex item is automatically determined by the content inside it. A flex item with a lot of text and pictures will be a lot wider than an item with just two words.

However, browsers apply different defaults when you explicitly assign the `flex` property to an item. The CSS `flex` property is actually shorthand for three other properties: `flex-grow`, `flex-shrink`, and `flex-basis`.

So the single line of code `flex: 1 1 400px;` is the same as

```
flex-grow: 1;
flex-shrink: 1;
flex-basis: 400px;
```

When you leave out the `flex-shrink` and `flex-basis` values—for example, `flex: 1;`—the browser assigns a default value of 1 to `flex-shrink`, but sets the default value of `flex-basis` to 0%. In other words, `flex: 1;` is the equivalent of:

```
flex-grow: 1;
flex-shrink: 1;
flex-basis: 0%;
```

These settings are very different from the default values a browser applies if you simply omit `flex` entirely. By setting the `flex-basis` to 0%, the width of each flex item is completely dictated by the `flex-grow` property: In other words, the amount of content inside each flex item has no effect on how wide the various items are.

For more information on the ins and outs of the flexbox (technically called the Flex Layout Box Module), visit the W3C: *http://dev.w3.org/csswg/css-flexbox/*.

```
flex-flow: row nowrap
```

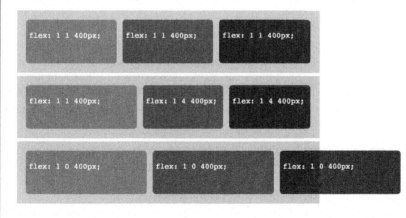

FIGURE 17-14

If the `flex-shrink` value is 0, and the container's wrap setting is `nowrap`, then the flex items in a row will extend outside the container (bottom). You probably want to avoid this predicament.

However, in the middle row in Figure 17-14, the first item has a `flex-shrink` value of 1, while the other two have flex-shrink values of 4. So the items aren't all the same widths. Unlike `flex-grow`, where the bigger the number the wider the item can be, the flex-shrink value determines how much *narrower* an item can become in rela-tion to other items in the same row. This means the larger the flex-shrink value, the narrower an item is allowed to be. So, in the middle row in Figure 17-14, two items on the right are narrower, because their flex-shrink values are larger.

The flex-shrink value adds another layer of complexity in trying to picture how flex items work. Because of this, and because it has no effect when the flex container allows items to wrap, you can simply use a flex-shrink value of 1 most of the time.

NOTE The flex-shrink property only comes into play when the container doesn't let items wrap into additional rows. In other words, when its flex-flow property is set like this:

```
.container {
    display: flex;
    flex-flow: row nowrap;
}
```

if the container allows wrapping, a flex item simply drops down to the next row, when it can no longer sit next to other items in a single row (see Figure 17-15).

Wrapping Flex Items

The real value of the flex-basis property comes into play when you set a flex container to allow wrapping:

```
.container {
    display: -webkit-flex;
    display: flex;
    -webkit-flex-flow: row wrap;
    flex-flow: row wrap;
}
```

When wrapping is enabled, flex items will drop to another row when they cannot fit within the container. For example, imagine you have a flex container with a width of 1000 pixels, and you have three flex items, each with a flex-basis of 400. Be-cause 400 + 400 + 400 is more than 1000 pixels, the three flex items can't all fit. However, since 400 + 400 is less than 1000 pixels, two of the items can fit side by side in a single row.

In this case, the browser will display the first two items in a single row and wrap the third item onto its own row (Figure 17-15, top). Because the three items each have a flex-grow property, they will fill the entire row, so the bottom item, which sits by itself, will stretch to fill the entire width of the container.

If the container shrinks so that no flex items can fit side by side, the browser then places each flex item on its own row (Figure 17-15, bottom).

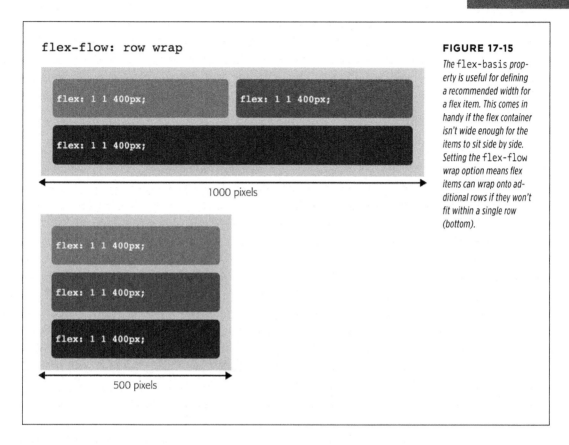

`flex-flow: row wrap`

FIGURE 17-15

The flex-basis prop-
erty is useful for defining
a recommended width for
a flex item. This comes in
handy if the flex container
isn't wide enough for the
items to sit side by side.
Setting the flex-flow
wrap option means flex
items can wrap onto ad-
ditional rows if they won't
fit within a single row
(bottom).

The Bottom Line

As you can see, there are a lot of things to keep track of when you begin combining
all three values of the flex property. They each interact in different ways, depending
upon the width of the container, and trying to keep track of every possible combination can be mind-bending. However, here are a few things that can help you guide
your understanding of when to use each property:

- Fit all flex items in a single row. If you simply want to create a row of items
  of various widths, set the flex container to not wrap and supply only a single
  value to the flex property. For example, say you have two sidebars and a main
  content item in a row. You want the main content area to take up half of the
  available width of the container, and each sidebar to take up 25%. You could
  simply do something like this:

```css
.container {
  display: -webkit-flex;
  display: flex;
  -webkit-flex-flow: row nowrap;
  flex-flow: row nowrap;
}
.sidebar1 {
  -webkit-flex: 1;
  flex: 1;
}
.sidebar2 {
  -webkit-flex: 1;
  flex: 1;
}
.main {
  -webkit-flex: 2;
  flex: 2;
}
```

You don't need to supply flex-shrink or flex-basis values at all, since you simply want a series of flexible containers whose widths stay in the same proportion to each other.

- Keep row proportions, but wrap when the container gets too small to display the items side by side. If you want the flex items to wrap onto new rows when their content can no longer be displayed in a single row, then set the wrap option on the container and the flex-basis value to a specific unit that matches the flex-grow ratios:

```css
.container {
  display: -webkit-flex;
  display: flex;
  -webkit-flex-flow: row wrap;
  flex-flow: row wrap;
}
.sidebar1 {
  -webkit-flex: 1 1 100px;
  flex: 1 1 100px;
}
.sidebar2 {
  -webkit-flex: 1 1 100px;
  flex: 1 1 100px;
}
.main {
  -webkit-flex: 2 1 200px;
  flex: 2 1 200px;
}
```

To make sure the flex items retain the same proportional widths dictated by the flex-grow property, you should set flex-basis values that match the flex-grow proportions. For example, in the above code there are three flex items. They have flex-grow values of 1, 1, and 2. So set their flex-basis values using the same proportions: 100px, 100px, and 200px, for example. The exact values you use will depend on the browser width at which you want the items to wrap. Given the code above, the flex container would have to get below 400 pixels before the items would wrap.

The flex-grow property is used to allocate leftover space once the widths of the flex items are totaled (see the box on page 549). So if you don't use flex-basis values that match the proportions of the flex-grow properties, you'll end up with some unexpected results. For example, in the bottom row in Figure 17-16, the middle item has a flex-grow value of 2. However, it's not twice as wide as either of the other items. That's because its flex-basis value is the same as those of the other two items—100px. So even though that item gets more of the leftover space added to its width than the other items, it simply adds that space to its 100-pixel width—the same width shared by the other items.

- Set flex-basis values to act as breakpoints to determine when items wrap onto new rows. You can use the flex-basis value as a way to simulate the breakpoints you learned about for responsive design on page 463. For example, if you have three items that you'd like to display side by side when the page is greater than 600 pixels wide, you could set the flex-basis for each item to 200px. When the browser gets narrower than 600 pixels, then the first and second items will sit side by side, while the third item drops to its own row. When the browser window is narrower than 400 pixels, each item will sit on its own row, creating three stacked rows.

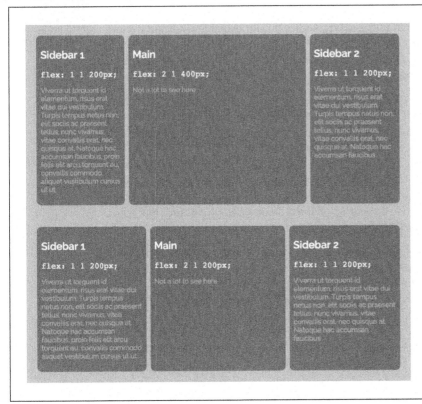

FIGURE 17-16

To keep flex items proportionally sized to each other, make sure your flex-basis *values— the base widths for your flex items—share the same proportions as their* flex-grow *values (top). If they don't, then you won't be able to accurately set consistent proportions for the width of your flex items in a row, as shown here in the bottom row.*

Tutorial: Build a Flexbox Layout

In this tutorial, you'll take a linear layout that stacks one div on top of another (Figure 17-17, left) and create columns using flexbox (Figure 17-17, right). In addition, you'll create a few visual effects that are extremely easy with flexbox but nearly impossible with other CSS techniques.

To get started, download the tutorial files located on this book's companion website at *https://github.com/sawmac/css_mm_4e*.

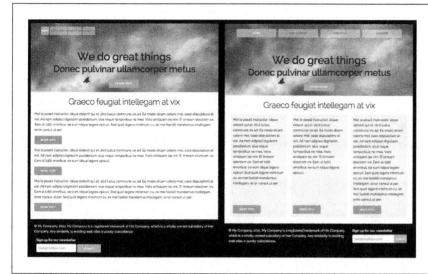

FIGURE 17-17

You can create multi-column layouts without using any floats with flexbox.

Styling the Navigation Bar

This design consists of three flex containers—one for the navigation button, one for the main content area, and one for the footer (Figure 17-18). Each container will hold a variable number of flex items: four buttons in the navigation bar, three content boxes in the main area, and two regions in the footer. The first step is create those flex containers.

1. **In your text editor, open the file *17→flexbox-layout→css→custom.css*.**

    This is an empty CSS file, to which you'll add the CSS for flexbox. The *index.html* page has two style sheets linked to it: this empty file and a file named *base.css*, which contains a lot of styling information to make the basic page elements look good.

    First, you'll set up the main flex containers.

2. **In the *custom.css* file add a group selector rule:**

    ```
    .nav, .boxes, .footer {
      display: -webkit-flex;
      display: flex;
      -webkit-flex-flow: row wrap;
      flex-flow: row wrap;
    }
    ```

    Each of those class names corresponds to a class that is applied to the three regions outlined in Figure 17-18. This basic rule turns those divs into flex containers and sets them up to display as a row of flex items that can wrap into additional rows. The –webkit vendor prefix is included so these styles will work in Safari as well as Chrome, Firefox, Opera, and Internet Explorer 11.

Next, you'll do something that's usually difficult to achieve. You'll spread out the navigation buttons evenly so that the leftmost button is on the left side of its container, the rightmost button touches the right side of the container, and the other two buttons are distributed evenly between.

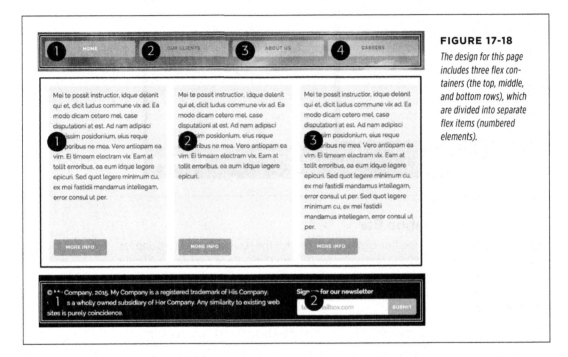

FIGURE 17-18

The design for this page includes three flex containers (the top, middle, and bottom rows), which are divided into separate flex items (numbered elements).

3. **Add another style following the one you added in the last step:**

```
.nav {
  -webkit-justify-content: space-between;
  justify-content: space-between;
}
```

The justify-content property applied to the flex container controls how the flex items are placed inside the container. In this case, the space-between value distributes all the flex items inside it evenly across the container. This is really cool, and usually difficult to do using other CSS techniques.

You can also give those buttons flexible widths by giving them percentage width values, so try that next.

4. **Style the links by adding one more style to the style sheet:**

```
.nav a {
  width: 23%;
}
```

This style makes each link take up 23% of the flex container's width. As the container shrinks, the buttons get narrower. The remaining space is evenly distributed between each button, thanks to the style you added in the previous step.

There you have it. A navigation bar made up of evenly distributed, variable-width buttons, and all done without floats or other difficult CSS.

Adding Three Columns

Now it's time to tackle the main content area. Currently, there are three divs, each containing a More Info button, stacked on top of each other. By adding a flex property, you can place them side by side. Remember that in step 1 on page 559, you turned the div that holds these three divs into a flex container. Now you'll turn the divs into flex items.

1. **At the bottom of the custom.css file add the following rule:**

```
.boxes div {
  -webkit-flex: 1 1 250px;
  flex: 1 1 250px;
}
```

This makes each of the divs take up an equal area of their flex container. They're each the same width, but currently they touch each other, and it's a bit hard to read that way (and the fact that the text is in Latin doesn't help either). The design should now look like the top image in Figure 17-19. To make the columns easier to read, you'll add a background color and a bit of space.

2. **Edit the style you added in the last step by adding four more properties to it (additions are in bold):**

```
.boxes div {
  -webkit-flex: 1 1 250px;
  flex: 1 1 250px;
  margin: 10px;
  border-radius: 5px;
  padding: 10px 10px 0 10px;
  background-color: rgba(0,0,0,.1);
}
```

The columns should now look like the middle image in Figure 17-19. Notice how each of the columns are the same height, even though the content inside them is of different lengths. This is another magic flexbox moment: By default, columns in a row are all the same height. That's really hard to do with regular CSS, and some designers even resort to using JavaScript to get this effect.

However, the buttons, which are so prominent in the design, are staggered at different vertical positions, which is distracting. It would be great if there were a way to force those buttons to the bottom of each column. Thanks to flexbox, there is!

Margins work slightly differently with flex items. For example, you can add auto margin to the top of each button to force it down to the bottom of its column. However, you can only use this margin magic on flex items. At this point, only the columns themselves are flex items; the buttons and paragraphs inside are regular elements.

Fortunately, the flexbox model lets you assign more than one role to a flex item. The columns can be flex items within their outer container (the row), *and* they can be flex containers holding flex items (the paragraph and button) inside them.

3. **Add four more lines of code to the** .boxes div **style:**

```
.boxes div {
  -webkit-flex: 1 1 250px;
  flex: 1 1 250px;
  margin: 10px;
  border-radius: 5px;
  padding: 10px 10px 0 10px;
  background-color: rgba(0,0,0,.2);
  display: -webkit-flex;
  display: flex;
  -webkit-flex-flow: column;
  flex-flow: column;
}
```

This defines the divs as flex containers, and it sets the flow direction of the flex items inside to column, which stacks the paragraph and buttons on top of each other. You may be saying to yourself, "Hey self, they're already stacked on top of each other, why do I need to do this?" Flex items can take advantage of auto margins, so you can force those buttons to the bottom of each div.

4. **Add another style after the** .boxes **div rule:**

```
.boxes .more {
  margin-top: auto;
}
```

Each button has the class of more applied to it, so this selector selects the buttons inside the columns. The top margin is set to auto, which tells the browser to automatically add whatever empty space is left inside the flex item above the top of the button. This auto-margin has the effect of pushing all of the buttons to the bottom of each column (Figure 17-19, bottom).

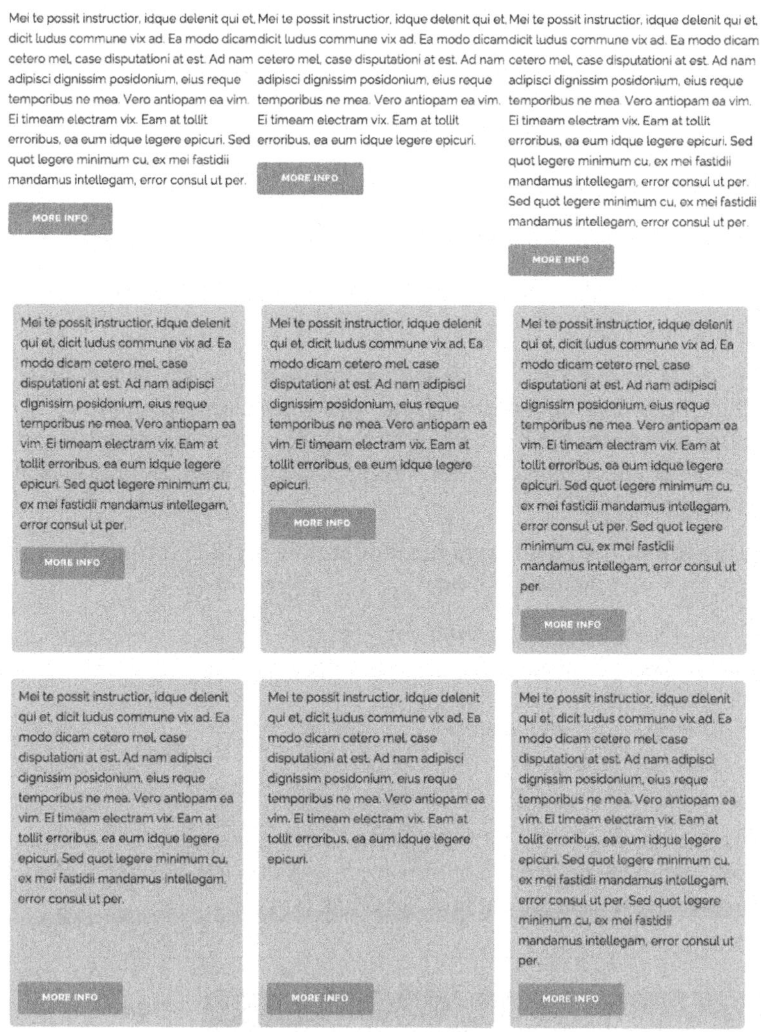

Mei te possit instructior, idque delenit qui et, dicit ludus commune vix ad. Ea modo dicam cetero mel, case disputationi at est. Ad nam adipisci dignissim posidonium, eius reque temporibus ne mea. Vero antiopam ea vim. Ei timeam electram vix. Eam at tollit erroribus, ea eum idque legere epicuri. Sed quot legere minimum cu, ex mei fastidii mandamus intellegam, error consul ut per.

MORE INFO

Mei te possit instructior, idque delenit qui et, dicit ludus commune vix ad. Ea modo dicam cetero mel, case disputationi at est. Ad nam adipisci dignissim posidonium, eius reque temporibus ne mea. Vero antiopam ea vim. Ei timeam electram vix. Eam at tollit erroribus, ea eum idque legere epicuri.

MORE INFO

Mei te possit instructior, idque delenit qui et, dicit ludus commune vix ad. Ea modo dicam cetero mel, case disputationi at est. Ad nam adipisci dignissim posidonium, eius reque temporibus ne mea. Vero antiopam ea vim. Ei timeam electram vix. Eam at tollit erroribus, ea eum idque legere epicuri. Sed quot legere minimum cu, ex mei fastidii mandamus intellegam, error consul ut per. Sed quot legere minimum cu, ex mei fastidii mandamus intellegam, error consul ut per.

MORE INFO

Mei te possit instructior, idque delenit qui et, dicit ludus commune vix ad. Ea modo dicam cetero mel, case disputationi at est. Ad nam adipisci dignissim posidonium, eius reque temporibus ne mea, Vero antiopam ea vim. Ei timeam electram vix. Eam at tollit erroribus, ea eum idque legere epicuri. Sed quot legere minimum cu, ex mei fastidii mandamus intellegam, error consul ut per.

MORE INFO

Mei te possit instructior, idque delenit qui et, dicit ludus commune vix ad. Ea modo dicam cetero mel, case disputationi at est. Ad nam adipisci dignissim posidonium, eius reque temporibus ne mea. Vero antiopam ea vim. Ei timeam electram vix. Eam at tollit erroribus, ea eum idque legere epicuri.

MORE INFO

Mei te possit instructior, idque delenit qui et, dicit ludus commune vix ad. Ea modo dicam cetero mel, case disputationi at est. Ad nam adipisci dignissim posidonium, eius reque temporibus ne mea. Vero antiopam ea vim. Ei timeam electram vix. Eam at tollit erroribus, ea eum idque legere epicuri. Sed quot legere minimum cu, ex mei fastidii mandamus intellegam, error consul ut per. Sed quot legere minimum cu, ex mei fastidii mandamus intellegam, error consul ut per.

MORE INFO

Mei te possit instructior, idque delenit qui et, dicit ludus commune vix ad. Ea modo dicam cetero mel, case disputationi at est. Ad nam adipisci dignissim posidonium, eius reque temporibus ne mea. Vero antiopam ea vim. Ei timeam electram vix. Eam at tollit erroribus, ea eum idque legere epicuri. Sed quot legere minimum cu, ex mei fastidii mandamus intellegam, error consul ut per.

MORE INFO

Mei te possit instructior, idque delenit qui et, dicit ludus commune vix ad. Ea modo dicam cetero mel, case disputationi at est. Ad nam adipisci dignissim posidonium, eius reque temporibus ne mea. Vero antiopam ea vim. Ei timeam electram vix. Eam at tollit erroribus, ea eum idque legere epicuri.

MORE INFO

Mei te possit instructior, idque delenit qui et, dicit ludus commune vix ad. Ea modo dicam cetero mel, case disputationi at est. Ad nam adipisci dignissim posidonium, eius reque temporibus ne mea. Vero antiopam ea vim. Ei timeam electram vix. Eam at tollit erroribus, ea eum idque legere epicuri. Sed quot legere minimum cu, ex mei fastidii mandamus intellegam, error consul ut per.

MORE INFO

FIGURE 17-19

Flex items have many virtues: Columns are, by default, the same height. That's normally very tricky to manage. In addition, you can distribute empty space automatically so that the browser can perform some magic—like aligning the buttons to the bottom of each column (bottom).

Formatting the Footer

You've worked your way to the bottom of this page. There's just the footer left to format. In the footer, there's a copyright notice and a signup form. This content would look good divided into two columns.

1. **Add two new styles to the bottom of the *custom.css* file:**

```
.footer .copyright {
  -webkit-flex: 2 1 500px;
  flex: 2 1 500px;
  margin-right: 30px;
}

.footer .signup {
  -webkit-flex: 1 1 250px;
  flex: 1 1 250px;
}
```

These styles set the copyright area to be around twice as wide as the signup form. A bit of right-margin helps to push the signup form away from the copyright notice (Figure 17-20, top).

The last thing to do is to organize the form elements. It would be great if the Submit button sat right next to the text field, perfectly aligned with it. You can do that with flexbox, but first you must turn the <form> tag into a flex container. Then, all of the elements inside—the label, the text field, and the button—can act like flex items.

2. **At the top of the *custom.css* file, update the style to include the selector** .footer form **(changes in bold):**

```
.nav, .boxes, .footer, .footer form {
  display: -webkit-flex;
  display: flex;
  -webkit-flex-flow: row wrap;
  flex-flow: row wrap;
}
```

This selector makes the form inside the footer a flex container, and turns the label, the text field, and the button inside the form into flex items. Next, you'll make the label span the entire width of the form.

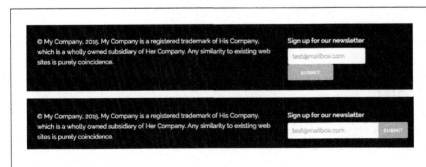

FIGURE 17-20

Using flexbox, it's easy to align form fields, like the text field and submit button in the bottom image. To see other great examples of using flexbox with forms, visit http:// philipwalton.github.io/ solved-by-flexbox/demos/ input-add-ons/.

3. **Add a style to the end of the *custom.css* file to make the label fill the column:**

```
.signup label {
  width: 100%;
}
```

In the previous step, you turned the form into a flex container that's set to wrap. Setting the width of the label in this rule to 100% forces the two input fields to wrap to another row. However, the text field and button are not sitting side by side. A couple of styles will fix that.

4. **Add two more rules to the end of the *custom.css* style sheet:**

```
.signup input[type="email"] {
  border-radius: 4px 0 0 4px;
  -webkit-flex: 1;
  flex: 1;
}
.signup input[type="submit"] {
  border-radius: 0 4px 4px 0;
  padding: 0 10px;
}
```

These rules use attribute selectors (page 59) to identify the text field for receiving the user's email address and the button for submitting the form. Setting the email field's flex value to 1 means the field grows to fill all the available space that's not occupied by the Submit button.

In addition, by using `border-radius` and rounding only the left corners of the text field and the right corners of the Submit button, you've created what looks like a unified form widget. The result looks like the bottom image in Figure 17-20.

Changing the Navigation Bar for Mobile

Thanks to the flexibility of flex items, the design you've created works really well at different browser widths. Go ahead and save the *custom.css* file; open the *index.html* file and resize the browser window. You'll see that the design shrinks to fit the browser window: The three columns in the middle of the page turn into two columns, and eventually one column.

The last thing worth adding is a simple media query to convert the navigation bar from side-by-side buttons to stacked buttons at small screen sizes.

1. **At the bottom of the *custom.css* file, add a media query:**

```
@media (max-width: 500px) {


}
```

This media query works when the page is 500 pixels wide or less. In other words, the styles you place inside it will apply only to devices whose screens are narrower than 501 pixels.

Inside this media query, add a style to change how the flex items (the nav buttons) are displayed inside the navigation bar.

2. **Add the following style to the media query you added in the last step (additions are in bold):**

```
@media (max-width: 500px) {
  .nav {
    -webkit-flex-flow: column;
    flex-flow: column;
  }
}
```

This changes the flow direction of the flex items. Instead of sitting next to each other in a row, the navigation buttons will sit one on top of the other in a column.

Finally, you can make the buttons fill the container.

3. **Add one last style to the media query so it looks like this:**

```
@media (max-width: 500px) {
  .nav {
    -webkit-flex-flow: column;
    flex-flow: column;
  }
  .nav a {
    width: 100%;
    margin-bottom: 2px;
  }
}
```

This last style forces each link to fill the width of the flex container. It also adds a bit of space below each link to add visual separation.

4. **Save the *custom.css* file and preview the *index.html* file in a browser. Resize the browser, first dragging it to fill your screen, and then dragging it to make it narrower.**

See how the design changes as you narrow the browser window (Figure 17-21)? First, at full width (#1) the main content area has three columns, and the footer has two. Then, at a slightly narrower size, the three columns turn into two, and the footer elements stack on top of each other (#2). Finally, at a width of less than 500 pixels, all the content appears in a single column, and the navigation bar turns into a series of stacked buttons (#3).

Flexbox is a fun and exciting addition to CSS. It makes many previously difficult (or almost impossible) layout chores simple. It simplifies responsive design and reduces the math you need to create proportionally designed columns. Its biggest drawback is that not all browsers understand the flexbox syntax, and simply ignore flex properties. However, with support in all current browsers including Internet Explorer, there's no reason not to start experimenting with flexbox in your web designs.

FIGURE 17-21

The CSS flexbox display mode lets you create designs that "flex," or change based on the width of the browser window. Used with media queries, flexbox lets you easily create responsive designs for all screen widths.

Advanced CSS

Improving Your CSS Habits

At this point, this book has covered most aspects of Cascading Style Sheets. With the addition of CSS-based layout, which you learned about in Part Three, you're now an unstoppable web-designing machine. But even after you've mastered all the properties CSS offers, nailed those annoying browser bugs, and learned great tricks for producing beautiful web pages, you can still stand to learn a few techniques that'll make your CSS easier to create, use, and maintain.

This chapter covers some recommendations for creating and using CSS. None of them count as "must know" CSS essentials, but they can make your CSS work go faster, leading to less frustration and greater productivity.

Adding Comments

When it's time to edit a style sheet weeks, months, or even years after creating it, you may find yourself wondering, "Why did I create that style? What does it do?" As with any project, when you're building a website, you should keep notes of what you did and why. Fortunately, you don't need a pad of paper to do this. You can embed your notes right into your style sheets using CSS comments.

A CSS comment is simply a note contained within two sets of characters, /* and */. As with HTML comments, CSS comments aren't read or acted on by a web browser, but they do let you add helpful reminders to your style sheets. You don't need to comment *everything* in your style sheets—after all, most properties like color, font-family, border-color, and so on are self-explanatory. But it's a good idea to add a comment for a style when it isn't immediately obvious what the style or property does. For example, you might reset the CSS box model so that the width and height of an element is calculated with the border and padding taken into account:

```
* {
  box-sizing: border-box;
}
```

At the time you wrote the style, you knew what you were doing, but will you still remember three months later? Or what if someone who's not familiar with this trick needs to edit your CSS at some point? Add a comment, and it'll be easy for you or someone else who needs to work on the site to figure out what the style does and why it was created:

```
/* Make width values include padding and borders */
* {
  box-sizing: border-box;
}
```

If you have a lot to say, comments can span multiple lines as well. Just begin with /*, type all the comments you'd like, then end with */. This is handy when adding background information at the beginning of a style sheet, as pictured in Figure 18-1.

Keep in mind that adding comments adds code to your files, making them larger and slower to download. In reality, you'd have to add a lot of comments before you'd see them significantly affect the file's download speed, but you can use online tools like CSS Minifier (*http://cssminifier.com*) to strip out comments when you want to create a CSS file that's ready to go onto your website. A better tool, however, is Sass. You'll learn about Sass in the next chapter, but one feature of this CSS coding tool is the ability to leave comments in the CSS you edit, but strip them out automatically in the CSS files that are used on your web pages (see the note on page 600 to learn this useful trick).

■ Organizing Styles

You've learned a lot in this book about creating styles and style sheets. But when you're designing a site that's meant to last, you can incorporate a few other steps to help you out in the future. The day will come when you need to change the look of the site, tweak a particular style, or hand off your hard work to someone else who'll be in charge. In addition to leaving notes for yourself and others, a little planning and organization within your CSS will make things go more smoothly down the road.

Name Classes Clearly

You've already learned the technical aspects of naming different types of selectors—class selectors begin with a . (period) to identify the styles as a class, and ID styles begin with the # symbol. In addition, the names you give IDs and classes must begin with a letter and can't contain symbols like &, *, or !. But beyond those requirements, following some rules of thumb can help you keep track of your styles and work more efficiently.

```
/*! normalize.css v3.0.2 | MIT License | git.io/normalize */

/**
 * 1. Set default font family to sans-serif.
 * 2. Prevent iOS text size adjust after orientation change, without disabling
 *    user zoom.
 */

html {
  font-family: sans-serif; /* 1 */
  -ms-text-size-adjust: 100%; /* 2 */
  -webkit-text-size-adjust: 100%; /* 2 */
}

/**
 * Remove default margin.
 */

body {
  margin: 0;
}

/* HTML5 display definitions
   ======================================================================= */

/**
 * Correct `block` display not defined for any HTML5 element in IE 8/9.
 * Correct `block` display not defined for `details` or `summary` in IE 10/11
 * and Firefox.
 * Correct `block` display not defined for `main` in IE 11.
 */

article,
aside,
details,
figcaption,
figure,
footer,
header,
hgroup,
main,
menu,
nav,
section,
summary {
  display: block;
}
```

FIGURE 18-1

CSS comments can help you identify your styles for later editing. You can also use them to provide helpful introductory information that lets you keep track of the version of the site or style sheets, add copyright information, and identify yourself as the CSS master behind it all.

■ NAME CLASSES BY PURPOSE NOT APPEARANCE

It's tempting to use a name like .redhighlight when creating a style to format eye-catching, fire-engine-red text. But what if you (or your boss or your client) decide that orange, blue, or chartreuse look better? Let's face it: a style named .redhighlight that's actually chartreuse is confusing. It's better to use a name that describes the *purpose* of the style. For example, if that "red" highlight is intended to indicate an error that a visitor made while filling out a form, then use the name .error. When the style needs to alert the visitor of some important information, a name like .alert would work. Either way, changing the color or other formatting options of the style won't cause confusion, because the style's still intended to point out an error or alert the visitor—regardless of its color.

Likewise, avoid names that provide exact sizes, like .font20px. While that font may be 20 pixels today, maybe you'll make it 24 pixels tomorrow, or switch from pixels to ems or percentages. Using a tag selector may be a better route: Apply the font size to an <h2> or <p> tag, or even a descendant selector like `.sidebar p`.

■ DON'T USE NAMES BASED ON POSITION

For the same reason you avoid naming styles by appearance, you should avoid naming them by position. Sometimes a name like `.leftSidebar` seems like an obvious choice—"I want all this stuff in a box placed at the left edge of the page!" But it's possible that you (or someone else) will want the left sidebar moved to the right, top, or even bottom of the page. All of a sudden, the name `.leftSidebar` makes no sense at all. A name more appropriate to the purpose of that sidebar—like `.news`, `.events`, `.secondaryContent`, or `.mainNav`—serves to identify the sidebar no matter where it gets moved. The names you've seen so far in this book—`.gallery`, `.figure`, `.banner`, `.wrapper`, and so on—follow this convention.

The temptation is to use names like `.header` and `.footer` (for elements that always appear at the top or bottom of the page, for example) since they're so easily understood, but you can often find names that are better at identifying the content of an element—for example, `.branding` instead of `.header`. On the other hand, sometimes using a name with position information does make sense. For example, say you wanted to create two styles, one for floating an image to the left side of a page and another for floating an image to the right side. Since these styles exist solely to place an image to the left or right, using that information in the style names makes sense. So `.floatLeft` and `.floatRight` are perfectly legitimate names.

■ AVOID CRYPTIC NAMES

Names like `.s`, `.s1`, and `.s2` may save you a few keystrokes and make your files a bit smaller, but they can cause trouble when you need to update your site. You could end up scratching your head, wondering what all those weird styles are for. Be succinct, but clear: `.sidebar`, `.copyright`, and `.banner` don't take all that much typing, and their purpose is immediately obvious.

> **NOTE** You can also learn a lot from checking out the naming conventions used on other sites. The web inspector built into most browsers gives you a quick way to reveal style names.

Don't Repeat Yourself

Typing the same code over and over wastes your time, and also adds extra code to your style sheets, making them slower to download for your site's visitors. When you create several page elements that look very similar with only slight visual differences, you'll probably find that you've typed the same CSS properties over and over again.

For example, say you have three different types of buttons—an orange button for adding a new item to a shopping cart, a red button for deleting an item from a shopping cart, and a green button for submitting an order. You could add different classes for each button in the HTML like this:

```
<button class="add">Add to Cart</button>
<button class="delete">Delete</button>
<button class="order">Submit Order</button>
```

You could then create three styles like this:

```
.add {
  border-radius: 3px;
  font: 12px Arial, Helvetica, sans-serif;
  color: #444;
  background-color: orange;
}
.delete {
  border-radius: 3px;
  font: 12px Arial, Helvetica, sans-serif;
  color: #444;
  background-color: red;
}
.order {
 border-radius: 3px;
  font: 12px Arial, Helvetica, sans-serif;
  color: #444;
  background-color: green;
}
```

Notice that most of the properties in these three styles are the same. Not only does that repeated code add to the file size, but if you decide to change the font for the buttons, you'll have to edit three styles instead of one.

A better approach is to create a "base" style that all the buttons share, as well as individual styles that just contain the differences between the buttons. For example, if you're using the HTML <button> element for these, you could create a style for that element, which would apply to all three buttons. Then create three more styles, one for each button, like this:

```
button {
  border-radius: 3px;
  font: 12px Arial, Helvetica, sans-serif;
  color: #444;
}
.add {
  background-color: orange;
}
.delete {
  background-color: red;
}
.order {
  background-color: green;
}
```

Not only is this less code, it's also more manageable. If you wanted to change the font on all of the buttons, you'd just change the font once in the button style.

Use Multiple Classes to Save Time

You can take the "Don't repeat yourself" motto even further by using multiple classes. For example, say you want some images to float to the left and have a right margin, while some photos float to the right and have a left margin. You also want those images to have the same border styles around them; however, you don't want all images on the page to have a border. See Figure 18-2 for an example.

The most obvious solution is to create two class styles, each having the same border properties but different float and margin properties. You then apply one class to the images that should float left and another to the images that should float right. But what if you need to update the border style for all of these images? You'll need to edit *two* styles, and if you forget one, the images on one side of the page will all have the wrong frames!

Bathtub Hydroponics

Lorem ipsum dolor sit amet, consectetuer adipiscing elit, sed diam nonummy nibh euismod tincidunt ut laoreet dolore magna aliquam erat volutpat. Ut wisi enim ad minim veniam, quis nostrud exerci tation ullamcorper suscipit lobortis nisl ut aliquip ex ea commodo consequat. Duis autem vel eum iriure dolor in hendrerit in vulputate velit esse molestie consequat, vel illum dolore eu feugiat nulla facilisis at vero eros et accumsan et iusto odio dignissim qui blandit praesent luptatum zzril delenit a

Lorem ipsum dolor sit amet, consectetuer adipiscing elit, sed diam nonummy nibh euismod tincidunt ut laoreet dolore magna aliquam erat volutpat. Ut wisi enim ad minim veniam, quis nostrud exerci tation ullamcorper suscipit lobortis nisl ut aliquip ex ea commodo consequat. Duis autem vel eum iriure dolor in hendrerit in vulputate velit esse molestie consequat, vel illum dolore eu feugiat nulla facilisis at vero eros et accumsan et iusto odio dignissim qui blandit praesent luptatum zzril delenit a

Lorem ipsum dolor sit amet, consectetuer adipiscing elit, sed diam nonummy nibh euismod tincidunt ut laoreet dolore magna aliquam erat volutpat. Ut wisi enim ad minim veniam, quis nostrud exerci tation ullamcorper suscipit lobortis nisl ut aliquip ex ea commodo consequat. Duis autem vel eum iriure dolor in hendrerit in vulputate velit esse molestie consequat, vel illum dolore eu feugiat nulla facilisis at vero eros et accumsan et iusto odio dignissim qui blandit praesent luptatum zzril delenit a

Copyright 2006, CosmoFarmer.com

FIGURE 18-2

The two photos pictured here have the same class style applied to them. This style provides the border around the image. In addition, the left image has a class style that merely floats the image left, whereas the right image has a different class that floats it to the right. In other words, each image has two classes applied to it.

There's a trick that works in all browsers that not all designers take advantage of—*multiple classes* applied to the same tag. This just means that when you use the class attribute for a tag, you add two (or more) class names like this: <div class="note alert">. In this example, the <div> tag receives formatting instructions from both the .note style and the .alert style.

Say you want to use the same border style for a group of images, but some of the images you want floating left and others you want floating right. You'd approach the problem like this:

1. **Create a class style that includes the formatting properties shared by all the images.**

   This style could be called `.imgFrame` and have a 2-pixel, solid black border around all four edges.

2. **Create two additional class styles, one for the left-floated images and another for the right-floated images.**

   For example, `.floatLeft` and `.floatRight`. One style would include properties unique to one set of images (floated left with a small right margin), while the other style includes properties specific to the second group of images.

3. **Apply both classes to each tag, like so:**

   ```
   <img src="photo1.jpg" height="100" class="imgFrame floatLeft">
   ```

   or

   ```
   <img src="photo1.jpg" height="100" class="imgFrame floatRight">
   ```

   At this point, two classes apply to each tag, and the web browser combines the style information for each class to format the tag. Now if you want to change the border style, then simply edit one style—`.imgFrame`—to update the borders around both the left and right floated images.

> **NOTE** You can list more than two classes with this method; just make sure to add a space between each class name.

This technique is useful when you need to tweak only a couple of properties of one element, while leaving other similarly formatted items unchanged. You may want a generic sidebar design that floats a sidebar to the right, adds creative background images, and includes carefully styled typography. You can use this style throughout your site, but the width of that sidebar varies in several instances. Perhaps it's 33 percent wide on some pages and 25 percent wide on others. In this case, create a single class style (like `.sidebar`) with the basic sidebar formatting and separate classes for defining just the width of the sidebar—for example, `.w33per` and `.w25per`. Then apply two classes to each sidebar: `<div class="sidebar w33per">`.

Use Shorthand Properties

Many CSS properties can be condensed into shorthand versions that require less code and less typing. For example, the `padding` property takes the place of four padding properties: `padding-top`, `padding-right`, `padding-bottom`, and `padding-left`. So, you can replace this code:

```
td {
  padding-top: 5px;
  padding-right: 10px;
  padding-bottom: 5px;
  padding-left: 10px;
}
```

with this:

```
td {
  padding: 5px 10px;
}
```

There are shorthand properties for font settings (page 165), borders (page 195), padding (page 189), margins (page 189), transitions (page 336), background (page 231), and lists (page 171). You'll get more done if you commit them to memory.

> **TIP** If the value for any property takes some kind of measurement value—30px, 40%, 10em, for example—you can leave off the unit if the value is a 0. In other words, you should use:

```
padding: 0;
```

And not:

```
padding: 0px
```

Grouping Related Styles

Adding one style after another is a common way to build a style sheet. But after a while, what was once a simple collection of five styles has ballooned into a massive 500-style CSS file. At that point, quickly finding the one style you need to change is like looking for a needle in a haystack. (Of course, haystacks don't have a Find command, but you get the point.) If you organize your styles from the get-go, you'll make your life a lot easier in the long run. There are no hard and fast rules for *how* to group styles together, but here are two common methods:

- **Group styles that apply to related parts of a page.** Group all the rules that apply to text, graphics, and links in the banner of a page in one place. Then group the rules that style the main navigation in another, and the styles for the main content in yet another.

- **Group styles with a related purpose.** Put all the styles for layout in one group, the styles for typography in another, the styles for links in yet another group, and so on.

■ USING COMMENTS TO SEPARATE STYLE GROUPS

Whichever approach you take, make sure to use CSS comments to introduce each grouping of styles. Say you collected all the styles that control the layout of your pages into one place in a style sheet. Introduce that collection with a comment like this:

```
/* *** Layout *** */
```

or

```
/* -------------------------
          Layout
------------------------- */
```

As long as you begin with /* and end with */, you can use whatever frilly combination of asterisks, dashes, or symbols you'd like to help make those comments easy to spot. You'll find as many variations on this as there are web designers.

Using Multiple Style Sheets

As you read in Chapter 17, you can create different style sheets for different types of displays—maybe one for a screen and another for a printer. But you may also want to have multiple onscreen style sheets, purely for organizational purposes. This takes the basic concept from the previous section—grouping related styles—one step further. When a style sheet becomes so big that it's difficult to find and edit styles, it may be time to create separate style sheets that each serve an individual function. You can put styles used to format forms in one style sheet, styles used for layout in another, styles that determine the color of things in a third, and so on. Keep the number of separate files reasonable, since having, say, 30 external CSS files to weed through may not save time at all. In addition, the more external CSS files, the more requests your web server has to answer. That's one source of slower website performance.

At first glance, it may seem like you'll end up with more code in each web page, since you'll have that many more external style sheets to link to or import—one line of code for each file. Ah, but there's a better approach: Create a single external style sheet that uses the @import directive to include multiple style sheets. Figure 18-3 illustrates the concept.

Here's how to set up this type of arrangement:

1. **Create external style sheets to format the different types of elements of your site.**

   For example, a *color.css* file with styles that control the color of the site, a *forms.css* file that controls form formatting, a *layout.css* file for layout control, and a *main.css* file that covers everything else (see the right side of Figure 18-3).

2. **Create an external style sheet and import each of the style sheets you created in step 1.**

   You can name this file *base.css*, *global.css*, *site.css*, or something generic like that. This CSS file won't contain any rules. Instead use the @import directive to attach the other style sheets like this:

   ```
   @import url(main.css);
   @import url(layout.css);
   @import url(color.css);
   @import url(forms.css);
   ```

That's the only code that needs to be in the file, though you may add some comments with a version number, site name, and so on to help identify this file.

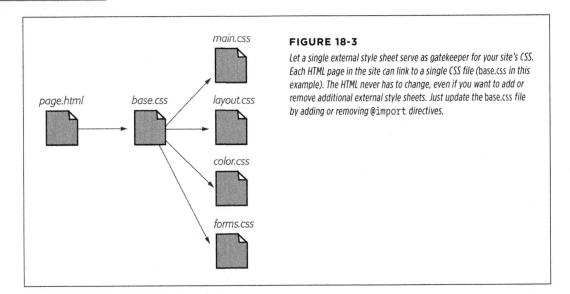

main.css

layout.css

page.html

base.css

color.css

forms.css

FIGURE 18-3

Let a single external style sheet serve as gatekeeper for your site's CSS. Each HTML page in the site can link to a single CSS file (base.css in this example). The HTML never has to change, even if you want to add or remove additional external style sheets. Just update the base.css file by adding or removing @import directives.

3. **Finally, attach the style sheet from step 2 to the HTML pages of your site using either the `<link>` tag or the `@import` method. (See page 26 for more on using these methods.) For example:**

   ```
   <link rel="stylesheet" href="base.css">
   ```

   Now, when a web page loads, the browser loads *base.css*, which in turn tells the browser to load the four other style sheets.

It may feel like there's a whole lot of loading going on here, but once the browser has downloaded those files and stored them in its cache, it won't have to retrieve them over the Internet again. (See the box on the next page.)

There's another benefit to using a single external style sheet to load several other style sheets: If you decide later to further divide your styles into additional style sheets, then you won't have to muck around with the HTML of your site. Instead, just add one more `@import` directive to that gatekeeper style sheet (see step 2). If you decide to take all the styles related to type out of the *main.css* file and put them in their own *type.css* file, then you won't need to touch the web pages on your site. Simply open the style sheet with all of the `@import` directives in it and add one more: `@import url(type.css)`.

This arrangement also lets you have some fun with your site by swapping in different style sheets for temporary design changes. Say you decide to change the color of your site for the day, month, or season. If you've already put the main color-defining styles into a separate *color.css* file, then you can create another file (like *summer_fun. css*) with a different set of colors. Then, in the gatekeeper file, change the `@import` directive for the *color.css* file to load the new color style file (for example, @import url(summer_fun.css)).

NOTE CSS preprocessors let you have the best of both worlds: They let you edit multiple CSS files, but then convert them into a single style sheet for your site, reducing download times. You'll learn about these advanced tools in the next chapter.

Eliminating Browser Style Interference

When you view a web page that hasn't been "CSS-ified" in a web browser, you can see that HTML tags already have some minimal formatting: Headings are bold, the <h1> tag is bigger than other text, links are underlined and blue, and so on. In some cases, different web browsers apply slightly different formatting to each of these elements. You may experience some frustrating "it *almost* looks the same in Internet Explorer and Firefox and Chrome" moments.

As discussed on page 109, to deal with these browser differences, it's a good idea to "zero out" the formatting for commonly used tags so your audience can see the beautiful styling you worked so hard to create (see Figure 18-4). All you have to do is set up some basic styles at the beginning of your style sheet that remove the offensive formatting.

Here are some things you may want to do to make browsers stop meddling with your designs:

- **Remove padding and margins.** Browsers add top and bottom margins to most block-level elements—the familiar space that appears between <p> tags, for example. This can cause some weird display issues, like when the exact margin amount is inconsistently applied across browsers. A better approach is to remove padding and margins from the block-level tags you use, and then purposely add the amount you want by creating new styles.

- **Apply consistent font sizes.** While text inside a <p> tag is displayed as 1 em, web browsers apply different sizes to other tags. You can force all tags to be 1 em to begin with, and then create additional styles with specific font sizes for the different tags. That way, you stand a much better chance of getting consistent font sizes across browsers.

- **Set a consistent line height.** Browsers can have subtle differences in the line height (page 163) values they use by default. By setting a multiplier on the <body> tag—body { line-height: 1.2; }—you make sure that browsers apply the same line height. The 1.2 value is equivalent to 120 percent of the tag's text size. You can, of course, change this value to match your design sense.

- **Improve table borders and create consistent table cells.** As you read on page 363, applying a border to a table cell usually creates an unpleasant gap between cell borders and doubles up the borders between cells. You should get rid of both the space and the extra borders. In addition, the `<th>` and `<td>` tag are given different alignments and font weights.

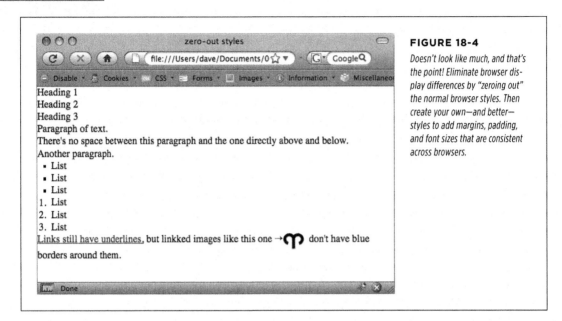

FIGURE 18-4

Doesn't look like much, and that's the point! Eliminate browser display differences by "zeroing out" the normal browser styles. Then create your own—and better—styles to add margins, padding, and font sizes that are consistent across browsers.

- **Remove borders from linked images.** Some browsers add a colored border around any image inside of a link. If you're like most people, you find this border both unattractive and unnecessary. Remove it and start fresh.

- **Set consistent list indents and bullet types.** Different browsers indent bulleted and numbered lists in different ways, and you'll even find the type of bullet used can vary between browsers. It's good to set a consistent indent and bullet type.

- **Remove quote marks from quoted material.** If you ever use the `<q>` tag to identify a quote (`<q>To err is human</q>`, for example), then you may have noticed that some browsers (Firefox, Safari) automatically add quote marks (' ') around the quote and some (Internet Explorer 6 and 7) don't. And even within the browsers that do add quote marks, the type of mark added varies; for example, IE8 inserts single quotes (' '), while Firefox adds double quotes (" "). For a consistent presentation, it's best to remove these quote marks.

To put these ideas into action, here are a few basic styles you can add at the beginning of your style sheet:

```
/* reset browser styles */

* { box-sizing: border-box; }

html, body, div, span, object, iframe, h1, h2, h3, h4, h5, h6, p, blockquote,
pre, a, abbr, acronym, address, big, cite, code, del, dfn, em, img, ins, kbd,
q, s, samp, small, strike, strong, sub, sup, tt, var, b, u, i, center, dl, dt,
```

```
dd, ol, ul, li, fieldset, form, label, legend, table, caption, tbody, tfoot,
thead, tr, th, td, article, aside, canvas, details, embed, figure, figcaption,
footer, header, hgroup, menu, nav, output, ruby, section, summary, time, mark,
audio, video {
    margin: 0;
    padding: 0;
    border: 0;
    font-size: 100%;
    vertical-align: baseline;
}

article, aside, details, figcaption, figure, footer, header, hgroup, menu,
nav, section {
    display: block;
}

body {
    line-height: 1.2;
}

table {
    border-collapse: collapse;
    border-spacing: 0;
}

ol {
    padding-left: 1.4em;
    list-style: decimal;
}

ul {
    padding-left: 1.4em;
    list-style: square;
}

blockquote, q {
    quotes: none;
}

blockquote:before, blockquote:after,
q:before, q:after {
    content: '';
    content: none;
}

/* end reset browser styles */
```

The first style changes how browsers treat the CSS width property (page 204). It makes sure that any widths you set also include the width of borders and padding—you can read about the box-sizing property on page 207.

The next two styles here are group selectors that apply the same formatting to every one of the tags listed. Add these styles to the beginning of your style sheet, and then, further down the style sheet, override them on a case-by-case basis. After zeroing out the margins and font size for the <h1> tag, you may want to give the <h1> tag a specific top margin value and font size. Just add another style, like so:

```
h1 {
    margin-top: 5px;
    font-size: 2.5em;
}
```

Thanks to the cascade (see Chapter 5), as long as this <h1> style appears in the style sheet *after* the group selector (the reset style that removes the margins and changes the font size), the new values take precedence.

You'll find the file *reset.css* in the *18* folder inside the *tutorials* folder. Just copy the code from that file into your own style sheets.

> **NOTE** Some designers take a different approach to the problem of inconsistent browser styles. The *normalize.css* project (*http://necolas.github.io/normalize.css/*) aims to provide consistent baseline styles while still retaining basic styling in HTML tags. For example, instead of making headlines and paragraphs the same size, *normalize.css* keeps headlines at varying sizes. It also includes many other styles aimed at fixing bugs present in some browsers.

■ Using Descendant Selectors

Classes and IDs are great for marking specific tags for styling. For example, you can add a class to a paragraph—<p class="intro">—and pinpoint just that one paragraph with its own look, as determined by the .intro class style. Trouble is, it's so easy to add a class or ID to a tag, lots of designers tend to add classes and IDs to *everything* (well, almost everything). The pros even have a diagnosis for this disease—*classitis*. Adding a class to every tag is not only a waste of your time, it also makes your HTML slower to download. Most important, there's a better way to exert pinpoint control over your tags without resorting to too many classes or IDs—descendant selectors.

A Pain in the Cache

The web browser's cache is usually every website owner's friend. As discussed on page 25, the cache makes sure frequent visitors to your site don't have to download the same file over and over again, which would slow down their experience and increase your web hosting bills. However, the cache can be a pain when it's time to update your site's appearance. For example, if all of the pages in your site reference an external style sheet named *main.css*, then visitors to your site will cache that file. However, when you update that file with all new styles and a completely new look and feel for your site, previous visitors to your site may continue to access the old style sheet from their hard drive instead of the new *main.css* file you've updated.

Eventually, a visitor's cache will clear and they'll get the new CSS file, but you have one simple way to defeat the cache—by updating the `<link>` tag on each HTML page. Normally a `<link>` tag to an external style sheet looks like this:

```
<link rel="stylesheet" href="main.css">
```

However, if you add a query string after the name of the .css file (for example, `main.css?v=1`), then a web browser will see the file as `main.css?v=1` and not just *main.css*. If you

change the number after the v= whenever you change the external style sheet, then browsers consider that a new file and will download the external style sheet from the web server instead of using the cached site.

For example, suppose when you launch your site, the *main.css* file is the first version of the site's CSS. You can then use this link:

```
<link rel="stylesheet" href="main.
css?v=1">
```

Then when you update the *main.css* file, you change the `<link>` to this:

```
<link rel="stylesheet" type="textcss"
href="main.css?v=2">
```

The web browser considers this different from the cached version of the *main.css* file and downloads the file from the web server. In reality, the `?v=1` doesn't do anything—it doesn't affect how your web server works, for example. It's a way of telling a web browser to redownload the file.

The downside of this technique is that you must update the `<link>` tag for every HTML file on your site.

Descendant selectors are a powerful tool for efficient website building. As discussed in Chapter 3, they let you pinpoint the tags you want to style with greater accuracy than tag styles, with less work than class styles. Most of the time you want to format *all* the links in a navigation bar the same way, but that doesn't mean you want to format all of the links in the entire *page* the same way. What you need is a way to say (in CSS), "Format *only* the links in the nav bar this way"—without having to apply a class style to each of those links. In other words, you need the ability to format the same HTML in different ways depending on where it's located—and that's exactly what descendant selectors offer (see Figure 18-5).

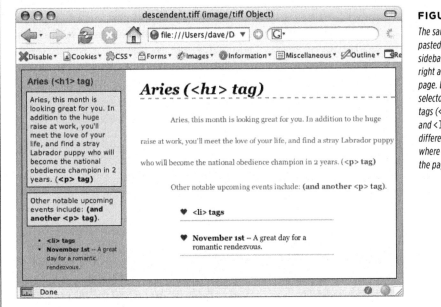

FIGURE 18-5

The same HTML was pasted into both the left sidebar and the larger right area of this web page. By using descendant selectors, identical HTML tags (<h1>, <p>, <ul>, and <li>) are formatted differently based solely on where they're located on the page.

Compartmentalize Your Pages

One of your biggest allies in using descendant selectors effectively is the <div> tag. Since this HTML tag lets you create logical *divisions* in a page, you can use it to identify different layout elements like a banner, a sidebar, a column of text, and so on. You can organize the content of your page into different areas by wrapping HTML in a <div> tag.

Group the title of a story and a list of links used to navigate the story's pages like this:

```
<div>
  <h2>The CosmoFarmer Revolution</h2>
  <ul>
    <li><a href="page1.html">page 1</a></li>
    <li><a href="page2.html">page 2</a></li>
    <li><a href="page3.html">page 3</a></li>
  </ul>
</div>
```

After adding the <div>, identify it for CSS purposes with a class attribute: <div class="pullQuote">. When you want to include the same type of layout element more than once on a page—multiple pull quotes in a single story perhaps—use a class.

Suppose the list of links in the HTML above appears twice on a page—at the beginning of the text and at the end. You'd apply a class to it like this:

```
<div class="storyNav">
  <h2>The CosmoFarmer Revolution</h2>
  <ul>
    <li><a href="page1.html">page 1</a></li>
    <li><a href="page2.html">page 2</a></li>
    <li><a href="page3.html">page 3</a></li>
  </ul>
</div>
```

> **NOTE** You don't always need to add a `<div>` tag to style a group of elements. If the preceding HTML had only an unordered list of links and didn't include the `<h2>` tag, then you could just as easily skip the `<div>` tag and simply add a class to the unordered list: `<ul class="storyNav">`. You could also wrap the `<ul>` tag in the HTML5 `<nav>` tag and apply the class to it.

Once you identify each div on a page, it becomes very easy to use a descendant selector to target tags inside a particular div. Say you want to create a unique look for each of the links in the above HTML. You'd create a descendant selector like this:

```
.storyNav a {
  color: red;
  background-color: #ccc;
}
```

Now links will appear as red text on a light gray background, but *only* when they appear *inside* another tag with the storyNav class applied to it. Best of all, if you want to add another link (like page4.html) to this list, then you don't have to lift a finger to format it like the other links. The browser handles all of that automatically when it applies the descendant selector.

Formatting other tags inside that `<div>` is a simple matter of creating a descendant selector that begins with the class name—.storyNav, for instance—followed by a space and the tag you want to style. To format the `<h2>` that appears inside the `<div>`, create the descendant selector .storyNav h2.

Identify the Body

Because descendant selectors provide such specific targeting of styles, you can easily create styles that not only apply to one particular area of a page, but also apply only to particular *types* of pages on your site. Say you want to style the `<h1>` tag differently on the home page than on other pages of the site. An easy way to distinguish `<h1>` tags on the home page is to add a class to the `<body>` tag of the home page:

```
<body class="home">
```

You can style the <h1> tag on the home page using a descendant selector: .home h1. With this technique, you can create entirely different looks for any tag on any particular page of your site (Figure 18-6). One approach is to identify the section of the site each page is in. Say your site is divided into four sections—news, events, articles, and links. On each page within a section, add either a class or ID to the <body> tag. So each page in the news section might have the following HTML: <body class="news">, while pages in the events section would have <body class="events">.

> **NOTE** Another common CSS technique is to use a class to identify the type of layout you want for a particular page (like a one-, two-, or three-column design).

One great use for identifying a page's section in the site is to highlight that section's button in a navigation bar. The highlighted button acts as a kind of "you are here" marker, as shown in Figure 18-6. If a page is in the news section of your site, you can highlight the "news" button so visitors can tell immediately which section they're in.

Here's how to format a navigation button differently depending on which section of your site it's in:

1. **Add a class to the <body> tag indicating the section the page is in.**

   For example, <body class="home">. Do the same thing for each section, so pages in the news section of the site would have code like this: <body class="news">.

2. **Add a navigation bar to the page.**

   Step-by-step instructions are on page 289.

3. **Identify each link within the navigation bar.**

   For a link to the home page, you might have this code: <a href="/index.html" class="homeLink">Home</a>. The class lets you identify that particular link as the one going to the home page. Repeat for the other links: <a href="/news/" class="newsLink">News</a> and so on.

   At this point, you have enough information in your HTML to uniquely format each section's link using CSS. In this example, you know that the Home page link is nested inside a <body> tag with the class of home *only* on the Home page.

4. **Create a descendant selector to format each section's link differently when the link is inside a page for that section.**

   For the home page in this example, the descendant selector would look like this:

   ```
   .home .homeLink
   ```

   This selector formats the .homeLink only when it's inside another tag with the ID #home. In most cases, you'll want the look of the "you are here" button to be the same for each section of the site, so you can use a group selector (page 49) to group all the descendant selectors for each section's button. That way, you can apply the same formatting to each button without creating separate rules for each button. A group selector to highlight the current section's navigation button with a light yellow background may look like this:

```
.home .homeLink,
.news .newsLink,
.articles .articlesLink,
.links .linksLink {
  background-color: #FBEF99;
}
```

FIGURE 18-6

Using descendant selectors, you can highlight a button in a navigation bar simply by changing the class applied to the <body> tag. In this example, when the <body> tag has the class home applied to it, the Home button lights up (circled, top). Change the class to about, and the About button highlights (circled, bottom).

TIP   When creating a group selector that includes several descendant selectors, keep each selector on its own line, as in this example. This way, it's easier to identify each selector in the group when you need to go back and edit your style sheet.

Using the same technique, make additional styles to apply different looks for the links when you hover over them or click them, or when they've been visited. See page 281 for the details.

These few examples are just some of the ways you can take advantage of descendant selectors. They can make your style sheets a little more complex. You'll have styles like `.home .navbar a`, for example, instead of a simple class like `.navLink`. But once the styles are set up, you'll need to do very little further formatting. HTML pasted into different areas of the page automatically gets formatted in strikingly different ways. Almost like magic.

POWER USERS' CLINIC

Object Oriented CSS

Object Oriented CSS is another approach to organizing and using CSS. The term was coined by CSS expert Nicole Sullivan, and the approach was developed to respond to the complexity of very large sites with a wide variety of HTML structures. On large sites, you might end up having really different HTML containing similar types of information.

For example, in one case you might use a bulleted list to display names, contact info, and photos for a list of contacts. But on another page you might use the `<article>` tag for each contact. Say you wanted to format those elements similarly, because they really are the same type of information. If you use CSS styles that depend on that HTML, you could end up with either duplicate styles or group selectors like this:

```
article img, li img {
    /* formatting info here */
}
```

Object Oriented CSS recommends abandoning any CSS that's tied to actual HTML elements and instead use classes. In other words, you'd apply class names throughout your HTML and then use CSS class styles to format then. In this way, it doesn't

matter what HTML tags you use. As long as they use the same classes, they'll look the same.

This may sound a lot like the classitis problem described on page 582, and in a sense, it is. Object Oriented CSS does require adding lots of class attributes to your HTML. If you're using a content management system like WordPress, then this might not be much work—you can add the class names into the template files. But if you're building every page by hand, this approach could add a lot of work.

For a quick introduction to Object Oriented CSS, read *http://coding.smashingmagazine.com/2011/12/12/an-introduction-to-object-oriented-css-oocss/*. You can find the OOCSS project at *https://github.com/stubbornella/oocss*.

Another related approach from Jonathon Snook, called Scalable and Modular Architecture for CSS (or SMACSS), is a simpler style guide for creating reusable CSS components. You can read more about it at *http://smacss.com*. You can also find a bunch of videos discussing SMACSS at *http://tv.adobe.com/watch/adc-presents/smacss-introduction-to-a-scalable-and-modular-architecture-for-css/*.

More Powerful Styling with Sass

Y ou've learned a lot about CSS so far in this book. In the last chapter you learned
techniques for being a better style sheet author. In this chapter, we'll look at
a very popular tool that makes it a lot easier to write CSS code.

▨ What is Sass?

Sass is known as a *CSS preprocessor*—that means you first write Sass code, then
process it into the CSS the browser understands. You can think of Sass—which
stands for "Syntactically awesome style sheets"—as a kind of shorthand for CSS
that lets you write less code.

When working with Sass, you have two different types of files: Sass files, which end
in .scss, and CSS files, which (as you know) end in .css. You actually only ever edit
the .scss files: Sass's preprocessor automatically converts the Sass file to a regular
.css file.

This may sound like a lot of extra work to simply produce the CSS code you've
learned about in this book. However, as your sites and their style sheets get larger
and more complex, Sass provides a number of benefits:

- It organizes your CSS code into smaller files. Currently, web designers are told
  to use as few CSS files as possible. The more files the browser has to load, the
  slower the site will feel to visitors who must wait for each file to transfer from
  the web server to their browser. Some web designers, therefore, stuff hundreds
  or even thousands of styles into a single style sheet. While this may be more
  efficient for your site visitors, it's not easy for you when you have to locate

that one style that's formatting the <h2> tag inside a sidebar on the About Us page. Sass lets you logically group your styles into smaller files, so that all of the styles for your site's forms, for example, can be found in one Sass file, while your typographic rules live in another. When Sass does its preprocessing magic, it can automatically combine these multiple files into one fast-loading CSS file. Even better, Sass can compress the final CSS file so it's much smaller than the same file you might create by hand.

- You can easily update shared values. You'll often find yourself using the same CSS value over and over. For example, your company may have a set of corporate colors that you use consistently in a web design for coloring text, backgrounds, borders, and so on. What if your marketing department decides that the colors need to change? Using a regular CSS file, you'd have to locate and change each instance of a changed color. With Sass, you can define the color value in one place and use it throughout your styles. If the color changes, update in a single spot in the Sass file, and Sass automatically updates the old color to the new one.

- You get to write less code. Sass provides some really powerful tools that let you write less code. Remember those vendor prefixes from page 321? Having to write multiple lines of code just to get the same property in multiple browsers is a drag. Sass *mixins* can take care of that chore for you. You can write just one line of code and have Sass convert it to all the different browser-prefixed versions you need. In addition, if you find yourself using the same set of CSS properties among many different styles, you can tell Sass to add that code automatically for you. Less writing for you, means faster production time, and fewer chances for errors.

There are many other advantages to using Sass that you'll learn about in this chapter, but the bottom line is that Sass can make you a more efficient web designer: You'll be able to work faster and spend more time thinking about design than typing code.

> **NOTE** You can find out much more about Sass at the official Sass website: *www.sass-lang.com* (Figure 19-1).

There are a couple of downsides, however. First, Sass introduces several new concepts as well as new syntax for writing your CSS. You'll get that in this chapter.

Second, to use Sass you need to install a few things on your computer. Sass relies on the Ruby programming language, so you need to install Ruby, as well as the basic Sass command files. In addition, Sass isn't a regular program that you just double-click to launch. You must use the command line (the command prompt in Windows or the Terminal application on Macs) to make Sass work. The command line intimidates a lot of web designers, but it shouldn't. It's actually pretty easy to set up, as you'll see in the next section.

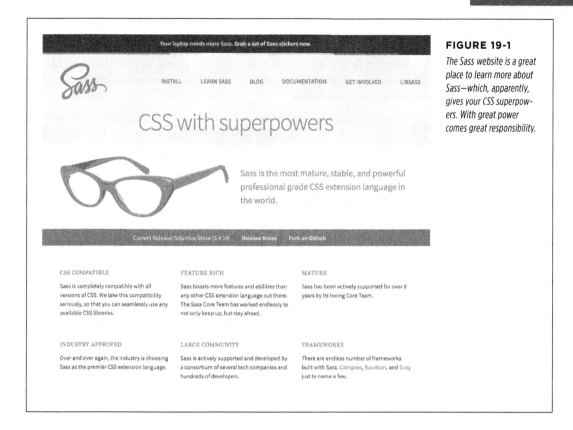

FIGURE 19-1

The Sass website is a great place to learn more about Sass—which, apparently, gives your CSS superpowers. With great power comes great responsibility.

Installing Sass

Sass was originally created using the Ruby programming language. It's the same language used to create many websites using the Ruby on Rails framework, including GitHub, Square, Airbnb, and the original Twitter site. The first step in installing Sass is to install Ruby. In Windows, you have to download Ruby and then install it. Macs come with a copy of Ruby, so installing it takes a few quick steps (Mac users can skip to page 594).

> **NOTE** Sass originally only worked with Ruby. However, a rewrite of Sass named libSass that uses the C/C++ programming languages is now available. libSass works with many different programming languages, and is often used with Node.js in conjunction with JavaScript build tools like Grunt (*http://gruntjs.com*) and Gulp (*http://gulpjs.com*).

Installing Sass on Windows

Installing Sass on Windows is a two step-process: First you must install Ruby, and then the Sass *gem* (a program written in the Ruby programming language).

1. **Download the Ruby installer from *http://rubyinstaller.org/downloads/*.**

   Download a recent version of Ruby by clicking one of the download links. If your machine uses 64-bit Windows, select the x64 version. The installer is a regular Windows .exe file.

   NOTE The author tested Ruby 2.2.2 version of the installer for this book. Sometimes, the newest version of Ruby may not be able to install Sass—if, for example, the Sass gem hasn't been updated to work with the latest version. In that case, install an older version of Ruby that does work.

2. **Open and run the installer.**

   You'll need to click through a couple of windows—selecting the language you use and accepting the license agreement—until you reach the installation destination window (Figure 19-2).

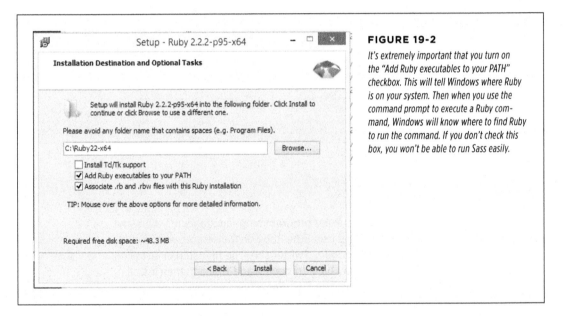

FIGURE 19-2

It's extremely important that you turn on the "Add Ruby executables to your PATH" checkbox. This will tell Windows where Ruby is on your system. Then when you use the command prompt to execute a Ruby command, Windows will know where to find Ruby to run the command. If you don't check this box, you won't be able to run Sass easily.

3. **In the "Installation Destination and Optional Tasks" window, accept the suggested installation location and check the "Add Ruby executables to your PATH" and "Associate .rb and .rbw files with this Ruby installation". Click the Install button.**

   The Windows installer will install Ruby, which may take a minute or so.

4. **After the installation is done, click the Finish button on the last installation screen.**

   Now that your system has the Ruby language installed, you can install Sass using the Windows command prompt. Read on.

5. **Open the Windows command prompt.**

   Here's a quick way to do so:

   a. **Press the Windows Key+R to open the Run window.**

      This window lets you run applications simply by typing the name.

   b. **Type *CMD* and click OK.**

      This runs the cmd.exe program and opens a command prompt window (see Figure 19-3).

   For other methods of opening a Windows command prompt, visit *http://pcsupport.about.com/od/windows-8/a/command-prompt-windows-8.htm*.

   The Command Prompt lets you type commands and run them directly in the console. This is the way computer science people worked back in the '70s (and many still do).

NOTE If you had the command prompt window open when you installed Ruby, Windows won't know how to get to the Ruby installation yet. You have to close the command prompt and then open it again—the new, refreshed prompt will have access to Ruby.

---

6. **Type** gem install sass **and press Enter.**

   The gem command is part of Ruby and is used to install different Ruby programs and libraries. It may take a few minutes for this command to run—it has to go onto the Internet and download and then install the correct files.

   If you have some kind of virus protection software installed, you might need to click a confirmation window to install Sass.

   In addition, if you didn't select the "Add Ruby executables to your PATH" box when installing Ruby (see Figure 19-2), then you'll get an error that looks something like "'gem' is not recognized as an internal or external command, operable program or batch file." This means Windows doesn't know where Ruby is and can't run the gem command. Just reinstall Ruby following the steps above, but make sure you check the "Add Ruby executables to your PATH" box this time.

   If all goes well, the command prompt should look something like Figure 19-3. You're ready to run Sass. You'll learn how to do that on page 597.

NOTE To update to a newer version of Sass, you can type gem update sass in the command prompt.

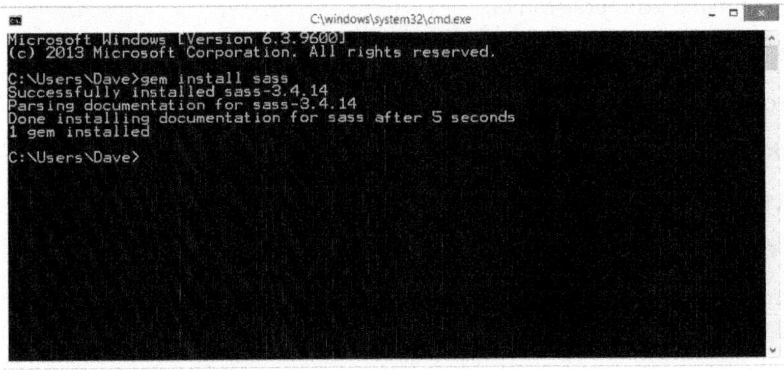

FIGURE 19-3

It's not pretty to look at, but the Windows command prompt is a simple way to install and run Sass. Here, you can see that we just installed version 3.4.14 of Sass. To see which version you have installed you can type sass -v in the command prompt.

Installing Sass on Mac

Since Ruby is preinstalled on Macs, the process for installing Sass is quite simple.

1. **Open the Terminal application.**

   You'll find this in the Applications→Utilities folder. You'll need to use the Terminal a lot, so add it to the Dock, by dragging its application icon there.

2. **In the Terminal window type** gem install sass **(see Figure 19-4).**

   The gem command is part of Ruby and is used to install different Ruby programs and libraries. It may take a few minutes for this command to run, since your Mac has to go onto the Internet and download and then install the correct files.

   In addition, depending on how permissions are set up on your Mac, you may need to execute this command as an administrator. To do that you must use the sudo command, like this:

       sudo gem install sass

   You'll then have to type an administrator username and password to install Sass.

   If all goes well, the Terminal window should look something like Figure 19-4. You're ready to run Sass. You'll learn how to do that on page 597.

   NOTE To update to a newer version of Sass, you can type gem update sass in the Terminal. If you don't have proper permissions, you may need to type sudo gem update sass then type in an administrator's username and password.

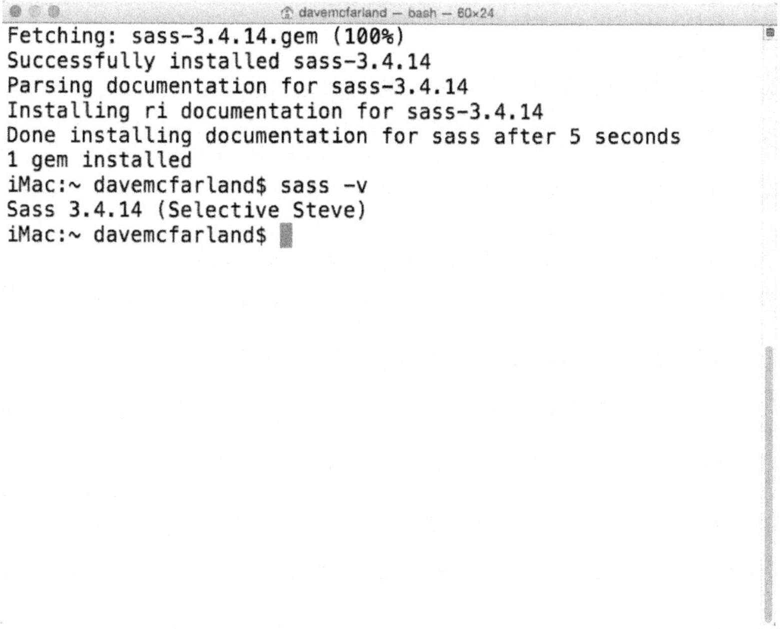

FIGURE 19-4

The Mac Terminal program is a command line utility. You'll use it all the time when working with Sass and many other common web development tools. To see which version of Sass you have installed, type sass -v *in the Terminal window.*

■ Sass Basics

Sass is both a *tool*—software that creates CSS files—and a *language* that adds features that don't currently exist in CSS. But don't worry; having spent this whole time learning about CSS, you won't need to spend another month learning a whole new language. Sass is completely compatible with plain CSS. In other words, you can start with a regular style sheet (like the ones you've been building throughout this book) and slowly improve that style sheet by adding time-saving Sass features to it.

In this chapter, you'll learn how to add many efficiency-boosting Sass features to your style sheets, but the important thing to keep in mind is that you can apply all of your hard-won knowledge about CSS when creating style sheets with Sass. In fact, you can take a regular style sheet—*styles.css*, for example—and turn it into a Sass style sheet simply by replacing .css with .scss—*styles.scss*, for example.

Sass Without the Command Line

If the idea of the Windows command prompt or the Mac Terminal gives you the shivers, there are other ways to harness the power of Sass.

Some text editors, like Sublime and WebStorm, let you install plugins that can compile Sass into CSS for you. In addition, there are several free and paid programs that can compile Sass files into CSS without having to install Ruby and Sass on your own.

These apps lets you specify which folder you'll put your Sass files into, and into which folder they should put the finished, processed CSS files. They can also detect changes you make to the Sass files and automatically generate new CSS files so you can instantly preview the changes you've made. Some even automatically refresh your browser window to reload the newly created CSS file.

- Scout (*http://mhs.github.io/scout-app/*) is a popular, free application, that runs on both Macs and Windows machines

- Koala (*http://koala-app.com/*) runs on Windows, Mac and Linux. It not only compiles Sass files, but also can convert Less (another CSS preprocessor language) and CoffeeScript (a JavaScript preprocessor language) for you.

- LiveReload (*http://livereload.com/*) is a commercial Mac app ($10), and a Windows version is under development. It can compile Sass, Less, Stylus, CoffeeScript, Jade and a bunch of other pre-processed languages web developers use.

- CodeKit (*http://incident57.com/codekit/*) is a powerful Mac app ($32) which not only handles Sass and a bunch of other languages, but also auto-refreshes your browser so you can instantly preview changes you make to your Sass files.

Organizing Your Files

When using Sass, you'll work with two different types of files: the ones you create (Sass files), and the ones the Sass preprocessor generates (plain CSS files for use by the browser). Sass files end in the extension .scss, and you'll add your CSS and Sass-specific code to these files.

Then, you'll use Sass—the software—to convert Sass files to a CSS file ending in .css. When using Sass you *never* edit the .css files themselves; you only edit the .scss files.

Because you have these two different types of files, the most common way to organize them is to create two separate directories at the root of your website: a css folder to hold the final CSS file that Sass creates, and another folder for your working Sass files. You can name this folder anything you want, but many web designers name it scss or sass. Inside this folder you'll create a Sass file, and name it based on what you'd like the final CSS file to be named. For example, if you're used to naming your CSS style sheets *styles.css*, then name your Sass file *styles.scss*. When Sass processes the *styles.scss* file, it automatically creates the file *styles.css*.

Converting Your Current Site to Sass

Because Sass understands plain CSS perfectly well, here's a simple process you can follow to start using Sass with a site you've already created.

1. **Add a folder named *sass* to the root level of your web site.**

   Make sure you also have a folder named *css* at the root of your site, and that *that* folder has the style sheet for your site.

2. **Move the site's style sheet from the *css* folder to the *sass* folder.**

   It's all right if the folder in your site isn't currently named *css*. Maybe you named it *styles* or something else. That's OK—you'll just have to use that folder name when running the Sass command, as described in the next section.

   In addition, if you have more than one style sheet in the *css* folder—for example, a *reset.css* file and a *styles.css* file—move both of them into the *sass* folder. As you'll see on page 600, you'll frequently use multiple Sass files in a project.

3. **Rename the style sheet in the *sass* folder so that its file extension is .scss.**

   For example, if the file's name is *site.css*, change its name to *site.scss*. If you have more than one CSS file—perhaps you have a *reset.css* file as well—then rename those files using the .scss extension also.

Of course, moving your CSS files to another folder in your site means your current web pages won't be able to find them, and the browser won't apply any styles to those web pages. But that's just temporary. When you run the Sass command, you'll get a new .css style sheet.

Running Sass

In order to convert a Sass file into a CSS file, you need to run the Sass command using the command line (the command prompt in Windows, or the Terminal app on Macs). The Sass command also includes a very special feature—called watch—that keeps a constant lookout for any changes you make to a .scss file. When the Sass command detects a change, it automatically regenerates the CSS file. This setup is particularly helpful as you're designing your site. Browsers don't understand Sass files, so simply changing the code in your Sass file doesn't let you see that change immediately. However, when the Sass command is in watch mode, you can instantly see any changes you make to a Sass file reflected in the web page just by refreshing the browser window to load the updated style sheet.

To run the Sass command:

1. **Open the command prompt on Windows, or Terminal on a Mac.**

   See step 5 on page 598 for a reminder on how to do this for Windows users, or step 1 on page 598 for Mac users.

2. **Using the command line, navigate to your site's root folder.**

   In order to run Sass, you need to get to the site's root folder—the folder where the *sass* and *css* folders are. However, you have to use language the command line understands. This involves typing a command like cd C:\Users\dave\Desktop\site or cd ~/Documents/site.

   If you're not sure how to navigate inside the command line, here's a simple trick that works for both Windows and Mac:

   a. **Open the command prompt or Terminal.**

   b. **In Windows Explorer or the Mac Finder, open a window that shows the directory with your site in it.**

      You need to be able to see both the command line and the window with your site's directory in it (see Figure 19-5).

   c. **On the command line, type** cd **followed by a space.**

      cd is a command that comes from Unix. It stands for "change directory," and it's used to travel from one folder to another using the command line. Don't forget to type a space character, since you need it to separate the cd command from the path you're about to add in the next step.

> **NOTE** Windows Note: To learn how to use the Windows command prompt to navigate your file system, visit *www.wikihow.com/Change-Directories-in-Command-Prompt*.

   d. **Drag the directory from the file window into the command line and release the mouse (#1 in Figure 19-5).**

      The *path*—the route to get from the top level of your computer's hard drive to the folder with your site—is added automatically to the command line.

> **NOTE** Mac Note: To learn how to use the Terminal to navigate your file system, visit *www.macworld.com/article/2042378/master-the-command-line-navigating-files-and-folders.html*.

   e. **Hit Enter.**

      The command-line prompt changes to the site's directory. It doesn't look like anything has happened, but according to the computer, you're now "in" that folder. Any commands you run on the command line at this point will use that folder as a point of reference.

3. **On the command line, type** sass --watch sass:css **and press Enter.**

   This starts the Sass preprocessor. It looks inside the *sass* folder for any files ending in .scss, converts them to regular CSS and then creates a CSS file inside the *css* folder. You should see output like that picture in #2 in Figure 19-5.

Because Sass is watching for any changes to Sass files, if you edit an .scss file inside the *sass* folder, a new .css file will be created automatically and deposited into the *css* folder.

If you're using a name other than *sass* for the folder containing your Sass files, use that in the command instead of *sass*. For example, if you named that folder *scss*, you would type sass --watch scss:css instead.

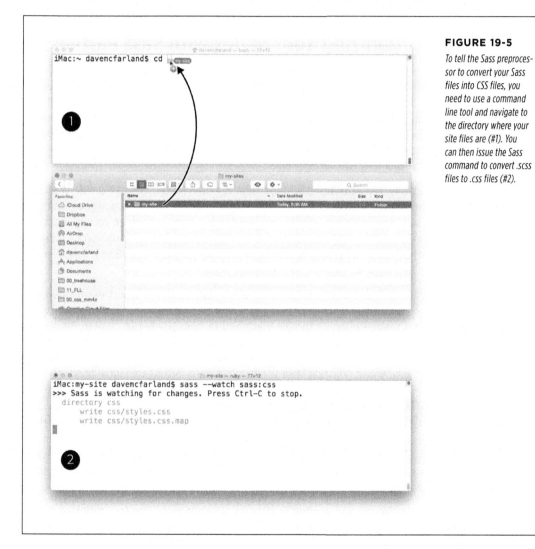

FIGURE 19-5

To tell the Sass preprocessor to convert your Sass files into CSS files, you need to use a command line tool and navigate to the directory where your site files are (#1). You can then issue the Sass command to convert .scss files to .css files (#2).

> **TIP** Sass can also compress the final CSS file—remove comments and extra spaces, and make other changes that shrink the file size of your CSS file. The result is a file that will load as quickly as possible for your site's visitors. To compress your CSS files when using Sass, type sass --watch scss:css --type compressed on the command line.

When you run Sass using the --watch option, Sass will run continuously. If you want to stop the watch command, type Ctrl-c in the command prompt or Terminal. If you close the command line window or restart your computer, you'll have to run the sass command again, following the instructions above.

As you can see, there's a fair amount of setup to get started using Sass. However, once you have Sass up and running, the fun begins.

▨ Organizing Your Styles with Sass Partials

Well-designed websites use lots of CSS. And the bigger and more complex a site gets, the larger and more complex the CSS. It's not difficult to create hundreds or even thousands of styles for a website, but that many styles make for a really big and long CSS file. Some web designers divide their CSS into smaller, more manageable files, but the more files you add to a site, the more time visitors' browsers will have to spend asking for and downloading files. Many web design pros recommend using as few CSS files as possible.

Fortunately, Sass can bring you the best of both worlds. You can divide your Sass rules into separate files organized in a logical way. For example, you could put your reset rules (page 109) in one file, your grid layout rules in another, your typographic rules in yet another file, and so on. You can then tell the Sass preprocessor to compile all of those files into a single CSS file, or even compress that CSS so it's smaller and faster to download (see the note on page 600).

In fact, even if you don't want to learn anything else about Sass, this one feature is reason enough to start using it. Being able to organize your CSS into separate files means it's easy to locate the file you need to edit: "I want to change the look of that form—the rules for that must be in the *forms.scss* file!" Remember, you can put regular CSS rules into any Sass file (see page 595), so you can simply use Sass as a way to divide and organize your regular CSS rules into manageable files.

Creating and Using Sass Partials

Sass lets you divide your CSS/Sass rules into multiple files and then combine them into a single CSS file. Sass calls these files *partials*, and there's a special way that you name and use them. To tell Sass that you *don't* want it to convert these partials into individual CSS files, you must begin the name of the partial file with an underscore (_) character.

For example, say you wanted to divide your style rules into four different files to make creating, finding, and updating them easier. You would begin the name of each file with an underscore: for example, *_reset.scss*, *_grid.scss*, *_layout.scss*, and *_forms.scss*. Now, when you run the Sass command, Sass won't convert this into four CSS files—*reset.css*, *grid.css*, *layout.css*, and *forms.css*—and place them into the css folder. In fact, Sass ignores these files until you explicitly call them into action.

Of course, you don't want those partial files to just sit there—you create them to include in the final CSS file that Sass outputs. You use an @import statement to load a Sass partial into another file, like this:

```
@import '_reset.scss';
```

The most common way to use partials is to have one main Sass file—the one that Sass converts to the finished CSS file—that includes nothing but these import statements. For example, say you wanted to produce a single CSS file named *styles.css*. You could then create a Sass file named *styles.scss* and place it in the *sass* folder. The contents of the Sass file would look like this:

```
@import '_reset.scss';
@import '_grid.scss';
@import '_layout.scss';
@import '_forms.scss';
```

Because the *styles.scss* file does *not* begin with an underscore character, Sass processes it and creates the file *styles.css* in the *css* folder. There's nothing particularly tricky happening here: Sass just copies the code from each of the partial files and then pastes that code into a single file. The order in which you list the partials dictates the order in which Sass adds the CSS, so in the above example the top of the CSS file will be the reset rules and the bottom of the CSS file will contain styles for forms. Remember that the order styles appear in a file can affect how the cascade works (page 99). Keep that in mind when ordering your @import directives.

Sass is pretty smart about partials, so you can use shorthand to identify them when importing them into another Sass file: You can leave off the _ and the .scss from the file name. The code above could be re-written more simply as:

```
@import 'reset';
@import 'grid';
@import 'layout';
@import 'forms';
```

The @import directive is your first taste of Sass syntax. Although @import is part of CSS, the way it's used here is purely Sass. If you tried to do this in a regular CSS file, a browser wouldn't know what to do with this, and it certainly couldn't combine all the files into a single CSS file.

Organizing Your Sass Partial Files

Many web designers who use Sass like to keep their files orderly. They'll create multiple Sass files and place them into subfolders grouped by function. There are as many ways to organize files as there are web designers, but here's a simple diagram for a basic Sass folder structure:

```
sass/
|
|-- helpers/              # special Sass files
|   |-- _variables.scss
```

```
|    |-- _mixins.scss
|
|-- base/                  # starter files for project
|    |-- _reset.scss
|    |-- _grid.scss
|    |-- _typography.scss
|
|-- layout/                # files to style page areas
|    |-- _header.scss
|    |-- _footer.scss
|    |-- _sidebar.scss
|    |-- _forms.scss
|
|-- components/            # file for UI components
|    |-- _buttons.scss
|    |-- _dropdown.scss
|    |-- _navigation.scss
|
`- styles.scss            # primary Sass file
```

Inside the main *sass* folder is the *styles.scss* file—the main file that Sass will convert to a CSS file. In addition, there are four subfolders to hold files that serve particular functions in the site design, as well as a few Sass-specific files that you'll learn about later in this chapter. To use all of these partial files, you need to import them into the *styles.scss* file. For this particular set of files, here's what you'd put in the *styles.scss* file:

```
@import 'helpers/variables';
@import 'helpers/mixins';
@import 'base/reset';
@import 'base/grid';
@import 'base/typography';
@import 'layout/header';
@import 'layout/footer';
@import 'layout/sidebar';
@import 'layout/forms';
@import 'components/buttons';
@import 'components/dropdown';
@import 'components/navigation';
```

Note that you have to list the folder name (so Sass knows to look in the correct subfolder), but you can leave off the underscore and the .scss extension for the file names.

NOTE For more ways to organize your Sass projects, check out these blog posts: *www.sitepoint.com/architecture-sass-project/*, *http://thesassway.com/beginner/how-to-structure-a-sass-project*, and *www.sitepoint.com/look-different-sass-architectures/*.

◼ Sass Variables

You've probably encountered times when you use the same value over and over and over again in your CSS. For example, say the main color of your company's logo is a deep blue: #083B91. The marketing department wants you to use this color a lot, so you use it as the background color for the navigation bar, the text color for <h1> tags, and the border color for sidebars.

So you create a few dozen CSS rules that use that color. But what happens if the logo color changes, or the marketing department decides to change the color by a single digit to #083B92? Sure, you can use search and replace to swap in a new color, but wouldn't it be great if you could just make a single change to a single file and have that color update everywhere in your CSS?

You can do just that using Sass variables. A *variable* is something that holds a value that might change or "vary"—just like your company's logo color. You store a value in the variable once, then use that variable multiple times. If you store a new value in the variable, the value is updated everywhere you used the variable in your Sass files: In other words, you make a change in one file, and Sass updates everything else for you.

There are two steps to using a Sass variable. First, you must define the variable, which means giving it a name and then giving it a value. In Sass, variable names begin with a dollar sign. You assign a value to the variable by using a colon (:) followed by the value. For example, to create a variable for your company's logo color, you'd add this to a Sass file:

```
$logo_color : #083B91;
```

Notice how this is formatted very much like a CSS declaration, except that $logo_color isn't a valid CSS property. It's Sass syntax, which means the Sass program identifies this particular line of code as a special Sass variable. Just as Sass converts Sass files to a CSS file, it replaces this variable name with the correct color value.

But to make Sass work this magic, you need to use that variable in a CSS rule. You use a variable anywhere you'd use a regular CSS value. For example, to assign that special logo color to <h1> tags, you'd write this style in a Sass file:

```
h1 {
  color: $logo_color;
}
```

When Sass finishes *compiling* (that is, converting) this code, the finished CSS file will have this perfectly valid CSS rule in it:

```
h1 {
  color: #083B91;
}
```

Organizing Your Sass Variables

You might start out with just a few uses for variables—maybe a couple of commonly used colors. However, as you start to use Sass more, you'll come up with dozens of good uses for them. To keep your variables in one place and accessible to all of your other Sass files, it's a good idea to create a separate file dedicated to just variables.

One way to do this is to create a file named _variables.scss and place it inside a folder dedicated to special Sass files like this one. Page 601 lists one possible way to organize all of your Sass files; a folder named something like *helpers* is a good solution.

Remember that beginning the name of a Sass file with the _ character means that file is a Sass partial; Sass creates a final CSS file by combining multiple partial files into one. The order in which you list the partial files in the main Sass file determines the order that Sass reads and processes those files. For example, say you had a file named *styles.scss*, and inside it you imported three partial files like this:

```
@import 'base/reset';
@import 'base/grid';
@import 'base/layout';
```

When you run the Sass command, Sass would first read the contents of a _reset. scss partial file. Sass would process its contents and add them to the beginning of a new file names *styles.css*. The rest of that CSS file would contain the contents of the _grid.scss partial, followed by the _layout.scss partial.

The point of a Sass variable is to set its value once and use it many, many times in your Sass files. Because other files will need to know the value you set the variable to, you must make sure the variables you create are loaded *first*, before any other Sass files. In other words, the best approach to including your variables is to import their partial file first, before any other partials, like this:

```
@import 'helpers/variables';
@import 'base/reset';
@import 'base/grid';
@import 'base/layout';
```

Common Uses for Sass Variables

Sass variables are commonly used to store color values. Based on marketing choices at your company, whims in web design, or your own change of mind, you may very well want to completely swap out the colors you're using on your site today with new colors tomorrow.

One simple approach is to define colors for different elements on a page, like text colors, headline colors, border colors, and background colors:

```
$text-color: #33333;
$headline-color: #ff0000;
$border-color: #0032ff;
$background-color: #FFEE99;
```

You'd put these styles in the _variables.scss file, and then you could use them in other Sass partial files. Many designers recommend using a two-step approach for color variables: Create a set of variables that defines a palette of colors, and then assign that variable to yet another variable that defines the particular use of the color.

Say your company has a set of five colors that make up its color palette. You could start by defining those color variables first. Then you could assign those colors to variables with functional names specific to the particular page elements or CSS properties, like this:

```scss
/* corporate color palette */
$primary-dark: #06888A;
$primary-light:  #FFEED5;
$primary-mid: #DC664A;
$secondary-dark: #5A3928;
$secondary-light: #FDC149;

/* functional variables */
$page-background: $primary-light;
$headline-color: $primary-dark;
$text-color: $primary-dark;
$border-light: $secondary-light;
$border-dark: $primary-dark;
```

This approach makes it easy to use the same color for multiple components. For example, in this code the text and headline colors are the same color: #06888A. But instead of setting that color twice, like this:

```scss
$headline-color: #06888A;
$text-color: #06888A;
```

You set it once, in the $primary-dark variable. If you decide to change your site's color palette, just change the value of the $primary-dark variable, and both the headline and text colors will change. In addition, if you later decide to use another color for the text color, it's easy to swap in one of the other variables you created in your color palette:

```scss
$headline-color: $primary-dark;
$text-color: $secondary-dark;
```

Variables are also useful for setting up your *font stacks*—the list of fonts you wish to use for different page elements like headlines and body text (see page 123). For example, a simple technique is to assign one font stack to a variable used for headline text, and another for body text, like this:

```scss
$headline-font: 'Varela Round', Helvetica, Arial, sans-serif;
$body-font: 'Palatino Linotype', Baskerville, serif;
```

You could then use those variables in other Sass partial files. For example, say you had a partial file named _typography.scss_. You could then use the font stack variables in other styles:

```
body {
  font-family: $body-font;
}
h1, h2, h3 {
  font-family: $headline-font;
}
```

If you later decide to use different fonts in those stacks, just update the $headline-font variable or the $body-font variable.

As you start to use Sass variables you'll discover many uses for them. For example, if you like rounded corners (page 199), you could set up a variable that controls how rounded those corners should be on your page elements like sidebars, images, and so on:

```
$border-radius: 6px;
```

If you find that the radius is too small or large, change the variable. All the styles will update, and the page elements will use the new radius value.

POWER USERS' CLINIC

Let Sass Do the Math

Sass can even do basic mathematical operations. No, you won't use Sass to replace your calculator, but you can use it to generate new values based on mathematical principles, and you'll often do this using Sass variables.

For example, say you wanted to set a standard margin for headlines: The bottom margin will always be half of the top margin. To give you flexibility so you can adjust these margins using a variable, you could start by defining a variable for the top margin:

```
$margin-top: 20px;
```

Then, instead of using a plain number like 10px for the bottom margin setting, create a new variable and use some math:

```
$margin-bottom: $margin-top / 2;
```

Using this mathematical approach offers a lot of flexibility. If 20 pixels isn't enough, change its value in the variable. The other variable's value will automatically change, keeping the same 1:2 proportions.

You need to use the same measurement units when adding or subtracting. For example, using the 20px value you just set for $margin-top;, you can't do this:

```
$margin-bottom: $margin-top + 1em;
```

Sass doesn't know how to add pixels to ems and will spit out an error when trying to compile the Sass code. However, you can add and subtract using the same units:

```
$margin-bottom: $margin-top – 5px;
```

There are lots of good uses for Sass math. You'll see one example on page 628 when you'll use Sass to create media queries. For other uses and more information on Sass math, check out _https://scotch.io/tutorials/getting-started-with-sass#math_, _https://css-tricks.com/video-screencasts/132-quick-useful-case-sass-math-mixins/_, _http://sass-lang.com/documentation/file.SASS_REFERENCE.html#operations_.

Nesting Selectors

Earlier in this book you read about descendant selectors (page 50) and some of the ways they can be useful (page 582). As you'll recall, a descendant selector is a selector composed of multiple selectors that indicate the nesting of elements. For example, the selector .nav a translates to "select all <a> tags that are inside another element with the class of nav."

Often you'll use descendant selectors to define the look of various elements inside a larger component. For example, say you use the following HTML to create a navigation bar:

```
<ul class="nav">
  <li><a href="index.html">Home</a></li>
  <li><a href="about.html">About</a></li>
  <li><a href="contact.html">Contact</a></li>
</ul>
```

You might create a series of selectors to format the different parts of this navigation bar. For example, there are three tags in use here, so you might have the following selectors:

```
.nav {
  display: flex;
  justify-content: space-around;
  list-style-type: none;
}
.nav li {
  width: 30%;
  background-color: #FFEED5;
  padding: 5px;
  text-align: center;
}
.nav a {
  text-decoration: none;
}
```

These styles use flexbox (Chapter 17) to lay out three buttons side by side. Don't worry about the properties listed: What's important for this discussion are the selectors. Here, descendant selectors make sure that not every list item (<li>) or anchor (<a>) tag is formatted using these rules; just the ones inside the navigation bar.

Sass provides a way to keep styles like this grouped together while also decreasing the amount of code you need to write to get the same output as above. To do that, you use Sass's *nested selector* feature. First, notice that all three of the selectors above begin with .nav. That becomes the *base* or main selector:

```
.nav {
  display: flex;
  justify-content: space-around;
  list-style-type: none;
}
```

Then, instead of creating two new styles with the selectors .nav li, and .nav a, you simply nest the li and a selectors inside like this:

```
.nav {
  display: flex;
  justify-content: space-around;
  list-style-type: none;

  li {
    width: 30%;
    background-color: #FFEED5;
    padding: 5px;
    text-align: center;
  }

  a {
    text-decoration: none;
  }
}
```

Notice that the CSS for the li and a goes inside the closing } for the .nav style: that's *nesting*. It's not valid CSS, but it *is* valid SCSS. In fact, when the Sass command compiles the above code, the final CSS will look like this:

```
.nav {
  display: flex;
  justify-content: space-around;
  list-style-type: none;
}
.nav li {
  width: 30%;
  background-color: #FFEED5;
  padding: 5px;
  text-align: center;
}
.nav a {
  text-decoration: none;
}
```

It's the same code as you saw on page 607, but it involves a little less typing, and it keeps the styles grouped within the outer .nav container.

Referencing the Parent Selector

In the examples directly above, you can see that Sass automatically adds the name of the outer selector—the one that wraps around the nested selectors—when generating the final CSS. For example, the `.nav` selector is added to the `li` in the Sass code to produce `.nav li` in the CSS code. By default, Sass uses the name of the parent selector, followed by a space and then the nested selector.

But there are times when you don't want that space. For example, say you wanted to use Sass nested selectors to create the pseudo-classes used for different link states. You might try to use this Sass code:

```
a {
  color: blue;
  :hover {
    color: green;
  }
}
```

Unfortunately, you'd end up with this CSS:

```
a {
  color: blue;
}
a :hover {
  color: green;
}
```

That might look OK at first glance, but see the space between the a and the `:hover`? This only changes the text color of an tag *inside* the <a> tag and not the <a> tag itself, and only when you hover over that nested tag. What you really want is a`:hover`, without the space. To do that, Sass provides the & (ampersand) symbol. When the Sass command encounters the &, it replaces that & with the parent selector name. So, to get the correct CSS output for the above example, you'd use this Sass code:

```
a {
  color: blue;
  &:hover {
    color: green;
  }
}
```

There's no space between the & and the `:hover`, so the final, output will be a`:hover`—the correct pseudo-class. If you wanted to style all four of the pseudo-classes for links, you could use this basic format for a Sass nested selector:

```
a {
  &:link {

  }
```

```
  &:visited {

  }
  &:hover {

  }
  &:active {

  }
}
```

Likewise, if you apply a class—button, for example—to certain links and want pseudo-classes like .button:link, .button:visited, .button:hover, and .button:active, start like this:

```
.button {
  &:link {

  }
  &:visited {

  }
  &:hover {

  }
  &:active {

  }
}
```

Because Sass literally replaces the & with the parent selector's name, you can use nesting to create a series of class names that are independent of the hierarchy of descendant selectors. For example, some designers don't like to worry about the exact nesting or type of HTML tags used to create page elements. They simply apply class names to every (or most) HTML tags. For example, instead of writing HTML like this:

```
<div class="main">
  <h1>Title</h1>
  <div>

  </div>
</div>
```

And, relying on CSS selectors like .main, .main h1, .main div, they'll write HTML like this:

```
<div class="main">
  <h1 class="main-title">Title</h1>
  <div class="main-content">
```

```
            </div>
        </div>
```

And create styles like .main, .main-title, and .main-content. Sass makes it easy to do that using nesting and the & character.

```
.main {
  &-title {

  }
  &-content {

  }
}
```

Multiple Levels of Nesting

Sass lets you nest selectors nearly infinitely. After all, it's just a computer program, and it can figure out what to do with 50 levels of nested selectors. But for mere humans, it's best to limit how much you nest your selectors—one or two levels is enough to handle most situations. More than that and it's easy to lose track of your selectors.

TIP Too many nested levels also indicates that you are depending too much on how your HTML tags are nested in your web pages. This makes your CSS "brittle," since a simple change to how you structure your HTML could mean that a complex descendant selector no longer applies.

To nest multiple levels of selectors, just place a selector inside an already nested selector. For instance, say in the example on page 607, you also wanted to add a :hover pseudo-class to each navigation bar link. You can nest the :hover style inside the a selector, which is itself nested inside the .nav selector, like this:

```
.nav {
  display: flex;
  justify-content: space-around;
  list-style-type: none;

  li {
    width: 30%;
    background-color: #FFEED5;
    padding: 5px;
    text-align: center;
  }
```

```
a {
  text-decoration: none;

  &:hover {
    text-decoration: underline;
  }
}
```

Note that you need to use the & character to reference the parent selector, and that the &:hover is nested inside the a selector.

In addition to the styles listed on page 608, Sass will compile the above code to produce a selector created by this multiple-level nest:

```
.nav a:hover {
  text-decoration: underline;
}
```

As you can probably see by now, nesting multiple levels of selectors with Sass can get very confusing very quickly. But used with care, Sass nested selectors will make it easier for you to write less CSS and keep your selectors organized and grouped together by function.

■ Inheriting (or Extending) Properties

On page 49, you learned how group selectors let you apply the same set of properties to multiple page elements. For example, to assign the same font and font color to all headings, you could use a group selector like this:

```
h1, h2, h3, h4, h5, h6 {
  font-family: "Raleway", Helvetica, Arial, sans-serif;
  color: #222;
}
```

Group selectors mean you don't have to repeat the same set of properties over and over again. Without a group selector, the single style above would turn into six styles like this:

```
h1 {
  font-family: "Raleway", Helvetica, Arial, sans-serif;
  color: #222;
}
h2 {
  font-family: "Raleway", Helvetica, Arial, sans-serif;
  color: #222;
}
```

```
h3 {
  font-family: "Raleway", Helvetica, Arial, sans-serif;
  color: #222;
}
h4 {
  font-family: "Raleway", Helvetica, Arial, sans-serif;
  color: #222;
}
h5 {
  font-family: "Raleway", Helvetica, Arial, sans-serif;
  color: #222;
}
h6 {
  font-family: "Raleway", Helvetica, Arial, sans-serif;
  color: #222;
}
```

Not only is that a lot of code, but if you want to change the font color for all six headlines, you need to update six lines of code instead of just one. Sass provides a way for a style to inherit the properties of another style. In the above example, basically the six different headings h1 through h6 share the same set of properties. In other words, they inherit, or what programmers call *extend*, a base set of properties.

Sass lets you take a current style and apply its properties to other styles by extending the original style. You can see a simple example in the headline styles above. Say you wanted to apply the same font-family and color to headings h1 through h3 (you can use as many as you want; this is just a quick example). You could start with the h1 style, and using Sass's @extend directive, apply those style to the other headings, like this:

```
h1 {
  font-family: "Raleway", Helvetica, Arial, sans-serif;
  color: #222;
}
h2 {
  @extend h1
}
h3 {
  @extend h1
}
```

By now you're probably wondering: Wouldn't a group selector be easier? Well, the power of the @extend directive comes when you add additional properties to each selector, so the particular styles share *some* properties, but are distinct in other ways. For example, say you wanted to add a borderline above <h2> tags, and indent <h3> tags. However, you still want the headlines to share the same font and color. In that case, you'd write the following Sass:

```
h1 {
  font-family: "Raleway", Helvetica, Arial, sans-serif;
  color: #222;
}
h2 {
  @extend h1;
  border-top: 1px solid #444;
}
h3 {
  @extend h1;
  margin-left: 20px;
}
```

When the Sass command does its magic, it converts the above code into the following CSS:

```
h1, h2, h3 {
  font-family: "Raleway", Helvetica, Arial, sans-serif;
  color: #222;
}
h2 {
  border-top: 1px solid #444;
}
h3 {
  margin-left: 20px;
}
```

Extending styles provides several benefits: First, you can limit the number of selectors you have to write. Using a group selector, you have two different styles for the same element. For example, above, in the CSS code, the h2 selector is used in both the group selector—h1, h2, h3—and in the unique h2 selector.

Another related benefit is that you can keep all of your CSS properties for an element in a single selector. This means if you want to change the look of <h2> tags, you don't have to hunt around for two styles—the group selector and the individual selector style. Just locate the h2 selector, and if you want to change the font and color, then remove the @extend directive. Or, even better, if you want to change the color for all of the headlines find the extending selector—the h1, in this example—and change it there.

> **NOTE** You can put the @extend directive anywhere within a style—on the first or the last line, for example. However, most designers add @extend first before any other properties. This approach makes it a lot easier to see that the style is based on another style.

Extending With Placeholder Selectors

Sass is pretty aggressive about extending selectors. It will extend not just the selector you specify, but other styles that reference that selector. This usually leads to unwanted consequences. For example, let's say I had the following Sass code in an .scss file:

```scss
#main h1 {
    background-color: blue;
}
h1 {
    font-family: "Raleway", Helvetica, Arial, sans-serif;
    color: #222;
}
h2 {
    @extend h1;
    border-top: 1px solid #444;
}
h3 {
    @extend h1;
    margin-left: 20px;
}
```

The first style—#main h1—adds a blue background to any <h1> tag inside an element with an ID value of main. Unfortunately, when the h2 and h3 styles extend the h1 style, they also extend to that #main h1 style producing the following CSS:

```css
#main h1, #main h2, #main h3 {
    background-color: blue;
}
h1, h2, h3 {
    font-family: "Raleway", Helvetica, Arial, sans-serif;
    color: #222;
}
h2 {
    border-top: 1px solid #444;
}
h3 {
    margin-left: 20px;
}
```

Notice that Sass produces a group selector for all <h1>, <h2>, and <h3> tags inside the main element. It gets worse if you have other styles that include the h1 selector, like h1 span or h1 a. Sass will create group selectors for those too! To work around that problem, Sass provides what it calls a *placeholder selector*. This placeholder's name begins with a % symbol; you can't use that symbol in a normal CSS selector name, but in Sass it indicates a style that you only want to use as the basis for other styles.

For example, to avoid the problem of *over*extending the h1 selector in the above example, you could create a placeholder selector and extend it like this:

```
#main h1 {
  background-color: blue;
}
%headline {
  font-family: "Raleway", Helvetica, Arial, sans-serif;
  color: #222;
}
h1 {
  @extend %headline;
}
h2 {
  @extend %headline;
  border-top: 1px solid #444;
}
h3 {
  @extend %headline;
  margin-left: 20px;
}
```

Now, %headline isn't a real CSS selector. It's a only Sass thing, so when the final CSS is generated, there won't be a %headline style in the CSS file. Because the other styles aren't extending the h1 selector, that top style—#main h1—won't be extended, and the final CSS output will look like what you'd hope for:

```
#main h1 {
  background-color: blue;
}
h1, h2, h3 {
  font-family: "Raleway", Helvetica, Arial, sans-serif;
  color: #222;
}
h2 {
  border-top: 1px solid #444;
}
h3 {
  margin-left: 20px;
}
```

Only Extend Related Elements

If you're not careful, extending styles using Sass can get out of hand quickly. You might be tempted to come up with a placeholder style for a particular border style—say blue, dotted, 1 pixel thick, with 5-pixel rounded corners—and then @extend that style on every style you'd like to have that border. That might sound like a good idea, but it will quickly lead to style sheets bloated with group selectors of unrelated elements.

A better approach is to only extend elements that are related by function. The headline example on page 612 is a good use case for the @extend directive. In addition, if you have a particular user-interface element—like a button or dialog box—that has different states, then create a base style and extend it.

The headline example on page 612

> **NOTE** Mixins (discussed next) provide another alternative to @extend. For a discussion on the key differences between the two and when to use which, read *http://csswizardry.com/2014/11/when-to-use-extend-when-to-use-a-mixin/*.

For example, you might create a style that applies to all the buttons on your site—like an Order Now, Delete, or Cancel button. They all share some similarities—font, shape, and so on—but could have unique properties as well, like a green background for the Order Now button and red for Delete. You can easily create a base style for all buttons and extend it into other styles with additional properties, like this:

```
%btn {
    display: inline-block;
    padding: 1em;
    border-radius: 3px;
}
.btn-order {
    @extend %btn;
    background-color: green;
    color: white;
}
.btn-delete {
    @extend %btn;
    background-color: red;
    color: white;
}
.btn-cancel {
    @extend %btn;
    background-color: #888;
    color: black;
}
```

The Sass command will compile that code into this:

```
.btn, .btn-order, .btn-delete, .btn-cancel {
  display: inline-block;
  padding: 1em;
  border-radius: 3px;
}
.btn-order {
    background-color: green;
    color: white;
}
```

```
.btn-delete {
    background-color: red;
    color: white;
}
.btn-cancel {
    background-color: #888;
    color: black;
}
```

Using and extending placeholders makes it easy for you to update the overall look of a generic user interface element like a button. In this example, if you wanted to remove rounded corners from all buttons, you'd simply delete the border-radius property from the placeholder selector, and all the buttons on your site would be updated.

There are many other user interface elements that benefit from placeholder selectors and the @extend directive, like dialog boxes used to alert the user, indicate an error, confirm an order, or indicate a successful transaction.

Mixins

Sass includes another powerful tool called *mixins* to streamline your CSS and save you time. Think of a mixin as akin to a macro in Word or Excel—it's like a mini program that does a lot of work so you don't have to. In the case of Sass, a mixin is a shortcut that refers to a group of CSS declarations that you'd like to use over and over again. In other words, mixins can write CSS code for you, saving your tired fingers the effort.

Creating a Mixin

In Chapter 17 you learned about flexbox and how you can turn any page element into a flex container simply by setting the display property to flex. Unfortunately, to get that to work in Safari, you also need a vendor prefix (page 321), so to turn a div with the class of container into a flex container, you have to write two lines of CSS:

```
.container {
  display: -webkit-flex;
  display: flex;
}
```

In other words, you have to write more than twice as much code as you should. A Sass mixin simplifies this chore by letting you write one line of code and giving you two in return. To create a mixin, first add the @mixin directive, followed by the name you want to assign to the mixin and a set of curly braces:

```
@mixin flex {

}
```

@mixin is a Sass keyword, but the name (flex in this example) is up to you. Because this mixin will create the CSS code to create a flex container, the name flex is a good choice.

Then, inside the curly braces, you add the code you want Sass to add to your final style sheet. In this case, it should output the same two lines of CSS code:

```
@mixin flex {
  display: -webkit-flex;
  display: flex;
}
```

Mixins are reusable bits of code, so they're like a function in programming languages like JavaScript: You can use a mixin over and over to insert CSS into your finished CSS file. Because you can reuse them, just as you can reuse Sass variables (page 603), it's a common practice to put your mixins into a separate Sass partial file named _mixins.scss and include this partial file near the top of your main Sass file (the one that inserts all the other partials). So as a general rule, it's best to import mixins just *after* variables (since you'll often use variables in mixins) but *before* any Sass file that might use your mixins. For example:

```
@import 'helpers/variables';
@import 'helpers/mixins';
@import 'base/reset';
@import 'base/grid';
@import 'base/layout';
```

Once you've created a mixin, you can use it in any styles you create.

Using a Mixin

To use a mixin, you use Sass's @include directive followed by the name of the mixin. For example, to turn a page element with the class of container into a flex container, you could use the mixin like this:

```
.container {
  @include flex;
}
```

After Sass compiles this code, you'll see the following code in the final CSS file:

```
.container {
  display: -webkit-flex;
  display: flex;
}
```

Of course, you can also include other properties as part of the style after you use the mixin. For example, if you wanted to assign a background color to the container and a border, just add that CSS after the mixin, like this:

```
.container {
  @include flex;
  background-color: #84F;
  border: 1px solid #444;
}
```

That code will turn into the following CSS:

```
.container {
  display: -webkit-flex;
  display: flex;
  background-color: #84F;
  border: 1px solid #444;
}
```

As you can see, mixins come in very handy for any properties that include vendor prefixes like the flex properties discussed in Chapter 17, or the CSS animations and transforms discussed in Chapter 10.

> **NOTE** Sass mixins are useful, but can get very complicated. For a complete reference to Sass mixins, visit the Sass documentation at *http://sass-lang.com/documentation/file.SASS_REFERENCE.html#mixins*.

Giving Mixins Information

Sass mixins can do more than just spit back CSS. They can also accept information and use it to control the information the mixin produces. As you just saw, mixins come in really handy for properties that include vendor prefixes. The CSS transform property (page 319), requires two vendor prefixes if you want to support Safari and Internet Explorer 9. For example, to rotate an element 10 degrees, you'd need three lines of CSS code

```
-webkit-transform: rotate(10deg);
-ms-transform: rotate(10deg);
transform: rotate(10deg);
```

This looks like a great place to use a Sass mixin, but notice that the rotation value is very specific: 10 degrees of rotation. You might want a particular element to rotate 5 degrees, or 45 degrees, or even -30 degrees; the exact amount will usually vary. For example, it would be great if, when you include the mixin, you could specify how much the element should rotate.

Fortunately, you can give a mixin some data, and it'll use that data when outputting its CSS. In this case, you want to create a mixin that takes a degree value. So start with the @mixin directive, the name of the mixin, a pair of parentheses with a variable name inside them, and a set of curly braces, like this:

```
@mixin rotate($deg) {

}
```

The $deg in the above code looks just like the Sass variables discussed on page 603. It begins with a dollar sign followed by some characters. In this example, the $deg inside the parentheses is called a *parameter*— it's a variable, but it's empty until you use the mixin and *pass* in (that is, assign it) a value. You'll see how to do that in a minute, but first you need to finish this mixin by adding the code Sass should output:

```
@mixin rotate($deg) {
  -webkit-transform: rotate($deg);
  -ms-transform: rotate($deg);
  transform: rotate($deg);
}
```

Note that the parameter $deg is used just as you would use any Sass variable. In this case, you're using it to set a specific amount of rotation. You'd add the above code to the _mixins.scss partial file, then use (or *call*) the mixin in your styles. For example, say you wanted to rotate every <h1> tag three degrees, and every <div> tag seven degrees. You could create this style:

```
h1 {
  @include rotate(3deg);
}
div {
  @include rotate(7deg);
}
```

The resulting Sass compiled CSS would look like this:

```
h1 {
  -webkit-transform: rotate(3deg);
  -ms-transform: rotate(3deg);
  transform: rotate(3deg);
}
div {
  -webkit-transform: rotate(7deg);
  -ms-transform: rotate(7deg);
  transform: rotate(7deg);
}
```

Don't Reinvent the Mixin

Sass mixins save you time by letting your write less CSS. Why not take that a step further and save even more time by using mixins that other people have already written? At their most complex, mixins look very much like straight computer programming: They can use variables, loops, and conditional statements to do some seemingly amazing things. Fortunately, there are many libraries of established Sass mixins to choose from:

- Bourbon (*http://bourbon.io*) is a small mixin library that adds vendor prefixes and performs other fancy magic for many CSS properties such as animation (page 338), transitions (page 330), font-face (page 131) and more. It's a great little set of tools.

- Neat (*http://neat.bourbon.io*), from the same people who

created Bourbon, is a set of mixins that make creating CSS grids (see Chapter 16) easier.

- Susy (*http://susy.oddbird.net*) is another set of mixins for creating CSS grids. This library is very popular with Sass folks.

- Breakpoint (*http://breakpoint-sass.com*) is a mixin library with a single purpose: to make writing media queries (page 460) fast and simple.

- Compass (*http://compass-style.org*) is actually a bit more than a mixin library. It does contain loads of useful mixins but it does a lot more, including helping you create CSS sprites (page 298). Compass is big, and offers so many features that the creators call it a *CSS authoring framework*.

Inserting Variables into Text

In the previous section, you created a handy rotate mixin. Every time you want to rotate an element, you simply include the mixin and give it a value, like 5deg, 7deg, or -45deg. Since mixins are all about doing less typing, wouldn't it be even better to just supply a number, instead of the full degree value—5 instead of 5deg, for example. After all, you'll always need the deg part in the final CSS code, so why not let Sass write it for you?

In other words, you could just write the rotation as:

```
h1 {
  @include rotate(3);
}
```

Then, add deg to the output in your mixin. You might think you could try something like this:

```
@mixin rotate($deg) {
  -webkit-transform: rotate($deg deg);
  -ms-transform: rotate($deg deg);
  transform: rotate($deg deg);
}
```

Unfortunately, Sass would add a space between the value you supply and deg, and the output would look something like this:

```
h1 {
  -webkit-transform: rotate(3 deg);
  -ms-transform: rotate(3 deg);
  transform: rotate(3 deg);
}
```

The space is invalid, so browsers won't rotate the element. But you can't just eliminate the space in the mixin like this:

```
@mixin rotate($deg) {
  -webkit-transform: rotate($degdeg);
  -ms-transform: rotate($degdeg);
  transform: rotate($degdeg);
}
```

If you do, Sass won't create any CSS. Instead it will spit out an error: Undefined variable: "$degdeg". That's because without the space, the variable is no longer $deg; it's $degdeg, which doesn't exist.

To combine a Sass variable with text strings, you have to use some special symbols that tell Sass where the real variable lives. This technique is called *interpolation*, and basically it says, "Hey Sass, here's the variable; spit out its value." To do so, you must wrap the variable inside some special characters, starting with #{ followed by the variable name and a closing }. For example, to get the above example to work, Sass has to interpolate the $deg variable, so you have to write the code like this:

```
@mixin rotate($deg) {
  -webkit-transform: rotate(#{$deg}deg);
  -ms-transform: rotate(#{$deg}deg);
  transform: rotate(#{$deg}deg);
}
```

Now you can use the above mixin, send a number value, and Sass will correctly connect the number with the text "deg" without complaining, so that @include rotate(3); will produce:

```
  -webkit-transform: rotate(3deg);
  -ms-transform: rotate(3deg);
  transform: rotate(3deg);
```

Passing More Information and Optional Values to Mixins

Mixins aren't just useful for vendor-prefixed properties or values, either. They come in handy anytime you have to write similar CSS over and over. For example, when assigning text properties to a heading, a paragraph, a copyright notice, or any piece of text, it's common to set values like font-size, line-height, font-weight, and color.

You can create a mixin that lets you write a single line of Sass code, but get four lines of CSS in return. The trick is providing all of that information to the mixin. Fortunately, Sass lets you supply more than one piece of information (also called an *argument*) to a mixin. Just provide the names of each of the variable (or *parameter*) in a comma-separated list inside the parentheses after the mixin name. For example, to create a mixin that accepts four font properties and produces four lines of CSS, you could write this:

```
@mixin text($size, $line-height, $weight, $color) {
  font-size: $size;
  line-height: $line-height;
  font-weight: $weight;
  color: $color;
}
```

In this example, the mixin is named text. To use it, you include the mixin and supply four values like this:

```
h1 {
  @include text(1.25em, 1.2, bold, #FF0000);
}
```

The resulting CSS that Sass creates would look like this:

```
h1 {
  font-size: 2em;
  line-height: 1.2;
  font-weight: bold;
  color: #FF000;
}
```

Mixins can really save you time and typing. But in this example, what if you don't want to supply a color or a font weight? You're only interested in setting the font size and line height. In that case you can't simply leave out the extra values like this:

```
h1 {
  @include text(1.25em, 1.2);
}
```

Because this mixin expects four values, if you only provide two, Sass will spit out an error and your Sass files won't compile into a CSS file. Fortunately, you can tell Sass that mixin values are optional. For instance, say you wanted to make the line-height, font-weight, and color values optional. You would assign null within the mixin definition for each of those parameters, like this:

```
@mixin text($size, $line-height: null, $weight: null, $color: null) {
  font-size: $size;
  line-height: $line-height;
  font-weight: $weight;
  color: $color;
}
```

The null value here tells Sass that it's okay if those values are empty. In other words you can leave those values out when using the mixin, so all of these styles will compile without errors:

```
h1 {
  @include text(2em);
}
h2 {
  @include text(1.25em, 1.2);
}
p {
  @include text(1em, 1,2, normal);
}
```

In addition, instead of using null, you can assign default values to mixin parameters, and Sass will use those values if you don't supply your own. For example, say you wanted the regular value of the line-height for most elements to be 1.2, and the weight property to be normal. You can assign those default values within the mixin like this:

```
@mixin text($size, $line-height: 1.2, $weight: normal, $color: null) {
  font-size: $size;
  line-height: $line-height;
  font-weight: $weight;
  color: $color;
}
```

Now, if you simply specify the font size when using the mixin like this:

```
h1 {
  @include text(2em);
}
```

Sass will create CSS using the default values for any properties you leave out:

```
h1 {
  font-size: 2em;
  line-height: 1.2;
  font-weight: normal;
}
```

There's one final wrinkle to using multiple parameters like this. What if you want to specify a font size and color, but not the two other parameters? When you include a mixin in a style, Sass expects the values you pass the mixin to come in the same order as they're listed in the mixin. For example, look at this use of the above mixin for an h2 rule:

```
h2 {
  @include text(2em, red);
}
```

Because Sass expects the second piece of information to be a `line-height` value, it will attempt to assign `red` to the `line-height` property. This isn't valid CSS and is clearly not what you want. However, you can explicitly tell Sass what values you want assigned to which parameters when you include the mixin in a style by listing the mixin parameter followed by a colon and the value you wish to assign:

```
h2 {
  @include text(2em, $color:red);
}
```

Sass mixins can be a real time-saver and are well worth the time it takes to learn how to use them.

Working with Media Queries

As you saw in Chapter 15, media queries are important for creating flexible designs that look and work well at a variety of screen sizes. Media queries let you make fonts larger for bigger screens, or eliminate unwanted margins and padding on small phone screens. Sass includes built-in support for media queries within selectors. For example, say you wanted all <h1> tags to be 2 ems in size normally, but when the screen width reached 1200 pixels, the headline should be larger—3 ems, for instance. You can do that in Sass like this:

```
h1 {
  font-size: 2em;
  @media (min-width: 1200px) {
    font-size: 3em;
  }
}
```

This looks a little like the nested selectors you read about on page 607; however, the final CSS looks very different. In this case, Sass creates one h1 style, and then generates a media query with another h1 style. The final, compiled CSS looks like this:

```
h1 {
  font-size: 2em;
}
@media (min-width: 1200px) {
  h1 {
    font-size: 3em;
  }
}
```

Pretty slick. The benefit of this approach is that you can group all of your h1 style information in one place. As you read on page 464, normally with media queries you divide your style sheet into multiple media queries and duplicate selectors within each media query. So, depending upon how many media queries you add to a CSS file, you may have h1 selectors in 2, 3, or 5 different parts of a file. With Sass, you can group all of the media queries with the selector, so you can see at a glance how the h1 tag will be formatted at each breakpoint.

NOTE The downside of the Sass approach is that it literally creates separate media queries for each selector, so a style sheet can become littered with extra media query code. There's a lot of debate about this, but many designers think that Sass's approach is easier for managing your styles and that it doesn't really add much code. Here's a good article explaining the pros and cons of *inline media queries* (the kind shown in the above example): *http://benfrain.com/inline-or-combined-media-queries-in-sass-fight/*.

Creating Media Query Mixins

While embedding your media queries inside a selector can help group an element's properties in a single spot in a Sass file, they're even more useful when combined with a mixin. As you can see in the code on the opposite page, the media query's specification is written directly in the code: `min-width: 1200px`. But what if you decide that 1200 pixels is too large a number, or too small? If you've added the query to hundreds of other page elements, then you'll need to make a lot of updates to your Sass files.

You can combine several Sass techniques—variables, mixins, and inline media queries—to create a very customizable method for adding media queries to your styles. There are many different ways to create media query mixins with Sass, and (as you read on page 460) there are also many different ways to use media queries.

In this section, you'll see one technique based on the mobile-first approach discussed on page 463. The basic strategy is to start with styles that work at all browser widths. That is, the basic styles (without media queries) present the mobile version and also set common properties shared at all screen widths, like the fonts used for headlines and text, or the colors used for backgrounds.

Then you add media queries for different breakpoints that modify the previous styles to accommodate different screen widths. For example, as the browser window gets wider, you could use a breakpoint to change the size of headlines, or to add space around a photo. In other words, each media query refines the original design by adding rules that improve the appearance at the new screen width.

In this example, you'll have three breakpoints: small, medium, and large. Small will cover devices like larger mobile phones—something like a Samsung Galaxy S6. Medium will be for most tablets, and large will work with desktop and laptop displays. In addition, you'll create media queries that work within *just* those ranges and ones that work for that breakpoint and greater.

To do so, you'll create Sass variables for the breakpoints; create mixins to generate the media queries based on those breakpoints; and use mixins in your code, using the `@include` directive.

■ SETTING BREAKPOINT VARIABLES.

Your design might adapt differently at different screen widths. For example, you might want that four-column design to turn into a three-column design when the screen is less than 760 pixels wide. Or maybe 780 is a better value. To get started, you can create Sass variables and provide values that you can later change if you need to:

```
$screen-small : 400px;
$screen-medium : 760px;
$screen-larger: 1000px;
```

Because these are Sass variables, it's a good idea to follow the advice on page 604, and store these inside a Sass partial file dedicated to just defining variables: _variables.scss is a good choice. You can use these variables in the mixins.

CREATING THE MEDIA QUERY MIXINS

The mixins will generate the necessary media query code using the breakpoint variables. To provide the most flexibility, you can create two different media queries for the small and medium breakpoints. The first media query will apply when the browser window is *at least* as wide as the breakpoint, but it can be wider than the next breakpoints as well. You'd use this media query when you want, for example, to add a style that works on both tablet and desktop displays.

The mixin for this media query would look like this:

```
@mixin mq-small-up {
  @media (min-width: $screen-small) {
    @content;
  }
}
```

Notice that there's a new Sass directive here: @content. This represents whatever code the designer places inside opening and closing braces following the @include directive. For example, to use the above mixin to increase the font size of paragraphs when the browser screen is wider than the smallest breakpoint, you could write this:

```
p {
  font-size: 1.5em;
  @include mq-small-up {
    font-size: 1.75em;
    margin-top: 10px;
  }
}
```

The code inside the braces—font-size: 1.75em; margin-top: 10px;—replaces the @content directive when the mixin does its magic. The CSS code that Sass would generate from the above example looks like this:

```
p {
  font-size: 1.5em;
}
@media (min-width: 500px) {
```

```
  p {
    font-size: 1.75em;
    margin-top: 10px;
  }
}
```

The second media query for the small breakpoint *only* applies when the screen is greater than that breakpoint *and also* narrower than the next breakpoint. That way you can create styles that only work within a specific range of screen sizes.

The "breakpoint-only" mixin for the small breakpoint would look like this:

```
@mixin mq-small {
  @media (min-width: $screen-small) and (max-width: $screen-medium - 1px) {
    @content;
  }
}
```

This code would generate a media query that looks something like this:

```
@media (min-width: 400px) and (max-width: 759px) {


}
```

Notice that there's a bit of math going on here: $screen-medium - 1px. Sass is actually programmed to perform basic math operations (see the box on page 606). In this case, Sass is subtracting 1 pixel from the $screen-medium variable, creating the value 759px. Because this media query should not apply at the next breakpoint—760px—so the max-width value needs to be 1 less than that breakpoint.

You'll create two mixins like this for each breakpoint except the last, so sticking with the example of three breakpoints, you could use these three mixins:

```
@mixin mq-small {
  @media (min-width: $screen-small) and (max-width: $screen-medium - 1px) {
    @content;
  }
}
@mixin mq-small-up {
  @media (min-width: $screen-small) {
    @content;
  }
}
@mixin mq-medium {
  @media (min-width: $screen-medium) and (max-width: $screen-large - 1px) {
    @content;
  }
}
```

```
@mixin mq-medium-up {
  @media (min-width: $screen-medium) {
    @content;
  }
}
@mixin mq-large-up {
  @media (min-width: $screen-large) {
    @content;
  }
}
```

■ USING THE MEDIA QUERY MIXINS

Finally, with the variables and mixins in place, you can start using them in your styles using the @include directive. Suppose you wanted the padding inside a sidebar to get larger at each breakpoint to add more white space and breathing room on progressively larger screens. In addition, you want the top and bottom margins of the sidebar to be 0 pixels at first, then change to 20 pixels when the browser window is at least as wide as the medium breakpoint. So if the sidebar has the class name sidebar, for example, you could write this Sass code to accomplish that goal:

```
.sidebar {
  padding: 0px;
  margin: 0px;
  @include mq-small {
    padding: 3px;
  }
  @include mq-medium {
    padding: 10px;
  }
  @include mq-medium-up {
    margin: 10px 0;
  }
  @include mq-large-up {
    padding: 15px;
  }
}
```

Although this code is a long way from writing the traditional media queries in Chapter 15, once you get used to this approach, you'll soon find the benefits of writing less code, and keeping all media queries bound with their elements will make it easier and more efficient to update your CSS.

> **NOTE** There are lots of other ways to use Sass to make writing media queries simpler. For a few other techniques read the following articles: *https://css-tricks.com/approaches-media-queries-sass/*, *http://davidwalsh.name/write-media-queries-sass*, *http://thesassway.com/intermediate/responsive-web-design-in-sass-using-media-queries-in-sass-32* and *www.sass-lang.com/documentation/file.SASS_REFERENCE.html#media*.

▓ Troubleshooting with CSS Source Maps

As you read in Chapters 5 and 6, CSS styles can interact in all sorts of fun, unusual, and frustrating ways. The box on page 104 explains one solution to determine how multiple styles affect a page element. Most browsers let you inspect a page element by right-clicking on a web page and choosing Inspect Element from the pop-up menu (circled in Figure 19-6). A browser's element inspector usually opens in the bottom half of the browser screen and shows HTML on the left and CSS styles on the right (see bottom section of Figure 19-6).

The information in the right-hand styles section shows all of the styles (including media queries) that affect the current selection. With this information you can see if there's a style that's doing something you don't want, and then fix it in your text editor. In addition, the style sheet containing each style is listed to the right of the style. For example, in Figure 19-6, the first style (beginning with `.button.button-primary:hover`) is located in the *skeleton.css* style sheet, while the two styles below that can be found in the *custom.css* file. This information lets you know where to go when you want to modify a style.

With Sass, however, the style sheet that the browser uses to format the HTML of a page isn't the same file in which you add and edit your styles. Knowing that a button's background color is defined in the *styles.css* file isn't a big help when you actually need to go to the *_buttons.scss* partial file to change that color. Fortunately, most browsers support a special feature called *source maps*, which can help you find the Sass file you need to edit in order to make changes.

A source map is just that: a map that a browser can follow to point from one style to its source. That is, it tells the browser how to get from a style in the compiled CSS file back to the original style inside a Sass file. Sass automatically generates these source maps for you, so when you run the `sass --watch` command (page 597), Sass produces both the final CSS file and its source map.

NOTE   In older versions of Sass you had to turn on source maps manually:

```
sass --watch --sourcemap sass:scss
```

Source map files end in .map—*styles.css.map*, for example. If you don't see one of those files in the folder where Sass puts your finished, compiled CSS file, try running the `sass` command above using the `--sourcemap` option.

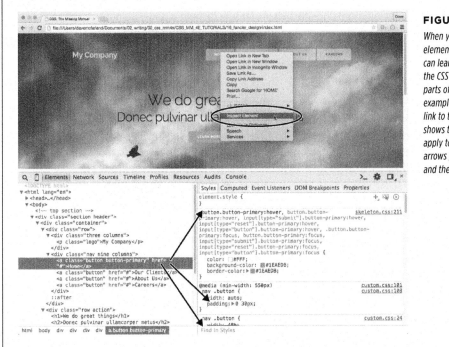

FIGURE 19-6

When you use a browser's element inspector, you can learn a lot about the CSS used to format parts of a web page. For example, inspecting the link to the home page shows that multiple styles apply to the link. The arrows point to the styles and their properties.

Internet Explorer 11, Firefox, Chrome, and Safari all support source maps, so inspecting page elements isn't really that different for Sass-generated CSS than it is for regular CSS. Simply right-click the element you wish to inspect, and then choose Inspect Element from the pop-up menu. The same element inspector appears in your browser window. However, now you'll see the names of the Sass partial files responsible for rules that format the element (circled in Figure 19-7).

FIGURE 19-7

A CSS source map makes it easy for you to locate the Sass partial files containing the rules that format elements of a web page. Here, you can see that a media query was generated by a mixin in the _mixins. scss file, and the actual style for this heading tag is in the _layout. scss file. To change that media query, you'd open the _mixins.scss file; to change the font-size value for the headline or add more properties to it, you'd open and edit the _layout.scss file.

Sass opens a lot of opportunities for you, the web designer. It makes it easy to organize your CSS into small, easily edited files; it can create much smaller CSS files; it can take the chore out of working with vendor prefixes; and, in general, it lets you work more quickly and efficiently.

> **NOTE** For creating a compressed, production-ready CSS file see the Tip on page 600.

Appendixes

CSS Property Reference

Mastering Cascading Style Sheets involves knowing how to use a large number of CSS properties that control the appearance of text, images, tables, and forms. To help you in your quest, this appendix gives you a summary of common properties and values you'll use to create your own styles. This list covers nearly all of the CSS 2.1 standard properties—the ones that most web browsers support—as well as a handful of the most useful and commonly supported newer CSS properties.

> **NOTE** The latest CSS specification is really quite large. In fact, to better manage the growth of CSS, the W3C split CSS into many modules, each of which describes a particular property or set of related properties. For full details straight from the horse's mouth, visit the latest CSS specifications from the World Wide Web Consortium at *www.w3.org/Style/CSS/current-work*. For a complete list of CSS properties, visit the Mozilla Developer Network's CSS Reference at *https://developer.mozilla.org/en-US/docs/Web/CSS/Reference*.

CSS Values

Every CSS property has a corresponding value. The `color` property, which formats font color, requires a color value to specify which color you want to use. The property `color: #FFFFFF;` creates white text. Different properties require different types of values, but they come in four basic categories: colors, lengths and sizes, keywords, and URLs.

Colors

You can assign colors to many different properties, including those for font, background, and borders. CSS provides several different ways to specify color.

■ KEYWORDS

A web color keyword is simply the name of the color, like white or black. There are currently 17 recognized web color keywords: aqua, black, blue, fuchsia, gray, green, lime, maroon, navy, olive, orange, purple, red, silver, teal, white, and yellow. Some browsers accept more keywords, and CSS 3 promises to offer many more in the future; for one example, RGBA color, see page 149. You can read a lot more about color keywords at *www.w3.org/TR/css3-color*.

■ RGB VALUES

Computer monitors create colors using a mixture of red, green, and blue light. These RGB values can create (nearly) the full spectrum of color. Almost every design, illustration, and graphics program lets you specify colors using RGB, so it's easy to transfer a color from one of those programs to a CSS property. CSS represents RGB values in several ways:

- **Hex values.** The method most commonly used on the Web for identifying color, hex color values consist of three two-character numbers in the hexadecimal (that is, base 16) system. #FF0033 represents an RGB value composed of red (FF, which equals 255 in normal, base 10 numbers), green (00), and blue (33). The # tells CSS to expect hex numbers ahead, and it's required. If you leave off the #, a web browser won't display the correct color.

> **TIP** If all three two-digit values are repeated pairs of digits, you can shorten the hex value by using just the first number of each pair. For example, #361 means the same thing as #336611.

- **RGB percentages.** You can also specify a color using percentage values, like this: rgb(100%, 0%, 33%). You can get these numbers from image-editing and design programs that can define colors using percentages (which is most of them).

- **Integer values.** Finally, you can use integer RGB values to specify a color. The format is similar to the percentage option, but you use a number from 0 to 255 to indicate each color: rgb(255, 0, 33).

- **RGBA adds transparency to the mix.** You can make the color see-through so the underlying background colors, images, or text shows through. You add a value of 0 (completely invisible) to 1 (totally opaque) to the end of an RGB color like this. You can use either the percentage or decimal values for the colors, but only decimal values for the transparency. For example, both of these options create a middle gray color that's 50% transparent:

  ```
  rgba(50%,50%,50%,.5)
  rgba(122,122,122,.5)
  ```

- **HSL** stands for hue, saturation, and lightness (also sometimes labeled *luminance*). It's yet another way to specify color. It's not supported by Internet Explorer 8 or earlier, but works in all other browsers. If you're used to RGB or hex colors, you may find the HSL syntax is a bit unusual. Here's an example of a bright red color:

  ```
  hsl(0, 100%, 50%);
  ```

The first number is a degree value from 0 to 360 representing the spectrum of colors in a color wheel. The number represents a hue, or what we normally think of as a color; for example, 360 is red, 240 is blue, and 180 is green. The second number is saturation, or how pure the color is, specified in a percentage from 0% (dull gray) to 100% (vibrant). The last value is lightness, and it's also specified as a percentage from 0% (completely black) to 100% (completely white). As with RGB color, there is a version of HSL that supports transparency, called HSLA: `hsla(0, 100%, 50%, .5)`.

It doesn't matter which method you use—they all work. For consistency, you may want to pick one way of specifying RGB values and stick with it. However, using keywords like `white` and `black` can be quick and convenient. The Windows and Mac operating systems both have color pickers that let you find the perfect color from a palette of millions, and then show you the RGB value. Alternatively, you can use this free online color picker: *www.ficml.org/jemimap/style/color/wheel.html*. Or for more advanced color picking (including the ability to create and save a palette of colors), check out *http://kuler.adobe.com*.

Lengths and Sizes

CSS provides many different ways to measure the size of type, the width of a box, or the thickness of a border line. To indicate type size, you can use inches, picas, points, centimeters, millimeters, em-heights, ex-heights, pixels, and percentages. However, even though there are a lot of options, most don't apply to the world of onscreen display, for reasons discussed on page 151. You really need to think about these three only—pixels, ems, and percentages.

■ PIXELS

A pixel is a single dot on a computer screen. Pixels give you a consistent method of identifying lengths and font sizes from computer to computer: 72 pixels on one monitor is 72 pixels on another monitor. That doesn't mean the actual, real-world length is the same for everyone, though. Since people set their monitors to different resolutions—800×600, 1024×768, 1600×1200, or whatever—72 pixels may take up 1 inch on one monitor, but only half an inch for someone else. Nevertheless, pixels give you the most consistent control over presentation.

> **NOTE** There's just one drawback to using pixels: Folks using Internet Explorer 6 or earlier can't resize any type that's sized using pixels. If your text is too small for someone's eyes, the visitor won't be able to enlarge it to make it more readable. (See page 151 for more on pixel measurements.)

■ EMS

Originally from the typographic world, an *em* is a unit that represents the height of the capital letter M for a particular font. In web pages, 1 em is the height of the web browser's base text size, which is usually 16 pixels. However, anyone can change that base size setting, so 1 em may be 16 pixels for one person, but 24 pixels in someone else's browser. In other words, ems are a relative unit of measurement.

In addition to the browser's initial font-size setting, ems can inherit size information from containing tags. A type size of .9em would make text about 14 pixels tall on most browsers with a 16-pixel base size. But if you have a <p> tag with a font size of .9 ems, and then a <strong> tag with a font size of .9 ems inside that <p> tag, that <strong> tag's em size isn't 14 pixels—it's 12 pixels (16 x .9 x .9). So keep inheritance in mind when you use em values.

PERCENTAGES

CSS uses percentages for many different purposes, like sizing text, determining the width or height of an element, and specifying the placement of an image in the background of a style, to name a few. Now, what you're taking a percentage *of* varies from property to property. For font sizes, the percentage is calculated based on the text's inherited value. Say the general font size for a paragraph is 16 pixels tall. If you created a style for one special paragraph and set its font size to 200 percent, that text is displayed at 32 pixels tall. When applied to width, however, percentages are calculated based on the width of the page or on the width of the nearest parent element. You specify a percentage with a number followed by the percent sign: *100%*.

REMS

The rem unit is a relative size based on the root element's font size—the font size you set on the html element. This value remains consistent in the document, so unlike an em unit, rem units do not change based on the font-size value inherited from parent elements.

VH

The vh unit stands for *viewport height*, and it's equivalent to 1/100 of the viewport, or browser window's, height. So 100vh is the height of the browser window. If a visitor resizes the browser window, the vh value changes accordingly.

VW

The vw unit stands for *viewport width*, and it's equivalent to 1/100 of the viewport, or browser window's, width. So 100vw is the full width of the browser window. If a visitor resizes the browser window, the vw value changes accordingly.

VMIN

Equal to the minimum of either vh or vw. In other words, if the browser window is taller than it is wide, then 1vmin is the same as 1vw. However, if the browser window is wider than it is tall, then 1vmin is the same as 1vh.

VMAX

Equal to the maximum of either vh or vw. In other words, if the browser window is taller than it is wide, then 1vmin is the same as 1vh. However, if the browser window is wider than it is tall, then 1vmin is the same as 1vw.

Keywords

Instead of color or size, many properties have their own specific values that affect how the properties display and are represented by keywords. The text-align property, which aligns text on screen, can take one of four keywords: right, left, center, and justify. Since keywords vary from property to property, read the property descriptions that follow to learn the keyword appropriate to each property.

One keyword, however, is shared by all properties—inherit. This keyword lets you force a style to inherit a value from a parent element. You can use the inherit keyword on any property. This keyword gives you the power to make styles inherit properties that aren't normally inherited from parent tags. For instance, say you use the border property to add a border around a paragraph. Other tags, such as <em> and <strong>, inside the <p> tag don't inherit this value, but you can force them to do so with the inherit keyword:

```
em, strong {
  border: inherit;
}
```

That way, the <em> and <strong> tags display the same border value as their parent <p> tag. So the <em> and <strong> elements of the paragraph each get their own borders, as does the entire paragraph, so you'd end up with boxes within boxes (a good reason why that property *isn't* inherited normally). If you change the <p> tag's border value to *a different color or thickness*, the <em> and <strong> tags inherit that value and display the same type of border, too.

URLs

URL values let you point to another file on the Web. For example, the background-image property accepts a URL—the path to the file on the Web—as its value, which lets you assign a graphic file as a background for a page element. This technique is handy for adding a tiling image in the background of a page or using your own graphic for bulleted lists (see page 231).

In CSS, you specify a URL like this: url(images/tile.gif). A style that adds an image called *tile.gif* to the background of the page would look like this:

```
body { background-image: url(images/tile.gif); }
```

Unlike in HTML, in CSS, quotes around the URL are optional, so url("images/tile. gif"), url('images/tile.gif'), and url(images/tile.gif) are equivalent.

NOTE The URL itself is just like the HTML href attribute used for links, meaning you can use an absolute URL like *http://www.missingmanuals.com/images/tile.gif*, a root-relative path like */images/tile.gif*, or a document-relative URL like *../../images/tile.gif*. See page 237 for the full story on these kinds of paths.

■ Text Properties

The following properties affect how text is formatted on a web page. Since most of the properties in this category are inherited, you don't necessarily have to apply them to tags specifically intended for text (like the <p> tag). You can apply these properties to the <body> tag, so that other tags inherit and use the same settings. This technique is a quick way to define an overall font, color, and so on for a page or section.

color (inherited)

Sets the color of text. Since it's inherited, if you set the color of the <body> tag to red, for example, all text inside of the body—and all other tags inside the <body> tag—is red, too.

- **Values:** Any valid color value

- **Example:** color: #FFFF33;

> **NOTE** The preset link colors for the <a> tag override color inheritance. In the above example, any links inside the <body> tag would still be standard hyperlink blue. See page 279 for ways to change preset link colors.

font (inherited)

This is a shortcut method for cramming the following text properties into a single style declaration: font-style, font-variant, font-weight, font-size, line-height, and font-family. (Read on for the individual descriptions.)

You must separate each value by a space and include at least font-size and font-family, *and* those two properties must be the last two items in the declaration. The others are optional. If you don't set a property, the browser uses its own preset value, potentially overriding inherited properties.

- **Values:** Any value that's valid for the specific font property. When including a line height, add a slash followed by the line height after the font size, like this: 1.25em/150%.

- **Example:** font: italic small-caps bold 1.25em/150% Arial, Helvetica, sans-serif;

font-family (inherited)

Specifies the font the browser should use to display text. Fonts are usually specified as a series of three to four options to accommodate the fact that a particular font may not be installed on a visitor's computer. See page 121.

- **Values:** A comma-separated list of font names. When a font has a space in its name, surround that font name with quotes. The last font listed is usually a generic font type instructing browsers to choose a suitable font if the other listed fonts aren't available: serif, sans-serif, monotype, fantasy, or cursive.

- **Example:** font-family: "Lucida Grande", Arial, sans-serif;

NOTE   All browsers let you specify additional fonts that you keep on your web server or that your site's visitors download from a web font service. See page 126 for a detailed description of using web fonts.

font-size (inherited)

Sets the size of text. This property is inherited, which can lead to some weird behaviors when using relative length measurements like percentages and ems.

- **Values:** Any valid CSS measurement unit plus the following keywords: xx-small, x-small, small, medium, large, x-large, xx-large, larger, and smaller. Medium represents the web browser's normal, preset font size; the other sizes are multiples of medium.

  Each of the other options decreases or increases the size by a different factor. While each size change is supposed to be a consistent increase or decrease from the previous size, it isn't. Basically, xx-small is the equivalent of 9 pixels (assuming you haven't adjusted the base font size in your browser); x-small is 10 pixels; small is 13 pixels; large is 18 pixels; x-large is 24 pixels; and xx-large is 32 pixels. Due to the uncertainty of how each browser handles these keywords, many designers use pixels, ems, or percentages instead.

- **Example:** font-size: 1.25em;

font-style (inherited)

Makes text italic. Applied to italic text, it turns it back to plain text. The options italic and oblique are functionally the same.

- **Values:** italic, oblique, normal
- **Example:** font-style: italic;

font-variant (inherited)

Makes text appear in small caps, like this: SPECIAL PRESENTATION. The value normal removes small caps from text already formatted that way.

- **Values:** small-caps, normal
- **Example:** font-variant: small-caps;

font-weight (inherited)

Makes text bold or removes bolding from text already formatted that way.

- **Values:** CSS actually provides 14 different font-weight keywords, but only a couple actually work with today's browsers and computer systems: bold and normal.
- **Example:** font-weight: bold;

letter-spacing (inherited)

Adjusts the space between letters to spread out letters (adding spacing between each) or cram letters together (removing space).

- **Values:** Any valid CSS measurement unit, though ems and pixels are most common. For this property, percentages don't work in most browsers. Use a positive value to increase the space between letters and a negative value to remove space (scrunch letters together). The value normal resets letter-spacing to its regular browser value of 0.

- **Examples:** letter-spacing: -1px; letter-spacing: 2em;

line-height (inherited)

Adjusts space between lines of text in a paragraph (often called *line spacing* in word-processing programs). The normal line height is 120 percent of the size of the text (page 163).

- **Values:** Most valid CSS lengths (page 151), though ems and pixels and percentages are most common.

- **Example:** line-height: 200%;

text-align (inherited)

Positions a block of text to the left, right, or center of the page or container element.

- **Values:** left, center, right, justify (the justify option often makes text difficult to read on monitors).

- **Example:** text-align: center;

text-decoration (inherited)

Adds lines above, under, and/or through text. Underlining is common with links, so it's usually a good idea *not* to underline text that isn't a link. The color of the underline, overline, or strikethrough line is the same as the font color of the tag being styled. The property also supports a blink value that makes text flash off and on obnoxiously (but most browsers ignore blink anyway).

- **Values:** underline, overline, line-through, blink, none. The none value turns off all decoration. Use this to hide the underline that normally appears under links. You can also add multiple decorations by listing the name of each type (except none) separated by a space.

- **Example:** text-decoration: underline overline line-through;

text-indent (inherited)

Sets the indent size of the first line of a block of text. The first line can be indented (as in many printed books) or outdented, so that the first line hangs off and over the left edge of the rest of the text.

- **Values:** Any valid CSS measurement unit. Ems and pixels are most common; percentages behave differently than with the font-size property. Here, percentages are based on the width of the box containing the text, which can be the width of the entire browser window. So 50% would indent the first line half of the way across the window. To outdent (hang the first line off the left edge), use a negative value. This technique works well in conjunction with a positive margin-left property (page 187), which indents the left side of the other lines of text a set amount.

- **Example:** text-indent: 3em;

text-shadow (inherited)

Lets you add a drop shadow to any text.

- **Values:** Two measurement values (ems or pixels) for horizontal and vertical offset; a value for the amount of blur applies to the text, and a color value. For the horizontal offset, a negative number places the shadow to the left of the text, a positive value to the right. For vertical offset, a negative number moves the shadow above the text, and positive value places it below. Each value is separated from the next by a space. You can also add multiple shadows by adding additional shadows values separated by a comma.

- **Example:**

```
text-shadow: -4px 4px 3px #999999;
text-shadow: -4px 4px 3px #999999, 2px 3px 10px #000;
```

text-transform (inherited)

Changes the capitalization of text, so text appears in all uppercase letters, all lowercase, or only the first letter of each word capitalized.

- **Values:** uppercase, lowercase, capitalize, none. The none option returns the text to whatever case is in the actual HTML code. If *aBCDefg* are the actual letters typed in HTML, then none removes any other inherited case set by an ancestor tag and displays *aBCDefg* onscreen.

- **Example:** text-transform: uppercase;

vertical-align

Sets the baseline of an inline element relative to the baseline of the surrounding contents. With it, you can make a character appear slightly above or below surrounding text. Use this to create superscript characters like ™, ®, or ©. When applied to a table cell, the values top, middle, bottom, and *baseline* control the vertical placement of content inside the cell (page 360).

- **Values:** baseline, sub, super, top, text-top, middle, bottom, text-bottom, a percentage value, or an absolute value (like pixels or ems). Percentages are calculated based on the element's line-height value (page 163).

- **Examples:**

```
vertical-align: top;
vertical-align: -5px;
vertical-align: 75%;
```

white-space

Controls how the browser displays space characters in the HTML code. Normally, if you include more than one space between words—"Hello   Dave"—a web browser displays only one space—"Hello Dave." You can preserve any white space exactly as is in the HTML using the pre value, which does the same as the HTML <pre> tag. In addition, web browsers will split a line of text at a space, if the line won't fit within the window's width. To prevent text from wrapping, use the nowrap value. But the nowrap value makes *all* of the paragraph's text stay on one line, so don't use it with long paragraphs (unless you like the idea of making your visitors scroll endlessly to the right).

- **Values:** nowrap, pre, normal. Two other values—pre-line and pre-wrap—don't work in many browsers.

- **Example:** white-space: pre;

word-spacing (inherited)

Works like the letter-spacing property (page 159), but instead of letters, it adjusts space between words.

- **Values:** Any valid CSS measurement unit, though ems and pixels are most common; percentages don't work in most browsers. Use a *positive* value to increase the space between words and a *negative* value to remove space (scrunch words together). The value normal resets word spacing to its regular browser value of 0.

- **Examples:** word-spacing: -1px; word-spacing: 2em;

■ List Properties

The following properties affect the formatting of bulleted lists (`<ul>`) and numbered lists (`<ol>`). (See page 168 for more on using CSS with lists.)

list-style (inherited)

This property is a shorthand method of specifying the three properties listed next. You can include a value for one or more of those properties, separating each by a space. You can even use this property as a shortcut for writing a single property and save a couple of keystrokes: `list-style: outside`, instead of `list-style-position: outside`. If you specify both a type and an image, a web browser will display the bullet type (disc, square, and so on) *only* if it can't find the image. This way, if the path to your custom bullet image doesn't work, you don't end up with a bulletless bulleted list.

- **Values:** Any valid value for `list-style-type`, `list-style-image`, and/or `list-style-position`.

- **Example:** `list-style: disc url(images/bullet.gif) inside;`

list-style-image (inherited)

Specifies an image to use for a bullet in a bulleted list.

- **Values:** A URL value (page 641) or none.

- **Example:** `list-style-image: url(images/bullet.gif);`

> **NOTE** The `background-image` property does the custom bullet job just as well and offers more control (see page 231).

list-style-position (inherited)

Positions the bullets or numbers in a list. These markers can appear outside of the text, hanging off to the left, or inside the text (exactly where the first letter of the first line normally begins). The `outside` position is how web browsers normally display bullets and numbers.

- **Values:** `inside`, `outside`

- **Example:** `list-style: inside;`

list-style-type (inherited)

Sets the type of bullet for a list—round, square, roman numeral, and so on. You can even turn an unordered (bulleted) list into an ordered (numbered) list by changing the `list-style-type` property. Use the `none` option to completely remove bullets or numbers from the list.

- **Values:** `disc`, `circle`, `square`, `decimal`, `decimal-leading-zero`, `upper-alpha`, `lower-alpha`, `upper-roman`, `lower-roman`, `lower-greek`, `none`

- **Example:** `list-style-type: square;`

▉ Padding, Borders, and Margins

The following properties control the space around an element, and let you add border lines to a style.

box-shadow

- **Values:** An optional value—inset—to add a drop shadow inside an element, followed by four measurement values and a color. The first two measurement values (ems or pixels) are for horizontal and vertical offset; the third value specifies the amount of blur applied to the box; the fourth value, which is optional, adds a "spread" to the shadow, making the shadow wider. For the horizontal offset, a negative number places the shadow to the left of the box, a positive value to the right. For vertical offset, a negative number moves the shadow above the box, and positive value places it below. Each value is separated from the next by a space. You can also add multiple shadows by adding additional shadows values separated by a comma.

- **Example:**

```
box-shadow: -4px 4px 3px #999999;
box-shadow: inset 4px 4px 3px 5px #999999;
box-shadow: inset 4px 4px 3px 5px #999999
            2px 2px 5px black;
```

border

Draws a line around the four edges of an element.

- **Values:** The width (thickness) of the border line in any valid CSS measurement unit (except percentages).

  You can also specify a style for the line: solid, dotted, dashed, double, groove, ridge, inset, outset, none, and hidden. The none and hidden values do the same thing—remove any border.

  Finally, you can specify a color using any valid CSS color type (a keyword like green or a hex number like #33fc44).

- **Example:** border: 2px solid #f33;

border-radius

Rounds the corners of an element. Only has a visual effect if the element has a border, background color, or image.

- **Values:** One, two, three, or four values (px, em, or %) that indicate the size of a radius of a circle drawn at the corners of an element's box. If you supply only one value, it applies the same size rounded corner to all four corners; with two values, the first specifies the top-left and bottom-right corner, while the second indicates the top-right and bottom-left corner radii. When using three values, the first specifies the top-left corner; the second, both the top-right and bottom-left, and the third the bottom-right corner. With four values, each value applies in order to the top-left corner, top-right corner, bottom-right corner, and bottom-left corner. You can add a / followed by a second value to create an elliptical corner rather than a perfectly circular one.

- **Example:**

```
border-radius: .5em;
border-radius: 15px 10px 25px 5px;
border-radius: 15px / 5px;
```

border-top, border-right, border-bottom, border-left

Adds a border to a single edge. For example, border-top adds a border to the top of the element.

- **Values:** Same as for border.

- **Example:** border-left: 1em dashed red;

border-color

Defines the color used for all four borders.

- **Values:** Any valid CSS color type (a keyword like green or a hex number like #33fc44).

- **Example:** border-color: rgb(255,34,100);

This property also supports a shorthand method, which lets you assign different colors to each of the four borders.

- **Values:** Any valid CSS color type for each border: top, right, bottom, left. If you include just two colors, the first color applies to the top and bottom, and the second color to the left and right.

- **Example:** border-color: #000 #F33 #030 #438F3C;

border-top-color, border-right-color, border-bottom-color, border-left-color

Functions just like the border-color property but sets color for only one edge. Use these properties to override the color set by the border property. In this way, you can customize the color for an individual edge while using a more generic border style to define the basic size and style of all four edges.

- **Values:** See border-color above.

- **Example:** border-left-color: #333;

border-style

Defines the style used for all four borders.

- **Values:** One of these keywords: solid, dotted, dashed, double, groove, ridge, inset, outset, none, and hidden. See Figure 7-7 on page 195 for an illustration of the different styles. The none and hidden values act identically—they remove any border.

- **Example:** border-style: inset;

This property also supports a shorthand method, which lets you assign different styles to each of the four borders.

- **Values:** One of the keywords mentioned above for each border: top, right, bottom, left. If you include just two keywords, then the first style applies to the top and bottom and the second style to the left and right.

- **Example:** border-style: solid dotted dashed double;

border-top-style, border-right-style, border-bottom-style, border-left-style

Functions just like the border-style property, but applies only to one edge.

- **Values:** See border-style above.

- **Example:** border-top-style: none;

border-width

Defines the width or thickness of the line used to draw all four borders.

- **Values:** Any valid CSS measurement unit except percentages. The most common are ems and pixels.

- **Example:** border-width: 1px;

This property also supports a shorthand method, which lets you assign different widths to each of the four borders.

- **Values:** Any valid CSS measurement unit (except percentages) for each border: top, right, bottom, left. If you include just two values, then the first value sets the width for the top and bottom border and the second value the width for the left and right borders.

- **Example:** border-width: 3em 1em 2em 3.5em;

border-top-width, border-right-width, border-bottom-width, border-left-width

Functions just like the border-width property but applies only to one edge.

- **Values:** See border-width above.

- **Example:** border-bottom-width: 3em;

box-sizing

Dictates how a browser measures the height and width of an element. Normally, browsers combine the border, padding, and CSS width properties to determine the amount of screen space an element takes up. This is often confusing, since you can specify an element's width to be 300 pixels, but, if the element also has padding and borders, the browser displays that element wider than 300 pixels on screen.

- **Values:** content-box, padding-box, or border-box. The content-box option is the normal way browsers do it. The padding-box option tells a browser to include the padding in with the CSS width and height values; border-box also includes the border width and height in its calculations. For example, if you have a <div> tag that you set to 300 pixels width, with 20 pixels of padding and a 2-pixel border, a browser will normally display that div in 344 pixels of screen space (300 + 20 + 20 + 2 +2); however, if you set the box-sizing property to padding-box, the browser would display that div in 304 pixels of space (300 + 2 +2), because the padding is considered part of that 300 pixels; the border-box setting would tell a browser to simply make the div 300 pixels wide. The border-box option is commonly used to make it easier to keep track of element widths.

- **Example:** box-sizing: border-box;

outline

This property is a shorthand way to combine outline-color, outline-style, and outline-width (listed next). An outline works just like a border, except the outline takes up no space (that is, it doesn't add to the width or height of an element), and it applies to all four edges. It's intended more as a way of highlighting something on a page than as a design detail.

- **Values:** The same as for border with one exception—see outline-color next.

- **Example:** outline: 3px solid #F33;

outline-color

Specifies the color for an outline (see outline above).

- **Values:** Any valid CSS color, plus the value invert, which merely reverses the color the outline is sitting on. If the outline is drawn on a white background, the invert value makes the outline black. Works just like border-color (page 649).

- **Example:** outline-color: invert;

outline-style

Specifies the type of line for the outline—dotted, solid, dashed, and so on.

- **Values:** Same as border-style (page 650).

- **Example:** outline-style: dashed;

outline-width

Specifies the thickness of the outline. Works just like `border-width`.

- **Values:** Any valid CSS measurement unit except percentages. The most common are ems and pixels.

- **Example:** `outline-width: 3px;`

padding

Sets the amount of space between the content, border, and edge of the background. Use it to add empty space around text, images, or other content. (See Figure 7-1 on page 186 for an illustration.)

- **Values:** Any valid CSS measurement unit, like pixels or ems. Percentage values are based on the width of the containing element. A headline that's a child of the `<body>` tag uses the width of the browser window to calculate a percentage value, so a padding of 20 percent adds 20 percent of the window's width. If the visitor resizes his browser, the padding size changes proportionately. For example, you can specify the padding for all four edges by using a single value, or set individual padding sizes per edge using this order: `top`, `right`, `bottom`, `left`.

- **Examples:** `padding: 20px; padding: 2em 3em 2.5em 0;`

padding-top

Works just like the `padding` property, but sets padding for top edge only.

- **Example:** `padding-top: 20px;`

padding-right

Works just like the `padding` property, but sets padding for right edge only.

- **Example:** `padding-right: 20px;`

padding-bottom

Works just like the `padding` property, but sets padding for bottom edge only.

- **Example:** `padding-bottom: 20px;`

padding-left

Works just like the `padding` property, but sets padding for left edge only.

- **Example:** `padding-left: 20px;`

margin

Sets the amount of space between an element's border and the margin of other elements (see Figure 7-1 on page 186). It lets you add white space between two elements—between one picture and another picture, or between a sidebar and the main content area of a page.

> **NOTE** Vertical margins between elements can *collapse*. That is, browsers use only the top or bottom margin and ignore the other, creating a smaller gap than expected (see page 189).

- **Values:** Any valid CSS measurement unit like pixels or ems. Percentage values are based on the width of the containing element. A headline that's a child of the <body> tag uses the width of the browser window to calculate a percentage value, so a margin of 10 percent adds 10 percent of the window's width to the edges of the headline. If the visitor resizes his browser, the margin size changes. As with padding, you specify the margin for all four edges using a single value, or set individual margins in this order: top, right, bottom, left.

- **Examples:** margin: 20px; margin: 2em 3em 2.5em 0;

margin-top

Works just like the margin property, but sets margin for top edge only.

- **Example:** margin-top: 20px;

margin-right

Works just like the margin property, but sets margin for right edge only.

- **Example:** margin-right: 20px;

margin-bottom

Works just like the margin property, but sets margin for bottom edge only.

- **Example:** margin-bottom: 20px;

margin-left

Works just like the margin property, but sets margin for left edge only.

- **Example:** margin-left: 20px;

■ Backgrounds

CSS provides several properties for controlling the background of an element, including coloring the background, placing an image behind an element, and controlling how that background image is positioned.

background

Provides a shorthand method of specifying properties that appear in the background of an element, like a color, an image, and the placement of that image. It combines the five background properties (described next) into one compact line, so you can get the same effect with much less typing. However, if you don't set one of the properties, browsers use that property's normal value instead. For example, if you don't specify how a background image should repeat, browsers will tile that image from left to right and top to bottom (see page 234).

- **Values:** The same values used for the background properties listed next. The order of the properties isn't important (except for positioning as described below), but usually follow the order of background-color, background-image, background-repeat, background-attachment, background-position.

- **Example:** background: #333 url(images/logo.gif) no-repeat fixed left top;

background-attachment

Specifies how a background image reacts when your visitor scrolls the page. The image either scrolls along with the rest of the content or remains in place. You can add a logo to the upper-left corner of a very long web page, using the background-attachment property's fixed value, and make that image stay in the upper-left corner even when the page is scrolled.

- **Values:** scroll or fixed. Scroll is the normal behavior: An image will scroll off the screen along with text. fixed locks the image in place.

- **Example:** background-attachment: fixed;

background-clip

This property limits the area in which a background-image appears. Normally a background image fills the entire area of an element including its borders, padding, and content. However, you may want a background image to only appear behind the padding area and exclude the borders. That effect is useful when you have a dotted or dashed border, to keep the image from appearing in the gaps of the border. Likewise, you might want to exclude the padding area so a tiled background appears only in the content area, and a solid color in the padding area.

- **Values:** border-box, padding-box, or content-box. The border-box option is the normal method—placing an image behind the border, padding and content. The padding-box option keeps a background image in the padding area only, so that it won't appear behind the border; content-box places a background image in the content area only, so it won't appear in the padding area or behind the border.

- **Example:**

```
background-clip: content-box;
background-clip: padding-box;
```

background-color

Adds a color to the background of a style. The background sits underneath the border and underneath a background image, a fact to keep in mind if you use one of the nonsolid border styles like dashed or dotted. In these cases, the background color shows through the gaps between the dashes or dots.

- **Values:** Any valid color value (page 637).

- **Example:** background-color: #FFF;

background-image

Places an image into the background of a style. Other page elements sit on top of the background image, so make sure that text is legible where it overlaps the image. You can always use padding to move content away from the image, too. The image tiles from left to right and top to bottom, unless you set the background-repeat property as well. CSS also lets you apply multiple background images (see page 249).

- **Values:** The URL of an image. Can also include a browser generated linear- or radial-gradient (see page 252).

- **Examples:**

```
background-image: url(images/photo.jpg);
background-image: url(http://www.example.org/photo.jpg);
background-image: url(http://www.example.org/photo.jpg),
                 url(images/photo.jpg);
```

background-origin

Tells a browser where to place a background image in relationship to the border, padding and content of an element. This is most useful for a non-repeating image, since this property lets you better control the image's position. This property is not supported by Internet Explorer 8 or earlier.

- **Values:** border-box, padding-box, or content-box. The border-box option is the normal method—placing an image in the top-left corner of the border. The padding-box option starts a background image in the padding area only, so that it won't appear behind the border; content-box places a background image in the content area only, so it won't appear in the padding area or behind the border. However, if the image is tiled, you'll still see the image behind the borders and padding—this property only controls where the image starts. Use the background-clip property (page 654) to keep a tiled image from appearing behind borders or padding.

- **Example:** background-origin: content-box;

background-position

Controls the placement of an image in the background of a page element. Unless you specify otherwise, an image begins in the element's top-left corner. If the image tiles, background-position controls the image's start point (see background-repeat next). If you position an image in the center of an element, the browser puts the image there, and then tiles the image up and to the left *and* down and to the right. In many cases, the exact placement of an image doesn't cause a visible difference in the background tiling, but it lets you make subtle changes to the positioning of a pattern in the background.

- **Values:** Any valid CSS measurement unit, like pixels or ems, as well as keywords or percentages. The values come in pairs, with the first being the horizontal position, and the second being the vertical. Keywords include left, center, and right for horizontal positioning and top, center, and bottom for vertical. Pixel and em values are calculated from the top-left corner of the element, so to place a graphic 5 pixels from the left edge and 10 pixels from the top, you'd use a value of 5px 10px.

  Percentage values map one point on the image to one point in the background of the element, calculated by the specified percentage from the left and top edges of the image and the specified percentage from the left and top edges of the element. 50% 50% places the point that's 50 percent across and 50 percent down the image on top of the point that's 50 percent across and 50 percent down the element. In other words, it puts the image directly in the middle of the element. You can mix and match these values: If you want, use a pixel value for horizontal placement and a percentage value for vertical placement.

- **Examples:** background-position: left top; background-position: 1em 3em; background-position: 10px 50%;

background-repeat

Controls whether or how a background image repeats. Normally, background images tile from the top left to the bottom right, filling the element's entire background.

- **Values:** repeat, no-repeat, repeat-x, repeat-y. The repeat option is the normal method—tiling left to right, top to bottom. The no-repeat places the image a single time in the background with no tiling; repeat-y tiles the image top to bottom only—perfect for adding a graphical sidebar. The repeat-x option tiles the image from left to right only, so you can add a graphical bar to an element's top, middle, or bottom.

- **Example:** background-repeat: no-repeat;

background-size

Lets you resize a background image scaling it up or down, or even distorting its proportions.

- **Values:** You can use specific values in pixels, ems or percentages, or one of two keywords: `contain` or `cover`. The `contain` keyword forces the image to resize to completely fit the entire element while still maintaining its aspect ratio; `cover` forces the width of the image to fit the width of the element and the height of the image to fit the height of the element. This usually distorts the image by stretching it or squishing it to fit within the element.

- **Example:**

```
background-size: 200px 400px;
background-size: contain;
```

■ Page Layout Properties

The following properties control the placement and size of elements on a web page.

bottom

This property is used with `absolute`, `relative`, and `fixed` positioning (see page 430). When used with absolute or fixed positioning, `bottom` determines the position of the bottom edge of the style relative to the bottom edge of its closest positioned ancestor. If the styled element isn't inside of any positioned tags, then the placement is relative to the bottom edge of the browser window. You can use this property to place a footnote at the bottom of the browser window. When used with relative positioning, the placement is calculated from the element's bottom edge (prior to positioning).

- **Values:** Any valid CSS measurement unit, like pixels, ems, or percentages. Percentages are calculated based on the width of the containing element.

- **Example:** `bottom: 5em;`

clear

Prevents an element from wrapping around a floated element. Instead, the cleared element drops below the bottom of the floated element.

- **Values:** `left`, `right`, `both`, `none`. The `left` option means the element can't wrap around left-floated elements. Similarly, `right` drops the element below any right-floated items. The `both` value prevents an element from wrapping around *either* left- or right-floated elements. The `none` value turns the property off, so you use it to override a previously set `clear` property. This trick comes in handy when a particular tag has a style that drops below a floated element, but you want the tag to wrap in just one case. Create a more specific style to override the float for that one tag.

- **Example:** `clear: both;`

clip

Creates a rectangular window that reveals part of an element. If you had a picture of your high-school graduating class, and the class bully was standing on the far right edge of the photo, you could create a display area that crops out the image of your tormentor. The full image is still intact, but the clipping area only displays the bully free portion of it. The clip property is most effective when used with JavaScript programming to animate the clip. You can start with a small clipping area and expand it until the full photo is revealed.

- **Values:** Coordinates of a rectangular box. Enclose the coordinates in parentheses and precede them by the keyword rect, like so: rect(5px,110px,40px,10px);.

  Here's how the order of these coordinates works: The first number indicates the top offset—the top edge of the clipping window. In this example, the offset is 5px, so everything in the first four rows of pixels is hidden. The last number is the left offset—the left edge of the clipping window. In this example, the offset is 10px, so everything to the left (the first 9 pixels of the element) is hidden. The second number is the width of the clipping window plus the last number; if the left edge of the clip is 10 pixels and you want the visible area to be 100 pixels, the second number would be 110px. The third number is the height of the clipping region plus the top offset (the first number). So, in this example, the clipping box is 35 pixels tall (35px + 5px = 40px).

- **Example:** clip: rect(5px,110px,40px,10px);

> **NOTE** Since the order of the coordinates is a little strange, most designers like to start with the first and last numbers, and then compute the two other numbers from them.

display

Determines the kind of box used to display a web page element—block-level or inline (page 192). Use it to override how a browser usually displays a particular element. You can make a paragraph (block-level element) display without line breaks above and below it—exactly like, say, a link (inline element).

- **Values:** block, inline, none. The display property accepts 17 values, most of which have no effect in the browsers available today. Block, inline, and none, however, work in almost all browsers. The block value forces a line break above and below an element, just like other block-level elements (like paragraphs and headers). The inline value causes an element to display on the same line as surrounding elements (just as text within a <strong> tag appears right on the same line as other text). The none value makes the element completely disappear from the page. Then, you can make the element reappear with some JavaScript programming or the :hover pseudo-class (see page 55).

- **Example:** display: block;

float

Moves an element to the left or right edge of the browser window, or, if the floated element is inside another element, to the left or right edge of that containing element. Elements that appear after the floated element move up to fill the space to the right (for left floats) or left (for right floats), and then wrap around the floated element. Use floats for simple effects—like moving an image to one side of the page—or for very complex layouts, like those described in Chapter 12.

- **Values:** left, right, none. To turn off floating entirely, use none. This comes in handy when a particular tag has a style with a left or right float applied to it and you want to create a more specific style to override the float for that one tag.

- **Example:** float: left;

height

Sets the height of the *content area*—the area of an element's box that contains content like text, images, or other tags. The element's actual onscreen height is the total of height, top and bottom margins, top and bottom padding, and top and bottom borders.

- **Values:** Any valid CSS measurement unit, such as pixels, ems, or percentages. Percentages are calculated based on the height of the containing element.

- **Example:** height: 50%;

> **NOTE** Sometimes, your content ends up taller than the set height—if you type a lot of text, for instance, or your visitor increases text size in her browser, the content extends outside the box flowing outside of a background color and over any borders. The overflow property controls what happens in this case (see page 208).

left

When used with absolute or fixed positioning (page 430), this property determines the position of the left edge of the style relative to the left edge of its closest-positioned ancestor. If the styled element isn't inside of any positioned tags, then the placement is relative to the left edge of the browser window. You can use this property to place an image 20 pixels from the left edge of the browser window. When used with relative positioning, the placement is calculated from the element's left edge (prior to positioning).

- **Values:** Any valid CSS measurement unit, such as pixels, ems, or percentages.

- **Example:** left: 5em;

max-height

Sets the maximum height for an element. That is, the element's box may be shorter than this setting, but it can't be any taller. If the element's contents are taller than the max-height setting, they overflow the box. You can control what happens to the excess using the overflow property. Internet Explorer 6 (and earlier) doesn't understand the max-height property.

- **Values:** Any valid CSS measurement unit, like pixels, ems, or percentages. Browsers calculate percentages based on the height of the containing element.

- **Example:** max-height: 100px;

max-width

Sets the maximum width for an element. The element's box can be narrower than this setting, but not wider. If the element's contents are wider than the max-width setting, they overflow the box, which you can control with the overflow property. You mostly use max-width in liquid layouts (page 386) to make sure a page design doesn't become unreadably wide on very large monitors.

- **Values:** Any valid CSS measurement unit, like pixels, ems, or percentages. Percentages are calculated based on the width of the containing element.

- **Example:** max-width: 950px;

min-height

Sets the minimum height for an element. The element's box may be taller than this setting, but it can't be shorter. If the element's contents aren't as tall as the min-height setting, the box's height shrinks to meet the min-height value.

- **Values:** Any valid CSS measurement unit, like pixels, ems, or percentages. Percentages are based on the containing element's height.

- **Example:** min-height: 20em;

min-width

Sets the minimum width for an element. The element's box may be wider than this setting, but it can't be narrower. If the element's contents aren't as wide as the min-width value, the box simply gets as thin as the min-width setting. You can also use min-width in liquid layouts, so that the design doesn't disintegrate at smaller window widths. When the browser window is thinner than min-width, it adds horizontal scroll bars.

- **Values:** Any valid CSS measurement unit, like pixels, ems, or percentages. Percentages are based on the containing element's width.

- **Example:** min-width: 760px;

NOTE You usually use the max-width and min-width properties in when creating responsive web designs like those discussed in Chapter 15.

overflow

Dictates what should happen to text that overflows its content area, like a photo that's wider than the value set for the width property.

- **Values:** visible, hidden, scroll, auto. The visible option makes the overflowing content extend outside the box—potentially overlapping borders and other elements on the page. The hidden value hides any content outside of the content area. The scroll value adds scroll bars to the element so a visitor can scroll to read any content outside the content area—sort of like a mini-frame. The auto option adds scrollbars *only* when they're necessary to reveal more content.

- **Example:** overflow: hidden;

position

Determines what type of positioning method a browser uses when placing an element on the page.

- **Values:** static, relative, absolute, fixed. The static value is the normal browser mode—one block-level item stacked on top of the next, with content flowing from the top to the bottom of the screen. The relative option positions an element in relation to where the element currently appears on the page—in other words, it can offset the element from its current position. The absolute value takes an element completely out of the page flow. Other items don't see the absolute element and may appear underneath it. It's used to position an element in an exact place on the page, or to place an element in an exact position relative to a parent element that's positioned with absolute, relative, or fixed positioning. The fixed option locks an element on the page, so that when the page is scrolled, the fixed element remains on the screen—much like HTML frames. Internet Explorer 6 (and earlier) ignores the fixed option.

- **Example:** position: absolute;

TIP You usually use relative, absolute, and fixed in conjunction with left, right, top, and bottom. See Chapter 13 for the full details on positioning.

---

right

When used with absolute or fixed positioning, this property determines the position of the right edge of the style relative to the right edge of its closest positioned ancestor. If the styled element isn't inside of any positioned tags, then the placement is relative to the right edge of the browser window. You can use this property to place a sidebar a set amount from the right edge of the browser window. When used with relative positioning, the placement is calculated from the element's right edge (prior to positioning).

- **Values:** Any valid CSS measurement unit, like pixels, ems, or percentages.

- **Example:** left: 5em;

top

Does the opposite of the bottom property. In other words, when used with absolute or fixed positioning, this property determines the position of the top edge of the style relative to the top edge of its closest positioned ancestor. If the styled element isn't inside of any positioned tags, then the placement is relative to the top edge of the browser window. You can use this property to place a logo a set amount from the top edge of the browser window. When used with relative positioning, the placement is calculated from the element's top edge (prior to positioning).

- **Values:** Any valid CSS measurement unit, like pixels, ems, or percentages.

- **Example:** top: 5em;

visibility

Determines whether a web browser displays the element. Use this property to hide part of the content of the page, such as a paragraph, headline, or <div> tag. Unlike the display property's none value—which hides an element and removes it from the flow of the page—the visibility property's hidden option doesn't remove the element from the page flow. Instead, it just leaves an empty hole where the element would have been. For this reason, you most often use the visibility property with absolutely positioned elements, which have already been removed from the flow of the page.

Hiding an element doesn't do you much good unless you can show it again. JavaScript programming is the most common way to toggle the visibility property to show and hide items on a page. You can also use the :hover pseudo-class (page 55) to change an element's visibility property when a visitor hovers over some part of the page.

- **Values:** visible, hidden. You can use the collapse value to hide a row or column in a table as well.

- **Example:** visibility: hidden;

width

Sets the width of the content area (the area of an element's box that contains text, images, or other tags). The amount of onscreen space actually dedicated to the element may be much wider, since it includes the width of the left and right margin, left and right padding, and left and right borders.

- **Values:** Any valid CSS measurement unit, like pixels, ems, or percentages. Percentages are based on the containing element's width.

- **Example:** width: 250px;

z-index

Controls the layering of positioned elements. Only applies to elements with a position property set to absolute, relative, or fixed (page 430). It determines where on the z-axis an element appears. If two absolutely positioned elements overlap, the one with the higher z-index appears to be on top.

- **Values:** An integer value, like 1, 2, or 10. You can also use negative values, but different browsers handle them differently. The larger the number, the more "on top" the element appears. An element with a z-index of 20 appears below an element with a z-index of 100 (if the two overlap). However, when the element is inside another positioned element, its "positioning context" changes and it may not appear above another element—no matter what its z-index value. (See Figure 14-6 on page 440.)

- **Example:** z-index: 12;

NOTE The values don't need be in exact integer order. If element A has a z-index of 1, you don't have to set element B's z-index to 2 to put it on top. You can use 5, 10, and so on to get the same effect, as long as it's a bigger number. So, to make sure an element *always* appears above other elements, simply give it a very large value, like 10000. However, Firefox can only handle a maximum value of 2147483647, so don't ever set your z-index above that number.

▟ Animation, Transform and Transition Properties

CSS has some spiffy properties (added in CSS3) to transform elements by scaling, rotating, skewing, and moving them, as well as the ability to animate changes from one CSS property to another.

@keyframes

The heart of CSS animations is the @keyframes rule. It lets you name an animation (which you can then apply to any element on a page) and set up a set of keyframes, or places within the animation where CSS properties change. For example, to fade the background of an element from black to white, you'd need two keyframes: The first keyframe sets the CSS background-color property to black, while the second keyframe sets it to white. You can have any number of keyframes and animate changes in a variety of CSS properties.

At the time of this writing, you need to use vendor prefixes for a @keyframes rule and animations with Safari, and they don't work at all in Internet Explorer 9 and earlier (see page 338).

- **Values:** The @keyframes rule isn't like any other CSS property—in fact, it's not a property at all. It's called an *at rule*, and it's more complex than a regular property. You need to supply a name (which you'll use later when you apply the animation to an element on the page) and then a set of braces: { }. Inside the braces are the keyframes, which can be as simple as the two keywords from and to to mark the first and last keyframes. Each keyframe has its own set of braces, in which you put CSS properties that you'd like to animate—background color, font size, position on the page, and so on. For detailed information on how animations work, turn to page 338.

- **Example:**

```
@keyframes myAnimation {
from {
  background-color: black;
}


to {
  background-color: white;
}
}
}
```

animation

This is the shorthand method of applying an animation to an element. It's a compact way to include the following properties into one: animation-name, animation-duration, animation-timing-function, animation-iteration-count, animation-direction, animation-delay, and animation-fill-mode, all of which are explained below. Safari requires a vendor prefix for this property, and animations don't work in IE9 and earlier.

- **Values:** A space-separated list of values that includes the animation properties listed in the previous paragraph. For the exact type of values you need to supply for each, read the following entries (animation-name, animation-duration, and so on). Only two values are required: animation-name and animation-duration. Animation requires vendor prefixes (page 321). You can apply multiple named animations to the same element by providing a comma-separated list of animation values.

- **Example:**

```
animation: myAnimation 2s;
animation: myAnimation 2s ease-in 2 alternate 5s forwards;
animation: fadeOut 2s ease-in-out 2 alternate 5s forwards,
           glow 5s;
```

animation-name

Use this property to assign an animation that you've created with the @keyframes rule. You add this property as part of a CSS selector that applies to one or more page elements. For example, adding this property to an <h1> tag style will tell a browser to run the specified animation on all <h1> tags when the page loads. You also need to assign the animation-duration property for this to work. This property requires a vendor prefix for Safari, and it doesn't work in IE9 or earlier.

- **Values:** A name from an @keyframes rule.

- **Example:** animation-name: myAnimation;

animation-duration

Specifies how long an animation specified by the animation-name property (above) takes to complete.

- **Values:** A value in seconds—1s—or milliseconds—1000ms.

- **Example:** animation-duration: 2s;

animation-timing-function

Dictates the speed of an animation within the allotted animation duration. For example, while you may set the duration of an animation to 5 seconds, you can also control how the animation plays back within that 5 seconds, such as starting slowly and finishing quickly. Safari requires a vendor prefix for this property and animations don't work in IE9 or earlier.

- **Values:** One of five keywords: linear, ease, ease-in, ease-out, and ease-in-out. Can also supply a cubic Bezier value for a custom timing function (page 332).

- **Example:**

```
animation-timing-function: ease-out;
animation-timing-function: cubic-bezier(.20, .96, .74, .07);
```

animation-delay

Specifies a time in seconds or milliseconds that an animation should wait before beginning to play. Safari requires a vendor prefix and this property doesn't work in IE9 or earlier.

- **Values:** A value in seconds—1s—or milliseconds—1000ms.

- **Example:** animation-delay: 1.5s;

animation-iteration-count

Specifies how many times an animation runs. Normally, an animation runs once and then is done, but you can make an animation run 4, 5, 100, or an infinite number of times. Safari requires a vendor prefix, and this property doesn't work in IE9 or earlier.

- **Values**: A positive integer or the keyword infinite.

- **Example:**

```
animation-iteration-count: 5;
animation-iteration-count: infinite;
```

animation-direction

When an animation runs more than once, this property specifies the starting point for each subsequent animation. Normally, a browser simply replays an animation from its original starting point, over and over. However, you can also make the animation forwards, then backwards, then forwards again. For example, if you have an animation that makes an element's background color progress from white to black, you may want to give it a pulsing quality by having it run many times and animate from white to black, then black back to white, then white to black, then black to white, and so on. Safari requires a vendor prefix, and this property doesn't work in IE9 or earlier.

- **Values:** The keyword normal or alternate. Normal is the way a browser already plays back animations, so you only need to use this property if you want to use the alternate keyword.

- **Example:** animation-direction: alternate;

animation-fill-mode

Dictates how an animated element should be styled at the beginning and/or end of an animation. Requires vendor prefixes for Safari, and doesn't work in IE9 or earlier.

- **Values:** One of three keywords: backwards, forwards, or both. forwards is the most common, as it leaves the element styled in the same way as the end of the animation, instead of reverting back to the styling before the animation began.

- **Example:** animation-fill-mode: backwards;

animation-play-state

Controls whether an animation is playing or not. You can use this property on a :hover pseudo-class to pause an animation when a visitor hovers over the element. Safari requires a vendor prefix, and this property doesn't work in IE9 or earlier.

- **Values:** One of two keywords: pause or running. The paused keyword stops the animation, while running makes it go. The default value is running.

- **Example:** animation-play-state: paused;

transform

Changes an element in one or more ways, including scaling, rotating, skewing, or moving the element. Safari requires a vendor prefix, and this property doesn't work in IE9 or earlier.

- **Values:** Keywords `rotate()`, `translate()`, `skew()`, or `scale()`. Each keyword takes its own kind of value. For example, `rotate()` requires a degree value, as in `180deg`, for example; `translate()` requires a measurement like percentage, ems or pixels; `skew()` takes two degree values; and `scale()` takes a number positive or negative. See page 319 for details. You can apply more than one type of transformation to an element.

- **Example:**

```
transform: rotate(45deg);
transform: scale(1.5);
transform: skew(45deg 0) rotate(200deg) translate(100px, 0) scale(.5);
```

transform-origin

Controls the point at which a transformation is applied. For example, normally when you rotate an element, you spin it around its center. However, you can also rotate it around one of its four corners.

- **Values:** Two values, one for the horizontal origin, the other for the vertical origin. You use the same keywords and values as for the `background-position` property (page 236).

- **Example:**

```
transform-origin: left top;
transform-origin: 0% 100%;
transform-origin: 10px -100px;
```

transition

A shorthand method to specify the `transition-property`, `transition-duration`, `transition-timing-function`, and `transition-delay` properties (discussed next). Transitions tell a browser to animate changes in CSS properties on an element. For example, you can animate the change of a navigation button's background color from red to green as a visitor mouses over that button.

- **Values:** A space-separated list of properties, which include the `transition-property` (optional, defaults to `all`), `transition-duration` (required), `transition-timing-function` (optional, defaults to `ease`), `transition-delay` (optional, defaults to `0`).

- **Example:** `transition: background-color 1.5s ease-in-out 500ms;`

transition-property

Specifies the specific CSS properties that should be animated when an element's CSS properties change.

- **Values:** An animatable CSS property (see page 331), or the keyword all.

- **Example:**

```
transition-property: width, left, background-color;
transition-property: all;
```

transition-duration

Specifies how long a transition animation takes to complete.

- **Values:** A value in seconds—1s—or milliseconds—1000ms.

- **Example:** transition-duration: 2s;

transition-timing-function

Dictates the speed of a transition animation within the specified duration. For example, while you may set the duration of a transition to 5 seconds, you can also control how the transition plays back within that 5 seconds, such as starting slowly and finishing quickly.

- **Values:** One of five keywords linear, ease, ease-in, ease-out, and ease-in-out. Can also supply a cubic Bezier value for a custom timing function (page 332).

- **Example:**

```
transition-timing-function: ease-out;
transition-timing-function: cubic-bezier(.20, .96, .74, .07);
```

transition-delay

Specifies a time in seconds or milliseconds that the transition animation should wait before beginning to play.

- **Values:** A value in seconds—1s—or milliseconds—1000ms.

- **Example:** transition-delay: 1.5s;

■ Table Properties

There are a handful of CSS properties that relate solely to HTML tables. Chapter 10 has complete instructions on using CSS with tables.

border-collapse

Determines whether the borders around the cells of a table are separated or collapsed. When they're separated, browsers put a space of a couple of pixels between each cell. Even if you eliminate this space by setting the cellspacing attribute for the HTML <table> tag to 0, browsers still display double borders. That is, the bottom border of one cell will appear above the top border of the cell below, causing a doubling of border lines. Setting the border-collapse property to collapse eliminates both the space between cells and this doubling up of border lines (page 363). This property works only when applied to a <table> tag.

- **Values:** collapse, separate
- **Example:** border-collapse: collapse;

border-spacing

Sets the amount of space between cells in a table. It replaces the <table> tag's cellspacing HTML attribute. However, Internet Explorer 7 and earlier doesn't understand the border-spacing property, so it's best to continue to use the cellspacing attribute in your <table> tags to guarantee space between cells in all browsers.

> **NOTE** If you want to eliminate the space browsers normally insert between cells, just set the border-collapse property to collapse.

- **Values:** Two CSS length values. The first sets the horizontal separation (the space on either side of each cell), and the second sets the vertical separation (the space separating the bottom of one cell from the top of the one below it).
- **Example:** border-spacing: 0 10px;

caption-side

When applied to a table caption, this property determines whether the caption appears at the top or bottom of the table. (Since, according to HTML rules, the <caption> tag must immediately follow the opening <table> tag, a caption would normally appear at the top of the table.)

- **Values:** top, bottom
- **Example:** caption-side: bottom;

empty-cells

Determines how a browser should display a table cell that's completely empty, which in HTML would look like this: <td></td>. The hide value prevents any part of the cell from being displayed. Instead, only an empty placeholder appears, so borders, background colors, and background images don't show up in an emptied cell. Apply this property to a style formatting the <table> tag.

- **Values:** show, hide
- **Example:** empty-cells: show;

> **NOTE** The empty-cells property has no effect in Internet Explorer 7 and earlier.

table-layout

Controls how a web browser draws a table and can slightly affect the speed at which the browser displays it. The fixed setting forces the browser to render all columns the same width as the columns in the first row, which (for complicated technical reasons) draws tables faster. The auto value is the normal "browser just do your thing" value, so if you're happy with how quickly your tables appear on a page, don't bother with this property. If you use it, apply table-layout to a style formatting the <table> tag.

- **Values:** auto, fixed
- **Example:** table-layout: fixed;

Miscellaneous Properties

CSS offers a few additional—and sometimes interesting—properties. They let you enhance your web pages with special content and cursors, offer more control over how a page prints, and so on.

content

Specifies text that appears either before or after an element. Use this property with the :after or :before pseudo-elements. You can add an opening quotation mark in front of quoted material and a closing quotation after the quote.

- **Values:** Text inside of quotes "like this", the keywords normal, open-quote, close-quote, no-open-quote, no-close-quote. You can also use the value of an HTML attribute.

- **Examples:**

```
p.advert:before { content: "And now a word from our sponsor…"; }
a:after { content: " (" attr(href) ") "; }
```

NOTE   Adding text in this way (like the opening and closing quote example) is called *generated content*. Read a simple explanation of the generated content phenomenon at *www.westciv.com/style_master/academy/ css_tutorial/advanced/generated_content.html.* For a deeper explanation, visit *www.w3.org/TR/CSS21/generate. html.*

---

cursor

Lets you change the look of the mouse pointer when it moves over a particular element. You can make a question mark appear next to the cursor when someone mouses over a link that provides more information on a subject (like a word definition).

- **Values:** auto, default, crosshair, pointer, move, e-resize, ne-resize, nw-resize, n-resize, se-resize, sw-resize, s-resize, w-resize, text, wait, help, progress. You can also use a URL value to use your own graphic as a cursor (but see the Note below). The look of a cursor when mousing over a link is pointer, so if you want to make some element on the page display the "click me" icon, you can add the declaration cursor: pointer to the style.

- **Example:** cursor: help; cursor: url(images/cursor.cur);

> **NOTE** Not all browsers recognize URL cursor values. For more information, visit *www.quirksmode.org/css/cursor.html*.

opacity

Lets you control the transparency of any element and all of its descendants. In this way, you can have underlying colors, images, and content show through an element. Note that if you apply opacity to a div, all of the items inside that div, headlines, images, paragraphs, and other divs will share the same opacity level. In other words, if you set a <div> tag to .5 opacity (50% transparent), an image inside that div will also be 50% transparent—even explicitly setting the opacity of that image to 1 won't override the 50% transparency.

- **Values:** A decimal value from 0 to 1. 0 is invisible, 1 is completely opaque.

- **Example:** opacity: .5;

orphans

Specifies the minimum number of lines of text that can be left at the bottom of a printed page. Suppose you're printing your web page on a laser printer, and a five-line paragraph is split between two pages, with just one line at the bottom of page one, and the four remaining lines at the top of page two. Because a single line all by itself looks odd (sort of like a lost *orphan*—get it?), you can tell the browser to break a paragraph *only* if at least, say, three lines are left on the bottom of the page. (At this writing, only the Opera browser understands this property.)

- **Values:** a number like 1, 2, 3, or 5.

- **Example:** orphans: 3;

page-break-inside

Prevents an element from being split across two printed pages. If you want to keep a photo and its caption together on a single page, wrap the photo and caption text in a `<div>` tag, and then apply a style with `page-break-inside` to that `<div>`.

- **Values:** avoid

- **Example:** `page-break-inside: avoid;`

widows

The opposite of `orphans`, it specifies the minimum number of lines that must appear at the *top* of a printed page. Say the printer can manage to fit four out of five lines of a paragraph at the bottom of a page and has to move the last line to the top of the next page. Since that line might look weird all by itself, use `widows` to make the browser move at least two or three (or whatever number of) lines together to the top of a printed page.

- **Values:** A number like 1, 2, 3, or 5.

- **Example:** `widows: 3;`

CSS Resources

N o one book—not even this one—can answer all of your CSS questions. Luck-
ily, CSS resources abound for both beginning and expert web designers. In
this appendix, you'll find resources to help you with general CSS concepts as
well as specific CSS tasks, like building a navigation bar or laying out a web page.

■ References

References that cover CSS properties range from the official to the obscure. There
are websites and online tutorials, of course, but you don't have to be on the Web to
learn about CSS. Some of these guides come on good old-fashioned paper.

World Wide Web Consortium (W3C)

- **CSS Current Work (***www.w3.org/Style/CSS/current-work***).** Here you'll find all
  of the CSS specifications, including the newest additions to CSS. The different
  specifications are organized by status, like Completed, Testing, Refining, Revising,
  or Abandoned. You can click any specification to dig into the nitty-gritty details,
  but just because a specification is listed as "Completed" doesn't necessarily mean
  it's been fully implemented in all web browsers. However, this site does provide
  the final (sometimes overly complex and hard-to-understand) word on CSS.

Other Online References

- **CSS Reference at the Mozilla Developer Network (***https://developer.mozilla.
  org/en-US/docs/Web/CSS/Reference***).** The Mozilla Developer Network (MDN)
  provides one of the most comprehensive references to CSS (as well as HTML5,
  JavaScript, and other web technologies).

- **The Codrops CSS Reference** (*http://tympanus.net/codrops/css_reference/*). This provides an extensive and detailed reference for most CSS properties. Includes many examples of properties in action as well as detailed descriptions with notes and trivia.

- **Can I use** (*http://caniuse.com*). This frequently updated site provides detailed information on CSS and browser compatibility. Here, you'll be able to determine if a particular CSS property works in Internet Explorer 9, for example.

- **CSS3 Files** (*http://www.css3files.com/*). This provides very good instruction and even better demonstrations of popular CSS3 properties like animation, shadows, gradients and more. Also includes blog posts on current CSS techniques.

◼ CSS Help

Even with the best references (like this book), sometimes you need to ask an expert. You can join a discussion list where CSS-heads answer questions by email, or peruse a wealth of information in an online forum.

Discussion Boards

- **Stack Overflow** (*http://stackoverflow.com*). One of the best resources for everything Web and programming. Thousands of experts answer questions on nearly every computer-related question. You can ask CSS questions here as well, and find questions tagged with the CSS keyword to find out what people are asking about: *http://stackoverflow.com/questions/tagged/css*.

- **CSS Creator Forum** (*www.csscreator.com/css-forum*). A very active online forum offering help and advice for everything from basic CSS to advanced layout.

- **SitePoint.com's HTML and CSS Forum** (*http://community.sitepoint.com/c/html-css*). Another helpful group of CSS addicts.

- **CSS-Tricks.com Forum** (*http://css-tricks.com/forums*). This small forum holds some good information. (If you like PHP and JavaScript, there's some good discussion on those topics here as well.)

◼ CSS Tips, Tricks, and Advice

The Web makes it easy for anyone to become a publisher. That's the good news. The bad news is, when everyone's a publisher, it's harder to sort through all the chaff to find the golden wheat of clear, concise, and accurate information. There's plenty of good CSS information on the Web—and a lot that's not good. Here are a few of the best destinations for CSS information:

- **CSS-Tricks.com** (*http://css-tricks.com*). This one-man blog is full of great CSS tips. You'll find frequently updated tips and tricks as well as comprehensive video tutorials.

- **SitePoint** (*www.sitepoint.com/html-css/*)**.** Lots of articles and tutorials on CSS techniques. You'll often find the latest news and information about CSS here too.

- **Smashing Magazine** (*www.smashingmagazine.com/tag/css*)**.** Smashing Magazine gathers some of the best resources on the Web, and in the CSS category you'll find a nearly endless number of links highlighting some of the most creative thinking on CSS and web design.

CSS Navigation

Chapter 9 shows you how to create navigation buttons for your website from scratch. But online tutorials are a great way to solidify your knowledge. Also, once you understand the process in detail, you don't have to do it yourself every single time. On the Web you can find examples of navigation features for inspiration.

Tutorials

- **Listutorial** (*http://css.maxdesign.com.au/listutorial*)**.** Step-by-step tutorials on building navigation systems from unordered lists.

- **Responsive, Fluid-Width, Variable-Item Navigation with CSS** (*www.sitepoint. com/responsive-fluid-width-variable-item-navigation-css/*)**.** Behind that really, really long title is a tutorial that provides step-by-step instructions for creating a responsive navigation bar.

- **How To Create A Responsive Navigation Menu Using Only CSS** (*http://medialoot.com/blog/how-to-create-a-responsive-navigation-menu-using-only-css/*)**.** Learn how to use only CSS to create a responsive, drop-down menu.

Online Examples

- **NavNav** (*http://navnav.co*) provides a showcase of navigation bar examples, demos and tutorials. The site lists both CSS and JavaScript solutions for creating exciting navigation options.

- **5 Examples of Patterns for Mobile Navigation Menus** (*www.sitepoint.com/5-examples-patterns-mobile-navigation-menus/*)**.** Learn different design patterns for mobile menus.

- **Pure CSS Off-screen Navigation Menu** (*http://www.sitepoint.com/pure-css-off-screen-navigation-menu/*)**.** What good is a nav menu that's not on screen? It saves screen real estate. This tutorial shows you how to create a menu that slides onto the screen when a visitor clicks a button. And it's all done with CSS!

- **The Priority+ Navigation Pattern** (*https://css-tricks.com/the-priority-navigation-pattern/*)**.** See how to adjust and prioritize your navigation menu buttons based on screen size.

CSS Layout

CSS layout is so flexible, you could spend a lifetime exploring the possibilities. And some people seem to be doing just that. You can gain from their labors by reading articles, checking out online examples, and experimenting with tools that can do some of the CSS work for you.

- **Learn CSS Layout** (*http://learnlayout.com/index.html*) provides an interactive set of lessons teaching different CSS layout techniques.

- **Free CSS Responsive Layouts** (*http://maxdesign.com.au/css-layouts/*) provides starter templates of HTML and CSS for a handful of common page layouts. The designs are responsive (Chapter 15) so they adjust to the visitor's screen size.

- **Pure Layouts** (*http://purecss.io/layouts/*) provides many sample, starter layouts based on Yahoo's CSS framework, Pure.

- **Twitter Bootstrap** (*http://getbootstrap.com*). A complete website toolkit— includes HTML, CSS and JavaScript components to make it easy to build a complete, responsive, grid-based page, with some fancy JavaScript thrown in.

- **Foundation** (*http://foundation.zurb.com*). Another take on the complete website toolkit. Very much like Twitter bootstrap, Foundation includes HTML, CSS and JavaScript. It has excellent documentation and is relatively easy to learn.

Showcase Sites

Knowing the CSS standard inside out is no help when your imagination is running dry. A great source of inspiration is the creative work of others. There are more CSS showcase sites than you can shake a search engine at, so here's a handful of sites where you can appreciate and study beautiful CSS designs.

- **CSS ZenGarden** (*www.csszengarden.com*). The mother of all CSS showcase sites: many different designs for the exact same HTML.

- **CSS Line** (*http://cssline.com*). A wonderful gallery of inspirational CSS designs, with innovative filtering options. Interested in websites that use a particular color? You can see just those sites. Or if you want to see sites with particular features like unique navigation and typography, you can filter the results to see just those.

- **The Awwwards** (*www.awwwards.com*). A site that awards great design despite having an awwwkwwward name.

- **CSS Design Awards** (*www.cssdesignawards.com*). This site highlights a new "winner" every day. It's unclear if the judges are really just teenagers surfing the Web in their bedrooms, but the site does highlight some very nicely designed sites.

Index

CSS

THE MISSING CD

There's no CD with this book; you just saved $5.00.

Instead, every single Web address, practice file, and piece of downloadable software mentioned in this book is available at *missingmanuals.com* (click the Missing CD icon). There you'll find a tidy list of links, organized by chapter.

Don't miss a thing!
Sign up for the free Missing Manual email announcement list at missingmanuals.com. We'll let you know when we release new titles, make free sample chapters available, and update the features and articles on the Missing Manual website.